RENAL DIET COOKBOOK FOR BEGINNERS 2023

850+

Easy and Delicious Recipes to Manage Low Potassium, Low Phosphorus, Low Sodium for a Living a Healthy Life

JUDITH PARKER

TABLE OF CONTENTS

INTRODUCTION

When renal function is impaired, a renal diet is one that is deficient in sodium, phosphorus, and potassium, three minerals that the body cannot adequately metabolize and flush out (in excess levels).

A renal diet adheres to a few basic principles. The first is that it must be a well-balanced, organic, and long-term diet that is high in whole grains, vitamins, fibers, carbohydrates, omega-3 fats, and fluids. Proteins should be enough, but not too many.

The Renal Diet Cookbook is for people who have been diagnosed with chronic kidney disease (CKD) and want to eat a balanced diet. The book contains basic, step-by-step, and easy-to-follow recipes, as well as instructions for kidney patients. This guide was created to assist those with CKD in regaining lost weight and enjoying their favorite foods. The terms kidney function and renal function are used to describe how well the kidneys work. A pair of kidneys is born with every healthy person. As a result, when one of the kidneys stopped working, it went unnoticed because the other kidney was still working. However, if the kidney functions continue to deteriorate and hit a level as low as 25%, the situation becomes dangerous for the patients. People with only one working kidney need adequate external therapy and, in the worst-case scenario, a kidney transplant.

Renal Diet Cookbook aided you in learning more about your condition, making good decisions, and staying on track with the basics. We hope you've learned a lot more about your Renal Diet as a result of this article. We recognize that the quality of our goods and services is just as critical as the quality of our knowledge at Renal Diet Cookbook.

When a number of renal cells called nephrons are partially or entirely impaired, they fail to filter blood entering the body properly, resulting in kidney disease. The progressive damage to kidney cells can be caused by a number of factors, including an acidic or toxic build-up within the kidney over time, genetics, or other kidney-damaging diseases such as hypertension (high blood pressure) or diabetes.

Chronic Kidney Disease (CKD) is a form of kidney disease (CKD)

Chronic kidney disease, or CKD, is a level of kidney failure in which the kidneys are unable to filter the blood properly. The term chronic is used to describe organ damage that occurs over time. As a result, such a stage must be avoided at all costs. As a result, early detection of the disease is critical. The earlier the patient recognizes the seriousness of the case, the more effective steps he will take to address it. If you need to limit potassium, consult your primary care physician or a dietitian. If you need to lower your potassium levels, you can use your food and drink choices to help.

Potassium levels in salt substitutes can be high. Examine the affixing label. If you want to use salt derivatives, talk to your supplier. Before eating canned foods, run them through a screening machine. More advice on how to keep the levels of potassium in your blood at a healthy level. Choose new, ground-grown foods and avoid salt derivatives or subsidiaries, as well as potassium-based seasonings. Phosphorus can be present in a variety of foods. Patients with reduced kidney function can consult with a renal dietitian to keep track of their phosphorus levels.

It is a way of eating that protects your kidneys from more harm. It entails limiting a few ingredients and liquids in order to prevent such minerals from developing in your body. However, as the infection worsens and kidney failure worsens, you must become more vigilant about what you eat and drink.

There are many foods that fit well in the renal diet, and once you see how many options there are, it won't seem as restrictive or difficult to stick to. The trick is to concentrate on foods that are rich in nutrients, as these make it easier for the kidneys to absorb waste by reducing the amount of waste that the body has to discard. Long-term renal function depends on maintaining and enhancing balance.

BREAKFAST

1. Raspberry Peach Breakfast Smoothie

Preparation time: 5 minutes
Cooking time: 1 minute
Servings: 2

Ingredients

- 1/3 cup of raspberries, (it can be frozen)
- 1/2 peach, skin and pit removed
- 1 tablespoon of honey
- 1 cup of coconut water

Directions

1. Mix all ingredients together and blend it until smooth.
2. Pour and serve chilled in a tall glass or Mason jar.

Nutrition: Calories: 86.3 kcal Carbohydrate: 20.6 g Protein: 1.4 g Sodium: 3 mg Potassium: 109 mg Phosphorus: 36.08 mg Dietary fiber: 2.6 g fat: 0.31 g

2. Fast Microwave Egg Scramble

Preparation time: 5 minutes
Cooking time: 1-2 minutes
Servings: 1

Ingredients

- 1 large egg
- 2 large egg whites
- 2 tablespoons of milk
- Kosher pepper, ground

Directions

1. Spray a coffee cup with a bit of cooking spray.
2. Whisk all the ingredients together and place into the coffee cup.
3. Place the cup with the eggs into the microwave and set to cook for approx. 45 seconds. Take out and stir.
4. Cook it for another 30 seconds after returning it to the microwave.
5. Serve.

Nutrition: Calories: 128.6 kcal Carbohydrate: 2.47 g Protein: 12.96 g Sodium: 286.36 mg Potassium: 185.28 mg Phosphorus: 122.22 mg Dietary fiber: 0 g fat: 5.96 g

3. Summer Veggie Omelet

Preparation time: 5 minutes
Cooking time: 5 minutes
Servings: 2

Ingredients

- 4 large egg whites
- ¼ cup of sweet corn, frozen
- 1/3 cup of zucchini, grated
- 2 green onions, sliced
- 1 tablespoon of cream cheese
- Kosher pepper

Directions

1. Grease a medium pan with some cooking spray and add the onions, corn and grated zucchini.
2. Sauté for a couple of minutes until softened.
3. Beat the eggs together with the water, cream cheese, and pepper in a bowl.
4. Add the eggs into the veggie mixture in the pan, and let cook while moving the edges from inside to outside with a spatula, to allow raw egg to cook through the edges.
5. Turn the omelet with the aid of a dish (placed over the pan and flipped upside down and then back to the pan).
6. Let sit for another 1-2 minutes.

7. Fold in half and serve.

Nutrition: calories: 90 kcal carbohydrate: 15.97 g protein: 8.07 g sodium: 227 mg potassium: 244.24 mg

phosphorus: 45.32 mg dietary fiber: 0.88 g fat: 2.44 g

4. Raspberry Overnight Porridge

Preparation time: overnight
Cooking time: 0 minute
Servings: 12
Ingredients
- 1/3 cup of rolled oats
- ½ cup almond milk
- 1 tablespoon of honey
- 5-6 raspberries, fresh or canned and unsweetened
- 1/3 cup of rolled oats
- ½ cup almond milk
- 1 tablespoon of honey
- 5-6 raspberries, fresh or canned and unsweetened

Directions
1. Combine the oats, almond milk, and honey in a Mason jar and place into the fridge for overnight.
2. Serve the next morning with the raspberries on top.

Nutrition: calories: 143.6 kcal Carbohydrate: 34.62 g Protein: 3.44 g Sodium: 77.88 mg Potassium: 153.25 mg Phosphorus: 99.3 mg Dietary fiber: 7.56 g Fat: 3.91 g

5. Baked Curried Apple Oatmeal Cups

Preparation time: 10 minutes
Cooking time: 20 minutes
Servings: 6
Ingredients
- 3½ cups old-fashioned oats

- 3 tablespoons brown sugar
- 2 teaspoons of your preferred curry powder
- 1/8 teaspoon salt
- 1 cup unsweetened almond milk
- 1 cup unsweetened applesauce
- 1 teaspoon vanilla
- ½ cup chopped walnuts

Directions
1. Preheat the oven to 375°f. Then spray a 12-cup muffin tin with baking spray then set aside.
2. Combine the oats, brown sugar, curry powder, and salt, and mix in a medium bowl.
3. Mix together the milk, applesauce, and vanilla in a small bowl,
4. Stir the liquid ingredients into the dry ingredients and mix until just combined. Stir in the walnuts.
5. Using a scant 1/3 cup for each divide the mixture among the muffin cups.
6. Bake this for 18 to 20 minutes until the oatmeal is firm. Serve.

Nutrition: Calories: 296; Total fat: 10g; Saturated fat: 1g; Sodium: 84mg; Phosphorus: 236mg;
Potassium: 289mg; Carbohydrates: 45g;Fiber: 6g; Protein: 8g; Sugar: 11g

6. Feta Mint Omelette

Preparation Time: 10 minutes
Cooking Time: 5 minutes
Servings: 1
Ingredients:
- 3 eggs
- 1/4 cup fresh mint, chopped
- 2 tbsp coconut milk
- 1/2 tsp olive oil
- 2 tbsp feta cheese, crumbled
- Pepper
- Salt

Directions:

1. In a bowl, whisk eggs with feta cheese, mint, milk, pepper, and salt.
2. Heat olive oil in a pan over low heat.
3. Pour egg mixture in the pan and cook until eggs are set.
4. Flip omelet and cook for 2 minutes more.
5. Serve and enjoy.

Nutrition: Calories 275 fat 20 g Carbohydrates 4 g Sugar 2 g Protein 20 g Cholesterol 505 mg Phosphorus: 215mg Potassium: 269mgSodium: 360mg Protein: 19g

7. Breakfast Maple Sausage

Preparation time: 15 minutes
Cooking time: 8 minutes
Servings: 12
Ingredients

- 1 pound of pork, minced
- ½ pound lean turkey meat, ground
- ¼ teaspoon of nutmeg
- ½ teaspoon black pepper
- ¼ all spice
- 2 tablespoon of maple syrup
- 1 tablespoon of water

Directions

1. Combine all the ingredients in a bowl.
2. Cover and refrigerate for 3-4 hours.
3. Take the mixture and form into small flat patties with your hand (around 10-12 patties).
4. Lightly grease a medium skillet with oil and shallow fry the patties over medium to high heat, until brown (around 4-5 minutes on each side).
5. Serve hot.

Nutrition: Calories: 53.85 kcal Carbohydrate: 2.42 g Protein: 8.5 g Sodium: 30.96 mg

Phosphorus: 83.49 mg Dietary fiber: 0.03 g Fat: 0.9 g

8. Mango Lassa Smoothie

Preparation time: 5 minutes
Cooking time: 0 minute
Servings: 2
Ingredients

- ½ cup of plain yogurt
- ½ cup of plain water
- ½ cup of sliced mango
- 1 tablespoon of sugar
- ¼ teaspoon of cardamom
- ¼ teaspoon cinnamon
- ¼ cup lime juice

Directions

1. Pulse all the above ingredients in a blender until smooth (around 1 minute).
2. Pour into tall glasses or mason jars and serve chilled immediately.

Nutrition: Calories: 89.02 kcal Carbohydrate: 14.31 g Protein: 2.54 g Sodium: 30 mg potassium: 185.67 mg
phosphorus: 67.88 mg Dietary fiber: 0.77 g Fat: 2.05 g

9. Sausage Cheese Bake Omelette

Preparation Time: 10 minutes
Cooking Time: 45 minutes
Servings: 8
Ingredients:

- 16 eggs
- 2 cups cheddar cheese, shredded
- 1/2 cup salsa
- 1 lb ground sausage
- 1 1/2 cups coconut milk
- Pepper
- Salt

Directions:

1. Preheat the oven to 350 F.

2. Add sausage in a pan and cook until browned. Drain excess fat.
3. In a large bowl, whisk eggs and milk. Stir in cheese, cooked sausage, and salsa.
4. Pour omelet mixture into the baking dish and bake for 45 minutes.
5. Serve and enjoy.

Nutrition: Calories 360 Fat 24 g Carbohydrates 4 g Sugar 3 g Protein 28 g Cholesterol 400 mg phosphorus: 165mg potassium: 370mg sodium: 135mg

10. Italian Breakfast Frittata

Preparation Time: 10 minutes
Cooking Time: 45 minutes
Servings: 4
Ingredients:
- 2 cups egg whites
- 1/2 cup mozzarella cheese, shredded
- 1 cup cottage cheese, crumbled
- 1/4 cup fresh basil, sliced
- 1/2 cup roasted red peppers, sliced
- Pepper
- Salt

Directions:
1. Preheat the oven to 375 F.
2. Add all ingredients into the large bowl and whisk well to combine.
3. Pour frittata mixture into the baking dish and bake for 45 minutes.
4. Slice and serve.

Nutrition: Calories 131 Fat 2 g Carbohydrates 5 g Sugar 2 g Protein 22 g Cholesterol 6 mg phosphorus: 110mg potassium: 117mg sodium: 75mg protein: 7g

11. American Blueberry Pancakes

Preparation time: 5 minutes
Cooking time: 10 minutes

Servings: 6
Ingredients
- 1 ½ cups of all-purpose flour, sifted
- 1 cup of buttermilk
- 3 tablespoons of sugar
- 2 tablespoons of unsalted butter, melted
- 2 teaspoon of baking powder
- 2 eggs, beaten
- 1 cup of canned blueberries, rinsed

Directions
1. Combine the baking powder, flour and sugar in a bowl.
2. Make a hole in the center and slowly add the rest of the ingredients.
3. Begin to stir gently from the sides to the center with a spatula, until you get a smooth and creamy batter.
4. With cooking spray, spray the pan and place over medium heat.
5. Take one measuring cup and fill 1/3rd of its capacity with the batter to make each pancake.
6. Use a spoon to pour the pancake batter and let cook until golden brown. Flip once to cook the other side.
7. Serve warm with optional agave syrup.

Nutrition: Calories: 251.69 kcal Carbohydrate: 41.68 g Protein: 7.2 g Sodium: 186.68 mg Potassium: 142.87 mg Phosphorus: 255.39 mg Dietary fiber: 1.9 g Fat: 6.47 g

12. Chicken Egg Breakfast Muffins

Preparation Time: 10 minutes
Cooking Time: 15 minutes
Servings: 12
Ingredients:
- 10 eggs
- 1 cup cooked chicken, chopped
- 3 tbsp green onions, chopped
- 1/4 tsp garlic powder
- Pepper

- Salt

Directions:
1. Preheat the oven to 400 F.
2. Spray a muffin tray with cooking spray and set aside.
3. In a large bowl, whisk eggs with garlic powder, pepper, and salt.
4. Add remaining ingredients and stir well.
5. Pour egg mixture into the muffin tray and bake for 15 minutes.
6. Serve and enjoy.

Nutrition: Calories 71 Fat 4 g Carbohydrates 0.4 g Sugar 0.3 g Protein 8 g Cholesterol 145 mg Phosphorus: 151mg Potassium: 127mg Sodium: 55mg

13. Mozzarella Cheese Omelette

Preparation Time: 10 minutes
Cooking Time: 5 minutes
Servings: 1

Ingredients:
- 4 eggs, beaten
- 1/4 cup mozzarella cheese, shredded
- 1/4 tsp. Italian seasoning
- 1/4 tsp. dried oregano
- Pepper
- Salt

Directions:
1. In a small bowl, whisk eggs with salt.
2. Spray pan with cooking spray and heat over medium heat.
3. Pour egg mixture into the pan and cook over medium heat.
4. Once eggs are set then sprinkle oregano and Italian seasoning on top.
5. Cook omelet for 1 minute.
6. Serve and enjoy.

Nutrition: Calories 285 Fat 19 g Carbohydrates 4 g Sugar 3 g Protein 25 g Cholesterol 655 mg Phosphorus: 110mg Potassium: 117mg Sodium: 75mg

14. Cherry Berry Bulgur Bowl

Preparation time: 15 minutes
Cooking time: 15 minutes
Servings: 4

Ingredients
- 1 cup medium-grind bulgur
- 2 cups water
- Pinch salt
- 1 cup halved and pitted cherries or 1 cup canned cherries, drained
- ½ cup raspberries
- ½ cup blackberries
- 1 tablespoon cherry jam
- 2 cups plain whole-milk yogurt

Directions
1. Mix the bulgur, water, and salt in a medium saucepan. Do this in a medium heat. Bring to a boil.
2. Reduce the heat to low and simmer, partially covered, for 12 to 15 minutes or until the bulgur is almost tender. Cover, and let stand for 5 minutes to finish cooking do this after removing the pan from the heat.
3. While the bulgur is cooking, combine the raspberries and blackberries in a medium bowl. Stir the cherry jam into the fruit.
4. When the bulgur is tender, divide among four bowls. Top each bowl with ½ cup of yogurt and an equal amount of the berry mixture and serve.

Nutrition per serving: Calories: 242; Total fat: 6g; Saturated fat: 3g;Sodium: 85mg; Phosphorus: 237mg; Potassium: 438mg; Carbohydrates: 44g; Fiber: 7g; Protein: 9g; Sugar: 13g

15. Mexican Scrambled Eggs in Tortilla

Preparation time: 5 minutes
Cooking time: 2 minutes
Servings: 2

Ingredients

- 2 medium corn tortillas
- 4 egg whites
- 1 teaspoon of cumin
- 3 teaspoons of green chilies, diced
- ½ teaspoon of hot pepper sauce
- 2 tablespoons of salsa
- ½ teaspoon salt

Directions

1. Spray some cooking spray on a medium skillet and heat for a few seconds.
2. Whisk the eggs with the green chilies, hot sauce, and comminute
3. Add the eggs into the pan, and whisk with a spatula to scramble. Add the salt.
4. Cook until fluffy and done (1-2 minutes) over low heat.
5. Open the tortillas and spread 1 tablespoon of salsa on each.
6. Distribute the egg mixture onto the tortillas and wrap gently to make a burrito.
7. Serve warm.

Nutrition: Calories: 44.1 kcal Carbohydrate: 2.23 g Protein: 7.69 g Sodium: 854 mg Potassium: 189 mg Phosphorus: 22 mg Dietary fiber: 0.5 g Fat: 0.39 g

16. Easy Turnip Puree

Preparation Time: 10 minutes
Cooking Time: 12 minutes
Servings: 4

Ingredients:

- 1 1/2 lbs. turnips, peeled and chopped
- 1 tsp. dill
- 3 bacon slices, cooked and chopped
- 2 tbsp. fresh chives, chopped

Directions:

1. Add turnip into the boiling water and cook for 12 minutes. Drain well and place in a food processor.
2. Add dill and process until smooth.
3. Transfer turnip puree into the bowl and top with bacon and chives.
4. Serve and enjoy.

Nutrition: Calories 127 Fat 6 g Carbohydrates 11.6 g Sugar 7 g Protein 6.8 g Cholesterol 16 mg Phosphorus: 110mg Potassium: 127mg Sodium: 86mg

17. Breakfast Tacos

Preparation time: 10 minutes
Cooking time: 10 minutes
Servings: 4

Ingredients

- 1 teaspoon olive oil
- ½ sweet onion, chopped
- ½ red bell pepper, chopped
- ½ teaspoon minced garlic
- 4 eggs, beaten
- ½ teaspoon ground cumin
- Pinch red pepper flakes
- 4 tortillas

Directions

1. Heat the oil in a large skillet in a medium heat only.
2. Add the onion, bell pepper, and garlic, and sauté until softened, about 5 minutes.
3. Add the eggs, cumin, and red pepper flakes, and scramble the eggs with the vegetables until cooked through and fluffy.
4. Spoon one-fourth of the egg mixture into the center of each tortilla, and top each with 1 tablespoon of salsa.
5. Serve immediately.

Nutrition per serving: Calories: 211; Total fat: 7g; Saturated fat: 2g; Cholesterol: 211mg;

Sodium: 346mg; Carbohydrates: 17g; Fiber: 1g; Phosphorus: 120mg; Potassium: 141mg; Protein: 9g

18. Spiced French toast

Preparation time: 15 minutes
Cooking time: 12 minutes
Servings: 4
Ingredients

- 4 eggs
- ½ cup homemade rice milk (here, or use unsweetened store-bought) or almond milk
- ¼ cup freshly squeezed orange juice
- 1 teaspoon ground cinnamon
- ½ teaspoon ground ginger
- Pinch ground cloves
- 1 tablespoon unsalted butter, divided
- 8 slices white bread

Directions

1. Whisk eggs, rice milk, orange juice, cinnamon, ginger, and cloves until well blended in a large bowl.
2. Melt half the butter in a large skillet. It should be in medium-high heat only.
3. Dredge four of the bread slices in the egg mixture until well soaked, and place them in the skillet.
4. Cook the toast until golden brown on both sides, turning once, about 6 minutes total.
5. Repeat with the remaining butter and bread.
6. Serve 2 pieces of hot French toast to each person.

Nutrition Calories: 236; Total fat: 11g; Saturated fat: 4g; Cholesterol: 220mg; Sodium: 84mg;
Carbohydrates: 27g; Fiber: 1g; Phosphorus: 119mg; Potassium: 158mg; Protein: 11g

19. Vegetable Tofu Scramble

Preparation Time: 10 minutes
Cooking Time: 7 minutes
Servings: 2
Ingredients:

- 1/2 block firm tofu, crumbled
- 1/4 tsp. ground cumin
- 1 tbsp. turmeric
- 1 cup spinach
- 1/4 cup zucchini, chopped
- 1 tbsp. olive oil
- 1 tbsp. chives, chopped
- 1 tbsp. coriander, chopped
- Pepper
- Salt

Directions:

1. Heat oil in a pan over medium heat.
2. Add zucchini, and spinach and sauté for 2 minutes.
3. Add tofu, cumin, turmeric, pepper, and salt and sauté for 5 minutes.
4. Top with chives, and coriander.
5. Serve and enjoy.

Nutrition: Calories 101 Fat 8.5 g Carbohydrates 5.1 g Sugar 1.4 g Protein 3.1 g Cholesterol 0 mg Phosphorus: 80mg Potassium: 119mg Sodium: 75mg

20. Keto Overnight Oats

Preparation Time: 5 minutes
Cooking Time: 5 minutes
Servings: 2
Ingredients:

- 1 tbsp chia seed
- 4 drops liquid stevia
- 1/2 cup hemp hearts
- 2/3 cup coconut milk
- 1/2 tsp vanilla
- Pinch of salt

Directions:

1. Add all ingredients into the bowl and mix well.
2. Cover and place in refrigerator for 8 hours.
3. Serve and enjoy.

Nutrition: Calories 289 Fat 22.5 g Carbohydrates 5 g Sugar 0.1 g Protein 14 g Cholesterol 0 mg
Phosphorus: 70mg Potassium: 87mg Sodium: 45mg

21. Coconut Breakfast Smoothie

Preparation Time: 5 minutes
Cooking Time: 5 minutes
Servings: 1

Ingredients:

- 1/4 cup whey protein powder
- 1/2 cup coconut milk
- 5 drops liquid stevia
- 1 tbsp coconut oil
- 1 tsp vanilla
- 2 tbsp coconut butter
- 1/4 cup water
- 1/2 cup ice

Directions:

1. Add all ingredients into the blender and blend until smooth.
2. Serve and enjoy.

Nutrition: Calories 560 Fat 45 g Carbohydrates 12 g Sugar 4 g Protein 25 g Cholesterol 60 mg Phosphorus: 160mg Potassium: 127mg Sodium: 85mg

22. Mexican Style Burritos

Preparation Time: 5 minutes
Cooking Time: 15 minutes
Servings: 2

Ingredients:

- 1 tbsp. Olive oil

- 2 Corn tortillas
- ¼ cup chopped Red onion
- ¼ cup chopped Red bell peppers
- ½, deseeded and chopped red chili
- 2 Eggs
- 1 lime juice
- 1 tbsp. chopped Cilantro

Directions:

1. Place the tortillas in medium heat for 1 to 2 minutes on each side or until lightly toasted.
2. Remove and keep the broiler on.
3. Heat the oil in a skillet and sauté onion, chili, and bell peppers for 5 to 6 minutes or until soft.
4. Crack the eggs over the top of the onions and peppers.
5. Place skillet under the broiler for 5 to 6 minutes or until the eggs are cooked.
6. Serve half the eggs and vegetables on top of each tortilla and sprinkle with cilantro and lime juice to serve.

Nutrition: Calories: 202 Fat: 13g Carb: 19g Protein: 9g Sodium: 77mg Potassium: 233mg Phosphorus: 184mg

23. Bulgur, Couscous, and Buckwheat Cereal

Preparation Time: 10 minutes
Cooking Time: 25 minutes
Servings: 4

Ingredients:

- 2 ¼ cups Water
- 1 ¼ cups Vanilla rice milk
- 6 Tbsps. Uncooked bulgur
- 2 Tbsps. Uncooked whole buckwheat
- 1 cup Sliced apple
- 6 Tbsps. Plain uncooked couscous
- ½ tsp. Ground cinnamon

Directions:

1. Heat the water and milk in the saucepan over medium heat. Let it boil.

2. Put the bulgur, buckwheat, and apple.
3. Reduce the heat to low and simmer, occasionally stirring until the bulgur is tender, about 20 to 25 minutes.
4. Remove the saucepan and stir in the couscous and cinnamon—cover for 10 minutes.
5. Put the cereal before serving.

Nutrition: Calories: 159 Fat: 1g Carb: 34g Protein: 4g Sodium: 33mg Potassium: 116m Phosphorus: 130mg

24. Blueberry Muffins

Preparation Time: 15 minutes
Cooking Time: 30 minutes
Servings: 12
Ingredients:
- 2 cups Unsweetened rice milk
- 1 Tbsp. Apple cider vinegar
- 3 ½ cups All-purpose flour
- 1 cup Granulated sugar
- 1 Tbsp. Baking soda substitute
- 1 tsp. Ground cinnamon
- ½ tsp. Ground nutmeg
- Pinch ground ginger
- ½ cup Canola oil
- 2 Tbsps. Pure vanilla extract
- 2 ½ cups Fresh blueberries

Directions:
1. Preheat the oven to 375F.
2. Prepare a muffin pan and set aside.
3. Stir together the rice milk and vinegar in a small bowl. Set aside for 10 minutes.
4. In a large bowl, stir together the sugar, flour, baking soda, cinnamon, nutmeg, and ginger until well mixed.
5. Add oil and vanilla to the milk and mix.
6. Put milk mixture to dry ingredients and stir well to combine.
7. Put the blueberries and spoon the muffin batter evenly into the cups.

8. Bake the muffins for 25 to 30 minutes or until golden and a toothpick inserted comes out clean.
9. Cool for 15 minutes and serve.

Nutrition: Calories: 331 Fat: 11g Carb: 52g Protein: 6g Sodium: 35mg Potassium: 89mg Phosphorus: 90mg

25. Cheesy Scrambled Eggs with Fresh Herbs

Preparation Time: 15 minutes
Cooking Time: 10 minutes
Servings: 4
Ingredients:
- 3 Eggs
- 2 Egg whites
- ½ cup Cream cheese
- ¼ cup Unsweetened rice milk
- 1 tbsp. green part only Chopped scallion
- 1 tbsp. Chopped fresh tarragon
- 2 tbsps. Unsalted butter
- Ground black pepper to taste

Directions:
1. Whisk the eggs, egg whites, cream cheese, rice milk, scallions, and tarragon. Mix until smooth.
2. Melt the butter in a skillet.
3. Put egg mixture and cook for 5 minutes or until the eggs are thick and curds creamy.
4. Season with pepper and serve.

Nutrition: Calories: 221 Fat: 19g Carb: 3g Protein: 8g Sodium: 193mg Potassium: 140mg Phosphorus: 119mg

26. Turkey and Spinach Scramble on Melba toast

Preparation Time: 5 minutes
Cooking Time: 15 minutes
Servings: 2
Ingredients:

- 1 tsp. Extra virgin olive oil
- 1 cup Raw spinach
- ½ clove, minced Garlic
- 1 tsp. grated Nutmeg
- 1 cup Cooked and diced turkey breast
- 4 slices Melba toast
- 1 tsp. Balsamic vinegar

Directions:
1. Heat a skillet over medium heat and add oil.
2. Add turkey and heat through for 6 to 8 minutes.
3. Add spinach, garlic, and nutmeg and stir-fry for 6 minutes more.
4. Plate up the Melba toast and top with spinach and turkey scramble.
5. Drizzle with balsamic vinegar and serve.

Nutrition: Calories: 301 Fat: 19g Carb: 12g Protein: 19g Sodium: 360mg Potassium: 269mg Phosphorus: 215mg

27. Berry Chia with Yogurt

Preparation Time: 35 minutes
Cooking Time: 5 minutes
Servings: 4
Ingredients:
- ½ cup chia seeds, dried
- 2 cup Plain yogurt
- 1/3 cup strawberries, chopped
- ¼ cup blackberries
- ¼ cup raspberries
- 4 teaspoons Splenda

Directions:
1. Mix up together Plain yogurt with Splenda, and chia seeds.
2. Transfer the mixture into the serving ramekins (jars) and leave for 35 minutes.
3. After this, add blackberries, raspberries, and strawberries. Mix up the meal well.
4. Serve it immediately or store it in the fridge for up to 2 days.

Nutrition: Calories: 150 Fat: 5g Carbs: 19g Protein: 6.8g Sodium: 65mg Potassium: 226mg Phosphorus: 75mg

28. Egg and Veggie Muffins

Preparation Time: 15 minutes
Cooking Time: 20 minutes
Servings: 4
Ingredients:
- 4 Eggs
- 2 Tbsp. Unsweetened rice milk
- ½ chopped Sweet onion
- ½ chopped Red bell pepper
- Pinch red pepper flakes
- Pinch ground black pepper

Directions:
1. Preheat the oven to 350F.
2. Spray 4 muffin pans with cooking spray. Set aside.
3. Whisk the milk, eggs, onion, red pepper, parsley, red pepper flakes, and black pepper until mixed.
4. Pour the egg mixture into prepared muffin pans.
5. Bake until the muffins are puffed and golden, about 18 to 20 minutes. Serve.

Nutrition: Calories: 84 Fat: 5g Carb: 3g Protein: 7g Sodium: 75mg Potassium: 117mg Phosphorus: 110mg

29. Cheese Coconut Pancakes

Preparation Time: 10 minutes
Cooking Time: 5 minutes
Servings: 1
Ingredients:
- 2 eggs
- 1 packet stevia
- 1/2 tsp. cinnamon
- 2 oz. cream cheese

- 1 tbsp. coconut flour
- 1/2 tsp. vanilla

Directions:
1. Add all ingredients into the bowl and blend until smooth.
2. Spray pan with cooking spray and heat over medium-high heat.
3. Pour batter on the hot pan and make two pancakes.
4. Cook pancake until lightly brown from both the sides.
5. Serve and enjoy.

Nutrition: Calories 386 Fat 30 g Carbohydrates 12 g Sugar 1 g Protein 16 g Cholesterol 389 mg Phosphorus: 110mg Potassium: 117mg Sodium: 75mg

30. Arugula Eggs with Chili Peppers

Preparation Time: 7 minutes
Cooking Time: 10 minutes
Servings: 4

Ingredients:
- 2 cups arugula, chopped
- 3 eggs, beaten
- ½ chili pepper, chopped
- 1 tablespoon butter
- 1 oz Parmesan, grated

Directions:
1. Toss butter in the skillet and melt it.
2. Add arugula and sauté it over medium heat for 5 minutes. Stir it from time to time.
3. Meanwhile, mix up together Parmesan, chili pepper, and eggs.
4. Pour the egg mixture over the arugula and scramble well.
5. Cook for 5 minutes more over medium heat.

Nutrition: Calories: 218 Fat: 15g Carbs: 2.8g Protein: 17g Sodium: 656mg Potassium: 243mg Phosphorus: 310mg

31. Eggplant Chicken Sandwich

Preparation Time: 10 minutes
Cooking Time: 15 minutes
Servings: 2
Ingredients:
- 1 eggplant, trimmed
- 10 oz chicken fillet
- 1 teaspoon Plain yogurt
- ½ teaspoon minced garlic
- 1 tablespoon fresh cilantro, chopped
- 2 lettuce leaves
- 1 teaspoon olive oil
- ½ teaspoon salt
- ½ teaspoon chili pepper
- 1 teaspoon butter

Directions:
1. Slice the eggplant lengthwise into 4 slices.
2. Rub the eggplant slices with minced garlic and brush with olive oil.
3. Grill the eggplant slices on the preheated to 375F grill for 3 minutes from each side.
4. Meanwhile, rub the chicken fillet with salt and chili pepper.
5. Place it in the skillet and add butter.
6. Roast the chicken for 6 minutes from each side over medium-high heat.
7. Cool the cooked eggplants gently and spread one side of them with Plain yogurt.
8. Add lettuce leaves and chopped fresh cilantro.
9. After this, slice the cooked chicken fillet and add over the lettuce.
10. Cover it with the remaining sliced eggplant to get the sandwich shape. Pin the sandwich with the toothpick if needed.

Nutrition: Calories: 276 Fat: 11g Carbs: 41g Protein: 13.8g Sodium: 775mg Potassium: 532mg Phosphorus: 187mg

32. Buckwheat and Grapefruit Porridge

Preparation Time: 5 minutes
Cooking Time: 20 minutes
Servings: 2
Ingredients:
- ½ cup Buckwheat
- ¼ chopped Grapefruit
- 1 Tbsp. Honey
- 1 ½ cups Almond milk
- 2 cups Water

Directions:
1. Let the water boil on the stove. Add the buckwheat and place the lid on the pan.
2. Lower heat slightly and simmer for 7 to 10 minutes, checking to ensure water does not dry out.
3. When most of the water is absorbed, remove, and set aside for 5 minutes.
4. Drain any excess water from the pan and stir in almond milk, heating through for 5 minutes.
5. Add the honey and grapefruit.
6. Serve.

Nutrition: Calories: 231 Fat: 4g Carb: 43g Protein: 13g Sodium: 135mg Potassium: 370mg Phosphorus: 165mg

33. Apple Pumpkin Muffins

Preparation time: 15 minutes
Cooking time: 20 minutes
Servings: 12
Ingredients
- 1 cup all-purpose flour
- 1 cup wheat bran
- 2 teaspoons phosphorus powder
- 1 cup pumpkin purée

- ¼ cup honey
- ¼ cup olive oil
- 1 egg
- 1 teaspoon vanilla extract
- ½ cup cored diced apple

Directions
1. Preheat the oven to 400°f.
2. Line 12 muffin cups with paper liners.
3. Stir together the flour, wheat bran, and baking powder, mix this in a medium bowl.
4. In a small bowl, whisk together the pumpkin, honey, olive oil, egg, and vanilla.
5. Stir the pumpkin mixture into the flour mixture until just combined.
6. Stir in the diced apple.
7. Spoon the batter in the muffin cups.
8. Bake for about 20 minutes, or until a toothpick inserted in the center of a muffin comes out clean.

Nutrition Calories: 125; Total fat: 5g; Saturated fat: 1g; Cholesterol: 18mg; Sodium: 8mg; Carbohydrates: 20g;
Fiber: 3g; Phosphorus: 120mg; Potassium: 177mg; Protein: 2g

34. Chorizo Bowl with Corn

Preparation Time: 10 minutes
Cooking Time: 15 minutes
Servings: 4

Ingredients:
- 9 oz chorizo
- 1 tablespoon almond butter
- ½ cup corn kernels
- ¾ cup heavy cream
- 1 teaspoon butter
- ¼ teaspoon chili pepper
- 1 tablespoon dill, chopped

Directions:

1. Chop the chorizo and place it in the skillet.
2. Add almond butter and chili pepper.
3. Roast the chorizo for 3 minutes.
4. After this, add corn kernels.
5. Add butter and chopped the dill. Mix up the mixture well—Cook for 2 minutes.
6. Close the lid and simmer for 10 minutes over low heat.
7. Transfer the cooked meal into the serving bowls.

Nutrition: Calories: 286 Fat: 15g Carbs: 26g Protein: 13g Sodium: 228mg Potassium: 255mg Phosphorus: 293mg

35. Panzanella Salad

Preparation Time: 10 minutes
Cooking Time: 5 minutes
Servings: 4
Ingredients:
- 2 cucumbers, chopped
- 1 red onion, sliced
- 2 red bell peppers, chopped
- ¼ cup fresh cilantro, chopped
- 1 tablespoon capers
- 1 oz whole-grain bread, chopped
- 1 tablespoon canola oil
- ½ teaspoon minced garlic
- 1 tablespoon Dijon mustard
- 1 teaspoon olive oil
- 1 teaspoon lime juice

Directions:
1. Pour canola oil into the skillet and bring it to boil.
2. Add chopped bread and roast it until crunchy (3-5 minutes).
3. Meanwhile, in the salad bowl, combine sliced red onion, cucumbers, bell peppers, cilantro, capers, and mix up gently.

4. Make the dressing: mix up together lime juice, olive oil, Dijon mustard, and minced garlic.
5. Put the dressing over the salad and stir it directly before serving.

Nutrition: Calories: 224.3 Fat: 10g Carbs: 26g Protein: 6.6g Sodium: 401mg Potassium: 324.9mg Phosphorus: 84mg

36. Poached Asparagus and Egg

Preparation time: 3 minutes
Cooking Time: 15 minutes
Servings: 1
Ingredients:
- 1 egg
- 4 spears asparagus
- Water

Directions:
1. Half-fill a deep saucepan with water set over high heat. Let the water come to a boil.
2. Dip asparagus spears in water. Cook until they turn a shade brighter, about 3 minutes. Remove from saucepan and drain on paper towels. Keep warm—lightly season before serving.
3. Use a slotted spoon to lower the egg into boiling water gently.
4. Cook for only 4 minutes. Remove from pan immediately. Place on egg holder.
5. Slice off the top. The egg should still be fluid inside.
6. Place asparagus spears on a small plate and serve egg on the side.
7. Dip asparagus into the egg and eat while warm.

Nutrition: Calories: 178 Fat: 13g Carbs: 1g Protein: 7.72g Calories 178 Sodium: 71mg Potassium: 203mg Phosphorus: 124mg

37. Egg Drop Soup

Preparation Time: 5 minutes
Cooking Time: 10 minutes
Servings: 4

Ingredients:

- ¼ cup minced fresh chives
- 4 cups unsalted vegetable stock
- 4 whisked eggs

Directions:

1. Pour unsalted vegetable stock into the oven set over high heat. Bring to a boil. Lower heat.
2. Pour in the eggs. Stir until ribbons form into the soup.
3. Turn off the heat immediately. The residual heat will cook eggs through.
4. Cool slightly before ladling the desired amount into individual bowls. Garnish with a pinch of parsley, if using.
5. Serve immediately.

Nutrition: Calories: 73 Fat: 3g Carbs: 1g Protein: 7g Sodium: 891mg Potassium: 53mg Phosphorus: 36mg

38. Breakfast Salad from Grains and Fruits

Preparation Time: 5 minutes
Cooking Time: 15 minutes
Servings: 6

Ingredients:

- 1 8 oz low fat vanilla yogurt
- 1 mango
- 1 Red delicious apple
- 1 Granny Smith apple
- ¾ cup bulgur
- ¼ teaspoon salt
- 3 cups water

Direction:

1. On high fire, place a large pot and bring water to a boil.
2. Add bulgur and rice. Lower fire to a simmer and cooks for ten minutes while covered.
3. Turn off fire, set aside for 2 minutes while covered.
4. In baking sheet, transfer and evenly spread grains to cool.
5. Meanwhile, peel mango and cut into sections. Chop and core apples.
6. Once grains are cool, transfer to a large serving bowl along with fruits.
7. Add yogurt and mix well to coat.
8. Serve and enjoy.

Nutrition: Calories: 187; Carbs: 4g; Protein: 6g; Fats: g; Phosphorus: 60 mg; Potassium: 55 mg; Sodium: 117mg

39. French toast with Applesauce

Preparation Time: 5 minutes
Cooking Time: 15 minutes
Servings: 6

Ingredients:

- ¼ cup unsweetened applesauce
- ½ cup almond milk
- 1 teaspoon ground cinnamon
- 2 eggs
- 2 tablespoon white sugar

Directions:

1. Mix well applesauce, sugar, cinnamon, almond milk and eggs in a mixing bowl.
2. Soak the bread, one by one into applesauce mixture until wet.
3. On medium fire, heat a nonstick skillet greased with cooking spray.
4. Add soaked bread one at a time and cook for 2-3 minutes per side or until lightly browned.
5. Serve and enjoy.

Nutrition: Calories: 57; Carbs: 6g; Protein: 4g; Fats: 4g; Phosphorus: 69mg; Potassium: 88mg; Sodium: 43mg

40. Bagels Made Healthy

Preparation Time: 5 minutes
Cooking Time: 25 minutes
Servings: 8
Ingredients:
- 2 teaspoon yeast
- 1 ½ tablespoon olive oil
- 1 ¼ cups bread flour
- 2 cups whole wheat flour
- 1 tablespoon vinegar
- 2 tablespoon honey
- 1 ½ cups warm water

Directions:
1. In a bread machine, mix all ingredients, and then process on dough cycle.
2. Once done or end of cycle, create 8 pieces shaped like a flattened ball.
3. In the center of each ball, make a hole using your thumb then create a donut shape.
4. In a greased baking sheet, place donut-shaped dough then covers and let it rise about ½ hour.
5. Prepare about 2 inches of water to boil in a large pan.
6. In a boiling water, drop one at a time the bagels and boil for 1 minute, then turn them once.
7. Remove them and return them to baking sheet and bake at 350oF (175oC) for about 20 to 25 minutes until golden brown.

Nutrition: Calories: 221; Crabs: 42g; Protein: 7g; Fats: g; Phosphorus: 130mg; Potassium: 166mg; Sodium: 47mg

41. Pasta with Indian Lentils

Preparation Time: 5 minutes
Cooking Time: 0 minutes
Servings: 6

Ingredients:
- ¼-½ cup fresh cilantro (chopped)
- 3 cups water
- 2 small dry red peppers (whole)
- 1 teaspoon turmeric
- 1 teaspoon ground cumin
- 2-3 cloves garlic (minced)
- 1 can (15 ounces) cubed Red bell peppers (with juice)
- 1 large onion (chopped)
- ½ cup dry lentils (rinsed)
- ½ cup orzo or tiny pasta

Directions:
1. In a skillet, combine all ingredients except for the cilantro then boil on medium-high heat.
2. Ensure to cover and slightly reduce heat to medium-low and simmer until pasta is tender for about 35 minutes.
3. Afterwards, take out the chili peppers then add cilantro and top it with low-fat sour cream.

Nutrition: Calories: 175; Carbs: 40g; Protein: 3g; Fats: 2g; Phosphorus: 139mg; Potassium: 513mg; Sodium: 61mg

42. Pineapple Bread

Preparation Time: 20 Minutes
Cooking Time: 1 Hour
Servings: 10
Ingredients:
- 1/3 cup Swerve
- 1/3 cup butter, unsalted
- 2 eggs
- 2 cups flour
- 3 teaspoons baking powder
- 1 cup pineapple, undrained
- 6 cherries, chopped

Directions:
1. Whisk the Swerve with the butter in a mixer until fluffy.
2. Stir in the eggs, then beat again.

3. Add the baking powder and flour, then mix well until smooth.
4. Fold in the cherries and pineapple.
5. Spread this cherry-pineapple batter in a 9x5 inch baking pan.
6. Bake the pineapple batter for 1 hour at 350 degrees F.
7. Slice the bread and serve.

Nutrition: Calories 197, Total Fat 7.2g, Sodium 85mg, Dietary Fiber 1.1g, Sugars 3 g, Protein 4g, Calcium 79mg, Phosphorous 316mg, Potassium 227mg

43. Garlic Mayo Bread

Preparation Time: 10 minutes
Cooking Time: 5 minutes
Servings: 16
Ingredients:
- 3 tablespoons vegetable oil
- 4 cloves garlic, minced
- 2 teaspoons paprika
- Dash cayenne pepper
- 1 teaspoon lemon juice
- 2 tablespoons Parmesan cheese, grated
- 3/4 cup mayonnaise
- 1 loaf (1 lb.) French bread, sliced
- 1 teaspoon Italian herbs

Directions:
1. Mix the garlic with the oil in a small bowl and leave it overnight.
2. Discard the garlic from the bowl and keep the garlic-infused oil.
3. Mix the garlic-oil with cayenne, paprika, lemon juice, mayonnaise, and Parmesan.
4. Place the bread slices in a baking tray lined with parchment paper.
5. Top these slices with the mayonnaise mixture and drizzle the Italian herbs on top.
6. Broil these slices for 5 minutes until golden brown.
7. Serve warm.

Nutrition: Calories 217, Total Fat 7.9g, Sodium 423mg, Dietary Fiber 1.3g, Sugars 2g, Protein 7g, Calcium 56mg, Phosphorous 347mg, Potassium 72mg

44. Strawberry Topped Waffles

Preparation Time: 15 minutes
Cooking Time: 20 minutes
Servings: 5
Ingredients:
- 1 cup flour
- 1/4 cup Swerve
- 1 ¾ teaspoons baking powder
- 1 egg, separated
- ¾ cup almond milk
- ½ cup butter, melted
- ½ teaspoon vanilla extract
- Fresh strawberries, sliced

Directions:
1. Prepare and preheat your waffle pan following the instructions of the machine.
2. Begin by mixing the flour with Swerve and baking soda in a bowl.
3. Separate the egg yolks from the egg whites, keeping them in two separate bowls.
4. Add the almond milk and vanilla extract to the egg yolks.
5. Stir the melted butter and mix well until smooth.
6. Now beat the egg whites with an electric beater until foamy and fluffy.
7. Fold this fluffy composition in the egg yolk mixture.
8. Mix it gently until smooth, then add in the flour mixture.
9. Stir again to make a smooth mixture.
10. Pour a half cup of the waffle batter in a preheated pan and cook until the waffle is done.

11. Cook more waffles with the remaining batter.
12. Serve fresh with strawberries on top.

Nutrition: Calories 342, Total Fat 20.5g, Sodium 156mg, Dietary Fiber 0.7g, Sugars 3.5g, Protein 4.8g, Calcium 107mg, Phosphorous 126mg, Potassium 233mg

45. Cheese Spaghetti Frittata

Preparation Time: 10 minutes
Cooking Time: 10 minutes
Servings: 6
Ingredients:

- 4 cups whole-wheat spaghetti, cooked
- 4 teaspoons olive oil
- 3 medium onions, chopped
- 4 large eggs
- 1/2 cup almond milk
- 1/3 cup Parmesan cheese, grated
- 2 tablespoons fresh parsley, chopped
- 2 tablespoons fresh basil, chopped
- 1/2 teaspoon black pepper
- 1 tomato, diced

Directions:
1. Set a suitable non-stick skillet over moderate heat and add in the olive oil.
2. Place the spaghetti in the skillet and cook by stirring for 2 minutes on moderate heat.
3. Whisk the eggs with almond milk, parsley, and black pepper in a bowl.
4. Pour this almond milky egg mixture over the spaghetti and top it all with basil, cheese, and tomato.
5. Cover the spaghetti frittata again with a lid and cook for approximately 8 minutes on low heat.
6. Slice and serve.

Nutrition: Calories 230, Total Fat 7.8g, Sodium 77mg, Dietary Fiber 5.6g, Sugars 4.5g, Protein 11.1g,
Calcium 88mg, Phosphorous 368 mg, Potassium 214mg,

46. Shrimp Bruschetta

Preparation Time: 15 minutes
Cooking Time: 10 minutes
Servings: 4
Ingredients:

- 13 oz. shrimps, peeled
- 1 tablespoon tomato sauce
- ½ teaspoon Splenda
- ¼ teaspoon garlic powder
- 1 teaspoon fresh parsley, chopped
- ½ teaspoon olive oil
- 1 teaspoon lemon juice
- 4 whole-grain bread slices
- 1 cup water, for cooking

Directions:
1. In the saucepan, pour water and bring it to boil.
2. Add shrimps and boil them over the high heat for 5 minutes.
3. After this, drain shrimps and chill them to the room temperature.
4. Mix up together shrimps with Splenda, garlic powder, tomato sauce, and fresh parsley.
5. Add lemon juice and stir gently.
6. Preheat the oven to 360f.
7. Coat the slice of bread with olive oil and bake for 3 minutes.
8. Then place the shrimp mixture on the bread. Bruschetta is cooked.

Nutrition: Calories 199, Fat 3.7, Fiber 2.1, Carbs 15.3, Protein 24.1 Calcium 79mg, Phosphorous 316mg, Potassium 227mg Sodium: 121 mg

47. Strawberry Muesli

Preparation Time: 10 minutes
Cooking Time: 30 minutes
Servings: 4
Ingredients:
- 2 cups Greek yogurt
- 1 ½ cup strawberries, sliced
- 1 ½ cup Muesli
- 4 teaspoon maple syrup
- ¾ teaspoon ground cinnamon

Directions:
1. Put Greek yogurt in the food processor.
2. Add 1 cup of strawberries, maple syrup, and ground cinnamon.
3. Blend the ingredients until you get smooth mass.
4. Transfer the yogurt mass in the serving bowls.
5. Add Muesli and stir well.
6. Leave the meal for 30 minutes in the fridge.
7. After this, decorate it with remaining sliced strawberries.

Nutrition: Calories 149, Fat 2.6, Fiber 3.6,Carbs 21.6, Protein 12 Calcium 69mg, Phosphorous 216mg, Potassium 227mg Sodium: 151 mg

48. Yogurt Bulgur

Preparation Time: 10 minutes
Cooking Time: 15 minutes
Servings: 3
Ingredients:
- 1 cup bulgur
- 2 cups Greek yogurt
- 1 ½ cup water
- ½ teaspoon salt
- 1 teaspoon olive oil

Directions:
1. Pour olive oil in the saucepan and add bulgur.

2. Roast it over the medium heat for 2-3 minutes. Stir it from time to time.
3. After this, add salt and water.
4. Close the lid and cook bulgur for 15 minutes over the medium heat.
5. Then chill the cooked bulgur well and combine it with Greek yogurt. Stir it carefully.
6. Transfer the cooked meal into the serving plates. The yogurt bulgur tastes the best when it is cold.

Nutrition: Calories 274, Fat 4.9, Fiber 8.5, Carbs 40.8, Protein 19.2Calcium 39mg, Phosphorous 216mg, Potassium 237mg Sodium: 131 mg

49. Grandma's Pancake Special

Preparation Time: 5 minutes
Cooking Time: 15 minutes
Servings: 3
Ingredients:
- 1 tablespoon oil
- 1 cup almond milk
- 1 egg
- 2 teaspoons sodium free baking powder
- 2 tablespoons sugar
- 1 ¼ cups flour

Directions:
1. Mix together all the dry ingredients such as the flour, sugar and baking powder.
2. Combine oil, almond milk and egg in another bowl. Once done, add them all to the flour mixture.
3. Make sure that as your stir the mixture, blend them together until slightly lumpy.

4. In a hot greased griddle, pour-in at least ¼ cup of the batter to make each pancake.
5. To cook, ensure that the bottom is a bit brown, then turn and cook the other side, as well.

Nutrition: Calories: 167; Carbs: 50g; Protein: 11g; Fats: 11g; Phosphorus: 176mg; Potassium: 215mg; Sodium: 70mg

50. Parmesan Zucchini Frittata

Preparation Time: 10 minutes
Cooking Time: 35 minutes
Servings: 6
Ingredients:
- 1 tablespoon olive oil
- 1 cup yellow onion, sliced
- 3 cups zucchini, chopped
- ½ cup Parmesan cheese, grated
- 8 large eggs
- 1/2 teaspoon black pepper
- 1/8 teaspoon paprika
- 3 tablespoons parsley, chopped

Directions:
1. Toss the zucchinis with the onion, parsley, and all other ingredients in a large bowl.
2. Pour this zucchini-garlic mixture in an 11x7 inches pan and spread it evenly.
3. Bake the zucchini casserole for approximately 35 minutes at 350 degrees F.
4. Cut in slices and serve.

Nutrition: Calories 142, Total Fat 9.7g, Saturated Fat 2.8g, Cholesterol 250mg, Sodium 123mg, Carbohydrate 4.7g, Dietary Fiber 1.3g, Sugars 2.4g, Protein 10.2g, Calcium 73mg, Phosphorous 375mg, Potassium 286mg

51. Green lettuce Bacon Breakfast Bake

Preparation Time: 10 minutes
Cooking Time: 45 minutes
Servings: 6
Ingredients:
- 10 eggs
- 3 cups baby green lettuce, chopped
- 1 tbsp. olive oil
- 8 bacon slices, cooked and chopped
- 2 Red bell peppers, sliced
- 2 tbsp. chives, chopped
- Pepper
- Salt

Directions:
1. Preheat the oven to 350 F.
2. Spray a baking dish with cooking spray and set aside.
3. Heat oil in a pan
4. Add green lettuce and cook until green lettuce wilted.
5. In a mixing bowl, whisk eggs and salt. Add green lettuce and chives and stir well.
6. Pour egg mixture into the baking dish.
7. Top with Red bell peppers and bacon and bake for 45 minutes.
8. Serve and enjoy.

Nutrition: Calories 273 Fat 20.4g Carbohydrates 3.1g Sugar 1.7g Protein 19.4g Cholesterol 301 mg

52. Mozzarella Cheese Omelet

Preparation Time: 10 minutes
Cooking Time: 5 minutes
Servings: 1
Ingredients:
- 4 eggs, beaten
- 1/4 cup mozzarella cheese, shredded
- 4 tomato slices

- 1/4 tsp. Italian seasoning
- 1/4 tsp. dried oregano
- Pepper
- Salt

Directions:
1. In a small bowl, whisk eggs with salt.
2. Spray pan with cooking spray and heat over medium heat.
3. Pour egg mixture into the pan and cook over medium heat.
4. Once eggs are set then sprinkle oregano and Italian seasoning on top.
5. Arrange tomato slices on top of the omelet and sprinkle with shredded cheese.
6. Cook omelet for 1 minute.
7. Serve and enjoy.

Nutrition: Calories 285 Fat 19g Carbohydrates 4g Sugar 3g Protein 25g Cholesterol 655 mg

53. Sun-Dried Tomato Frittata

Preparation Time: 10 minutes
Cooking Time: 20 minutes
Servings: 8
Ingredients:
- 12 eggs
- 1/2 tsp. dried basil
- 1/4 cup parmesan cheese, grated
- 2 cups baby green lettuce, shredded
- 1/4 cup sun-dried Red bell peppers, sliced
- Pepper
- Salt

Directions:
1. Preheat the oven to 425 F. In a large bowl, whisk eggs with pepper and salt.
2. Add remaining ingredients and stir to combine. Spray oven-safe pan with cooking spray.

3. Pour egg mixture into the pan and bake for 20 minutes.
4. Slice and serve.

Nutrition: Calories 115 Fat 7g Carbohydrates 1g Sugar 1g Protein 10g Cholesterol 250 mg

54. Sausage Cheese Bake Omelet

Preparation Time: 10 minutes
Cooking Time: 45 minutes
Servings: 8
Ingredients:
- 16 eggs
- 2 cups cheddar cheese, shredded
- 1/2 cup salsa
- 1 lb. ground sausage
- 1 1/2 cups coconut almond milk
- Pepper
- Salt

Directions:
1. Preheat the oven to 350 F.
2. Add sausage in a pan and cook until browned. Drain excess fat.
3. In a large bowl, whisk eggs and almond milk. Stir in cheese, cooked sausage, and salsa.
4. Pour omelet mixture into the baking dish and bake for 45 minutes.
5. Serve and enjoy.

Nutrition: Calories 360 Fat 24g Carbohydrates 4g Sugar 3g Protein 28g Cholesterol 400 mg

55. Cornbread with Southern Twist

Preparation Time: 15 minutes
Cooking Time: 60 minutes
Servings: 8
Ingredients:
- 2 tablespoons shortening
- 1 ¼ cups skim almond milk
- ¼ cup egg substitute

- 4 tablespoons sodium free baking powder
- ½ cup flour
- 1 ½ cups cornmeal

Directions:
1. Prepare 8 x 8-inch baking dish or a black iron skillet then add shortening.
2. Put the baking dish or skillet inside the oven on 425oF, once the shortening has melted that means the pan is hot already.
3. In a bowl, add almond milk and egg then mix well.
4. Take out the skillet and add the melted shortening into the batter and stir well.
5. Pour all mixed ingredients into skillet.
6. For 15 to 20 minutes, cook in the oven until golden brown.

Nutrition: Calories: 166; Carbs: 35g; Protein: 5g;
Fats: 1g; Phosphorus: 79mg; Potassium: 122mg; Sodium: 34mg

56. Greek Egg Scrambled

Preparation Time: 10 minutes
Cooking Time: 10 minutes
Servings: 2
Ingredients:
- 4 eggs
- 1/2 cup grape Red bell peppers, sliced
- 2 tbsp. green onions, sliced
- 1 bell pepper, diced
- 1 tbsp. olive oil
- 1/4 tsp. dried oregano
- 1/2 tbsp. capers
- Pepper
- Salt

Directions:
1. Heat oil in a pan over medium heat
2. Add green onions and bell pepper and cook until pepper is softened.

3. Add eggs and stir until eggs are cooked. Season it with oregano, pepper, and salt.
4. Serve and enjoy.

Nutrition: Calories 230 Fat 17g Carbohydrates 8g Sugar 5g Protein 12g Cholesterol 325 mg

57. Feta Mint Omelet

Preparation Time: 10 minutes
Cooking Time: 5 minutes
Servings: 1
Ingredients:
- 3 eggs
- 1/4 cup fresh mint, chopped
- 2 tbsp. coconut almond milk
- 1/2 tsp. olive oil
- 2 tbsp. feta cheese, crumbled
- Pepper
- Salt

Directions:
1. In a bowl, whisk eggs with feta cheese, mint, almond milk, pepper, and salt.
2. Heat olive oil in a pan over low heat. Pour egg mixture in the pan and cook until eggs are set.
3. Flip omelet and cook for 2 minutes more.
4. Serve and enjoy.

Nutrition: Calories 275 Fat 20g Carbohydrates 4g Sugar 2g Protein 20g Cholesterol 505 mg

58. Sausage Breakfast Casserole

Preparation Time: 10 minutes
Cooking Time: 50 minutes
Servings: 8
Ingredients:
- 12 eggs
- 1 lb. ground Italian sausage
- 2 1/2 Red bell peppers, sliced
- 3 tbsp. coconut flour
- 1/4 cup coconut almond milk

- 2 small zucchinis, shredded
- Pepper
- Salt

Directions:
1. Preheat the oven to 350 F.
2. Spray casserole dish with cooking spray and set aside.
3. Cook sausage in a pan until brown.
4. Transfer sausage to a mixing bowl.
5. Add coconut flour, almond milk, eggs, zucchini, pepper, and salt. Stir well.
6. Add eggs and whisk to combine.
7. Transfer bowl mixture into the casserole dish and top with tomato slices.
8. Bake for 50 minutes.
9. Serve and enjoy.

Nutrition: Calories 305 Fat 21.8g Carbohydrates 6.3g Sugar 3.3g Protein 19.6g Cholesterol 286 mg

59. Healthy Green lettuce Tomato Muffins

Preparation Time: 10 minutes
Cooking Time: 20 minutes
Servings: 12
Ingredients:
- 12 eggs
- 1/2 tsp. Italian seasoning
- 1 cup Red bell peppers, chopped
- 4 tbsp. water
- 1 cup fresh green lettuce, chopped
- Pepper
- Salt

Directions:
1. Preheat the oven to 350 F. Spray a muffin tray with cooking spray and set aside.
2. In a mixing bowl, whisk eggs with water, Italian seasoning, pepper, and salt.
3. Add green lettuce and Red bell peppers and stir well.

4. Pour egg mixture into the prepared muffin tray and bake for 20 minutes.
5. Serve and enjoy.

Nutrition: Calories 67 Fat 4.5g Carbohydrates 1g Sugar 0.8g Protein 5.7g Cholesterol 164 mg

60. Breakfast Egg Salad

Preparation Time: 10 minutes
Cooking Time: 5 minutes
Servings: 4
Ingredients:
- 6 eggs, hard-boiled, peeled and chopped
- 1 tbsp. fresh dill, chopped
- 4 tbsp. mayonnaise
- Pepper
- Salt

Directions:
1. Add all ingredients into the large bowl and stir to mix. Serve and enjoy.

Nutrition: Calories 140 Fat 10g Carbohydrates 4g Sugar 1g Protein 8g Cholesterol 245 mg

61. Turkey and Green Lettuce Scramble on Melba toast

Preparation Time: 2 minutes
Cooking Time: 15 minutes
Servings: 2
Ingredients:
- Extra virgin olive oil – 1 tsp.
- Raw green lettuce – 1 cup
- Garlic – 1/2 clove, minced
- Nutmeg – 1 tsp. grated
- Cooked and diced turkey breast – 1 cup
- Melba toast – 4 slices
- Balsamic vinegar – 1 tsp.

Directions:
1. Heat a skillet over medium heat and add oil.

2. Add turkey and heat through for 6 to 8 minutes.
3. Add green lettuce, garlic, and nutmeg and stir-fry for 6 minutes more.
4. Plate up the Melba toast and top with green lettuce and turkey scramble.
5. Drizzle with balsamic vinegar and serve.

Nutrition: Calories: 301 Fat: 19g Carb: 12g Phosphorus: 215mg Potassium: 269mg Sodium: 360mg Protein: 19g

62. Breakfast Smoothie

Preparation Time: 15 minutes
Cooking Time: 0 minutes
Servings: 2
Ingredients:
- Frozen blueberries – 1 cup
- Pineapple chunks – 1/2 cup
- English cucumber – 1/2 cup
- Apple – 1/2
- Water – 1/2 cup

Directions:
1. Put the pineapple, blueberries, cucumber, apple, and water in a blender and blend until thick and smooth.
2. Pour into 2 glasses and serve.

Nutrition: Calories: 87 Fat: g Carb: 22g Phosphorus: 28mg Potassium: 192mg Sodium: 3mg Protein: 0.7g

63. Salad with Vinaigrette

Preparation Time: 25 minutes
Cooking Time: 0 minutes
Servings: 4
Ingredients:
For the vinaigrette:
- Olive oil – 1/2 cup
- Balsamic vinegar - 4 Tbsps.
- Chopped fresh oregano – 2 Tbsps.
- Pinch red pepper flakes
- Ground black pepper

For the salad
- Shredded green leaf lettuce – 4 cups
- Carrot – 1, shredded
- Fresh green beans – ¾ cup, cut into 1-inch pieces
- Large radishes – 3, sliced thin

Directions:
1. To make the vinaigrette: put the vinaigrette Ingredients in a bowl and whisk.
2. To make the salad, in a bowl, toss together the carrot, lettuce, green beans, and radishes.
3. Add the vinaigrette to the vegetables and toss to coat.
4. Arrange the salad on plates and serve.

Nutrition: Calories: 273 Fat: 27g Carb: 7g Phosphorus: 30mg Potassium: 197mg Sodium: 27mg Protein: 1g

64. Shrimp with Salsa

Preparation Time: 15 minutes
Cooking Time: 10 minutes
Servings: 4
Ingredients:
- Olive oil – 2 Tbsp.
- Large shrimp – 6 ounces, peeled and deveined, tails left on
- Minced garlic – 1 tsp.
- Chopped English cucumber – 1/2 cup
- Chopped mango – 1/2 cup
- Zest of 1 lime
- Juice of 1 lime
- Ground black pepper
- Lime wedges for garnish

Directions:
1. Soak 4 wooden skewers in water for 30 minutes.
2. Preheat the barbecue to medium heat.
3. In a bowl, toss together the olive oil, shrimp, and garlic.

4. Thread the shrimp onto the skewers, about 4 shrimp per skewer.
5. In a bowl, stir together the mango, cucumber, lime zest, and lime juice, and season the salsa lightly with pepper. Set aside.
6. Grill the shrimp for 10 minutes, turning once or until the shrimp is opaque and cooked through.
7. Season the shrimp lightly with pepper.
8. Serve the shrimp on the cucumber salsa with lime wedges on the side.

Nutrition: Calories: 120 Fat: 8g Carb: 4g Phosphorus: 91mg Potassium: 129mg Sodium: 60mg Protein: 9g

65. Scrambled Eggs and Pesto

Preparation Time: 5 minutes
Cooking Time: 5 minutes
Servings: 2
Ingredients:
- 3 large whole eggs
- 1 tablespoon almond butter
- 1 tablespoon pesto
- 2 tablespoons creamed coconut almond milk
- Salt and pepper as needed

Directions:
1. Take a bowl and crack open your egg
2. Flavor with a salt and pepper
3. Pour eggs into a pan
4. Add butter and introduce heat
5. Cook on low heat and gently add pesto
6. Once the egg is cooked and scrambled, remove from the heat
7. Spoon in coconut cream and mix well
8. Turn on the heat and cook on LOW until you have a creamy texture
9. Serve and enjoy!

Nutrition: Calories: 467 Fat: 41g Carbohydrates: 3g Protein: 20g

66. Vegetable Omelet

Preparation Time: 15 minutes
Cooking Time: 10 minutes
Servings: 3
Ingredients:
- Egg whites – 4
- Egg – 1
- Chopped fresh parsley – 2 Tbsps.
- Water – 2 Tbsps.
- Olive oil spray
- Chopped and boiled red bell pepper – 1/2 cup
- Chopped scallion – 1/4 cup, both green and white parts
- Ground black pepper

Directions:
1. Whisk together the egg, egg whites, parsley, and water until well blended. Set aside.
2. Spray a skillet with olive oil spray and place over medium heat.
3. Sauté the peppers and scallion for 3 minutes or until softened.
4. Pour the egg mixture into the skillet over vegetables and cook, swirling the skillet, for 2 minutes or until the edges start to set. Cook until set.
5. Season with black pepper and serve.

Nutrition: Calories: 77 Fat: 3g Carb: 2g Phosphorus: 67mg Potassium: 194mg Sodium: 229mg Protein: 12g

67. Pesto Pork Chops

Preparation Time: 20 minutes
Cooking Time: 20 minutes
Servings: 4
Ingredients:
- Pork top-loin chops – 4 (3-ounce) boneless, fat trimmed
- Herb pesto – 8 tsps.
- Breadcrumbs – 1/2 cup

- Olive oil – 1 Tbsp.

Directions:
1. Preheat the oven to 450F.
2. Line a baking sheet with foil. Set aside.
3. Rub 1 tsp. of pesto evenly over both sides of each pork chop.
4. Lightly dredge each pork chop in the breadcrumbs.
5. Heat the oil in a skillet.
6. Brown the pork chops on each side for 5 minutes.
7. Place the pork chops on the baking sheet.
8. Bake for 10 minutes or until pork reaches 145F in the center.

Nutrition: Calories: 210 Fat: 7g Carb: 10g Phosphorus: 179mg Potassium: 220mg Sodium: 148mg Protein: 24g

68. Turkey Burgers

Preparation Time: 15 minutes
Cooking Time: 8 minutes
Servings: 5
Ingredients:
- 1 ripe pear, peeled, cored and chopped roughly
- 1-pound lean ground turkey
- 1 teaspoon fresh ginger, grated finely
- 2 minced garlic cloves
- 1 teaspoon fresh rosemary, minced
- 1 teaspoon fresh sage, minced
- Salt, to taste
- Freshly ground black pepper, to taste
- 1-2 tablespoons coconut oil

Directions:
1. In a blender, add pear and pulse till smooth.
2. Transfer the pear mixture in a large bowl with remaining ingredients except for oil and mix till well combined.
3. Make small equal sized 10 patties from the mixture.

4. In a heavy-bottomed frying pan, heat oil on medium heat.
5. Add the patties and cook for around 4-5 minutes.
6. Flip the inside and cook for approximately 2-3 minutes.

Nutrition: Calories: 477 Fat: 15g Carbohydrates: 26g Fiber: 11g Protein: 35g

69. Simple Zucchini BBQ

Preparation Time: 10 minutes
Cooking Time: 10 minutes
Servings: 2
Ingredients:
- Olive oil as needed
- 3 zucchini
- ½ teaspoon black pepper
- ½ teaspoon mustard
- ½ teaspoon cumin
- 1 teaspoon paprika
- 1 teaspoon garlic powder
- 1 tablespoon of sea salt
- 1-2 stevia
- 1 tablespoon chili powder

Directions:
1. Preheat your oven to 300°F
2. Take a small bowl and add cayenne, black pepper, salt, garlic, mustard, paprika, chili powder, and stevia
3. Mix well
4. Slice zucchini into 1/8 inch slices and spray them with olive oil
5. Sprinkle spice blend over zucchini and bake for 40 minutes
6. Remove and flip, spray with more olive oil and leftover spice
7. Bake for 20 minutes more
8. Serve!

Nutrition: Calories: 163 Fat: 14g Carbohydrates: 3g Protein: 8g

70. Sweet Pancakes

Preparation Time: 10 minutes
Cooking Time: 5 minutes
Servings: 5
Ingredients:
- All-purpose flour – 1 cup
- Granulated sugar – 1 Tbsp.
- Baking powder – 2 tsps.
- Egg whites – 2
- Almond milk - 1 cup
- Olive oil - 2 Tbsps.
- Maple extract – 1 Tbsp.

Directions:
1. Mix the flour, sugar and baking powder in a bowl.
2. Make a well in the center and place to one side.
3. In another bowl, mix the egg whites, almond milk, oil, and maple extract.
4. Add the egg mixture to the well and gently mix until a batter is formed.
5. Heat skillet over medium heat.
6. Add 1/5 of the batter to the pan and cook 2 minutes on each side or until the pancake is golden.
7. Repeat with the remaining batter and serve.

Nutrition: Calories: 178 Fat: 6g Carb: 25g Phosphorus: 116mg Potassium: 126mg Sodium: 297mg Protein: 6g

71. Angel Eggs

Preparation Time: 15 minutes
Cooking Time: 10 minutes
Servings: 2
Ingredients:
- 4 eggs, hardboiled and peeled
- 1 tablespoon vanilla bean sweetener, sugar-free
- 2 tablespoons Keto-Friendly mayonnaise
- 1/8 teaspoon cinnamon

Directions:
1. Halve the boiled eggs and scoop out the yolk
2. Place in a bowl
3. Add egg whites on a plate
4. Add sweetener, cinnamon, mayo to the egg yolks and mash them well
5. Transfer the yolk mix to white halves

Nutrition: Calories: 184 Fat: 15g Carbohydrates: 1g Protein: 12g

72. Collard Greens Dish

Preparation Time: 10 minutes
Cooking Time: 60 minutes
Servings: 6
Ingredients:
- 1 tablespoon olive oil
- 3 slices of bacon, sliced
- 1 large onion, chopped
- 2 garlic cloves, minced
- 1 teaspoon salt
- 3 cups chicken broth
- 1 red pepper flake
- 1-pound fresh collard greens, cut into 2-inch pieces

Directions:
1. Take a large-sized pan
2. Put oil and allow the oil to heat it up
3. Add bacon and cook it until crispy and remove it, crumble the bacon and add the crumbled bacon to the pan
4. Add onion and keep cooking for 5 minutes
5. Add garlic and cook until you have a nice fragrance
6. Add collard greens and keep frying until wilted, add chicken broth and season with pepper, salt, and red pepper flakes
7. Lessening the heat and cover with a lid, simmer for 45 minutes
8. Enjoy!

Nutrition: Calories: 127 Fat: 10g Carbohydrates: 8g Protein: 4g

73. Denver Omelets

Preparation Time: 4 minutes
Cooking Time: 1 minute
Servings: 2
Ingredients:

- 2 tablespoons almond butter
- ¼ cup onion, chopped
- ¼ cup green bell pepper, diced
- 2 whole eggs
- ¼ cup ham, chopped

Directions:

1. Put a skillet and place it over medium heat
2. Add butter and wait until the butter melts
3. Add onion and bell pepper and sauté for a few minutes
4. Take a bowl and whip eggs
5. Add the remaining ingredients and stir
6. Add sautéed onion and pepper, stir
7. Microwave the egg mix for 1 minute

Nutrition: Calories: 605 Fat: 46g Carbohydrates: 6g Protein: 39g

74. Salad with Lemon Dressing

Preparation Time: 10 minutes

Cooking Time: 0 minutes
Servings: 4
Ingredients:

- Heavy cream – 1/4 cup
- Freshly squeezed lemon juice – 1/4 cup
- Granulated sugar – 2 Tbsps.
- Chopped fresh dill – 2 Tbsps.
- Finely chopped scallion – 2 Tbsps. green part only
- Ground black pepper – 1/4 tsp.
- English cucumber – 1, sliced thin
- Shredded green cabbage – 2 cups

Directions:

1. In a small bowl, stir together the lemon juice, cream, sugar, dill, scallion, and pepper until well blended.
2. In a large bowl, toss together the cucumber and cabbage.
3. Place the salad in the refrigerator and chill for 1 hour.
4. Stir before serving.

Nutrition: Calories: 99 Fat: 6g Carb: 13g Phosphorus: 38mg Potassium: 200mg Sodium: 14mg
Protein: 2g

75. Scrambled Turkey Eggs

Preparation Time: 15 minutes
Cooking Time: 15 minutes
Servings: 2
Ingredients:

- 1 tablespoon coconut oil
- 1 medium red bell pepper, diced
- ½ medium yellow onion, diced
- ¼ teaspoon hot pepper sauce
- 3 large free-range eggs
- ¼ teaspoon black pepper, freshly ground
- ¼ teaspoon salt

Directions:

1. Put a pan to medium-high heat and add coconut oil, let it heat up
2. Add onions and Saute
3. Add turkey and red pepper
4. Cook until turkey is cooked
5. Take a bowl and beat eggs, stir in salt and pepper
6. Pour eggs in the pan with turkey and gently cook and scramble eggs
7. Top with hot sauce and enjoy!

Nutrition: Calories: 435 Fat: 30g Carbohydrates: 34g Protein: 16g

76. Pineapple Oatmeal

Preparation Time: 10 minutes
Cooking Time: 4-8 hours
Servings: 5
Ingredients:

- 1 cup steel-cut oats
- 4 cups unsweetened almond almond milk
- 2 medium apples, slashed
- 1 teaspoon coconut oil
- 1 teaspoon cinnamon
- ¼ teaspoon nutmeg
- 2 tablespoons maple syrup, unsweetened
- A drizzle of lemon juice

Directions:
1. Add the listed ingredients to a cooking pan and mix well
2. Cook on a very low flame for 8 hours or on high flame for 4 hours
3. Gently stir
4. Add your desired toppings
5. Stock in the fridge for later use, make sure to add a splash of almond almond milk after re-heating for added flavor

Nutrition: Calories: 180 Fat: 5g Carbohydrates: 31g Protein: 5g

77. Lemon Broccoli

Preparation Time: 10 minutes
Cooking Time: 15 minutes
Servings: 4
Ingredients:

- 2 heads broccoli, separated into florets
- 2 teaspoons extra virgin olive oil
- 1 teaspoon salt
- ½ teaspoon pepper
- 1 garlic clove, minced
- ½ teaspoon lemon juice

Directions:
1. Pre-heat your oven to a temperature of 400 °F
2. Take a large-sized bowl and add broccoli florets with some extra virgin olive oil, pepper, sea salt and garlic
3. Spread the broccoli out in a single even layer on a fine baking sheet
4. Bake in your pre-heated oven for about 15-20 minutes until the florets are soft enough so that they can be pierced with a fork
5. Squeeze lemon juice over them generously before serving
6. Enjoy!

Nutrition: Calories: 49 Fat: 2g Carbohydrates: 4g Protein: 3g

78. Pepperoni Omelet

Preparation Time: 5 minutes
Cooking Time: 20 minutes
Servings: 2
Ingredients:

- 3 eggs
- 7 pepperoni slices
- 1 teaspoon coconut cream
- Salt and ground black pepper, to taste
- 2 tablespoon almond butter

Directions:

1. Take a bowl and whisk eggs with all the remaining ingredients
2. Then take a skillet and heat the butter
3. Pour one quarter of the egg mixture into your skillet
4. After that, cook for 2 minutes per side
5. Repeat to use the entire batter

Nutrition: Calories: 141 Fat: 11.5g Carbohydrates: 0.6g Protein: 8.9g

79. Eggplant Fries

Preparation Time: 15 minutes
Cooking Time: 10 minutes
Servings: 8
Ingredients:

- 2 eggs
- 2 cups almond flour
- 2 tablespoons coconut oil, spray
- 2 eggplants, peeled and cut thinly
- Salt and pepper

Directions:
1. Preheat your oven to 400 °F
2. Take a bowl and mix with salt and black pepper in it
3. Take another bowl and beat eggs until frothy
4. Dip the eggplant pieces into the eggs
5. Then coat them with the flour mixture
6. Add another layer of flour and egg
7. Then, take a baking sheet and grease with coconut oil on top
8. Bake for about 15 minutes

Nutrition: Calories: 212 Fat: 15.8g Carbohydrates: 12.1g Protein: 8.6g

80. Simple Chia Porridge

Preparation Time: 10 minutes
Cooking Time: 5-10 minutes
Servings: 2
Ingredients:

- 1 tablespoon chia seeds
- 1 tablespoon ground flaxseed

- 1/3 cup coconut cream
- ½ cup of water
- 1 teaspoon vanilla extract
- 1 tablespoon almond butter

Directions:
1. Add chia seeds, coconut cream, flaxseed, water and vanilla to a small pot
2. Mix and let it sit for 7 minutes
3. Put almond butter and place pot over low heat
4. Keep stirring as almond butter melts
5. Once the porridge is hot/not boiling, pour into a bowl
6. Add a few berries or a dash of cream for extra flavor

Nutrition: Calories: 410 Fat: 38g Carbohydrates: 10g Protein: 6g

81. Cranberry and Apple Oatmeal

PreparationTime:10minutes
CookingTime:25Minutes
Servings: 2
Ingredients:

- 1 apple – diced
- ¼ teaspoon nutmeg
- ¼ cup cranberry – fresh
- 2/3 cup oatmeal – you can use quick oatmeal with no added sodium and extra potassium – avoid whole grain if not on dialysis
- ½ teaspoon cinnamon
- 2 cup water

Direction:

1. You need to prepare all the ingredients and cut the apple in small pieces. Pour two cups of water into a saucepan and add the diced apple, cranberries, nutmeg and cinnamon.
2. Seal the saucepan and bring the water with ingredients to boil. Cook until the fruit is tender, which shouldn't take more than 5 to 10 minutes.
3. Check if apples are tender then add 2/3 cup oatmeal to the boiling water. Stir in and cook for around one minute before serving the oatmeal. Based on your doctor's recommendations you can serve the oatmeal with an adequate dose of milk or add milk substitute to the oatmeal when serving.

Nutrition: Potassium 170 mg Sodium 59 mg Phosphorus 187 mg Calories 173

82. Apple Sauce Cream Toast

PreparationTime:5minutes
CookingTime:10Minutes
Servings: 1
Ingredients:
- 2 tablespoons applesauce
- 2 slices of toast or white bread
- 1 egg white – uncooked, scrambled
- Cinnamon

Direction:
1. Whip the liquid uncooked egg white until foamy and take a skillet that doesn't stick. Heat the skillet then soak one side of the toast into the egg white whip.
2. Bake the toast on the side where the toast is soaked into the egg white and while you are doing so, soak another piece of toast into the egg white whip and as you are baking the second toast piece and applesauce on the second piece and seal with the first piece of toast once the outside crust is well baked.
3. Sprinkle with cinnamon to taste and serve.

Nutrition: Potassium 294 mg Sodium 366 mg Phosphorus 158 mg Calories 256

83. Breakfast Casserole

PreparationTime:10minutes
CookingTime:60Minutes
Servings: 8
Ingredients:
- 200 grams of ground lean beef – fresh and grass-fed if possible
- 4 slices of bread – white, cut in cubes
- 5 eggs
- 1 teaspoon of mustard – dry
- ½ teaspoon garlic powder with no added sodium

Direction:
1. Preheat your oven to 350 degrees F as you are preparing ingredients for breakfast casserole.

2. Cube bread sliced and place it aside while you are taking care of the ground beef. As you prepare the beef, add a tablespoon of olive oil to the skillet and add the beef.
3. Cook the beef with occasional stirring as you are breaking the meat parts to bits. Once the meat is browned, set aside and add garlic powder, stirring it well to combine.
4. Beat the five eggs in a bowl, combine all ingredients in the egg bowl, and mix to get a homogenous mass out of the egg mixture. Pour the mixture into the mildly greased baking dish and place it in the oven. Bake for 50 minutes or until ready.

Nutrition: Potassium 176 mg Sodium 201 mg Phosphorus 119 mg Calories 220

84. Asparagus Frittata

Preparation Time: 5 minutes
Cooking Time: 30 minutes
Servings: 2 servings

Ingredients:

- 10 medium asparagus spears, ends trimmed
- 2 teaspoons extra-virgin olive oil, divided
- Freshly ground black pepper
- 4 large eggs
- ½ teaspoon onion powder
- ¼ cup chopped parsley

Directions:

1. heat the oven to 350°F.

2. Mix the asparagus with 1 teaspoon of olive oil and season with pepper. Place to a baking pan and roast, stirring occasionally, for 20 minutes, until the spears are browned and tender.
3. In a small bowl, beat the eggs with the onion powder and parsley. Season with pepper.
4. Cut the asparagus spears into 1-inch pieces and arrange in a medium skillet. Drizzle with the remaining oil, and shake the pan to distribute.
5. Pour the egg mixture into the skillet, and cook over medium heat. When the egg is well set on the bottom and nearly set on the top, cover it with a plate, invert the pan so the frittata is on the plate, and then slide it back into the pan with the cooked-side up. Continue to cook for about 30 more seconds, until firm.

Nutrition: Calories: 102; Total Fat: 8g; Saturated Fat: 2g; Cholesterol: 104mg; Carbohydrates: 4g; Fiber: 2g; Protein: 6g; Phosphorus: 103mg; Potassium: 248mg; Sodium: 46mg

85. Poached Eggs with Cilantro Butter

Preparation Time: 5 minutes
Cooking Time: 10 minutes
Servings: 2 servings

Ingredients:

- 2 tablespoons unsalted butter
- 1 tablespoon chopped parsley
- 1 tablespoon chopped cilantro
- 4 large eggs

- Dash vinegar
- Freshly ground black pepper

Directions:

1. In a small pan over low heat, melt the butter. Add the parsley and cilantro, and cook for about 1 minute, stirring constantly. Remove from the heat, and pour into a small dish.
2. In a small saucepan, bring about 3 inches of water to a simmer. Add the dash of vinegar.
3. Crack 1 egg into a cup or ramekin. Using a spoon, create a whirlpool in the simmering water, and then pour the egg into the water. Use the spoon to draw the white together until just starting to set. Repeat with the remaining eggs. Cook for 4 to 7 minutes, depending on how set you like your yolk.
4. With a slotted spoon, remove the eggs.
5. Serve the eggs topped with 1 tablespoon of the herbed butter and some pepper.

Nutrition: Calories: 261; Total Fat: 22g; Saturated Fat: 7g; Cholesterol: 429mg; Carbohydrates: 1g; Fiber: 0g; Protein: 14g; Phosphorus: 226mg; Potassium: 173mg; Sodium: 164mg

86. Blueberry Breakfast Smoothie

PreparationTime:10minutes
CookingTime:10Minutes
Servings: 1

Ingredients:

- 1/3 cup vanilla almond milk – no sugar added
- 2 tablespoons protein powder of your choice
- ¼ cup of Greek yogurt - look for brands with low sodium and low potassium
- 3 strawberries - fresh, sliced
- 6 raspberries
- 1 cup blueberries – frozen or fresh
- 1 tablespoon cereal – avoid whole grain due to high levels of potassium

Direction:

1. First, you need to blend one cup of blueberries in a food processor, blending the fruit on low speed for around a minute.
2. After a minute, add almond milk, protein powder and Greek yogurt to blended blueberries and blend the mixture for another minute or until the blueberry smoothie turns into a homogeneous mass.
3. Pour the smoothie in a bowl, add cereals, raspberries, sliced strawberries, and serve.

Nutrition: Potassium 270 mg Sodium 108 mg Phosphorus 114 mg Calories 225

87. Blackberry Pudding

Preparation Time: 45 minutes
Cooking Time: 30 minutes
Servings: 2

Ingredients:

- ¼ cup chia seeds
- ½ cup blackberries, fresh
- 1 teaspoon liquid sweetener
- 1 cup coconut almond milk, full fat and unsweetened

- 1 teaspoon vanilla extract

Directions:
1. Take the vanilla, liquid sweetener and coconut almond milk and add to blender
2. Process until thick
3. Add blackberries and process until smooth
4. Divide the mixture between cups and chill for 30 minutes
5. Serve and enjoy!

Nutrition: Calories: 437 Fat: 38g Carbohydrates: 8g Protein: 8g

88. Hungarian's Porridge

Preparation Time: 10 minutes
Cooking Time: 10 minutes
Servings: 2
Ingredients:
- 1 tablespoon chia seeds
- 1 tablespoon ground flaxseed
- 1/3 cup coconut cream
- ½ cup of water
- 1 teaspoon vanilla extract
- 1 tablespoon almond butter

Directions:
1. Add chia seeds, coconut cream, flaxseed, water and vanilla to a small pot
2. Mix and let it sit for 6 minutes
3. Put butter and place pot over low heat
4. Keep stirring as butter melts
5. Once the porridge is hot/not boiling, pour into a bowl
6. Add a few berries or a dash of cream for extra flavor

Nutrition: Calories: 410 Fat: 38g Carbohydrates: 10g Protein: 6g

89. Chorizo and Egg Tortilla

Preparation Time: 10 minutes
Cooking Time: 13 minutes
Servings: 1 tortilla
Ingredients:
- 1 flour tortilla, about 6-inches
- 1/3 cup chorizo meat, chopped
- 1 egg

Directions:
1. Take a medium-sized skillet pan, place it over medium heat and when hot, add chorizo.
2. When the meat has cooked, drain the excess fat, whisk an egg, pour it into the pan, stir until combined, and cook for 3 minutes, or until eggs have cooked.
3. Spoon egg onto the tortilla and then serve.

Nutrition: Calories: 223 Fat: 11 g Protein: 16 g Carbohydrates: 15 g Fiber: 1.5 g

90. Egg in a Hole

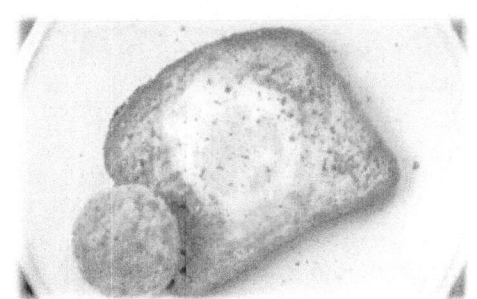

Preparation Time: 5 minutes
Cooking Time: 5 minutes
Servings: 1 slice
Ingredients:
- 1 slice of white bread
- ¼ teaspoon lemon pepper seasoning, salt-free
- 1 egg

Directions:
1. Prepare the bread by making a hole in the middle: use a cookie cutter for cutting out the center.
2. Brush the slice with oil on both sides, then take a medium-sized skillet pan, place it over medium heat and when hot, add bread slice in it, crack the egg in the center of the slice sprinkle with lemon pepper seasoning.
3. Cook the egg for 2 minutes, then carefully flip it along with the slice and continue cooking for an additional 2 minutes.

Nutrition: Calories – 159 Fat – 7 g Protein – 9 g Carbohydrates – 15 g Fiber – 0.8 g

91. Open-Faced Bagel Breakfast Sandwich

Preparation Time: 5 minutes
Cooking Time: 5 minutes
Servings: 2 servings
Ingredients:
- 1 multigrain bagel, halved
- 2 slices tomato

- 1 slice red onion
- Freshly ground black pepper
- 1 cup microgreens

Directions:
1. Lightly toast the bagel.
2. Place the bagel halves, top each half with 1 slice of tomato and a coupleof onion ringsn.
3. Season with the black pepper. Top each half with ½ cup of microgreens and serve.

Nutrition: Calories: 156; Total Fat: 6g; Saturated Fat: 3g; Cholesterol: 18mg; Carbohydrates: 22g; Fiber: 3g; Protein: 5g; Protein: 5g; Phosphorus: 98mg; Potassium: 163mg; Sodium: 195mg

92. Bulgur Bowl with Strawberries and Walnuts

Preparation Time: 10 minutes
Cooking Time: 15 minutes
Servings: 4 servings
Ingredients:
- 1 cup bulgur
- 1 cup strawberries, sliced
- 4 tablespoons (¼ cup) homemade rice milk or unsweetened store-bought rice milk
- 4 teaspoons brown sugar
- 4 teaspoons extra-virgin olive oil
- 4 tablespoons (¼ cup) walnut pieces

- 4 tablespoons (¼ cup) cacao nibs (optional)

Directions:

1. In a small pot, combine the bulgur with 2 cups of water. Bring to a boil, lower the heat and let simmer, covered, for 12 to 15 minutes, until tender.
2. In each of four bowls, add a quarter of the bulgur and top with ¼ cup of strawberries, 1 tablespoon of rice milk, 1 teaspoon of brown sugar, 1 teaspoon of olive oil, 1 tablespoon of walnut pieces, and 1 tablespoon of cacao nibs (if using).

Nutrition: Calories: 190; Total Fat: 9g; Saturated Fat: 1g; Cholesterol: 0mg; Carbohydrates: 26g; Fiber: 5g; Protein: 4g; Phosphorus: 66mg; Potassium: 153mg; Sodium: 13mg

93. Cauliflower Tortilla

PreparationTime:15minutes
CookingTime:25Minutes
Servings: 4

Ingredients:

- 4 cups cauliflower
- 1 cup onion – chopped
- 2 garlic cloves – minced
- 1 cup egg substitute - liquefied
- ¼ teaspoon nutmeg
- 1 tablespoon parsley – fresh, chopped
- ½ teaspoon allspice

Direction:

1. Prepare the cauliflower by cutting it into small cubes, then place the cauliflower bits in a bowl with a tablespoon of water and microwave it for 5 minutes until cauliflower is crisped.
2. While you are waiting for the cauliflower bits to get ready in the microwave, you may start preparing the onion.
3. Sauté chopped onions with 2 tablespoons of olive oil until browned, which should take around 5 minutes, then add garlic, nutmeg and allspice to the pan. Stir in and cook for another 1 to 2 minutes then add the cauliflower and egg substitute.
4. Stir in all ingredients to combine the mixture then seal the pan and lower the heat. Cook for another 10 to 15 minutes, until cauliflower tortilla is browned. Serve by slicing the tortilla into 4 pieces.

Nutrition: Potassium 272 mg Sodium 148 mg Phosphorus 78 mg Calories 102

94. Eggs Benedict

PreparationTime:20minutes
CookingTime:35Minutes
Servings: 4

Ingredients:

- 2 pieces of toasted bread - white flour
- 4 eggs
- 3 egg yolks
- 1 tablespoon lemon juice

- ½ teaspoon of cayenne pepper
- ½ teaspoon of paprika
- 1 tablespoon apple cider vinegar
- 2 tablespoons of unsalted butter

Direction:
1. Slice the two toasted bread pieces in two, so you can end up with four pieces where each piece represents one serving.
2. Take a large skillet or a pot and pour one cup of water in it. Add a tablespoon of vinegar and bring the water to boil. When the water starts to boil, break four eggs, one at the time, and poach the eggs by covering the skillet. Eggs should be done between 3 and 5 minutes of poaching, depending on how you like your eggs cooked.
3. Next place poached eggs on top of bread pieces. Take a skillet and add the butter to melt it then add cayenne and paprika to the melted butter. Beat the egg yolks over medium heat then add the eggs to the mixture with butter. Add lemon juice and whisk it into the egg and butter mixture. Once the sauce reaches an adequate thickness, remove from the heat and pour over the eggs and toasted bread.

Nutrition: Potassium 146 mg Sodium 206 mg Phosphorus 114 mg Calories 316

95. Peach Berry Parfait

Preparation Time: 5 minutes
Cooking Time: 5 minutes
Servings: 2 servings
Ingredients:
- 1 cup plain, unsweetened yogurt, divided
- 1 teaspoon vanilla extract
- 1 small peach, diced
- ½ cup blueberries
- 2 tablespoons walnut pieces

Directions:
1. In a small bowl, combine the yogurt and vanilla.
2. Put 2 tablespoons of yogurt to each of 2 cups. Divide the diced peach and the blueberries between the cups, and top with the remaining yogurt.
3. Sprinkle each cup with 1 tablespoon of walnut pieces.

Nutrition: Calories: 191; Total Fat: 10g; Saturated Fat: 3g; Cholesterol: 15mg; Carbohydrates: 14g; Fiber: 14g; Protein: 12g; Phosphorus: 189mg; Potassium: 327mg; Sodium: 40mg

96. Waffles

PreparationTime:20minutes
CookingTime:15Minutes
Servings: 8
Ingredients:
- 1 and ½ teaspoons yeast for baking
- 8 tablespoons butter – unsalted
- 2 eggs
- 1 and ¾ cups of milk – 2% milkfat
- Sugar substitute to taste
- 1 teaspoon almond extract
- 2 cups flour – all-purpose

Direction:
1. Heat a saucepan and place the butter and milk in it. Wait for the butter to melt with occasional stirring. As you are waiting for the milk and butter mixture to cool off a bit so that the saucepan is warm to touch, you will take a bowl and whisk sugar substitute, yeast and flour.

Once combined, you will add the warm milk and butter mixture to the flour bowl and whisk some more until the mass is well combined.

2. Take another bowl and whisk the eggs with almond extract, adding the flour batter's whipped egg mixture. Stir in well to combine until you get a smooth, homogenous mass. The best option is to prepare the mixture a day ahead as you will need to keep the dough in the fridge for at least 12 hours before baking.
3. Once you are ready to bake your waffles, you will set the oven to 200 degrees F and keep the waffle bowl near so that the dough is kept warm. Prepare your waffle maker and start making waffles by pouring the dough.

Nutrition: Potassium 131 mg Sodium 208 mg Phosphorus 113 mg Calories 223

97. Overnight oats three ways

Preparation Time: 5 minutes
Cooking Time: 5 minutes
Servings: 2 servings
Ingredients:
- ¾ cup homemade rice milk or unsweetened store-bought rice milk
- ½ cup plain, unsweetened yogurt
- ½ cup rolled oats
- 1 tablespoon ground flaxseed
- 1 teaspoon vanilla extract
- 2 teaspoons honey

Directions:

1. In a medium bowl, mix the rice milk, yogurt, oats, flaxseed, vanilla, and honey.
2. Add the ingredients to make your preferred variation, and stir to blend.
3. Divide between two jars, cover, and refrigerate for at least 4 hours or overnight.

Nutrition: Calories: 196; Total Fat: 7g; Saturated Fat: 2g; Cholesterol: 7mg; Carbohydrates: 25g; Fiber: 3g; Protein: 8g; Phosphorus: 99mg; Potassium: 114mg; Sodium: 63mg

98. Buckwheat Pancakes

Preparation Time: 10 minutes
Cooking Time: 15 minutes
Servings: 4 servings
Ingredients:
- 1¾ cups homemade or unsweetened store-bought rice milk
- 2 teaspoons white vinegar
- 1 cup buckwheat flour
- ½ cup all-purpose flour
- 1 tablespoon sugar
- 1 large egg
- 2 teaspoons Phosphorus-Free baking powder
- 1 teaspoon vanilla extract
- 2 tablespoons butter, for the skillet

Directions:

1. combine the rice milk and vinegar. Let sit for 5 minutes.
2. Meanwhile, in a large bowl, mix the buckwheat flour and all-purpose

flour. Add the sugar and baking powder, stirring to blend.

3. Add the egg and vanilla to the rice milk and stir to blend. Add the wet ingredients to the dry, and stir until just mixed.

4. melt 1½ teaspoons of butter. Use a ¼-cup measuring cup to scoop the batter into the skillet. Cook for 2 to 3 minutes, until small bubbles form on the surface of the pancakes. Flip and cook on the opposite side for 1 to 2 minutes.

5. Transfer the pancakes to a serving platter, and in batches, continue cooking the remaining batter in the skillet, adding more butter as needed.

Nutrition: Calories: 264; Total Fat: 9g; Saturated Fat: 3g; Cholesterol: 58mg; Carbohydrates: 39g; Fiber: 3g; Protein: 7g; Phosphorus: 147mg; Potassium: 399mg; Sodium: 232mg

99. Lemon Curd

Preparation Time: 5 minutes
Cooking Time: 75 minutes
Serving: 6
Ingredients:
- Freshly squeezed lemon juice 150 ml
- Freshly squeezed mango juice 100 ml
- Butter 100 gr.
- Sifted corn starch 30 gr.
- White wine dry 150 ml
- Sugar 150 gr.
- Grated lemon peel 1 pc.

Direction:
1. Melt the butter and heat the corn-starch while stirring until it is light yellow. Add lemon and mango juice and the white wine. Please make sure that there are no lumps.

2. Now add the sugar and lemon zest and let it cook for another 2 minutes. Fill everything into glasses immediately.

3. The lemon curd unfortunately only lasts about 3 days in the refrigerator.

Nutrition: 239 calories 0.3g protein 28mg potassium 171mg sodium

100. Egg Whites and Veggie Bake

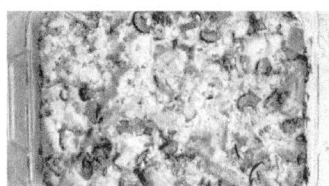

PreparationTime:20minutes
CookingTime:50Minutes
Servings: 4
Ingredients:
- 1 cup broccoli florets
- 1 cup cauliflower florets
- 1 garlic clove - minced
- 6 egg whites – liquid, uncooked
- ½ cup bell pepper – diced
- 1 small onion – finely diced
- ½ cup low-sodium cheese

Direction:
1. Take care of the veggies, wash and dice the cauliflower, broccoli and onion. While you are sautéing onion with a tablespoon of olive oil, place broccoli and cauliflower in a bowl with a tablespoon water and place the bowl in the microwave.

2. Microwave florets for 5 minutes before taking the bowl out of the microwave. The onions should be ready within 5 minutes, when you should add the minced garlic and peppers. Sauté for another 3 to 4 minutes.

3. Combine broccoli and cauliflower florets with garlic, peppers and onion and let the veggie mixture cool off a bit

as you are whisking egg whites. Egg whites should be whisked until foamy. Whisk in the cheese with the egg whites then add the veggie mixture to your egg whites, stirring the ingredients to combine it into a homogenous mass.

4. Take a medium baking dish and pour in the mixture. Preheat the oven to 350 degrees F and place the baking dish into the oven, baking the egg white veggie bake for 20 minutes or until the mixture settles.

Nutrition: Potassium 163 mg Sodium 89 mg Phosphorus 105 mg Calories 258

101. Crispy Lemon Chicken

Preparation Time: 10 minutes
Cooking Time: 10 minutes
Servings: 6

Ingredients:

- 1 lb. boneless and skinless chicken breast
- ½ cup of all-purpose flour
- 1 large egg
- ½ cup of lemon juice
- 2 tbsp. of water
- ¼ tsp salt
- ¼ tsp lemon pepper
- 1 tsp of mixed herb seasoning
- 2 tbsp. of olive oil
- A few lemon slices for garnishing
- 1 tbsp. of chopped parsley (for garnishing)
- 2 cups of cooked plain white rice

Directions:

1. Slice the chicken breast into thin and season with the herb, salt, and pepper.
2. In a small bowl, whisk together the egg with the water.
3. Keep the flour in a separate bowl.
4. Dip the chicken slices in the egg bath and then into the flour.
5. Heat your oil in a medium frying pan.
6. Shallow fry the chicken in the pan until golden brown.
7. Add the lemon juice and cook for another couple of minutes.
8. Taken the chicken out of the pan and transfer on a wide dish with absorbing paper to absorb any excess oil.
9. Garnish with some chopped parsley and lemon wedges on top.
10. Serve with rice.

Nutrition: Calories: 232 Carbohydrate: 24g Protein: 18g Fat: 8g Sodium: 100g Potassium: 234mg Phosphorus: 217mg

102. Colorful Bean Salad

Preparation Time: 11 minutes
Cooking Time: 0 minute
Serving: 4

Ingredients:

- 200 g green beans
- 1 onion
- 1 bell pepper
- 1 small can (drained weight 250 g) white beans
- 1 small can (drained weight 250 g) kidney beans
- 2 tbsp wine vinegar
- 2 tbsp sour cream
- 1/2 teaspoon mustard
- 1/2 teaspoon tomato ketchup
- 1/2 teaspoon horseradish
- salt
- pepper
- 1 tbsp oil
- chopped thyme

Direction:

1. Clean and wash the green beans and cook in salted boiling water for 6-8 minutes until they are firm to the bite. Pour into a sieve, rinse in cold water and drain well. Transfer to a large bowl.
2. Skin the onion and cut into thin rings. Halve and core the peppers lengthways, wash and cut into cubes. Drain the kidney beans and white beans each into a sieve, rinse with cold water and drain well. Then add the onion, bell pepper,

kidney beans, and white beans to the green beans.

3. For the dressing mix together vinegar, sour cream, mustard, tomato ketchup, horseradish, oil, and thyme, season with salt and pepper. Mix with the salad ingredients and let the bean salad steep for about 5 minutes before serving.

Nutrition: 210 calories7g protein 29mg potassium 132mg sodium

103. Mexican Steak Tacos

Preparation Time: 10 minutes
Cooking Time: 15 minutes
Servings: 8
Ingredients:
- 1 pound of flank or skirt steak
- ¼ cup of fresh cilantro, chopped
- ¼ cup white onion, chopped
- 3 limes, juiced
- 3 cloves of garlic, minced
- 2 tsp of garlic powder
- 2 tbsp. of olive oil
- ½ cup of Mexican or mozzarella cheese, grated
- 1 tsp of Mexican seasoning
- 8 medium-sized (6") corn flour tortillas

Directions:
1. Combine the juice from two limes, Mexican seasoning, and garlic powder in a dish or bowl and marinate the steak with it for at least half an hour in the fridge.
2. In a separate bowl, combine the chopped cilantro, garlic, onion, and juice from one lime to make your salsa. Cover and keep in the fridge.
3. Slice steak into thin strips and cook for approximately 3 minutes on each side.
4. Preheat your oven to 350F/180C.
5. Distribute evenly the steak strips in each tortilla. Top with a tablespoon of the grated cheese on top.
6. Wrap each taco in aluminum foil and bake in the oven for 7-8 minutes or until cheese is melted.
7. Serve warm with your cilantro salsa.

Nutrition: Calories: 230 Carbohydrate: 19.5 g Protein: 15 g Fat: 11 g Sodium: 486.75 g Potassium: 240 mg Phosphorus: 268 mg

104. Mexican Chorizo Sausage

Ingredients:
- 2 pounds of boneless pork but coarsely ground

3 tbsp. of red wine Preparation Time: 10 minutes
Cooking Time: 15 minutes
Servings: 1
- vinegar
- 2 tbsp. of smoked paprika
- ½ tsp of cinnamon
- ½ tsp of ground cloves
- ¼ tsp of coriander seeds
- ¼ tsp ground ginger
- 1 tsp of ground cumin
- 3 tbsp. of brandy

Directions:
1. In a large mixing bowl, combine the ground pork with the seasonings, brandy, and vinegar and mix with your hands well.
2. Place the mixture into a large Ziploc bag and leave in the fridge overnight.
3. Form into 15-16 patties of equal size.
4. Heat the oil in a large pan and fry the patties for 5-7 minutes on each side, or until the meat inside is no longer pink and there is a light brown crust on top.
5. Serve hot.

Nutrition: Calories: 134 Carbohydrate: 0 g Protein: 10 g Fat: 7 g Sodium: 40 mg Potassium: 138 mg Phosphorus: 128 mg

105. Eggplant Casserole

Ingredients: Preparation Time: 10 minutes
Cooking Time: 25 – 30 minutes
Servings: 4

- 3 cups of eggplant, peeled and cut into large chunks
- 2 egg whites
- 1 large egg, whole
- ½ cup of unsweetened vegetable
- ¼ tsp of sage
- ½ cup of breadcrumbs
- 1 tbsp. of margarine, melted
- 1/4 tsp garlic salt

Directions:
1. Preheat the oven at 350F/180C.
2. Place the eggplants chunks in a medium pan, cover with a bit of water and cook with the lid covered until tender. Drain from the water and mash with a tool or fork.
3. Beat the eggs with the non-dairy vegetable cream, sage, salt, and pepper. Whisk in the eggplant mush.
4. Combine the melted margarine with the breadcrumbs.
5. Bake in the oven for 20-25 minutes or until the casserole has a golden-brown crust.

Nutrition: Calories: 186 Carbohydrate: 19 g Protein: 7 g Fat: 9 g Sodium: 503 mg Potassium: 230 mg Phosphorus: 62 mg

106. Grilled Corn on the Cob

Preparation Time: 5 minutes
Cooking Time: 20 minutes
Servings: 4
Ingredients:
- 4 frozen corn on the cob, cut in half
- ½ tsp of thyme
- 1 tbsp. of grated parmesan cheese
- ¼ tsp of black pepper

Directions:

1. Combine the oil, cheese, thyme, and black pepper in a bowl.
2. Place the corn in the cheese/oil mix and roll to coat evenly.
3. Fold all 4 pieces in aluminum foil, leaving a small open surface on top.
4. Place the wrapped corns over the grill and let cook for 20 minutes.
5. Serve hot.

Nutrition: Calories: 125 Carbohydrate: 29.5 g Protein: 2 g Fat: 1.3 g Sodium: 26 g Potassium: 145 mg Phosphorus: 91.5 mg

107. Beer Pork Ribs

Ingredients:
2 pounds of pork ribs, cut Preparation Time: 10 minutes
Cooking Time: 8 hours
Servings: 1
- into two units/racks
- 18 oz. of root beer
- 2 cloves of garlic, minced
- 2 tbsp. of onion powder
- 2 tbsp. of vegetable oil (optional)

Directions:
1. Wrap the pork ribs with vegetable oil and place one unit on the bottom of your slow cooker with half of the minced garlic and the onion powder.
2. Place the other rack on top with the rest of the garlic and onion powder.
3. Pour over the root beer and cover the lid.
4. Let simmer for 8 hours on low heat.
5. Take off and finish optionally in a grilling pan for a nice sear.

Nutrition: Calories: 301 Carbohydrate: 36 g Protein: 21 g Fat: 18 g Sodium: 729 mg Potassium: 200 mg Phosphorus: 209 mg

108. Couscous with Veggies

Preparation Time: 10 minutes
Cooking Time: 10 minutes

Servings: 5

Ingredients:

- ½ cup of uncooked couscous
- ¼ cup of white mushrooms, sliced
- ½ cup of red onion, chopped
- 1 garlic clove, minced
- ½ cup of frozen peas
- 2 tbsp. of dry white wine
- ½ tsp of basil
- 2 tbsp. of fresh parsley, chopped
- 1 cup water or vegetable stock
- 1 tbsp. of margarine or vegetable oil

Directions:

1. Thaw the peas by setting them aside at room temperature for 15-20 minutes.
2. In a medium pan, heat the margarine or vegetable oil.
3. Add the onions, peas, mushroom, and garlic and sauté for around 5 minutes. Add the wine and let it evaporate.
4. Add all the herbs and spices and toss well. Take off the heat and keep aside.
5. In a small pot, cook the couscous with 1 cup of hot water or vegetable stock. Bring to a boil, take off the heat, and sit for a few minutes with a lid covered.
6. Add the sauté veggies to the couscous and toss well.
7. Serve in a serving bowl warm or cold.

Nutrition: Calories: 110.4 Carbohydrate: 18 g Protein: 3 g Fat: 2 g Sodium: 112.2 mg Potassium: 69.6 mg Phosphorus: 46.8 mg

109. Easy Egg Salad

Preparation Time: 5 minutes
Cooking Time: 8 minutes
Servings: 4

Ingredients:

- ¼ cup of celery, chopped
  - 1 tbsp. of yellow mustard
  - 1 tsp of smoked paprika
  - 3 tbsp. of mayo

Directions:

1. Hard boil the eggs in a small pot filled with water for approx. 7-8 minutes. Leave the eggs in the water for an extra couple of minutes before peeling.
2. Peel the eggs and chop finely with a knife or tool.
3. Combine all the chopped veggies with the mayo and mustard. Add in the eggs and mix well.
4. Sprinkle with some smoked paprika on top.
5. Serve cold with pitta, white bread slices, or lettuce wraps.

Nutrition: Calories: 127 Carbohydrate: 6 g Protein: 7 g Fat: 13 g Sodium: 170.7 mg Potassium: 87.5 mg Phosphorus: 101 mg

110. Shrimp Quesadilla

Preparation Time: 10 minutes
Cooking Time: 10 minutes
Servings: **2**

Ingredients:

- 5 oz. of shrimp, shelled and deveined
- 4 tbsp. of Mexican salsa
- 2 tbsp. of fresh cilantro, chopped
- 1 tbsp. of lemon juice
- 1 tsp of ground cumin
- 1 tsp of cayenne pepper
- 2 tbsp. of unsweetened soy yogurt or creamy tofu
- 2 medium corn flour tortillas
- 2 tbsp. of low-fat cheddar cheese

Directions:

1. Mix the cilantro, cumin, lemon juice, and cayenne in a Ziploc bag to make your marinade.
2. Put the shrimps and marinate for 10 minutes.
3. Heat a pan over medium heat with some olive oil and toss in the shrimp with the marinade. Let cook for a couple of

minutes or as soon as shrimps have turned pink and opaque.

4. Add the soy cream or soft tofu to the pan and mix well. Remove from the heat and keep the marinade aside.
5. Heat tortillas in the grill or microwave for a few seconds.
6. Place 2 tbsp. of salsa on each tortilla. Top one tortilla with the shrimp mixture and add the cheese on top.
7. Stack one tortilla against each other (with the spread salsa layer facing the shrimp mixture).
8. Transfer this on a baking tray and cook for 7-8 minutes at 350F/180C to melt the cheese and crisp up the tortillas.
9. Serve warm.

Nutrition: Calories: 255 Carbohydrate: 21 g Fat: 9 g Protein: 24 g Sodium: 562 g Potassium: 235 mg Phosphorus: 189 mg

111. Pizza with Chicken and Pesto

Preparation Time: 10 minutes
Cooking Time: 25 minutes
Servings: 4
Ingredients:

- 1 ready-made frozen pizza dough
- 2/3 cup cooked chicken, chopped
- 1/2 cup of mango bell pepper, diced
- 1/2 cup of green bell pepper, diced
- 1/4 cup of purple onion, chopped
- 2 tbsp. of green basil pesto
- 1 tbsp. of chives, chopped
- 1/3 cup of parmesan or Romano cheese, grated
- 1/4 cup of mozzarella cheese
- 1 tbsp. of olive oil

Directions:

1. Thaw the pizza dough according to instructions on the package.

2. Heat the olive oil in a pan and sauté the peppers and onions for a couple of minutes. Set aside
3. Once the pizza dough has thawed, spread the Bali pesto over its surface.
4. Top with half of the cheese, the peppers, the onions, and the chicken. Finish with the rest of the cheese.
5. Bake at 350F/180C for approx. 20 minutes (or until crust and cheese are baked).
6. Slice in triangles with a pizza cutter or sharp knife and serve.

Nutrition: Calories: 225 Carbohydrate: 13.9 g Protein: 11.1 g Fat: 12 g Sodium: 321 mg Potassium: 174 mg Phosphorus: 172 mg

112. Cucumber Sandwich

Preparation Time: 1 hour
Cooking Time: 5 minutes
Servings: 2
Ingredients:

- 6 tsp. of cream cheese
- 1 pinch of dried dill weed
- 3 tsp. of mayonnaise
- .25 tsp. dry Italian dressing mix
- 4 slices of white bread
- .5 of a cucumber

Directions:

1. Prepare the cucumber and cut it into slices.
2. Mix cream cheese, mayonnaise, and Italian dressing. Chill for one hour.
3. Distribute the mixture onto the white bread slices.
4. Place cucumber slices on top and sprinkle with the dill weed.
5. Cut in halves and serve.

Nutrition: Calories: 143 Fat: 6g Carbs: 16.7g Protein: 4g Sodium: 255mg Potassium: 127mg Phosphorus: 64mg

113. Salad al Tonno

Preparation Time: 15 minutes
Cooking Time: 0 minutes
Servings: 2
Ingredients:

- 1 ½ cup lettuce leaves, teared
- ½ cup cherry Red bell peppers, halved
- ½ teaspoon garlic powder
- ½ teaspoon salt
- ½ teaspoon ground black pepper
- 1 tablespoon lemon juice
- 6 oz. tuna, canned, drained

Directions:

1. Chop the tuna roughly and put it in the salad bowl.
2. Add cherry Red bell peppers, lettuce leaves, salt, garlic powder, ground black pepper. Lemon juice, and olive oil.
3. Give a good shake to the salad.
4. Salad can be stored in the fridge for up to 3 hours.

Nutrition: calories 235, fat 12, fiber 1, carbs 6.5, protein 23.4 Phosphorus: 120mg Potassium: 217mg Sodium: 75mg

114. Arlecchino Rice Salad

Preparation Time: 10 minutes
Cooking Time: 15 minutes
Servings: 3
Ingredients:

- ½ cup white rice, dried
- 1 cup chicken stock
- 1 zucchini, shredded
- 2 tablespoons capers
- 1 carrot, shredded
- 1 tomato, chopped
- 1 tablespoon apple cider vinegar
- ½ teaspoon salt
- 2 tablespoons fresh parsley, chopped
- 1 tablespoon canola oil

Directions:

1. Put rice in the pan.
2. Add chicken stock and boil it with the closed lid for 15-20 minutes or until rice absorbs all water.
3. Meanwhile, in the mixing bowl combine together shredded zucchini, capers, carrot, and tomato.
4. Add fresh parsley.
5. Make the dressing: mix up together canola oil, salt, and apple cider vinegar.
6. Chill the cooked rice little and add it in the salad bowl to the vegetables.
7. Add dressing and mix up salad well.

Nutrition: calories 183, fat 5.3, fiber 2.1, carbs 30.4, protein 3.8 Phosphorus: 110mg Potassium: 117mg Sodium: 75mg

115. Traditional Black Bean Chili

Preparation Time: 10 minutes
Cooking Time: 4 hours
Servings: 4
Ingredients:

- 1 ½ cups red bell pepper, chopped
- 1 cup yellow onion, chopped
- 1 ½ cups mushrooms, sliced
- 1 tablespoon olive oil
- 1 tablespoon chili powder
- 2 garlic cloves, minced
- 1 teaspoon chipotle chili pepper, chopped
- ½ teaspoon cumin, ground
- 16 ounces canned black beans, drained and rinsed
- 2 tablespoons cilantro, chopped
- 1 cup Red bell peppers, chopped

Directions:

1. Add red bell peppers, onion, dill, mushrooms, chili powder, garlic, chili pepper, cumin, black beans, and Red bell peppers to your Slow Cooker.

2. Stir well.
3. Place lid and cook on HIGH for 4 hours.
4. Sprinkle cilantro on top.
5. Serve and enjoy!

Nutrition: Calories: 211 Fat: 3g Carbohydrates: 22g Protein: 5g Phosphorus: 90mg Potassium: 107mg Sodium: 75mg

116. Dolmas Wrap

Preparation Time: 10 minutes
Cooking Time: 5 minutes
Servings: 2
Ingredients:
- 2 whole wheat wraps
- 6 dolmas (stuffed grape leaves)
- 1 tomato, chopped
- 1 cucumber, chopped
- 2 oz. Greek yogurt
- ½ teaspoon minced garlic
- ¼ cup lettuce, chopped
- 2 oz. Feta, crumbled

Directions:
1. In the mixing bowl combine together chopped tomato, cucumber, Greek yogurt, minced garlic, lettuce, and Feta.
2. When the mixture is homogenous transfer it in the center of every wheat wrap.
3. Arrange dolma over the vegetable mixture.
4. Carefully wrap the wheat wraps.

Nutrition: calories 341, fat 12.9, fiber 9.2, carbs 52.4, protein 13.2 Phosphorus: 110mg Potassium: 117mg Sodium: 75mg

117. Sauteed Chickpea and Lentil Mix

Preparation Time: 10 minutes
Cooking Time: 50 minutes
Servings: 4

Ingredients:
- 1 cup chickpeas, half-cooked
- 1 cup lentils
- 5 cups chicken stock
- ½ cup fresh cilantro, chopped
- 1 teaspoon salt
- ½ teaspoon chili flakes
- ¼ cup onion, diced
- 1 tablespoon tomato paste

Directions:
1. Place chickpeas in the pan.
2. Add water, salt, and chili flakes.
3. Boil the chickpeas for 30 minutes over the medium heat.
4. Then add diced onion, lentils, and tomato paste. Stir well.
5. Close the lid and cook the mix for 15 minutes.
6. After this, add chopped cilantro, stir the meal well and cook it for 5 minutes more.
7. Let the cooked lunch chill little before serving.

Nutrition: calories 370, fat 4.3, fiber 23.7, carbs 61.6, protein 23.2 Phosphorus: 110mg Potassium: 117mg Sodium: 75mg

118. Crazy Japanese Potato and Beef Croquettes

Preparation Time: 10 minutes
Cooking Time: 20 minutes
Servings: 10
Ingredients:
- 3 medium russet carrots, peeled and chopped
- 1 tablespoon almond butter
- 1 tablespoon vegetable oil
- 3 onions, diced
- ¾ pound ground beef
- 4 teaspoons light coconut aminos
- All-purpose flour for coating

- 2 eggs, beaten
- Panko bread crumbs for coating
- ½ cup oil, frying

Directions:

1. Take a saucepan and place it over medium-high heat; add carrots and sunflower seeds water, boil for 16 minutes.
2. Remove water and put carrots in another bowl, add almond butter and mash the carrots.
3. Take a frying pan and place it over medium heat, add 1 tablespoon oil and let it heat up.
4. Add onions and stir fry until tender.
5. Add coconut aminos to beef to onions.
6. Keep frying until beef is browned.
7. Mix the beef with the carrots evenly.
8. Take another frying pan and place it over medium heat; add half a cup of oil.
9. Form croquettes using the mashed potato mixture and coat them with flour, then eggs and finally breadcrumbs.
10. Fry patties until golden on all sides.
11. Enjoy!

Nutrition: Calories: 239 Fat: 4g Carbohydrates: 20g Protein: 10g Phosphorus: 120mg Potassium: 107mg Sodium: 75mg

119. Green Palak Paneer

Preparation Time: 5 minutes
Cooking Time: 10 minutes
Servings: 4
Ingredients:

- 1-pound green lettuce
- 2 cups cubed paneer (vegan)
- 2 tablespoons coconut oil
- 1 teaspoon cumin
- 1 chopped up onion
- 1-2 teaspoons hot green chili minced up
- 1 teaspoon minced garlic

- 15 cashews
- 4 tablespoons almond milk
- 1 teaspoon Garam masala
- Flavored vinegar as needed

Directions:

1. Add cashews and almond milk to a blender and blend well.
2. Set your pot to Sauté mode and add coconut oil; allow the oil to heat up.
3. Add cumin seeds, garlic, green chilies, ginger and sauté for 1 minute.
4. Add onion and sauté for 2 minutes.
5. Add chopped green lettuce, flavored vinegar and a cup of water.
6. Lock up the lid and cook on HIGH pressure for 10 minutes.
7. Quick-release the pressure.
8. Add ½ cup of water and blend to a paste.
9. Add cashew paste, paneer and Garam Masala and stir thoroughly.
10. Serve over hot rice!

Nutrition: Calories: 367 Fat: 26g Carbohydrates: 21g Protein: 16g Phosphorus: 110mg Potassium: 117mg Sodium: 75mg

120. Pizza Pitas

Preparation Time: 10 minutes
Cooking Time: 10 minutes
Servings: 1
Ingredients:

- .33 cup of mozzarella cheese
- 2 pieces of pita bread, 6 inches in size
- 6 tsp. of chunky tomato sauce
- 2 cloves of garlic (minced)
- .25 cups of onion, chopped small
- .25 tsp. of red pepper flakes
- .25 cup of bell pepper, chopped small
- 2 ounces of ground pork, lean
- No-stick oil spray
- .5 tsp. of fennel seeds

Directions:

1. Preheat oven to 400.
2. Put the garlic, ground meat, pepper flakes, onion, and bell pepper in a pan. Sauté until cooked.
3. Grease a flat baking pan and put pitas on it. Use the mixture to spread on the pita bread.
4. Spread one tablespoon of the tomato sauce and top with cheese.
5. Bake for five to eight minutes, until the cheese is bubbling.

Nutrition: Calories: 284 Fat: 10g Carbs: 34g Protein: 16g Sodium: 795mg Potassium: 706mg Phosphorus: 416mg

121. Turkey Pinwheels

Preparation Time: 10 minutes
Cooking Time: 15 minutes
Servings: 6
Ingredients:

- 6 toothpicks
- 8 oz. of spring mix salad greens
- 1 ten-inch tortilla
- 2 ounces of thinly sliced deli turkey
- 9 tsp. of whipped cream cheese
- 1 roasted red bell pepper

Directions:
1. Cut the red bell pepper into ten strips about a quarter-inch thick.
2. Spread the whipped cream cheese on the tortilla evenly.
3. Add the salad greens to create a base layer and then lay the turkey on top of it.
4. Space out the red bell pepper strips on top of the turkey.
5. Tuck the end and begin rolling the tortilla inward.
6. Use the toothpicks to hold the roll into place and cut it into six pieces.
7. Serve with the swirl facing upward.

Nutrition: Calories: 206 Fat: 9g Carbs: 21g Protein: 9g Sodium: 533mg Potassium: 145mg Phosphorus: 47mg

122. Tuna Twist

Preparation Time: 10 minutes
Cooking Time: 30 minutes
Servings: 4
Ingredients:

- 1 can of unsalted or water packaged tuna, drained
- 6 tsp. of vinegar
- .5 cup of cooked peas
- .5 cup celery (chopped)
- 3 tsp. of dried dill weed
- 12 oz. cooked macaroni
- .75 cup of mayonnaise

Directions:
1. Stir together the macaroni, vinegar, and mayonnaise together until blended and smooth.
2. Stir in remaining ingredients.
3. Chill before serving.

Nutrition: Calories: 290 Fat: 10g Carbs: 32g Protein: 16g Sodium: 307mg Potassium: 175mg Phosphorus: 111mg

123. Ciabatta Rolls with Chicken Pesto

Preparation Time: 10 minutes
Cooking Time: 20 minutes
Servings: 2
Ingredients:

- 6 tsp. of Greek yogurt
- 6 tsp. of pesto
- 2 small ciabatta rolls
- 8 oz. of a shredded iceberg or romaine lettuce
- 8 oz. of cooked boneless and skinless chicken breast, shredded
- .125 tsp. of pepper

Directions:

1. Combine the shredded chicken, pesto, pepper, and Greek yogurt in a medium-sized bowl.
2. Slice and toast the ciabatta rolls.
3. Divide the shredded chicken and pesto mixture in half and make sandwiches with the ciabatta rolls.
4. Top with shredded lettuce if desired.

Nutrition: Calories: 374 Fat: 10g Carbs: 40g Protein: 30g Sodium: 522mg Potassium: 360mg Phosphorus: 84mg

124. Peanut Butter and Jelly Grilled Sandwich

Preparation Time: 5 minutes
Cooking Time: 5 minutes
Servings: 1
Ingredients:
- 2 tsp. butter (unsalted)
- 6 tsp. butter (peanut)
- 3 tsp. of flavored jelly
- 2 pieces of bread

Directions:
1. Put the peanut butter evenly on one bread. Add the layer of jelly.
2. Butter the outside of the pieces of bread.
3. Add the sandwich to a frying pan and toast both sides.

Nutrition: Calories: 300 Fat: 7g Carbs: 49g Protein: 8g Sodium: 460mg Potassium: 222mg Phosphorus: 80mg

125. Aromatic Carrot Cream

Preparation Time: 15 minutes
Cooking Time: 25 minutes
Servings: 4
Ingredients:
- 1 tablespoon olive oil
- ½ sweet onion, chopped
- 2 teaspoons fresh ginger, peeled and grated

- 1 teaspoon fresh garlic, minced
- 4 cups water
- 3 carrots, chopped
- 1 teaspoon ground turmeric
- ½ cup coconut almond milk

Directions:
1. Heat the olive oil into a big pan over medium-high heat.
2. Add the onion, garlic and ginger. Softly cook for about 3 minutes until softened.
3. Include the water, turmeric and the carrots. Softly cook for about 20 minutes (until the carrots are softened).
4. Blend the soup adding coconut almond milk until creamy.
5. Serve and enjoy!

Nutrition: Calories 112 Fat 10 g Cholesterol 0 mg Carbohydrates 8 g Sugar 5 g Fiber 2 g Protein 2 g Sodium 35 mg Calcium 32 mg Phosphorus 59 mg Potassium 241 mg

126. Lettuce Wraps with Chicken

Preparation Time: 10 minutes
Cooking Time: 15 minutes
Servings: 4
Ingredients:
- 8 lettuce leaves
- .25 cups of fresh cilantro
- .25 cups of mushroom
- 1 tsp. of five spices seasoning
- .25 cups of onion
- 6 tsp. of rice vinegar
- 2 tsp. of hoisin
- 6 tsp. of oil (canola)
- 3 tsp. of oil (sesame)
- 2 tsp. of garlic
- 2 scallions
- 8 ounces of cooked chicken breast

Directions:
1. Mince together the cooked chicken and the garlic. Chop up the onions, cilantro, mushrooms, and scallions.

2. Use a skillet overheat, combine chicken to all remaining ingredients, minus the lettuce leaves. Cook for fifteen minutes, stirring occasionally.
3. Place .25 cups of the mixture into each leaf of lettuce.
4. Wrap the lettuce around like a burrito and eat.

Nutrition: Calories: 84 Fat: 4g Carbs: 9g Protein: 5.9g Sodium: 618mg Potassium: 258mg Phosphorus: 64mg

127. Chicken Tacos

Preparation Time: 5 minutes
Cooking Time: 20 minutes
Servings: 4
Ingredients:
- 8 corn tortillas
- 1.5 tsp. of Sodium-free taco seasoning
- 1 juiced lime
- .5 cups of cilantro
- 2 green onions, chopped
- 8 oz. of iceberg or romaine lettuce, shredded or chopped
- .25 cup of sour cream
- 1 pound of boneless and skinless chicken breast

Directions:
1. Cook chicken, by boiling, for twenty minutes. Shred or chop cooked chicken into fine bite-sized pieces.
2. Mix the seasoning and lime juice with the chicken.
3. Put chicken mixture and lettuce in tortillas.
4. Top with the green onions, cilantro, and sour cream.

Nutrition: Calories: 260 Fat: 3g Carbs: 36g Protein: 23g Sodium: 922mg Potassium: 445mg Phosphorus: 357mg

128. Marinated Shrimp Pasta Salad

Ingredients: Preparation Time: 15 minutes
Cooking Time: 5 hours
Servings: 1

- 1/4 cup of honey
- 1/4 cup of balsamic vinegar
- 1/2 of an English cucumber, cubed
- 1/2 pound of fully cooked shrimp
- 15 baby carrots
- 1.5 cups of dime-sized cut cauliflower
- 4 stalks of celery, diced
- 1/2 large yellow bell pepper (diced)
- 1/2 red onion (diced)
- 1/2 large red bell pepper (diced)
- 12 ounces of uncooked tri-color pasta (cooked)
- 3/4 cup of olive oil
- 3 tsp. of mustard (Dijon)
- 1/2 tsp. of garlic (powder)
- 1/2 tsp. pepper

Directions:
1. Cut vegetables and put them in a bowl with the shrimp.
2. Whisk together the honey, balsamic vinegar, garlic powder, pepper, and Dijon mustard in a small bowl. While still whisking, slowly add the oil and whisk it all together.
3. Add the cooked pasta to the bowl with the shrimp and vegetables and mix it.
4. Toss the sauce to coat the pasta, shrimp, and vegetables evenly.
5. Cover and chill for a minimum of five hours before serving. Stir and serve while chilled.

Nutrition: Calories: 205 Fat: 13g Carbs: 10g Protein: 12g Sodium: 363mg Potassium: 156mg Phosphorus: 109mg

129. Mushrooms Velvet Soup

Preparation Time: 40 minutes
Cooking Time: 40 minutes
Servings: 6
Ingredients:

- 1 teaspoon olive oil
- ½ teaspoon fresh ground black pepper
- 3 medium (85g) shallots, diced
- 2 stalks (80g) celery, chopped
- 1 clove garlic, diced
- 12-ounces cremini mushrooms, sliced
- 5 tablespoons flour
- 4 cups low sodium vegetable stock, divided
- 3 sprigs fresh thyme
- 2 bay leaves
- ½ cup regular yogurt

Directions:

1. Heat oil in a large pan.
2. Add ground pepper, shallots and celery. Cook over medium-high heat.
3. Sauté for 2 minutes until golden.
4. Add garlic and stir.
5. Include the sliced mushrooms. Stir and cook until the mushrooms give out their liquid.
6. Sprawl the flour on the mushrooms and toast for about 2 min.
7. Add one cup of hot stock, thyme sprigs and bay leaves. Stir and add the second cup of stock
8. Stir until well combined.
9. Add the remaining cups of stock.
10. Slowly cook for 15 minutes.
11. Take out bay leaves and thyme sprigs.
12. Blend until mixture is smooth.
13. Include the yogurt and stir well.
14. Slowly cook for 4 minutes.
15. Serve and enjoy!

Nutrition: Calories 126 Fat 8 g Cholesterol 0 mg Carbohydrate 14 g Sugar 4 g Fiber 2 g Protein 3 g Sodium 108 mg Calcium 55 mg Phosphorus 70 mg Potassium 298 mg

130. Grilled Onion and Pepper Jack Grilled Cheese Sandwich

Preparation Time: 5 minutes
Cooking Time: 5 minutes
Servings: 2
Ingredients:

- 1 tsp. of oil (olive)
- 6 tsp. of whipped cream cheese
- 1/2 of a medium onion
- 2 ounces of pepper jack cheese
- 4 slices of rye bread
- 2 tsp. of unsalted butter

Directions:

1. Set out the butter so that it becomes soft. Slice up the onion into thin slices.
2. Sauté onion slices. Continue to stir until cooked. Remove and put it to the side.
3. Spread one tablespoon of the whipped cream cheese on two of the slices of bread.
4. Then add grilled onions and cheese to each slice. Then top using the other two bread slices.
5. Spread the softened butter on the outside of the slices of bread.
6. Use the skillet to toast the sandwiches until lightly brown and the cheese is melted.

Nutrition: Calories: 350 Fat: 18g Carbs: 34g Protein: 13g Sodium: 589mg Potassium: 184mg Phosphorus: 226mg

131. Lemon Chicken

Preparation Time: 20 minutes
Cooking Time: 24 minutes
Servings: 4

Ingredients:

- 2 lemons
- 12 ounces' boneless skinless chicken breasts, cubed
- 2 tablespoons extra-virgin olive oil
- 1/8 teaspoon salt
- 1/8 teaspoon freshly ground black pepper
- ½ large onion, chopped
- 1 cup 2-inch green bean pieces
- 1 cup 2-inch asparagus pieces

Directions:

1. Zest one of the lemons and place the zest into a medium bowl. Juice that lemon and add the juice to the bowl. Slice the remaining lemon, remove the seeds, and set aside.
2. In the bowl with the lemon juice, place the cubed chicken and set aside for 10 minutes to marinate.
3. When ready to cook, in a large skillet, heat the olive oil over medium heat.
4. Using a slotted spoon, remove the chicken from the lemon juice, reserving the lemon juice mixture. Add the chicken to the pan and cook for 3 to 4 minutes, stirring, until the chicken is lightly browned. It doesn't have to be completely cooked. Transfer the chicken to a clean plate and sprinkle with the salt and pepper.
5. Add the sliced lemon to the skillet and cook for 3 minutes on each side, turning once, until it is slightly caramelized. Transfer to the plate with the chicken.
6. Add the onion to the skillet and cook for 3 to 4 minutes, until the onion is tender-crisp, stirring to loosen the chicken drippings from the skillet.
7. Add the green beans and sauté for 2 minutes. Add the asparagus and sauté for 1 minute.
8. Return the chicken to the skillet and add the reserved lemon juice. Simmer for 4 to 6 minutes or until the chicken is thoroughly cooked to 165°F, the vegetables are tender, and the sauce has slightly thickened.
9. Add the caramelized lemon slices to the skillet and cook for 1 to 2 minutes, stirring, until hot. Serve.

Nutrition: Calories: 207; Total fat: 9g; Saturated fat: 1g; Sodium: 121mg; Phosphorus: 245mg; Potassium: 593mg; Carbohydrates: 11g; Fiber: 4g; Protein: 22g; Sugar: 5g

132. Easy Lettuce Wraps

Preparation Time: 15 minutes
Cooking Time: 0 minutes
Servings: 4

Ingredients:

- 8 ounces cooked chicken, shredded
- 1 scallion, chopped
- ½ cup seedless red grapes, halved
- 1 celery stalk, chopped
- ¼ cup mayonnaise
- A pinch ground black pepper
- 4 large lettuce leaves

Directions:

1. In a mixing bowl add the scallion, chicken, celery, grapes and mayonnaise.
2. Stir well until incorporated.
3. Season with pepper.
4. Place the lettuce leaves onto serving plates.
5. Place the chicken salad onto the leaves.
6. Serve and enjoy!

Nutrition: Calories 146 Fat 5 g Cholesterol 35 mg Carbohydrates 8 g Sugar 4 g Fiber 0 g Protein 16 g Sodium 58 mg Calcium 18 mg Phosphorus 125 mg Potassium 212 mg

133. Fish Taco Filling

Preparation Time: 15 minutes
Cooking Time: 10 minutes

Servings: 4

Ingredients:

- 2 tablespoons extra-virgin olive oil
- 2 shallots, minced
- 3 (6-ounce) sole fillets, cut into strips
- 2 teaspoons chili powder
- 1 lime, zested and juiced
- 3 cups cabbage coleslaw mix with carrots

Directions:

1. In a large skillet, heat the olive oil over medium heat.
2. Add the shallots and cook for 3 minutes, stirring, until softened.
3. Add the sole fillets and sprinkle with the chili powder. Cook for 3 to 5 minutes, stirring gently, until the fish flakes when tested with a fork. Remove the skillet from the heat.
4. Drizzle the lime zest and juice over the fish.
5. Serve with the coleslaw in tacos or over rice.
6. Increase Protein Tip: To make this a medium-protein recipe, add one more 6-ounce sole fillet. The protein content will increase to 18g per serving.

Ingredient Tip: If you like spicy food, you can add 1 diced medium jalapeño pepper to the shallots or add ½ teaspoon of red pepper flakes to the fish mixture along with the lime juice and zest.

Nutrition: Calories: 176; Total fat: 9g; Saturated fat: 1g; Sodium: 315mg; Phosphorus: 265mg; Potassium: 451mg; Carbohydrates: 14g; Fiber: 4g; Protein: 13g; Sugar: 6g

134. Roasted Cod with Plums

Preparation Time: 10 minutes
Cooking Time: 20 minutes
Servings: 4

Ingredients:

- 6 red plums, halved and pitted
- 1½ pounds cod fillets
- 3 tablespoons extra-virgin olive oil
- 2 tablespoons freshly squeezed lemon juice
- ½ teaspoon dried thyme leaves
- 1/8 teaspoon salt
- 1/8 teaspoon freshly ground black pepper
- ¾ cup plain whole-almond milk yogurt, for serving

Directions:

1. Preheat the oven to 375°F. Line a baking sheet with parchment paper.
2. Arrange the plums, cut-side up, along with the fish on the prepared baking sheet. Drizzle with the olive oil and lemon juice and sprinkle with the thyme, salt, and pepper.
3. Roast for 15 to 20 minutes or until the fish flakes when tested with a fork and the plums are tender.
4. Serve with the yogurt.
5. Ingredient Tip: There's no need to measure out exactly 2 tablespoons of lemon juice. A standard-size lemon has approximately 2 tablespoons juice in it. Simply squeeze all the juice from the lemon, being careful to avoid squeezing in the seeds.

Nutrition: Calories: 230; Total fat: 9g; Saturated fat: 2g; Sodium: 154mg; Phosphorus: 197mg; Potassium: 437mg; Carbohydrates: 10g; Fiber: 1g; Protein: 27g; Sugar: 8g

135. Spaghetti with Pesto

Preparation Time: 10 minutes
Cooking Time: 10 minutes
Servings: 4

Ingredients:

- 8 ounces spaghetti (package pasta)
- 2 cups packed basil leaves

- 2 cups packed arugula leaves
- 1/3 cup walnut pieces
- 3 cloves of garlic
- ¼ cup extra-virgin olive oil
- Black pepper

Directions:
1. Cook pasta with boiling water. Drain.
2. Add the basil, garlic, olive oil, walnuts, pepper and arugula in a blender and mix until creamy.
3. Mix pesto mixture into pasta in a large bowl.
4. Serve and enjoy!

Nutrition: Calories 400 Fat 21 g Cholesterol 0 mg Carbohydrates 46 g Sugar 2 g Fiber 3 g Protein 11 g Sodium 6 mg Calcium 64 mg Phosphorus 113 mg Potassium 202 mg

136. Corn and Shrimp Quiche

Preparation Time: 15 minutes
Cooking Time: 50 minutes
Servings: 6

Ingredients:
- 1 cup small cooked shrimp
- 1½ cups frozen corn, thawed and drained
- 5 large eggs, beaten
- 1 cup unsweetened almond milk
- Pinch salt
- 1/8 teaspoon freshly ground black pepper

Directions:
1. Preheat the oven to 350°F. Spray a 9-inch pie pan with nonstick baking spray.
2. In the prepared pan, combine the shrimp and corn.
3. In a medium bowl, beat the eggs, almond milk, salt, and pepper. Gently pour into the pan.

4. Bake for 45 to 55 minutes or until the quiche is puffed, set to the touch, and light golden brown on top. Let stand for 10 minutes before cutting into wedges to serve.
5. Ingredient Tip: Shrimp are measured according to the number per pound. So bigger shrimp have a lower number per pound. For this recipe, small shrimp should be about 50 per pound. Medium shrimp are usually 36 to 40 per pound. You can cut larger shrimp into small pieces instead of buying small shrimp if you'd like.

Nutrition: Calories: 198; Total fat: 10g; Saturated fat: 4g; Sodium: 238mg; Phosphorus: 260mg; Potassium: 261mg; Carbohydrates: 9g; Fiber: 1g; Protein: 20g; Sugar: 2g

137. Ginger-Mango Tuna Pasta Salad

Preparation Time: 20 minutes
Cooking Time: 9 minutes
Servings: 6

Ingredients:
- 3 cups whole-wheat ziti pasta
- 1 large navel mango, zested and juiced
- ¼ cup extra-virgin olive oil
- 2 tablespoons yellow prepared mustard
- ¼ teaspoon ground ginger
- Pinch salt
- 1 large navel mango, peeled and segmented
- 1 (6-ounce) can light low-sodium tuna, drained

Directions:
1. Bring a large pot of water to a boil. Add the pasta and cook according to package directions, until the pasta is al dente. Drain and set aside.
2. In a large bowl, whisk the mango juice and zest, olive oil, mustard, ginger, and

salt until combined. Add the mango segments and tuna and stir to coat.

3. When the pasta is done, drain and add to the bowl with the dressing and other ingredients. Toss to coat.
4. Cover and chill the salad for 2 to 3 hours, stirring once.
5. Increase Protein Tip: To make this a medium-protein recipe, add one more can of drained tuna. The protein content will increase to 19g per serving.

Nutrition: Calories: 305; Total fat: 11g; Saturated fat: 2g; Sodium: 105mg; Phosphorus: 218mg; Potassium: 379mg; Carbohydrates: 43g; Fiber: 6g; Protein: 13g; Sugar: 7g

138. Pineapple-Soy Salmon Stir-Fry

Preparation Time: 15 minutes
Cooking Time: 15 minutes
Servings: 4
Ingredients:

- 1 (8-ounce) can crushed pineapple, strained, reserving juice
- 2 tablespoons low-sodium soy sauce
- 1 tablespoon cornstarch
- 1/8 teaspoon freshly ground black pepper
- 2 tablespoons extra-virgin olive oil
- 2 (6-ounce) salmon fillets without skin, cubed
- 1 (16-ounce) bag frozen stir-fry vegetables

Directions:

1. In a small bowl, whisk the reserved pineapple juice, soy sauce, cornstarch, and pepper and set aside.
2. In a large wok or skillet, heat the olive oil. Add the salmon cubes and stir-fry for 3 to 4 minutes, or until the salmon flakes with a fork. Using a slotted

spoon, transfer the salmon to a plate and set aside.
3. Add the frozen vegetables to the wok and stir-fry for another 3 to 4 minutes, or until the vegetables are hot and tender.
4. Return the salmon to the wok and add the pineapple.
5. Whisk the sauce again and add to the wok; stir-fry for 3 to 4 minutes or until the sauce bubbles and has thickened. Serve.
6. Ingredient Tip: You can make this recipe with just about any protein, such as cubed boneless skinless chicken breasts, cod or sole, or peeled and deveined shrimp. To make this recipe gluten-free, use low-sodium tamari instead of soy sauce.

Nutrition: Calories: 280; Total fat: 13g; Saturated fat: 2g; Sodium: 361mg; Phosphorus: 271mg; Potassium: 599mg; Carbohydrates: 21g; Fiber: 3g; Protein: 22g; Sugar: 11g

139. Ginger Shrimp with Snow Peas

Preparation Time: 20 minutes
Cooking Time: 12 minutes
Servings: 4
Ingredients:

- 2 tablespoons extra-virgin olive oil
- 1 tablespoon minced peeled fresh ginger
- 2 cups snow peas
- 1½ cups frozen baby peas
- 3 tablespoons water
- 1-pound medium shrimp, shelled and deveined
- 2 tablespoons low-sodium soy sauce
- 1/8 teaspoon freshly ground black pepper

Directions:

1. In a large wok or skillet, heat the olive oil over medium heat.
2. Add the ginger and stir-fry for 1 to 2 minutes, until the ginger is fragrant.
3. Add the snow peas and stir-fry for 2 to 3 minutes, until they are tender-crisp.
4. Add the baby peas and the water and stir. Cover the wok and steam for 2 to 3 minutes or until the vegetables are tender.
5. Stir in the shrimp and stir-fry for 3 to 4 minutes, or until the shrimp have curled and turned pink.
6. Add the soy sauce and pepper; stir and serve.
7. Ingredient Tip: Snow peas can have a tough string along one side that won't soften very well during the stir-fry process. Just pinch the curly end of the pod and pull to remove it. Discard the string.

Nutrition: Calories: 237; Total fat: 7g; Saturated fat: 1g; Sodium: 469mg; Phosphorus: 350mg; Potassium: 504mg; Carbohydrates: 12g; Fiber: 4g; Protein: 32g; Sugar: 5g

140. Curried Chicken Stir-Fry

Preparation Time: 20 minutes
Cooking Time: 15 minutes
Servings: 6
Ingredients:

- 12 ounces' boneless skinless chicken breasts, cut into 1-inch cubes
- 2 teaspoons curry powder
- 1/8 teaspoon salt
- 1/8 teaspoon freshly ground black pepper
- 1 (20-ounce) can pineapple tidbits, strained, reserving juice
- 2 tablespoons extra-virgin olive oil
- 1 yellow onion, chopped
- 2 red bell peppers, chopped

Directions:
1. In a medium bowl, toss the chicken, curry powder, salt, and pepper and set aside.
2. In a small saucepan, heat the reserved pineapple juice over low heat. Let it reduce, stirring occasionally, while you make the rest of the stir-fry.
3. In a large skillet, heat the olive oil over medium heat. Add the chicken. Stir-fry for 3 for 4 minutes or until the chicken is light brown; it doesn't have to cook completely. Transfer the chicken to a plate.
4. Add the onion to the skillet and cook for 3 minutes, stirring, until the onion is crisp-tender. Check to make sure the pineapple liquid isn't burning and continue to stir it. Add the bell peppers and stir-fry for another 3 minutes, until crisp tender.
5. Return the chicken to the skillet, add the pineapple tidbits and cook, stirring, for 3 to 4 minutes or until the chicken is cooked through.
6. Add the thickened pineapple juice to the skillet and stir. Serve.
7. Increase Protein Tip: To make this a high-protein recipe, increase the chicken to 1 pound. The protein content will increase to 25g per serving.

Nutrition: Calories: 215; Total fat: 7g; Saturated fat: 1g; Sodium: 98mg; Phosphorus: 146mg; Potassium: 374mg; Carbohydrates: 19g; Fiber: 2g; Protein: 19g; Sugar: 16g

141. Juicy Salmon Dish

Preparation Time: 5 minutes
Cooking Time: 6 minutes
Serving: 3
Ingredients:

- ¾ cup of water

- Few sprigs of parsley, basil, tarragon, basil
- 1 pound of salmon, skin on
- 3 teaspoons of ghee
- ¼ teaspoon of salt
- ½ teaspoon of pepper
- ½ of lemon, thinly sliced
- 1 whole carrot, julienned

Directions:
1. Set your pot to Sauté mode and add water and herbs
2. Place a steamer rack inside your pot and place salmon
3. Drizzle ghee on top of the salmon and season with salt and pepper
4. Cover with lemon slices
5. Cook on HIGH pressure with locked lid for 3 minutes
6. Release the pressure naturally over 10 minutes
7. Transfer the salmon to a serving platter
8. Set your pot to Sauté mode and add vegetables
9. Cook for 1-2 minutes
10. Serve with vegetables and salmon
11. Enjoy!

Nutrition Values Calories: 464 Fat: 34g Carbohydrates: 3g Protein: 34g

142. Chicken with Quinoa and Wild Rice

Preparation Time: 10 minutes
Cooking Time: 40 minutes
Servings: 4

Ingredients:
- ½ cup kale
- 1 cup red onion
- 10 garlic cloves
- 1 tablespoon olive oil
- 6 tablespoons lemon juice
- 1 tablespoon black pepper

- 1 cup quinoa, uncooked
- 1 cup white rice, uncooked
- 4 cups low-sodium chicken broth
- 2 pounds boneless, skinless chicken breast
- 5 tablespoons fresh basil

Directions:
1. Preheat oven to 375°F.
2. Chop kale. Chop the red onion and garlic.
3. Add olive oil, 4 tablespoons of lemon juice, pepper, onion, garlic, quinoa and rice and chicken broth to a 9-inch x 13-inch baking pan. Mix ingredients together.
4. Add kale on top of rice mixture.
5. Add chicken breast on top of kale.
6. Cover with foil and bake for 45 minutes or until chicken is done and the majority of chicken broth has been absorbed.
7. Let sit for 5-10 minutes. While dish is cooling, chop fresh parsley and combine with remaining 2 tablespoon lemon juice. Sprinkle on top and enjoy!

Nutrition: Calories 146, Total Fat 2.7g, Saturated Fat 0.4g, Cholesterol 11mg, Sodium 40mg, Total Carbohydrate 21.8g, Dietary Fiber 2.4g, Total Sugar 1g, Protein 8.7g, Calcium 27mg, Iron 1mg, Potassium 270mg, Phosphorus 206 mg

143. BlackBerry Chicken Wings

Preparation Time: 35 minutes
Cooking Time: 50 minutes
Serving: 4
Ingredients:
- 3 pounds chicken wings, about 20 pieces
- ½ cup blackberry chipotle jam
- Salt and pepper to taste
- ½ cup of water

Directions:

1. Add water and jam to a bowl and mix well
2. Place chicken wings in a zip bag and add two-thirds of the marinade
3. Season with salt and pepper
4. Let it marinate for 30 minutes
5. Preheat your oven to 400°F
6. Prepare a baking sheet and wire rack, place chicken wings in a wire rack and bake for 15 minutes
7. Brush remaining marinade and bake for 30 minutes more
8. Enjoy!

Nutrition Calories: 502 Fat: 39g Carbohydrates: 01.8g Protein: 34g

144. Platter-O-Brussels

Preparation Time: 10 minutes
Cooking Time: 20 minutes
Serving: 4
Ingredients:

- 2 tablespoons olive oil
- 1 yellow onion, chopped
- 2 pounds Brussels sprouts, trimmed and halved
- 4 cups chicken stock
- ¼ cup coconut cream

Directions:

1. Take a pot and place over medium heat
2. Add oil and let it heat up
3. Add onion and stir cook for 3 minutes
4. Add Brussels sprouts and stir, cook for 2 minutes
5. Add stock and black pepper, stir and bring to a simmer
6. Cook for 20 minutes more
7. Blend until creamy.
8. Add coconut cream and stir well
9. Ladle into soup bowls and serve
10. Enjoy!

Nutrition Calories: 200 Fat: 11g Carbohydrates: 6g Protein: 11g

145. Ratatouille

Preparation Time: 5 minutes
Cooking Time: 15 minutes
Servings: 4
Ingredients:

- 1 cup Water
- 3 tbsp. oil
- 2 Zucchinis, sliced in rings
- 2 Eggplants, sliced in rings
- 1 medium Red Onion, sliced in thin rings
- 3 cloves Garlic, minced
- 2 sprigs Fresh Thyme
- Salt to taste
- Black Pepper to taste
- 4 tsp Plain Vinegar

Directions:

1. Place all veggies in a bowl, sprinkle with salt and pepper; toss. Line foil in a spring form tin and arrange 1 slice each of the vegetables in, one after the other in a tight circular arrangement.
2. Fill the entire tin. Sprinkle the garlic over, some more black pepper and salt, and arrange the thyme sprigs on top. Drizzle olive oil and vinegar over the veggies.
3. Place a trivet to fit in the Instant Pot, pour the water in and place the veggies on the trivet. Seal the lid, secure the pressure valve and select Manual mode on High Pressure for 6 minutes. Once ready, quickly release the pressure. Carefully remove the tin and serve ratatouille.

Nutrition: Calories 152, Protein 2g, Net Carbs 4g, Fat 12g Potassium: 220 mg; Sodium: 86 mg;

146. Vegetable Casserole

Preparation Time: 15 minutes
Cooking Time: 15 minutes

Servings: 8
Ingredients:

- 1 teaspoon olive oil
- 1 sweet onion, chopped
- 1 teaspoon garlic, minced
- 2 zucchinis, chopped
- 1 red bell pepper, diced
- 2 carrots, chopped
- 2 cups low-sodium vegetable stock
- 2 large Red bell peppers, chopped
- 2 cups broccoli florets
- 1 teaspoon ground coriander
- ½ teaspoon ground comminutes
- Black pepper

Directions:

1. Heat the olive oil into a big pan over medium-high heat.
2. Add onion and garlic. Softly cook for about 3 minutes until softened.
3. Include the zucchini, carrots, bell pepper and softly cook for 5-6 minutes.
4. Pour the vegetable stock, Red bell peppers, broccoli, coriander, cumin, pepper and stir well.
5. Softly cook for about 5 minutes over medium-high heat until the vegetables are tender.
6. Serve hot and enjoy!

Nutrition: Calories 47 Fat 1 g Cholesterol 0 g Carbohydrates 8 g Sugar 6 g Fiber 2 g Protein 2 g Sodium 104 mg Calcium 36 mg Phosphorus 52 mg Potassium 298 mg

147. Almond Chicken

Preparation Time: 15 minutes
Cooking Time: 15 minutes
Serving: 3
Ingredients:

- 2 large chicken breasts, boneless and skinless
- 1/3 cup lemon juice
- 1 ½ cups seasoned almond meal
- 2 tablespoons coconut oil
- Lemon pepper, to taste
- Parsley for decoration

Directions:

1. Slice chicken breast in half
2. Pound out each half until ¼ inch thick
3. Take a pan and place over medium heat, add oil and heat it up
4. Dip each chicken breast slice into lemon juice and let it sit for 2 minutes
5. Turnover and let the other side sit for 2 minutes as well
6. Transfer to almond meal and coat both sides
7. Add coated chicken and fry for 4 minutes per side, making sure to sprinkle lemon pepper liberally
8. Transfer to a paper-lined sheet and repeat until all chicken is fried
9. Garnish with parsley and enjoy!

Nutrition Calories: 325 Fat: 24g Carbohydrates: 3g Protein: 16g

148. Spiced Up Pork Chops

Preparation Time: 4 hours 10 minutes
Cooking Time: 15 minutes
Serving: 4
Ingredients:

- ¼ cup lime juice
- 4 pork rib chops
- 1 tablespoon coconut oil, melted
- 2 garlic cloves, peeled and minced
- 1 tablespoon chili powder
- 1 teaspoon ground cinnamon
- 2 teaspoons cumin
- Salt and pepper to taste
- ½ teaspoon hot pepper sauce
- Mango, sliced

Directions:

1. Take a bowl and mix in lime juice, oil, garlic, cumin, cinnamon, chili powder, salt, pepper, hot pepper sauce
2. Whisk well
3. Add pork chops and toss
4. Keep it on the side and refrigerate for 4 hours
5. Pre-heat your grill to medium and transfer pork chops to a pre-heated grill
6. Grill for 7 minutes both sides
7. Divide between serving platters and serve with mango slices
8. Enjoy!

Nutrition Calories: 200 Fat: 8g Carbohydrates: 3g Protein: 26g

149. Beef Stir-Fry

Preparation Time: 5 minutes
Cooking Time: 15 minutes
Servings: 4

Ingredients:

- 4 cups water
- 2 tablespoons cornstarch
- 2 teaspoons honey
- 6 tablespoons Worcestershire sauce
- 1 tablespoon minced fresh ginger
- 1-pound boneless beef round steak, cut into thin strips
- 1 tablespoon olive oil
- 3 cups broccoli florets
- 2 carrots, thinly sliced
- 1 (6 ounce) package frozen pea pods, thawed
- 2 tablespoons chopped onion
- 1 (8 ounce) can sliced water chestnuts, untrained
- 1 cup cabbage
- ½ cup kale, chopped
- 1 tablespoon olive oil

Directions:

1. Combine corn-starch, honey, and Worcestershire sauce, in a small bowl

until smooth. Stir in ginger; toss beef in sauce to coat.
2. Heat 1 tablespoon oil in a large skillet over medium-high heat. Cook and stir broccoli, carrots, pea pods, and onion for 1 minute. Stir in water chestnuts, cabbage, and kale; cover and simmer until vegetables are tender, about 4 minutes. Remove from skillet and keep warm.
3. In same skillet, heat 1 tablespoon oil over medium-high heat. Cook and stir beef until desired degree of doneness, about 2 minutes per side for medium. Return vegetables to skillet; cook and stir until heated through, about 3 minutes.

Nutrition: Calories 139, Total Fat 3.9g, Saturated Fat 0.8g, Cholesterol 12mg, Sodium 972mg, Total Carbohydrate 18.7g, Dietary Fiber 4g, Total Sugar 5.8g,

150. Appetizing Rice Salad

Preparation Time: 20 minutes
Cooking Time: 1 hour
Servings: 8

Ingredients:

- 1 cup wild rice
- 2 cups water
- 1 tablespoon olive oil
- 2/3 cup walnuts, chopped
- 1 (4 inches) celery rib, sliced
- 4 scallions, thinly sliced
- 1 medium red apple, cored and diced
- ½ cup pomegranate seeds
- ½ tablespoon lemon zest
- 3 tablespoons lemon juice
- Black pepper
- 1/3 cup olive oil

Directions:

1. In a big pot place the wild strained rice together with water and olive oil.

2. Bring to a boil and simmer for about 50 minutes until rice is tender.
3. In a mixing bowl add celery, walnuts, apple, scallions, pomegranate seeds and lemon zest.
4. Mix well with a blender the lemon juice, pepper, and olive oil.
5. Spread half of this dressing on the apple mixture and mix well.
6. When the rice is cooked, let it cool and incorporate with the fruit mixture
7. Season with the remaining dressing.
8. Serve at room temperature and enjoy!

Nutrition: Calories 300 Fat 19 g Cholesterol 0 mg Carbohydrates 34 g Sugar 11 g Fiber 5 g Protein 6 g Sodium 6 mg Calcium 30 mg Phosphorus 144 mg Potassium 296 mg

151. Couscous and Sherry Vinaigrette

Preparation Time: 10 minutes
Cooking Time: 30 minutes
Servings: 6
Ingredients:

- For Sherry Vinaigrette: (makes 2/3 cup)
- 2 tablespoons sherry vinegar
- ¼ cup lemon juice
- 1 clove garlic, pressed
- 1/3 cup olive oil
- For Roasted Carrots, Cranberries and Couscous:
- 1 medium onion, sliced
- 2 large carrots, sliced
- 2 tablespoons extra-virgin olive oil
- 2 cups pearl couscous
- 2 ½ to 3 cups no sodium vegetable broth
- ½ cup dried cranberries
- ¼ cup Sherry vinaigrette

Directions:
1. For Sherry Vinaigrette:

2. Beat the vinegar with garlic and lemon juice.
3. Slowly whisk in olive oil.
4. Store refrigerated in a glass jar.
5. For Carrots, Cranberries and Couscous:
6. Preheat oven to 400°F.
7. Spray a baking dish with cooking spray (olive oil) and place the carrots and onions on it.
8. Roast the vegetables in oven for about 20 minutes until starting to brown. Stir halfway cooking.
9. Heat the couscous in a pan over medium-high heat.
10. Toast the couscous until light brown (about 10 minutes). Stir well.
11. Check the package instructions for the amount of liquid needed for couscous.
12. Bring to a boil the added vegetable stock. Cover and reduce for about 10 minutes. The vegetable stock has to be absorbed.
13. In a mixing bowl, incorporate the couscous with the onions, carrots, cranberries, and sherry vinaigrette.
14. Serve and enjoy!

Nutrition: Calories 365 Fat 11 g Cholesterol 0 mg Carbohydrate 58 g Sugar 11 g Fiber 4 g Protein 9 g Sodium 95 mg Calcium 41 mg Phosphorus 119 mg Potassium 264 mg

152. Spiced Wraps

Preparation Time: 30 minutes
Cooking Time: 0 minutes
Servings: 8
Ingredients:

- 6 ounces cooked chicken breast, minced
- 1 scallion, chopped
- ½ red apple, cored and chopped
- ½ cup bean sprouts
- ¼ cucumber, chopped
- Juice of 1 lime
- Zest of 1 lime

- 2 tablespoons fresh cilantro, chopped
- ½ teaspoon Chinese five-spice powder
- 8 lettuce leaves

Directions:
1. Combine the chicken, apple, bean sprouts, cucumber, lime juice, lime zest, cilantro, five-spice powder and scallions.
2. Place the lettuce leaves onto 8 serving plates.
3. Spoon the chicken mixture onto lettuce leaves.
4. Wrap the lettuce around the chicken mixture.
5. Serve and enjoy!

Nutrition: Calories 53 Fat 3 g Cholesterol 19 mg Carbohydrates 3 g Sugar 3 g Fiber 2 g Protein 7 g Sodium 19 mg Calcium 16 mg Phosphorus 58 mg Potassium 134

153. Maple-Brined Pork Loin

Preparation Time: 15 minutes
Cooking Time: 60 minutes
Servings: 4
Ingredients:
- 1-quart cold water
- 1/3 cup maple syrup
- 3 cloves garlic, crushed
- 3 tablespoons chopped fresh ginger
- 2 teaspoons dried rosemary
- 1 tablespoon cracked black pepper
- 1 boneless pork loin roast
- salt and freshly ground black pepper
- 1 tablespoon olive oil
- 2 tablespoons maple syrup
- 2 tablespoons Dijon mustard

Directions:
1. Mix water, salt, 1/3 cup maple syrup, garlic, ginger, rosemary, and black pepper, in a large bowl. Place pork loin in brine mixture and refrigerate for 8 to 10 hours.

2. Remove pork from brine, pat dry, and season all sides with salt and black pepper.
3. Preheat oven to 325 degrees F.
4. Heat olive oil in an oven-proof skillet over high heat. Cook pork, turning to brown each side, about 10 minutes' total.
5. Transfer skillet to the oven and roast until pork is browned, about 40 minutes.
6. Mix 2 tablespoons maple syrup and Dijon mustard together in a small bowl.
7. Remove pork roast from the oven and spread maple syrup mixture on all sides. Cook for an additional 15 minutes, until the pork is no longer pink in the center. An instant-read thermometer inserted into the center should read 145 degrees F.

Nutrition: Calories 158, Total Fat 5g, Saturated Fat 0.9g, Cholesterol 16mg, Sodium 106mg, Total Carbohydrate 23.1g, Dietary Fiber 1.5g, Total Sugar 15.9g,

154. Rump Roast

Ingredients:
1- Preparation Time: 10 minutes
Cooking Time: 5 hours
Servings: 8
- pound rump roast
- ½ teaspoon black pepper
- 1 tablespoon olive oil
- ½ small onion, chopped
- 2 teaspoons garlic, minced
- 1 teaspoon dried thyme
- 1 cup + 3 tablespoons water
- 2 tablespoons cornstarch

Directions:
1. Heat the olive oil into a big saucepan over medium heat.
2. Add the peppered meat and brown the roast all over. Set aside the meat.

3. Softly cook the garlic and onion in the same saucepan for about 3 minutes until they are tendered.
4. Incorporate the roast to the saucepan, add 1 cup of water and the thyme.
5. Cover, simmer until the meat is tender or for 4 and half hours.
6. In a mixing bowl, stir the cornstarch with 3 tablespoons water to form a slurry.
7. Beat the slurry into the liquid in the pan and cook for about 15 minutes to thicken the sauce.
8. Serve and enjoy!

Nutrition: Calories 156 Fat 12 g Cholesterol 42 mg Carbohydrates 4 g Sugar 2 g Fiber 0 g Protein 14 g Sodium 48 mg Calcium 18 mg Phosphorus 114 mg Potassium 220 mg

155. Pineapple and Mint Lamb Chops

Preparation Time: 10 minutes
Cooking Time: 10 minutes
Servings: 4
Ingredients:
- 1/2 tablespoon olive oil
- 2 tablespoons pineapple juice
- ¼ tablespoon chopped fresh mint
- Salt and pepper to taste
- 4 lamb chops

Directions:
1. Stir together olive oil, pineapple juice, and mint in a small bowl. Season with salt and pepper to taste. Place lamb chops in a shallow dish, and brush with the olive oil mixture. Marinate in the refrigerator for 1 hour.
2. Preheat grill for high heat.
3. Lightly oil grill grate. Place lamb chops on grill, and discard marinade. Cook for 10 minutes, turning once, or to desired doneness.

Nutrition: Calories 137, Total Fat 6.4g, Saturated Fat 1.9g, Cholesterol 57mg, Sodium 49mg, Total Carbohydrate 0.8g, Dietary Fiber 0g, Total Sugar 0.7g,

156. Stir-Fried Vegetables

Preparation Time: 15 minutes
Cooking Time: 15 minutes
Servings: 4
Ingredients:
- 2 teaspoons of olive oil
- ½ medium red onion, sliced
- 1 tablespoon of grated peeled fresh ginger
- 2 teaspoons of minced garlic
- 2 cups of broccoli florets
- 2 cups of cauliflower florets
- 1 red bell pepper, diced
- 1 cup of sliced carrots

Directions:
1. In a large skillet over medium-high heat, heat the olive oil.
2. Add the onion, ginger, and garlic and sauté until softened, about 3 minutes.
3. Add the broccoli, cauliflower, bell pepper, carrots, and sauté until tender, about 10 minutes.
4. Serve hot.

Nutrition: Calories: 50 Total fat: 1g Saturated fat: 0g Cholesterol: 0mg Sodium: 26mg Carbohydrates: 6g Fiber: 2g Phosphorus: 36mg Potassium: 198mg Protein: 1g

157. Lime Asparagus Spaghetti

Preparation Time: 5 minutes
Cooking Time: 20 minutes
Servings: 6
Ingredients:
- 1 pound of asparagus spears, trimmed and cut into 2-inch pieces

- 2 teaspoons of olive oil
- 2 teaspoons of minced garlic
- 2 teaspoons of all-purpose flour
- 1 cup of Homemade Rice Almond milk (here, or use unsweetened store-bought) or almond milk
- Juice and zest of ½ lemon
- 1 tablespoon of chopped fresh thyme
- Freshly ground black pepper
- 2 cups of cooked spaghetti
- ¼ cup of grated Parmesan cheese

Directions:

1. Fill a large saucepan with water and bring to a boil over high heat. Add the asparagus and blanch until crisp-tender, about 2 minutes. Drain and set aside.
2. In a large skillet over medium-high heat, heat the olive oil. Add the garlic, and sauté until softened, about 2 minutes. Whisk in the flour to create a paste, about 1 minute. Whisk in the rice almond milk, lemon juice, lemon zest, and thyme.
3. Reduce the heat to medium and cook the sauce, whisking constantly, until thickened and creamy, about 3 minutes.
4. Season the sauce with pepper.
5. Stir in the spaghetti and the asparagus.
6. Serve the pasta topped with the Parmesan cheese.

Nutrition: Calories: 127 Total fat: 3g Saturated fat: 1g Cholesterol: 4mg Sodium: 67mg Carbohydrates: 19g Fiber: 2g Phosphorus 109mg Potassium: 200mg Protein: 6g

158. Garden Crustless Quiche

Preparation Time: 25 minutes
Cooking Time: 20 minutes
Servings: 6
Ingredients:

- 6 eggs
- 2 egg whites
- ¼ cup of Homemade Rice Almond milk (here or use unsweetened store-bought)
- ¼ cup of shredded Swiss cheese, divided
- ¼ teaspoon of freshly ground black pepper
- 1 teaspoon of unsalted butter, plus more for the pie plate
- 1 teaspoon of minced garlic
- 1 scallion, white and green parts, chopped
- 1 yellow zucchini, chopped
- ½ cup of shredded stemmed kale

Directions:

1. In a medium bowl, beat the eggs, egg whites, rice almond milk, half the Swiss cheese, and the pepper until well blended, and set aside.
2. Preheat the oven to 350°F.
3. Grease a 9-inch pie plate with butter and set aside.
4. In a medium skillet over medium-high heat, melt 1 teaspoon of butter. Add the garlic and scallion, and sauté until softened, about 2 minutes.
5. Add the zucchini and kale, and sauté until wilted, about 3 minutes.
6. Transfer the vegetables from the skillet to the pie plate and spreading the vegetables evenly across the bottom.
7. Pour the egg mixture into the pie plate, and sprinkle with the remaining half of the Swiss cheese.
8. Bake until the quiche is puffed and lightly browned, 15 to 20 minutes.
9. Serve hot, warm, or cold.
10. Ingredient tip Yellow zucchini, sometimes called summer squash, is usually lined up in a bin next to the more common green variety. You can interchange green with yellow in this dish.

Nutrition: calories: 120 Total fat: 8g Saturated fat: 4g Cholesterol: 221mg Sodium: 93mg Carbohydrates: 3g Fiber: 0g Phosphorus 120mg Potassium: 189mg Protein: 9g

159. Lentil Veggie Burgers

Preparation Time: 15 minutes
Cooking Time: 10 minutes
Servings: 4
Ingredients:

- 2½ cups cooked white rice
- ½ cup cooked red lentils, drained and rinsed
- 2 eggs, lightly beaten
- 2 tablespoons chopped fresh parsley
- 2 teaspoons chopped fresh basil leaves
- Juice and zest of 1 lime
- 1 teaspoon minced garlic
- 1 tablespoon olive oil

Directions:

1. In a food processor (or blender), pulse the rice, lentils, eggs, parsley, basil, lime juice, lime zest, and garlic until the mixture holds together.
2. Transfer the rice mixture to a medium bowl, and set in the refrigerator until it firms up, about 1 hour.
3. Form the rice mixture into 4 patties.
4. In a large skillet over medium-high heat, heat the olive oil.
5. Add the veggie patties and cook until golden, about 5 minutes. Flip the patties over. Cook the other side for 5 minutes.
6. Transfer the burgers to a paper towel-lined plate.
7. Serve the veggie burgers hot with your favorite toppings.

Nutrition: calories: 247 Total fat: 7g Saturated fat: 2g Cholesterol: 106mg Sodium: 36mg Carbohydrates: 31g Fiber: 3g Phosphorus 120mg Potassium: 183mg Protein: 8g

160. Baked Cauliflower Rice Cakes

Preparation Time: 20 minutes
Cooking Time: 10 minutes
Servings: 6
Ingredients:

- Olive oil for the pan
- 2 cups of chopped blanched cauliflower (see Cooking tip)
- 2 cups of cooked white basmati rice
- ¼ cup of plain yogurt
- 2 eggs, lightly beaten
- ½ cup of grated Cheddar cheese
- ¼ teaspoon of ground nutmeg
- Freshly ground black pepper

Directions:

1. Preheat the oven to 350°f.
2. Lightly coat 6 cups of a standard muffin tin with olive oil.
3. In a large bowl, mix the cauliflower, rice, yogurt, eggs, cheese, and nutmeg.
4. Season the mixture with pepper.
5. Evenly divide the cauliflower mixture among the 6 prepared muffin cups.
6. Bake until golden and slightly puffy, about 20 minutes.
7. Let them stand for 5 minutes, then run a knife around the edges to loosen.
8. Serve hot, warm, or cold.

Nutrition: Calories: 141 Total fat: 5g Saturated fat: 3g Cholesterol: 82mg Sodium: 98mg Carbohydrates: 18g Fiber: 1g Phosphorus 119mg Potassium: 178mg Protein: 7g

161. Marinated Paprika Chicken

Preparation Time: 25 minutes
Cooking Time: 3 hours
Servings: 4
Ingredients:

- 1/2 cup chopped onion, sweet

- 1/4 cup oil, olive
- 2 tbsp. lemon juice, fresh squeezed if available
- 1 tbsp. chopped oregano, fresh
- 1 tsp. minced garlic
- 1 tsp. paprika, smoked
- 4 x 3-oz. chicken thighs, skinless, boneless

Directions:
1. Add lemon juice, oil, onion, paprika, oregano and garlic to food processor. Puree.
2. Next, pour mixture in large zipper-top plastic bag. Add chicken.
3. Press air from bag and seal. Place in refrigerator, then allow to marinate for about two hours. Turn bag a few times while marinating.
4. Preheat oven to 400F. Place chicken thighs in baking dish. Discard leftover marinade.
5. Roast chicken till cooked fully through, 30-35 minutes. Serve while hot.

Nutrition: For each serving (1 chicken thigh) 196 calories 11 g fat 47 mg cholesterol 3 g carbs 2 g sugar 2 g fiber 18 g protein 60 mg sodium 17 mg calcium 166 mg phosphorus 232 mg potassium

162. Zucchini Noodles with Spring Vegetables

Preparation Time: 20 minutes
Cooking Time: 10 minutes
Servings: 6
Ingredients:
- 6 zucchinis, cut into long noodles
- 1 cup of halved snow peas
- 1 cup (3-inch pieces) of asparagus
- 1 tablespoon of olive oil
- 1 teaspoon of minced fresh garlic
- 1 tablespoon of freshly squeezed lemon juice

- 2 tablespoons of chopped fresh basil leaves

Directions:
1. Fill a medium saucepan with water, place over medium-high heat, and bring to a boil.
2. Reduce the heat to medium, and blanch the zucchini ribbons, snow peas, and asparagus by submerging them in the water for 1 minute. Drain and rinse immediately under cold water.
3. Pat the vegetables dry with paper towels, and transfer to a large bowl.
4. Place a medium skillet over medium heat, and add the olive oil. Add the garlic, and sauté until tender, about 3 minutes.
5. Add the lemon juice
6. Add the zucchini mixture, and basil and toss until well combined.
7. Serve immediately.

Nutrition: calories: 52 Total fat: 2g Saturated fat: 0g Cholesterol: 0mg Sodium: 7mg Carbohydrates: 4g Fiber: 1g Phosphorus: 40mg Potassium: 197mg Protein: 2g

163. Cool Cucumber Salad

Preparation Time: 25 minutes
Cooking Time: 10 minutes
Servings: 6
Ingredients:
- 2 cups of 1/4"-thick sliced cucumbers, fresh, peeled or unpeeled
- 2 tbsp. of salad dressing, Caesar or Italian, no sodium
- Pepper, ground, as desired

Directions:
1. In medium bowl with secure lid, combine sliced cucumbers with salad dressing.
2. Cover the bowl with the lid, then shake, coating cucumbers.

3. Sprinkle using pepper. Place in refrigerator. Serve chilled.

Nutrition: 26 calories 1.5 g fat 0 mg cholesterol 73 mg sodium 2 g carbs 0 g protein 12 mg phosphorus 88 mg potassium 0 g fiber 11 mg calcium

164. Sautéed Butternut Squash

Preparation Time: 25 minutes
Cooking Time: 10 minutes
Servings: 8
Ingredients:

- 1 tbsp. of oil, olive
- 4 cups of peeled, de-seeded, cubed squash, butternut
- 1/2 chopped onion, sweet
- 1 tsp. of chopped thyme, fresh
- A pinch pepper, ground

Directions:

1. Heat oil in large-sized skillet on med-high heat.
2. Add squash. Sauté till tender, 15-17 minutes.
3. Add thyme and onion. Sauté for five minutes more.
4. Season using ground pepper. Serve while hot.

Nutrition: For each serving (1 serving) 50 calories 1.5 g fat 0 mg cholesterol 8 g carbs 2 g sugar 2 g fiber 2 g protein 3 mg sodium 36 mg calcium 20 mg phosphorus 243 mg potassium

165. Herb Roasted Chicken

Preparation Time: 25 minutes
Cooking Time: 20 minutes
Servings: 4
Ingredients:

- 1 lb. of chicken breasts, skinless, boneless
- 1 onion, medium

- 1 or 2 cloves of garlic, fresh
- 2 tbsp. of herb & garlic seasoning
- 1 tsp. of pepper, ground
- 1/4 cup of oil, olive

Directions:

1. Chop the garlic and onion. Place in bowl. Add oil, seasoning and pepper.
2. Add chicken to marinade and cover. Then, place in refrigerator for four hours or overnight.
3. Preheat oven to 375F.
4. Cover cookie sheet with aluminum foil. Place marinated chicken on foil.
5. Pour remainder of marinade over chicken. Bake in 375F oven for 18-20 minutes.
6. Broil for five extra minutes to brown, if desired. Serve.

Nutrition: For each serving (4 ounces) 268 calories 16 g fat 82 mg cholesterol 52 mg sodium 2 g carbs 25 g protein 250 mg phosphorus 489 mg potassium 0.5 g fiber 16 mg calcium

166. Seared Scallops

Preparation Time: 25 minutes
Cooking Time: 20 minutes
Servings: 4
Ingredients:

- 1 tbsp. of oil, olive
- 12 oz. of rinsed, patted dry sea scallops
- Pepper, ground, as desired
- 2 tbsp. of lemon juice, freshly squeezed if available
- 1 tsp. each of fresh chopped parsley, thyme and chives

Directions:

1. Heat oil in large-sized skillet on med-high.
2. Season scallops lightly using pepper. Add to skillet.

3. Sea scallops and turn once till just cooked fully through and lightly browned, three to four minutes.
4. Add and stir in lemon juice, chives, parsley and thyme.
5. Turn scallops, coating in herb sauce. Serve while hot.

Nutrition: For each serving (3 scallops) 119 calories 4 g fat 26 mg cholesterol 2 g carbs 0 g sugar 4 g fiber 12 g protein 288 mg sodium 7 mg calcium 245 mg phosphorus 199 mg potassium

167. Falafel

Preparation Time: 10 minutes
Cooking time: 6 minutes
Servings: 4 servings
Ingredients:
- 1 cup chickpeas, soaked, cooked
- 1/3 cup white onion, diced
- 3 garlic cloves, chopped
- 3 tablespoons fresh parsley, chopped
- 1 tablespoon chickpea flour
- ½ teaspoon salt
- ½ teaspoon ground cumin
- ¾ teaspoon ground coriander
- ½ teaspoon chili flakes
- ½ teaspoon cayenne pepper
- ½ teaspoon ground cardamom
- 3 tablespoons olive oil

Directions:
1. Blend chickpeas, onion, garlic cloves, parsley, chickpea flour, salt, ground cumin, ground coriander, chili flakes, and cayenne pepper ground cardamom.
2. When the chickpea mixture is homogenous and smooth transfer it in the mixing bowl.
3. Make the medium balls from the chickpea mixture.
4. Pour olive oil in the skillet and heat it.

5. Fry the chickpea balls for 2 minutes from each side over the medium heat.
6. The cooked falafel should have a light brown color.
7. Dry the falafel with a paper towel if needed.

Nutrition: Calories 283, Fat 13.7, Fiber 9.2, Carbs 32.6, Protein 10.1

168. Greek Salad

Preparation Time: 10 minutes
Cooking time: 0 minutes
Servings: 2 servings
Ingredients:
- 2 cups lettuce leaves
- 2 cucumbers
- 1 tablespoon lemon juice
- 1 teaspoon olive oil
- ¼ teaspoon dried oregano
- ½ teaspoon salt
- ¼ teaspoon chili flakes
- 4 oz. Feta cheese

Directions:
1. Chop Feta cheese into the small cubes.
2. Chop the lettuce leaves roughly put them in the salad bowl.
3. Then chop cucumbers into the cubes. Add them in the lettuce bowl.
4. For the dressing: whisk together chili flakes, salt, dried oregano, olive oil, and lemon juice.
5. Pour the dressing over the lettuce mixture and mix up well.
6. Sprinkle the salad with Feta cubes and shake gently.

Nutrition: Calories 312, Fat 21.2, Fiber 5.3, Carbs 23.5, Protein 11.9

169. Baked Vegetables Soup

Preparation Time: 15 minutes

Cooking time: 5 hours
Servings: 2 servings
Ingredients:

- 1 carrot, peeled
- 1 onion, peeled
- 1 eggplant, peeled
- 2 oz. asparagus, peeled
- 2 tablespoons sour cream
- 1 teaspoon salt
- ½ teaspoon ground black pepper
- 1 tablespoon dried dill
- 2 cups of water

Directions:

1. Place all vegetables in the tray and bake them for 30 minutes at 360F.
2. When the vegetables are tender, chop them roughly and put in the pan.
3. Add water, dried dill, ground black pepper, salt, and close the lid.
4. Simmer the soup for 10 minutes.
5. After this, gently blend the soup. It should have a soft but not smooth texture.
6. Simmer the soup for 2-3 minutes and remove from the heat.
7. Add more salt if needed.

Nutrition: Calories 128, Fat 3.1, Fiber 11, Carbs 24.4, Protein 4.5

170. Peas Soup

Preparation Time: 10 minutes
Cooking Time: 10 minutes
Servings: 4
Ingredients:

- 1 white onion, chopped
- 1 quart veggie stock
- 2 eggs
- 3 tablespoons lemon juice
- 2 cups peas
- 2 tablespoons parmesan, grated
- Salt and black pepper to the taste

Directions:

1. Heat up a pot with the oil over medium-high heat, add the onion and sauté for 4 minutes.
2. Add the rest of the ingredients except the eggs, bring to a simmer and cook for 4 minutes.
3. Add whisked eggs, stir the soup, cook for 2 minutes more, divide into bowls and serve.

Nutrition: Calories 293, Fat 11.2 Fiber 3.4, Carbs 27, Protein 4.45

171. Minty Lamb Stew

Preparation Time: 10 minutes
Cooking Time: 1 hour and 45 minutes
Servings: 4
Ingredients:

- ½ cup mint, chopped
- Salt and black pepper to the taste
- 2 pounds lamb shoulder, boneless and cubed
- 3 tablespoons oil
- 1 carrot, chopped
- 1 yellow onion, chopped
- 1 celery rib, chopped
- 1 tablespoon ginger, grated
- 1 tablespoon garlic, minced
- ½ cup mint, chopped
- 15 ounces canned chickpeas, drained
- 6 tablespoons Greek yogurt

Directions:

1. Heat up a pot with 2 tablespoons oil over medium-high heat, add the meat and brown for 5 minutes.
2. Add the carrot, onion, celery, garlic and the ginger, stir and sauté for 5 minutes more.
3. Add the rest of the ingredients except the yogurt, bring to a simmer and cook over medium heat for 1 hour and 30 minutes.

4. Divide the stew into bowls, top each serving with the yogurt and serve.

Nutrition: Calories 355, fat 14.3, fiber 6.7, carbs 22.6, protein 15.4

172. Pesto Chicken Salad

Ingredients:
1-pound Preparation Time: 15 minutes
Cooking time: 15 minutes
Servings: 4 servings
- chicken breast, skinless, boneless
- 1 teaspoon salt
- 1 teaspoon ground black pepper
- 1 teaspoon olive oil
- 2 cucumbers, chopped
- 1 cup lettuce, chopped
- 1 red onion, sliced
- 3 tablespoons fresh basil
- 2 oz. Parmesan, grated
- 1 tablespoon walnut
- ½ teaspoon minced garlic
- 1 tablespoon canola oil
- 1 tablespoon lemon juice

Directions:
1. Preheat the grill to 360F.
2. Rub the chicken breast with salt, ground black pepper, and olive oil.
3. Grill the chicken for 7 minutes from each side. The cooked chicken breast should have a crunchy crust.
4. Meanwhile, mix up cucumbers, lettuce, red onion, and mix up the mixture well. Add lemon juice and canola oil. Mix up the salad well again.
5. Make pesto sauce: blend in the blender minced garlic, walnuts, Parmesan, and basil.
6. Chop the cooked grilled chicken breast roughly and put over salad.
7. Drizzle the salad with pesto sauce.

Nutrition: calories 293, fat 13.9, fiber 2.9, carbs 12.3, protein 31.1

173. Israeli Pasta Salad

Preparation Time: 10 minutes
Cooking time: 15 minutes
Servings: 2 servings
Ingredients:
- 2 bell peppers, chopped
- 3 oz. Feta cheese, chopped
- 1 red onion, chopped
- 1 tomato, chopped
- 1 cucumber, chopped
- ½ cup elbow macaroni, dried
- 1 teaspoon dried oregano
- 1 tablespoon lemon juice
- 1 teaspoon olive oil
- 1 cup water for macaroni

Directions:
1. Pour water in the pan, add macaroni and boil them according to the
2. Directions of the manufacturer (appx. 15 minutes).
3. Then drain water and chill the macaroni little.
4. Meanwhile, in the salad bowl mix up together Feta cheese, bell peppers, onion, tomato, and cucumber.
5. Make the dressing for the salad: combine dried oregano, lemon juice, and olive oil.
6. Add cooked macaroni in the salad bowl and mix up well.
7. Drizzle the salad with dressing and shake gently.

Nutrition: calories 328, fat 14.8, fiber 5.6, carbs 40.3, protein 12.2

174. Artichoke Matzo Mina

Preparation Time: 10 minutes
Cooking time: 45 minutes
Servings: 6 servings
Ingredients:
- 4 sheets matzo

- ½ cup artichoke hearts
- 1 cup cream cheese
- ½ teaspoon salt
- 1 teaspoon ground black pepper
- 3 tablespoons fresh dill, chopped
- 3 eggs, beaten
- 1 teaspoon canola oil
- ½ cup cottage cheese

Directions:
1. In the bowl combine, salt, ground black pepper, dill, and cottage cheese.
2. Pour canola oil in the skillet, add artichoke hearts and roast them for 2-3 minutes over the medium heat. Stir them from time to time.
3. Then add roasted artichoke hearts in the cheese mixture.
4. Add eggs and stir until homogenous.
5. Place one sheet of matzo in the casserole mold.
6. Then spread it with cheese mixture generously.
7. Cover the cheese layer with the second sheet of matzo.
8. Repeat the steps till you use all ingredients.
9. Then preheat oven to 360F.
10. Bake matzo mina for 40 minutes.
11. Cut the cooked meal into the.

Nutrition: calories 272, fat 17.3, fiber 4.3, carbs 20.2, protein 11.8

175. Sautéed Chickpea and Lentil Mix

Preparation Time: 10 minutes
Cooking Time: 50 minutes
Servings: 4
Ingredients:
- 1 cup chickpeas, half-cooked
- 1 cup lentils
- 5 cups chicken stock
- ½ cup fresh cilantro, chopped
- 1 teaspoon salt
- ½ teaspoon chili flakes
- ¼ cup onion, diced
- 1 tablespoon tomato paste

Directions:
1. Place chickpeas in the pan. Add water, salt, and chili flakes.
2. Boil the chickpeas for 30 minutes over the medium heat.
3. Then add diced onion, lentils, and tomato paste. Stir well.
4. Close the lid and cook the mix for 15 minutes.
5. After this, add chopped cilantro, stir the meal well and cook it for 5 minutes more.
6. Let the cooked lunch chill little before serving.

Nutrition: Calories 370 Fat 4.3 Fiber 23.7 Carbs 61.6 Protein 23.2

176. Beef Enchiladas

Preparation Time: 10 minutes
Cooking Time: 30 minutes
Servings: 1
Ingredients:
- 1 pound of lean beef
- 12 whole-wheat tortillas
- 1 can of low-sodium enchilada sauce
- ½ cup of onion (diced)
- ½ tsp of black pepper
- 1 garlic clove
- 1 tbsp of olive oil
- 1 tsp of cumin

Directions:
1. Heat the oven to 375 degrees-Fahrenheit
2. In a medium-sized frying pan, cook the beef in olive oil until completely cooked.
3. Add the minced garlic, diced onion, cumin, and black pepper to the pan and mix everything in with the beef.
4. In a separate pan, cook the tortillas in olive oil and dip each cooked tortilla in the enchilada sauce.
5. Fill the tortilla with the meat mixture and roll it up.
6. Put the finished product in a slightly heated pan with cheese on top.
7. Bake the tortillas in the pan until crispy, golden brown, and the cheese is melted.

Nutrition: Calories: 177 Fat: 6g Carbs: 15g Protein: 15g Sodium: 501mg Potassium: 231mg Phosphorus: 98mg

177. Eggplant and Red Pepper Soup

Preparation Time: 20 minutes
Cooking Time: 40 minutes
Servings: 1
Ingredients:
- 1 small, cut into quarters Sweet onion
- 2, halved Small red bell peppers
- 2 cups Cubed eggplant
- 2 cloves, crushed Garlic
- 1 tbsp. Olive oil
- 1 cup Chicken stock
- Water
- ¼ cup Chopped fresh basil
- Ground black pepper

Directions:
1. Preheat the oven to 350f.
2. Put the onions, red peppers, eggplant, and garlic in a baking dish.
3. Drizzle the vegetables with the olive oil.
4. Cook vegetables for 30 minutes or until they are slightly charred and soft.
5. Cool the vegetables slightly and remove the skin from the peppers.
6. Puree the vegetables with a hand mixer (with the chicken stock).
7. Transfer the soup to a medium pot and add enough water to reach the desired thickness.
8. Heat the soup to a simmer and add the basil.
9. Season with pepper and serve.

Nutrition: Calories: 61 Fat: 2g Carb: 9g Protein: 2g Sodium: 98mg Potassium: 198mg Phosphorus: 33mg

178. Baked Flounder

Preparation Time: 20 minutes
Cooking Time: 5 minutes
Servings: 4
Ingredients:

- ¼ cup Homemade mayonnaise
- Juice of 1 lime
- Zest of 1 lime
- ½ cup Chopped fresh cilantro
- 4 (3-ounce) Flounder fillets
- Ground black pepper

Directions:
1. Preheat the oven to 400f.
2. In a bowl, stir together the cilantro, lime juice, lime zest, and mayonnaise.
3. Prepare foil on a clean work surface.
4. Place a flounder fillet in the center of each square.
5. Top the fillets evenly with the mayonnaise mixture.
6. Season the flounder with pepper.
7. Fold the foil's sides over the fish, and place on baking sheet.
8. Bake for 4 - 5 minutes.
9. Unfold the packets and serve.

Nutrition: Calories: 92 Fat: 4g Carb: 2g Protein: 12g Sodium: 267mg Potassium: 137mg Phosphorus: 208mg

179. Chicken and Broccoli Casserole

Preparation Time: 15 minutes
Cooking Time: 45 minutes – 1 hour
Servings: 1
Ingredients:
- 2 cups of rice (cooked)
- 3 chicken breasts
- 2 cups of broccoli
- 1 onion (diced)
- 2 eggs
- 2 cups of cheddar cheese
- 2 tbsp of butter
- 1-2 tbsp of parmesan cheese

Directions:
1. Heat the oven to 350 degrees-Fahrenheit

2. Add the broccoli to a bowl and cover it with plastic wrap. Microwave the broccoli for 2-3 minutes.
3. Dice the onion and add it with the chicken and the butter in the pa.
4. Cook the chicken for 15 minutes.
5. Once the chicken is cooked, mix it, broccoli, and rice together, and add to a greased casserole dish.
6. Add the grated cheese into the casserole dish and stir well.
7. Add the parmesan cheese on top.
8. Place the casserole dish in the oven for 30-45 minutes.

Nutrition: Calories: 349 Fat: 12g Carbs: 14g Protein: 44g Sodium: 980mg Potassium: 713mg Phosphorus: 451mg

180. Baked Macaroni & Cheese

Preparation Time: 10 minutes
Cooking Time: 40 – 45 minutes
Servings: 1
Ingredients:
- 3 cups of macaroni
- 2 cups of milk
- 2 tbsp of butter (unsalted)
- 2 tbsp of flour (all-purpose)
- 2 ½ cups of cheddar
- 2 tbsp of blanched almonds
- 1 tbsp of thyme
- 1 tbsp of olive oil
- 1 cheese sauce (quick make packets)

Directions:
1. Preheat the oven to 350 degrees-Fahrenheit.
2. Prepare a medium-sized pot on the stove and fill it up with water.
3. Add the macaroni to the pot with a tbsp of olive oil for 8-10 minutes. Stir until cooked.

4. In a measuring cup, measure your butter and flour and mix it. Place it in the microwave for 1 minute. Then stir in the milk, spices, and herbs—microwave for 2-3 minutes, or until the mixture is thick.
5. Drain the noodles and add to a casserole dish that has been sprayed with cooking spray, the sauce, and cheese. Mix it well, followed with more cheese on top.
6. Put and bake casserole dish into the oven for 15-20 minutes.
7. Serve with blanched almonds on top.

Nutrition: Calories: 314 Fat: 14g Carbs: 34g Protein: 19g Sodium: 373mg Potassium: 120mg Phosphorus: 222mg

181. Persian Chicken

Preparation Time: 10 minutes
Cooking Time: 20 minutes
Servings: 5
Ingredients:
- ½, chopped Sweet onion
- ¼ cup Lemon juice
- 1 tbsp. Dried oregano
- 1 tsp. Minced garlic
- 1 tsp. Sweet paprika
- ½ tsp. Ground cumin
- ½ cup Olive oil
- 5 Boneless, skinless chicken thighs

Directions:
1. Put the cumin, paprika, garlic, oregano, lemon juice, and onion in a food processor and pulse to mix the ingredients.
2. Put olive oil until the mixture is smooth.
3. Put chicken thighs in a large Ziploc and add the marinade for 2 hours.
4. Remove the thighs from the marinade.
5. Preheat the barbecue to medium.
6. Grill the chicken for about 20 minutes, turning once, until it reaches 165F.

Nutrition: Calories: 321 Fat: 21g Carb: 3g Protein: 22g Sodium: 86mg Potassium: 220mg Phosphorus: 131mg

182. Korean Pear Salad

Preparation Time: 5 minutes
Cooking Time: 15 minutes
Servings: 2
Ingredients:
- 6 cups green lettuce
- 4 medium-sized pears (peeled, cored, and diced)
- ½ cup of sugar
- ½ cup of pecan nuts
- ½ cup of water
- 2 oz of blue cheese
- ½ cup of cranberries
- ½ cup of dressing

Directions:
1. Dissolve the water and sugar in a frying pan (non-stick).
2. Heat the mixture until it turns into a syrup, and then add the nuts immediately.
3. Place the syrup with the nuts on a piece of parchment paper and separate the nuts while the mixture is hot. Let it cool down.
4. Prepare lettuce in a salad bowl and add the pears, blue cheese, and cranberries to the salad.
5. Add the caramelized nuts to the salad and serve it with a dressing of choice on the side.

Nutrition: Calories: 112 Fat: 9g Carbs: 5.5g Protein: 2g Sodium: 130mg Potassium: 160mg Phosphorus: 71.7mg

183. Pumpkin Bites

Preparation Time: 10 minutes
Cooking Time: 5 minutes
Servings: 12
Ingredients:

- 8 oz cream cheese
- 1 tsp vanilla
- 1 tsp pumpkin pie spice
- 1/4 cup coconut flour
- 1/4 cup erythritol
- 1/2 cup pumpkin puree
- 4 oz butter

Directions:
1. Add all ingredients into the mixing bowl and beat using hand mixer until well combined.
2. Scoop mixture into the silicone ice cube tray and place it in the refrigerator until set.
3. Serve and enjoy.

Nutrition: Calories 149 Fat 14.6 g Carbohydrates 8.1 g Sugar 5.4 g Protein 2 g Cholesterol 41 mg Phosphorus: 66mg Potassium: 77mg Sodium: 55mg

184. Ground Beef and Rice Soup

Preparation time: 15 minutes
Cooking time: 40 minutes
Servings: **1**
Ingredients:
- ½ pound Extra-lean ground beef
- ½, chopped Small sweet onion
- 1 tsp. Minced garlic
- 2 cups Water
- 1 cup Low-sodium beef broth
- ½ cup, uncooked Long-grain white rice
- 1, chopped Celery stalk
- ½ cup, cut into – 1-inch pieces Fresh green beans
- 1 tsp. Chopped fresh thyme
- Ground black pepper

Directions:
1. Sauté the ground beef in a saucepan for 6 minutes or until the beef is completely browned.

2. Drain off the excess fat and add the onion and garlic to the saucepan.
3. Sauté the vegetables for about 3 minutes, or until they are softened.
4. Add the celery, rice, beef broth, and water.
5. Let it boil, reduce the heat to low, and simmer for 30 minutes or until the rice is tender.
6. Add the green beans and thyme and simmer for 3 minutes.
7. Remove the soup from the heat and season with pepper.

Nutrition: Calories: 154 Fat: 7g Carb: 14g Protein: 9g Sodium: 133mg Potassium: 179mg Phosphorus: 76mg

185. Feta Bean Salad

Preparation Time: 5 minutes
Cooking Time: 20 minutes
Servings: 2
Ingredients:
- 1 tbsp of olive oil
- 2 egg whites (boiled)
- 1 cup of green beans (8 oz)
- 1 tbsp of onion
- 1/2 red chili
- 1/8 cup of cilantro
- 1 1/2 tbsp lime juice
- 1/4 tbsp of black pepper

Directions:
1. Remove the ends off the green beans and cut them into small pieces.
2. Chop the onion, cilantro, and chili and mix it.
3. Use a steamer to cook green beans for 5- 10 minutes and rinse with cold water once done.
4. Place all the mixed dry ingredients together in two serving bowls.
5. Chop the egg whites up and place them on top of the salad with crumbled feta.

6. Drizzle a pinch of olive oil with black pepper on top.

Nutrition: Calories: 255 Fat: 24g Carbs: 8g Protein: 5g Sodium: 215.6mgPotassium: 211mg Phosphorus: 125mg

186. Seafood Casserole

Preparation Time: 20 minutes
Cooking Time: 45 minutes
Servings: 1
Ingredients:

- 2 cups, peeled and diced into 1-inch pieces Eggplant
- Butter, for greasing the baking dish
- 1 tbsp. Olive oil
- ½, chopped Sweet onion
- 1 tsp. Minced garlic
- 1 chopped Celery stalk
- ½ boiled and chopped Red bell pepper
- 3 tbsps. Freshly squeezed lemon juice
- 1 tsp. Hot sauce
- ¼ tsp. Creole seasoning mix
- ½ cup, uncooked White rice
- 1 large Egg
- 4 ounces Cooked shrimp
- 6 ounces Queen crab meat

Directions:
1. Preheat the oven to 350f.
2. Boil the eggplant in a saucepan for 5 minutes. Drain and set aside.
3. Grease a 9-by-13-inch baking dish with butter and set aside.
4. Heat the olive oil in a large skillet over medium heat.
5. Sauté the garlic, onion, celery, and bell pepper for 4 minutes or until tender.
6. Add the sautéed vegetables to the eggplant, along with the lemon juice, hot sauce, seasoning, rice, and egg.
7. Stir to combine.
8. Fold in the shrimp and crab meat.
9. Spoon the casserole mixture into the casserole dish, patting down the top.
10. Bake for 25 to 30 minutes or until casserole is heated through and rice is tender. Serve warm.

Nutrition: Calories: 118 Fat: 4g Carb: 9g Protein: 12g Sodium: 235mg Potassium: 199mg Phosphorus: 102mg

187. Slow-Cooked BBQ Beef

Preparation Time: 10 minutes
Cooking Time: 30 minutes
Servings: 4
Ingredients:

- 4-pound pot roast
- 2 cups of water
- ¾ cup ketchup
- 1/4 cup brown sugar
- 1/3 cup vinegar
- 1/2 teaspoon allspice
- 1/4 cup onion

Directions:
1. Add 2 cups water and roast to a Crockpot and cover it.
2. Cook for 10 hours on LOW setting, then drain it while keeping 1 cup of its liquid.
3. Transfer the cooked meat to a 9x13 pan and set it aside.
4. Whisk 1 cup liquid, ketchup, vinegar, brown sugar, minced onion, and allspice in a bowl.
5. Add beef to the marinade and mix well to coat, then marinate overnight in the refrigerator.
6. Spread it on a baking pan then bake for 30 minutes at 350°F.
7. Serve.

Nutrition: Calories: 303 kcal Total Fat: 17 g Saturated Fat: 0 g Cholesterol: 71 mg Sodium: 207 mg Total Carbs: 7 g

188. Beef Chili

Preparation Time: 10 minutes
Cooking Time: 30 minutes
Servings: 2
Ingredients:
- 1 diced Onion
- 1 diced Red bell pepper
- 2 cloves, minced Garlic
- 6 oz. Lean ground beef
- 1 tsp. Chili powder
- 1 tsp. Oregano
- 2 tbsps. Extra virgin olive oil
- 1 cup Water
- 1 cup Brown rice
- 1 tbsp. Fresh cilantro to serve

Directions:
1. Soak vegetables in warm water.
2. Boil pan of water and add rice for 20 minutes.
3. Meanwhile, add the oil to a pan and heat on medium-high heat.
4. Add the pepper, onions, and garlic and sauté for 5 minutes until soft.
5. Remove and set aside.
6. Add the beef to the pan and stir until browned.
7. Put and stir vegetables back into the pan.
8. Now add the chili powder and herbs and the water, cover, and turn the heat down a little to simmer for 15 minutes.
9. Meanwhile, drain the water from the rice and the lid and steam while the chili is cooking.
10. Serve hot with the fresh cilantro sprinkled over the top.

Nutrition: Calories: 459 Fat: 22g Carb: 36g Protein: 22g Sodium: 33mg Potassium: 360mg Phosphorus: 332mg

189. Pork Meatloaf

Preparation Time: 10 minutes
Cooking Time: 50 minutes
Servings: 1
Ingredients:
- 1-pound lean ground beef
- ½ cup Breadcrumbs
- ½ cup Chopped sweet onion
- 1 Egg
- 2 tbsps. Chopped fresh basil
- 1 tsp. Chopped fresh thyme
- 1 tsp. Chopped fresh parsley
- ¼ tsp. Ground black pepper
- 1 tbsp. Brown sugar
- 1 tsp. White vinegar
- ¼ tsp. Garlic powder

Directions:
1. Preheat the oven to 350f.
2. Mix well the breadcrumbs, beef, onion, basil, egg, thyme, parsley, and pepper.
3. Stir the brown sugar, vinegar, and garlic powder in a small bowl.
4. Put the brown sugar mixture evenly over the meat.
5. Bake the meatloaf for about 50 minutes or until it is cooked through.
6. Let the meatloaf stand for 10 minutes and then pour out any accumulated grease.

Nutrition: Calories: 103 Fat: 3g Carb: 7g Protein: 11g Sodium: 87mg Potassium: 190mg Phosphorus: 112mg

190. Apple & Cinnamon Spiced Honey Pork Loin

Preparation time: 20 minutes
Cooking time: 6 hours
Servings: 6
Ingredients
- 1 2-3lb boneless pork loin roast
- ½ teaspoon low-sodium salt

- ¼ teaspoon pepper
- 1 tablespoon canola oil
- 3 medium apples, peeled and sliced
- ¼ cup honey
- 1 small red onion, halved and sliced
- 1 tablespoon ground cinnamon

Directions

1. Season the pork with salt and pepper.
2. Heat the oil in a skillet and brown the pork on all sides.
3. Arrange half the apples in the base of a 4 to 6-quart slow cooker.
4. Top with the honey and remaining apples.
5. Sprinkle with cinnamon and cover.
6. Cover and cook on low for 6-8 hours until the meat is tender.

Nutrition: Calories 290, Fat 10g, Carbs 19g, Protein 29g, Fiber 2g, Potassium 789mg, Sodium 22mg

191. Baked Pork Chops

Ingredients:

1/2 cup Preparation Time: 15 minutes
Cooking Time: 40 minutes
Servings: 6

- flour
- 1 large egg
- 1/4 cup water
- 3/4 cup breadcrumbs
- 6 (3 1/2 oz.) pork chops
- 2 tablespoons butter, unsalted
- 1 teaspoon paprika

Directions:

1. Begin by switching the oven to 350 degrees F to preheat.
2. Mix and spread the flour in a shallow plate.
3. Whisk the egg with water in another shallow bowl.
4. Spread the breadcrumbs on a separate plate.

5. Firstly, coat the pork with flour, then dip in the egg mix and then in the crumbs.
6. Grease a baking sheet and place the chops in it.
7. Drizzle the pepper on top and bake for 40 minutes.
8. Serve.

Nutrition: Calories: 221 kcal Total Fat: 7.8 g Saturated Fat: 1.9 g Cholesterol: 93 mg Sodium: 135 mg Total Carbs: 11.9 g

192. Beef Kabobs with Pepper

Preparation Time: 5 Minutes
Cooking Time: 10 Minutes
Servings: 8

Ingredients:

- 1 Pound of beef sirloin
- 1/2 Cup of vinegar
- 2 tbsp. of salad oil
- 1 Medium, chopped onion
- 2 tbsp. of chopped fresh parsley
- 1/4 tsp. of black pepper
- 2 Cut into strips green peppers

Directions:

1. Trim the fat from the meat; then cut it into cubes of 1 and 1/2 inches each
2. Mix the vinegar, the oil, the onion, the parsley and the pepper in a bowl
3. Place the meat in the marinade and set it aside for about 2 hours; make sure to stir from time to time.
4. Remove the meat from the marinade and alternate it on skewers instead with green pepper
5. Brush the pepper with the marinade and broil for about 10 minutes 4 inches from the heat
6. Serve and enjoy your kabobs

Nutrition: Calories: 357 kcal Total Fat: 24 g Saturated Fat: 0 g Cholesterol: 9 mg Sodium: 60 mg Total Carbs: 0 g

193. Chicken Stew

Preparation Time: 20 minutes
Cooking Time: 50 minutes
Servings: 1
Ingredients:

- 1 tbsp. Olive oil
- 1 pound, cut into 1-inch cubes Boneless, skinless chicken thighs
- ½, chopped Sweet onion
- 1 tbsp. Minced garlic
- 2 cups Chicken stock
- 1 cup, plus 2 tbsps. Water
- 1 sliced Carrot
- 2 stalks, sliced Celery
- 1, sliced thin Turnip
- 1 tbsp. Chopped fresh thyme
- 1 tsp. Chopped fresh rosemary
- 2 tsp. Cornstarch
- Ground black pepper to taste

Directions:
1. Prepare a large saucepan on medium heat and add the olive oil.
2. Sauté the chicken for 6 minutes or until it is lightly browned, stirring often.
3. Add the onion and garlic, and sauté for 3 minutes.
4. Add 1-cup water, chicken stock, carrot, celery, and turnip and bring the stew to a boil.
5. Simmer for 30 minutes or until cooked and tender.
6. Add the thyme and rosemary and simmer for 3 minutes more.
7. In a small bowl, stir together the 2 tbsps. Of water and the cornstarch.
8. Add the mixture to the stew.
9. Stir to incorporate the cornstarch mixture and cook for 3 to 4 minutes or until the stew thickens.
10. Remove from the heat once done and season with pepper.

Nutrition: Calories: 141 Fat: 8g Carb: 5g Protein: 9g Sodium: 214mg Potassium: 192mg Phosphorus: 53mg

194. Cabbage and Beef Fry

Preparation Time: 5 minutes
Cooking Time: 15 minutes
Servings: 4
Ingredients:

- 1 pound beef, ground
- 1/2 pound bacon
- 1 onion
- 1 garlic cloves, minced
- 1/2 head cabbage
- Salt and pepper to taste

Directions:
1. Take a skillet and place it over medium heat
2. Add chopped bacon, beef and onion until slightly browned
3. Transfer to a bowl and keep it covered
4. Add minced garlic and cabbage to the skillet and cook until slightly browned
5. Return the ground beef mixture to the skillet and simmer for 3-5 minutes over low heat
6. Serve and enjoy!

Nutrition: Calories: 360 kcal Total Fat: 22 g Saturated Fat: 0 g Cholesterol: 0 mg Sodium: 0 mg Total Carbs: 5 g

195. California Pork Chops

Preparation Time: 10 minutes
Cooking Time: 10 minutes
Servings: 2
Ingredients:

- 1 tbsp. fresh cilantro, chopped
- 1/2 cup chives, chopped
- 2 large green bell peppers, chopped
- 1 lb. 1" thick boneless pork chops
- 1 tbsp. fresh lime juice

- 2 cups cooked rice
- 1/8 tsp. dried oregano leaves
- 1/4 tsp. ground black pepper
- 1/4 tsp. ground cumin
- 1 tbsp. butter
- 1 lime

Directions:
1. Start by seasoning the pork chops with lime juice and cilantro.
2. Place them in a shallow dish.
3. Toss the chives with pepper, cumin, butter, oregano and rice in a bowl.
4. Stuff the bell peppers with this mixture and place them around the pork chops.
5. Cover the chop and bell peppers with a foil sheet and bake them for 10 minutes in the oven at 375 degrees f.
6. Serve warm.

Nutrition: Calories: 265 kcal Total Fat: 15 g Saturated Fat: 0 g Cholesterol: 86 mg Sodium: 70 mg Total Carbs: 24 g Fiber: 1 g Sugar: 0 g Protein: 34 g

196. Chicken Fajitas

Preparation Time: 10 minutes
Cooking Time: 10 minutes
Servings: 8
Ingredients:
- 8 flour tortillas, 6" size
- 1/4 cup green pepper, cut in strips
- 1/4 cup red pepper, cut in strips
- 1/2 cup onion, sliced
- 1/2 cup cilantro
- 2 tbsp. canola oil
- 12 oz. boneless chicken breasts
- 1/4 tsp. black pepper
- 2 tsp. chili powder
- 1/2 tsp. cumin
- 2 tbsp. lemon juice

Directions:
1. Start by wrapping the tortillas in a foil.

2. Warm them up for 10 minutes in a preheated oven at 300 degrees f.
3. Add oil to a nonstick pan.
4. Add lemon juice chicken and seasoning
5. Stir fry for 5 minutes then add onion and peppers.
6. Continue cooking for 5 minutes or until chicken is tender.
7. Stir in cilantro, mix well and serve in tortillas.

Nutrition: Calories: 343 kcal Total Fat: 13 g Saturated Fat: 0 g Cholesterol: 53 mg Sodium: 281 mg Total Carbs: 33 g

197. Chicken and Apple Curry

Preparation Time: 10 minutes
Cooking Time: 1 hour and 11 minutes
Servings: 8
Ingredients:
- 8 boneless skinless chicken breasts
- 1/4 teaspoon black pepper
- 2 medium apples, peeled, cored, and chopped
- 2 small onions, chopped
- 1 garlic clove, minced
- 3 tablespoons butter
- 1 tablespoon curry powder
- 1/2 tablespoon dried basil
- 3 tablespoons flour
- 1 cup chicken broth
- 1 cup of rice almond milk

Directions:
1. Preheat oven to 350°F.
2. Set the chicken breasts in a baking pan and sprinkle black pepper over it.
3. Place a suitably-sized saucepan over medium heat and add butter to melt.
4. Add onion, garlic, and apple, then sauté until soft.
5. Stir in basil and curry powder, and then cook for 1 minute.

6. Add flour and continue mixing for 1 minute.
7. Stir in rice almond milk and chicken broth, then stir cook for 5 minutes.
8. Pour this sauce over the chicken breasts in the baking pan.
9. Bake the chicken for 60 minutes then serve.

Nutrition: Calories: 232 kcal Total Fat: 8 g Saturated Fat: 0 g Cholesterol: 85 mg Sodium: 118 mg Total Carbs: 11 g

198. Sirloin with Squash and Pineapple

Preparation Time: 10 minutes
Cooking Time: 9 minutes
Servings: 2
Ingredients:
- 8 ounces canned pineapple slices
- 2 garlic cloves, minced
- 2 teaspoons ginger root, minced
- 3 teaspoons olive oil
- 1 pound sirloin tips
- 1 medium zucchini, diced
- 1 medium yellow squash, diced
- 1/2 medium red onion, diced

Directions:
1. Mix pineapple juice with 1 teaspoon olive oil, ginger, and garlic in a Ziplock bag.
2. Add sirloin tips to the pineapple juice marinade and seal the bag.
3. Place the bag in the refrigerator overnight.
4. Preheat oven to 450°F.
5. Layer 2 sheet pans with foil and grease it with 1 teaspoon olive oil.
6. Spread the squash, onion, and pineapple rings in the prepared pans.
7. Bake them for 5 minutes then transfer to the serving plate.

8. Place the marinated sirloin tips on a baking sheet and bake for 4 minutes in the oven.
9. Transfer the sirloin tips to the roasted vegetables.
10. Serve.

Nutrition: Calories: 264 kcal Total Fat: 12 g Saturated Fat: 0 g Cholesterol: 74 mg Sodium: 150 mg Total Carbs: 14 g

199. Golden Eggplant Fries

Preparation Time: 10 minutes
Cooking Time: 15 minutes
Servings: 8
Ingredients:
- 2 eggs
- 2 cups almond flour
- 2 tablespoons coconut oil, spray
- 2 eggplant, peeled and cut thinly
- Sunflower seeds and pepper

Directions:
1. Preheat your oven to 400 degrees F.
2. Take a bowl and mix with sunflower seeds and black pepper.
3. Take another bowl and beat eggs until frothy.
4. Dip the eggplant pieces into the eggs.
5. Then coat them with the flour mixture.
6. Add another layer of flour and egg.
7. Then, take a baking sheet and grease with coconut oil on top.
8. Bake for about 15 minutes.
9. Serve and enjoy!

Nutrition: Calories: 212 Fat: 15.8g Carbohydrates: 12.1g Protein: 8.6g Phosphorus: 150mg Potassium: 147mg Sodium: 105mg

200. Very Wild Mushroom Pilaf

Preparation Time: 10 minutes
Cooking Time: 3 hours
Servings: 4

Ingredients:
- 1 cup wild rice
- 2 garlic cloves, minced
- 6 green onions, chopped
- 2 tablespoons olive oil
- ½ pound baby Bella mushrooms
- 2 cups water

Directions:
1. Add rice, garlic, onion, oil, mushrooms and water to your Slow Cooker.
2. Stir well until mixed.
3. Place lid and cook on LOW for 3 hours.
4. Stir pilaf and divide between serving platters.
5. Enjoy!

Nutrition: Calories: 210 Fat: 7g Carbohydrates: 16g Protein: 4g Phosphorus: 110mg Potassium: 117mg Sodium: 75mg

201. Caribbean Turkey Curry

Preparation Time: 10 minutes
Cooking Time: 1 hour an 30 minutes
Servings: 6

Ingredients:
- 3 1/2 lbs. turkey breast, with skin
- 1/4 cup butter, melted
- 1/4 cup honey
- 1 tbsp. mustard
- 2 tsp. curry powder
- 1 tsp. garlic powder

Directions:
1. Place the turkey breast in a shallow roasting pan.
2. Insert a meat thermometer to monitor the temperature.
3. Bake the turkey for 1.5 hours at 350 degrees f until its internal temperature reaches 170 degrees f.
4. Meanwhile, thoroughly mix honey, butter, curry powder, garlic powder, and mustard in a bowl.
5. Glaze the cooked turkey with this mixture liberally.
6. Let it sit for 15 minutes for absorption.
7. Slice and serve.

Nutrition: Calories: 275 kcal Total Fat: 13 g Saturated Fat: 0 g Cholesterol: 82 mg Sodium: 122 mg Total Carbs: 90 g

202. Chicken Veronique

Preparation Time: 10 minutes
Cooking Time: 10 minutes
Servings: 4

Ingredients:
- 2 boneless skinless chicken breasts
- 1/2 shallot, chopped
- 2 tablespoons butter
- 2 tablespoons dry white wine
- 2 tablespoons chicken broth
- 1/2 cup green grapes, halved
- 1 teaspoon dried tarragon
- 1/4 cup cream

Directions:
1. Place an 8-inch skillet over medium heat and add butter to melt.
2. Sear the chicken in the melted butter until golden-brown on both sides.
3. Place the boneless chicken on a plate and set it aside.
4. Add shallot to the same skillet and stir until soft.
5. Whisk cornstarch with broth and wine in a small bowl.
6. Pour this slurry into the skillet and mix well.
7. Place the chicken in the skillet and cook it on a simmer for 6 minutes.
8. Transfer the chicken to the serving plate.
9. Add cream, tarragon, and grapes.
10. Cook for 1 minute, and then pour this sauce over the chicken.
11. Serve.

Nutrition: Calories: 306 kcal Total Fat: 18 g Saturated Fat: 0 g Cholesterol: 124 mg Sodium: 167 mg Total Carbs: 9 g

203. Marinated Shrimp and Pasta

Preparation Time: 10 minutes
Cooking Time: 20 minutes
Servings: 10
Ingredients:

- 12 oz. of three-colored penne pasta
- ½ pound of cooked shrimp
- ½ red bell pepper, diced
- ½ cup of red onion, chopped
- 3 stalks of celery
- 12 baby carrots, cut into thick slices
- 1 cup of cauliflower, cut into small round pieces
- ¼ cup of honey
- ¼ cup balsamic vinegar
- ½ tsp. of black pepper
- ½ tsp. garlic powder
- 1 tbsp. of French mustard
- ¾ cup of olive oil

Directions:

1. Cook pasta for around 10 minutes (or according to packaged instructions).
2. While pasta is boiling, cut all your veggies and place into a large mixing bowl. Add the cooked shrimp.
3. In a mixing bowl, add the honey, vinegar, black pepper, garlic powder, and mustard. While you whisk, slowly incorporate the oil and stir well.
4. Add in the drained pasta with the veggies and shrimp and gently combine everything. Pour the liquid marinade over the pasta and veggies and toss to coat everything evenly.
5. Refrigerate for 3-5 hours before serving. Serve chilled.

Nutrition: Calories: 256kcal Carbohydrate: 41g Protein: 6.55g Sodium: 242.04mg Potassium: 131.88mg Phosphorus: 86.03mg Dietary Fiber: 2.28g Fat: 16.88g

204. Exotic Palabok

Preparation Time: 25 minutes
Cooking Time: 15 minutes
Servings: 6
Ingredients:

- 12 oz. rice noodles.
- 1 ½ cups of medium shrimp, peeled and deveined
- 2/3 cup of white onion, chopped
- 1 spring onion, sliced
- 3 tbsp. of canola oil
- 1-pound, lean ground turkey
- 2 cups of firm tofu, chopped
- 2 packs of shrimp or ordinary gravy mix
- 5 hard-boiled eggs
- 1 lemon
- ½ cup of pork rinds (optional)

Directions:

1. Boil rice noodles until nice and soft. Keep aside.
2. Boil the peeled shrimp for 2-3 minutes in a pot with plain water.
3. In a wok or shallow pan, saute the garlic and onion with the oil. Add the ground turkey, tofu, and shrimps.
4. Dissolve the gravy mix in water or as per package instructions.
5. Combine the rice noodles, tofu, onions, and the gravy mix with ½ cup of pork rind (optional).
6. Slice the egg and lemons.
7. Serve with egg and lemons on top.

Nutrition: Calories: 305 kcal Carbohydrate: 39.14g Protein: 17.6g Sodium: 536mg Potassium: 243.52 mg Phosphorus: 180.41mg Dietary Fiber: 0.9g

205. Creamy Chicken with Cider

Preparation Time: 25 minutes
Cooking Time: 20 minutes
Servings: 4
Ingredients:
- 4 bone-in chicken breasts
- 2 tbsp. of lightly salted butter
- ¾ cup of apple cider vinegar
- 2/3 cup of rich unsweetened coconut almond milk or cream
- Kosher pepper

Directions:
1. Melt the butter in a skillet over medium heat.
2. Season the chicken with the pepper and add to the skillet. Cook over low heat for approx. 20 minutes.
3. Remove the chicken from the heat and set aside in a dish.
4. In the same skillet, add the cider and bring to a boil until most of it has evaporated.
5. Add the coconut cream and let cook for 1 minute until slightly thickened.
6. Pour the cider cream over the cooked chicken and serve.

Nutrition: Calories: 86.76kcal Carbohydrate: 1.88g Protein: 1.5g Sodium: 93.52mg Potassium: 74.65mg Phosphorus: 36.54mg Dietary Fiber: 0.1g Fat: 8.21g

206. Beef Bulgogi

Preparation Time: 10 minutes
Cooking Time: 5 minutes
Servings: 4
Ingredients:
- 1-pound flank steak, thinly sliced
- 5 tablespoons Worcestershire sauce
- 2 1/2 tablespoons honey
- 1/4 cup chopped green onion
- 2 tablespoons minced garlic
- 2 tablespoons olive oil
- 1/2 teaspoon ground black pepper

Directions:
1. Place the beef in a shallow dish. Combine Worcestershire sauce, honey, green onion, garlic, olive oil, and ground black pepper in a small bowl. Pour over beef. Cover and refrigerate for at least 1 hour or overnight.
2. Preheat an outdoor grill for high heat, and lightly oil the grate.
3. Quickly grill beef on hot grill until slightly charred and cooked through, 1 to 2 minutes per side

Nutrition: Calories 348, Total Fat 16.5g, Saturated Fat 4.9g, Cholesterol 62mg, Sodium 272mg, TotalCarbohydrate 16.6g, Dietary Fiber 0.4g, Total Sugar 14.7g,

207. Steak and Onion Sandwich

Preparation Time: 25 minutes
Cooking Time: 8 minutes
Servings: 4
Ingredients:
- 4 flank steaks (around 4 oz. each)
- 1 medium red onion, sliced
- 1 tbsp. of lemon juice
- 1 tbsp. of Italian seasoning
- 1 tsp. of black pepper
- 1 tbsp. of vegetable oil
- 4 sandwich/burger buns

Directions:
1. Wrap the steak with the lemon juice, the Italian seasoning, and pepper to taste. Cut into 4 pieces Heat the vegetable oil in a medium skillet over medium heat.
2. Cook steaks around 3 minutes on each side until you get a medium to well-done result. Take off and transfer onto a dish with absorbing paper.

3. In the same skillet, saute the onions until tender and transparent (around 3 minutes).
4. Cut the sandwich bun into half and place 1 piece of steak in each topped with the onions. Serve or wrap with paper or foil and keep in the fridge for the next day.

Nutrition: calories: 315.26 kcal Carbohydrate: 8.47g Protein: 38.33g Sodium: 266.24mg Potassium: 238.2mg Phosphorus: 364.25mg Dietary Fiber: 0.76g Fat: 13.22g

208. Zesty Crab Cakes

Preparation Time: 25 minutes
Cooking Time: 6 minutes
Servings: 6
Ingredients:

- 9 oz. (250 grams) of crab meat
- 1/3 cup of green or red bell pepper, thinly chopped
- 1/3 cup of low salt crackers, crushed
- ¼ cup of low-fat mayonnaise
- 1 tbsp. of dry mustard
- ½ tsp. of pepper
- 2 tbsp. of lemon juice
- ½ tsp. of lemon zest
- 1 tsp. of garlic powder
- 2 tbsp. of vegetable oil

Directions:
1. Mix all the ingredients except for the oil until uniform. Divide into 6 flat patties (around 5 inches in diameter).
2. Heat the vegetable oil in the skillet and shallow fry the patties for 2-3 minutes on each side (or until golden brown).
3. Serve warm on a dish with absorbing paper.

Nutrition: calories: 144.42kcal Carbohydrate: 5.12g Protein: 8.47g Sodium: 212.31mg Potassium: 195mg Phosphorus: 127.42mg Dietary Fiber: 1.02g Fat: 9.2g

209. London broil

Preparation Time: 10 minutes
Cooking Time: 5 minutes
Servings: 4
Ingredients:

- 2 pounds flank steak
- 1/4 teaspoon meat tenderizer
- 1 tablespoon sugar
- 2 tablespoons lemon juice
- 2 tablespoons soy sauce
- 1 tablespoon honey
- 1 teaspoon herb seasoning blend

Directions:
1. Pound the meat with a mallet then place it in a shallow dish.
2. Sprinkle meat tenderizer over the meat.
3. Whisk rest of the ingredients and spread this marinade over the meat.
4. Marinate the meat for 4 hours in the refrigerator.
5. Bake the meat for 5 minutes per side at 350°F.
6. Slice and serve.

Nutrition: Calories: 184 kcal Total Fat: 8 g Saturated Fat: 0 g Cholesterol: 43 mg Sodium: 208 mg Total Carbs: 3 g

210. Garden Salad

Preparation Time: 5 minutes
Cooking Time: 20 minutes
Servings: 6
Ingredients:

- 1-pound raw peanuts in shell
- 1 bay leaf
- 2 medium-sized chopped up Red bell peppers
- ½ cup diced up green pepper
- ½ cup diced up sweet onion
- ¼ cup finely diced hot pepper
- ¼ cup diced up celery
- 2 tablespoons olive oil

- ¾ teaspoon flavored vinegar
- ¼ teaspoon freshly ground black pepper

Directions:
1. Boil your peanuts for 1 minute and rinse them.
2. The skin will be soft, so discard the skin.
3. Add 2 cups of water to the Instant Pot.
4. Add bay leaf and peanuts.
5. Lock the lid and cook on HIGH pressure for 20 minutes.
6. Drain the water.
7. Take a large bowl and add the peanuts, diced up vegetables.
8. Whisk in olive oil, lemon juice, pepper in another bowl.
9. Pour the mixture over the salad and mix.
10. Enjoy!

Nutrition: Calories: 140 Fat: 4g Carbohydrates: 24g Protein: 5g Phosphorus: 110mg Potassium: 117mg Sodium: 75mg

211. Sporty Baby Carrots

Preparation Time: 5 minutes
Cooking Time: 5 minutes
Servings: 4
Ingredients:
- 1-pound baby carrots
- 1 cup water
- 1 tablespoon clarified ghee
- 1 tablespoon chopped up fresh mint leaves
- Sea flavored vinegar as needed

Directions:
1. Place a steamer rack on top of your pot and add the carrots.
2. Add water.
3. Lock the lid and cook at HIGH pressure for 2 minutes.
4. Do a quick release.
5. Pass the carrots through a strainer and drain them.

6. Wipe the insert clean.
7. Return the insert to the pot and set the pot to Sauté mode.
8. Add clarified butter and allow it to melt.
9. Add mint and sauté for 30 seconds.
10. Add carrots to the insert and sauté well.
11. Remove them and sprinkle with bit of flavored vinegar on top.
12. Enjoy!

Nutrition: Calories: 131 Fat: 10g Carbohydrates: 11g Protein: 1g Phosphorus: 130mg Potassium: 147mg Sodium: 85mg

212. Saucy Garlic Greens

Preparation Time: 5 minutes
Cooking Time: 20 minutes
Servings: 4
Ingredients:
- 1 bunch of leafy greens
- Sauce
- ½ cup cashews soaked in water for 10 minutes
- ¼ cup water
- 1 tablespoon lemon juice
- 1 teaspoon coconut aminos
- 1 clove peeled whole clove
- 1/8 teaspoon of flavored vinegar

Directions:
1. Make the sauce by draining and discarding the soaking water from your cashews and add the cashews to a blender.
2. Add fresh water, lemon juice, flavored vinegar, coconut aminos, and garlic.
3. Blitz until you have a smooth cream and transfer to bowl.
4. Add ½ cup of water to the pot.
5. Place the steamer basket to the pot and add the greens in the basket.
6. Lock the lid and steam for 1 minute.
7. Quick-release the pressure.

8. Transfer the steamed greens to strainer and extract excess water.
9. Place the greens into a mixing bowl.
10. Add lemon garlic sauce and toss.
11. Enjoy!

Nutrition: Calories: 77 Fat: 5g Carbohydrates: 0g Protein: 2g Phosphorus: 120mg Potassium: 137mg Sodium: 85mg

213. Tofu Hoisin Sauté

Preparation Time: 15 minutes
Cooking Time: 20 minutes
Servings: 4
Ingredients:
- 2 tablespoons of hoisin sauce
- 2 tablespoons of rice vinegar
- 1 teaspoon of cornstarch
- 2 tablespoons of olive oil
- 1 (15-ounce) package extra-firm tofu, cut into 1-inch cubes
- 2 cups of unpeeled cubed eggplant
- 2 scallions, white and green parts, sliced
- 2 teaspoons of minced garlic
- 1 jalapeño pepper, minced
- 2 tablespoons of chopped fresh cilantro

Directions:
1. In a small bowl, whisk together the hoisin sauce, rice vinegar, and cornstarch and set aside.
2. In a large skillet over medium-high heat, heat the olive oil. Add the tofu, and sauté gently until golden brown, about 10 minutes, and transfer to a plate.
3. Reduce the heat to medium. Add the eggplant, scallions, garlic, jalapeño pepper, and sauté until tender and fragrant, about 6 minutes.
4. Stir in the reserved sauce, and toss until the sauce thickens about 2 minutes. Stir in the tofu and cilantro, and serve hot.
5. Low-sodium tip Hoisin sauce is made with soy sauce, containing a hefty amount of sodium per serving. This recipe would still be tasty, while slightly less intensely flavored if you use 1 tablespoon of hoisin sauce instead of 2 tablespoons.

Nutrition: Calories: 105 Total fat: 4g Saturated fat: 1g Cholesterol: 0mg Sodium: 234mg Carbohydrates: 9g Fiber: 2g Phosphorus: 105mg Potassium: 192mg Protein: 8g

214. Vegetarian Gobi Curry

Preparation Time: 25 minutes
Cooking Time: 15 minutes
Servings: 4
Ingredients:
- 2 cups of cauliflower florets
- 2 tbsp. of unsalted butter
- 1 medium dry white onion, thinly chopped
- ½ cup of green peas (frozen if wish)
- 1 tsp. of fresh ginger, chopped
- 1/2 tsp. of turmeric
- 1 tsp of garam masala
- ¼ tsp. cayenne pepper
- 1 tbsp. of water

Directions:
1. Heat a skillet over medium heat with the butter and sauté the onions until caramelized (golden brown).
2. Add the spices e.g. ginger, garam masala turmeric, and cayenne.
3. Add the cauliflower and the (frozen) peas and stir.
4. Add the water and cover with a lid. Reduce the heat to a low temperature and let cook covered for 10 minutes.
5. Serve with whsite rice.

Nutrition: Calories: 91.04kcal Carbohydrate: 7.3g Protein: 2.19g Sodium: 39.38mg Potassium: 209.58mg Phosphorus: 42mg Dietary Fiber: 3g Fat: 6.4g

215. Spicy Chili Crackers

Preparation Time: 15 minutes
Cooking Time: 60 minutes
Servings: 30 crackers
Ingredients:
- ¾ cup almond flour
- ¼ cup coconut four
- ¼ cup coconut flour
- ½ teaspoon paprika
- ½ teaspoon cumin
- 1 ½ teaspoons chili pepper spice
- 1 teaspoon onion powder
- ½ teaspoon sunflower seeds
- 1 whole egg
- ¼ cup unsalted almond butter

Directions:
1. Preheat your oven to 350 degrees F.
2. Line a baking sheet with parchment paper and keep it on the side.
3. Add ingredients to your food processor and pulse until you have a nice dough.
4. Divide dough into two equal parts.
5. Place one ball on a sheet of parchment paper and cover with another sheet; roll it out.
6. Cut into crackers and repeat with the other ball.
7. Transfer the prepped dough to a baking tray and bake for 8-10 minutes.
8. Remove from oven and serve.
9. Enjoy!

Nutrition: Carbs: 2.8g Fiber: 1g Protein: 1.6g Fat: 4.1g

216. Spicy Cabbage Dish

Preparation Time: 10 minutes
Cooking Time: 4 hours
Servings: 4
Ingredients:
- 2 yellow onions, chopped
- 10 cups red cabbage, shredded
- 1 cup plums, pitted and chopped
- 1 teaspoon cinnamon powder
- 1 garlic clove, minced
- 1 teaspoon cumin seeds
- ¼ teaspoon cloves, ground
- 2 tablespoons red wine vinegar
- 1 teaspoon coriander seeds
- ½ cup water

Directions:
1. Add cabbage, onion, plums, garlic, cumin, cinnamon, cloves, vinegar, coriander and water to your Slow Cooker.
2. Stir well.
3. Place lid and cook on LOW for 4 hours.
4. Divide between serving platters.
5. Enjoy!

Nutrition: Calories: 197 Fat: 1g Carbohydrates: 14g Protein: 3g Phosphorus: 115mg Potassium: 119mg Sodium: 75mg

217. Roasted Chicken and Vegetables

Preparation Time: 10 minutes
Cooking Time: 45 minutes
Servings: 2
Ingredients:
- 8 oz chicken strips
- 1 ½ cups baby potatoes
- 5 oz green beans
- 2 tbsp sesame seed oil
- 1 tsp of Cajun chicken spice
- ½ tbsp Italian herb dressing

Directions:
1. Heat the oven to 400 degrees-Fahrenheit
2. Fill up a large pot with water until it is ¾ full. Add the baby potatoes to the pot and cook for 10 minutes.
3. Drain the baby potatoes.
4. Chop off the tips of the green beans.

5. Line a 9 x 13-inch oven tray with parchment paper or spray the oven tray with cooking spray.
6. Place the chicken strips on the tray side, with the green beans and baby potatoes.
7. Add Cajun chicken spice to the chicken breasts and drizzle sesame seed oil over the chicken and vegetables.
8. Roast for 20 minutes.
9. Drizzle Italian herb dressing on top of the chicken and vegetables and roast for another 5-10 minutes.

Nutrition: Calories: 263 Fat: 6g Sodium: 366mg Potassium: 879mg Phosphorus: 275mg Carbs: 28.6g Protein: 23g

218. Extreme Balsamic Chicken

Preparation Time: 10 minutes
Cooking Time: 35 minutes
Servings: 4
Ingredients:
- 3 boneless chicken breasts, skinless
- Sunflower seeds to taste
- ¼ cup almond flour
- 2/3 cups low-fat chicken broth
- 1 ½ teaspoons arrowroot
- ½ cup low sugar raspberry preserve
- 1 ½ tablespoons balsamic vinegar

Directions:
1. Cut chicken breast into bite-sized pieces and season them with seeds.
2. Dredge the chicken pieces in flour and shake off any excess.
3. Take a non-stick skillet and place it over medium heat.
4. Add chicken to the skillet and cook for 15 minutes, making sure to turn them half-way through.
5. Remove chicken and transfer to platter.
6. Add arrowroot, broth, raspberry preserve to the skillet and stir.

7. Stir in balsamic vinegar and reduce heat to low, stir-cook for a few minutes.
8. Transfer the chicken back to the sauce and cook for 15 minutes more.
9. Serve and enjoy!

Nutrition: Calories: 546 Fat: 35g Carbohydrates: 11g Protein: 44g Phosphorus: 120mg Potassium: 117mg Sodium: 85mg

219. Enjoyable Green lettuce and Bean Medley

Servings: 4
Preparation Time: 10 minutes
Cooking Time: 4 hours
Ingredients:
- 5 carrots, sliced
- 1 ½ cups great northern beans, dried
- 2 garlic cloves, minced
- 1 yellow onion, chopped
- Pepper to taste
- ½ teaspoon oregano, dried
- 5 ounces baby green lettuce
- 4 ½ cups low sodium veggie stock
- 2 teaspoons lemon peel, grated
- 3 tablespoon lemon juice

Directions:
1. Add beans, onion, carrots, garlic, oregano and stock to your Slow Cooker.
2. Stir well.
3. Place lid and cook on HIGH for 4 hours.
4. Add green lettuce, lemon juice and lemon peel.
5. Stir and let it sit for 5 minutes.
6. Divide between serving platters and enjoy!

Nutrition: Calories: 219 Fat: 8g Carbohydrates: 14g Protein: 8g Phosphorus: 210mg Potassium: 217mg Sodium: 85mg

220. Tantalizing Cauliflower and Dill Mash

Preparation Time: 10 minutes
Cooking Time: 6 hours
Servings: 6
Ingredients:

- 1 cauliflower head, florets separated
- 1/3 cup dill, chopped
- 6 garlic cloves
- 2 tablespoons olive oil
- Pinch of black pepper

Directions:

1. Add cauliflower to Slow Cooker.
2. Add dill, garlic and water to cover them.
3. Place lid and cook on HIGH for 5 hours.
4. Drain the flowers.
5. Season with pepper and add oil, mash using potato masher.
6. Whisk and serve.
7. Enjoy!

Nutrition: Calories: 207 Fat: 4g Carbohydrates: 14g Protein: 3g Phosphorus: 130mg Potassium: 107mg Sodium: 105mg

221. Green Tuna Salad

Preparation Time: 10 minutes
Cooking Time: 15 -20 minutes
Servings: 2
Ingredients:

- 5 ounces of tuna (in freshwater only)
- 2-3 cups of lettuce
- 1 cup of baby marrows
- 1/2 cup of red bell pepper
- 1/4 cup of red onion
- 1/4 cup of fresh thyme
- 2 tbsp olive oil
- 1/8 tsp of black pepper
- 2 tbsp of red wine vinegar

Directions:

1. Chop the bell pepper, onion, baby marrow, and thyme into small pieces.

2. Add a 3/4 cup of water to a saucepan and add the bell pepper, onion, baby marrow, and thyme to the pan. Let it boil, steam the vegetables by adding a lid on top of the saucepan—steam for 10 minutes.
3. Remove the vegetables and drain them.
4. Combine the vegetables (once cooled down) with the chopped tomatoes and tuna.
5. Mix olive oil, red wine vinegar, and black pepper to create a salad dressing.
6. Add the mixture on a bed of lettuce and drizzle the dressing on top.

Nutrition: Calories: 210 Fat: 1.5g Carbs: 4g Protein: 43.3g Sodium: 726mg Potassium: 582mg Phosphorus: 296mg

222. Sirloin Medallions, Green Squash, and Pineapple

Preparation Time: 10 minutes
Cooking Time: 40 minutes
Servings: 4
Ingredients:

- 1 lb. of sirloin medallions
- 1 medium baby marrows
- 1 yellow squash
- ½ onion
- 8 oz of thinly sliced pineapple
- 3 tbsp of olive oil
- 2 tsp of ginger
- ½ tsp of salt
- 1 garlic clove

Directions:

1. Retrieve thinly sliced pineapple rings from a can and drain. Set the juice aside.
2. Slice garlic and ginger into fine pieces.
3. Mix the pineapple juice, ginger, garlic, salt, and olive oil together in a bowl to create a dressing for the sirloin medallions.

4. Add the sirloin medallions to the marinade and let it sit for 10-15 minutes.
5. Heat the oven to 450 degrees-Fahrenheit and line 2 oven trays with parchment paper.
6. Chop the squash into little ½-inch circles and place it on the parchment paper—drizzle 1tbsp of olive oil on top of it.
7. Cut the onion into small wedges, add to the tray and drizzle with olive oil.
8. Add pineapple rings next to the squash on the first tray and roast for 6 minutes.
9. Remove the pan and turn the squash and pineapple over. Add the onion onto the tray and roast it for another 5 minutes. Close the fruit and vegetables with foil to lock in the heat and set aside.
10. Remove sirloin medallions from the marinade. Line another oven tray pan with parchment paper and place the sirloin medallions on top.
11. Cook for 5 minutes and flip the sirloin to cook for another 5 minutes on the other side.
12. Serve the sirloin medallions with the vegetables and pineapple on a platter.

Nutrition: Calories: 264 Fat: 12g Carbs: 14g Protein: 25g Sodium: 150mg Potassium: 685mg Phosphorus: 257mg

223. Chicken and Savory Rice

Preparation Time: 15 minutes
Cooking Time: 45 minutes
Servings: 4
Ingredients:
- 4 medium chicken breasts
- 1 baby marrow (chopped)
- 1 red bell pepper (chopped)
- 3 tbsp olive oil
- 1 onion
- 1 garlic clove (minced)

- ½ tsp of black pepper
- 1 tbsp of cumin
- ¼ tsp cayenne pepper
- 2 cups of brown rice

Directions:
1. Add 2 tbsp of olive oil to medium heat and place the chicken breasts into the pan. Cook for 15 minutes and remove from the pan.
2. Add another tbsp of olive oil to the pan, and add the baby marrow, onion, red pepper, and corn.
3. Sauté the vegetables on medium heat for 10 minutes or until golden brown.
4. Add minced garlic, black pepper, cumin, and cayenne pepper to the vegetables. Stir the vegetables and spices together well.
5. Cut the chicken into cube and add it back to the pan. Mix it with the vegetables for 5 minutes.
6. In a medium pot, fill it up with water until it is 2/3 full. Add the rice to the pot and cook it for 35-40 minutes.
7. Serve the chicken and vegetable mixture on a bed of rice with extra black pepper.

Nutrition: Calories: 374 Fat: 6.2g Carbs: 65g Protein: 15g Sodium: 520mg Potassium: 645mg Phosphorus: 268mg

224. Salmon and Green Beans

Preparation Time: 10 minutes
Cooking Time: 20 minutes
Servings: 4
Ingredients:
- 3 oz x 4 salmon fillets
- ½ lb. of green beans
- 2 tbsp of dill
- 2 tbsp of coriander
- 2 lemons
- 2 tbsp olive oil
- 4 tbsp of mayonnaise

Directions:

1. Rinse and salmon fillets and wait for it to dry. Don't remove the skin.
2. Wash green beans and chop the tips of the green beans.
3. Heat the oven up to 425 degrees-Fahrenheit.
4. Spray an oven sheet pan with cooking spray and place the salmon fillets on the sheet pan.
5. Chop up the dill and combine it with the mayonnaise.
6. Put mayo mixture on top of the salmon fillets.
7. Place the green beans next to the salmon fillets and drizzle olive oil on top of everything.
8. Place the oven baking sheet in the middle of the oven and cook for 15 minutes.
9. Slice the lemons into wedges and serve with the salmon fillets and green beans.

Nutrition: Calories: 399 Fat: 21g Carbs: 8g Protein: 38g Sodium: 229mg Potassium: 1000mg Phosphorus: 723mg

225. Cranberry and Raisins Granola

Preparation Time: 15 minutes
Cooking Time: 20 minutes
Servings: 4
Ingredients:

- 4 cups old-fashioned rolled oats
- 1/4 cup sesame seeds
- 1 cup dried cranberries
- 1 cup golden raisins
- 1/8 teaspoon nutmeg
- 2 tablespoons olive oil
- 1/2 cup almonds, slivered
- 2 tablespoons warm water
- 1 teaspoon vanilla extract
- 1 teaspoon cinnamon
- 1/4 teaspoon of salt
- 6 tablespoons maple syrup
- 1/3 cup of honey

Directions:

1. In a bowl, mix the sesame seeds, nutmeg, almonds, oats, salt, and cinnamon.
2. In another bowl, mix the oil, water, vanilla, honey, and syrup. Gradually pour the mixture into the oats mixture. Toss to combine. Spread the mixture into a greased jelly-roll pan. Bake in the oven at 300°F for at least 55 minutes. Stir and break the clumps every 10 minutes.
3. Once you get it from the oven, stir the cranberries and raisins. Allow cooling. This will last for a week when stored in an airtight container and up to a month when stored in the fridge.

Nutrition: Calories: 698 kcal Protein: 21.34 g Fat: 20.99 g Carbohydrates: 148.59 g

MAIN DISHES

226. Almond Scones

Preparation Time: 10 minutes
Cooking Time: 20 minutes
Servings: 6
Ingredients:
- 1 cup almonds
- 1 1/3 cups almond flour
- ¼ cup arrowroot flour
- 1 tablespoon coconut flour
- 1 teaspoon ground turmeric
- Salt, to taste
- Freshly ground black pepper, to taste
- 1 egg
- ¼ cup essential olive oil
- 3 tablespoons raw honey
- 1 teaspoon vanilla flavoring

Directions:
1. In a mixer, put almonds then pulse till chopped roughly
2. Move the chopped almonds in a big bowl.
3. Put flours and spices and mix well.
4. In another bowl, put the remaining ingredients and beat till well combined.
5. Put the flour mixture into the egg mixture then mix till well combined.
6. Arrange a plastic wrap over the cutting board.
7. Place the dough over the cutting board.
8. Using both of your hands, pat into 1-inch thick circle.
9. Cut the circle in 6 wedges.
10. Set the scones onto a cookie sheet in a single layer.
11. Bake for at least 15-20 minutes.

Nutrition: Calories: 304 Fat: 3g
Carbohydrates: 22g Fiber: 6g Protein: 20g

227. Spicy Marble Eggs

Preparation Time: 15 minutes
Cooking Time: 2 hours
Servings: 12
Ingredients:
- 6 medium-boiled eggs, unpeeled, cooled
- For the Marinade
- 2 oolong black tea bags
- 3 Tbsp. brown sugar
- 1 thumb-sized fresh ginger, unpeeled, crushed
- 3 dried star anise, whole
- 2 dried bay leaves
- 3 Tbsp. light soy sauce
- 4 Tbsp. dark soy sauce
- 4 cups of water
- 1 dried cinnamon stick, whole
- 1 tsp. salt
- 1 tsp. dried Szechuan peppercorns

Directions:
1. Using the back of a metal spoon, crack eggshells in places to create a spider web effect. Do not peel. Set aside until needed.
2. Pour marinade into large Dutch oven set over high heat. Put lid partially on. Bring water to a rolling boil, about 5 minutes. Turn off heat.
3. Secure lid. Steep ingredients for 10 minutes.
4. Using a slotted spoon, fish out and discard solids. Cool marinade completely to room proceeding.
5. Place eggs into an airtight non-reactive container just small enough to snugly fit all these in.
6. Pour in marinade. Eggs should be completely submerged in liquid. Discard

leftover marinade, if any. Line container rim with generous layers of saran wrap. Secure container lid.

7. Chill eggs for 24 hours before using.
8. Extract eggs and drain each piece well before using, but keep the rest submerged in the marinade.

Nutrition: Calories: 75 kcal Protein: 4.05 g Fat: 4.36 g Carbohydrates: 4.83 g

228. Almond Pancakes with Coconut Flakes

Preparation: Time: 5 minutes
Cooking Time: 10 minutes
Servings: 6

Ingredients:

- 1 overripe banana, mashed
- 2 eggs, yolks, and whites separated
- ½ cup unsweetened applesauce
- 1 cup almond flour, finely milled
- ¼ cup of water
- ¼ tsp. coconut oil
- Garnish
- 2 Tbsp. blanched almond flakes
- Dash of cinnamon powder
- ¼ cup coconut flakes, sweetened
- Pinch of sea salt
- Pure maple syrup, use sparingly

Directions:

1. Whisk egg whites until soft peaks form.
2. Except for egg whites and coconut oil, combine remaining ingredients in another bowl. Mix until batter comes together.
3. Gently fold in egg whites. Make sure that you don't over mix, or the pancake will become dense and chewy.
4. Pour oil into a nonstick skillet set over medium heat.
5. Wait for the oil to heat up before dropping in approximately ½ cup of batter. Cook until each side are set, and bubbles form in the center. Turn on the other side then cook for another 2 minutes.
6. Transfer flapjacks to a plate. Repeat step until all batter is cooked. Pour in more oil into the skillet only if needed. This recipe should yield between 4 to 6 medium-sized pancakes.
7. Stack pancakes. Pour the desired amount of pure maple syrup on top. Garnish each stack with cinnamon-flavored almond-coconut flakes just before serving.
8. For the garnish, set the oven to 350°F for at least 10 minutes before use. Line a baking sheet with parchment paper. Set aside.
9. Mix almond and coconut flakes together in a bowl. Spread mixture evenly on a prepared baking sheet.
10. Bake for 7 to 10 minutes until flakes turn golden brown. Stir almond and coconut flakes once midway through roasting to prevent over-browning.
11. Remove the baking sheet from the oven. Cool almond and coconut flakes for at least 10 minutes before sprinkling in cinnamon powder and salt. Toss to combine. Set aside.

Nutrition: Calories: 62 kcal Protein: 2.24 g Fat: 4.01 g Carbohydrates: 4.46 g

229. Bake Apple Turnover

Preparation Time: 30 minutes
Cooking Time: 25 minutes
Servings: 4

Ingredients:

- For the turnovers
- 4 apples, peeled, cored, diced into bite-sized pieces
- 1 Tbsp. almond flour
- All-purpose flour, for rolling out the dough
- 1 frozen puff pastry, thawed
- ½ cup palm sugar, crumbled by hand to loosen granules
- ½ tsp. cinnamon powder

- For the egg wash
- 1 egg white, whisked in
- 2 Tbsp. water

Directions:

1. For the filling: combine almond flour, cinnamon powder, and palm sugar until these resemble coarse meal. Toss in diced apples until well coated. Set aside.
2. On a lightly floured surface, roll the puff pastry until ¼ inch thin. Slice into 8 pieces of 4" x 4" squares.
3. Divide prepared apples into 8 equal portions. Spoon on individual puff pastry squares. Fold in half diagonally. Press edges to seal.
4. Place each filled pastry on a baking tray lined with parchment paper. Make sure there is ample space between pastries.
5. Freeze for at least 20 minutes, or till ready to bake.
6. Preheat oven to 400°F or 205°C for at 10 minutes.
7. Brush frozen pastries with egg wash. Bring in a hot oven, and cook for 12 to 15 minutes, or until these turn golden brown all over.
8. Take off the baking tray in the oven immediately. Cool slightly for easier handling.
9. Place 1 apple turnover on a plate. Serve warm.

Nutrition: Calories: 203 kcal Protein: 5.29 g Fat: 4.4 g Carbohydrates: 38.25 g

230. Nutty Oats Pudding

Preparation Time: 5 minutes
Cooking Time: 0 minutes
Servings: 3 -5
Ingredients:

- ¼ cup rolled oats
- 1 tablespoon yogurt, fat-free
- 1 ½ tablespoon natural peanut butter
- ¼ cup dry almond milk

- 1 teaspoon peanuts, finely chopped
- ½ cup of water

Directions:

1. Using a microwaveable-safe bowl, put together peanut butter and dry almond milk. Whisk well. Add in water to achieve a smooth consistency. Add in oats.
2. Cover bowl with plastic wrap. Create a small hole for the steam to escape.
3. Place inside the microwave oven for 1 minute on high powder.
4. Continue heating, this time on medium power for 90 seconds. Let sit for 5 minutes.
5. To serve, spoon an equal amount of cereals in a bowl top with peanuts and yogurt.

Nutrition: Calories: 70 kcal Protein: 4.25 g Fat: 3.83 g Carbohydrates: 6.78 g

231. Quinoa and Cauliflower Congee

Preparation Time: 10 minutes
Cooking Time: 1 hour
Servings: 8
Ingredients:

- 1 cauliflower head, minced
- 2 tablespoons red quinoa
- 2 leeks, minced
- 1 tablespoon fresh ginger, grated
- 2 garlic cloves, grated
- 6 cups of water
- 2 tablespoons white rice
- 1 tablespoon olive oil
- 1 tablespoon fish sauce
- 2 onions, minced
- Pinch of white pepper
- For Garnish
- 4 eggs, soft-boiled
- 2 red chili, minced

- 1 lime, sliced into wedges
- ¼ cup packed basil leaves, torn
- ¼ cup loosely packed cilantro leaves, torn
- ¼ cup loosely packed spearmint leaves, torn

Directions:
1. Put olive oil into a huge skillet on medium heat. Sauté shallots, garlic, and ginger until limp and aromatic; pour into a slow cooker set at medium heat.
2. Except for garnishes, pour remaining ingredients into slow cooker; stir. Put the lid on. Cook for 6 hours. Turn off heat. Taste; adjust seasoning if needed.
3. Ladle congee into individual bowls. Garnish with basil leaves, cilantro leaves, red chilli, and spearmint leaves. Add 1 piece of soft-boiled egg on top of each; serve with a wedge of lime on the side. Slice egg just before eating so yolk runs into congee. Squeeze lime juice into congee just before eating.

Nutrition: Calories: 138 kcal Protein: 7.23 g Fat: 7.65 g Carbohydrates: 10.76 g

232. Breakfast Arrozcaldo

Preparation Time: 20 minutes
Cooking Time: 30 minutes
Servings: 5
Ingredients:
- 6 eggs, white only
- 1½ cups white rice, cooked
- For the filling
- ¼ cup raisins
- ½ cup frozen peas, thawed
- 1 white onion, minced
- 1 garlic clove, minced
- oil, for greasing

Directions:
1. For the filling, spray a small amount of oil into a skillet set over medium heat.

Add in onion and garlic. Stir-fry until former is limp and transparent.
2. Stir-fry while breaking up clumps, about 2 minutes. Add in remaining ingredients. Stir-fry for another minute.
3. Turn down the heat, and let filling cook for 10 to 15 minutes, or until juices are greatly reduced. Stir often. Turn off heat. Divide into 6 equal portions.
4. For the eggs, spray a small amount of oil into a smaller skillet set over medium heat. Cook eggs. Discard yolk. Transfer to holding the plate.
5. To serve, place 1 portion of rice on a plate, 1 portion of filling, and 1 egg white. Serve warm.

Nutrition: Calories: 53 kcal Protein: 6.28 g Fat: 1.35 g Carbohydrates: 3.59 g

233. Apple Bruschetta with Almonds and Blackberries

Preparation Time: 20 minutes
Cooking Time: 30 minutes
Servings: 5
Ingredients:
- 1 apple, sliced into ¼-inch thick half-moons
- ¼ cup blackberries, thawed, lightly mashed
- ½ tsp. fresh lemon juice
- 1/8 cup almond slivers, toasted

Sea salt
Directions:
1. Drizzle lemon juice on apple slices. Put these on a tray lined with parchment paper.
2. Spread a small number of mashed berries on top of each slice. Top these off with the desired amount of almond slivers.
3. Sprinkle sea salt on "bruschetta" just before serving.

Nutrition: Calories: 56 kcal Protein: 1.53 g Fat: 1.43 g Carbohydrates: 9.87 g

234. Oven-Poached Eggs

Preparation Time: 2minutes
Cooking Time: 11minutes
Servings: 4
Ingredients:

- 6 eggs, at room temperature
- Water
- Ice bath
- 2 cups water, chilled
- 2 cups of ice cubes

Directions:

1. Set the oven to 350°F. Put 2 cups of water into a deep roasting tin, and place it into the lowest rack of the oven.
2. Place one egg into each cup of cupcake/muffin tins, along with one tablespoon of water.
3. Carefully place muffin tins into the middle rack of the oven.
4. Bake eggs for 45 minutes.
5. Turn off the heat immediately. Take off the muffin tins from the oven and set on a cake rack to cool before extracting eggs.
6. Pour ice bath ingredients into a large heat-resistant bowl.
7. Bring the eggs into an ice bath to stop the cooking process. After 10 minutes, drain eggs well. Use as needed.

Nutrition: Calories: 357 kcal Protein: 17.14 g Fat: 24.36 g Carbohydrates: 16.19 g

235. Hash Browns

Preparation Time: 15 minutes
Cooking Time: 15 minutes
Servings: 4
Ingredients:

- 1 pound Russet carrots, peeled, processed using a grater
- Pinch of sea salt
- Pinch of black pepper, to taste
- 3 Tbsp. olive oil

Directions:

1. Line a microwave safe-dish with paper towels. Spread shredded carrots on top. Microwave veggies on the highest heat setting for 2 minutes. Remove from heat.
2. Pour 1 tablespoon of oil into a non-stick skillet set over medium heat.
3. Cooking in batches, place a generous pinch of carrots into the hot oil. Press down using the back of a spatula.
4. Cook for 3 minutes every side, or until brown and crispy. Drain on paper towels. Repeat step for remaining carrots. Add more oil as needed.
5. Season with salt and pepper. Serve.

Nutrition: Calories: 200 kcal Protein: 4.03 g Fat: 11.73 g Carbohydrates: 20.49 g

236. Frittata

Preparation Time: 10 minutes
Cooking Time: 40 minutes
Servings: 4
Ingredients:

- 4 large eggs
- 6 egg whites
- 450g button mushrooms
- 450g baby spinach
- 125g firm tofu
- 1 onion, chopped
- 1 tbsp. minced garlic
- ½ tsp. ground turmeric
- ½ tsp. cracked black pepper
- ¼ cup water
- Kosher salt to taste

Directions:

1. Set your oven to 350F.
2. Sauté the mushrooms in a little bit of extra virgin olive oil in a large non-stick

ovenproof pan over medium heat. Add the onions once the mushrooms start turning golden and cook for 3 minutes until the onions become soft.

3. Stir in the garlic then cook for at least 30 seconds until fragrant before adding the spinach. Pour in water, cover, and cook until the spinach becomes wilted for about 2 minutes.

Take off the lid and continue cooking up to the water evaporates. Now, combine the eggs, egg whites, tofu, pepper, turmeric, and salt in a bowl. When all the liquid has evaporated, pour in the egg mixture, let cook for about 2 minutes until the edges start setting, then transfer to the oven and bake for about 25 minutes or until cooked.

Take off from the oven then let sit for at least 5 minutes before cutting it into quarters and serving.

Enjoy!

Baby spinach and mushrooms boost the nutrient profile of the eggs to provide you with amazing anti-inflammatory benefits.

Nutrition: Calories: 521 kcal Protein: 29.13 g Fat: 10.45 g Carbohydrates: 94.94 g

237. Sun-Dried Tomato Garlic Bruschetta

Preparation Time: 10 minutes
Cooking Time: 5 minutes
Servings: 6
Ingredients:

- 2 slices sourdough bread, toasted
- 1 tsp. chives, minced
- 1 garlic clove, peeled
- 2 tsp. sun-dried bell pepper in olive oil, minced
- 1 tsp. olive oil

Directions:

1. Vigorously rub garlic clove on 1 side of each of the toasted bread slices

2. Spread equal portions of sun-dried bell pepper on the garlic side of bread. Sprinkle chives and drizzle olive oil on top.
3. Pop both slices into oven toaster, and cook until well heated through.
4. Place bruschetta on a plate. Serve warm.

Nutrition: Calories: 149 kcal Protein: 6.12 g Fat: 2.99 g Carbohydrates: 24.39 g

238. Mushroom Crêpes

Preparation Time: 1 hour 30 minutes
Cooking Time: 30 minutes
Servings: 6
Ingredients:

- 2 eggs
- 3/4 cup almond milk
- 1/2 cup all-purpose flour
- 1/4 teaspoon salt
- For the filling
- 3 tablespoons all-purpose flour
- 2 cups of cremini mushrooms, sliced
- 3/4 cup chicken broth
- 1/2 cup Parmesan cheese, grated
- 1/8 teaspoon cayenne
- 1/8 teaspoon nutmeg
- ¾ cup almond milk
- 3 garlic cloves, minced
- 2 tablespoons of parsley (chopped)
- 6 slices of deli-sliced cooked lean ham
- 1/4 teaspoon of salt
- Freshly ground pepper

Directions:

1. Put and combine the salt and flour in a bowl. In another bowl, whisk the eggs and almond milk. Gradually combine the two mixtures until smooth. Leave for 15 minutes.
2. Spray a skillet using non-stick cooking spray and put over medium heat. Stir the batter a little. Add 1/4 of the batter into the skillet. Tilt the skillet to form a thin

and even crêpe. Cook for 1-2 minutes or until the bottom is golden and the top is set. Flip and cook for 20 seconds. Transfer to a plate.

3. Repeat the steps with the remaining batter. Loosely cover the cooked crêpes with plastic wrap.

4. For the filling. Put all together the ingredients for filling in a saucepan on medium heat – flour, almond milk, cayenne, nutmeg, and pepper. Constantly whisk until thick or around 7 minutes. Remove from the stove. Stir in a tablespoon of parsley and cheese. Loosely cover to keep warm.

5. Spray a skillet using non-stick cooking spray and put over medium heat. Cook the garlic and mushrooms. Season with salt. Cook for 6 minutes or until the mushrooms are soft. Add 2 tablespoons of sherry. Cook for a couple of minutes. Remove from the stove. Add the remaining parsley and stir.

6. Put the crêpes side by side on a flat surface. Spread a tablespoon of the sauce and 2 tablespoons of the cooked mushrooms. Roll up the crêpes and transfer them to a greased baking dish. Put all the sauce on top. Bake in the oven at 450°F for 15 minutes.

Nutrition: Calories: 232 kcal Protein: 16.51 g Fat: 10.8 g Carbohydrates: 16.25 g

239. Oat Porridge with Cherry & Coconut

Preparation Time: 10 minutes
Cooking Time: 0 minutes
Servings: 3
Ingredients:
- 1 ½ cups regular oats
- 3 cups coconut almond milk
- 4 tbsp. chia seed
- 3 tbsp. raw cacao

- Coconut shavings
- Dark chocolate shavings
- Fresh or frozen tart cherries
- A pinch of stevia, optional
- Maple syrup, to taste (optional)

Directions:
1. Combine the oats, almond milk, stevia, and cacao in a medium saucepan over medium heat and bring to a boil. Lower the heat, then simmer until the oats are cooked to desired doneness.

2. Divide the porridge among 3 serving bowls and top with dark chocolate and coconut shavings, cherries, and a little drizzle of maple syrup.

Nutrition: Calories: 343 kcal Protein: 15.64 g Fat: 12.78 g Carbohydrates: 41.63 g

240. Gingerbread Oatmeal Breakfast

Preparation Time: 10 minutes
Cooking Time: 0 minutes
Servings: 4
Ingredients:
- 1 cup steel-cut oats
- 4 cups drinking water
- Organic Maple syrup, to taste
- 1 tsp ground cloves
- 1 ½ tbsp. ground cinnamon
- 1/8 tsp nutmeg
- ¼ tsp ground ginger
- ¼ tsp ground coriander
- ¼ tsp ground allspice
- ¼ tsp ground cardamom
- Fresh mixed berries

Directions:
1. Cook the oats based on the package instructions. When it comes to a boil, reduce heat and simmer.

2. Stir in all the spices and continue cooking until cooked to desired doneness.
3. Serve in four serving bowls and drizzle with maple syrup and top with fresh berries.
4. Enjoy!

Nutrition: Calories: 87 kcal Protein: 5.82 g Fat: 3.26 g Carbohydrates: 18.22 g

241. Apple, Ginger, and Rhubarb Muffins

Preparation Time: 15 minutes
Cooking Time: 25 minutes
Servings: 4
Ingredients:
- ½ cup finely ground almonds
- ¼ cup white rice flour
- ½ cup buckwheat flour
- 1/8 cup unrefined raw sugar
- 2 tbsp. arrowroot flour
- 1 tbsp. linseed meal
- 2 tbsp. crystallized ginger, finely chopped
- ½ tsp. ground ginger
- ½ tsp. ground cinnamon
- 2 tsp. gluten-free baking powder
- A pinch of fine sea salt
- 1 small apple, peeled and finely diced
- 1 cup finely chopped rhubarb
- 1/3 cup almond/ rice almond milk
- 1 large egg
- ¼ cup extra virgin olive oil
- 1 tsp. pure vanilla extract

Directions:
1. Set your oven to 350Fgrease an eight-cup muffin tin and line with paper cases.
2. Combine the almond four, linseed meal, ginger and sugar in a mixing bowl. Sieve this mixture over the other flours, spices and baking powder and use a whisk to combine well.
3. Stir in the apple and rhubarb in the flour mixture until evenly coated.
4. In a separate bowl, whisk the almond milk, vanilla, and egg then pour it into the dry mixture. Stir until just combined – don't overwork the batter as this can yield very tough muffins.
5. Scoop the mixture into the arrange muffin tin and top with a few slices of rhubarb. Bake for at least 25 minutes, till they start turning golden or when an inserted toothpick emerges clean.
6. Take off from the oven and let sit for at least 5 minutes before transferring the muffins to a wire rack for further cooling.
7. Serve warm with a glass of squeezed juice.
Enjoy!

Nutrition: Calories: 325 kcal Protein: 6.32 g Fat: 9.82 g Carbohydrates: 55.71 g

242. Breakfast Sausage and Mushroom Casserole

Preparation Time: 20 minutes
Cooking Time: 45 minutes
Servings: 4
Ingredients:
- 450g of Italian sausage, cooked and crumbled
- Three-fourth cup of coconut almond milk
- 8 ounces of white mushrooms, sliced
- 1 medium onion, finely diced
- 2 Tablespoons of organic ghee
- 6 free-range eggs
- 600g of carrots
- 1 red bell pepper, roasted
- 3/4 tsp. of ground black pepper, divided

- 1 ½ tsp. of sea salt, divided

Directions:
1. Peel and shred the carrots.
2. Take a bowl, fill it with ice-cold water, and soak the carrots in it. Set aside.
3. Peel the roasted bell pepper, remove its seeds and finely dice it.
4. Set the oven 375°F.
5. Get a casserole baking dish and grease it with the organic ghee.
6. Put a skillet over medium flame and cook the mushrooms in it. Cook until the mushrooms are crispy and brown.
7. Take the mushrooms out and mix them with the crumbled sausage.
8. Now sauté the onions in the same skillet. Cook up to the onions are soft and golden. This should take about 4 – 5 minutes.
9. Take the onions out and mix them in the sausage-mushroom mixture.
10. Add the diced bell pepper to the same mixture.
11. Mix well and set aside for a while.
12. Now drain the soaked shredded carrots, put them on a paper towel, and pat dry.
13. Bring the carrots in a bowl and add about a teaspoon of salt and half a teaspoon of ground black pepper to it. Mix well and set aside.
14. Now take a large bowl and crack the eggs in it.
15. Break the eggs and then blend in the coconut almond milk.
16. Stir in the remaining black pepper and salt.
17. Take the greased casserole dish and spread the seasoned carrots evenly in the base of the dish.
18. Next, spread the sausage mixture evenly in the dish.
19. Finally, spread the egg mixture.
20. Now cover the casserole dish using a piece of aluminum foil.
21. Bake for 20 - 30 minutes. To check if the casserole is baked properly, insert a tester in the middle of the casserole, and it should come out clean.
22. Uncover the casserole dish and bake it again, uncovered for 5 - 10 minutes, until the casserole is a little golden on the top.
23. Allow it to cool for 10 minutes.
24. Enjoy!

Nutrition: Calories: 598 kcal Protein: 28.65 g Fat: 36.75 g Carbohydrates: 48.01 g

243. Yummy Steak Muffins

Preparation Time: 10 minutes
Cooking Time: 20 minutes
Servings: 4

Ingredients:
- 1 cup red bell pepper, diced
- 2 Tablespoons of water
- 8 ounce thin steak, cooked and finely chopped
- ¼ teaspoon of sea salt
- Dash of freshly ground black pepper
- 8 free-range eggs
- 1 cup of finely diced onion

Directions:
1. Set the oven to 350°F
2. Take 8 muffin tins and line then with parchment paper liners.
3. Get a large bowl and crack all the eggs in it.
4. Beat well the eggs.
5. Blend in all the remaining ingredients.
6. Spoon the batter into the arrange muffin tins. Fill three-fourth of each tin.
7. Put the muffin tins in the preheated oven for about 20 minutes, until the muffins are baked and set in the middle.
8. Enjoy!

Nutrition: Calories: 151 kcal Protein: 17.92 g Fat: 7.32 g Carbohydrates: 3.75 g

244. White and Green Quiche

Preparation Time: 10 minutes
Cooking Time: 40 minutes
Servings: 3
Ingredients:

- 3 cups of fresh spinach, chopped
- 15 large free-range eggs
- 3 cloves of garlic, minced
- 5 white mushrooms, sliced
- 1 small sized onion, finely chopped
- 1 ½ teaspoon of baking powder
- Ground black pepper to taste
- 1 ½ cups of coconut almond milk
- Ghee, as required to grease the dish
- Sea salt to taste

Directions:
1. Set the oven to 350°F.
2. Get a baking dish then grease it with the organic ghee.
3. Break all the eggs in a huge bowl then whisk well.
4. Stir in coconut almond milk. Beat well
5. While you are whisking the eggs, start adding the remaining ingredients in it.
6. When all the ingredients are thoroughly blended, pour all of it into the prepared baking dish.
7. Bake for at least 40 minutes, up to the quiche is set in the middle.
8. Enjoy!

Nutrition: Calories: 608 kcal Protein: 20.28 g
Fat: 53.42 g Carbohydrates: 16.88 g

245. Beef Breakfast Casserole

Preparation Time: 10 minutes
Cooking Time: 30 minutes
Servings: 5
Ingredients:

- 1 pound of ground beef, cooked

- 10 eggs
- ½ cup Pico de Gallo
- 1 cup baby spinach
- ¼ cup sliced black capers
- Freshly ground black pepper

Directions:
1. Preheat oven to 350 degrees Fahrenheit. Prepare a 9" glass pie plate with non-stick spray.
2. Whisk the eggs until frothy. Season with salt and pepper.
3. Layer the cooked ground beef, Pico de Gallo, and spinach in the pie plate.
4. Slowly pour the eggs over the top.
5. Top with black capers.
6. Bake for at least 30 minutes, until firm in the middle.
7. Slice into 5 pieces and serve.

Nutrition: Calories: 479 kcal Protein: 43.54 g
Fat: 30.59 g Carbohydrates: 4.65 g

246. Ham and Veggie Frittata Muffins

Preparation Time: 10 minutes
Cooking Time: 25 minutes
Servings: 12
Ingredients:

- 5 ounces thinly sliced ham
- 8 large eggs
- 4 tablespoons coconut oil
- ½ yellow onion, finely diced
- 8 oz. frozen spinach, thawed and drained
- 8 oz. mushrooms, thinly sliced
- 1 cup cherry bell pepper, halved
- ¼ cup coconut almond milk (canned)
- 2 tablespoons coconut flour
- Sea salt and pepper to taste

Directions:
1. Preheat oven to 375 degrees Fahrenheit.

2. In a medium skillet, warm the coconut oil on medium heat. Add the onion and cook until softened.
3. Add the mushrooms, spinach, and cherry bell pepper. Season with salt and pepper. Cook until the mushrooms have softened. About 5 minutes. Remove from heat and set aside.
4. In a huge bowl, beat the eggs together with the coconut almond milk and coconut flour. Stir in the cooled the veggie mixture.
5. Line each cavity of a 12 cavity muffin tin with the thinly sliced ham. Pour the egg mixture into each one and bake for 20 minutes.
6. Remove from oven and allow to cool for about 5 minutes before transferring to a wire rack.
7. To maximize the benefit of a vegetable-rich diet, it's important to eat a variety of colors, and these veggie-packed frittata muffins do just that. The onion, spinach, mushrooms, and cherry bell pepper provide a wide range of vitamins and nutrients and a healthy dose of fiber.

Nutrition: Calories: 125 kcal Protein: 5.96 g Fat: 9.84 g Carbohydrates: 4.48 g

247. Tomato and Almond Omelet

Preparation Time: 5 minutes
Cooking Time: 5 minutes
Servings: 1
Ingredients:
- 2 eggs
- ¼ almond, diced
- 4 cherry bell pepper, halved
- 1 tablespoon cilantro, chopped
- Squeeze of lime juice
- Pinch of salt

Directions:

1. Put together the almond, bell pepper, cilantro, lime juice, and salt in a small bowl, then mix well and set aside.
2. Warm a medium nonstick skillet on medium heat. Whisk the eggs until frothy and add to the pan. Move the eggs around gently with a rubber spatula until they begin to set.
3. Scatter the almond mixture over half of the omelet. Remove from heat, and slide the omelet onto a plate as you fold it in half.
4. Serve immediately.

Nutrition: Calories: 433 kcal Protein: 25.55 g Fat: 32.75 g Carbohydrates: 10.06 g

248. Vegan-Friendly Banana Bread

Preparation Time: 15 minutes
Cooking Time: 40 minutes
Servings: 4-6
Ingredients:
- 2 ripe apple, mashed
- 1/3 cup brewed coffee
- 3 tbsp. chia seeds
- 6 tbsp. water
- ½ cup soft vegan butter
- ½ cup maple syrup
- 2 cups flour
- 2 tsp. baking powder
- 1 tsp. cinnamon powder
- 1 tsp. allspice
- ½ tsp. salt

Directions:
1. Set oven at 350F.
2. Bring the chia seeds in a small bowl then soak it with 6 tbsp. of water. Stir well and set aside.
3. In a mixing bowl, mix using a hand mixer the vegan butter and maple syrup until it turns fluffy. Add the chia seeds along with the mashed apple.

4. Mix well and then add the coffee.
5. Meanwhile, sift all the dry ingredients (flour, baking powder, cinnamon powder, all spice, and salt) and then gradually add into the bowl with the wet ingredients.
6. Combine the ingredients well and then pour over a baking pan lined with parchment paper.
7. Place in the oven to bake for at least 30-40 minutes, or until the toothpick comes out clean after inserting in the bread.
8. Allow the bread to cool before serving.

Nutrition: Calories: 371 kcal Protein: 5.59 g Fat: 16.81 g Carbohydrates: 49.98 g

249. Mango Granola

Preparation Time: 10 minutes
Cooking Time: 30 minutes
Servings: 4
Ingredients:
- 2 cups rolled oats
- 1 cup dried mango, chopped
- ½ cup almonds, roughly chopped
- ½ cup nuts
- ½ cup dates, roughly chopped
- 3 tbsp. sesame seeds
- 2 tsp. cinnamon
- 2/3 cup agave nectar
- 2 tbsp. coconut oil
- 2 tbsp. water

Directions:
1. Set oven at 320F
2. In a large bowl, put the oats, almonds, nuts, sesame seeds, dates, and cinnamon then mix well.
3. Meanwhile, heat a saucepan over medium heat, pour in the agave syrup, coconut oil, and water.
4. Stir and let it cook for at least 3 minutes or until the coconut oil has melted.

5. Gradually pour the syrup mixture into the bowl with the oats and nuts and stir well, ensure that all the ingredients are coated with the syrup.
6. Transfer the granola on a baking sheet lined with parchment paper and place in the oven to bake for 20 minutes.
7. After 20 minutes, take off the tray from the oven and lay the chopped dried mango on top. Put back in the oven then bake again for another 5 minutes.
8. Let the granola cool to room temperature before serving or placing it in an airtight container for storage. The shelf life of the granola will last up to 2-3 weeks.

Nutrition: Calories: 434 kcal Protein: 13.16 g Fat: 28.3 g Carbohydrates: 55.19 g

250. Sautéed Veggies on Hot Bagels

Preparation Time: 10 minutes
Cooking Time: 16 minutes
Servings: 2
Ingredients:
- 1 yellow squash, diced
- 1 zucchini, sliced thin
- ½ onion, sliced thin
- 2 pcs. bell pepper, sliced
- 1 clove of garlic, chopped
- salt and pepper to taste
- 1 tbsp. olive oil
- 2 pcs. vegan bagels
- vegan butter for spread

Directions:
1. Heat the olive oil on the medium temperature in a cast-iron skillet.
2. Lower the heat to medium-low and sauté the onions for 10 minutes or until the onions start to brown.
3. Turn the heat again to medium and then add the diced squash and zucchini to the

pan and cook for 5 minutes. Add the clove of garlic and cook for another minute.

4. Throw in the tomato slices to the pan and cook for 1 minute. Season with pepper and salt and turn off the heat.
5. Toast the bagels and cut in half.
6. Spread the bagels lightly with butter and serve with the sautéed veggies on top.

Nutrition: Calories: 375 kcal Protein: 14.69 g Fat: 11.46 g Carbohydrates: 54.61 g

251. Honey Pancakes

Preparation Time: 10 minutes
Cooking Time: 5 minutes
Servings: 2
Ingredients:
- ½ cup almond flour
- 2 tablespoons coconut flour
- 1 tablespoon ground flaxseeds
- ¼ tsp baking soda
- ½ tablespoon ground ginger
- ½ tablespoon ground nutmeg
- ½ tablespoon ground cinnamon
- ½ teaspoon ground cloves
- Pinch of salt
- 2 tablespoons organic honey
- ¾ cup organic egg whites
- ½ teaspoon organic vanilla extract
- Coconut oil, as required

Directions:
1. In a big bowl, mix together flours, flax seeds, baking soda, spices, and salt.
2. In another bowl, add honey, egg whites and vanilla and beat till well combined.
3. Put the egg mixture into the flour mixture then mix till well combined.
4. Lightly, grease a big nonstick skillet with oil and heat on medium-low heat.
5. Add about ¼ cup of mixture and tilt the pan to spread it evenly inside the skillet.
6. Cook for about 3-4 minutes.

7. Carefully, customize the side and cook approximately 1 minute more.
8. Repeat with the remaining mixture.
9. Serve along with your desired topping.

Nutrition: Calories: 291 Fat: 8g Carbohydrates: 26g Fiber: 4g Protein: 23g

252. Coco-Tapioca Bowl

Preparation Time: 10 minutes
Cooking Time: 20 minutes
Servings: 2
Ingredients:
- ¼ cup tapioca pearls, small sized
- 1 can light coconut almond milk
- ¼ cup maple syrup
- 1 ½ tsp. lemon juice
- ½ cup unsweetened coconut flakes, toasted
- 2 cups water

Directions:
1. Place the tapioca in a saucepan and pour over the 2 cups of water. Let it stand for at least 30 minutes.
2. Pour in the coconut almond milk and syrup and heat the saucepan over medium temperature. Bring to a boil while stirring constantly.
3. Add the lemon juice and stir and then garnish with coconut flakes.

Nutrition: Calories: 309 kcal Protein: 3.93 g Fat: 9.02 g Carbohydrates: 54.55 g

253. Choco-Banana Oats

Preparation Time: 5 minutes
Cooking Time: 8 minutes
Servings: 2
Ingredients:
- 2 cups oats
- 2 cups almond milk
- ¾ cup water
- 2 ripe apple, sliced

- ¼ tsp. Vanilla
- ¼ tsp. almond extract
- 2 tbsp. cocoa powder, unsweetened
- 2 tbsp. agave nectar
- 1/8 tsp. cinnamon
- 1/8 tsp. salt
- 1/3 cup toasted walnuts, chopped
- 2 tbsp. vegan chocolate chips, semisweet

Directions:
1. In a large saucepan, pour the almond milk, water, apple, vanilla, and almond extract. Add the salt, stir, and heat over high temperature.
2. Mix the oats in the pan along with the unsweetened cocoa powder, 1 tbsp. agave nectar and lower the temperature to medium. Cook for 7-8 minutes, or until the oats are cooked to your liking. Stir frequently.
3. Scoop the cooked oats into serving bowls and garnish with the chopped walnuts, chocolate chips, and drizzle with the remaining agave nectar.

Nutrition: Calories: 522 kcal Protein: 30.17 g Fat: 27.01 g Carbohydrates: 79.09 g

254. Savory Bread

Preparation Time: 10 minutes
Cooking Time: 20-25 minutes
Servings: 8-10
Ingredients:
- ½ cup plus 1tablespoon almond flour
- 1 tsp. baking soda
- 1 teaspoon ground turmeric
- Salt, to taste
- 2 large organic eggs
- 2 organic egg whites
- 1 cup raw cashew butter
- 1 tablespoon water
- 1 tablespoon apple cider vinegar

Directions:

1. Set the oven to 350F. Grease a loaf pan.
2. In a big pan, mix together flour, baking soda, turmeric, and salt.
3. In another bowl, add eggs, egg whites, and cashew butter and beat till smooth.
4. Gradually, add water and beat till well combined.
5. Add flour mixture and mix till well combined.
6. Stir in apple cider vinegar treatment.
7. Place a combination into prepared loaf pan evenly.
8. Bake for around twenty minutes or till a toothpick inserted within the center is released clean.

Nutrition: Calories: 347 Fat: 11g Carbohydrates: 29g Fiber: 6g Protein: 21g

255. Savory Veggie Muffins

Preparation Time: 15 minutes
Cooking Time: 18-23 minutes
Servings: 5
Ingredients:
- ¾ cup almond meal
- ½ tsp baking soda
- ¼ cup concentrate powder
- 2 teaspoons fresh dill, chopped
- Salt, to taste
- 4 large organic eggs
- 1½ tablespoons nutritional yeast
- 2 teaspoons apple cider vinegar
- 3 tablespoons fresh lemon juice
- 2 tablespoons coconut oil, melted
- 1 cup coconut butter, softened
- 1 bunch scallion, chopped
- 2 medium carrots, peeled and grated
- ½ cup fresh parsley, chopped

Directions:
1. Set the oven to 350F. Grease 10 cups of your large muffin tin.
2. In a large bowl, mix together flour, baking soda, Protein powder, and salt.

3. In another bowl, add eggs, nutritional yeast, vinegar, lemon juice, and oil and beat till well combined.
4. Add coconut butter and beat till the mixture becomes smooth.
5. Put egg mixture into the flour mixture and mix till well combined.
6. Fold in scallion, carts, and parsley.
7. Place the amalgamation into prepared muffin cups evenly.
8. Bake for about 18-23 minutes or till a toothpick inserted inside center comes out clean.

Nutrition: Calories: 378 Fat: 13g Carbohydrates: 32g Fiber: 11g Protein: 32g

256. Crepes with Coconut Cream & Strawberry Sauce

Preparation Time: 15 minutes
Cooking Time: 8 minutes
Servings: 4
Ingredients:

- For Sauce:
- 12-ounces frozen strawberries, thawed and liquid reserved
- 1½ teaspoons tapioca starch
- 1 tablespoon honey
- For the Coconut cream:
- 1 (13½-ounce) can chilled coconut almond milk
- 1 teaspoon organic vanilla flavoring
- 1 tablespoon organic honey
- For Crepes:
- 2 tablespoons tapioca starch
- 2 tablespoons coconut flour
- ¼ cup almond milk
- 2 organic eggs
- Pinch of salt
- Almond oil, as required

Directions:

1. For sauce inside a bowl, mix together some reserved strawberry liquid and tapioca starch.
2. Add remaining ingredients and mix well.
3. Transfer a combination inside a pan on medium-high heat.
4. Bring to a boil, stirring continuously.
5. Cook for at least 2-3 minutes, till the sauce, becomes thick.
6. Remove from heat and aside, covered till serving.
7. For coconut cream, carefully, scoop your cream from your surface of a can of coconut almond milk.
8. In a mixer, add coconut cream, vanilla flavoring, and honey and pulse for around 6-8 minutes or till fluffy.
9. For crepes in a blender, add all ingredients and pulse till well combined and smooth.
10. Lightly, grease a substantial nonstick skillet with almond oil as well as heat on medium-low heat.
11. Add a modest amount of mixture and tilt the pan to spread it evenly inside the skillet.
12. Cook approximately 1-2 minutes.
13. Carefully change the side and cook for approximately 1-1½ minutes more.
14. Repeat with the remaining mixture.
15. Divide the coconut cream onto each crepe evenly and fold into quarters.
16. Place strawberry sauce ahead and serve.

Nutrition: Calories: 364 Fat: 9g Carbohydrates: 26g Fiber: 7g Protein: 15g

257. Spicy Ginger Crepes

Preparation Time: 15 minutes
Cooking Time: 20-30 seconds
Servings: 8
Ingredients:

- 1 1/3 cups chickpea flour
- ½ teaspoon red chili powder

- Salt, to taste
- 1 (1-inch) fresh ginger piece, grated finely
- 1 cup fresh cilantro leaves, chopped
- 1 green chili, seeded and chopped finely
- 1 cup water
- Cooking spray, as required

Directions:
1. In a sizable bowl, mix together flour, chili powder, and salt.
2. Add ginger, cilantro, and chili and mix well.
3. Add water and mix till an even mixture form.
4. Keep aside, covered for approximately ½-120 minutes.
5. Lightly, grease a substantial nonstick skillet with cooking spray and heat on medium-high heat.
6. Add the desired volume of the mixture and tilt the pan to spread it evenly inside the skillet.
7. Cook approximately 10-15 seconds per side.
8. Repeat while using the remaining mixture.

Nutrition: Calories: 73 Fat: 1.3 Carbohydrates: 11g Fiber: 2.1g, Protein: 4.3g

258. Cilantro Pancakes

Preparation Time: 10 minutes
Cooking Time: 6-8 minutes
Servings: 6
Ingredients:
- ½ cup tapioca flour
- ½ cup almond flour
- ½ teaspoon chili powder
- ¼ teaspoon ground turmeric
- Salt, to taste
- Freshly ground black pepper, to taste
- 1 cup full- fat coconut almond milk
- ½ of red onion, chopped

- 1 (½-inch) fresh ginger piece, grated finely
- 1 Serrano pepper, minced
- ½ cup fresh cilantro, chopped
- Oil, as required

Directions:
1. In a big bowl, put together the flours and spices then mix.
2. Put the coconut almond milk and mix till well combined.
3. Fold within the onion, ginger, Serrano pepper, and cilantro.
4. Lightly, grease a sizable nonstick skillet with oil and warmth on medium-low heat.
5. Add about ¼ cup of mixture and tilt the pan to spread it evenly inside the skillet.
6. Cook for around 3-4 minutes from either side.
7. Repeat with all the remaining mixture.
8. Serve along with your desired topping.

Nutrition: Calories: 331 Fat: 10g Carbohydrates: 37g Fiber: 6g Protein: 28g

259. Zucchini Pancakes

Preparation Time: 15 minutes
Cooking Time: 6-10 min
Servings: 8
Ingredients:
- 1 cup chickpea flour
- 1½ cups water, divided
- ¼ teaspoon cumin seeds
- ¼ tsp cayenne
- ¼ teaspoon ground turmeric
- Salt, to taste
- ½ cup zucchini, shredded
- ½ cup red onion, chopped finely
- 1 green chile, seeded and chopped finely
- ¼ cup fresh cilantro, chopped

Directions:
1. In a large bowl, add flour and ¾ cup with the water and beat till smooth.

2. Add remaining water and beat till a thin
3. Fold inside the onion, ginger, Serrano pepper, and cilantro.
4. Lightly, grease a substantial nonstick skillet with oil and heat on medium-low heat.
5. Add about ¼ cup of mixture and tilt the pan to spread it evenly in the skillet.
6. Cook for around 4-6 minutes.
7. Carefully, alter the side and cook for approximately 2-4 minutes.
8. Repeat while using the remaining mixture.
9. Serve together with your desired topping.

Nutrition: Calories: 389 Fat: 13g Carbohydrates: 25g Fiber: 4g Protein: 21g

260. Leek & Spinach Frittata

Preparation Time: 10 minutes
Cooking Time: 15 minutes
Servings: 4
Ingredients:
- 2 Leeks, Chopped Fine
- 2 Tablespoons Almond Oil
- 8 Eggs
- ½ Teaspoon Garlic Powder
- ½ Teaspoon Bail, Dried
- 1 Cup Baby Spinach, Fresh & Packed
- 1 Cup Cremini Mushrooms, Sliced
- Sea Salt & Black Pepper to Taste

Directions:
1. Set the oven to 400°F then get an ovenproof skillet. Place it over medium-high heat, sautéing your leeks in your almond oil until soft. It should take roughly five minutes

Get out a bowl, and whisk the eggs with your garlic, basil, and salt. Add them to the skillet with your leeks, cooking for five minutes. You'll need to stir frequently.

Stir in your mushrooms and spinach, seasoning with pepper.

Place the skillet in the oven then bake for 10 minutes. Serve warm.

Nutrition: Calories: 276 Protein: 19 Grams Fat: 17 Grams Carbs: 15 Grams

261. Cherry Chia Oats

Preparation Time: 10 minutes
Cooking Time: 20 minutes
Servings: 2
Ingredients:
- ¼ Teaspoon Vanilla Extract, Pure
- 2 Tablespoons Almond Butter
- 8 Cherries, Fresh, Pitted & Halved
- 1 Cup Quick Cook Oats
- 2 Tablespoons Chia Seeds
- ¼ Cup Whole Almond milk Yogurt, Plain
- 1 ¼ Cup Almond milk

Directions:
2. Mix all of together the ingredients until they're combined well.
3. Seal in two jars and refrigerate for twenty-five minutes before serving.

Nutrition: Calories: 564 Protein: 22 Grams Fat: 32 Grams Carbs: 27 Grams

262. Banana Pancakes

Preparation Time: 5 minutes
Cooking Time: 15 minutes
Servings: 2
Ingredients:
- 2 Eggs
- 1 Egg White
- 1 Banana, Ripe
- 1 Cup Rolled Oats
- 2 Teaspoons Ground Cinnamon
- 1 Tablespoon Coconut Oil, Divided
- 1 Teaspoon Vanilla Extract, Pure
- ½ Teaspoon Sea Salt

Directions:

1. Get out a food processor, grinding your oats until they make a coarse flour.
2. Add your cinnamon, egg whites, eggs, banana, vanilla, and salt. Blend until it forms a smooth batter, and then heat a small skillet over medium heat. Heat a half a tablespoon of coconut oil, and then pour your batter in. Cook for two minutes per side, and continue until all of your batter has been used.

Nutrition: Calories: 306 Protein: 15 Grams Fat: 15 Grams Carbs: 17 Grams

263. Baked French Toast Casserole

Ingredients: Preparation Time: 20 minutes
Cooking Time: 45 minutes
Servings: 12

- 1 lb. French bread
- 1 cup of egg white liquid
- 6 eggs
- 1/3 cup maple syrup
- 1-1/2 cups of rice almond milk,
- ½ lb. raspberries
- ½ lb. blueberries
- 1 teaspoon of vanilla extract
- ¾ cup strawberries

Directions:

1. Slice the bread into small cubes. Keep them in a greased casserole dish.
2. Add all the berries. Only leave a few for the topping.
3. Whisk together the egg whites, eggs, rice almond milk, and maple syrup in a bowl.
4. Combine well.
5. Put the egg mixture on the top of the bread. Press the bread down. All pieces should be soaked well.
6. Add berries on the top. Fill up the holes, if any.

7. Refrigerate covered for a couple of hours at least.
8. Take out the casserole half an hour before baking.
9. Set your oven to 350 degrees F.
10. Now, bake your casserole uncovered for 30 minutes.
11. Bake for another 15 minutes covered with a foil.
12. Let it rest for 15 minutes.
13. Serve it warm with maple syrup.

Nutrition: Calories 200 Carbohydrates 31g Cholesterol 93mg Total Fat 4g Protein 10g Fiber 2g
Sodium 288mg Sugar 10g

264. Whole Grain Blueberry Scones

Preparation Time: 10 minutes
Cooking Time: 25 minutes
Servings: 8

Ingredients:

- 2 cups of whole-wheat flour
- ¼ cup maple syrup
- 6 tablespoons of olive oil
- 2-1/2 teaspoons baking powder
- ½ teaspoon sea salt
- 2 tablespoons of coconut almond milk
- 1 teaspoon vanilla extract
- 1 cup blueberries

Directions:

1. Set the oven 400°F. Keep parchment paper on your baking sheet.
2. Add the syrup, flour, salt, and baking powder in a bowl. Combine well by whisking together.
3. Pour the olive oil into a bowl with the dry ingredients.
4. Work the oil into your flour mix.
5. Stir the vanilla extract and coconut almond milk into the dry ingredients bowl.

6. Fold in the blueberries gently. Your dough should be sticky and thick.
7. Put some flour on your hand then shape the dough into a circle.
8. Take a knife and create triangle slices.
9. Keep them on the baking sheet. Maintain an 8-inch gap.
10. Bake for 25 minutes. Set aside on the baking sheet for cooling once done.

Nutrition: Calories 331 Carbohydrates 27g Cholesterol 0mg Total Fat 23g Protein 4g Fiber 4g Sugar 8g

265. Weekend Breakfast Salad

Preparation Time: 30 minutes
Cooking Time: 0 minutes
Servings: 4
Ingredients:
- 4 Eggs, hard-boiled
- 1 Lemon
- 10 cups Arugula
- 1 cup Quinoa, cooked and cooled
- 2 tbsp. Olive oil
- ½ cup Dill, chopped
- 1 cup Almonds, chopped
- 1 Large Almond, sliced thin
- ½ cup Cucumber, chopped
- 1 Large Tomato, cut in wedges

Directions:
1. Mix together the quinoa, cucumber, bell pepper, and arugula. Toss these ingredients lightly together with olive oil, salt, and pepper. Divide the salad into 4 plates and arrange the egg and almond on top. Top each salad with almonds and herbs. Drizzle with juice from the lemon.

Nutrition: Calories 336 7.7 grams fat 12.3 grams protein 54.6 grams carbs 5.5 grams sugar 5.2 grams fiber

266. Egg Muffins with Feta and Quinoa

Preparation Time: 15 minutes
Cooking Time: 30 minutes
Servings: 6-12
Ingredients:
- 8 Eggs
- 1 cup Bell pepper, chopped
- ¼ tsp. Salt
- 1 cup Feta cheese
- 1 cup Quinoa, cooked
- 2 tsp. Olive oil
- 1 tbsp. Oregano, fresh chop
- ¼ cup Black capers, chopped
- ¼ cup Onion, chopped
- 2 cups baby spinach, chopped

Directions:
1. Heat oven to 350. Spray oil a muffin pan with twelve cups. Cook spinach, oregano, capers, onion, and bell pepper for five minutes in the olive oil over medium heat. Beat eggs. Add the cooked mix of veggies to the eggs with the cheese and salt. Spoon mix into muffin cups. Bake thirty minutes. These will remain fresh in the fridge for two days. To eat, just wrap in a paper towel and warm in the microwave for thirty seconds.

Nutrition: Calorie 113 5 grams carbs 6 grams protein 7 grams fat 1-gram sugar

267. Tomato Omelet

Preparation Time: 2 minutes
Cooking Time: 8 minutes
Servings: 1
Ingredients:
- 2 Eggs
- ½ cup Basil, fresh
- ½ cup Cherry bell pepper
- 1 tsp. Black pepper

- ¼ cup Cheese, any type, shredded
- ½ tsp. Salt
- 2 tbsp. Olive oil

Directions:
1. Cut the bell pepper into quarters. Fry the bell pepper for 3 hours. Set the bell pepper off to the side. Add the salt and pepper to the eggs in a small bowl and beat together well. Pour the mix of beaten egg into the pan and use a spatula to gently work around the edges under the omelet, letting the eggs fry unmoved for three minutes.
2. When just the center third of the egg mix is still runny, add on the basil, bell pepper, and cheese. Fold over half of the omelet onto the other half. Cook two more minutes and serve.

Nutrition: Calories 342 8 grams carbs 20 grams protein 25.3 grams fat

268. Quinoa Breakfast Bowl

Preparation Time: 30 minutes
Cooking Time: 0 minutes
Servings: 6
Ingredients:
- 2 cups Quinoa, cooked
- 12 Eggs
- ¼ cup Greek yogurt, plain
- ½ tsp. Salt
- 1 cup Feta cheese
- 1 Pint Cherry bell pepper, cut in halves
- 1 tsp. Black pepper
- 1 tsp. Garlic, minced
- 1 cup Baby spinach, chopped
- 1 tsp. Olive oil

Directions:
1. Mix together the eggs, salt, pepper, garlic, onion powder, and yogurt. Cook the spinach and bell pepper for five minutes in the olive oil over medium heat.

2. Pour in the egg mix and stir until eggs have set to your preferred doneness. Mix in quinoa and feta until they are hot. This will store in the fridge for two to three days.

Nutrition: Calories 340 7.3 grams fat 59.4 grams carbs 6.2 grams fiber 21.4 grams sugar 10.5 grams protein.

269. Cream Cheese Salmon Toast

Preparation Time: 15 minutes
Cooking Time: 5 minutes
Servings: 2
Ingredients:
- Whole grain or rye toast, two slices
- 1 tbsp. Red onion, chopped fine
- 2 tbsp. Cream cheese, low-fat
- ½ tsp. Basil flakes
- ½ cup Arugula or spinach, chopped
- 2 oz. Smoked salmon

Directions:
1. Toast the wheat bread. Mix cream cheese and basil and spread this mixture on the toast. Add salmon, arugula, and onion.

Nutrition: Calories 291 15.2 grams fat (8.5 saturated) 17.8 grams carbohydrates 3 grams of sugar

270. Kale Turmeric Scramble

Preparation Time: 5 minutes
Cooking Time: 10 minutes
Servings: 1
Ingredients:
- 2 tbsp. Olive oil
- ½ cup Kale, shredded
- ½ cup Sprouts
- 1 tbsp. Garlic, minced
- ¼ tsp. Black pepper

- 1 tbsp. Turmeric, ground
- 2 Eggs

Directions:
1. Beat the eggs and add in the turmeric, black pepper, and garlic. Sauté the kale into the olive oil over medium heat for five minutes, and then pour this egg mixture into the pan with the kale.
2. Continue cooking, often stirring, until the eggs are cooked to your preference. Top with raw sprouts and serve.

Nutrition: Calories 137 8.4 grams fat 7.9 grams carbs 4.8 grams fiber 1.8grams sugar 13.2 grams protein

271. Carrot Cake Overnight Oats

Preparation Time: 5 minutes + overnight
Cooking Time: 0 minutes
Servings: 1
Ingredients:
- 1 cup Coconut or almond milk
- 1 tbsp. Chia seeds
- 1 tsp. Cinnamon, ground
- ½ cup Raisins
- 2 tbsp. Cream cheese, low fat, at room temperature
- 1 Large Carrot, peel, and shred
- 2 tbsp. Honey
- 1 tsp. Vanilla

Directions:
1. Mix together all of the listed ingredients and store them in a safe refrigerator container overnight. Eat cold in the morning. If you choose to warm this, just microwave for one minute and stir well before eating.

Nutrition: Calories 340 32 grams sugar 8 grams protein 4 grams fat 9 grams fiber 70 grams carbs

272. Mediterranean Frittata

Preparation Time: 5 minutes
Cooking Time: 20 minutes
Servings: 6
Ingredients:
- 6 Eggs
- ¼ cup Feta cheese, crumbled
- ¼ tsp. Black pepper
- Oil, spray or olive
- 1 tsp. Oregano
- ¼ cup Almond milk, almond or coconut
- 1 tsp. Sea salt
- ¼ cup Black capers, chopped
- ¼ cup Green capers, chopped
- ¼ cup Bell pepper, diced

Directions:
1. Heat oven to 400. Oil one eight by eight-inch baking dish. Beat the almond milk into the eggs, and then add other ingredients. Pour all of this mixture into the baking dish and bake for twenty minutes.

Nutrition: Calories 107 2 grams sugars 7 fat grams 3 carb grams 7 grams protein

273. Poached Salmon Egg Toast

Preparation Time: 10 minutes
Cooking Time: 4 minutes
Servings: 2
Ingredients:
- Bread, two slices rye or whole-grain toasted
- ¼ tsp. Lemon juice
- 2 tbs. Almond, mashed
- ¼ tsp. Black pepper
- 2 Eggs, poached
- 4 oz. Salmon, smoked
- 1 tbsp. Scallions, sliced thin

- 1/8 tsp. Salt

Directions:

1. Add lemon juice to almond with pepper and salt. Spread the mixed almond over the toasted bread slices. Lay smoked salmon over toast and top with a poached egg. Top with sliced scallions

Nutrition: Calories 389 17.2 grams fat 33.5 grams protein 31.5 grams carbs 1.3 grams sugar 9.3 grams fiber

274. Maple Oatmeal

Preparation Time: 5 minutes
Cooking Time: 20 minutes
Servings: 4

Ingredients:

- 1 tsp. Maple flavoring
- 1 tsp. Cinnamon
- 3 tbsp. Sunflower seeds
- ½ cup Pecans, chopped
- ¼ cup Coconut flakes, unsweetened
- ½ cup Walnuts, chopped
- ½ cup Almond milk, almond or coconut
- 4 tbsp. Chia seeds

Directions:

1. Pulse the sunflower seeds, walnuts, and pecans in a food processor to crumble. Or you can just put the nuts in a sturdy plastic bag, wrap the bag with a towel, lay it on a sturdy surface, and beat the towel with a hammer until the nuts are crumbled. Mix the crushed nuts with the rest of the ingredients and pour them into a large pot.
2. Simmer this mixture over low heat for thirty minutes. Stir often, so the mix does not stick to the bottom. Serve garnished with fresh fruit or a sprinkle of cinnamon if desired.

Nutrition: Calories 374 3.2 grams carbs 9.25 grams protein 34.59 grams fat

275. Tuna & Sweet Potato Croquettes

Preparation Time: 15 minutes
Cooking Time: 12 minutes
Servings: 8

Ingredients:

- 1 tablespoon coconut oil
- ½ large onion, chopped
- 1 (1-inch piece fresh ginger, minced
- 3 garlic cloves, minced
- 1 Serrano pepper, seeded and minced
- ½ teaspoon ground coriander
- ¼ teaspoon ground turmeric
- ¼ teaspoon red chili powder
- ¼ teaspoon garam masala
- Salt, to taste
- Freshly ground black pepper, to taste
- 2 (5 oz.) cans tuna
- 1 cup sweet potato, peeled and mashed
- 1 egg
- ¼ cup tapioca flour
- ¼ cup almond flour
- Olive oil, as required

Directions:

1. In a frying pan, warm the coconut oil on medium heat.
2. Put onion, ginger, garlic, and Serrano pepper and sauté for approximately 5-6 minutes.
3. Stir in spices and sauté approximately 1 minute more.
4. Transfer the onion mixture in a bowl.
5. Add tuna and sweet potato and mix till well combined.
6. Make equal sized oblong shaped patties in the mixture.
7. Arrange the croquettes inside a baking sheet in a very single layer and refrigerate for overnight.
8. In a shallow dish, beat the egg.

9. In another shallow dish, mix together both flours.
10. In a big skillet, heat the enough oil.
11. Add croquettes in batches and shallow fry for around 2-3 minutes per side.

Nutrition: Calories: 404   Fat: 9g   Carbohydrates: 20g Fiber: 4g Protein: 30g

276. Quinoa & Veggie Croquettes

Preparation Time: 15 minutes
Cooking Time: 9 minutes
Servings: 12-15
Ingredients:
- 1 tbsp. essential olive oil
- ½ cup frozen peas, thawed
- 2 minced garlic cloves
- 1 cup cooked quinoa
- 2 large boiled carrots, peeled and mashed
- ¼ cup fresh cilantro leaves, chopped
- 2 teaspoons ground cumin
- 1 teaspoon garam masala
- ¼ teaspoon ground turmeric
- Salt, to taste
- Freshly ground black pepper, to taste
- Olive oil, for frying

Directions:
1. In a frying pan, warm oil on medium heat.
2. Add peas and garlic and sauté for about 1 minute.
3. Transfer the pea mixture into a large bowl.
4. Add the remainder ingredients and mix till well combined.
5. Make equal sized oblong shaped patties from your mixture.
6. In a huge skillet, heat oil on medium-high heat.
7. Add croquettes and fry for about 4 minutes per side.

Nutrition: Calories: 367   Fat: 6g   Carbohydrates: 17g Fiber: 5g Protein: 22g

277. Peaches with Honey Almond Ricotta

Preparation Time: 15 minutes
Cooking Time: 0 minutes
Servings: 4-6
Ingredients:
- Spread
- 1 cup Ricotta, skim almond milk
- 1 tsp. Honey
- ½ cup Almonds, thin slices
- ¼ cup Almond extract
- To Serve
- ¼ cup Peaches, sliced
- Bread, whole grain bagel or toast

Directions:
1. Mix the almond extract, honey, ricotta, and almonds. Spread one tablespoon of this mix on toasted bread and cover with peaches.

Nutrition: Calories 230   9 grams protein 8 grams fat 37 carbs grams 3 fiber grams 34 sugar grams

278. Salmon Burgers

Preparation Time: 15 minutes
Cooking Time: 8 minutes
Servings: 3
Ingredients:
- 1 (6-oz. can) skinless, boneless salmon, drained
- 1 celery rib, chopped
- ½ of a medium onion, chopped
- 2 large eggs
- 1 tablespoon plus 1 teaspoon coconut flour
- 1 tablespoon dried dill, crushed
- 1 teaspoon lemon

- Salt, to taste
- Freshly ground black pepper, to taste
- 3 tablespoons coconut oil

Directions:

1. In a substantial bowl, add salmon and which has a fork, break it into small pieces.
2. Add remaining ingredients excluding the for oil and mix till well combined.
3. Make 6 equal sized small patties from the mixture.
4. In a substantial skillet, melt coconut oil on medium-high heat.
5. Cook the patties for around 3-4 minutes per side.

Nutrition: Calories: 39 Fat: 12g Carbohydrates: 19g Fiber: 5g Protein: 24g

279. Quinoa & Beans Burgers

Preparation Time: 15 minutes
Cooking Time: 55 minutes
Servings: 12

Ingredients:

- ½ cup dry quinoa
- 1½ cups water
- 1 cup cooked corn kernels
- 1 (15 oz.) can black beans, drained
- 1 small boiled potato, peeled
- 1 small onion, chopped
- ½ teaspoon fresh ginger, grated finely
- 1 teaspoon garlic, minced
- ½ cup fresh cilantro, chopped
- 1 teaspoon flax meal
- 1 teaspoon ground cumin
- 1 teaspoon paprika
- 1 teaspoon chili flakes
- ½ teaspoon ground turmeric
- Salt, to taste
- Freshly ground black pepper, to taste

Directions:

1. In a pan, add water and quinoa on high heat and provide to a boil.
2. Lower the heat to medium and simmer for around 15-twenty or so minutes.
3. Drain excess water.
4. Set the oven to 375°F. Line a sizable baking sheet that has a parchment paper.
5. In a sizable bowl, add quinoa and remaining ingredients.
6. With a fork, mix till well combined.
7. Make equal-sized patties from the mixture.
8. Arrange the patties onto the prepared baking sheet in the single layer.
9. Bake for around 20-25 minutes.
10. Carefully, alter the side and cook for about 8-10 minutes.

Nutrition: Calories: 400 Fat: 9 Carbohydrates: 27g Fiber: 12g Protein: 38g

280. Veggie Balls

Preparation Time: 15 minutes
Cooking Time: 25 minutes
Servings: 5-6

Ingredients:

- 2 medium carrots, cubed into ½-inch size
- 2 tablespoons coconut almond milk
- 1 cup fresh kale leaves, trimmed and chopped
- 1 medium shallot, chopped finely
- 1 tsp. ground cumin
- ½ teaspoon granulated garlic
- ¼ tsp. ground turmeric
- Salt, to taste
- Freshly ground black pepper, to taste
- Ground flax seeds, as required

Directions:

1. Set the oven to 400°F. Line a baking sheet with parchment paper.

2. In a pan of water, arrange a steamer basket.
3. Bring the sweet potato in a steamer basket and steam approximately 10-15 minutes.
4. In a sizable bowl, put the sweet potato.
5. Add coconut almond milk and mash well.
6. Add remaining ingredients except for flax seeds and mix till well combined.
7. Make about 1½-2-inch balls from your mixture.
8. Arrange the balls onto the prepared baking sheet inside a single layer.
9. Sprinkle with flax seeds.
Bake for around 20-25 minutes.

Nutrition: Calories: 464 Fat: 12g Carbohydrates: 20g Fiber: 8g Protein: 27g

281. Coconut & Banana Cookies

Preparation Time: 15 minutes
Cooking Time: 25 minutes
Servings: 7
Ingredients:
- 2 cups unsweetened coconut, shredded
- 3 medium apple, peeled
- ½ tsp. ground cinnamon
- ½ tsp. ground turmeric
- Pinch of salt, to taste
- Freshly ground black pepper

Directions:
1. Set the oven to 350°F. Line a cookie sheet a lightly greased parchment paper.
2. In a mixer, put all together ingredients and pulse till a dough-like mixture forms.
3. Form small balls through the mixture and set onto a prepared cookie sheet in a single layer.

4. Using your fingers, press along the balls to create the cookies.
5. Bake for at least 15-20 minutes or till golden brown.

Nutrition: Calories: 370 Fat: 4g Carbohydrates: 28g Fiber: 11g Protein: 33g

282. Fennel Seeds Cookies

Preparation Time: 10 minutes
Cooking Time: 20 minutes
Servings: 5
Ingredients:
- 1/3 cup coconut flour
- ¼ teaspoon whole fennel seeds
- ½ teaspoon fresh ginger, grated finely
- ¼ cup coconut oil, softened
- 2 tablespoons raw honey
- 1 teaspoon vanilla extract
- Pinch of ground cinnamon
- Pinch of salt
- Pinch freshly ground black pepper

Directions:
1. Set the oven to 360°F. Line a cookie sheet that has a parchment paper.
2. In a substantial bowl, add all together the ingredients and mix till an even dough form.
3. Form a small balls in the mixture make onto a prepared cookie sheet inside a single layer.
4. Using your fingers, gently press along the balls to create the cookies.
5. Bake for at least 9 minutes or till golden brown.

Nutrition: Calories: 353 Fat: 5g Carbohydrates: 19g Fiber: 3g Protein: 25g

SNACKS

283. Veggie Snack

Preparation Time: 5 minutes
Cooking Time: 10 minutes
Servings: 1
Ingredients:
- 1 large yellow pepper
- 5 carrots
- 5 stalks celery

Directions:
1. Clean the carrots and rinse under running water.
2. Rinse celery and yellow pepper. Remove seeds of pepper and chop the veggies into small sticks.
3. Put in a bowl and serve.

Nutrition: Calories: 189 Fat: 0.5 g Carbs: 44.3 g Protein: 5 g Sodium: 282 mg Potassium: 0mg Phosphorus: 0mg

284. Roasted Asparagus

Preparation Time: 5 minutes
Cooking Time: 10 minutes
Servings: 4
Ingredients:
- 1 tbsp. extra virgin olive oil
- 1-pound fresh asparagus
- 1 medium lemon, zested
- 1/2 tsp. freshly grated nutmeg
- 1/2 tsp. kosher salt
- ½ tsp. black pepper

Directions:
1. Preheat your oven to 500 degrees F.
2. Put asparagus on an aluminum foil and add extra virgin olive oil.
3. Prepare asparagus in a single layer and fold the edges of the foil.

4. Cook in the oven for 5 minutes. Continue roasting until browned.
5. Add the roasted asparagus with nutmeg, salt, zest, and pepper before serving.

Nutrition: Calories: 55 Fat: 3.8 g Carbs: 4.7 g Protein: 2.5 g Sodium: 98mg Potassium: 172mg Phosphorus: 35mg

285. Cinnamon Apple Fries

Preparation Time: 5 minutes
Cooking Time: 15 minutes
Servings: 1
Ingredients:
- 1 apple, sliced thinly
- Dash of cinnamon
- Stevia

Directions:
1. Coat apple slices with cinnamon and stevia.
2. Bake for 15 minutes or until tender and crispy at 325 degrees F.

Nutrition: Calories: 146 Fat: 0.7 g Carbs: 36.4 g Protein: 1.6 g Sodium: 10 mg Potassium: 100mg Phosphorus: 0mg

286. Vinegar & Salt Kale

Preparation Time: 10 minutes
Cooking Time: 12 minutes
Servings: 2
Ingredients:
- 1 head kale, chopped
- 1 teaspoon extra virgin olive oil
- 1 tablespoon apple cider vinegar
- ½ teaspoon of sea salt

Directions:
1. Prepare kale in a bowl and put vinegar and extra virgin olive oil.

2. Sprinkle with salt and massage the ingredients with hands.
3. Spread the kale out onto two paper-lined baking sheets and bake at 375°F for about 12 minutes or until crispy.
4. Let cool for about 10 minutes before serving.

Nutrition: Calories: 152 Fat: 8.2 g Carbs: 15.2 g Protein: 4 g Sodium: 170mg Potassium: 304mg Phosphorus: 37mg

287. Lemon Pops

Preparation Time: 5 minutes
Cooking Time: 5 minutes
Servings: 1
Ingredients:
- 4 tablespoons fresh lemon juice
- Powdered stevia

Directions:
1. Mix mango or lemon juice and stevia and pour into molds.
2. Freeze until firm.

Nutrition: Calories: 46 Fat: 0.2g Carbs: 16g Protein: 0.9g Sodium: 3.7mg Potassium: 104mg Phosphorus: 11mg

288. Apple & Strawberry Snack

Preparation Time: 5 minutes
Cooking Time: 2 minutes
Servings: 1
Ingredients:
- ½ apple, cored and sliced
- 2-3 strawberries
- dash of ground cinnamon
- 2-3 drops stevia 2-3 drops

Directions:
1. In a bowl, mix strawberries and apples and sprinkle with stevia and cinnamon.
2. Microwave for about 1-2 minutes. Serve warm.

Nutrition: Calories: 145 Fat: 0.8 g Carbs: 34.2 g Protein: 1.6 g Sodium: 20 mg Potassium: 0mg Phosphorus: 0mg

289. Candied Macadamia Nuts

Preparation Time: 5 minutes
Cooking Time: 15 minutes
Servings: 2
Ingredients:
- 2 cups macadamia nuts
- 1 tablespoon extra-virgin olive oil
- 2 tablespoons honey

Directions:
1. Toss ingredients in bowl and spread into a baking dish.
2. Bake for 15 minutes at 350°F.
3. Let cool before serving.

Nutrition: Calories: 200 Fat: 18 g Carbs: 10g Protein: 1g Sodium: 5 mg Potassium: 55mg Phosphorus: 10mg

290. Healthy Spiced Nuts

Preparation Time: 10 minutes
Cooking Time: 10 minutes
Servings: 4
Ingredients:
- 1 tbsp. extra virgin olive oil
- ¼ cup walnuts
- ¼ cup pecans
- ¼ cup almonds
- ½ tsp. sea salt
- ½ tsp. cumin
- ½ tsp. pepper
- 1 tsp. chili powder

Directions:
1. Put the skillet on medium heat and toast the nuts until lightly browned.
2. Prepare the spice mixture and add black pepper, cumin, chili, and salt.

3. Put extra virgin olive oil and sprinkle with spice mixture to the toasted nuts before serving.

Nutrition: Calories: 88 Fat: 8g Carbs: 4g Protein: 2.5g Sodium: 51mgPotassium: 88mg Phosphorus: 6.3mg

291. Low-Fat Mango Salsa

Preparation Time: 10 minutes
Cooking Time: 10 minutes
Servings: 4
Ingredients:
- 1 cup cucumber, chopped
- 2 cups mango, diced
- ½ cup cilantro, minced
- 2 tablespoons fresh lime juice
- 1 tablespoon scallions, minced
- ¼ teaspoon chipotle powder
- ¼ teaspoon sea salt

Directions
1. Mix the ingredients in a bowl and serve or refrigerate.

Nutrition: Calories: 155 Fat: 0.6 g Carbs: 38.2 g Protein: 1.4 g Sodium: 3.2 mg Potassium: 221mg Phosphorus: 27mg

292. Easy No-Bake Coconut Cookies

Preparation Time: 5 minutes
Cooking Time: 10 minutes
Servings: 20
Ingredients:
- 3 cups finely shredded coconut flakes
- 1 cup melted coconut oil
- 1 teaspoon liquid stevia

Directions:
1. Prepare all ingredients in a large bowl; stir until well blended.
2. Form the mixture into small balls and arrange them on a paper-lined baking tray.

3. Press each cookie down with a fork and refrigerate until firm. Enjoy!

Nutrition: Calories: 99 Fat: 10 g Carbs: 2 g Protein: 3 Sodium: 7 m Potassium: 105mg Phosphorus: 11mg

293. Roasted Chili-Vinegar Peanuts

Preparation Time: 5 minutes
Cooking Time: 10 minutes
Servings: 4
Ingredients:
- 1 tablespoon coconut oil
- 2 cups raw peanuts, unsalted
- 2 teaspoon sea salt
- 2 tablespoon apple cider vinegar
- 1 teaspoon chili powder
- 1 teaspoon fresh lime zest

Directions:
1. Preheat oven to 350°F.
2. In a large bowl, toss together coconut oil, peanuts, and salt until well coated.
3. Transfer to a rimmed baking sheet and roast in the oven for about 15 minutes or until fragrant.
4. Transfer the roasted peanuts to a bowl and add vinegar, chili powder, and lime zest.
5. Toss to coat well and serve.

Nutrition: Calories: 447 Fat: 39.5g Carbs: 12.3 g Protein: 18.9 g Sodium: 160 mg Potassium: 200mg Phosphorus: 0mg

294. Carrot and Parsnips French Fries

Preparation Time: 15 minutes
Cooking Time: 20 minutes
Servings: 2
Ingredients:
- 6 large carrots

- 6 large parsnips
- 2 tablespoons extra virgin olive oil
- ½ teaspoon of sea salt

Directions:
1. Chop the carrots and parsnips into 2-inch slices and then cut each into thin sticks.
2. Toss together the carrots and parsnip sticks with extra virgin olive oil and salt in a bowl and spread into a baking sheet lined with parchment paper.
3. Bake the sticks at 425° for about 20 minutes or until browned.

Nutrition: Calories: 179 Fat: 4g Carbs: 14g Protein: 11g Sodium: 27.3mg Potassium: 625mg Phosphorus: 116mg

295. Popcorn with Sugar and Spice

Preparation Time: 10 minutes
Cooking Time: 10 minutes
Servings: 2
Ingredients:
- 8 cups hot popcorn
- 2 tablespoons unsalted butter
- 2 tablespoons sugar
- 1/2 teaspoon cinnamon
- 1/4 teaspoon nutmeg

Directions:
1. Popping the corn; put aside.
2. Heat the butter, sugar, cinnamon, and nutmeg in the microwave or saucepan over a range fire until the butter is melted, and the sugar dissolved.
3. Sprinkle the corn with the spicy butter, mix well.
4. Serve immediately for optimal flavor.

Nutrition: Calories: 120 Fat: 7g Carbs: 12g Protein: 2g Sodium: 2mg Potassium: 56mg Phosphorus: 60mg

296. Sesame-Garlic Edamame

Preparation time: 10 minutes
Cooking time: 10 minutes
Servings: 4
Ingredients:
- 1 (14-ounce) package frozen edamame in their shells
- 1 tablespoon canola or sunflower oil
- 1 tablespoon toasted sesame oil
- 3 garlic cloves, minced
- ½ teaspoon kosher salt
- ¼ teaspoon red pepper flakes (or more)

Directions:
1. Bring a large pot of water to a boil over high heat. Add the edamame, and cook just long enough to warm them up, 2 to 3 minutes.
2. Meanwhile, heat the canola oil, sesame oil, garlic, salt, and red pepper flakes in a large skillet over medium heat for 1 to 2 minutes, then remove the pan from the heat.
3. Drain the edamame and add them to the skillet, tossing to combine.

Nutrition: Calories: 173; Total Fat: 12g; Saturated Fat: 1g; Cholesterol: 0mg; Sodium: 246mg;Carbohydrates: 8g; Fiber: 5g; Added Sugars: 0g; Protein: 11g; Potassium: 487mg; Vitamin K: 34mcg

297. Mixes of Snacks

Preparation Time: 15 minutes
Cooking Time: 1 hour
Servings: 1
Ingredients:
- 6 c. margarine
- 2 tbsp. Worcestershire sauce
- 1 ½ tbsp. spice salt
- ¾ c. garlic powder
- ½ tsp. onion powder

- 3 cups Cheerios
- 3 cups corn flakes
- 1 cup pretzel
- 1 cup broken bagel chip into 1-inch pieces

Directions:
1. Preheat the oven to 250F (120C)
2. Melt the margarine in a large roasting pan. Stir in the seasoning. Gradually add the ingredients remaining by mixing so that the coating is uniform.
3. Cook 1 hour, stirring every 15 minutes.
4. Spread on paper towels to let cool. Store in a tightly closed container.

Nutrition: Calories: 150 Fat: 6g Carbs: 20g Protein: 3g Sodium: 300mg Potassium: 93mg Phosphorus: 70mg

298. Baked Pita Fries

Preparation Time: 5 minutes
Cooking Time: 15 minutes
Servings: 6
Ingredients:
- 3 pita loaves (6 inches)
- 3 tablespoons olive oil
- Chili powder

Directions:
1. Separate each bread in half with scissors to obtain 6 round pieces.
2. Cut each piece into eight points. Brush each with olive oil and sprinkle with chili powder.
3. Bake at 350 degrees F for about 15 minutes until crisp.

Nutrition: Calories: 120 Fat: 2.5g Carbs: 22g Protein: 3g Sodium: 70mg Potassium: 0mg Phosphorus: 0mg

299. Eggplant and Chickpea Bites

Preparation Time: 15 minutes
Cooking Time: 50 minutes

Servings: 6
Ingredients:
- 3 large aubergine cut in half (make a few cuts in the flesh with a knife)
- 2 large cloves garlic, peeled and deglazed
- 2 tbsp. coriander powder
- 2 tbsp. cumin seeds
- 400 g canned chickpeas, rinsed and drained
- 2 Tbsp. chickpea flour
- Zest and juice of 1/2 lemon
- 1/2 lemon quartered for serving
- 3 tbsp. tablespoon of polenta

Directions:
1. Heat the oven to 200°C. Spray the eggplant halves generously with oil and place them on the meat side up on a baking sheet.
2. Sprinkle with coriander and cumin seeds, and then place the cloves of garlic on the plate.
3. Season and roast for 40 minutes until the flesh of eggplant is completely tender. Reserve and let cool a little.
4. Scrape the flesh of the eggplant in a bowl with a spatula and throw the skins in the compost. Thoroughly scrape and make sure to incorporate spices and crushed roasted garlic.
5. Add chickpeas, chickpea flour, zest, and lemon juice. Crush roughly and mix well.
6. Check to season. Do not worry if the mixture seems a bit soft - it will firm up in the fridge.
7. Form about twenty pellets and place them on a baking sheet covered with parchment paper. Refrigerate for at least 30 minutes.
8. Preheat oven to 180°C. Remove the meatballs from the fridge and coat them by rolling them in the polenta.

9. Place them back on the baking sheet and spray a little oil on each. Roast for 20 minutes until golden and crisp.
10. Serve with lemon wedges. You can also serve these dumplings with a spicy yogurt dip.

Nutrition: Calories: 72 Fat: 1g Carbs: 18g Protein: 3g Sodium: 63mg Potassium: 162mg Phosphorus: 36mg

300. Spicy Crab Dip

Preparation Time: 10 minutes
Cooking Time: 20 minutes
Servings: 1
Ingredients:
- 1 can of 8 oz. softened cream cheese
- 1 tbsp. finely chopped onions
- 1 tbsp. lemon juice
- 2 tbsp. Worcestershire sauce
- 1/8 tsp. black pepper Cayenne pepper to taste
- 2 tbsp. to s. of almond milk or non-fortified rice drink
- 1 can of 6 oz. of crabmeat

Directions:
1. Preheat the oven to 375 degrees F.
2. Pour the cheese cream into a bowl. Add the onions, lemon juice, Worcestershire sauce, black pepper, and cayenne pepper. Mix well. Stir in the almond milk/rice drink.
3. Add the crabmeat and mix until you obtain a homogeneous mixture.
4. Pour the mixture into a baking dish. Cook without covering for 15 minutes or until bubbles appear. Serve hot with triangle cut pita bread.
5. Microwave until bubbles appear, about 4 minutes, stirring every 1 to 2 minutes.

Nutrition: Calories: 42 Fat: 0.5g Carbs: 2g Protein: 7g Sodium: 167mg Potassium: 130mg Phosphorus: 139mg

301. Baba Ghanouj

Preparation Time: 10 minutes
Cooking Time: 1 hour and 20 minutes
Servings: 1
Ingredients:
- 1 large aubergine, cut in half lengthwise
- 1 head of garlic, unpeeled
- 30 ml (2 tablespoons) of olive oil
- Lemon juice to taste

Directions:
1. Preheat the oven to 350 degrees F.
2. Place the eggplant on the plate, skin side up. Roast until the meat is very tender and detaches easily from the skin, about 1 hour depending on the eggplant's size. Let cool.
3. Meanwhile, cut the tip of the garlic cloves. Put garlic cloves in a square aluminum foil. Fold the edges of the sheet and fold together to form a tightly wrapped foil.
4. Roast with the eggplant until tender, about 20 minutes. Let cool. Purée the pods with a garlic press.
5. With a spoon, scoop out the eggplant's flesh and place it in the bowl of a food processor. Add the garlic puree, the oil, and the lemon juice. Stir until purée is smooth and pepper.
6. Serve with mini pita bread.

Nutrition: Calories: 110 Fat: 12g Carbs: 5g Protein: 1g Sodium: 180mg Potassium: 207mg Phosphorus: 81mg

302. Herbal Cream Cheese Tartines

Preparation Time: 15 minutes
Cooking Time: 15 minutes
Servings: 2
Ingredients:
- 1 clove garlic, halved
- 1 cup cream cheese spread

- ¼ cup chopped herbs such as chives, dill, parsley, tarragon, or thyme
- 2 tbsp. minced French shallot or onion
- ½ tsp. black pepper
- 2 tbsp. tablespoons water

Directions:

1. In a medium-sized bowl, combine the cream cheese, herbs, shallot, pepper, and water with a hand blender.
2. Serve the cream cheese with the rusks.

Nutrition: Calories: 476 Fat: 9g Carbs: 75g Protein: 23g Sodium: 885mg Potassium: 312mg Phosphorus: 165mg

303. Garlicky Cale Chips

Preparation time: 5 minutes
Cooking time: 25 minutes
Servings: 4

Ingredients:

- 1 bunch curly kale
- 2 teaspoons extra-virgin olive oil
- ¼ teaspoon kosher salt
- ¼ teaspoon garlic powder (optional)

Direction

1. Preheat the oven to 325°F. Line a rimmed baking sheet with parchment paper.
2. Remove the tough stems from the kale, and tear the leaves into squares about big potato chips (they'll shrink when cooked).
3. Transfer the kale to a large bowl, and drizzle with the oil. Massage with your fingers for 1 to 2 minutes to coat well. Spread out on the baking sheet.
4. Cook for 8 minutes, then toss and cook for another 7 minutes and check them. Take them out as soon as they feel crispy, likely within the next 5 minutes.
5. Sprinkle with salt and garlic powder (if using). Enjoy immediately.

Nutrition: Calories: 28; Total Fat: 2g; Saturated Fat: 0g; Cholesterol: 0mg; Sodium:

126mg; Carbohydrates: 2g; Fiber: 1g; Added Sugars: 0g; Protein: 1g; Potassium: 81mg; Vitamin K: 114mcg

304. Baked Tortilla Chips

Preparation time: 5 minutes
Cooking time: 20 minutes
Servings: 4

Ingredients:

- 1 tablespoon canola or sunflower oil
- 4 medium whole-wheat tortillas
- 1/8 teaspoon coarse salt

Direction

1. Preheat the oven to 350°F.
2. Brush the oil onto both sides of each tortilla. Stack them on a large cutting board, and cut the entire stack at once, cutting the stack into 8 wedges of each tortilla. Transfer the tortilla pieces to a rimmed baking sheet. Sprinkle a little salt over each chip.
3. Bake for 10 minutes, and then flip the chips. Bake for another 3 to 5 minutes, until they're just starting to brown.

Nutrition: Calories: 194; Total Fat: 11g; Saturated Fat: 2g; Cholesterol: 0mg; Sodium: 347mg; Carbohydrates: 20g; Fiber: 4g; Added Sugars: 0g; Protein: 4g; Potassium: 111mg; Vitamin K: 7mcg

305. Spicy Guacamole

Preparation time: 15 minutes
Cooking time: 15 minutes
Servings: 4 (about 3 tablespoons per serving)

Ingredients:

- 1½ tablespoons freshly squeezed lime juice
- 1 tablespoon minced jalapeño pepper, or to taste
- 1 tablespoon minced red onion
- 1 tablespoon chopped fresh cilantro
- 1 garlic clove, minced

- 1/8 to ¼ teaspoon kosher salt
- Freshly ground black pepper

Direction

1. Combine the lime juice, jalapeño, onion, cilantro, garlic, salt, and pepper in a large bowl, and mix well.

Nutrition: Calories: 61; Total Fat: 5g; Saturated Fat: 1g; Cholesterol: 0mg; Sodium: 123mg; Carbohydrates: 4g; Fiber: 2g; Added Sugars: 0g; Protein: 1g; Potassium: 195mg; Vitamin K: 8mcg

306. Marinated Berries

Preparation time: 5 minutes
Cooking time: 30 minutes
Servings: 4

Ingredients:

- 2 cups fresh strawberries, hulled and quartered
- 1 cup fresh blueberries (optional)
- 2 tablespoons sugar
- 1 tablespoon balsamic vinegar
- 2 tablespoons chopped fresh mint (optional)
- 1/8 teaspoon freshly ground black pepper

Direction

1. Gently toss the strawberries, blueberries (if using), sugar, vinegar, mint (if using), and pepper in a large nonreactive bowl.
2. Let the flavors blend for at least 25 minutes, or as long as 2 hours.

Nutrition: Calories: 73; Total Fat: 8g; Saturated Fat: 8g; Cholesterol: 0mg; Sodium: 4mg; Carbohydrates: 18g; Fiber: 2g; Added Sugars: 6g; Protein: 1g; Potassium: 162mg; Vitamin K: 9mcg

307. Roasted Broccoli and Cauliflower

Preparation Time: 7 minutes
Cooking Time: 23 minutes
Serving: 6

Ingredients:

- 2 cups broccoli florets
- 2 cups cauliflower florets
- 2 tablespoons olive oil
- 1 tablespoon freshly squeezed lemon juice
- 2 teaspoons Dijon mustard
- ¼ teaspoon garlic powder
- Pinch salt
- 1/8 teaspoon freshly ground black pepper

Direction

1. Preheat the oven to 425°F.
2. On a baking sheet with a lip, combine the broccoli and cauliflower florets in one even layer.
3. In a small bowl, combine the olive oil, lemon juice, mustard, garlic powder, salt, and pepper until well blended and drizzle the mixture over the vegetables. Toss to coat and spread the vegetables out in a single layer again.
4. Roast for 22 minutes. Serve immediately.

Nutrition: 63 Calories 74mg Sodium 39mg Phosphorus 216mg Potassium 2g Protein

308. Pumpkin-Turmeric Latte

Preparation time: 10 minutes
Cooking time: 10 minutes
Servings: 1

Ingredients:

- ½ cup brewed espresso or 1 cup brewed strong coffee
- ¼ cup pumpkin purée

- 1 teaspoon vanilla extract
- 1 teaspoon sugar
- ½ teaspoon ground turmeric
- ½ teaspoon ground cinnamon, plus more if needed
- 1 cup 1% almond milk

Direction

1. Combine the espresso, pumpkin, vanilla, sugar, turmeric, and cinnamon in a medium saucepan over medium heat, whisking occasionally.
2. Warm the almond milk over low heat in a small pan. When it is warm (not hot), whisk it vigorously (or mix with a blender or handheld frother) to make it foamy.
3. Pour the hot coffee mixture into a mug, then top with the frothy almond milk. Sprinkle with more cinnamon, if desired.

Nutrition: Calories: 169; Total Fat: 3g; Saturated Fat: 2g; Cholesterol: 12mg; Sodium: 128mg; Carbohydrates: 26g; Fiber: 3g; Added Sugars: 5g; Protein: 9g; Potassium: 665mg; Vitamin K: 11mcg

309. Dark Hot Chocolate

Preparation time: 5 minutes
Cooking time: 5 minutes
Servings: 2
Ingredients:

- 1¾ cups vanilla soy almond milk
- 1-ounce dark chocolate (70% cacao or more), broken into small pieces

Direction:

1. Heat the soy almond milk in a small saucepan over medium-high heat and add the chocolate. When the almond milk starts bubbling, turn the heat to low.
2. Whisk until the chocolate is melted and fully incorporated. Tip the pot to make sure there is no remaining chocolate on the bottom.

Nutrition: Calories: 149; Total Fat: 8g; Saturated Fat: 3g; Cholesterol: 0mg; Sodium: 105mg; Carbohydrates: 14g; Fiber: 2g; Added Sugars: 5g; Protein: 6g; Potassium: 351mg; Vitamin K: 4mcg

310. Chocolate-Cashew Spread

Preparation time: 10 minutes
Cooking time: 10 minutes
Servings: Makes ½ cup (2 tablespoons per serving)
Ingredients:

- ¼ cup unsalted cashew butter
- 3 tablespoons water
- 1½ tablespoons unsweetened cocoa powder
- 2 teaspoons honey
- 1 teaspoon extra-virgin olive oil
- ½ teaspoon vanilla extract
- Pinch of ground cinnamon
- Pinch of salt

Direction

1. Stir together the cashew butter, water, cocoa powder, honey, olive oil, vanilla, cinnamon, and salt in a large bowl until smooth, 2 to 3 minutes.

Nutrition: Calories: 108; Total Fat: 9g; Saturated Fat: 2g; Cholesterol: 0mg; Sodium: 93mg; Carbohydrates: 8g; Fiber: 1g; Added Sugars: 3g; Protein: 2g; Potassium: 92mg; Vitamin K: 5mcg

311. Rosemary and White Bean Dip

Preparation time: 10 minutes
Cooking time: 10 minutes
Servings: 10 (¼ cup per serving)

Ingredients:

- 1 (15-ounce) can cannellini beans, rinsed and drained
- 2 tablespoons extra-virgin olive oil
- 1 garlic clove, peeled
- 1 teaspoon finely chopped fresh rosemary
- Pinch cayenne pepper
- Freshly ground black pepper
- 1 (7.5-ounce) jar marinated artichoke hearts, drained

Direction:
2. Blend the beans, oil, garlic, rosemary, cayenne pepper, and black pepper in a food processor until smooth.
3. Add the artichoke hearts, and pulse until roughly chopped but not puréed.

Nutrition: Calories: 75; Total Fat: 5g; Saturated Fat: 1g; Cholesterol: 0mg; Sodium: 139mg; Carbohydrates: 6g; Fiber: 3g; Added Sugars: 0g; Protein: 2g; Potassium: 75mg; Vitamin K: 1mcg

312. Chickpea Fatteh

Preparation time: 25 minutes
Cooking time: 25 minutes
Servings: 8

Ingredients:
- 2 (4-inch) whole-wheat pitas
- 4 tablespoons extra-virgin olive oil, divided
- 1 (15-ounce) can no-salt-added chickpeas, rinsed and drained
- 1/3 cup pine nuts
- 1 cup plain 1% yogurt
- 2 garlic cloves, minced
- ¼ teaspoon salt
- ½ cup pomegranate seeds (optional)

Directions:
1. Preheat the oven to 375°F.
2. Cut the pitas into 1-inch squares (no need to separate the two halves), and toss with 2 tablespoons of oil in a large bowl. Spread onto a rimmed baking sheet and bake, occasionally shaking the sheet until golden brown, about 10 minutes.
3. Meanwhile, gently warm the chickpeas and 1 tablespoon of oil in a small saucepan over medium-low heat, 4 to 5 minutes.
4. Toast the pine nuts in a skillet with the remaining 1 tablespoon of oil over medium heat until golden brown, 4 to 5 minutes.
5. Mix the yogurt with the garlic and salt in a small bowl.
6. Transfer the toasted pitas to a wide serving bowl. Top with the chickpeas. Drizzle with the yogurt mixture, then top with the pine nuts and pomegranate seeds (if using).

Nutrition: Calories: 198; Total Fat: 12g; Saturated Fat: 2g; Cholesterol: 2mg; Sodium: 144mg; Carbohydrates: 18g; Fiber: 3g; Added Sugars: 0g; Protein: 6g; Potassium: 236mg; Vitamin K: 9mcg

313. Dark Chocolate and Cherry Trail Mix

Preparation time: 5 minutes
Cooking time: 5 minutes
Servings: Makes 3 cups (¼ cup per serving)

Ingredients:
- 1 cup unsalted almonds
- 2/3 cup dried cherries
- ½ cup walnuts
- ½ cup sweet cinnamon-roasted chickpeas
- ¼ cup dark chocolate chips

Directions:
1. Combine the almonds, cherries, walnuts, chickpeas, and chocolate chips in an airtight container.

2. Store at room temperature for up to 1 week or in the freezer for up to 3 months.

Nutrition: Calories: 174; Total Fat: 12g; Saturated Fat: 2g; Cholesterol: 0mg; Sodium: 18mg; Carbohydrates: 16g; Fiber: 4g; Added Sugars: 7g; Protein: 5g; Potassium: 134mg; Vitamin K: 0mcg

314. Happy Heart Energy Bites

Preparation time: 20 minutes
Cooking time: 30 min
Servings: Makes 30 (2 balls per serving)
Ingredients:

- 1 cup rolled oats
- ¾ cup chopped walnuts
- ½ cup natural peanut butter
- ½ cup ground flaxseed
- ¼ cup honey
- ¼ cup dried cranberries

Directions:

1. Combine the oats, walnuts, peanut butter, flaxseed, honey, and cranberries in a large bowl. Refrigerate for 10 to 20 minutes, if you can, to make them easier to roll.
2. Roll into ¾-inch balls. Store in the fridge or freezer, if they don't disappear first.

Nutrition: Calories: 174; Total Fat: 10g; Saturated Fat: 1g; Cholesterol: 0mg; Sodium: 43mg; Carbohydrates: 17g; Fiber: 3g; Added Sugars: 7g; Protein: 5g; Potassium: 169mg; Vitamin K: 1mcg

315. Mango Chiller

Preparation time: 5 minutes
Cooking time: 5 minutes
Servings: 4 (½ cup per serving)
Ingredients:

- 2 cups frozen mango chunks
- ½ cup plain 2% Greek yogurt
- ¼ cup 1% almond milk
- 2 teaspoons honey (optional)

Direction

1. Mix the mango and yogurt in a food processor or blender. Add the almond milk, a bit at a time, to get it to soft ice cream consistency.
2. Taste, and add honey if you like. Enjoy immediately.

Nutrition: Calories: 85; Total Fat: 1g; Saturated Fat: 1g; Cholesterol: 4mg; Sodium: 17mg; Carbohydrates: 16g; Fiber: 1g; Added Sugars: 3g; Protein: 4g; Potassium: 197mg; Vitamin K: 3mcg

316. Roasted Asparagus with Pine Nuts

Preparation Time: 10 minutes
Cooking Time: 13 minutes
Serving: 4
Ingredients:

- 1-pound fresh asparagus, woody ends removed
- 1 tablespoon olive oil
- 1 tablespoon balsamic vinegar
- 3 garlic cloves, minced
- ½ teaspoon dried thyme leaves
- ¼ cup pine nuts

Direction

1. Preheat the oven to 400°F.
2. Rinse the asparagus and arrange in a single layer on a baking sheet.
3. Blend olive oil, balsamic vinegar, garlic, and thyme until well mixed.
4. Drizzle the dressing over the asparagus and toss to coat.
5. Roast the asparagus for 10 minutes and remove the baking sheet from the oven.
6. Sprinkle the pine nuts over the asparagus and return the baking sheet to the oven. Roast for another 5 to 7

minutes or until the pine nuts are toasted and the asparagus is tender and light golden brown. Serve.

Nutrition: 116 Calories 4mg Sodium 112mg Phosphorus 294mg Potassium 4g Protein

317. Herbed Garlic Cauliflower Mash

Preparation Time: 10 minutes
Cooking Time: 20 minutes
Serving: 6
Ingredients:

- 4 cups cauliflower florets
- 4 garlic cloves, peeled
- 4 ounces cream cheese, softened
- ¼ cup unsweetened almond milk
- 2 tablespoons unsalted butter
- Pinch salt
- 2 tablespoons minced fresh chives
- 2 tablespoons chopped flat-leaf parsley
- 1 tablespoon fresh thyme leaves

Direction

1. Boil water at high heat. Add the cauliflower and garlic and cook, stirring occasionally, until the cauliflower is tender, about 8 to 10 minutes.
2. Drain the cauliflower and garlic into a colander in the sink and shake the colander well to remove excess water.
3. Using a paper towel, blot the vegetables to remove any remaining water. Return the florets to the pot and place over low heat for 1 minute to remove as much water as possible.
4. Mash the florets and garlic with a potato masher until smooth.
5. Beat in the cream cheese, almond milk, butter, salt, chives, parsley, and thyme with a spoon. Serve.

Nutrition: 124 Calories 115mg Sodium 59mg Phosphorus 266mg Potassium 3g Protein

318. Sautéed Spicy Cabbage

Preparation Time: 15 minutes
Cooking Time: 5 minutes
Serving: 6
Ingredients:

- 3 tablespoons olive oil
- 3 cups chopped green cabbage
- 3 cups chopped red cabbage
- 2 garlic cloves, minced
- 1/8 teaspoon cayenne pepper
- Pinch salt

Direction

1. Cook olive oil in a large skillet over medium heat.
2. Stir in red and green cabbage and the garlic; sauté until the leaves wilt and are tender, about 4 to 5 minutes.
3. Sprinkle the vegetables with the cayenne pepper and salt, toss, and serve.

Nutrition: 86 Calories 46mg Sodium 27mg Phosphorus 189mg Potassium 1g Protein

319. Fragrant Thai-Style Eggplant

Preparation Time: 10 minutes
Cooking Time: 20 minutes
Serving: 6
Ingredients:

- 1 eggplant, cut into ½-inch slices
- ¼ teaspoon salt
- 1 tablespoon extra-virgin olive oil
- 1 tablespoon peeled and grated fresh ginger root
- 1 garlic clove, minced
- 2 tablespoons freshly squeezed lime juice
- 1 tablespoon water
- 2 tablespoons chopped fresh basil

Direction

1. Preheat the oven to 400°F.

2. On a baking sheet with a lip, arrange the eggplant slices and sprinkle evenly with the salt. Drizzle with the olive oil.
3. Bake the eggplant for 10 minutes, then remove the baking sheet from the oven and turn the slices over. Return the baking sheet to the oven and bake for 10 to 15 minutes longer or until the eggplant is tender.
4. Meanwhile, stir together the ginger, garlic, lime juice, water, and basil in a small bowl until well mixed.
5. Situate the eggplant on a serving plate and drizzle with the ginger mixture. Serve warm or cool.

Nutrition: 52 Calories 101mg Sodium 30mg Phosphorus 280mg Potassium 1g Protein

320. Brussels Sprout Chips

Preparation Time: 10 minutes
Cooking Time: 10 minutes
Servings: 4
Ingredients:
- 2 cups Brussels sprout leaves
- 2 tablespoons ghee
- Kosher salt
- Lemon zest

Directions:
1. Set the oven to 350F, then cover two cookie sheets with parchment paper.
2. Put the leaves in a huge bowl and pour melted ghee over the top, and add salt.
3. Bake for at least 8 to 10 minutes or until the leaves are crispy. If they are soft at all, put them back in the oven.
4. While still hot, sprinkle the lemon zest over the leaves. Serve warm.

Nutrition: Calories: 42 kcal Protein: 3.13 g Fat: 1.68 g Carbohydrates: 4.77 g

321. Roasted Radishes

Preparation Time: 10 minutes

Cooking Time: 20 minutes
Serving: 6
Ingredients:
- 3 bunches whole small radishes
- 3 tablespoons olive oil, divided
- 1 tablespoon freshly squeezed lemon juice
- 1 tablespoon Dijon mustard
- ½ teaspoon dried marjoram leaves
- 1/8 teaspoon white pepper
- Pinch salt
- 2 tablespoons chopped flat-leaf parsley

Direction
1. Preheat the oven to 425°F. Prep a baking sheet with a lip with parchment paper and set aside.
2. Scrub the radishes, remove the stem and root, and cut each in half or thirds, depending on the size. The radishes should be similarly sized, so they cook evenly.
3. Toss the radishes and 1 tablespoon olive oil on the baking sheet to coat and arrange the radishes in a single layer.
4. Roast the radishes for 18 to 20 minutes or until they are slightly golden and tender, but still crisp on the outside.
5. While the radishes are roasting, whisk together the remaining 2 tablespoons of olive oil with the lemon juice, mustard, marjoram, pepper, and salt in a small bowl.
6. Once done, take them from the baking sheet and place them in a serving bowl. Drizzle the vegetables with the dressing and toss. Sprinkle with the parsley. Serve warm or cool.

Nutrition: 79 Calories 123mg Sodium 23mg Phosphorus 232mg Potassium 1g Protein

322. Grilled Peppers in Chipotle Vinaigrette

Preparation Time: 15 minutes
Cooking Time: 6 minutes
Serving: 4
Ingredients:
- 1 red bell pepper
- 1 yellow bell pepper
- 1 mango bell pepper
- 2 tablespoons extra-virgin olive oil
- Juice of 1 lemon
- 1 tsp. minced chipotle peppers in adobo sauce

Direction
1. Prepare and preheat the grill to medium coals and set a grill 6 inches from the coals. If grilling indoors, heat the grill pan over medium-high heat. For charcoal grills, medium coals mean you can hold your palm 6 inches above the grill rack for 3 to 4 seconds before you have to take it away. For gas and propane grills, medium coals are 350°F to 375°F.
2. Wash the bell peppers, remove the seeds, and cut them into 1-inch strips.
3. Blend olive oil, lemon juice, and chipotle peppers in adobo sauce.
4. Place the peppers on the grill and brush with some of the sauce. Grill the peppers for 2 to 3 minutes per side, brushing with the sauce occasionally, until the vegetables are tender and have defined grill marks. Serve.

Nutrition: 66 Calories 90mg Sodium 22mg Phosphorus 201mg Potassium 1g Protein

323. Hummus Deviled Eggs

Preparation Time: 10 minutes
Cooking Time: 0 minutes
Servings: 6
Ingredients:

- 6 hard-boiled eggs
- 1/2 cup hummus
- Paprika

Directions:
1. Slice the hardboiled eggs in half lengthwise and remove the yolk.
2. Fill the egg whites with hummus and sprinkle with paprika before serving.

Nutrition: Calories: 179 kcal Protein: 11.03 g Fat: 12.41 g Carbohydrates: 5.14 g

324. Hummus with Celery

Preparation Time: 15 minutes
Cooking Time: 0 minutes
Servings: 4
Ingredients:
- 1/4 cup lemon juice
- 1/4 cup tahini
- 3 cloves of garlic, crushed
- 2 tablespoons extra virgin olive oil
- 1/2 teaspoon salt
- 1/2 teaspoon cumin
- 1 (15–ounce) can chickpeas
- 2 to 3 tablespoons water
- Dash of paprika
- 6 stalks celery, cut into 2-inch pieces
- 3 tablespoons salsa

Directions:
1. Using a food processor mix the lemon juice and tahini for about a minute, until it is smooth. Scrape the sides down and process for 30 more seconds.
2. Add the garlic, olive oil, salt, and cumin. Blend for about 1 minute.
3. Drain the chickpeas, put the half of them on the food processor, and blend for another minute. Scrape down the sides, add the other half of the chickpeas, and process until smooth, about 2 minutes. If it like a little too thick, add water, 1 tablespoon at a time until you reach the desired consistency.

4. Fill the celery sticks with hummus and sprinkle paprika on top.
5. Serve with salsa for dipping.

Nutrition: Calories: 240 kcal Protein: 9.27 g Fat: 14.51 g Carbohydrates: 21.01 g

325. Lemony Ginger Cookies

Preparation Time: 15 minutes + 30 minutes chill time
Cooking Time: 10-12 minutes
Servings: 25
Ingredients:

- 1/2 cup arrowroot flour
- 1 1/2 cups stevia
- 3/4 teaspoon salt
- 1/2 teaspoon baking soda
- 1 teaspoon nutritional yeast
- 3 inches of ginger root, peeled and diced
- 1 1/2 cup coconut butter, softened
- Zest of 1 lemon
- 2 teaspoons vanilla

Directions:

1. Set the oven to 350F, then line two or three cookie sheets with parchment paper.
2. Mix the arrowroot flour, stevia, salt, soda, and yeast in a bowl.
3. In another bowl, put the remaining ingredients and mix well.
4. Put in the dry ingredients gradually until well combined. If the dough is too soft, put an additional 1 to 2 tablespoons of arrowroot powder. The dough will stiffen when chilled, so be careful.
5. Wrap the dough in parchment and press it flat. Chill for 30 minutes.
6. Take a chunk of the chilled dough and flatten it between two pieces of parchment until it is 1/8 inch thick. Dust with a little arrowroot powder and cut into shapes.

7. Place on baking sheets about 1 inch apart and bake 10 to 12 minutes. Cool on cookie sheets for 15 minutes before removing.

Nutrition: Calories: 112 kcal Protein: 0.44 g Fat: 11.3 g Carbohydrates: 2.49 g

326. Mandarin Cottage Cheese

Preparation Time: 5 minutes
Cooking Time: 0 minutes
Servings: 1
Ingredients:

- 1/2 cup low-fat cottage cheese
- 1/2 cup canned mandarin mangos
- 1 1/2 tablespoons slivered almonds

Directions:

1. Place the cottage cheese in a bowl.
2. Drain the mandarin mangos, place them atop the cottage cheese, and sprinkle with almonds.

Nutrition: Calories: 360 kcal Protein: 26.24 g Fat: 21.37 g Carbohydrates: 15.22 g

327. Double Corn Muffins

Preparation Time: 10 minutes
Cooking Time: 20 minutes
Serving: 6
Ingredients:

- ¾ cup all-purpose flour
- ¼ cup yellow cornmeal
- 2 tablespoons brown sugar
- 1 teaspoon cream of tartar
- ½ teaspoon baking soda
- Pinch salt
- 1 large egg
- ½ cup unsweetened almond milk
- ½ cup whole kernel corn
- 3 tablespoons unsalted butter, melted

Direction

1. Preheat the oven to 350°F. Prep a 6-cup muffin pan with paper liners and set aside.
2. Scourge flour, cornmeal, brown sugar, cream of tartar, baking soda, and salt until well blended.
3. In a small bowl, stir together the egg, almond milk, corn, and melted butter.
4. Add the liquid ingredients to the dry ingredients and stir just until combined.
5. Split the batter among the prepared muffin cups, filling each about ¾ full.
6. Bake for 18 to 20 minutes or until the muffins are set and light golden brown.
7. Remove the muffins from the muffin tin and set on a wire rack to cool. Serve warm.

Nutrition: 165 Calories 160mg Sodium 55mg Phosphorus 168mg Potassium 4g Protein

328. Cucumber Yogurt

Preparation Time: 5 minutes
Cooking Time: 0 minutes
Servings: 1
Ingredients:
- 1 cup cucumbers, skin removed and chopped in chunks
- 2 tablespoons chopped cashews
- 1/4 cup fat-free Greek yogurt
- 2 teaspoons fresh-squeezed lemon juice
- 1 teaspoon fresh dill, chopped fine

Directions:
1. Peel and chop the cucumbers, then place them in a bowl.
2. Add the cashews, yogurt, lemon juice, and dill.
3. Mix well, grab a spoon, and enjoy.

Nutrition: Calories: 300 kcal Protein: 11.35 g Fat: 23.55 g Carbohydrates: 14.13 g

329. Cauliflower Snacks

Preparation Time: 10 minutes
Cooking Time: 60 minutes
Servings: 4
Ingredients:
- 1 head of cauliflower
- 4 tablespoons extra virgin olive oil
- 1 teaspoon salt

Directions:
1. Set the oven to 425F, then prepare two cookie sheets by lining them with parchment paper.
2. Trim off the cauliflower florets and discard the core. Cut the florets into golf-ball-sized pieces.
3. Place the cauliflower in a bowl, and pour olive oil over them and sprinkle with salt. Mix to coat. Spread in a single layer, not touching.
4. Roast about 1 hour, turning the cauliflower three to four times until golden brown. Serve warm.

Nutrition: Calories: 91 kcal Protein: 2.93 g Fat: 7.7 g Carbohydrates: 3.29 g

330. Mushroom Chips

Preparation Time: 10 minutes
Cooking Time: 45-60 minutes
Servings: 2-4
Ingredients:
- 16 ounces of king oyster mushrooms
- 2 tablespoons ghee
- Kosher salt and ground pepper to taste

Directions:
1. Set the oven to 300F, then line two cookie sheets with parchment paper.
2. Cut every mushroom in half lengthwise, then cut with a mandolin into 1/8 inch slices or strips. Place them on cookie sheets with some room in between. Melt the ghee and brush it over the

mushrooms, then season with the salt and pepper.

3. Bake for at least 45 minutes to 1 hour, until they are completely crisp. Store in airtight containers.

Nutrition: Calories: 62 kcal Protein: 5.58 g Fat: 2 g Carbohydrates: 7.97 g

331. Buttered Banana Chickpea Cookies

Preparation Time: 10 minutes
Cooking Time: 12 minutes
Servings: 8
Ingredients:

- 15-oz. chickpeas, rinsed and drained
- ½-cup creamy peanut butter
- 1-pc small banana, very ripe
- 2-tsp vanilla extract
- 1/3-cup coconut sugar
- 2-Tbsps ground flaxseed
- 1-tsp baking powder
- ¼-tsp salt
- ¼-tsp cinnamon
- 1/3-cup chocolate chips

Directions:
1. Preheat your oven to 350F. Grease a baking pan with cooking spray.
2. Stir in all the ingredients except the chocolate chips in your blender. Blend the batter for two minutes, or until turning into a smooth consistency.
3. Stir in the chocolate chips. Spoon the batter to form cookies. Place the cookies in the pan, and bake for 12 minutes.

Nutrition: Calories: 372 Fat: 12.4g Protein: 18.6g Sodium: 174mg Total Carbs: 58.1g Dietary Fiber: 11.6g Net Carbs: 46.5g

332. Toasted Pumpkin Seeds

Preparation Time: 5 minutes
Cooking Time: 30 minutes
Servings:2-4
Ingredients:

- 1 to 2 cups pumpkin seeds
- Water
- 1 teaspoon salt
- 1/2 teaspoon extra virgin olive oil
- Sea salt

Directions:
1. Put seeds in a saucepan and cover with water. Add salt.
2. Bring it to a boil and boil for 10 minutes.
3. Simmer uncovered for 10 more minutes. This makes the seeds very crispy when baked. Drain the seeds and pat dry using a paper towel.
4. Cover a baking sheet with parchment paper and spread out the seeds in a single layer.
5. Dust with salt, then bake in an oven at 325F for at least 10 minutes, stirring halfway through.
6. Cool, then store in an airtight container.

Nutrition: Calories: 192 kcal Protein: 10.41 g Fat: 16.23 g Carbohydrates: 4.34 g

333. Tofu Pudding

Preparation Time: 10 minutes
Cooking Time: 0 minutes
Servings: 4
Ingredients:

- 12 ounces silken tofu, softened and well-drained
- 2 scoops of protein powder
- 3/4 cup blueberries
- 1 cup strawberries
- 1 teaspoon honey
- 1 teaspoon pumpkin pie spice

- 1 teaspoon vanilla
- 4 almonds
- Fresh mint leaves

Directions:
1. Blend the tofu and protein powder in a blender until well mixed.
2. Add the blueberries, strawberries, honey, pumpkin pie spice, and vanilla. Blend until smooth.
3. Cover and place on the fridge to chill for at least 2 hours.
4. Spoon into four dessert bowls and top with an almond and a mint leaf before serving.

Nutrition: Calories: 371 kcal Protein: 23.31 g Fat: 21.1 g Carbohydrates: 27.17 g

334. Turmeric Gummies

Preparation Time: 5 minutes
Cooking Time: 4 hours and 10 minutes
Servings: 4
Ingredients:
- 6 tbsp. Maple syrup
- 3 ½ cups Water
- 8 tbsp. Unflavored gelatin powder
- 1 tsp. Ground turmeric
- ¼ tsp. Ground pepper

Directions:
1. Mix the ground turmeric, maple syrup, and water in a pot set over medium heat. Stir constantly for 5 minutes before removing from heat and pouring in the gelatin powder. Stir with a wooden spoon to dissolve the gelatin.
2. Put back the pan on the heat and stir for another 2 minutes.
3. Turn off the heat and take the mixture to a deep bowl that you will seal with plastic wrap right after.
4. Refrigerate the mixture for about 4 hours.
5. It should be firm now, cut it into small squares, and serve or store.

Nutrition: Calories: 123 kcal Protein: 2.15 g Fat: 1.56 g Carbohydrates: 25.67 g

335. Paleo Ginger Spiced Mixed Nuts

Preparation Time: 5 minutes
Cooking Time: 40 minutes
Servings: 8
Ingredients:
- 1 tsp. Grated fresh ginger
- 2 Large Egg,
- Egg whites
- ½ tsp. Vietnamese cinnamon
- 2 cups Mix nuts; Cashew, goji berries, raw almonds, pumpkin seeds, etc.
- Coconut oil spray
- ½ tsp. Fine sea salt

Directions:
1. Prepare the oven by preheating to 250°F.
2. Whisk egg whites in a bowl until it gets fluffy. Pour in sea salt, grated ginger, and Vietnamese cinnamon. Whisk until its one large mix.
3. Pour in the mixed nuts and stir to mix.
4. Coat the parchment-lined baking sheet with coconut oil spray and spread the nut mixture all across the baking sheet.
5. Let it bake for about 20 minutes, rotate the sheet then bake for an additional 20 minutes.
6. Take off the baking sheet from the oven and leave to cool.
7. Once it's completely cool and hard, break them into bits with clean hands.
8. Serve or store.

Nutrition: Calories: 212 kcal Protein: 6.92 g Fat: 17.3 g Carbohydrates: 10.05 g

336. Easy Peasy Ginger Date

Preparation Time: 20 minutes
Cooking Time: 10 minutes
Servings: 8
Ingredients:
- ¾ cup Dates
- 1 tsp. Ground ginger
- 1 or 1 ½ cup Almonds or almond flour
- ¼ cup Almond milk

Directions:
1. Prep oven by preheating it to 350°F.
2. If you're using fresh almonds, put it through a blender to turn it to almond flour. Blitz for 2 minutes or so until it looks and feels smooth.
3. Don't blitz for too long, or you might end up making nut butter. Now that you have your almond powder put it in a bowl and set it aside.
4. Pour the dates and almond milk into the blender and pulse for 5 minutes. If it doesn't resemble a paste, pulse for another 2 minutes.
5. Pour in the ground ginger and almond flour. Pulse for 3 to 4 minutes to mix.
6. Put the mixture to a baking dish and bake for about 20 minutes.
7. Remove from the oven and leave to cool before cutting into bits.
8. Serve or store.

Nutrition: Calories: 55 kcal Protein: 1.24 g Fat: 0.99 g Carbohydrates: 11.24 g

337. Baked Veggie Turmeric Nuggets

Preparation Time: 10 minutes
Cooking Time: 25 minutes
Servings: 24
Ingredients:
- 2 cups Broccoli florets
- ¼ tsp. Sea salt
- 2 cups Cauliflower florets
- 1 tsp. Minced garlic
- ½ cup Almond meal
- 1 cup Chopped carrots
- ½ tsp. Turmeric powder
- 1 large Whole egg
- ¼ tsp. Black pepper powder

Directions:
1. Prep oven by preheating to 400°F.
2. Get a parchment-lined baking sheet ready.
3. Pour cauliflower, turmeric, broccoli, carrots, black pepper, garlic, and sea salt in the blender and blitz until it's smooth.
4. Pour in the egg and almond meal and mix until it's incorporated.
5. Pour the paste into a mixing bowl. Scoop out a bit onto your hand and form a circular disc. Place this disc on the baking sheet and repeat the process until the mixing bowl is empty.
6. Slide into the oven then bake for at least 15 minutes on one before flipping and baking for 10 minutes on the other side.
7. Serve with a side of Paleo ranch sauce.

Nutrition: Calories: 12 kcal Protein: 0.88 g Fat: 0.52 g Carbohydrates: 1.12 g

338. Ginger Flour Banana Ginger Bars

Preparation Time: 10 minutes
Cooking Time: 40 minutes
Servings: 4-6
Ingredients:
- 1 cup Coconut flour
- 1 ½ tbsp. Grated ginger
- 2 large Ripe apple
- 1 tsp. Baking soda
- 1/3 cup melted butter
- 2 tsp. Cinnamon
- 2 tsp. Apple cider vinegar

- 1/3 cup Honey or maple syrup
- 1 tsp. Ground cardamom
- 6 medium While eggs

Directions:
1. Prep the oven by preheating to 350°F.
2. Line a glass baking dish with parchment paper. If you don't have any paper, just grease the pan.
3. Put all the ingredients except the baking soda and apple cider vinegar through a food processor and blend until it's all mixed up.
4. Now add the last two ingredients and blitz once before pouring the mix into the glass dish.
5. Bake up to a toothpick inserted into the center comes out clean. This usually takes 40 minutes.

Nutrition: Calories: 1407 kcal Protein: 42.18 g Fat: 100.26 g Carbohydrates: 88.33 g

339. Turmeric Coconut Flour Muffins

Preparation Time: 5 minutes
Cooking Time: 25 minutes
Servings: 8
Ingredients:
- ½ cup Unsweetened coconut almond milk
- ¾ cup & 2 tbsp. Coconut flour
- 1 tsp. Vanilla extract
- 6 large Whole eggs
- ½ tsp. Baking soda
- 1/3 cup Maple syrup
- 2 tsp. Turmeric
- Pepper and salt
- ½ tsp. Ginger powder

Directions:
1. Prep oven by preheating to 350°F.
2. Line 8 muffin tins with 8 muffin liners.

3. Whisk eggs, maple syrup, almond milk, and vanilla extract in a mixing bowl until the egg starts to form bubbles.
4. In a different bowl, mix the coconut flour, turmeric powder, pepper, baking soda, ginger powder, and salt.
5. Put the dry mixture into the wet mixture then stir until it's all mixed and thick.
6. Spoon out the batter into prepared muffin tins.
7. Leave to bake for 25 minutes or until it looked golden.
8. Let the muffins cool for 1-2 minutes before transferring them to a rack.

Nutrition: Calories: 143 kcal Protein: 6.18 g Fat: 8 g Carbohydrates: 11.8 g

340. Tangy Turmeric Flavored Florets

Preparation Time: 10 minutes
Cooking Time: 55 minutes
Servings: 1
Ingredients:
- 1-head cauliflower, chopped into florets
- 1-Tbsp olive oil
- 1-Tbsp turmeric
- A pinch of cumin
- A dash of salt

Directions:
1. Set the oven to 400°F.
2. Put all together the ingredients in a baking pan. Mix well until thoroughly combined.
3. Cover the pan with foil. Roast for 40 minutes. Remove the foil cover and roast additionally for 15 minutes.

Nutrition: Calories: 90 Fat: 3g Protein: 4.5g Sodium: 87mg Total Carbs: 16.2g Dietary Fiber: 5g Net Carbs: 11.2g

341. Cereal Chia Chips

Preparation Time: 10 minutes

Cooking Time: 30 minutes
Servings: 10

Ingredients:

- ¼-cup rolled oats, gluten-free
- ½-cup white quinoa, uncooked
- ¾-cup pecans, chopped
- 2-Tbsps chia seeds
- 2-Tbsps coconut sugar
- A pinch of sea salt (optional)
- 2-Tbsps coconut oil
- ½-cup maple syrup

Directions:

1. Preheat your oven to 325°F. Line a baking pan with parchment paper.
2. Stir in the first six ingredients in a mixing bowl. Mix well until thoroughly combined. Set aside.
3. Pour the oil and syrup in a small saucepan placed over medium-low heat. Heat the mixture for 3 minutes, stirring occasionally.
4. Fold in the dry ingredients; stir well to coat thoroughly.
5. Pour the mixture in the baking pan, and spread to an even layer using a spoon.
6. Put the pan in the oven. Bake for 15 minutes. Turn the pan around to cook evenly. Bake for 8-10 minutes until the mixture turns golden brown.
7. Allow cooling entirely before breaking the chips into bite-size pieces.

Nutrition: Calories: 157 Fat: 5.2g Protein: 7.8g S Sodium: 25mg Total Carbs: 22.1g Dietary Fiber: 2.5g Net Carbs: 19.6g

342. Coco Cherry Bake-less Bars

Preparation Time: 10 minutes
Cooking Time: 0 minutes
Servings: 6

Ingredients:

- 1-cup old-fashioned oats
- 1/3-cup ground flaxseed
- 1/3-cup coconut, unsweetened and shredded
- 3-scoops vanilla plant-based protein powder
- ½-cup almond butter
- ¼-cup pure maple syrup
- 1-Tbsp almond milk
- 1-Tbsp vanilla extract
- 1/3-cup dried cherries or cranberries

Directions:

1. Line a loaf pan with parchment paper.
2. Stir in the first four ingredients in your blender. Blend until the mixture becomes powdery.
3. Transfer the mixture in a mixing bowl. Add in all the remaining ingredients. Mix well until thoroughly combined.
4. Place the mixture in the pan, and press down onto a uniformly flat surface.

Freeze for 30 minutes before slicing into six bars.

Nutrition: Calories: 193 Fat: 6.4g Protein: 9.6g Sodium: 200mg Total Carbs: 27.1g Dietary Fiber: 3g Net Carbs: 24.1g

343. Flourless & Flaky Muffin Munchies

Preparation Time: 25 minutes
Cooking Time: 20 minutes
Servings: 4

Ingredients:

- ½-cup quick oats or quinoa flakes, loosely packed
- ¾-tsp baking powder
- ¼-tsp salt
- 1/8-tsp baking soda
- 1-pc medium mashed banana, very ripe
- 1-cup white beans, cooked
- ¼-cup peanut butter or allergy-friendly substitution

- ¼-cup pure maple syrup or honey
- 2-tsp pure vanilla extract
- A handful of mini chocolate chips, crushed walnuts, shredded coconut, pinch cinnamon, etc. (optional)

Directions:
1. Preheat the oven to 350 F. Line 8-muffin cups with glassine.
2. Combine all the ingredients in your blender. Blend to a smooth consistency. Pour the mixture into the muffin cups at 2/3 full.
3. Put the cups in the oven, and bake for 20 minutes.
4. Allow the muffins to sit and cool for 20 minutes.

Nutrition: Calories: 119 Fat: 3.9g Protein: 8.9g Sodium: 102mg Total Carbs: 14.4g Dietary Fiber: 2.5g Net Carbs: 11.9g

344. Sweet Sunup Seeds

Preparation Time: 5 minutes
Cooking Time: 60 minutes
Servings: 8
Ingredients:
- 4-cups rolled oats
- 1-cup raw pumpkin seeds
- ½-cup flaxseed
- ¼-sesame seeds
- 3-tsp cinnamon
- 1/3-cup honey
- ¼-cup pure maple syrup
- ¼-cup sunflower oil
- 1-tsp vanilla extract
- 1-cup dried cranberries

Directions:
1. Preheat the oven to 350°F. Prepare two units of baking sheets by lining them with parchment paper.
2. In a large-sized mixing bowl, combine the rolled oats, pumpkin seeds, flaxseed,

sesame seeds, and cinnamon. Mix gently until thoroughly combined.
3. Pour all the liquid ingredients into the mixture and stir until blended well.
4. On the baking sheets, spread the mixture evenly. Put the sheets in the oven. Cook for at least an hour. While baking, stir the mixture every quarter of an hour to achieve uniform color on its surfaces.
5. Remove the sheets from the oven. Allow cooling completely. Add the cup of dried cranberries, and mix well.
6. Store the granola in an airtight container to maintain its freshness and crunchiness.

Nutrition: Calories: 189 Fat: 6.3g Protein: 9.4g Sodium: 5mg Total Carbs: 27.6g Dietary Fiber: 4g Net Carbs: 23.6g

345. Sweet savory meatballs

Preparation time: 10 minutes
Cooking time: 20 minutes
Servings: 12
Ingredients
- 1-pound ground turkey
- 1 large egg
- 1/4 cup bread crumbs
- 2 tablespoon onion, finely chopped
- 1 teaspoon garlic powder
- 1/2 teaspoon black pepper
- 1/4 cup canola oil
- 6-ounce grape jelly
- 1/4 cup chili sauce

Directions
1. Place all ingredients except chili sauce and jelly in a large mixing bowl.
2. Mix well until evenly mixed then make small balls out of this mixture.

3. It will make about 48 meatballs. Spread them out on a greased pan on a stovetop.
4. Cook them over medium heat until brown on all the sides.
5. Mix chili sauce with jelly in a microwave-safe bowl and heat it for 2 minutes in the microwave.
6. Pour this chili sauce mixture onto the meatballs in the pan.
7. Transfer the meatballs in the pan to the preheated oven.
8. Bake the meatballs for 20 minutes in an oven at 375 degrees f.
9. Serve fresh and warm.

Nutrition: calories 127. Protein 9 g. Carbohydrates 14 g. Fat 4 g. Cholesterol 41 mg. Sodium 129 mg. Potassium 148 mg. Phosphorus 89 mg. Calcium 15 mg. Fiber 0.2 g.

346. Buffalo chicken dip

Preparation time: 10 minutes
Cooking time: 3 hours
Servings: 4
Ingredients
- 4-ounce cream cheese
- 1/2 cup bottled roasted red peppers
- 1 cup reduced-fat sour cream
- 4 teaspoon hot pepper sauce
- 2 cups cooked, shredded chicken

Directions
1. Blend half cup of drained red peppers in a food processor until smooth.
2. Now, thoroughly mix cream cheese, and sour cream with the pureed peppers in a bowl.
3. Stir in shredded chicken and hot sauce then transfer the mixture to a slow cooker.
4. Cook for 3 hours on low heat.
5. Serve warm with celery, carrots, cauliflower, and cucumber.

Nutrition: calories 73. Protein 5 g. Carbohydrates 2 g. Fat 5 g. Cholesterol 25 mg. Sodium 66 mg. Potassium 81 mg. Phosphorus 47 mg. Calcium 31 mg. Fiber 0 g.

347. Mixes of snack

Preparation time: 10 minutes
Cooking time: 1 hours and 15 minutes
Servings: 4
Ingredients
- 6 cup margarine
- 2 tablespoon Worcestershire sauce
- 1 ½ tablespoon spice salt
- ¾ cup garlic powder
- ½ teaspoon onion powder
- 3 cups crispi
- 3 cups cheerios
- 3 cups corn flakes
- 1 cup kixe
- 1 cup pretzels
- 1 cup broken bagel chips into 1-inch pieces

Directions
1. Preheat the oven to 250f (120c)
2. Melt the margarine in a pan. Stir in the seasoning. Gradually add the ingredients remaining by mixing so that the coating is uniform.
3. Cook 1 hour, stirring every 15 minutes. Spread on paper towels to let cool. Store in a tightly-closed container.

Nutrition: calories: 200 kcal total fat: 9 g saturated fat: 3.5 g cholesterol: 0 mg sodium: 3.5 mg total carbs: 27 g fiber: 2 g sugar: 0 g protein: 3 g

348. Chicken pepper bacon wraps

Preparation time: 10 minutes
Cooking time: 15 minutes
Servings: 4

Ingredients

- 1 medium onion, chopped
- 12 strips bacon, halved
- 12 fresh jalapenos peppers
- 12 fresh banana peppers
- 2 pounds boneless, skinless chicken breast

Directions

1. How to prepare:
2. Grease a grill rack with cooking spray and preheat the grill on low heat.
3. Slice the peppers in half lengthwise then remove their seeds.
4. Dice the chicken into small pieces and divide them into each pepper.
5. Now spread the chopped onion over the chicken in the peppers.
6. Wrap the bacon strips around the stuffed peppers.
7. Place these wrapped peppers in the grill and cook them for 15 minutes.
8. Serve fresh and warm.

Nutrition: calories 71. Protein 10 g. Carbohydrates 1 g. Fat 3 g. Cholesterol 26 mg. Sodium 96 mg. Potassium 147 mg. Phosphorus 84 mg. Calcium 9 mg. Fiber 0.8 g.

349. Garlic oyster crackers

Preparation time: 10 minutes
Cooking time: 45 minutes
Servings: 4

Ingredients

- 1/2 cup butter-flavored popcorn oil
- 1 tablespoon garlic powder
- 7 cups oyster crackers
- 2 teaspoon dried dill weed

Directions

1. How to prepare:
2. Preheat oven to 250 degrees f.
3. Mix garlic powder with oil in a large bowl.
4. Toss in crackers and mix well to coat evenly.

5. Sprinkle the dill weed over the crackers and toss well again.
6. Spread the crackers on the baking sheet and bake them for 45 minutes.
7. Toss them every 15 minutes.
8. Serve fresh.

Nutrition: calories 118. Protein 2 g. Carbohydrates 12 g. Fat 7 g. Cholesterol 0 mg. Sodium 166 mg. Potassium 21 mg. Phosphorus 15 mg. Calcium 4 mg. Fiber 3 g.

350. Dried Dates & Turmeric Truffles

Preparation Time: 15 minutes
Cooking Time: 0 minutes
Servings: 4

Ingredients:

- 1/3-cup walnuts
- ½-cup rolled oats
- 1-Tbsp turmeric powder + more for rolling
- ¼-tsp black pepper
- ¾-cup dates, pitted

Directions:

1. Stir in all the ingredients, excluding the dates in a food processor. Blend until thoroughly combined.
2. Add the dates gradually until forming into the dough.
3. Shape and roll balls from the mixture. Roll each ball with the additional turmeric powder until coating fully.
4. Store the truffles in an airtight jar until ready to serve.

Nutrition: Calories: 95 Fat: 3.1g Protein: 4.7g Sodium: 62mg Total Carbs: 13.8g Dietary Fiber: 2g Net Carbs: 11.8g

351. Ants on a Log

Preparation Time: 5 minutes
Cooking Time: 0 minutes
Servings: 2

Ingredients:
- 6 celery sticks
- 3 tablespoons of almond butter
- 3 tablespoons of raisins

Directions:
1. Spread half a tablespoon of almond butter on each celery stick.
2. Top with half a tablespoon of raisins on each celery stick.
3. Divide the celery sticks between two plates, and enjoy!

Nutrition: Total Carbohydrates: 17g Dietary Fiber: 2g Net Carbs: Protein: 4g Total Fat: 14g Calories: 201

352. Cranberry dip with fresh fruit

Preparation time: 10 minutes
Cooking time: 0 minutes
Servings: 8

Ingredients
- 8-ounce sour cream
- 1/2 cup whole berry cranberry sauce
- 1/4 teaspoon nutmeg
- 1/4 teaspoon ground ginger
- 4 cups fresh pineapple, peeled, cubed
- 4 medium apples, peeled, cored and cubed
- 4 medium pears, peeled, cored and cubed
- 1 teaspoon lemon juice

Directions
1. Start by adding cranberry sauce, sour cream, ginger, and nutmeg to a food processor.
2. Blend the mixture until its smooth then transfer it to a bowl.
3. Toss the pineapple, with pears, apples, and lemon juice in a salad bowl.
4. Thread the fruits onto mini skewers.
5. Serve them with the sauce.

Nutrition: calories 70. Protein 0 g. Carbohydrates 13 g. Fat 2 g. Cholesterol 4 mg. Sodium 8 mg. Potassium 101 mg. Phosphorus 15 mg. Calcium 17 mg. Fiber 1.5 g.

353. Cucumbers with sour cream

Preparation time: 10 minutes
Cooking time: 0 minutes
Servings: 4

Ingredients
- 2 medium cucumbers, peeled and sliced thinly
- 1/2 medium sweet onion, sliced
- 1/4 cup white wine vinegar
- 1 tablespoon canola oil
- 1/8 teaspoon black pepper
- 1/2 cup reduced-fat sour cream

Directions
1. Toss in cucumber, onion, and all other ingredients in a medium-size bowl.
2. Mix well and refrigerate for 2 hours.
3. Toss again and serve to enjoy.

Nutrition: calories 64. Protein 1 g. Carbohydrates 4 g. Fat 5 g. Cholesterol 3 mg. Sodium 72 mg. Potassium 113 mg. Phosphorus 24 mg. Calcium 21 mg. Fiber 0.8 g.

354. Shrimp spread with crackers

Preparation time: 10 minutes
Cooking time: 0 minutes
Servings: 6

Ingredients
- 1/4 cup light cream cheese
- 2 1/2-ounce cooked, shelled shrimp, minced
- 1 tablespoon no-salt-added ketchup
- 1/4 teaspoon hot sauce
- 1 teaspoon Worcestershire sauce
- 1/2 teaspoon herb seasoning blend

- 24 matzo cracker miniatures
- 1 tablespoon parsley

Directions

1. Start by tossing the minced shrimp with cream cheese in a bowl.
2. Stir in Worcestershire sauce, hot sauce, herb seasoning, and ketchup.
3. Mix well and garnish with minced parsley.
4. Serve the spread with the crackers.

Nutrition: calories 57. Protein 3 g. Carbohydrates 7 g. Fat 1 g. Cholesterol 21 mg. Sodium 69 mg. Potassium 54 mg. Phosphorus 30 mg. Calcium 15 mg. Fiber 0.2 g.

355. Chia Cashew Cream

Preparation Time: 2 hours and 5 minutes
Cooking Time: 0 minutes
Servings: 1

Ingredients:

- 2-Tbsps maple syrup or a dash of liquid stevia
- 2-Tbsps hemp hearts
- 2-Tbsps chia seeds
- ¾-cup cashew almond milk
- ¼-tsp vanilla powder
- ¼-cup quinoa, cooked
- A pinch of cinnamon

Directions:

1. Combine all the ingredients in a jar. Mix well until thoroughly combined. Cover the jar and refrigerate for 2 hours.
2. To serve, top with your desired toppings.

Nutrition: Calories: 258 Fat: 8.6g Protein: 12.9g Sodium: 123mg Total Carbs: 34.2g Dietary Fiber: 2g Net Carbs: 32.2g

356. Spicy corn bread

Preparation time: 10 minutes
Cooking time: 30 minutes
Servings: 8

Ingredients

- 1 cup all-purpose white flour
- 1 cup plain cornmeal
- 1 tablespoon sugar
- 2 teaspoon baking powder
- 1 teaspoon chili powder
- 1/4 teaspoon black pepper
- 1 cup rice milk, unenriched
- 1 egg
- 1 egg white
- 2 tablespoon canola oil
- 1/2 cup scallions, finely chopped
- 1/4 cup carrots, finely grated
- 1 garlic clove, minced

Directions

1. Preheat your oven to 400 degrees f.
2. Now start by mixing the flour with baking powder, sugar, cornmeal, pepper and chili powder in a mixing bowl.
3. Stir in oil, milk, egg white, and egg.
4. Mix well until its smooth then stir in carrots, garlic, and scallions.
5. Stir well then spread the batter in an 8-inch baking pan greased with cooking spray.
6. Bake for 30 minutes until golden brown.
7. Slice and serve fresh.

Nutrition: calories 188. Protein 5 g. Carbohydrates 31 g. Fat 5 g. Cholesterol 26 mg. Sodium 155 mg. Potassium 100 mg. Phosphorus 81 mg. Calcium 84 mg. Fiber 2 g.

357. Fluffy mock pancakes

Preparation time: 5 minutes
Cooking time: 10 minutes
Servings: 2

Ingredients

- 1 egg
- 1 cup ricotta cheese
- 1 teaspoon cinnamon
- 2 tablespoons honey, add more if needed

Directions

1. Using a blender, put together egg, honey, cinnamon, and ricotta cheese. Process until all ingredients are well combined.
2. Pour an equal amount of the blended mixture into the pan. Cook each pancake for 4 minutes on both sides. Serve.

Nutrition: calories: 188.1 kcal total fat: 14.5 g saturated fat: 4.5 g cholesterol: 139.5 mg sodium: 175.5 mg total carbs: 5.5 g fiber: 2.8 g sugar: 0.9 g protein: 8.5 g

358. Sweet and spicy tortilla chips

Preparation time: 10 minutes
Cooking time: 8 minutes
Servings: 6
Ingredients

- 1/4 cup butter
- 1 teaspoon brown sugar
- 1/2 teaspoon ground chili powder
- 1/2 teaspoon garlic powder
- 1/2 teaspoon ground cumin
- 1/4 teaspoon ground cayenne pepper
- 6 flour tortillas, 6" size

Directions

1. Preheat oven to 425 degrees f.
2. Grease a baking sheet with cooking spray.
3. Add all spices, brown sugar, and melted butter to a small bowl.
4. Mix well and set this mixture aside.
5. Slice the tortillas into 8 wedges and brush them with the sugar mixture.
6. Spread them on the baking sheet and bake them for 8 minutes.
7. Serve fresh.

Nutrition: calories 115. Protein 2 g. Carbohydrates 11 g. Fat 7 g. Cholesterol 15 mg. Sodium 156 mg. Potassium 42 mg. Phosphorus 44 mg. Calcium 31 mg. Fiber 0.6 g.

359. Addictive pretzels

Preparation time: 10 minutes
Cooking time: 1 hour
Servings: 6
Ingredients

- 32-ounce bag unsalted pretzels
- 1 cup canola oil
- 2 tablespoon seasoning mix
- 3 teaspoon garlic powder
- 3 teaspoon dried dill weed

Directions

1. Preheat oven to 175 degrees f.
2. Place the pretzels on a cooking sheet and break them into pieces.
3. Mix garlic powder and dill in a bowl and reserve half of the mixture.
4. Mix the remaining half with seasoning mix and ¾ cup of canola oil.
5. Pour this oil over the pretzels and brush them liberally
6. Bake the pieces for 1 hour then flip them to bake for another 15 minutes.
7. Allow them to cool then sprinkle the remaining dill mixture and drizzle more oil on top.
8. Serve fresh and warm.

Nutrition: calories 184. Protein 2 g. Carbohydrates 22 g. Fat 8 g. Cholesterol 0 mg. Sodium 60 mg. Potassium 43 mg. Phosphorus 28 mg. Calcium 2 mg. Fiber 1.0 g.

360. Parmesan quinoa with peas

Preparation time: 5 minutes
Cooking time: 20 minutes
Servings: 2
Ingredients

- Quinoa – .75 cup
- Water – 1.5 cups
- Green peas, thawed if frozen - .75 cup
- Black pepper, ground - .25 teaspoon

- Olive oil – 1.5 tablespoons
- Parmesan cheese, grated – 3 tablespoons

Directions

1. Place the uncooked quinoa in a fine metal sieve and rinse it well with water until there is no debris running off.
2. Place the quinoa and water in a metal saucepan and bring it to a boil over medium heat. Once it attains a boil, reduce it to a light simmer, cover the pot with a lid, and allow cooking until the water has all been absorbed. This should take fifteen to twenty minutes.
3. Allow the quinoa to sit with the lid on for five minutes after turning off the heat. Once it has set, use a fork to fluff the quinoa and stir in the green peas, olive oil, and quinoa. Close the lid once again, allowing it to sit for five additional minutes to warm the peas and melt the cheese. Enjoy the quinoa while warm.

Nutrition: calories in individual servings: 386 protein grams: 13 phosphorus milligrams: 378 potassium milligrams: 465 sodium milligrams: 144 fat grams: 16 total carbohydrates grams: 47 net carbohydrates grams: 41

SOUP AND STEW

361. Easy Zucchini Soup

Preparation Time: 10 minutes
Cooking Time: 25 minutes
Servings: 4
Ingredients:
- 5 zucchinis, sliced
- 8 oz. cream cheese, softened
- 5 cups vegetable stock
- Pepper
- Salt

Directions:
1. Add zucchini and stock into the stockpot and bring to boil over high heat.
2. Turn heat to medium and simmer for 20 minutes.
3. Add cream cheese and stir until cheese is melted.
4. Puree soup using an immersion blender until smooth.
5. Season with pepper and salt.
6. Serve and enjoy.

Nutrition: Calories 245 Fat 20.3 g Carbohydrates 10.9 g Sugar 5.2 g Protein 7.7 g Cholesterol 62 mg Phosphorus: 110mg Potassium: 117mg Sodium: 75mg

362. Quick Tomato Soup

Preparation Time: 10 minutes
Cooking Time: 5 minutes
Servings: 4
Ingredients:
- 28 oz. can tomato, diced
- 1 tbsp. balsamic vinegar
- 1 tbsp. dried basil
- 1 tbsp. dried oregano
- 1 tsp garlic, minced

- 2 tbsp. olive oil
- Pepper
- Salt

Directions:
1. Heat oil in a saucepan over medium heat.
2. Add basil, oregano, and garlic and saute for 30 seconds.
3. Add Red bell peppers, vinegar, pepper, and salt and simmer for 3 minutes.
4. Stir well and serve hot.

Nutrition: Calories 108 Fat 7.1 g Carbohydrates 11.2 g Sugar 6.8 g Protein 2 g Cholesterol 0 mg Phosphorus: 130mg Potassium: 127mg Sodium: 75mg

363. Creamy Chicken Green lettuce Soup

Preparation Time: 10 minutes
Cooking Time: 10 minutes
Servings: 6
Ingredients:
- 3 cups cooked chicken, shredded
- 1/8 tsp nutmeg
- 4 cup chicken broth
- 1/2 cup parmesan cheese, shredded
- 8 oz. cream cheese
- 1/4 cup butter
- 4 cup baby green lettuce, chopped
- 1 tsp garlic, minced
- Pepper
- Salt

Directions:
1. Melt butter in a saucepan over medium heat.
2. Add green lettuce and garlic and cook until green lettuce is wilted.

3. Add parmesan cheese and cream cheese and stir until cheese is melted.
4. Add remaining ingredients and stir everything well and cook for 5 minutes.
5. Season soup with pepper and salt.
6. Serve and enjoy.

Nutrition: Calories 361 Fat 25.6 g Carbohydrates 2.8 g Sugar 0.6 g Protein 29.5 g Cholesterol 121 mg Phosphorus: 110mg Potassium: 117mg Sodium: 75mg

364. Spicy Chicken Soup

Preparation Time: 10 minutes
Cooking Time: 5 minutes
Servings: 4
Ingredients:
- 2 cups cooked chicken, shredded
- 1/2 cup half and half
- 4 cups chicken broth
- 1/3 cup hot sauce
- 3 tbsp. butter
- 4 oz. cream cheese
- Pepper
- Salt

Directions:
1. Add half and half, broth, hot sauce, butter, and cream cheese into the blender and blend until smooth.
2. Pour blended mixture into the saucepan and cook over medium heat until just hot.
3. Add chicken stir well. Season soup with pepper and salt.
4. Serve and enjoy.

Nutrition: Calories 361 Fat 25.6 g Carbohydrates 3.3 g Sugar 1.1 g Protein 28.4 g Cholesterol 119 mg Phosphorus: 110mg Potassium: 117mg Sodium: 75mg

365. Tasty Pumpkin Soup

Preparation Time: 10 minutes
Cooking Time: 30 minutes

Servings: 6
Ingredients:
- 2 cups pumpkin puree
- 1 cup coconut cream
- 4 cups vegetable broth
- 1/2 tsp ground ginger
- 1 tsp curry powder
- 2 shallots, chopped
- 1/2 onion, chopped
- 4 tbsp. butter
- Pepper
- Salt

Directions:
1. Melt butter in a saucepan over medium heat.
2. Add shallots and onion and sauté until softened.
3. Add ginger and curry powder and stir well.
4. Add broth, pumpkin puree, and coconut cream and stir well. Simmer for 10 minutes.
5. Puree the soup using an immersion blender until smooth.
6. Season with pepper and salt.
7. Serve and enjoy.

Nutrition: Calories 229 Fat 18.4 g Carbohydrates 13 g Sugar 4.9 g Protein 5.6 g Cholesterol 20 mg Phosphorus: 120mg Potassium: 137mg Sodium: 95mg

366. Delicious Curried Chicken Soup

Preparation Time: 10 minutes
Cooking Time: 35 minutes
Servings: 10
Ingredients:
- 5 cups cooked chicken, chopped
- 1/4 cup fresh parsley, chopped
- 1/2 cup sour cream
- 1/4 cup apple cider
- 3 cups celery, chopped

- 1 1/2 tbsp. curry powder
- 10 cups chicken broth
- Pepper
- Salt

Directions:
1. Add all ingredients except sour cream and parsley into the stockpot and stir well.
2. Bring to boil over medium-high heat.
3. Turn heat to medium and simmer for 30 minutes.
4. Add parsley and sour cream and stir well.
5. Season with pepper and salt.
6. Serve and enjoy.

Nutrition: Calories 180 Fat 6.1 g Carbohydrates 3.7 g Sugar 1.9 g Protein 28.9 g Cholesterol 59 mg Phosphorus: 160mg Potassium: 107mg Sodium: 75mg

367. Amazing Zucchini Soup

Preparation Time: 10 minutes
Cooking Time: 20 minutes
Servings: 4

Ingredients:
- 1 onion, chopped
- 3 zucchinis, cut into medium chunks
- 2 tablespoons coconut almond milk
- 2 garlic cloves, minced
- 4 cups chicken stock
- 2 tablespoons coconut oil
- Pinch of salt
- Black pepper to taste

Directions:
1. Take a pot and place over medium heat.
2. Add oil and let it heat up.
3. Add zucchini, garlic, onion and stir.
4. Cook for 5 minutes.
5. Add stock, salt, pepper and stir.
6. Bring to a boil and reduce the heat.
7. Simmer for 20 minutes.

8. Remove from heat and add coconut almond milk.
9. Use an immersion blender until smooth.
10. Ladle into soup bowls and serve.
11. Enjoy!

Nutrition: Calories: 160 Fat: 2g Carbohydrates: 4g Protein: 7g Phosphorus: 110mg Potassium: 117mg Sodium: 75mg

368. Sesame cucumber salad

Preparation time: 5 minutes
Cooking time: 0 minute
Servings: 2

Ingredients
- Cucumbers, thinly sliced – 1
- Sesame seeds - .5 teaspoon
- Rice wine vinegar – 1 tablespoon
- Sugar - .5 tablespoon
- Sesame seed oil – 1.5 tablespoons
- Red pepper flakes - .25 teaspoon

Directions
1. You want the cucumbers sliced as thinly as you can get them. While you can certainly do this with a knife, it is quicker and easier if you use a mandolin.
2. In a medium to a small bowl, whisk together the sesame seeds, rice wine vinegar, sugar, sesame seed oil, and red pepper flakes. Once well combined, add in the cucumbers and toss the vegetables in the vinaigrette. Serve immediately.

Nutrition: calories in individual servings: 92 protein grams: 1 phosphorus milligrams: 46 potassium milligrams: 250 sodium milligrams: 117 fat grams: 5

369. Carrot Cauliflower Soup

Preparation Time: 10 minutes

Cooking Time: 25 minutes
Servings: 8
Ingredients:

- 4 carrots, shredded
- 1 cauliflower head, chopped
- 8 cups chicken broth
- 1 onion, diced
- 5 oz. coconut almond milk
- 1 tbsp. olive oil
- 1 tbsp. curry powder
- 1/2 tsp turmeric powder
- 1/2 tbsp. ginger, grated
- Pepper
- Salt

Directions:

1. Heat oil in a saucepan over medium heat.
2. Add onion and sauté for 5 minutes.
3. Add cauliflower, carrots, and broth and bring to boil.
4. Turn heat to medium-low and simmer until veggie is softened.
5. Add curry powder, turmeric, and ginger and stir well.
6. Blend the soup using a blender until smooth.
7. Add coconut almond milk and stir well.
8. Season soup with pepper and salt.
9. Serve and enjoy.

Nutrition: Calories 125 Fat 7.5 g Carbohydrates 8.7 g Sugar 4.2 g Protein 6.5 g Cholesterol 0 mg Phosphorus: 210mg Potassium: 187mg Sodium: 105mg

370. Creamy Cauliflower Soup

Preparation Time: 10 minutes
Cooking Time: 4 hours
Servings: 5
Ingredients:

- 6 cups cauliflower florets
- 4 oz. mascarpone cheese
- 1 1/2 cup cheddar cheese, shredded
- 1/4 tsp mustard powder
- 3 cups of water
- 1 tsp garlic, minced
- Pepper
- Salt

Directions:

1. Add cauliflower, mustard powder, water, and garlic into the slow cooker and stir well.
2. Cover and cook on low for 4 hours.
3. Stir in cheddar cheese and mascarpone cheese.
4. Puree the soup using an immersion blender until smooth.
5. Season soup with pepper and salt.
6. Serve and enjoy.

Nutrition: Calories 208 Fat 14.3 g Carbohydrates 7.7 g Sugar 3.1 g Protein 13.5 g Cholesterol 47 mg Phosphorus: 210mg Potassium: 157mg Sodium: 85mg

371. Thai Chicken Soup

Preparation Time: 10 minutes
Cooking Time: 30 minutes
Servings: 6
Ingredients:

- 4 chicken breasts, slice into 1/4-inch strips
- 1 tbsp. fresh basil, chopped
- 1 tsp ground ginger
- 1 oz. fresh lime juice
- 1 tbsp. coconut aminos
- 2 tbsp. chili garlic paste
- 1/4 cup fish sauce
- 28 oz. water
- 14 oz. chicken broth
- 14 oz. coconut almond milk

Directions:

1. Add coconut almond milk, basil, ginger, lime juice, coconut aminos, chili garlic paste, fish sauce, water, and broth into

the stockpot. Stir well and bring to boil over medium-high heat.
2. Add chicken and stir well. Turn heat to medium-low and simmer for 30 minutes.
3. Stir well and serve.

Nutrition: Calories 357 Fat 23.4 g Carbohydrates 5.5 g Sugar 2.9 g Protein 31.7 g Cholesterol 87 mg Phosphorus: 110mg Potassium: 117mg Sodium: 75mg

372. White Fish Stew

Preparation Time: 10 minutes
Cooking Time: 35 minutes
Servings: 3
Ingredients:
- 4 white fish fillets
- 1 cup of water
- 1 onion, sliced
- 1/2 tsp paprika
- 1/4 cup olive oil
- 1/4 tsp pepper
- 1 tsp salt

Directions:
1. Add olive oil, paprika, onion, water, pepper, and salt into the saucepan. Stir well and bring to boil over medium-high heat.
2. Turn heat to medium-low and simmer for 15 minutes.
3. Add white fish fillets and cook until fish is cooked.
4. Serve and enjoy.

Nutrition: Calories 513 Fat 32.3 g Carbohydrates 3.7 g Sugar 1.6 g Protein 50.7 g Cholesterol 158 mg Phosphorus: 120mg Potassium: 117mg Sodium: 75mg

373. Pumpkin, Coconut and Sage Soup

Preparation Time: 10 minutes
Cooking Time: 30 minutes

Servings: 3
Ingredients:
- 1 cup pumpkin, canned
- 6 cups chicken broth
- 1 cup low fat coconut almond milk
- 1 teaspoon sage, chopped
- 3 garlic cloves, peeled
- Sunflower seeds and pepper to taste

Directions:
1. Take a stockpot and add all the ingredients except coconut almond milk into it.
2. Place stockpot over medium heat.
3. Let it bring to a boil.
4. Reduce heat to simmer for 30 minutes.
5. Add the coconut almond milk and stir.
6. Serve bacon and enjoy!

Nutrition: Calories: 145 Fat: 12g Carbohydrates: 8g Protein: 6g Phosphorus: 110mg Potassium: 117mg Sodium: 75mg

374. The Kale and Green lettuce Soup

Preparation Time: 5 minutes
Cooking Time: 10 minutes
Servings: 4
Ingredients:
- 3 ounces coconut oil
- 8 ounces kale, chopped
- 4 1/3 cups coconut almond milk
- Sunflower seeds and pepper to taste

Directions:
1. Take a skillet and place it over medium heat.
2. Add kale and sauté for 2-3 minutes
3. Add kale to blender.
4. Add water, spices, coconut almond milk to blender as well.
5. Blend until smooth and pour mix into bowl.
6. Serve and enjoy!

Nutrition: Calories: 124 Fat: 13g Carbohydrates: 7g Protein: 4.2g Phosphorus: 110mg Potassium: 117mg Sodium: 105mg

375. Delicious Tomato Basil Soup

Preparation Time: 10 minutes
Cooking Time: 20 minutes
Servings: 6
Ingredients:

- 28 oz. can tomato, diced
- 1 1/2 cups chicken stock
- 1/2 tsp Italian seasoning
- 1/2 tsp garlic, minced
- 1 onion, chopped
- 1/4 cup fresh basil leaves
- 1/2 cup heavy cream
- 2 tbsp. butter
- Pepper
- Salt

Directions:

1. Melt butter in a saucepan over medium-high heat.
2. Add onion and garlic sauté for 5 minutes.
3. Add Red bell peppers, Italian seasoning, and broth. Stir well and bring to boil over high heat.
4. Turn heat to medium-low and simmer for 8-10 minutes.
5. Blend the soup using an immersion blender until smooth.
6. Add heavy cream and basil and stir well. Season soup with pepper and salt.
7. Stir and serve.

Nutrition: Calories 108 Fat 7.8 g Carbohydrates 9.1 g Sugar 5.5 g Protein 1.9 g Cholesterol 24 mg Phosphorus: 110mg Potassium: 137mg Sodium: 95mg

376. Shredded Pork Soup

Preparation Time: 10 minutes
Cooking Time: 8 hours
Servings: 8
Ingredients:

- 1 lb. pork loin
- 8 cups chicken broth
- 2 tsp fresh lime juice
- 1 1/2 tsp garlic powder
- 1 1/2 tsp onion powder
- 1 1/2 tsp chili powder
- 1 1/2 tsp cumin
- 1 jalapeno pepper, minced
- 1 cup onion, chopped
- 3 Red bell peppers, chopped

Directions:

1. Add Red bell peppers, jalapeno, and onion into the slow cooker and stir well.
2. Place meat on top of the tomato mixture.
3. Pour remaining ingredients on top of the meat.
4. Cover slow cooker and cook on low for 8 hours.
5. Remove meat from slow cooker and shred using a fork.
6. Return shredded meat to the slow cooker and stir well.
7. Serve and enjoy.

Nutrition: Calories 199 Fat 9.6 g Carbohydrates 6.3 g Sugar 3.1 g Protein 21.2 g Cholesterol 45 mg Phosphorus: 140mg Potassium: 127mg Sodium: 95mg

377. Creamy Mushroom Soup

Preparation Time: 10 minutes
Cooking Time: 15 minutes
Servings: 6
Ingredients:

- 1 lb. mushrooms, sliced

- 1/2 cup heavy cream
- 4 cups chicken broth
- 1 tbsp. sage, chopped
- 1/4 cup butter
- Pepper
- Salt

Directions:
1. Melt butter in a large pot over medium heat.
2. Add sage and saute for 1 minute.
3. Add mushrooms and cook for 3-5 minutes or until lightly browned.
4. Add broth and stir well and simmer for 5 minutes.
5. Puree the soup using an immersion blender until smooth.
6. Add heavy cream and stir well. Season soup with pepper and salt.
7. Serve hot and enjoy.

Nutrition: Calories 145 Fat 12.5 g Carbohydrates 3.6 g Sugar 1.8 g Protein 5.9 g Cholesterol 34 mg Phosphorus: 140mg Potassium: 127mg Sodium: 75mg

378. Pork Soup

Preparation Time: 10 minutes
Cooking Time: 4 hours 15 minutes
Servings: 8
Ingredients:
- 2 lbs. country pork ribs, boneless and cut into 1-inch pieces
- 2 cups cauliflower rice
- 1 1/2 tbsp. fresh oregano, chopped
- 1 cup of water
- 2 cups Red bell peppers, chopped
- 1 cup chicken stock
- 1/2 cup dry white wine
- 1 onion, chopped
- 3 garlic cloves, chopped
- 1 tbsp. olive oil
- Pepper

- Salt

Directions:
1. Heat oil in a saucepan over medium heat.
2. Season pork with pepper and salt. Add pork into the saucepan and cook until lightly brown from all the sides.
3. Add onion and garlic and saute for 2 minutes.
4. Add Red bell peppers, water, stock, and white wine and stir well. Bring to boil.
5. Pour saucepan mixture into the slow cooker.
6. Cover and cook on high for 4 hours.
7. Add cauliflower rice and oregano in the last 20 minutes of cooking.
8. Stir well and serve.

Nutrition: Calories 263 Fat 15.1 g Carbohydrates 5.8 g Sugar 2.6 g Protein 23.4 g Cholesterol 85 mg Phosphorus: 130mg Potassium: 117mg Sodium: 105mg

379. Mexican Bean Soup

Preparation time 20mins
Cooking time 25mins,
Serving 4
Ingredients:
- 4 Red bell peppers
- 150 g green beans
- 1 onion
- 1 clove of garlic
- 1 red chili pepper
- 2 tbsp. olive oil
- 2 tbsp. tomato paste
- 1 tsp paprika noble sweet
- 1 tsp ground cumin
- 1 tsp ground coriander
- 1 l vegetable broth
- 240 g kidney beans (can; drained weight)
- 240 g white beans (can; drained weight)
- Salt
- Pepper

- Coriander greens for garnish

Directions:
1. Scald, quench, peel, remove the stalk and roughly chop the Red bell peppers with hot water. Wash the green beans, clean them, and cut them into small pieces.
2. Wash and clean the chili, remove the seeds and, if desired, finely chop it.
3. Sauté onion garlic and chilly. Sauté the tomato paste and add paprika, cumin, and cilantro to the mixture. Put the broth in and bring it to a boil. Add the green beans and Red bell peppers and simmer over low heat for about 10 minutes. The kidney and white beans are drained, washed, and added.
4. Let it simmer more for 5 minutes. Serve in bowls with coriander leaves and season with salt and pepper.

Nutrition: Calories 205 kcal Protein 13 g, Fat 6 g, Carbohydrates 23 g,

380. Chickpea Curry Soup

Preparation Time: 10 minutes
Cooking Time: 25 minutes
Servings: 4

Ingredients:
- ¼ cup extra-virgin olive oil or coconut oil
- 1 medium onion, finely chopped
- 2 garlic cloves, sliced
- 1 large apple, cored, peeled, and cut into ¼-inch dice
- 2 teaspoons curry powder
- 1 teaspoon salt
- 3 cups peeled butternut squash cut into ½-inch dice
- 3 cups vegetable broth
- 1 cup full-fat coconut almond milk
- 1 (15-ounce) can chickpeas, drained and rinsed

- 2 tablespoons finely chopped fresh cilantro

Directions:
1. In a huge pot, heat the oil on high heat.
2. Add the onion and garlic and sauté until the onion begins to brown, 6 to 8 minutes.
3. Put the apple, curry powder, and salt and sauté to toast the curry powder, 1 to 2 minutes.
4. Put the squash and broth then bring to a boil.
5. Lower the heat then cook until the squash is tender about 10 minutes.
6. Stir in the coconut almond milk.
7. Using an immersion blender, purée the soup in the pot until smooth.
8. Stir in the chickpeas and cilantro, heat through for 1 to 2 minutes, and serve.

Nutrition: Calories: 469 Total Fat: 30g Total Carbohydrates: 45g Sugar: 14g Fiber: 10g Protein: 12g Sodium: 1174mg

381. Onion, Kale and White Bean Soup

Preparation Time: 15 minutes
Cooking Time: 25 minutes
Servings: 4

Ingredients:
- ¼ cup extra-virgin olive oil
- 1 large onion, thinly sliced
- 2 garlic cloves, thinly sliced
- 1 teaspoon salt
- ¼ teaspoon freshly ground black pepper
- 1/8 Teaspoon red pepper flakes (optional)
- 3 cups stemmed kale leaves cut into ½-inch pieces
- 4 cups vegetable broth
- 1 (15½-ounce) can white beans, drained and rinsed

- 1 teaspoon finely chopped fresh rosemary

Directions:
1. In a huge pot, heat the oil on high heat.
2. Reduce the heat to medium, and add the onion, garlic, salt, pepper, and red pepper flakes (if using). Sauté until the onion is golden, about 10 minutes.
3. Add the kale, and sauté until wilted, 1 to 2 minutes.
4. Pour the broth then bring to a boil.
5. Reduce the heat to simmer, and cook until the kale is soft about 5 minutes.
6. Add the beans and rosemary. Cook until the beans are warmed through at least 2 to 3 minutes and serve.

Nutrition: Calories: 285 Total Fat: 15g Total Carbohydrates: 28g Sugar: 3g Fiber: 9g Protein: 13g Sodium: 1368mg

382. White rice and Shitake Miso Soup with Scallion

Preparation Time: 10 minutes
Cooking Time: 45 minutes
Servings: 4
Ingredients:
- 2 tablespoons sesame oil
- 1 cup thinly sliced shiitake mushroom caps
- 1 garlic clove, minced
- 1 (1½-inch) piece fresh ginger, peeled and sliced
- 1 cup medium-grain white rice
- ½ teaspoon salt
- 1 tablespoon white miso
- 2 scallions, thinly sliced
- 2 tablespoons finely chopped fresh cilantro

Directions:
1. In a huge pot, heat the oil on medium-high heat.

2. Add the mushrooms, garlic, and ginger and sauté until the mushrooms begin to soften, about 5 minutes.
3. Put the rice and stir to evenly coat with the oil.
4. Add 2 cups of water and salt and place it to a boil.
5. Lower the heat then cook until the rice is tender, 30 to 40 minutes.
6. Use a little of the soup broth to soften the miso, then stir it into the pot until well blended.
7. Mix in the scallions and cilantro, then serve.

Nutrition: Calories: 265 Total Fat: 8g Total Carbohydrates: 43g Sugar: 2g Fiber: 3g Protein: 5g Sodium: 456mg

383. Garlic and Lentil Soup

Preparation Time: 15 minutes
Cooking Time: 15 minutes
Servings: 4
Ingredients:
- 2 tablespoons extra-virgin olive oil
- 2 medium carrots, thinly sliced
- 1 small white onion, cut into ¼-inch dice
- 2 garlic cloves, thinly sliced
- 1 teaspoon ground cinnamon
- 1 teaspoon salt
- ¼ teaspoon freshly ground black pepper
- 3 cups vegetable broth
- 1 (15-ounce) can lentils, drained and rinsed
- 1 tablespoon minced or grated mango zest
- ¼ cup chopped walnuts (optional)
- 2 tablespoons finely chopped fresh flat-leaf parsley

Directions:

1. In a huge pot, heat the oil over high heat.
2. Add the carrots, onion, and garlic and sauté until softened, 5 to 7 minutes.
3. Put the cinnamon, salt, and pepper and stir to evenly coat the vegetables, 1 to 2 minutes.
4. Pour the broth then bring to a boil.
5. Lower the heat to a simmer, add the lentils and cook until they are heated through about 1 minute.
6. Stir in the mango zest and serve, sprinkled with the walnuts (if using) and parsley.

Nutrition: Calories: 201 Total Fat: 8g; Total Carbohydrates 22g Sugar: 4g Fiber: 8g Protein: 11g Sodium: 1178mg

384. Italian Summer Squash Soup

Preparation Time: 10 minutes
Cooking Time: 15 minutes
Servings: 4
Ingredients:

- 3 tablespoons extra-virgin olive oil
- 1 small red onion, thinly sliced
- 1 garlic clove, minced
- 1 cup shredded zucchini
- 1 cup shredded yellow squash
- ½ cup shredded carrot
- 3 cups vegetable broth
- 1 teaspoon salt
- 2 tablespoons finely chopped fresh basil
- 1 tablespoon finely chopped fresh chives
- 2 tablespoons pine nuts

Directions:
1. In a huge pot, heat the oil over high heat.
2. Add the onion and garlic and sauté until softened, 5 to 7 minutes.
3. Add the zucchini, yellow squash, and carrot and sauté until softened, 1 to 2 minutes.
4. Pour the broth and salt then bring to a boil.
5. Lower the heat and cook until the vegetables are soft, 1 to 2 minutes.
6. Stir in the basil and chives and serve, sprinkled with the pine nuts.

Nutrition: Calories: 172 Total Fat: 15g Total Carbohydrates: 6g Sugar: 3g Fiber: 2g Protein: 5g Sodium: 1170mg

385. Leek, Chicken and Spinach Soup

Preparation Time: 10 minutes
Cooking Time: 15 minutes
Servings: 4
Ingredients:

- 3 tablespoons unsalted butter
- 2 leeks, white parts only, thinly sliced
- 4 cups baby spinach
- 4 cups chicken broth
- 1 teaspoon salt
- ¼ teaspoon freshly ground black pepper
- 2 cups shredded rotisserie chicken
- 1 tablespoon thinly sliced fresh chives
- 2 teaspoons grated or minced lemon zest

Directions:
1. In a huge pot, melt the butter on high heat.
2. Add the leeks and sauté until softened and beginning to brown, 3 to 5 minutes.
3. Add the spinach, broth, salt, and pepper and bring to a boil.
4. Lower the heat and cook till the spinach wilts, 1 to 2 minutes.
5. Put the chicken and cook until warmed through 1 to 2 minutes.

6. Sprinkle with the chives and lemon zest and serve.

Nutrition: Calories: 256 Total Fat: 12g Total Carbohydrates: 9g Sugar: 3g Fiber: 2g Protein: 27g
Sodium: 1483mg

386. Saffron and Salmon Soup

Preparation Time: 10 minutes
Cooking Time: 20 minutes
Servings: 4
Ingredients:
- ¼ cup extra-virgin olive oil
- 2 leeks, white parts only, thinly sliced
- 2 medium carrots, thinly sliced
- 2 garlic cloves, thinly sliced
- 4 cups vegetable broth
- 1 lb. salmon fillets, cut into 1-inch pieces
- 1 tsp. salt
- ¼ tsp. freshly ground black pepper
- ¼ tsp. saffron threads
- 2 cups baby spinach
- ½ cup dry white wine
- 2 tablespoons chopped scallions, both white and green parts
- 2 tablespoons finely chopped fresh flat-leaf parsley

Directions:
1. In a huge pot, heat the oil over high heat.
2. Add the leeks, carrots, and garlic and sauté until softened, 5 to 7 minutes.
3. Pour the broth then bring to a boil.
4. Lower the heat to a simmer then add the salmon, salt, pepper, and saffron. Cook until the salmon is cooked through, at least 8 minutes.
5. Add the spinach, wine, scallions, and parsley and cook until the spinach has wilted, 1 to 2 minutes, and serve.

Nutrition: Calories: 418 Total Fat: 26g Total Carbohydrates: 13g Sugar: 4g Fiber: 2g Protein: 29g Sodium: 1455mg

387. Sweet Potato and Corn Soup

Preparation Time: 10 minutes
Cooking Time: 20 minutes
Servings: 4
Ingredients:
- ¼ cup extra-virgin olive oil or coconut oil
- 1 medium zucchini, cut into ¼-inch dice
- 1 cup broccoli florets
- 1 cup thinly sliced mushrooms
- 1 small onion, cut into ¼-inch dice
- 4 cups vegetable broth
- 2 cups peeled carrots cut into ¼-inch dice
- 1 cup frozen corn kernels
- 1 cup coconut almond milk or almond milk
- 2 tablespoons finely chopped fresh flat-leaf parsley
- 1 teaspoon salt
- ¼ teaspoon freshly ground black pepper

Directions:
1. In a huge pot, heat the oil on high heat.
2. Add the zucchini, broccoli, mushrooms, and onion and sauté until softened, 5 to 8 minutes.
3. Pour the broth and carrots and place it to a boil.
4. Reduce the heat to a simmer and cook until the carrots are tender, 5 to 7 minutes.
5. Add the corn, coconut almond milk, parsley, salt, and pepper. Cook on low heat up to the corn is heated through and serve.

Nutrition: Calories: 402 Total Fat: 29gTotal Carbohydrates: 31g Sugar: 9g Fiber: 6g Protein: 10g Sodium: 1406mg

388. Butternut Squash Soup with Shrimp

Preparation Time: 10 minutes
Cooking Time: 20 minutes
Servings: 4
Ingredients:

- 3 tablespoons unsalted butter
- 1 small red onion, finely chopped
- 1 garlic clove, sliced
- 1 teaspoon turmeric
- 1 teaspoon salt
- ¼ teaspoon freshly ground black pepper
- 3 cups vegetable broth
- 2 cups peeled butternut squash cut into ¼-inch dice
- 1 pound cooked peeled shrimp, thawed if necessary
- 1 cup unsweetened almond milk
- ¼ cup slivered almonds (optional)
- 2 tablespoons finely chopped fresh flat-leaf parsley
- 2 teaspoons grated or minced lemon zest

Directions:
1. In a huge pot, melt the butter on high heat.
2. Add the onion, garlic, turmeric, salt, and pepper and sauté until the vegetables are soft and translucent, 5 to 7 minutes.
3. Add the broth and squash and bring to a boil.
4. Lower the heat and cook until the squash has softened, about 5 minutes.
5. Add the shrimp and almond milk and cook until heated through, about 2 minutes.
6. Sprinkle with the almonds (if using), parsley, and lemon zest and serve.

Nutrition: Calories: 275 Total Fat: 12g Total Carbohydrates: 12g Sugar: 3g Fiber: 2g; Protein: 30g Sodium: 1665mg

389. Clear Clam Chowder

Preparation Time: 10 minutes
Cooking Time: 15 minutes
Servings: 4
Ingredients:

- 2 tablespoons unsalted butter
- 2 medium carrots, cut into ½-inch pieces
- 2 celery stalks, thinly sliced
- 1 small red onion, cut into ¼-inch dice
- 2 garlic cloves, sliced
- 2 cups vegetable broth
- 1 (8-ounce) bottle clam juice
- 1 (10-ounce) can clams
- ½ teaspoon dried thyme
- ½ teaspoon salt
- ¼ teaspoon freshly ground black pepper

Directions:
1. In a huge pot, melt the butter on high heat.
2. Add the carrots, celery, onion, and garlic and sauté until slightly softened 2 to 3 minutes.
3. Pour the broth and clam juice, then bring it to a boil.
4. Lower the heat and cook until the carrots are soft, 3 to 5 minutes.
5. Stir in the clams and their juices, thyme, salt, and pepper, heat through for 2 to 3 minutes, and serve.

Nutrition: Calories: 156 Total Fat: 7g Total Carbohydrates: 7g Sugar: 3g Fiber: 1g Protein: 14g Sodium: 981mg

390. Clear Soup with Vegetables

Preparation time 20mins,
Cooking time 20 mins
Serving 4

Ingredients:

- 200 g waxy carrots
- 2 poles celery
- 4 spring onions
- 1 onion
- 2 garlic cloves
- 2 yellow peppers
- 2 tbsp. olive oil
- 1 tbsp. tomato paste
- 1 l vegetable broth
- 400 g kidney beans can
- 2 fresh bay leaves
- salt
- pepper

Directions:

1. Peel and dice the carrots, clean and wash the celery and spring onions and cut into rings. Peel and chop the onion and garlic. Clean the peppers, cut in half, remove the seeds and white skins, wash and cut into thin strips.
2. Heat the oil in a hot saucepan and sauté the vegetables for 2-3 minutes over medium heat.
3. Fry the tomato paste briefly, then pour in the stock and bring to the boil once. In the meantime, drain the beans and wash them.
4. Add to the clear soup together with the bay leaf.
5. Season
6. Simmer over low heat for about 15 minutes.
7. Season the soup again to taste and serve in bowls.

Nutrition: Calories 227 kcal, Protein 12 g, Fat 6 g, Carbohydrates 30 g,

391. Bean Stew with Beef Fillet

Preparation time 20mins
Cooking time 25mins,
Serving 4

Ingredients:

- 50 g kidney beans (can; drained weight)
- 50 g small white beans (can; drained weight)
- ½ onion
- 1 small clove of garlic
- ½ red pepper
- 2 tsp olive oil
- 1 branch thyme
- 1 bay leaf
- 200 chunky Red bell peppers (can)
- salt
- pepper
- cayenne pepper
- ¼ tsp ground coriander
- 150 g beef fillet
- 1 stem basil

Directions:

1. In a sieve, rinse both types of beans and let them drain. Peel the garlic and onion and cut them into fine cubes. Wash, clean, core, and slice the peppers.
2. In a casserole, heat one teaspoon of oil. Sauté the onion and garlic in it over medium heat for 2 minutes. Wash the thyme and the bay leaves and add the beans and Red bell peppers to the saucepan, season with salt, pepper, cayenne pepper, and coriander and cook for about 15-17 minutes over medium heat, stirring occasionally.
3. Cut the beef into thin strips about 20 minutes before cooking time ends. In a pan, heat the remaining oil. For 2-3 minutes, fry the beef fillet strips over high heat. With salt and pepper, season.

4. Wash the basil, shake it dry, and finely chop it. Top the bean stew with the meat and basil.

Nutrition: Calories 393 kcal, Protein 40 g, Fat 17 g, Carbohydrates 19 g,

392. Nutmeg Pumpkin Soup with Kidney Beans

Preparation Time: 20 mins
Cooking Time: 0 mins
Serving 4
Ingredients:
- 1 kg nutmeg pumpkin
- 2 dice vegetable broth
- 1 tbsp. olive oil
- 1 lemon
- 400 g kidney beans (1 can, drained weight)
- 2 stems parsley
- pepper
- salt

Directions:
1. The pumpkin is cleaned and peeled, the core removed and the pulp cut into cubes. In a saucepan, put the pumpkin cubes in. Add sufficient water just to cover the pumpkin.
2. When boiling add 2 cubes of stock. Cook for 20 minutes over medium heat until the pumpkin is tender.
3. Squeeze the juice of the lemon.
4. In a colander drain the kidney beans and rinse with hot water.
5. Wash the parsley, shake it dry and, except for a few leaves, chop finely.
6. Add the oil to the pumpkin at the end of the cooking time and finely puree it with a hand blender. Season with lemon juice, pepper, and a little salt if necessary. Distribute the beans and pour hot soup over them on 4 soup plates. Serve with parsley, sprinkled.

Nutrition: Calories 197 kcal, Protein 12 g, Fat 4 g, Carbohydrates 27 g,

393. Zucchini Soup

Preparation time 20mins
Cooking time 20mins
Servings 4
Ingredients:
- 2 large zucchinis
- 1 onion
- 2 carrots
- 2 carrots
- 1 tbsp. (sesame oil, coconut fat, refined rapeseed or olive oil) frying oil
- 500 ml vegetable broth
- 100 g (natural, 15% fat in dry matter) cream cheese
- ½ bunch of parsley
- Salt and pepper

Direction:
1. Wash and dice the zucchini. Peel the onion, carrots, and carrots, then dice them.
2. Heat the oil in a pot. Sweat the onion cubes in it until they are golden yellow. Add the rest of the vegetables and fry briefly.
3. Deglaze with the vegetable stock
4. Simmer for about 10 minutes.
5. Puree the soup.
6. Stir the cream cheese into the warm soup and season with salt and pepper. Wash and finely chop the parsley and serve on top of the soup.

Nutrition: Calories/Energy: 36.04 Kcal, Carbs: 4.07 g Lipids: 1.68 g Protein: 2.38 g

394. Quick Pea Soup

Preparation Time: 5 mins
Cooking time 15 mins
Serving 3
Ingredients:

- 300 g Carrots
- 1 onion
- 1 toe garlic
- 30 g butter
- 200 g cream
- 1 Bay leaf
- 400 g frozen peas
- Salt
- Pepper
- Nutmeg
- Cumin
- As required: smoked salmon

Direction:
1. Peel the carrots, onion, and garlic and cut into cubes.
2. Melt the butter and sauté carrots, onions, and garlic in it.
3. Deglaze with cream, fill the cup twice with water and add this as well. Season with salt, pepper, freshly grated nutmeg, and cumin.
4. Add the bay leaf and cook everything until the carrots are done. Take out the bay leaf and add the peas.
5. Bring to the boil again and then puree with a hand blender. If the soup is still too thick, add 1 more shot of water.
6. Season again to taste and serve. Add smoked salmon strips to the soup to taste.

Nutritional values: Calories/Energy: 61 Kcal, Protein: 3.2 g Carbs: 9.88 g Calcium: 12 mg, Phosphorous: 47 mg, Potassium: 71 mg, Sodium: 336 mg

395. Chickpea Soup with Croutons

Preparation time 20 mins
Cooking time 45 mins
Serving: 1 – 4
Ingredients:
- Dried chickpeas 60 g

- Common bread without salt 80 g
- Extra virgin olive oil 20 g
- Rosemary
- Sage
- Garlic
- Bay leaf
- Chili

Direction:
1. Soak the chickpeas the night before.
2. Bring to a boil to pots of water.
3. Meanwhile, prepare a sauté with chopped rosemary, a bit of garlic, oil, sage, a few bay leaves, and a little chili. When the garlic is golden, it should be removed.
4. Pour the chickpeas into boiling water, drain them after a quarter of an hour and dip them back into the second pot of boiling water. Leave to cook for another quarter of an hour.
5. Add some chickpeas to the mixture and place them in a small pan with some of their water. The others must be blended to create a cream that we can make more or less thick with your water. Add the whole chickpeas, bring to the boil again and add the common pasta.
6. Serve accompanied with common wood baked toasted bread, adding a drizzle of extra virgin olive oil.

Nutrition: Protein: 23 g, Phosphorous: 241mg, Potassium: 609 mg, Carbs: 81 g, Sodium: 8 mg, Calories: 594 kcal

396. Tomato Soup Made from Fresh Red bell peppers

Preparation Time: 20mins
Cooking Time: 20mins
Servings 2
Ingredients:
- 1 kg of Red bell peppers

- 200 ml of water
- ½ teaspoon salt
- 1 sprig of rosemary
- 1 sprig of thyme
- 2 tbsp. cream
- 2 tbsp. sour cream

Direction:
1. Wash the Red bell peppers and put them in a saucepan with water and salt. Bring to a boil. Simmer for until the peel starts to peel off the Red bell peppers and the Red bell peppers are soft.
2. In the meantime, wash the herbs and let them dry on kitchen paper.
3. Drain the Red bell peppers, collecting the cooking water if necessary. Strain or strain the soft Red bell peppers through a sieve. Let the pureed Red bell peppers simmer for about 10 minutes. Then stir with the cream until smooth. Dilute with some of the collected cooking water as desired.
4. Strip off the rosemary and thyme needles and chop finely. Pour the soup into two bowls, put a dollop of sour cream on top and sprinkle everything with the herbs.

Nutrition: Calories186 kcal, Protein 6g Fat 8 g Carbohydrates 21g

397. Chicken Noodle Soup

Preparation Time: 10 minutes
Cooking Time: 25 minutes
Servings: 2

Ingredients:
- 1 1/2 cups low-sodium vegetable broth
- 1 cup of water
- 1/4 tsp poultry seasoning
- 1/4 tsp black pepper
- 1 cup chicken strips
- 1/4 cup carrot
- 2 oz. egg noodles, uncooked

Direction:
1. Cook soup on high heat for 25 minutes in a slow cooker.
2. Serve warm.

Nutrition: Calories 103. Protein 8 g. Carbohydrates 11 g. Fat 3 g. Cholesterol 4 mg. Sodium 355 mg.
Potassium 264 mg. Phosphorus 128 mg. Calcium 46 mg. Fiber 4.0 g.

398. Curried Carrot and Beet Soup

Preparation Time: 10 minutes
Cooking Time: 50 minutes
Servings: 4

Ingredients:
- 1 large red beet
- 5 carrots, chopped
- 1 tablespoon curry powder
- 3 cups Homemade Rice Almond milk or unsweetened store-bought rice almond milk
- Freshly ground black pepper
- Yogurt, for serving

Directions:
1. Preheat the oven to 400°F.
2. Wrap the beet in aluminum foil and roast for 45 minutes, until the vegetable is tender when pierced with a fork. Remove from the oven and let cool.
3. Add the carrots and cover with water. Bring to a boil, reduce the heat, cover, and simmer for 10 minutes, until tender.

4. Transfer the carrots and beet to a food processor, and process until smooth. Add the curry powder and rice almond milk. Season with pepper. Serve topped with a dollop of yogurt.
5. Substitution tip: Carrots are high in potassium. If you need to reduce your potassium further, use 2 carrots instead of 5. The soup will be a little thinner but still have a carrot flavor and just 322mg of potassium.

Nutrition: Calories: 112; Total Fat: 1g; Saturated Fat: 0g; Cholesterol: 0mg; Carbohydrates: 24g; Fiber: 7g; Protein: 3g; Phosphorus: 57mg; Potassium: 468mg; Sodium: 129mg

399. Cauliflower Soup

Preparation Time: 15 minutes
Cooking Time: 10 minutes
Servings: 4
Ingredients:
- Unsalted butter – 1 tsp.
- Sweet onion – 1 small, chopped
- Minced garlic – 2 tsps.
- Small head cauliflower – 1, cut into small florets
- Curry powder – 2 tsps.
- Water to cover the cauliflower
- Light sour cream – ½ cup
- Chopped fresh cilantro – 3 Tbsps.

Directions:
1. Heat the butter over a medium-high heat and sauté the onion-garlic for about 3 minutes or until softened.
2. Add the cauliflower, water, and curry powder.
3. Bring the soup to a simmer, then decrease the heat to low and simmer for 20 minutes or until the cauliflower is tender.
4. Puree the soup until creamy and smooth with a hand mixer.

5. Transfer the soup back into a saucepan and stir in the sour cream and cilantro.
6. Heat the soup on medium heat for 5 minutes or until warmed through.

Nutrition: Calories: 33 Fat: 2g Carb: 4g Phosphorus: 30mg Potassium: 167mg Sodium: 22mg Protein: 1g

400. Cabbage Stew

Preparation Time: 20 minutes
Cooking Time: 35 minutes
Servings: 6
Ingredients:
- Unsalted butter – 1 tsp.
- Large sweet onion - ½, chopped
- Minced garlic – 1 tsp.
- Shredded green cabbage – 6 cups
- Celery stalks - 3, chopped with leafy tops
- Scallion – 1, both green and white parts, chopped
- Chopped fresh parsley – 2 Tbsps.
- Freshly squeezed lemon juice – 2 Tbsps.
- Chopped fresh thyme – 1 Tbsp.
- Chopped savory – 1 tsp.
- Chopped fresh oregano – 1 tsp.
- Water
- Fresh green beans – 1 cup, cut into 1-inch pieces
- Ground black pepper

Directions:
1. Melt the butter in a pot.
2. Sauté the onion and garlic in the melted butter for 3 minutes, or until the vegetables are softened.
3. Add the celery, cabbage, scallion, parsley, lemon juice, thyme, savory, and oregano to the pot, add enough water to cover the vegetables by 4 inches.
4. Bring the soup to a boil. Reduce the heat to low and simmer the soup for 25

minutes or until the vegetables are tender.

5. Season with pepper.

Nutrition: Calories: 33 Fat: 1g Carb: 6g Phosphorus: 29mg Potassium: 187mg Sodium: 20mg
Protein: 1g

401. Roasted Red Pepper Soup

Preparation time: 30 minutes
Cooking time: 35 minutes
Servings: 4
Ingredients:

- 4 - Cups low-sodium chicken broth
- 3 - Red peppers
- 2 - Medium onions
- 3 - tbsp. lemon juice
- 1 - tbsp. finely minced lemon zest
- A pinch cayenne pepper
- ¼ - tsp. cinnamon
- ½ - cup finely minced fresh cilantro

Directions:

1. In a medium stockpot, consolidate each one of the fixings except for the cilantro and warmth to the point of boiling over excessive warm temperature.

2. Diminish the warmth and stew, ordinarily secured, for around 30 minutes, till thickened. Cool marginally. Utilizing a hand blender or nourishment processor, puree the soup. Include the cilantro and tenderly heat.

Nutrition: Calories 266, Fat 8, Fiber 6, Carbs 6, Protein 31

402. Golden Beet Soup

Preparation Time: 10 minutes
Cooking Time: 35 minutes
Servings: 4
Ingredients:

- 3 tablespoons unsalted butter
- 4 golden beets, cut into ½-inch cubes
- ½ sweet onion, chopped
- 1-inch piece ginger, minced
- Zest and juice of 1 lemon
- 4 cups Simple Chicken Broth or low-sodium store-bought chicken stock
- Freshly ground black pepper
- ¼ cup pomegranate seeds, for serving
- ¼ cup crème fraîche, for serving (see Substitution tip)
- 10 sage leaves, for serving

Directions:

1. In a medium saucepan over medium heat, melt the butter.

2. Add the beets, onion, ginger, and lemon zest, and cover. Cook, stirring occasionally, for 15 minutes. Add the broth, and continue to cook for 20 more minutes, until the beets are very tender.

3. In batches, transfer the soup to a blender and purée, or use an immersion blender.

4. Return the soup to the saucepan, and season with the pepper and lemon juice.

5. Serve topped with the pomegranate seeds, crème fraîche, and sage leaves.

6. Substitution tip: You can buy crème fraîche at many grocery stores, or make your own. If you don't have crème fraîche, a dollop of whole-almond milk yogurt is a fine substitute.

Nutrition: Calories: 186; Total Fat: 11g; Saturated Fat: 7g; Cholesterol: 26mg; Carbohydrates: 17g; Fiber: 3g; Protein: 7g; Phosphorus: 125mg; Potassium: 557mg; Sodium: 148mg

403. Creamy Vinaigrette

Preparation time: 15 minutes
Cooking time: 25 minutes
Servings: 4

Ingredients:

- 2 - tbsp. cider vinegar
- 2 - tbsp. lime or lemon juice
- 1 - Garlic clove, minced
- 1 - tsp. Dijon mustard
- 1 - tsp. ground cumin
- ½ - cup sour cream
- 2 - tbsp. olive oil
- ¼ - tsp. black pepper

Directions:

1. Consolidate all fixings and blend well. Fill serving of mixed greens carafe. Chill.

Nutrition: Calories 188, Fat 15, Fiber 8, Carbs 35, Protein 25

404. Chicken Wild Rice Soup

Preparation Time: 10 minutes
Cooking Time: 15 minutes
Servings: 6

Ingredients:

- 2/3 cup wild rice, uncooked
- 1 tbsp. onion, chopped finely
- 1 tbsp. fresh parsley, chopped
- 1 cup carrots, chopped
- 8 oz. chicken breast, cooked
- 2 tbsp. butter
- 1/4 cup all-purpose white flour
- 5 cups low-sodium chicken broth
- 1 tbsp. slivered almonds

Direction:

1. Start by adding rice and 2 cups broth along with ½ cup water to a cooking pot.
2. Cook until the rice soft and set it aside.
3. Melt butter in a saucepan.
4. Stir in onion and sauté until soft then add the flour and the remaining broth.
5. Cook while stirring for 1 minute then add the chicken, cooked rice, and carrots.
6. Cook for 5 minutes on simmer.
7. Garnish with almonds.
8. Serve fresh.

Nutrition: Calories 287 Protein 21 g. Carbohydrates 35 g. Fat 7 g. Cholesterol 42 mg. Sodium 182 mg. Potassium 384 mg. Phosphorus 217 mg. Calcium 45 mg. Fiber 1.6 g.

405. Herbed Soup with Black Beans

Preparation time: 10 minutes
Cooking time: 10 minutes
Servings: 4

Ingredients:

- 2 tbsp tomato paste
- 1/3 cup Poblano pepper, charred, peeled, seeded and chopped
- 2 cups vegetable stock
- ¼ tsp cumin
- ½ tsp paprika
- ½ tsp dried oregano
- 2 tsp fresh garlic, minced
- 1 cup onion, small diced
- 1 tbsp extra-virgin olive oil
- 1 15-oz can black beans, drained and rinsed

Directions:

1. On medium fire, place a soup pot and heat oil. Add onion and sauté until translucent and soft, around 4-5 minutes. Add garlic, cook for 2 minutes.
2. Add the rest of the ingredients and bring to a simmer. Once simmering, turn off the fire and transfer to a blender. Puree ingredients until smooth.

Nutrition: Calories 98, Fat 21 g, Fiber 10 g, Carbs 20 g, Protein 19 g

406. Cauliflower and Chive Soup

Preparation Time: 10 minutes
Cooking Time: 20 minutes
Servings: 4
Ingredients:

- 2 tablespoons extra-virgin olive oil
- ½ sweet onion, chopped
- 2 garlic cloves, minced
- 2 cups Simple Chicken Broth or low-sodium store-bought chicken stock
- 1 cauliflower head, broken into florets
- Freshly ground black pepper
- 4 tablespoons (¼ cup) finely chopped chives

Directions:

1. Heat the olive oil.
2. Add the onion and cook, stirring frequently, for 3 to 5 minutes, until it begins to soften. Add the garlic and stir until fragrant.
3. Add the broth and cauliflower, and bring to a boil. Reduce the heat and simmer until the cauliflower is tender, about 15 minutes.
4. Transfer the soup in batches to a blender or food processor and purée until smooth, or use an immersion blender.

5. Return the soup to the pot, and season with pepper. Before serving, top each bowl with 1 tablespoon of chives.

Nutrition: Calories 132; Total Fat: 8g; Saturated Fat: 1g; Cholesterol: 0mg; Carbohydrates: 13g; Fiber: 3g; Protein: 6g; Phosphorus: 116mg; Potassium: 607mg; Sodium: 84mg

407. Creamy Broccoli Soup

Preparation Time: 10 minutes
Cooking Time: 15 minutes
Servings: 4
Ingredients:

- 1 teaspoon extra-virgin olive oil
- ½ sweet onion, roughly chopped
- 2 cups chopped broccoli
- 4 cups low-sodium vegetable broth
- Freshly ground black pepper
- 1 cup Homemade Rice Almond milk or unsweetened store-bought rice almond milk
- ¼ cup grated Parmesan cheese

Directions:

1. Heat the olive oil. Add the onion and cook for 3 to 5 minutes, until it begins to soften. Add the broccoli and broth, and season with pepper.
2. Bring to a boil, reduce the heat, and simmer open for 10 minutes, until the broccoli is just tender but still bright green.
3. Transfer the soup mixture to a blender. Add the rice almond milk, and process until smooth. Return to the saucepan, stir in the Parmesan cheese, and serve.

Nutrition: Calories: 88;Total Fat: 3g;Saturated Fat: 1g; Cholesterol: 6mg; Carbohydrates: 12g; Fiber: 3g; Protein: 4g; Phosphorus: 87mg; Potassium: 201mg; Sodium: 281mg

408. Creamy Pumpkin Soup

Preparation time: 10 minutes
Cooking time: 20 minutes
Servings: 4
Ingredients:
- 1 onion, chopped
- 1 slice of bacon
- 2 tsp ground ginger
- 1 tsp cinnamon
- 1 cup applesauce
- 3 ½ cups low sodium chicken broth
- 1 29-oz can pumpkin
- Pepper to taste
- ½ cup light sour cream

Directions:
1. On medium high fire, place a soup pot and add bacon once hot. Sauté until crispy, around 4 minutes. Discard bacon fat, before continuing to cook.
2. Add ginger, applesauce, chicken broth and pumpkin. Lightly season with pepper. Bring to a simmer and cook for 11 minutes. Taste and adjust seasoning. Turn off fire, stir in sour cream and mix well.

Nutrition: Calories 220, Fat 8 g, Fiber 10 g, Carbs 36 g, Protein 10 g

409. Lemony Lentil Salad with Salmon

Preparation time: 10 minutes
Cooking time: 0 minutes
Servings: 3
Ingredients:
- ¼ tsp salt
- ½ cup chopped red onion
- 1 cup diced seedless cucumber
- 1 medium red bell pepper, diced
- 1/3 cup extra virgin olive oil
- 1/3 cup fresh dill, chopped
- 1/3 cup lemon juice
- 2 15oz cans of lentils
- 2 7oz cans of salmon, drained and flaked
- 2 tsp Dijon mustard
- Pepper to taste

Directions:
1. In a bowl, mix, lemon juice, mustard, dill, salt and pepper. Gradually add the oil, bell pepper, onion, cucumber, salmon flakes and lentils. Toss to coat evenly.

Nutrition: Calories 450, Fat 22 g, Fiber 10 g, Carbs 62 g, Protein 55 g

410. Spaghetti Squash & Yellow Bell-Pepper Soup

Preparation Time: 10 minutes
Cooking Time: 45 minutes
Servings: 4
Ingredients:
- 2 diced yellow bell peppers
- 2 chopped large garlic cloves
- 1 peeled and cubed spaghetti squash
- 1 quartered and sliced onion
- 1 tbsp. dried thyme
- 1 tbsp. coconut oil
- 1 tsp. curry powder
- 4 cups water

Directions:
1. Heat the oil in a large pan over medium-high heat before sweating the onions and garlic for 3-4 minutes.
2. Sprinkle over the curry powder.
3. Add the stock and bring to a boil over a high heat before adding the squash, pepper and thyme.
4. Turn down the heat, cover and allow to simmer for 25-30 minutes.
5. Continue to simmer until squash is soft if needed.

6. Allow to cool before blitzing in a blender/food processor until smooth.
7. Serve!

Nutrition: Calories 103, Protein 2 g, Carbs 17 g, Fat 4 g, Sodium (Na) 32 mg, Potassium (K) 365 mg, Phosphorus 50 mg

411. Red Pepper & Brie Soup

Preparation Time: 10 minutes
Cooking Time: 35 minutes
Servings: 4
Ingredients:

- 1 tsp. paprika
- 1 tsp. cumin
- 1 chopped red onion
- 2 chopped garlic cloves
- ¼ cup crumbled brie
- 2 tbsps. Extra virgin olive oil
- 4 chopped red bell peppers
- 4 cups water

Directions:
1. Heat the oil in a pot over medium heat.
2. Sweat the onions and peppers for 5 minutes.
3. Add the garlic cloves, cumin and paprika and sauté for 3-4 minutes.
4. Add the water and allow to boil before turning the heat down to simmer for 30 minutes.
5. Remove from the heat and allow to cool slightly.
6. Put the mixture in a food processor and blend until smooth.
7. Pour into serving bowls and add the crumbled brie to the top with a little black pepper.
8. Enjoy!

Nutrition: Calories 152, Protein 3 g, Carbs 8 g, Fat 11 g, Sodium (Na) 66 mg, Potassium (K) 270 mg, Phosphorus 207 mg

412. Turkey & Lemon-Grass Soup

Preparation Time: 5 minutes
Cooking Time: 40 minutes
Servings: 4
Ingredients:

- 1 fresh lime
- ¼ cup fresh basil leaves
- 1 tbsp. cilantro
- 1 cup chestnuts
- 1 tbsp. coconut oil
- 1 thumb-size minced ginger piece
- 2 chopped scallions
- 1 finely chopped green chili
- 4oz. skinless and sliced turkey breasts
- 1 minced garlic clove, minced
- ½ finely sliced stick lemon-grass
- 1 chopped white onion, chopped
- 4 cups water

Directions:
1. Crush the lemon-grass, cilantro, chili, 1 tbsp oil and basil leaves in a blender or pestle and mortar to form a paste.
2. Heat a large pan/wok with 1 tbsp olive oil on high heat.
3. Sauté the onions, garlic and ginger until soft.
4. Add the turkey and brown each side for 4-5 minutes.
5. Add the broth and stir.
6. Now add the paste and stir.
7. Next add the chestnuts, turn down the heat slightly, and simmer for 25-30 minutes or until turkey is thoroughly cooked through.
8. Serve hot with the green onion sprinkled over the top.

Nutrition: Calories 123, Protein 10 g, Carbs 12 g, Fat 3 g, Sodium (Na) 501 mg, Potassium (K) 151 mg, Phosphorus 110 mg

413. Paprika pork soup

Preparation time: 5 minutes
Cooking time: 35 minutes
Servings: 2

Ingredients
- 4-ounce sliced pork loin
- 1 teaspoon black pepper
- 2 minced garlic cloves
- 3 cups water
- 1 tablespoon extra-virgin olive oil
- 1 chopped onion
- 1 tablespoon paprika

Directions
1. Add in the oil, chopped onion and minced garlic.
2. Sauté for 5 minutes on low heat.
3. Add the pork slices to the onions and cook for 7-8 minutes or until browned.
4. Add the water to the pan and bring to a boil on high heat.
5. Reduce heat and simmer for a further 20 minutes or until pork is thoroughly cooked through.
6. Season with pepper to serve.

Nutrition: calories 165, protein 13 g, carbs 10 g, fat 9 g, sodium (na) 269 mg, potassium (k) 486 mg, phosphorus 158 mg

414. Mediterranean vegetable soup

Preparation time: 5 minutes
Cooking time: 30 minutes
Servings: 4

Ingredients
- 1 tablespoon oregano
- 2 minced garlic cloves
- 1 teaspoon black pepper
- 1 diced zucchini
- 1 cup diced eggplant
- 4 cups water
- 1 diced red pepper
- 1 tablespoon extra-virgin olive oil
- 1 diced red onion

Directions
1. Soak the vegetables in warm water prior to use.
2. Add in the oil, chopped onion and minced garlic.
3. Sweat for 5 minutes on low heat.
4. Add the other vegetables to the onions and cook for 7-8 minutes.
5. Add the stock to the pan and bring to a boil on high heat.
6. Stir in the herbs, reduce the heat, and simmer for a further 20 minutes or until thoroughly cooked through.
7. Season with pepper to serve.

Nutrition: calories 152, protein 1 g, carbs 6 g, fat 3 g, sodium (na) 3 mg, potassium (k) 229 mg, phosphorus 45 mg

415. Tofu soup

Preparation time: 5 minutes
Cooking time: 10 minutes
Servings: 2

Ingredients
- 1 tablespoon miso paste
- 1/8 cup cubed soft tofu
- 1 chopped green onion
- ¼ cup sliced shiitake mushrooms
- 3 cups renal stock
- 1 tablespoon soy sauce

Directions
1. Take a saucepan, pour the stock into this pan and let it boil on high heat. Reduce heat to medium and let this stock simmer. Add mushrooms in this stock and cook for almost 3 minutes.
2. Take a bowl and mix soy sauce (reduced salt) and miso paste together in this bowl. Add this mixture and tofu in stock. Simmer for nearly 5 minutes and serve with chopped green onion.

Nutrition: calories 129, fat 7.8g, sodium (na) 484mg, potassium (k) 435mg, protein 11g, carbs 5.5g, phosphorus 73.2mg

416. Onion soup

Preparation time: 15 minutes
Cooking time: 45 minutes
Servings: 6
Ingredients

- 2 tablespoons. Chicken stock
- 1 cup chopped shiitake mushrooms
- 1 tablespoon minced chives
- 3 teaspoons. Beef bouillon
- 1 teaspoon grated ginger root
- ½ chopped carrot
- 1 cup sliced Portobello mushrooms
- 1 chopped onion
- ½ chopped celery stalk
- 2 quarts water
- ¼ teaspoon minced garlic

Directions

1. Take a saucepan and combine carrot, onion, celery, garlic, mushrooms (some mushrooms) and ginger in this pan. Add water, beef bouillon and chicken stock in this pan. Put this pot on high heat and let it boil. Decrease flame to medium and cover this pan to cook for almost 45 minutes.
2. Put all remaining mushrooms in one separate pot. Once the boiling mixture is completely done, put one strainer over this new bowl with mushrooms and strain cooked soup in this pot over mushrooms. Discard solid-strained materials.
3. Serve delicious broth with yummy mushrooms in small bowls and sprinkle chives over each bowl.

Nutrition: calories 22, fat 0g, sodium (na) 602.3mg, potassium (k) 54.1mg, carbs 4.9g, protein 0.6g, phosphorus 15.8mg

417. Stuffed bell pepper soup

Preparation time: 5 minutes
Cooking time: 20 minutes
Servings: 2
Ingredients

- Chicken broth, low-sodium – 2 cups
- Bell pepper, red, diced – 1
- Garlic, minced – 4 cloves
- Onion, diced - .5 cup
- Ground turkey – 4 ounces
- Olive oil – 2 teaspoons
- Italian seasoning – 1 teaspoon
- White rice, cooked – 1 cup
- Parsley, fresh, chopped – 1 tablespoon

Directions

1. Cook the ground turkey with the onion, olive oil, and garlic until the turkey is fully cooked and no pink is remaining about five to seven minutes.
2. Add the black pepper, Italian seasoning, and bell pepper to the soup pot, allowing it to cook for three more minutes.
3. Into the pot, pour the low-sodium chicken broth, simmer the soup for fifteen minutes, until the bell peppers are tender. Stir in the cooked rice and parsley before serving.

Nutrition: calories in individual servings: 283 protein grams: 16 phosphorus milligrams: 183 potassium milligrams: 369 sodium milligrams: 85 fat grams: 9 total carbohydrates grams: 32 net carbohydrates grams: 30

418. Italian chicken stew

Preparation time: 20 minutes
Cooking time: 8 hours
Servings: 1
Ingredients

- 1/2-pound chicken breast, boneless, skinless, cubed
- 1/3 cup celery, chopped
- 1/2 cup carrot, chopped
- 1/2 cup onion, chopped
- 2 ounce any kind of mushrooms, sliced
- 1/4 teaspoon dill weed
- 1/2 teaspoon italian seasoning
- 1/4 teaspoon basil
- 1/4 teaspoon black pepper
- 1 tomato, diced – limit this

Directions
1. Place chicken breast cubes into the slow cooker.
2. Add in onion, carrot, italian seasoning, mushrooms, celery, basil, dill weed, and black pepper.
3. Cover and cook for 8 to 9 hours on low. Secure the lid.
4. After the 8-hour cooking cycle, turn off the heat. Adjust seasoning according to your preferred taste.
5. Serve warm.

Nutrition: protein: 29.9 g potassium: 89.6 mg sodium: 56.3 mg

419. Turkey pasta stew

Preparation time: 10 minutes
Cooking time: 8 hours
Servings: 1
Ingredients
- 1/2-pound ground turkey
- 1/2 cup carrots, sliced
- 1/2 fennel bulb, chopped
- 1/4 cup celery, sliced
- 1 cup chicken broth, low sodium
- 1/3 teaspoon garlic, minced
- 1/2 teaspoon oregano
- 1/2 teaspoon basil
- 1/2 cup shell pasta, uncooked

- 1 cup navy beans, unsalted, cooked

Directions
1. Cook turkey in a non-stick skillet set over medium heat until browned on all sides. Transfer to the slow cooker.
2. Add in garlic, carrots, chicken broth, navy beans, basil celery, pasta, oregano, and fennel. Stir well to combine.
3. Cover and cook for 8 to 9 hours on low. Secure the lid.
4. After the 8-hour cooking cycle, turn off the heat. Adjust seasoning according to your preferred taste. Serve warm.

Nutrition: protein: 18.8 g potassium: 84.6 mg sodium: 68.5 mg

420. Steakhouse soup

Preparation time: 15 minutes
Cooking time: 25 minutes
Servings: 4
Ingredients
- 2 tablespoons. Soy sauce
- 2 boneless and cubed chicken breasts.
- ¼ pound halved and trimmed snow peas
- 1 tablespoon minced ginger root
- 1 minced garlic clove
- 1 cup water
- 2 chopped green onions
- 3 cups chicken stock
- 1 chopped carrot
- 3 sliced mushrooms

Directions
1. Take a pot and combine ginger, water, chicken stock, soy sauce (reduced salt) and garlic in this pot. Let them boil on medium heat, mix in chicken pieces, and let them simmer on low heat for almost 15 minutes to tender chicken.
2. Stir in carrot and snow peas and simmer for almost 5 minutes. Add mushrooms in this blend and continue cooking to

tender vegetables for nearly 3 minutes. Mix in the chopped onion and serve hot.

Nutrition: calories 319, carbs 14g, fat 15g, potassium (k) 225 mg, protein 29g, sodium (na) 389 mg, phosphorous 190 mg

421. Chinese-style beef stew

Preparation time: 15 minutes
Cooking time: 6-8 hours
Servings: 6
Ingredients

- 2 medium carrots
- 2 green onions
- 2 celery stalks
- 1 medium green bell pepper, sliced
- 1 garlic clove
- 8 ounce of canned bean sprouts
- 8 ounce of canned water chestnuts
- 2 tablespoon of coconut oil
- 12ounce lean casserole beef, cut into cubes
- ½ cup low-sodium beef stock
- 1 tablespoon brown sugar
- 1/4 cup white wine vinegar
- 1 red chili, finely diced
- 1 ½ cups of water
- 3 cups cooked white rice

Directions

1. Slice the carrots, green onions, celery and green pepper.
2. Crush the garlic. (hint: use the flat edge of a knife to do this easily.)
3. Rinse and slice the bamboo shoots and water chestnuts.
4. Heat the coconut oil and just brown the beef all over.
5. Transfer the beef to the slow cooker.
6. Add all the ingredients except the water.
7. Stir, it and then cover and cook on low for 6 to 8 hours.

8. Turn the slow cooker up to high.
9. Add the cold water to the slow cooker.
10. Stir it in to make it smooth, and leave the cooker lid slightly open.
11. Cook for a further 15 minutes.
12. Serve your dish over a bed of rice.

Nutrition: per serving: calories: 267protein: 14gcarbohydrates: 31g fat: 9g cholesterol: 35mg sodium: 166mg potassium: 319mg phosphorus: 148mg calcium: 41mg fiber: 3g

422. Meatball Soup

Preparation Time: 20 minutes
Cooking Time: 40 minutes
Servings: 6
Ingredients:

- ½ pound lean ground beef
- 2 tablespoons breadcrumbs
- 1 tablespoon chopped fresh parsley
- 1 teaspoon minced garlic
- 1 teaspoon olive oil
- ½ sweet onion, chopped
- 5 cups of water
- 2 celery stalks with the greens, chopped
- 1 carrot, diced
- Freshly ground black pepper

Directions:

1. Mix the ground beef, breadcrumbs, parsley, and garlic in a large bowl. Roll the meat mixture into small (1-inch) meatballs.
2. Add the onion in a large saucepan, and sauté until softened, about 3 minutes.
3. Add the water, celery, and carrot, and bring to a boil. Add the meatballs, reduce the heat to medium-low, and simmer until the vegetables are tender and the meatballs are cooked through about 35 minutes.
4. Season the soup with pepper and serve hot.

Nutrition: Calories: 106 Total fat: 3g Carbohydrates: 4g Protein: 9g Sodium: 53mg Phosphorus: 92mg Potassium: 200mg

423. Pesto Green Vegetable Soup

Preparation Time: 10 minutes
Cooking Time: 15 minutes
Servings: 1

Ingredients:

- 2 teaspoons olive oil
- 1 sliced leek, white and light green
- 2 celery stalks, diced
- 1 teaspoon minced garlic
- 2 cups sodium-free chicken stock
- 1 cup chopped snow peas
- 1 tablespoon chopped fresh thyme
- Juice and zest of ½ lemon
- ¼ teaspoon freshly ground black pepper
- 1 tablespoon Basil Pesto

Directions:

1. Add olive oil in a large saucepan.
2. Add the leek, celery, and garlic, and sauté until tender, about 3 minutes.
3. Stir in the stock and bring to a boil.
4. Stir in the snow peas, and thyme, and simmer for about 5 minutes.
5. Remove the pan from the heat, and stir in the lemon juice, lemon zest, pepper, and pesto.
6. Serve immediately.

Nutrition: Calories: 170 Fat: 13g Carbohydrates: 8g Protein: 3g Sodium: 333mg Phosphorus: 42mg Potassium: 200mg

424. One-pot chicken pie stew

Preparation time: 15 minutes
Cooking time: 1 hour 15 minutes
Servings: 8

Ingredients

- Fresh chicken breast (skinless and boneless) – 1½ pounds
- Low-sodium chicken stock – 2 cups
- Canola oil – ¼ cup
- Flour – ½ cup
- Fresh carrots (diced) – ½ cup
- Fresh onions (diced) – ½ cup
- Fresh celery (diced) – ¼ cup
- Black pepper – ½ teaspoon
- Italian seasoning (sodium-free) – 1 tablespoon
- Low-sodium better than bouillon® chicken base – 2 teaspoons
- Frozen sweet peas (thawed) – ½ cup
- Heavy cream – ½ cup
- Frozen piecrust (cooked, broken into bite-sized pieces) – 1
- Cheddar cheese (low-fat) – 1 cup

Directions

1. Start by pounding the chicken to tenderize it. Cut into small equal-sized cubes.
2. Place it over a medium-high flame. Add in the stock and the chicken. Cook for about 30 minutes.
3. Add in the flour and oil, while the chicken is cooking, mix well to combine.
4. Stir the flour and oil mixture into the broth mixture. Keep stirring until the chicken broth starts to thicken.
5. Reduce the flame to low and cook for another 15 minutes.
6. Now add in the carrots, celery, onions, italian seasoning, bouillon, and black pepper. Cook for another 15 minutes.
7. Add in the cream and peas after turning off the flame. Keep stirring to mix well.
8. Transfer into soup mugs and top with the cheese and broken pie crust pieces.

Nutrition: protein – 26 g carbohydrates – 22 g fat – 21 g cholesterol – 82 mg sodium – 424 mg potassium – 209 mg phosphorus – 290 mg calcium – 88 mg fiber – 2 g

425. Easy Low-Sodium Chicken Broth

Preparation Time: 10 minutes
Cooking Time: 4 hours
Servings: 1
Ingredients:

- 2 pounds skinless whole chicken, cut into pieces
- 4 garlic cloves, lightly crushed
- 2 celery stalks, with greens, roughly chopped
- 2 carrots, roughly chopped
- 1 sweet onion, cut into quarters
- 10 peppercorns
- 4 fresh thyme sprigs
- 2 bay leaves
- Water

Directions:

1. In a large stockpot, place the chicken, garlic, celery, carrots, onion, peppercorns, thyme, and bay leaves, and cover with water by about 3 inches.
2. Let the water boil over high heat. Simmer for about 4 hours in low heat.
3. Skim off any foam on top of the stock and pour the stock through a fine-mesh sieve.
4. Pick off all the usable chicken meat for another recipe, discard the bones and other solids, and allow the stock to cool for about 30 minutes before transferring it to sealable containers.
5. You can put the stock in the refrigerator for 1 week or up to 2 months in the freezer.

Nutrition: Calories: 32 Carbohydrates: 8g Protein: 1g Sodium: 57mg Potassium: 187mg Phosphorus: 50mg

426. Vegetable Minestrone

Preparation Time: 20 minutes
Cooking Time: 20 minutes
Servings: 6
Ingredients:

- 1 teaspoon olive oil
- ½ sweet onion, chopped
- 1 celery stalk, diced
- 1 teaspoon minced garlic
- 2 cups sodium-free chicken stock
- 1 zucchini, diced
- ½ cup shredded stemmed kale
- Freshly ground black pepper
- 1-ounce grated Parmesan cheese

Directions:

1. Prepare a large saucepan over medium-high heat.
2. Add the onion, celery, and garlic. Sauté until softened, about 5 minutes.
3. Stir in the stock, zucchini, and bring to a boil. Let it simmer for 15 minutes.
4. Stir in the kale and season with pepper.
5. Garnish with the parmesan cheese and serve.

Nutrition: Calories: 100 Fat: 3g Carbohydrates: 6g Protein: 4g Sodium: 195mg Phosphorus: 70mg
Potassium: 200mg

427. Mushroom Mock Miso Soup

Preparation Time: 10 minutes
Cooking Time: 35 minutes
Servings: 6
Ingredients:

- 6 cups water, divided
- 2 ounces dried mixed mushrooms
- ¼ cup of seasoned rice vinegar
- 1 teaspoon low-sodium soy sauce
- 1 tablespoon grated peeled fresh ginger

- 1 cup julienned snow peas
- ½ cup grated carrot
- 2 scallions, green and white parts, chopped

Directions:
1. Prepare 2 cups of water in a small saucepan over high heat and bring to a boil.
2. Place the dried mushrooms in a medium bowl and pour the boiling water over them. Let the mushrooms reconstitute for 30 minutes, then remove them from the water and slice them thinly.
3. Transfer the mushroom water, the remaining 4 cups of water, vinegar, soy sauce, ginger to a large saucepan, and place over medium-high heat.
4. Bring to a boil, then put mushrooms, snow peas, and carrot. Reduce the heat to low, and simmer for 5 minutes.
5. Serve hot, topped with the scallions.

Nutrition: Calories: 56 Fat: 0g Carbohydrates: 9g Protein: 2g Sodium: 118mg Phosphorus: 43mg
Potassium: 198mg

428. Cream of pepper Soup

Preparation Time: 15 minutes
Cooking Time: 30 minutes
Servings: 4
Ingredients:
- 1 tablespoon olive oil
- ½ sweet onion, chopped
- 2 teaspoons minced garlic
- 4 cups fresh pepper
- ¼ cup chopped fresh parsley
- 3 cups of water
- ¼ cup heavy (whipping) cream
- 1 tablespoon freshly squeezed lemon juice
- Freshly ground black pepper

Directions:

1. On a heated olive oil, sauté the onion and garlic in a large saucepan for 3 minutes.
2. Add the pepper and parsley, and sauté for 5 minutes.
3. Stir in the water, bring to a boil, and then reduce the heat to low. Simmer the soup until the vegetables are tender, about 20 minutes.
4. Let it cool for 5 minutes, then, along with the heavy cream, purée the soup in batches in a food processor (or a blender or a handheld immersion blender).
5. Return the soup to the pot and cook through on low heat.
6. Add the lemon juice, season with pepper, and stir to combine. Serve hot.

Nutrition: Calories: 141 Fat: 14g Carbohydrates: 3g Protein: 2g Sodium: 36mg Phosphorus: 38mg
Potassium: 200mg

429. Spring Veggie Soup

Preparation Time: 20 minutes
Cooking Time: 45 minutes
Servings: 5
Ingredients:
- 2 tablespoons olive oil
- 1/2 cup onion, diced
- 1/2 cup mushrooms, sliced
- 1/8 cup celery, chopped
- 1 tomato, diced
- 1/2 cup carrots, diced
- 1 cup green beans, trimmed
- 1/2 cup frozen corn
- 1 teaspoon garlic powder
- 1 teaspoon dried oregano leaves
- 4 cups low-sodium vegetable broth

Directions:
1. In a pot, pour the olive oil and cook the onion and celery for 2 minutes.

2. Add the rest of the ingredients.
3. Bring to a boil.
4. Reduce heat and simmer for 45 minutes.

Nutrition: Calories: 136 Fat: 11g Carbohydrates: 17g Protein: 7g Sodium: 138mg Potassium: 527mg Phosphorus: 125mg

430. Chicken Alphabet Soup

Preparation Time: 15 minutes
Cooking Time: 35 minutes
Servings: 6
Ingredients:
- 1 tablespoon olive oil
- ½ sweet onion, diced
- 2 teaspoons minced garlic
- 4 cups of water
- 1½ cups chopped cooked chicken breast
- 1 cup sodium-free chicken stock
- 2 celery stalks, chopped
- 1 carrot, peeled and diced
- ½ cup dried alphabet noodles
- Freshly ground black pepper
- 2 tablespoons chopped fresh parsley

Directions:
1. Put olive oil in a large saucepan with medium-high heat.
2. Add the onion and garlic. Cook until softened, about 3 minutes.
3. Add the water, chicken, chicken stock, celery, and carrot. Bring to a boil, then reduce the heat to medium-low and simmer until the vegetables are tender-crisp about 15 minutes.
4. Add the noodles, stir, and simmer the soup until the noodles are tender about 15 minutes.
5. Season with pepper. Serve hot with topped parsley.

Nutrition: Calories: 132 Fat: 3g Carbohydrates: 10g Protein: 13g Sodium: 95mg Phosphorus: 116mg

Potassium: 200mg

431. Vegetable Stew

Preparation Time: 15 minutes
Cooking Time: 15 minutes
Servings: 8
Ingredients:
- 1 teaspoon olive oil
- 1 sweet onion, chopped
- 1 teaspoon minced garlic
- 2 zucchinis, chopped
- 1 red bell pepper, diced
- 2 carrots, chopped
- 2 cups low-sodium vegetable stock
- 2 cups broccoli florets
- 1 teaspoon ground coriander
- ½ teaspoon ground cumin
- Pinch cayenne pepper
- Freshly ground black pepper
- 2 tablespoons chopped fresh cilantro

Directions:
1. Cook garlic and onion in a saucepan until softened.
2. Put zucchini, bell pepper, and carrots, and sauté for 5 minutes.
3. Mix vegetable stock, broccoli, coriander, cumin, and cayenne pepper.
4. Let it boil and simmer to medium-low until the vegetables are tender, often stirring about 5 minutes.
5. Add pepper and serve hot, topped with the cilantro.

Nutrition: Calories: 45 Fat: 1g Carbohydrates: 5g Protein: 1g Sodium: 194mg Phosphorus: 21mg
Potassium: 184mg

432. Vibrant Carrot Soup

Preparation Time: 15 minutes
Cooking Time: 25 minutes
Servings: 4

189

Ingredients:

- 1 tablespoon olive oil
- ½ sweet onion, chopped
- 2 teaspoons grated peeled fresh ginger
- 1 teaspoon minced fresh garlic
- 4 cups of water
- 3 carrots, chopped
- 1 teaspoon ground turmeric
- ½ cup of coconut milk
- 1 tablespoon chopped fresh cilantro

Directions:

1. Heat the olive oil in a saucepan.
2. Sauté the onion, ginger, and garlic until softened.
3. Stir in the water, carrots, and turmeric. Bring the soup to a boil, reduce the heat to low, and simmer until the carrots are tender about 20 minutes.
4. Transfer the soup in batches to a food processor (or blender) and process with the coconut milk until the soup is smooth.
5. Reheat the soup in a pan.
6. Serve topped with the cilantro.

Nutrition: Calories: 113 Fat: 10g Protein: 1g Carbohydrates: 7g Sodium: 30mg Phosphorus: 50mg Potassium: 200mg;

433. Simple Cabbage Soup

Preparation Time: 20 minutes
Cooking Time: 35 minutes
Servings: 8
Ingredients:

- 1 tablespoon olive oil
- ½ sweet onion, chopped
- 2 teaspoons minced garlic
- 6 cups of water
- 1 cup sodium-free chicken stock
- ½ head green cabbage, shredded
- 2 carrots, diced
- Freshly ground black pepper
- 2 tablespoons chopped fresh thyme

Directions:

1. Prepare olive oil in a large saucepan over medium-high heat.
2. Sauté the onion and garlic until softened.
3. Add water, chicken stock, cabbage, carrots Let it bring it to a boil.
4. In medium-low heat, simmer the vegetables for 30 minutes or until tender.
5. Season the soup with black pepper. Serve hot, topped with the thyme.

Nutrition: Calories: 62 Fat: 2g Carbohydrates: 6g Protein: 2g Sodium: 61mg Phosphorus: 32mg Potassium: 200mg

434. Fennel Cauliflower Soup

Preparation Time: 20 minutes
Cooking Time: 30 minutes
Servings: 1
Ingredients:

- 1 teaspoon olive oil

- 1 small sweet onion, chopped
- 2 teaspoons minced garlic
- ½ small head cauliflower, cut into small florets
- 2 cups chopped fresh fennel
- 4 cups of water
- 2 teaspoons chopped fresh thyme
- ¼ cup heavy (whipping) cream

Directions:

1. Prepare a saucepan and heat the olive oil.
2. Put onion and garlic. Sauté until softened, about 3 minutes.
3. Add the cauliflower, fennel, and water. Let it boil, then reduce the heat to medium-low and simmer until the cauliflower is tender, about 20 minutes.
4. In batches, pour the soup into a food processor (or blender), and purée until smooth and creamy.
5. Return the soup to the pan. Stir in the thyme and cream—heat on medium-low until warmed through, about 5 minutes. Serve.

Nutrition: Calories: 105 Fat: 8g Carbohydrates: 5g Protein: 1g Sodium: 30mg Phosphorus: 41mg Potassium: 200mg

VEGETABLE

435. Thai Tofu Broth

Preparation time: 5 minutes
Cooking time: 15 minutes
Servings: 4 servings

Ingredients:

- 1 cup rice noodles
- ½ sliced onion
- 6 oz. drained, pressed and cubed tofu
- ¼ cup sliced scallions
- ½ cup water
- ½ cup chestnuts
- ½ cup rice almond milk
- 1 tbsp. lime juice
- 1 tbsp. coconut oil
- ½ finely sliced chili
- 1 cup snow peas

Directions:

1. Heat the oil in a wok on a high heat and then sauté the tofu until brown on each side.
2. Add the onion and sauté for 2-3 minutes.
3. Add the rice almond milk and water to the wok until bubbling.
4. Lower to medium heat and add the noodles, chili and water chestnuts.
5. Allow to simmer for 10-15 minutes and then add the sugar snap peas for 5 minutes.
6. Serve with a sprinkle of scallions.

Nutrition: Calories: 304 kcal; Total Fat: 13 g; Saturated Fat: 0 g; Cholesterol: 0 mg; Sodium: 36 mg; Total Carbs: 38 g; Fiber: 0 g; Sugar: 0 g; Protein: 9 g

436. Chinese Tempeh Stir Fry

Preparation time: 5 minutes
Cooking time: 15 minutes
Servings: 2 servings

Ingredients:

- 2 oz. sliced tempeh
- 1 cup cooked rice
- 1 minced garlic clove
- ½ cup green onions
- 1 tsp. minced fresh ginger
- 1 tbsp. coconut oil
- ½ cup corn

Directions:

1. Heat the oil in a skillet or wok on a high heat and add the garlic and ginger.
2. Sauté for 1 minute.
3. Now add the tempeh and cook for 5-6 minutes before adding the corn for a further 10 minutes.
4. Now add the green onions and serve over rice.

Nutrition: Calories: 304 kcal; Total Fat: 4 g; Saturated Fat: 0 g; Cholesterol: 0 mg; Sodium: 91 mg; Total Carbs: 35 g; Fiber: 0 g; Sugar: 0 g; Protein: 10 g

437. Roasted Peach Open-Face Sandwich

Preparation Time: 5 minutes
Cooking Time: 15 minutes
Servings: 4

Ingredients:

- 2 fresh peaches, peeled and sliced
- 1 tablespoon of extra-virgin olive oil
- 1 tablespoon of freshly squeezed lemon juice
- 1/8 teaspoon of salt
- 1/8 teaspoon of freshly ground black pepper
- 4 ounces of cream cheese, at room temperature
- 2 teaspoons of fresh thyme leaves
- 4 bread slices

Directions:

1. Preheat the oven to 400°F.
2. Arrange the peaches on a rimmed baking sheet. Brush them with olive oil on both sides.
3. Roast the peaches for 10 to 15 minutes, until they are lightly golden brown around the edges. Sprinkle with lemon juice, salt, and pepper.
4. In a small bowl, combine the cream cheese and thyme and mix well.
5. Toast the bread. Get the toasted bread and spread it with the cream cheese mixture. Top with the peaches and serve.

Nutrition: Calories: 250   Total fat: 13g Saturated fat: 6g Sodium: 376mg Phosphorus: 163mg Potassium: 260mg Carbohydrates: 28g Fiber: 3g Protein: 6g Sugar: 8g

438. Vegetable Fried Rice

Preparation time: 20 minutes
Cooking time: 20 minutes
Servings: 6 servings

Ingredients:

- Olive oil – 1 tbsp.
- Sweet onion – ½, chopped
- Grated fresh ginger – 1 tbsp.
- Minced garlic - 2 tsp
- Sliced carrots – 1 cup
- Chopped eggplant – ½ cup
- Peas – ½ cup
- Green beans – ½ cup, cut into 1-inch pieces
- Chopped fresh cilantro – 2 tbsp.
- Cooked rice – 3 cups

Directions:

1. Heat the olive oil in a skillet.
2. Sauté the ginger, onion, and garlic for 3 minutes or until softened.
3. Stir in carrot, eggplant, green beans, and peas and sauté for 3 minutes more.
4. Add cilantro and rice.
5. Sauté, constantly stirring, for about 10 minutes or until the rice is heated through.
6. Serve.

Nutrition: Calories: 189 kcal; Total Fat: 7 g; Saturated Fat: 0 g; Cholesterol: 0 mg; Sodium: 13 mg; Total Carbs: 28 g; Fiber: 0 g; Sugar: 0 g; Protein: 6 g

439. Couscous Burgers

Preparation time: 20 minutes
Cooking time: 10 minutes
Servings: 4 servings

Ingredients:
- chickpeas – ½ cup
- Chopped fresh cilantro – 2 tbsp.
- Chopped fresh parsley
- Lemon juice - 1 tbsp.
- Lemon zest – 2 tsp
- Minced garlic – 1 tsp
- Cooked couscous – 2 ½ cups
- Eggs – 2, lightly beaten
- Olive oil – 2 tbsp.

Directions:
1. Put the cilantro, chickpeas, parsley, lemon juice, lemon zest, and garlic in a food processor and pulse until a paste form.
2. Transfer the chickpea mixture to a bowl, and add the eggs and couscous. Mix well.
3. Chill the mixture in the refrigerator for 1 hour.
4. Form the couscous mixture into 4 patties.
5. Heat olive oil in a skillet.
6. Place the patties in the skillet, 2 at a time, gently pressing them down with the fork of a spatula.
7. Cook for 5 minutes or until golden, and flip the patties over.
8. Cook the other side for 5 minutes and transfer the cooked burgers to a plate covered with a paper towel.
9. Repeat with the remaining 2 burgers.

Nutrition: Calories: 242 kcal; Total Fat: 10 g; Saturated Fat: 0 g; Cholesterol: 0 mg; Sodium: 43 mg; Total Carbs: 29 g; Fiber: 0 g; Sugar: 0 g; Protein: 9 g

440. Egg White Frittata with Penne

Preparation time: 15 minutes
Cooking time: 30 minutes
Servings: 4 servings

Ingredients:
- Egg whites- 6
- Rice almond milk – ¼ cup
- Chopped fresh parsley – 1 tbsp.
- Chopped fresh thyme – 1 tsp
- Chopped fresh chives – 1 tsp
- Ground black pepper
- Olive oil – 2 tsp.
- Small sweet onion – ¼, chopped
- Minced garlic – 1 tsp
- Boiled and chopped red bell pepper – ½ cup
- Cooked penne – 2 cups

Directions:
1. Preheat the oven to 350f.
2. In a bowl, whisk together the egg whites, rice almond milk, parsley, thyme, chives, and pepper.
3. Heat the oil in a skillet.
4. Sauté the onion, garlic, red pepper for 4 minutes or until they are softened.
5. Add the cooked penne to the skillet.
6. Pour the egg mixture over the pasta and shake the pan to coat the pasta.
7. Leave the skillet on the heat for 1 minute to set the frittata's bottom and then transfer the skillet to the oven.
8. Bake the frittata for 25 minutes, or until it is set and golden brown.
9. Serve.

Nutrition: Calories: 170 kcal; Total Fat: 3 g; Saturated Fat: 0 g; Cholesterol: 0 mg; Sodium: 90 mg; Total Carbs: 25 g; Fiber: 0 g; Sugar: 0 g; Protein: 10 g

441. Curried Cauliflower

Preparation time: 5 minutes
Cooking time: 20 minutes
Servings: 4 servings

Ingredients:
- 1 tsp. turmeric
- 1 diced onion

- 1 tbsp. chopped fresh cilantro
- 1 tsp. cumin
- ½ diced chili
- ½ cup water
- 1 minced garlic clove
- 1 tbsp. coconut oil
- 1 tsp. garam masala
- 2 cups cauliflower florets

Directions:
1. Add the oil to a skillet on medium heat.
2. Sauté the onion and garlic for 5 minutes until soft.
3. Add the cumin, turmeric and garam masala and stir to release the aromas.
4. Now add the chili to the pan along with the cauliflower.
5. Stir to coat.
6. Pour in the water and reduce the heat to a simmer for 15 minutes.
7. Garnish with cilantro to serve.

Nutrition: Calories: 108 kcal; Total Fat: 7 g; Saturated Fat: 0 g; Cholesterol: 0 mg; Sodium: 35 mg; Total Carbs: 11 g; Fiber: 0 g; Sugar: 0 g; Protein: 2 g

442. Chili Tofu Noodles

Preparation time: 5 minutes
Cooking Time: 15 minutes
Servings: 4 servings

Ingredients:
- ½ diced red chili
- 2 cups rice noodles
- ½ juiced lime
- 6 oz. pressed and cubed silken firm tofu
- 1 tsp. grated fresh ginger
- 1 tbsp. coconut oil
- 1 cup green beans
- 1 minced garlic clove

Directions:
1. Steam the green beans for 10-12 minutes or according to package directions and drain.

2. Cook the noodles in a pot of boiling water for 10-15 minutes or according to package directions.
3. Meanwhile, heat a wok or skillet on a high heat and add coconut oil.
4. Now add the tofu, chili flakes, garlic and ginger and sauté for 5-10 minutes.
5. Drain the noodles and add to the wok along with the green beans and lime juice.
6. Toss to coat.
7. Serve hot!

Nutrition: Calories: 246 kcal; Total Fat: 12 g; Saturated Fat: 0 g; Cholesterol: 0 mg; Sodium: 25 mg; Total Carbs: 28 g; Fiber: 0 g; Sugar: 0 g; Protein: 10 g

443. Roasted Veggie Sandwiches

Preparation Time: 20 minutes
Cooking Time: 35 minutes
Servings: 6

Ingredients:
- 3 bell peppers, assorted colors, sliced
- 1 cup of sliced yellow summer squash
- 1 red onion, sliced
- 2 tablespoons of extra-virgin olive oil
- 2 tablespoons of balsamic vinegar
- 1/8 teaspoon of salt
- 1/8 teaspoon of freshly ground black pepper

- 3 large whole-wheat pita breads, halved

Directions:

1. Preheat the oven to 400°F.
2. Prepare a parchment paper and line it in a rimmed baking sheet.
3. Spread the bell peppers, squash, and onion on the prepared baking sheet. Sprinkle with the olive oil, vinegar, salt, and pepper.
4. Roast for 30 to 40 minutes, turning the vegetables with a spatula once during cooking, until they are tender and light golden brown.
5. Pile the vegetables into the pita breads and serve.

Nutrition Calories: 18 Total fat: 5g Saturated fat: 1g Sodium: 234mg Phosphorus: 106mg Potassium: 289mg Carbohydrates: 31g Fiber: 4g Protein: 5g Sugar: 6g

444. Curried Veggie Stir-Fry

Preparation Time: 20 minutes
Cooking Time: 10 minutes
Servings: 6

Ingredients:

- 2 tablespoons of extra-virgin olive oil
- 1 onion, chopped
- 4 garlic cloves, minced
- 4 cups of frozen stir-fry vegetables
- 1 cup unsweetened full-fat coconut almond milk
- 1 cup of water
- 2 tablespoons of green curry paste

Directions:

1. In a wok or non-stick, heat the olive oil over medium-high heat. Stir-fry the onion and garlic for 2 to 3 minutes, until fragrant.
2. Add the frozen stir-fry vegetables and continue to cook for 3 to 4 minutes longer, or until the vegetables are hot.
3. Meanwhile, in a small bowl, combine coconut almond milk, water, and curry paste. Stir until the paste dissolves.
4. Add the broth mixture to the wok and cook for another 2 to 3 minutes, or until the sauce has reduced slightly and all the vegetables are crisp-tender.
5. Serve over couscous or hot cooked rice.

Nutrition: Calories: 293 Total fat: 18g Saturated fat: 10g Sodium: 247mg Phosphorus: 138mg Potassium: 531mg Carbohydrates: 28g Fiber: 7g Protein: 7 Sugar: 4g

445. Delicious Vegetarian Lasagne

Preparation time: 10 minutes
Cooking time: 1 hour
Servings: 4 servings

Ingredients:

- 1 tsp. basil
- 1 tbsp. olive oil
- ½ sliced red pepper
- 3 lasagna sheets
- ½ diced red onion
- ¼ tsp. black pepper
- 1 cup rice almond milk
- 1 minced garlic clove
- 1 cup sliced eggplant
- ½ sliced zucchini
- ½ pack soft tofu
- 1 tsp. oregano

Directions:

1. Preheat oven to 325°F/Gas Mark 3.

2. Slice zucchini, eggplant and pepper into vertical strips.
3. Add the rice almond milk and tofu to a food processor and blitz until smooth. Set aside.
4. Heat the oil in a skillet over medium heat and add the onions and garlic for 3-4 minutes or until soft.
5. Sprinkle in the herbs and pepper and allow to stir through for 5-6 minutes until hot.
6. Into a lasagne or suitable oven dish, layer 1 lasagna sheet, then 1/3 the eggplant, followed by 1/3 zucchini, then 1/3 pepper before pouring over 1/3 of tofu white sauce.
7. Repeat for the next 2 layers, finishing with the white sauce.
8. Add to the oven for 40-50 minutes or until veg is soft and easily be sliced into servings.

Nutrition: Calories: 235 kcal; Total Fat: 9 g; Saturated Fat: 0 g; Cholesterol: 0 mg; Sodium: 35 mg; Total Carbs: 10 g; Fiber: 0 g; Sugar: 0 g; Protein: 5 g

446. Creamy Veggie Casserole

Preparation Time: 25 minutes
Cooking Time: 35 minutes
Servings: 4
Ingredients:
- 1/3 cup extra-virgin olive oil, divided
- 1 onion, chopped
- 2 tablespoons flour
- 3 cups low-sodium vegetable broth
- 3 cups frozen California blend vegetables
- 1 cup crushed crisp rice cereal

Directions:
1. Preheat the oven to 375°F.
2. Next is heat 2 tablespoons of olive oil in a large skillet over medium heat. Add the onion and cook for 3 to 4 minutes, stirring, until the onion is tender.
3. Add the flour and stir for 2 minutes.
4. Add the broth to the saucepan, stirring for 3 to 4 minutes, or until the sauce starts to thicken.
5. Add the vegetables to the saucepan. Simmer and cook until vegetables are tender (for six to eight minutes).
6. When the vegetables are done, pour the mixture into a 3-quart casserole dish.
7. Sprinkle the vegetables with the crushed cereal.
8. Bake for 20 to 25 minutes or until the cereal is golden brown and the filling is bubbling. Let cool for 5 minutes and serve.

Nutrition: Calories: 234 Total fat: 18g Saturated fat: 3g Sodium: 139mg Phosphorus: 21mg Potassium: 210mg Carbohydrates: 16g Fiber: 3g Protein: 3g Sugar: 5g

447. Pasta Fagioli

Preparation Time: 25 minutes
Cooking Time: 25 minutes
Servings: 6
Ingredients:
- 1 (15-ounce) can low-sodium great northern beans, drained and rinsed, divided

- 2 cups frozen peppers and onions, thawed, divided
- 5 cups low-sodium vegetable broth
- 1/8 teaspoon salt
- 1/8 teaspoon freshly ground black pepper
- 1 cup whole-grain orecchiette pasta
- 2 tablespoons extra-virgin olive oil
- 1/3 cup grated Parmesan cheese

Directions:

1. In a large saucepan, place the beans and cover with water. Bring to a boil over high heat and boil for 10 minutes. Drain the beans.
2. In a food processor or blender, combine 1/3 cup of beans and 1/3 cup of thawed peppers and onions. Process until smooth.
3. In the same saucepan, combine the pureed mixture, the remaining 12/3 cups of peppers and onions, the remaining beans, the broth, and the salt and pepper and bring to a simmer.
4. Add the pasta to the saucepan. Make sure to stir it and bring it to boil, reduce the heat to low, and simmer for 8 to 10 minutes, or until the pasta is tender.
5. Serve drizzled with olive oil and topped with Parmesan cheese.

Nutrition: Calories: 245 Total fat: 7g Saturated fat: 2g Sodium: 269mg Phosphorus: 188mg Potassium: 592mg Carbohydrates: 36g Fiber: 7g Protein: 12g Sugar: 4g

448. Spicy Corn and Rice Burritos

Preparation Time: 10 minutes
Cooking Time: 20 minutes
Servings: 4

Ingredients:

- 3 tablespoons of extra-virgin olive oil, divided
- 1 (10-ounce) package of frozen cooked rice
- 1½ cups of frozen yellow corn
- 1 tablespoon of chili powder
- 1 cup of shredded pepper jack cheese
- 4 large or 6 small corn tortillas

Directions:

1. Put the skillet in over medium heat and put 2 tablespoons of olive oil. Add the rice, corn, and chili powder and cook for 4 to 6 minutes, or until the ingredients are hot.
2. Transfer the ingredients from the pan into a medium bowl. Let cool for 15 minutes.
3. Stir the cheese into the rice mixture.
4. Heat the tortillas using the directions from the package to make them pliable. Fill the corn tortillas with the rice mixture, then roll them up.
5. At this point, you can serve them as is, or you can fry them first. Heat the

remaining tablespoon of olive oil in a large skillet. Fry the burritos, seam-side down at first, turning once, until they are brown and crisp, about 4 to 6 minutes per side, then serve.

Nutrition: Calories: 386 Total fat: 21 Saturated fat: 7g Sodium: 510mg Phosphorus: 304mg Potassium: 282mg Carbohydrates: 41g Fiber: 4g Protein: 11g Sugar: 2g

449. Marinated Tofu Stir-Fry

Preparation time: 20 minutes
Cooking time: 20 minutes
Servings: 4 servings
Ingredients:
For the tofu:
- Lemon juice – 1 tbsp.
- Minced garlic – 1 tsp
- Grated fresh ginger – 1 tsp
- Pinch red pepper flakes
- Extra-firm tofu- 5 ounces, pressed well and cubed

For the stir-fry:
- Olive oil – 1 tbsp.
- Cauliflower florets – ½ cup
- Thinly sliced carrots – ½ cup
- Julienned red pepper – ½ cup
- Fresh green beans – ½ cup
- Cooked white rice – 2 cups

Directions:
1. In a bowl, mix the lemon juice, garlic, ginger, and red pepper flakes.
2. Add the tofu and toss to coat.
3. Place the bowl in the refrigerator and marinate for 2 hours.
4. To make the stir-fry, heat the oil in a skillet.
5. Sauté the tofu for 8 minutes or until it is lightly browned and heated through.

6. Add the carrots, and cauliflower and sauté for 5 minutes. Stirring and tossing constantly.
7. Add the red pepper and green beans, sauté for 3 minutes more.
8. Serve over white rice.

Nutrition: Calories: 190 kcal; Total Fat: 6 g; Saturated Fat: 0 g; Cholesterol: 0 mg; Sodium: 22 mg; Total Carbs: 30 g; Fiber: 0 g; Sugar: 0 g; Protein: 6 g

450. Crust less Cabbage Quiche

Preparation Time: 10 minutes
Cooking Time: 40 minutes
Servings: 6
Ingredients:
- Olive oil cooking spray
- 2 tablespoons of extra-virgin olive oil
- 3 cups of coleslaw blend with carrots
- 3 large eggs, beaten
- 3 large egg whites, beaten
- ½ cup of half-and-half
- 1 teaspoon of dried dill weed
- 1/8 teaspoon of salt
- 1/8 teaspoon of freshly ground black pepper
- 1 cup of grated Swiss cheese

Directions:

1. Preheat the oven to 350°F. Spray pie plate (9-inch) with cooking spray and set aside.
2. In a skillet, put an oil and put it in medium heat. Add the coleslaw mix and cook for 4 to 6 minutes, stirring, until the cabbage is tender. Transfer the vegetables from the pan to a medium bowl to cool.
3. Meanwhile, in another medium bowl, combine the eggs and egg whites, half-and-half, dill, salt, and pepper and beat to combine.
4. Stir the cabbage mixture into the egg mixture and pour into the prepared pie plate.
5. Sprinkle with the cheese.
6. Bake for 30 to 35 minutes, or until the mixture is puffed, set, and light golden brown. Let stand for 5 minutes, then slice to serve.

Nutrition: Calories: 203 Total fat: 16g Saturated fat: 6g Sodium: 321mg Phosphorus: 169mg Potassium: 155mg Carbohydrates: 5g Fiber: 1g Protein: 11g Sugar: 4g

451. Chilaquiles

Preparation Time: 20 minutes
Cooking Time: 20 minutes
Servings: 4
Ingredients:

- 3 (8-inch) corn tortillas, cut into strips
- 2 tablespoons of extra-virgin olive oil
- 12 tomatillos, papery covering removed, chopped
- 3 tablespoons for freshly squeezed lime juice
- 1/8 teaspoon of salt
- 1/8 teaspoon of freshly ground black pepper
- 4 large egg whites
- 2 large eggs
- 2 tablespoons of water
- 1 cup of shredded pepper jack cheese

Directions:
1. In a dry nonstick skillet, toast the tortilla strips over medium heat until they are crisp, tossing the pan and stirring occasionally. This should take 4 to 6 minutes. Remove the strips from the pan and set aside.
2. In the same skillet, heat the olive oil over medium heat and add the tomatillos, lime juice, salt, and pepper. Cook and frequently stir for about 8 to 10 minutes until the tomatillos break down and form a sauce. Transfer the sauce to a bowl and set aside.
3. In a small bowl, beat the egg whites, eggs, and water and add to the skillet. Cook the eggs for 3 to 4 minutes, stirring occasionally until they are set and cooked to 160°F.
4. Preheat the oven to 400°F.
5. Toss the tortilla strips in the tomatillo sauce and place in a casserole dish. Top with the scrambled eggs and cheese.
6. Bake for 10 to 15 minutes, or until the cheese starts to brown. Serve.

Nutrition: Calories: 312 Total fat: 20g Saturated fat: 8g Sodium: 345mg Phosphorus: 280mg Potassium: 453mg Carbohydrates: 19g Fiber: 3g Protein: 15g Sugar: 5g

452. Vegetable Confetti

Preparation Time: 25 minutes
Cooking Time: 15 minutes
Servings: 1

Ingredients:

- ½ red bell pepper
- ½ green pepper, boiled and chopped
- 4 scallions, thinly sliced
- ½ tsp. of ground cumin
- 3 tbsp. of vegetable oil
- 1 ½ tbsp. of white wine vinegar
- Black pepper to taste

Directions:

1. Join all fixings and blend well.
2. Chill in the fridge.
3. You can include a large portion of slashed jalapeno pepper for an increasingly fiery blend

Nutrition: Calories: 230   Fat: 25g Fiber: 3g Carbs: 24g Protein: 43g

453. Vegetable Green Curry

Preparation Time: 20 minutes
Cooking Time: 20 minutes
Servings: 6

Ingredients:

- 2 tablespoons extra-virgin olive oil
- 1 head broccoli, cut into florets
- 1 bunch asparagus, cut into 2-inch lengths
- 3 tablespoons water
- 2 tablespoons green curry paste

- 1 medium eggplant
- 1/8 teaspoon salt
- 1/8 teaspoon freshly ground black pepper
- 2/3 cup plain whole-almond milk yogurt

Directions:

1. Put olive oil in a large saucepan in a medium heat. Add the broccoli and stir-fry for 5 minutes. Add the asparagus and stir-fry for another 3 minutes.
2. Meanwhile, in a small bowl, combine the water with the green curry paste.
3. Add the eggplant, curry-water mixture, salt, and pepper. Stir-fry or until vegetables are all tender.
4. Add the yogurt. Heat through but avoid simmering. Serve.

Nutrition: Calories: 113 Total fat: 6g Saturated fat: 1g Sodium: 174mg Phosphorus: 117mg Potassium: 569mg Carbohydrates: 13g Fiber: 6g Protein: 5g Sugar: 7g

454. Zucchini Bowl

Preparation Time: 10 minutes
Cooking Time: 20 minutes
Servings: 4

Ingredients:

- 1 onion, chopped
- 3 zucchini, cut into medium chunks

- 2 tablespoons coconut almond milk
- 2 garlic cloves, minced
- 4 cups chicken stock
- 2 tablespoons coconut oil
- Pinch of salt
- Black pepper to taste

Directions:
1. Take a pot and place it over medium heat
2. Add oil and let it heat up
3. Add zucchini, garlic, onion, and stir
4. Cook for 5 minutes
5. Add stock, salt, pepper, and stir
6. Bring to a boil and lower down the heat
7. Simmer for 20 minutes.
8. Remove heat and add coconut almond milk
9. Use an immersion blender until smooth
10. Ladle into soup bowls and serve
11. Enjoy!

Nutrition: Calories: 160 Fat: 2g
Carbohydrates: 4g Protein: 7g

455. Nice Coconut Haddock

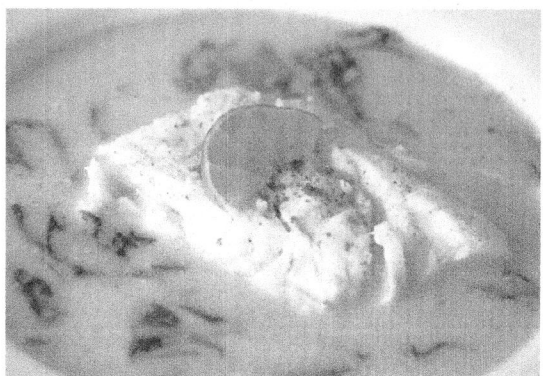

Preparation Time: 10 minutes
Cooking Time: 12 minutes
Servings: 3
Ingredients:
- 4 haddock fillets, 5 ounces each, boneless
- 2 tablespoons coconut oil, melted

- 1 cup coconut, shredded and unsweetened
- ¼ cup hazelnuts, ground
- Salt to taste

Directions:
1. Preheat your oven to 400 °F
2. Line a baking sheet with parchment paper
3. Keep it on the side
4. Pat fish fillets with a paper towel and season with salt
5. Take a bowl and stir in hazelnuts and shredded coconut
6. Drag fish fillets through the coconut mix until both sides are coated well
7. Transfer to a baking dish
8. Brush with coconut oil
9. Bake for about 12 minutes until flaky
10. Serve and enjoy!

Nutrition: Calories: 299 Fat: 24g
Carbohydrates: 1g Protein: 20g

456. Vegetable Rice Casserole

Preparation Time: 10 minutes
Cooking Time: 50 minutes
Servings: 4
Ingredients:
- 1 teaspoon of olive oil
- ½ small sweet onion, chopped
- ½ teaspoon of minced garlic
- ½ cup of chopped red bell pepper
- ¼ cup of grated carrot
- 1 cup of white basmati rice
- 2 cups of water
- ¼ cup of grated Parmesan cheese
- Freshly ground black pepper

Directions:
1. Preheat the oven to 350°f.
2. In a medium skillet over medium-high heat, heat the olive oil.

3. Add the onion and garlic, and sauté until softened, about 3 minutes.
4. Transfer the vegetables to a 9-by-9-inch baking dish, and stir in the rice and water.
5. Cover the dish and bake until the liquid is absorbed 35 to 40 minutes.
6. Sprinkle the cheese on top and bake an additional 5 minutes to melt.
7. Season the casserole with pepper, and serve.
8. Substitution tip: Not surprisingly, the cheesy topping on this casserole elevates it to a truly sublime experience. You can also try feta, Cheddar cheese, and goat cheese for different tastes and textures.

Nutrition: Calories: 224 total fat: 3g Saturated fat: 1g Cholesterol: 6mg Sodium: 105mg Carbohydrates: 41g Fiber: 2g Phosphorus: 118mg Potassium: 176mg Protein: 6g Kidney Disease Stage 1

457. Curried Veggies and Rice

Preparation Time: 12 minutes
Cooking Time: 18 minutes
Servings: 4
Ingredients:
- 1/4 cup olive oil
- 1 cup long-grain white basmati rice
- 4 garlic cloves, minced
- 2 1/2 teaspoons curry powder
- 1/2 cup sliced shiitake mushrooms
- 1 red bell pepper, chopped
- 1 cup frozen, shelled edamame
- 2 cups low-sodium vegetable broth
- 1/8 teaspoon freshly ground black pepper

Directions:
1. Heat the olive oil on medium heat.

2. Add the rice, garlic, curry powder, mushrooms, bell pepper, and edamame; cook, stirring, for 2 minutes.
3. Add the broth and black pepper and bring to a boil.
4. Reduce the heat to low, partially cover the pot, and simmer for 15 to 18 minutes or until the rice is tender. Stir and serve.

Nutrition: Calories: 347 Fat: 16g Carbohydrates: 44g Protein: 8g Sodium: 114mg Phosphorus: 131mg Potassium: 334mg

458. Spicy Veggie Pancakes

Preparation Time: 10 minutes
Cooking Time: 10 minutes
Servings: 4
Ingredients:
- 3 tablespoons olive oil, divided
- 2 small onions, finely chopped
- 1 jalapeño pepper, minced
- 3/4 cup carrot, grated
- 3/4 cup cabbage, finely chopped
- 11/2 cups quick-cooking oats
- 3/4 cup of water
- ½ cup whole-wheat flour
- 1 large egg
- 1 large egg white
- 1 teaspoon baking soda
- 1/4 teaspoon cayenne pepper

Directions:
1. In a skillet, heat 2 teaspoons oil over medium heat.
2. Sauté the onion, jalapeño, carrot, and cabbage for 4 minutes.
3. While the veggies are cooking, combine the oats, rice, water, flour, egg, egg white, baking soda, and cayenne pepper in a medium bowl until well mixed.
4. Add the cooked vegetables to the mixture and stir to combine.

5. Heat the remaining oil in a large skillet over medium heat.
6. Drop the mixture into the skillet, about 1/3 cup per pancake. Cook for 4 minutes, or until bubbles form on the pancakes' surface and the edges look cooked, then carefully flip them over.
7. Repeat with the remaining mixture and serve.

Nutrition: Calories: 323 Fat: 11g Carbohydrates: 48g Protein: 10g Sodium: 366mg Potassium: 381mg Phosphorus: 263mg

459. Vegetable Biryani

Preparation Time: 10 minutes
Cooking Time: 15 minutes
Servings: 4
Ingredients:
- 2 tablespoons olive oil
- 1 onion, diced
- 4 garlic cloves, minced
- 1 tbsp. peeled and grated fresh ginger root
- 1 cup carrot, grated
- 2 cups chopped cauliflower
- 1 cup thawed frozen baby peas
- 2 teaspoons curry powder
- 1 cup low-sodium vegetable broth
- 3 cups of frozen cooked white rice

Directions:
1. Get a skillet and heat the olive oil on medium heat.
2. Add onion, garlic, and ginger root. Sauté, frequently stirring, until tender-crisp, 2 minutes.
3. Add the carrot, cauliflower, peas, and curry powder and cook for 2 minutes longer.
4. Put vegetable broth. Cover the skillet partially, and simmer on low for 6 to 7 minutes or until the vegetables are tender.

5. Meanwhile, heat the rice as directed on the package.
6. Stir the rice into the vegetable mixture and serve.

Nutrition: Calories: 378 Fat 16g Carbohydrates: 53g Protein: 8g Sodium: 113mg Potassium: 510mg Phosphorus: 236mg

460. Pesto Pasta Salad

Preparation Time: 15 minutes
Cooking Time: 15 minutes
Servings: 4
Ingredients:
- 1 cup fresh basil leaves
- ½ cup packed fresh flat-leaf parsley leaves
- ½ cup arugula, chopped
- 2 tablespoons Parmesan cheese, grated
- ¼ cup extra-virgin olive oil
- 3 tablespoons mayonnaise
- 2 tablespoons water
- 12 ounces whole-wheat rotini pasta
- 1 red bell pepper, chopped
- 1 medium yellow summer squash, sliced
- 1 cup frozen baby peas

Directions:
1. Boil water in a large pot.
2. Meanwhile, combine the basil, parsley, arugula, cheese, and olive oil in a blender or food processor. Process until the herbs are finely chopped. Add the mayonnaise and water, then process again. Set aside.
3. Prepare the pasta to the pot of boiling water; cook according to package directions, about 8 to 9 minutes. Drain well, reserving ¼ cup of the cooking liquid.
4. Combine the pesto, pasta, bell pepper, squash, and peas in a large bowl and toss gently, adding enough reserved pasta cooking liquid to make a sauce on the

salad. Serve immediately or cover and chill, then serve.

5. Store covered in the refrigerator for up to 3 days.

Nutrition: Calories: 378 Fat: 24g Carbohydrates: 35g Protein: 9g Sodium: 163mg Potassium: 472mg Phosphorus: 213mg

461. Spicy Mushroom Stir-Fry

Preparation Time: 10 minutes
Cooking Time: 10 minutes
Servings: 4
Ingredients:

- 1 cup low-sodium vegetable broth
- 2 tablespoons cornstarch
- 1 teaspoon low-sodium soy sauce
- 1/2 teaspoon ground ginger
- 1/8 teaspoon cayenne pepper
- 2 tablespoons olive oil
- 2 (8-ounce) packages sliced button mushrooms
- 1 red bell pepper, chopped
- 1 jalapeño pepper, minced
- 2 tablespoons sesame oil

Directions:

1. In a small bowl, whisk together the broth, cornstarch, soy sauce, ginger, and cayenne pepper and set aside.
2. Heat the olive oil in a wok or heavy skillet over high heat.
3. Add the mushrooms and peppers and stir-fry for 3 to 5 minutes or until the vegetables are tender-crisp.
4. Stir the broth mixture and add it to the wok; stir-fry for 3 to 5 minutes longer or until the vegetables are tender and the sauce has thickened.
5. Serve

Nutrition: Calories: 361 Fat: 16g Carbohydrates: 49g Protein: 8g Sodium: 95mg Phosphorus: 267mg Potassium: 582mg

462. Barley Blueberry Salad

Preparation Time: 15 minutes
Cooking Time: 15 minutes
Servings: 4
Ingredients:

- 1 cup quick-cooking barley
- 3 cups low-sodium vegetable broth
- 3 tablespoons extra-virgin olive oil
- 2 tablespoons freshly squeezed lemon juice
- 1 teaspoon yellow mustard
- 1 teaspoon honey
- 2 cups blueberries
- ¼ cup crumbled feta cheese

Directions:

1. Combine the barley and vegetable broth in a medium saucepan and bring to a simmer.
2. Reduce the heat to low, partially cover the pan, and simmer for 10 to 12 minutes or until the barley is tender.
3. Meanwhile, whisk together the olive oil, lemon juice, mustard, and honey in a serving bowl until blended.
4. Drain the barley if necessary and add to the bowl; toss to combine.
5. Add the blueberries, and feta and toss gently. Serve.

Nutrition: Calories: 345 Fat 16g Carbohydrates: 44g Protein: 7g Sodium: 259mg Potassium: 301mg Phosphorus: 152mg

463. Garlic Mashed Carrots

Preparation Time: 5 minutes
Cooking Time: 20 minutes
Servings: 4
Ingredients:

- 2 medium carrots, peeled and sliced
- ¼ cup butter
- ¼ cup 1% low-fat almond milk

- 2 garlic cloves

Directions:
1. Double-boil or soak the carrots to reduce potassium if you are on a low potassium diet.
2. Boil carrots and garlic until soft. Drain.
3. Beat the carrots and garlic with butter and almond milk until smooth.

Nutrition: Calories 168 Carbs 29g Protein 5g Sodium 59 Potassium 161g Phosphorous 57mg

464. Egg and Veggie Fajitas

Preparation Time: 15 minutes
Cooking Time: 10 minutes
Servings: 4
Ingredients:
- 3 large eggs
- 3 egg whites
- 2 teaspoons chili powder
- 1 tablespoon unsalted butter
- 1 onion, chopped
- 2 garlic cloves, minced
- 1 jalapeño pepper, minced
- 1 red bell pepper, chopped
- 1 cup frozen corn, thawed and drained
- 8 (6-inch) corn tortillas

Directions:
1. Whisk the eggs, egg whites, and chili powder in a small bowl until well combined. Set aside.
2. Prepare a large skillet and melt the butter on medium heat.
3. Sauté the onion, garlic, jalapeño, bell pepper, and corn until the vegetables are tender, 3 to 4 minutes.
4. Add the beaten egg mixture to the skillet. Cook, occasionally stirring, until the eggs form large curds and are set, 3 to 5 minutes.
5. Meanwhile, soften the corn tortillas as directed on the package.

6. Divide the egg mixture evenly among the softened corn tortillas. Roll the tortillas up and serve.

Nutrition: Calories: 316 Fat 14g Carbohydrates: 35g Protein: 14g Sodium: 167mg Potassium: 408mg Phosphorus: 287mg

465. Vegetarian Taco Salad

Preparation Time: 15 minutes
Cooking Time: 15 minutes
Servings: 2
Ingredients:
- 1½ cups canned low-sodium or no-salt-added pinto beans, rinsed and drained
- 1 (10-ounce) package frozen white rice, thawed
- 1 red bell pepper, chopped
- 3 scallions, white and green parts, chopped
- 1 jalapeño pepper, minced
- 1 cup frozen corn, thawed and drained
- 1 tablespoon chili powder
- 1 cup chopped romaine lettuce
- 2 cups chopped butter lettuce
- ½ cup Powerhouse Salsa
- ½ cup grated pepper Jack cheese

Directions:
1. In a medium bowl, combine the beans, rice, bell pepper, scallions, jalapeño, and corn.
2. Sprinkle with the chili powder and stir gently.
3. Stir in the romaine and butter lettuce.
4. Serve topped with Powerhouse Salsa and cheese.

Nutrition: Calories: 254 Fat: 7g Carbohydrates: 39g Protein: 11g Sodium: 440mg Potassium: 599mg Phosphorus: 240mg

466. Double-Boiled Country Style Fried Carrots

Preparation Time: 20 minutes
Cooking Time: 20 minutes
Servings: 4
Ingredients:

- ½ cup canola oil
- ¼ tsp ground cumin
- ¼ tsp paprika
- ¼ tsp white pepper
- 3 tbsp. ketchup

Directions:
1. Soak or double boil the carrots if you are on a low potassium diet.
2. Heat oil over medium heat in a skillet.
3. Fry the carrots for around 10 minutes until golden brown.
4. Drain carrots, then sprinkle with cumin, pepper, and paprika.
5. Serve with ketchup or mayo.

Nutrition: Calories 156 Fat 0.1g Carbs 21g Protein 2gSodium 3mg Potassium 296mg Phosphorous 34mg

467. Double-Boiled Stewed Carrots

Preparation Time: 20 minutes
Cooking Time: 30 minutes
Servings: 4
Ingredients:

- 2 cup carrots, diced into ½ inch cubes
- ½ cup hot water
- ½ cup liquid non-dairy creamer
- ¼ tsp garlic powder
- ¼ tsp black pepper
- 2 tbsp. margarine
- 2 tsp all-purpose white flour

Directions:
1. Soak or double boil the carrots if you are on a low potassium diet.
2. Boil carrots for 15 minutes.

3. Drain carrots and return to pan. Add half a cup of hot water, the creamer, garlic powder, pepper, and margarine. Heat to a boil.
4. Mix the flour with a tablespoon of water and then stir this into the carrots. Cook for 3 minutes until the mixture has thickened and the flour has cooked.

Nutrition: Calories 184 Carbs 25g Protein 2g Potassium 161mg Phosphorous 65mg

468. Sautéed Green Beans

Preparation Time: 10 minutes
Cooking Time: 15 minutes
Servings: 4
Ingredients:

- 2 cup frozen green beans
- ½ cup red bell pepper
- 4 tsp margarine
- ¼ cup onion
- 1 tsp dried dill weed
- 1 tsp dried parsley
- ¼ tsp black pepper

Directions:
1. Cook green beans in a large pan of boiling water until tender, then drain.
2. 2. While the beans are cooking, melt the margarine in a skillet and fry the other vegetables.
3. Add the beans to sautéed vegetables.
4. Sprinkle with freshly ground pepper and serve with meat and fish dishes.

Nutrition: Calories 67 Carbs 8g Protein 4g Sodium 5mg Potassium 179mg Phosphorous 32mg

469. Garlicky Penne Pasta with Asparagus

Preparation Time: 10 minutes
Cooking Time: 10 minutes
Servings: 4
Ingredients:

- 2 tbsp. butter
- 1lb asparagus, cut into 2-inch pieces
- 2 tsp lemon juice
- 4 cup whole wheat penne pasta, cooked
- ¼ cup shredded Parmesan cheese
- ¼ tsp Tabasco® hot sauce

Directions:
1. Add olive oil and butter in a skillet over medium heat.
2. Fry garlic and red pepper flakes for 2-3 minutes.
3. Add asparagus, Tabasco sauce, lemon juice, and black pepper to skillet and cook for a further 6 minutes.
4. Add hot pasta and cheese. Toss and serve.

Nutrition: Calories 387 Carbs 49g Protein 13gSodium 93 Potassium 258mg Phosphorous 252mg

470. Asparagus Fried Rice

Preparation Time: 10 minutes
Cooking Time: 10 minutes
Servings: 1
Ingredients:
- 3 large eggs, beaten
- ½ teaspoon ground ginger
- 2 teaspoons low-sodium soy sauce
- 2 tablespoons olive oil
- 1 onion, diced
- 4 garlic cloves, minced
- 1 cup sliced cremini mushrooms
- 1 (10-ounce) package frozen white rice, thawed
- 8 ounces fresh asparagus, about 15 spears, cut into 1-inch pieces
- 1 teaspoon sesame oil

Directions:
1. Whisk the eggs, ginger, and soy sauce in a small bowl and set aside.
2. Heat the olive oil in a medium skillet or wok over medium heat.

3. Add the onion and garlic and sauté for 2 minutes until tender crisp.
4. Add the mushrooms and rice; stir-fry for 3 minutes longer.
5. Put asparagus and cook for 2 minutes.6.
6. Pour in the egg mixture. Stir the eggs until cooked through, 2 to 3 minutes, and stir into the rice mixture.
7. Sprinkle the fried rice with the sesame oil and serve.

Nutrition: Calories: 247 Fat: 13g Carbohydrates: 25g Protein: 9g Sodium: 149mg Potassium: 367mg Phosphorus: 206mg

471. Pasta with Creamy Broccoli Sauce

Preparation Time: 15 minutes
Cooking Time: 15 minutes
Servings: 4
Ingredients:
- 2 tablespoons olive oil
- 1-pound broccoli florets
- 3 garlic cloves, halved
- 1 cup low-sodium vegetable broth
- ½ pound whole-wheat spaghetti pasta
- 4 ounces cream cheese
- 1 teaspoon dried basil leaves
- ½ cup grated Parmesan cheese

Directions:
1. Prepare a large pot of water to a boil.
2. Put olive oil in a large skillet. Sauté the broccoli and garlic for 3 minutes.
3. Add the broth to the skillet and bring to a simmer. Reduce the heat to low, partially cover the skillet, and simmer until the broccoli is tender about 5 to 6 minutes.
4. Cook the pasta according to package directions. Drain when al dente, reserving 1 cup pasta water.

5. When the broccoli is tender, add the cream cheese and basil—purée using an immersion blender.
6. Put mixture into a food processor, about half at a time, and purée until smooth and transfer the sauce back into the skillet.
7. Add the cooked pasta to the broccoli sauce. Toss, adding enough pasta water until the sauce coats the pasta completely. Sprinkle with the Parmesan and serve.

Nutrition: Calories: 302 Fat 14g Carbohydrates: 36g Protein: 11g Sodium: 260mg Potassium: 375mg Phosphorus: 223mg

472. Ginger Glazed Carrots

Preparation Time: 10 minutes
Cooking Time: 20 minutes
Servings: 4
Ingredients:
- 2 cups carrots, sliced into 1-inch pieces
- ¼ cup apple juice
- 2 tbsp. margarine, melted
- ¼ cup boiling water
- 1 tbsp. sugar
- 1 tsp cornstarch
- ¼ tsp salt
- ¼ tsp ground ginger

Directions:
1. Cook carrots until tender.
2. Mix sugar, cornstarch, salt, ginger, apple juice, and margarine together
3. Pour mixture over carrots and cook for 10 minutes until thickened.

Nutrition: Calories 101 Fat 3 Carbs 14g Protein 1g Sodium 87 Potassium 202g Phosphorous 26mg

473. Carrot-Apple Casserole

Preparation Time: 15 minutes
Cooking Time: 50 minutes

Servings: 8
Ingredients:
- 6 large carrots, peeled and sliced
- 4 large apples, peeled and sliced
- 3 tbsp. butter
- ½ cup apple juice
- 5 tbsp. all-purpose flour
- 2 tbsp. brown sugar
- ½ tsp ground nutmeg

Directions:
1. Preheat oven to 350° F.
2. Let the carrots boil for 5 minutes or until tender. Drain.
3. Arrange the carrots and apples in a large casserole dish.
4. Mix the flour, brown sugar, and nutmeg in a small bowl.
5. Rub in butter to make a crumb topping.
6. Sprinkle the crumb over the carrots and apples, then drizzle with juice.
7. Bake until bubbling and golden brown.

Nutrition: Calories 245 Fat 6g Carbs 49g Protein 1g Sodium 91mg Potassium 169mg Phosphorous 17mg

474. Creamy Shells with Peas and Bacon

Preparation Time: 15 minutes
Cooking Time: 15 minutes
Servings: 4
Ingredients:
- 1 cup part-skim ricotta cheese
- ½ cup grated Parmesan cheese
- 3 slices bacon, cut into strips
- 1 cup onion, chopped
- ¾ cup of frozen green peas
- 1 tbsp. olive oil
- ¼ tsp black pepper
- 3 garlic cloves, minced
- 3 cup cooked whole-wheat small shell pasta

- 1 tbsp. lemon juice
- 2 tbsp. unsalted butter

Directions:
1. Place ricotta, Parmesan cheese, butter, and pepper in a large bowl.
2. Cook bacon in a skillet until crisp. Set aside.
3. Add the garlic and onion to the same skillet and fry until soft. Add to bowl with ricotta.
4. Cook the peas and add to the ricotta.
5. Add half a cup of the reserved cooking water and lemon juice to the ricotta mixture and mix well.
6. Add the pasta, bacon, and peas to the bowl and mix well.
7. Put freshly ground black pepper and serve.

Nutrition: Calories 429 Fat 14g Carbs 27g Protein 13g Sodium 244mg Potassium 172mg Phosphorous 203mg

475. Rutabaga Latkes

Preparation Time: 15 minutes
Cooking Time: 7 minutes
Servings: 4
Ingredients:
- 1 teaspoon hemp seeds
- 1 teaspoon ground black pepper
- 7 oz. rutabaga, grated
- ½ teaspoon ground paprika
- 2 tablespoons coconut flour
- 1 egg, beaten
- 1 teaspoon olive oil

Directions:
1. Mix up together hemp seeds, ground black pepper, ground paprika, and coconut flour.
2. Then add grated rutabaga and beaten egg.
3. With the help of the fork combine together all the ingredients into the smooth mixture.
4. Preheat the skillet for 2-3 minutes over the high heat.
5. Then reduce the heat till medium and add olive oil.
6. With the help of the fork, place the small amount of rutabaga mixture in the skillet. Flatten it gently in the shape of latkes.
7. Cook the latkes for 3 minutes from each side.
8. After this, transfer them in the plate and repeat the same steps with remaining rutabaga mixture.

Nutrition: Calories 64, Fat 3.1, Fiber 3, Carbs 7.1, Protein 2.8

476. Glazed Snap Peas

Preparation Time: 10 minutes
Cooking Time: 5 minutes
Servings: 2
Ingredients:
- 1 cup snap peas
- 2 teaspoon Erythritol
- 1 teaspoon butter, melted
- ¾ teaspoon ground nutmeg
- ¼ teaspoon salt
- 1 cup water, for cooking

Directions:
1. Pour water in the pan. Add snap peas and bring them to boil.
2. Boil the snap peas for 5 minutes over the medium heat.
3. Then drain water and chill the snap peas.
4. Meanwhile, whisk together ground nutmeg, melted butter, salt, and Erythritol.
5. Preheat the mixture in the microwave oven for 5 seconds.
6. Pour the sweet butter liquid over the snap peas and shake them well.
7. The side dish should be served only warm.

Nutrition: Calories 80, Fat 2.5, Fiber 3.9, Carbs 10.9, Protein 4

477. Steamed Collard Greens

Preparation Time: 10 minutes
Cooking Time: 5 minutes
Servings: 2
Ingredients:

- 2 cups Collard Greens
- 1 tablespoon lime juice
- 1 teaspoon olive oil
- 1 teaspoon sesame seeds
- ½ teaspoon chili flakes
- 1 cup water, for the steamer

Directions:
1. Chop collard greens roughly.
2. Pour water in the steamer and insert rack.
3. Place the steamer bowl, add collard greens, and close the lid.
4. Steam the greens for 5 minutes.
5. After this, transfer the steamed collard greens in the salad bowl.
6. Sprinkle it with the lime juice, olive oil, sesame seeds, and chili flakes.
7. Mix up greens with the help of 2 forks and leave to rest for 10 minutes before serving.

Nutrition: Calories 43, Fat 3.4, Fiber 1.7, Carbs 3.4, Protein 1.3

478. Baked Eggplants Slices

Preparation Time: 15 minutes
Cooking Time: 15 minutes
Servings: 3
Ingredients:

- 1 large eggplant, trimmed
- 1 tablespoon butter, softened
- 1 teaspoon minced garlic
- 1 teaspoon salt

Directions:
1. Slice the eggplant season it with salt. Mix up well and leave for 10 minutes to make the vegetable "give" bitter juice.
2. After this, dry the eggplant with the paper towel.
3. In the shallow bowl, mix up together minced garlic and softened butter.
4. Brush every eggplant slice with the garlic mixture.
5. Line the baking tray with baking paper. Preheat the oven to 355F.
6. Place the sliced eggplants in the tray to make 1 layer and transfer it in the oven.
7. Bake the eggplants for 15 minutes. The cooked eggplants will be tender but not soft!

Nutrition: Calories 81, Fat 4.2, Fiber 6.5, Carbs 11.1, Protein 1.9

479. Fast Cabbage Cakes

Preparation Time: 15 minutes
Cooking Time: 10 minutes
Servings: 2
Ingredients:

- 1 cup cauliflower, shredded
- 1 egg, beaten
- 1 teaspoon salt
- 1 teaspoon ground black pepper
- 2 tablespoons almond flour
- 1 teaspoon olive oil

Directions:
1. Blend the shredded cabbage in the blender until you get cabbage rice.
2. Then, mix up cabbage rice with the egg, salt, ground black pepper, and almond flour.
3. Pour olive oil in the skillet and preheat it.
4. Then make the small cakes with the help of 2 spoons and place them in the hot oil.

5. Roast the cabbage cakes for 4 minutes from each side over the medium-low heat.

Nutrition: Calories 227, Fat 18.6, Fiber 4.5, Carbs 9.5, Protein 9.9

480. Cauliflower Rice

Preparation Time: 5 minutes
Cooking Time: 10 minutes
Servings: 1
Ingredients:

- 1 small head cauliflower cut into florets
- 1 tbsp. butter
- ¼ tsp black pepper
- ¼ tsp garlic powder
- ¼ tsp salt-free herb seasoning blend

Directions:
1. Blitz cauliflower pieces in a food processor until it has a grain-like consistency.
2. Melt butter in a saucepan and add spices.
3. Add the cauliflower rice grains and cook over low-medium heat for approximately 10 minutes.
4. Use a fork to fluff the rice before serving.
5. Serve as an alternative to rice with curries, stews, and starch to accompany meat and fish dishes.

Nutrition: Calories 47 Fat Carbs 4g Protein 1g Sodium 300mg Potassium 206mg Phosphorous 31mg

481. Cranberry Cabbage

Preparation Time: 10 minutes
Cooking Time: 20 minutes
Servings: 8
Ingredients:

- 10 ounces canned whole-berry cranberry sauce
- 1 tablespoon fresh lemon juice

- 1 medium head red cabbage
- 1/4 teaspoon ground cloves

Directions:
1. Place the cranberry sauce, lemon juice, and cloves in a large pan and bring to the boil.
2. Add the cabbage and reduce it to a simmer.
3. Cook until the cabbage is tender, occasionally stirring to make sure the sauce does not stick.
4. Delicious served with beef, lamb, or pork.

Nutrition: Calories 73 Fat 0g Carbs 18g Protein 1g Sodium 32mg Potassium 138mg Phosphorous 18mg

482. Cilantro Chili Burgers

Preparation Time: 10 minutes
Cooking Time: 15 minutes
Servings: 3
Ingredients:

- 1 cup red cabbage
- 3 tablespoons almond flour
- 1 tablespoon cream cheese
- 1 oz. scallions, chopped
- ½ teaspoon salt
- ½ teaspoon chili powder
- ½ cup fresh cilantro

Directions:
1. Chop red cabbage roughly and transfer in the blender.
2. Add fresh cilantro and blend the mixture until very smooth.
3. After this, transfer it in the bowl.
4. Add cream cheese, scallions, salt, chili powder, and almond flour.
5. Stir the mixture well.
6. Make 3 big burgers from the cabbage mixture or 6 small burgers.
7. Line the baking tray with baking paper.
8. Place the burgers in the tray.

9. Bake the cilantro burgers for 15 minutes at 360F.
10. Flip the burgers onto another side after 8 minutes of cooking.

Nutrition: Calories 182, Fat 15.3, Fiber 4.1, Carbs 8.5, Protein 6.8

483. Jicama Noodles

Preparation Time: 15 minutes
Cooking Time: 7 minutes
Servings: 6
Ingredients:
- 1-pound jicama, peeled
- 2 tablespoons butter
- 1 teaspoon chili flakes
- 1 teaspoon salt
- ¾ cup of water

Directions:
1. Spiralize jicama with the help of spiralizer and place in jicama spirals in the saucepan.
2. Add butter, chili flakes, and salt.
3. Then add water and preheat the ingredients until the butter is melted.
4. Mix up it well.
5. Close the lid and cook noodles for 4 minutes over the medium heat.
6. Stir the jicama noodles well before transferring them in the serving plates.

Nutrition: Calories 63, Fat 3.9, Fiber 3.7, Carbs 6.7, Protein 0.6

484. Vegetable Masala

Preparation Time: 10 minutes
Cooking Time: 18 minutes
Servings: 4
Ingredients:
- 2 cups green beans, chopped
- 1 cup white mushroom, chopped
- ¾ cup Red bell peppers, crushed
- 1 teaspoon minced garlic
- 1 teaspoon minced ginger
- 1 teaspoon chili flakes
- 1 tablespoon garam masala
- 1 tablespoon olive oil
- 1 teaspoon salt

Directions:
1. Line the tray with parchment and preheat the oven to 360F.
2. Place the green beans and mushrooms in the tray.
3. Sprinkle the vegetables with crushed Red bell peppers, minced garlic and ginger, chili flakes, garam masala, olive oil, and salt.
4. Mix up well and transfer in the oven.
5. Cook vegetable masala for 18 minutes.

Nutrition: Calories 60, Fat 30.7, Fiber 2.5, Carbs 6.4,

485. Crack Slaw

Preparation Time: 15 minutes
Cooking Time: 10 minutes
Servings: 6
Ingredients:
- 1 cup cauliflower rice
- 1 tablespoon sriracha
- 1 teaspoon tahini paste
- 1 teaspoon sesame seeds
- 1 tablespoon lemon juice
- 1 teaspoon olive oil
- 1 teaspoon butter
- ½ teaspoon salt
- 2 cups coleslaw

Directions:
1. Toss the butter in the skillet and melt it.
2. Add cauliflower rice and sprinkle it with sriracha and tahini paste.
3. Mix up the vegetables and cook them for 10 minutes over the medium heat. Stir them from time to time.
4. When the cauliflower is cooked, transfer it into the big plate.

5. Add coleslaw and stir gently.
6. Then sprinkle the salad with sesame seeds, lemon juice, olive oil, and salt.
7. Mix up well.

Nutrition: Calories 76, Fat 5.8, Fiber 0.6, Carbs 6, Protein 1.1

486. Vegan Chili

Preparation Time: 10 minutes
Cooking Time: 20 minutes
Servings: 4
Ingredients:

- 1 cup cremini mushrooms, chopped
- 1 zucchini, chopped
- 1 bell pepper, diced
- 1/3 cup crushed Red bell peppers
- 1 oz. celery stalk, chopped
- 1 teaspoon chili powder
- 1 teaspoon salt
- ½ teaspoon chili flakes
- ½ cup of water
- 1 tablespoon olive oil
- ½ teaspoon diced garlic
- ½ teaspoon ground black pepper
- 1 teaspoon of cocoa powder
- 2 oz. Cheddar cheese, grated

Directions:

1. Pour olive oil in the pan and preheat it.
2. Add chopped mushrooms and roast them for 5 minutes. Stir them from time to time.
3. After this, add chopped zucchini and bell pepper.
4. Sprinkle the vegetables with the chili powder, salt, chili flakes, diced garlic, and ground black pepper.
5. Stir the vegetables and cook them for 5 minutes more.
6. After this, add crushed Red bell peppers. Mix up well.
7. Bring the mixture to boil and add water and cocoa powder.

8. Then add celery stalk.
9. Mix up the chili well and close the lid.
10. Cook the chili for 10 minutes over the medium-low heat.
11. Then transfer the cooked vegan chili in the bowls and top with the grated cheese.

Nutrition: Calories 123, Fat 8.6, Fiber 2.3, Carbs 7.6, Protein 5.6

487. Broccoli-Onion Latkes

Preparation Time: 15 minutes
Cooking Time: 20 minutes
Servings: 4
Ingredients:

- 3 cups broccoli florets, diced
- ½ cup onion, chopped
- 2 large eggs, beaten
- 2 tbsp. all-purpose white flour
- 2 tbsp. olive oil

Directions:

1. Cook the broccoli for around 5 minutes until tender. Drain.
2. Mix the flour into the eggs.
3. Combine the onion, broccoli, and egg mixture and stir through.
4. Prepare olive oil in a skillet on medium-high heat.
5. Drop a spoon of the mixture onto the pan to make 4 latkes.
6. Cook each side until golden brown.
7. Drain on a paper towel and serve.

Nutrition: Calories 140 Fat Carbs 7g Protein 6g Sodium 58mg Potassium 276mg Phosphorous 101mg

488. Chow Mein

Preparation Time: 10 minutes
Cooking Time: 10 minutes
Servings: 6
Ingredients:

- 7 oz. kelp noodles

- 5 oz. broccoli florets
- 1 tablespoon tahini sauce
- ¼ teaspoon minced ginger
- 1 teaspoon Sriracha
- ½ teaspoon garlic powder
- 1 cup of water

Directions:
1. Boil water in a sauce pan.
2. Add broccoli and boil for 4 minutes over the high heat.
3. Then drain water into the bowl and chill it tills the room temperature.
4. Soak the kelp noodles in the "broccoli water".
5. Meanwhile, place tahini sauce, sriracha, minced ginger, and garlic in the saucepan.
6. Bring the mixture to boil. Add oil if needed.
7. Then add broccoli and soaked noodles.
8. Add 3 tablespoons of "broccoli water".
9. Mix up the noodles and bring to boil.
10. Switch off the heat and transfer chow Mein in the serving bowls.

Nutrition: Calories 18, Fat 0.8, Fiber 0.7, Carbs 2.8, Protein 0.9

489. Carrot casserole

Preparation time: 10 minutes
Cooking time: 20 minutes
Serving: 8
Ingredients
- 1-pound carrots, sliced into rounds
- 12 low-sodium crackers
- 2 tablespoons butter
- 2 tablespoons onion, chopped
- 1/4 cup cheddar cheese, shredded

Directions
1. Preheat your oven to 350 degrees f.
2. Boil carrots in a pot of water until tender.

3. Drain the carrots and reserve ¼ cup liquid.
4. Mash carrots.
5. Add all the ingredients into the carrots except cheese.
6. Place the mashed carrots in a casserole dish.
7. Sprinkle cheese on top and bake in the oven for 15 minutes.

Nutrition: calories 97 protein 2 g carbohydrates 9 g fat 7 g cholesterol 13 mg sodium 174 mg potassium 153 mg phosphorus 47 mg calcium 66 mg fiber 1.8 g

490. Mushroom Tacos

Preparation Time: 10 minutes
Cooking Time: 15 minutes
Servings: 6
Ingredients:
- 6 collard greens leave
- 2 cups mushrooms, chopped
- 1 white onion, diced
- 1 tablespoon Taco seasoning
- 1 tablespoon coconut oil
- ½ teaspoon salt
- ¼ cup fresh parsley
- 1 tablespoon mayonnaise

Directions:
1. Put the coconut oil in the skillet and melt it.
2. Add chopped mushrooms and diced onion. Mix up the ingredients.
3. Close the lid and cook them for 10 minutes.
4. After this, sprinkle the vegetables with Taco seasoning, salt, and add fresh parsley.
5. Mix up the mixture and cook for 5 minutes more.
6. Then add mayonnaise and stir well.
7. Chill the mushroom mixture little.
8. Fill the collard green leaves with the mushroom mixture and fold up them.

Nutrition: Calories 52, Fat 3.3,Fiber 1.2, Carbs 5.1, Protein 1.4

491. Lime Green lettuce and Chickpeas Salad

Preparation Time: 10 minutes
Cooking Time: 0 minutes
Servings: 4
Ingredients:

- 16 ounces canned chickpeas, drained and rinsed
- 2 cups baby green lettuce leaves
- ½ tablespoon lime juice
- 2 tablespoons olive oil
- 1 teaspoon cumin, ground
- Sea salt and black pepper
- ½ teaspoon chili flakes

Directions:
1. In a bowl, mix the chickpeas with the green lettuce and the rest of the ingredients, toss and serve cold.

Nutrition: Calories 240, Fat 8.2, Fiber 5.3, Carbs 11.6, Protein 12

492. Stir-Fried Gingery Veggies

Preparation Time: 10 minutes
Cooking Time: 10 minutes
Servings: 4
Ingredients:

- 1 tablespoon oil
- 3 cloves of garlic, minced
- 1 onion, chopped
- 1 thumb-size ginger, sliced
- 1 tablespoon water
- 1 large carrots, peeled and julienned and seedless
- 1 large green bell pepper, julienned and seedless

- 1 large yellow bell pepper, julienned and seedless
- 1 large red bell pepper, julienned and seedless
- 1 zucchini, julienned
- Salt and pepper to taste

Directions:
1. Heat oil in a nonstick saucepan over a high flame and sauté the garlic, onion, and ginger until fragrant.
2. Stir in the rest of the ingredients.
3. Keep on stirring for at least 5 minutes until vegetables are tender.
4. Serve and enjoy.

Nutrition: Calories 70 Total Fat 4g Saturated Fat 1g Total Carbs 9g Net Carbs 7gProtein 1g Sugar: 4g Fiber2g Sodium 173mg Potassium 163mg

493. Minty Olives Salad

Preparation time: 10 minutes
Cooking time: 0 minutes
Servings: 4
Ingredients:

- 1 cup kalamata olives, pitted and sliced
- 1 cup black olives, pitted and halved
- 1 red onion, chopped
- 2 tablespoons oregano, chopped
- 1 tablespoon mint, chopped
- 2 tablespoons balsamic vinegar
- ¼ cup olive oil
- 2 teaspoons Italian herbs, dried
- A pinch of sea salt and black pepper

Directions:
1. In a salad bowl, mix the olives and the rest of the ingredients, toss and serve cold.

Nutrition: calories 190, fat 8.1, fiber 5.8, carbs 11.6, protein 4.6 Phosphorus: 110mg Potassium: 117mg Sodium: 75mg

494. Beans and Cucumber Salad

Preparation time: 10 minutes
Cooking time: 0 minutes
Servings: 4

Ingredients:

- 15 ounces canned great northern beans, drained and rinsed
- 2 tablespoons olive oil
- ½ cup baby arugula
- 1 cup cucumber, sliced
- 1 tablespoon parsley, chopped
- A pinch of sea salt and black pepper
- 2 tablespoon balsamic vinegar

Directions:

2. In a bowl, mix the beans with the cucumber and the rest of the ingredients, toss and serve cold.

Nutrition: calories 233, fat 9, fiber 6.5, carbs 13, protein 8 Phosphorus: 210mg Potassium: 127mg Sodium: 85mg

495. Roasted Mint Carrots

Preparation Time: 20 minutes
Cooking Time: 5 minutes
Servings: 6
Ingredients:
- 1 pound carrots, trimmed
- 1 tablespoon extra-virgin olive oil
- Freshly ground black pepper
- ¼ cup thinly sliced mint

Directions:
1. Preheat the oven to 425°F.
2. Assemble the carrots in a single layer on a rimmed baking sheet. Drizzle with the olive oil, and shake the carrots on the sheet to coat. Season with pepper.
3. Cook for 20 minutes, or until tender and browned, stirring twice while cooking. Sprinkle with the mint and serve.
4. Substitution tip: To lower the potassium in this dish, use 8 ounces of carrots and 8 ounces of turnips cut into cubes. This will cut the potassium to 193mg.

Nutrition: Calories: 51; Total Fat: 2g; Saturated Fat: 0g; Cholesterol: 0mg; Carbohydrates: 7g; Fiber: 2g; Protein: 1g; Phosphorus: 26mg; Potassium: 242mg; Sodium: 52mg

496. Braised Cabbage

Preparation Time: 10 minutes
Cooking Time: 10 minutes
Servings: 4
Ingredients:
- 1 small cabbage head, shredded
- 2 tablespoons water
- A drizzle of olive oil
- 6 ounces shallots, cooked and chopped
- A pinch of black pepper
- A pinch of sweet paprika
- 1 tablespoon dill, chopped

Directions:
3. Heat up a pan with the oil over medium heat, add the cabbage and the water, stir and sauté for 5 minutes.
4. Add the rest of the ingredients, toss, cook for 5 minutes more, divide everything between plates and serve as a side dish!
5. Enjoy!

Nutrition: Calories 91, fat 0, 5, fiber 5, 8, carbs 20, 8, protein 4, 1 Phosphorus: 120mg Potassium: 127mg Sodium: 75mg

497. Roasted Red Pepper Hummus

Preparation Time: 10 minutes
Cooking Time: 10 minutes
Servings: 28
Ingredients:
- 1 red bell pepper
- 1 (15-ounce) can chickpeas, drained and rinsed
- Juice of 1 lemon
- 2 tablespoons tahini
- 2 garlic cloves
- 2 tablespoons extra-virgin olive oil

Directions:
1. Change an oven rack to the highest position. Heat the broiler to high.
2. Core the pepper and cut it into three or four large pieces. Arrange them on a baking sheet, skin-side up.
3. Broil the peppers for 5 to 10 minutes, until the skins are charred.

4. Cover with plastic wrap and let them steam for 10 to 15 minutes, until cool enough to handle.
5. Peel the skin off the peppers, and place the peppers in a blender.
6. Add the chickpeas, lemon juice, tahini, garlic, and olive oil.
7. Process until smooth, adding up to 1 tablespoon of water to adjust consistency as desired.
8. Substitution tip: This hummus can also be made without the red pepper if desired. To do this, simply follow Step 5. This will cut the potassium to 59mg per serving.

Nutrition: Total Fat: 6g; Saturated Fat: 1g; Cholesterol: 0mg; Carbohydrates: 10g; Fiber: 3g; Protein: 3g; Phosphorus: 58mg; Potassium: 91mg; Sodium: 72mg

498. Roasted Root Vegetables

Preparation Time: 10 minutes
Cooking Time: 25 minutes
Servings: 6
Ingredients:
- 1 cup chopped turnips
- 1 cup chopped rutabaga
- 1 cup chopped parsnips
- 1 tablespoon extra-virgin olive oil
- 1 teaspoon fresh chopped rosemary
- Freshly ground black pepper

Directions:
1. Preheat the oven to 420°F.
2. Toss the turnips, rutabaga, and parsnips with the olive oil and rosemary.
3. Assemble in a single layer on a baking sheet, and season with pepper.
4. Roast until the vegetables are tender and browned, 20 to 25 minutes, stirring once.

Nutrition: Calories: 52; Total Fat: 2g; Saturated Fat: 0g; Cholesterol: 0mg; Carbohydrates: 7g;

Fiber: 2g; Protein: 1g; Phosphorus: 35mg; Potassium: 205mg; Sodium: 22mg

499. Collard Salad Rolls with Peanut Dipping Sauce

Preparation Time: 10 minutes
Cooking Time: 10 minutes
Servings: 4
Ingredients:
FOR THE DIPPING SAUCE
- ¼ cup peanut butter
- 2 tablespoons honey
- Juice of 1 lime
- ¼ teaspoon red chili flakes
FOR THE SALAD ROLLS
- 4 ounces' extra-firm tofu
- 1 bunch collard greens
- 1 cup thinly sliced purple cabbage
- 1 cup bean sprouts
- 2 carrots, cut into matchsticks
- ½ cup cilantro leaves and stems

Directions:
To Make The Dipping Sauce
1. In a blender, combine the peanut butter, honey, lime juice, chili flakes, and process until smooth. Put 1 to 2 tablespoons of water as desired for consistency.

To Make The Salad Rolls
1. Using paper towels, press the excess moisture from the tofu. Cut into ½-inch-thick matchsticks.
2. Remove any tough stems from the collard greens and set aside.
3. Arrange all of the ingredients within reach. Cup one collard green leaf in your hand, and add a couple pieces of the tofu and a small amount each of the cabbage, bean sprouts, and carrots. Top with a couple cilantro sprigs, and roll into a cylinder. Place each roll, seam-

side down, on a serving platter while you assemble the rest of the rolls. Serve with the dipping sauce.

4. Substitution tip: To lower the potassium, omit the cabbage and use only 1 carrot, which will drop the potassium to 208mg.

Nutrition: Calories: 174; Total Fat: 9g; Saturated Fat: 2g; Cholesterol: 0mg; Carbohydrates: 20g; Fiber: 5g;Protein: 8g; Phosphorus: 56mg; Potassium: 284mg; Sodium: 42mg

500. Thai-Style Eggplant Dip

Preparation Time: 10 minutes
Cooking Time: 30 minutes
Servings: 4
Ingredients:

- 1 pound Thai eggplant (or Japanese or Chinese eggplant)
- 2 tablespoons rice vinegar
- 2 teaspoons sugar
- 1 teaspoon low-sodium soy sauce
- 1 jalapeño pepper
- 2 garlic cloves
- ¼ cup chopped basil
- Cut vegetables for serving

Directions:

1. Preheat the oven to 475°F
2. Pierce the eggplant in several places with a skewer or knife. Place on a rimmed baking sheet and cook until soft, about 30 minutes.
3. Let cool, cut in half, and scoop out the flesh of the eggplant into a blender.
4. Add the rice vinegar, sugar, soy sauce, jalapeño, garlic, and basil to the blender. Process until smooth. Serve with cut vegetables

5. Lower sodium tip: If you need to lower your sodium further, omit the soy sauce to lower the sodium to 3mg.

Nutrition: Calories: 40; Total Fat: 0g; Saturated Fat: 0g; Cholesterol: 0mg; Carbohydrates: 10g; Fiber: 4g;Protein: 2g; Phosphorus: 34mg; Potassium: 284mg; Sodium: 47mg

501. Vegetable Couscous

Preparation Time: 10 minutes
Cooking Time: 51 minutes
Servings: 6
Ingredients:

- 1 tablespoon extra-virgin olive oil
- ½ sweet onion, diced
- 1 carrot, diced
- 1 celery stalk, diced
- ½ cup diced red or yellow bell pepper
- 1 small zucchini, diced
- 1 cup couscous
- 1½ cups Simple Chicken Broth or low-sodium store-bought chicken stock
- ½ teaspoon garlic powder
- Freshly ground black pepper

Directions:

1. Place the onion, carrot, celery, bell pepper, and cook, stirring occasionally, until the vegetables are just becoming tender, about 5 to 7 minutes.
2. Add the zucchini, couscous, broth, and garlic powder.
3. Stir to blend, and bring to a boil.
4. Cover and remove from the heat. Let stand for 5 to 8 minutes. Fluff with a fork, season with pepper, and serve.

Nutrition: Calories: 154; Total Fat: 3g; Saturated Fat: 1g; Cholesterol: 0mg;Carbohydrates: 27g; Fiber: 2g;Protein: 5g; Phosphorus: 83mg; Potassium: 197mg;Sodium: 36mg

502. Garlic Cauliflower Rice

Preparation Time: 10 minutes
Cooking Time: 5 minutes
Servings: 8
Ingredients:
- 1 medium head cauliflower
- 1 tablespoon extra-virgin olive oil
- 4 garlic cloves, minced
- Freshly ground black pepper

Directions:
1. Using a sharp knife, remove the core of the cauliflower, and separate the cauliflower into florets.
2. In a food processor, pulse the florets until they are the size of rice, being careful not to over process them to the point of becoming mushy.
3. In a large skillet over medium heat, heat the olive oil. Add the garlic, and stir until just fragrant.
4. Add the cauliflower, stirring to coat. Add 1 tablespoon of water to the pan, cover, and reduce the heat to low. Steam for 7 to 10 minutes, until the cauliflower is tender. Season with pepper and serve.

Nutrition: Calories: 37; Total Fat: 2g; Saturated Fat: 0g; Cholesterol: 0mg; Carbohydrates: 4g; Fiber: 2g; Protein: 2g; Phosphorus: 35mg; Potassium: 226mg; Sodium: 22mg

503. Eggplant and Mushroom Sauté

Preparation Time: 10 minutes
Cooking Time: 30 minutes
Servings: 4
Ingredients:
- 2 pounds oyster mushrooms, chopped
- 6 ounces shallots, peeled, chopped
- 1 yellow onion, chopped
- 2 eggplants, cubed
- 3 celery stalks, chopped
- 1 tablespoon parsley, chopped
- A pinch of sea salt
- Black pepper to taste
- 1 tablespoon savory, dried
- 3 tablespoons coconut oil, melted

Directions:
1. Heat up a pan with the oil over medium high heat, add onion, stir and cook for 4 minutes.
2. Add shallots, stir and cook for 4 more minutes.
3. Add eggplant pieces, mushrooms, celery, savory and black pepper to taste, stir and cook for 15 minutes.
4. Add parsley, stir again, cook for a couple more minutes, divide between plates and serve.
5. Enjoy!

Nutrition: calories 1013, fat 10, 9, fiber 35, 5, carbs 156, 5, protein 69, 1 Phosphorus: 210mg Potassium: 217mg Sodium: 105mg

504. Simple Roasted Broccoli

Preparation Time: 5 minutes
Cooking Time: 20 minutes
Servings: 6
Ingredients:
- 2 small heads broccoli, cut into florets
- 1 tablespoon extra-virgin olive oil
- 3 garlic cloves, minced

Directions:
1. Preheat the oven to 425°F.
2. Toss the broccoli with the olive oil and garlic.
3. Arrange in a single layer on a baking sheet.
4. Roast for 10 minutes, then flip the broccoli and roast an additional 10 minutes. Serve.
5. Cooking tip: Roasted broccoli makes for great leftovers—throw them in a

quick salad for added flavor and bulk. To save leftovers, refrigerate in an airtight container for three to five days.
Nutrition: Calories: 38; Total Fat: 2g; Saturated Fat: 0g; Cholesterol: 0mg; Carbohydrates: 4g; Fiber: 1g; Protein: 1g;Phosphorus: 32mg; Potassium: 150mg; Sodium: 15mg

505. Bok Choy and Beets

Preparation Time: 10 minutes
Cooking Time: 30 minutes
Servings: 4
Ingredients:
- 1 tablespoon coconut oil
- 4 cups bok choy, chopped
- 3 beets, cut into quarters and thinly sliced
- 2 tablespoons water
- A pinch of cayenne pepper

Directions:
1. Put water in a large saucepan, add the beets, bring to a boil over medium heat, cover, and cook for 20 minutes and drain.
2. Heat up a pan with the oil over medium high heat, add the bok choy and the water, stir and cook for 10 minutes.
3. Add beets and cayenne pepper, stir, cook for 2 minutes more, divide between plates and serve as a side dish!
4. Enjoy!

Nutrition: Calories 71, fat 3,7, fiber 2,2, carbs 9, protein 2,3 Phosphorus: 110mg Potassium: 117mg Sodium: 75mg

506. Broccoli and Almonds Mix

Preparation Time: 10 minutes
Cooking Time: 11 minutes
Servings: 4
Ingredients:
- 1 tablespoon olive oil

- 1 garlic clove, minced
- 1 pound broccoli florets
- 1/3 cup almonds, chopped
- Black pepper to taste

Directions:
1. Heat up a pan with the oil over medium-high heat, add the almonds, stir, cook for 5 minutes and transfer to a bowl,
2. Heat up the same pan again over medium-high heat, add broccoli and garlic, stir, cover and cook for 6 minutes more.
3. Add the almonds and black pepper to taste, stir, divide between plates and serve.
4. Enjoy!

Nutrition: Calories 116, fat 7,8, fiber 4, carbs 9,5, protein 4,9 Phosphorus: 110mg Potassium: 117mg Sodium: 75mg

507. Cinnamon Apple Chips

Preparation Time: 5 minutes
Cooking Time: 2 to 3 hours
Servings: 4
Ingredients:
- 4 apples
- 1 teaspoon ground cinnamon

Directions:
1. Preheat the oven to 200°F. Line a baking sheet with parchment paper.
2. Core the apples and cut into 1/8-inch slices.
3. In a medium bowl, toss the apple slices with the cinnamon. Spread the apples in a single layer on the prepared baking sheet.
4. Cook for 2 to 3 hours, until the apples are dry. They will still be soft while hot, but will crisp once completely cooled.
5. Store in an airtight container for up to four days.

6. Cooking tip: If you don't have parchment paper, use cooking spray to prevent sticking.

Nutrition: Calories: 96; Total Fat: 0g; Saturated Fat: 0g; Cholesterol: 0mg; Carbohydrates: 26g; Fiber: 5g; Protein: 1g; Phosphorus: 0mg; Potassium: 198mg; Sodium: 2mg

508. Ginger Cauliflower Rice

Preparation Time: 10 minutes
Cooking Time: 10 minutes
Servings: 4

Ingredients:

- 5 cups cauliflower florets
- 3 tablespoons coconut oil
- 4 ginger slices, grated
- 1 tablespoon coconut vinegar
- 3 garlic cloves, minced
- 1 tablespoon chives, minced
- A pinch of sea salt
- Black pepper to taste

Directions:

1. Put cauliflower florets in a food processor and pulse well.
2. Heat up a pan with the oil over medium-high heat, add ginger, stir and cook for 3 minutes.
3. Add cauliflower rice and garlic, stir and cook for 7 minutes.
4. Add salt, black pepper, vinegar, and chives, stir, cook for a few seconds more, divide between plates and serve.
5. Enjoy!

Nutrition: Calories 125, fat 10, 4, fiber 3, 2, carbs 7, 9, protein 2, 7 Phosphorus: 110mg Potassium: 117mg Sodium: 75mg

509. Basil Zucchini Spaghetti

Preparation Time: 1 hour and 10 minutes

Cooking Time: 10 minutes
Servings: 4

Ingredients:

- 1/3 cup coconut oil, melted
- 4 zucchinis, cut with a spiralizer
- ¼ cup basil, chopped
- A pinch of sea salt
- Black pepper to taste
- ½ cup walnuts, chopped
- 2 garlic cloves, minced

1. **Directions:**

1. In a bowl, mix zucchini spaghetti with salt and pepper, toss to coat, leave aside for 1 hour, drain well and put in a bowl.
2. Heat up a pan with the oil over medium-high heat, add zucchini spaghetti and garlic, stir and cook for 5 minutes.
3. Add basil and walnuts and black pepper, stir and cook for 3 minutes more.
4. Divide between plates and serve as a side dish
5. Enjoy!

Nutrition: Calories 287, fat 27, 8, fiber 3, 3, carbs 8, 7, protein 6, 3 Phosphorus: 110mg Potassium: 117mg Sodium: 75mg

510. Cauliflower and Leeks

Preparation Time: 10 minutes
Cooking Time: 20 minutes
Servings: 4

Ingredients:

- 1 and ½ cups leeks, chopped
- 1 and ½ cups cauliflower florets
- 2 garlic cloves, minced
- 1 and ½ cups artichoke hearts
- 2 tablespoons coconut oil, melted
- Black pepper to taste

Directions:

1. Heat up a pan with the oil over medium-high heat, add garlic, leeks, cauliflower florets and artichoke hearts, stir and cook for 20 minutes.
2. Add black pepper, stir, divide between plates and serve.
3. Enjoy!

Nutrition: Calories 192, fat 6, 9, fiber 8, 2, carbs 35, 1, protein 5, 1 Phosphorus: 110mg Potassium: 117mg Sodium: 75mg

511. Mint Zucchini

Preparation Time: 10 minutes
Cooking Time: 7 minutes
Servings: 4
Ingredients:
- 2 tablespoons mint
- 2 zucchinis, halved lengthwise and then slice into half moons
- 1 tablespoon coconut oil, melted
- ½ tablespoon dill, chopped
- A pinch of cayenne pepper

Directions:
1. Heat up a pan with the oil over medium-high heat, add zucchinis, stir and cook for 6 minutes.
2. Add cayenne, dill and mint, stir, cook for 1 minute more, divide between plates and serve.
3. Enjoy!

Nutrition: Calories 46, fat 3, 6, fiber 1, 3, carbs 3, 5, protein 1, 3 Phosphorus: 120mg Potassium: 127mg Sodium: 75mg

512. Celery and Kale Mix

Preparation Time: 10 minutes
Cooking Time: 20 minutes
Servings: 4
Ingredients:
- 2 celery stalks, chopped
- 5 cups kale, torn
- 1 small red bell pepper, chopped

- 3 tablespoons water
- 1 tablespoon coconut oil, melted

Directions:
1. Heat up a pan with the oil over medium-high heat, add celery, stir and cook for 10 minutes.
2. Add kale, water, and bell pepper, stir and cook for 10 minutes more.
3. Divide between plates and serve.
4. Enjoy!

Nutrition: Calories 81, fat 3, 5, fiber 1, 8, carbs 11, 3, protein 2, 9 Phosphorus: 120mg Potassium: 147mg Sodium: 75mg

513. Kale, Mushrooms and Red Chard Mix

Preparation Time: 10 minutes
Cooking Time: 17 minutes
Servings: 4
Ingredients:
- ½ pound brown mushrooms, sliced
- 5 cups kale, roughly chopped
- 1 and ½ tablespoons coconut oil
- 3 cups red chard, chopped
- 2 tablespoons water
- Black pepper to taste

Directions:
1. Heat up a pan with the oil over medium high heat, add mushrooms, stir and cook for 5 minutes.
2. Add red chard, kale and water, stir and cook for 10 minutes.
3. Add black pepper to taste, stir and cook 2 minutes more.
4. Divide between plates and serve.
5. Enjoy!

Nutrition: Calories 97, fat 3, 4, fiber 2, 3, carbs 13, 3, protein 5, 4 Phosphorus: 110mg Potassium: 117mg Sodium: 75mg

514. Squash and Cranberries

Preparation Time: 10 minutes
Cooking Time: 30 minutes
Servings: 2
Ingredients:

- 1 tablespoon coconut oil
- 1 butternut squash, peeled and cubed
- 2 garlic cloves, minced
- 1 small yellow onion, chopped
- 12 ounces coconut almond milk
- 1 teaspoon curry powder
- 1 teaspoon cinnamon powder
- ½ cup cranberries

Directions:

1. Spread squash pieces on a lined baking sheet, place in the oven at 425 degrees F, bake for 15 minutes and leave to one side.
2. Heat up a pan with the oil over medium high heat, add garlic and onion, stir and cook for 5 minutes.
3. Add roasted squash, stir and cook for 3 minutes.
4. Add coconut almond milk, cranberries, cinnamon and curry powder, stir and cook for 5 minutes more.
5. Divide between plates and serve as a side dish!
6. Enjoy!

Nutrition: Calories 518, fat 47, 6, fiber 7, 3, carbs 24, 9, protein 5, 3 Phosphorus: 110mg Potassium: 117mg Sodium: 75mg

515. Dill Carrots

Preparation Time: 10 minutes
Cooking Time: 30 minutes
Servings: 4
Ingredients:

- 1 tablespoon coconut oil, melted
- 2 tablespoons dill, chopped
- 1 pound baby carrots
- 1 tablespoon coconut sugar
- A pinch of black pepper

Directions:

1. Put carrots in a large saucepan, add water to cover, bring to a boil over medium-high heat, cover and simmer for 30 minutes.
2. Drain the carrots, put them in a bowl, add melted oil, black pepper, dill, and the coconut sugar, stir very well, divide between plates and serve.
3. Enjoy!

Nutrition: Calories 85, fat 3, 6, fiber 3, 5, carbs 13, 4, protein 1 Phosphorus: 140mg Potassium: 147mg Sodium: 65mg

516. Tofu Stir-Fry

Preparation Time: 20 minutes
Cooking Time: 20 minutes
Servings: 4
Ingredients:

- Ingredients for the tofu
- Lemon juice – 1 Tbsp.
- Minced garlic – 1 tsp.
- Grated fresh ginger – 1 tsp.
- Pinch red pepper flakes
- Extra-firm tofu- 5 ounces, pressed well and cubed
- For the stir-fry
- Olive oil – 1 Tbsp.
- Cauliflower florets – ½ cup
- Thinly sliced carrots – ½ cup
- Julienned red pepper – ½ cup
- Fresh green beans – ½ cup
- Cooked white rice – 2 cups

Directions:

1. Mix the lemon juice, garlic, ginger, and red pepper flakes.
2. Add the tofu and toss to coat.
3. Put the bowl in the refrigerator and soak for 2 hours.

4. To make the stir-fry, heat the oil in a skillet.
5. Sauté the tofu for 8 minutes or until it is lightly browned and heated through.
6. Add the carrots, and cauliflower and sauté for 5 minutes. Stirring and tossing constantly.
7. Add the red pepper and green beans, sauté for 3 minutes more.
8. Serve over white rice.

Nutrition: Calories: 190 Fat: 6g Carb: 30g Phosphorus: 90mg Potassium: 199mg Sodium: 22mg
Protein: 6g

517. Vegetable Rolls

Preparation Time: 30 minutes
Cooking Time: 0 minute
Servings: 8
Ingredients:

- Finely shredded red cabbage – ½ cup
- Grated carrot – ½ cup
- Julienne red bell pepper – ¼ cup
- Julienned scallion – ¼ cup, both green and white parts
- Chopped cilantro – ¼ cup
- Olive oil – 1 Tbsp.
- Ground cumin – ¼ tsp.
- Freshly ground black pepper – ¼ tsp.
- English cucumber – 1, sliced very thin strips

Directions:

1. In a bowl, toss together the black pepper, cumin, olive oil, cilantro, scallion, red pepper, carrot, and cabbage. Mix well.
2. Evenly divide the vegetable filling among the cucumber strips, placing the filling close to one end of the strip.
3. Roll up the cucumber strips around the filling and secure with a wooden pick.

4. Repeat with each cucumber strip.

Nutrition: Calories: 26 Fat: 2g Carb: 3g Phosphorus: 14mg Potassium: 95mg Sodium: 7mg Protein: 0g

518. Frittata with Penne

Preparation Time: 15 minutes
Cooking Time: 30 minutes
Servings: 4
Ingredients:

- Egg whites- 6
- Rice almond milk – ¼ cup
- Chopped fresh parsley – 1 Tbsp.
- Chopped fresh thyme – 1 tsp.
- Chopped fresh chives – 1 tsp.
- Ground black pepper
- Olive oil – 2 tsps.
- Small sweet onion – ¼, chopped
- Minced garlic – 1 tsp.
- Boiled and chopped red bell pepper – ½ cup
- Cooked penne – 2 cups

Directions:

1. Preheat the oven to 350F.
2. Whisk together the egg whites, rice almond milk, parsley, thyme, chives, and pepper.
3. Heat the oil in a skillet.
4. Sauté the onion, garlic, red pepper for 4 minutes or until they are softened.
5. Add the cooked penne to the skillet.
6. Transfer the egg mixture over the pasta and shake the pan to coat the pasta.
7. Leave the skillet on the heat for 1 minute to set the bottom of the frittata
8. Bake, the frittata for 25 minutes or until it is set and golden brown.
9. Serve.

Nutrition: Calories: 170 Fat: 3g Carb: 25g Phosphorus: 62mg Potassium: 144mg Sodium: 90mg Protein: 10g

519. Cauliflower Patties

Preparation Time: 5 minutes
Cooking Time: 8 minutes
Servings: 4
Ingredients:

- Eggs – 2
- Egg whites – 2
- Onion – ½, diced
- Cauliflower – 2 cups, frozen
- All-purpose white flour – 2 Tbsps.
- Black pepper – 1 tsp.
- Coconut oil – 1 Tbsp.
- Curry powder – 1 tsp.
- Fresh cilantro – 1 Tbsp.

Directions:

1. Soak vegetables in warm water before cooking.
2. Steam cauliflower over a pan of boiling water for 10 minutes.
3. Blend eggs and onion in a food processor before adding cooked cauliflower, spices, cilantro, flour, and pepper and blast in the processor for 30 seconds.
4. Heat a skillet on a high heat and add oil.
5. Enjoy with a salad.

Nutrition: Calories: 227 Fat: 12g Carb: 15g
Phosphorus: 193mg Potassium: 513mgSodium: 158mg
Protein: 13g

520. Tortilla Chips

Preparation Time: 15 minutes
Cooking Time: 10 minutes
Servings: 6
Ingredients:

- Granulated sugar – 2 tsps.
- Ground cinnamon – ½ tsp.
- Pinch ground nutmeg
- Flour tortillas – 3 (6-inch)
- Cooking spray

Directions:

1. Preheat the oven to 350F.
2. Line a baking sheet with parchment paper.
3. Mix the sugar, cinnamon, and nutmeg.
4. Lay the tortillas on a clean work surface and spray both sides of each lightly with cooking spray.
5. Sprinkle the cinnamon sugar evenly over both sides of each tortilla.
6. Cut the tortillas into 16 wedges each and place them on the baking sheet.
7. Bake the tortilla wedges, turning once, for about 10 minutes or until crisp.
8. Cool the chips serve.

Nutrition: Calories: 51 Fat: 1g Carb: 9g
Phosphorus: 29mg Potassium: 24mg Sodium: 103 mg
Protein: 1g

521. Beef stew pasta

Preparation time: 15 minutes
Cooking time: 8 hours
Servings: 2
Ingredients

- 1 tablespoon olive oil
- 3/4-pound beef round roast, sliced into bite-sized pieces
- 1/2 cup onion, chopped
- 1/2 cup carrots, chopped
- 1/2 cup celery, chopped
- 2 cups beef broth, no salt
- 1/2 teaspoon oregano
- 1/4 cup red wine
- 1/4 teaspoon thyme
- 1/4 teaspoon black pepper
- 1/4 cup whole wheat pasta

Directions

1. Pour olive oil into non-stick skillet. Cook beef round roast, in batches, for 5 minutes or until browned all over. Transfer meat to the slow cooker.

2. Add in onion, carrots, celery, beef broth, oregano, red wine, thyme, black pepper, and pasta. Stir mixture well.
3. Cover and cook for 8 to 9 hours on low. Secure the lid.
4. After the 8-hour cooking cycle, turn off the heat. Adjust seasoning according to your preferred taste.
5. To serve, place pasta into plates. Pour sauce all over.

Nutrition: protein: 12.8 g potassium: 128.5mg sodium: 95.8 mg

522. Kale Chips

Preparation Time: 20 minutes
Cooking Time: 25 minutes
Servings: 6
Ingredients:
- Kale – 2 cups
- Olive oil – 2 tsp.
- Chili powder – ¼ tsp.
- Pinch cayenne pepper

Directions:
1. Preheat the oven to 300F.
2. Line 2 baking sheets with parchment paper; set aside.
3. Remove the stems from the kale and tear the leaves into 2-inch pieces.
4. Wash the kale and dry it completely.
5. Handover the kale to a large bowl and drizzle with olive oil.
6. Use your hands to toss the kale with oil, taking care to coat each leaf evenly.
7. Season the kale with chili powder and cayenne pepper and toss to combine thoroughly.
8. Spread the seasoned kale in a single layer on each baking sheet. Do not overlap the leaves.
9. Bake the kale, rotating the pans once, for 20 to 25 minutes until it is crisp and dry.

10. Take out the oven trays and allow the chips to cool on the trays for 5 minutes.
11. Serve.

Nutrition: Calories: 24 Fat: 2g Carb: 2g Phosphorus: 21mg Potassium: 111mg Sodium: 13mg Protein: 1g

523. Creamy Chard

Preparation Time: 10 minutes
Cooking Time: 10 minutes
Servings: 2
Ingredients:
- Juice of ½ lemon
- 1 tablespoon coconut oil
- 12 ounces coconut almond milk
- 1 bunch chard
- A pinch of sea salt
- Black pepper to taste

Directions:
1. Heat up a pan with the oil over medium-high heat, add chard, stir and cook for 5 minutes.
2. Add lemon juice, a pinch of salt, black pepper, and coconut almond milk, stir and cook for 5 minutes more.
3. Divide between plates and serve as a side.
4. Enjoy!

Nutrition: Calories 453, fat 47, 4, fiber 4, carbs 10, 1, protein 4, 2 Phosphorus: 130mg Potassium: 1127mg Sodium: 85mg

524. Corn Bread

Preparation Time: 10 minutes
Cooking Time: 20 minutes
Servings: 10
Ingredients:
- Cooking spray for greasing the baking dish
- Yellow cornmeal – 1 ¼ cups
- All-purpose flour – ¾ cup

- Baking soda substitute – 1 tbsp.
- Granulated sugar – ½ cup
- Eggs – 2
- Unsweetened, unfortified rice almond milk – 1 cup
- Olive oil – 2 Tbsps.

Directions:

1. Preheat the oven to 425F.
2. Lightly spray an 8-by-8-inch baking dish with cooking spray. Set aside.
3. In a medium bowl, stir together the cornmeal, flour, baking soda substitute, and sugar.
4. In a small bowl, whisk together the eggs, rice almond milk, and olive oil until blended.
5. Place the wet ingredients to the dry ingredients and stir until well combined.
6. Pour the batter into the baking dish and bake for 20 minutes or until golden and cooked through.
7. Serve warm.

Nutrition: Calories: 198 Fat: 5g Carb: 34g Phosphorus: 88mg Potassium: 94mg Sodium: 25mg Protein: 4g

525. Turnip Chips

Preparation Time: 5 minutes
Cooking Time: 50 minutes
Servings: 2
Ingredients:

- Turnips – 2, peeled and sliced
- Extra virgin olive oil – 1 Tbsp.
- Onion – 1 chopped
- Minced garlic – 1 clove
- Black pepper – 1 tsp.
- Oregano – 1 tsp.
- Paprika - 1 1 tsp.

Directions:

1. Preheat oven to 375F. Grease a baking tray with olive oil.
2. Add turnip slices in a thin layer.

3. Dust over herbs and spices with an extra drizzle of olive oil.
4. Bake 40 minutes. Turning once.

Nutrition: Calories: 136 Fat: 14g Carb: 30g Phosphorus: 50mg Potassium: 356mg Sodium: 71mg Protein: g

526. Chicken and Mandarin Salad

Preparation time: 40 minutes
Cooking time: 30 minutes
Servings: 3
Ingredients:

- 1 ½ - cup Chicken
- ½ - cup Celery
- ½ - cup Green pepper
- ¼ - cup Onion, finely sliced
- ¼ - cup Light mayonnaise
- ½ - tsp. freshly ground pepper

Directions:

1. Hurl chicken, celery, green pepper and onion to blend. Include mayo and pepper. Blend delicately and serve.

Nutrition: Calories 375, Fat 15, Fiber 2, Carbs 14, Protein 28

527. Salmon chowder

Preparation time: 20 minutes
Cooking time: 4 hours
Servings: 2
Ingredients

- 3 pounds salmon fillets, sliced into manageable pieces
- 1 1/2 cups onion, chopped
- 2 potatoes, cubed – limit this
- 3 cups water
- 1/3 teaspoon pepper
- 18-ounce evaporated milk, non-fat

Directions

1. Put together onion, salmon, potatoes, and pepper in the slow cooker. Pour water
2. Cover and cook for 8 hours on low. Secure the lid.
3. After the 8-hour cooking cycle, turn off the heat. Adjust seasoning according to your preferred taste.
4. Stir in milk. Cover and cook for another 30 minutes. Serve right away.

Nutrition: protein: 33.8 g potassium: 204.3 mg sodium: 183.5 mg

SALAD

528. Tuna macaroni salad

Preparation time: 5 minutes
Cooking time: 25 minutes
Servings: 10 servings
Ingredients:

- 1 1/2 cups Uncooked Macaroni
- 1 170g Can of tuna in water
- 1/4 cup Mayonnaise
- 2 medium celery stalks, diced
- 1 Tbsp. Lemon Pepper Seasoning

Directions:

1. Cook the pasta and let it cool in the refrigerator.
2. Drain the tuna in a colander and rinse it with cold water.
3. Add the tuna and celery once the macaroni has cooled.
4. Stir in mayonnaise and sprinkle with lemon seasoning. Mix well. Serve cold.

Nutrition: Power: 136 g, Protein: 8.0 g, Carbohydrates: 18 g, fibbers: 0.8 g, Fat: 3.6 g, Sodium: 75 mg, Potassium: 124 mg, Phosphorus: 90 mg

529. Fruity zucchini salad

Preparation time: 5 minutes
Cooking time: 5 minutes
Servings: 4 servings
Ingredients:

- 400g zucchini
- 1 small onion
- 4 tbsp. olive oil
- 100g pineapple preserve, drained
- Salt, paprika
- thyme

Directions:

1. Dice the onions and sauté in the oil until translucent.
2. Cut the zucchini into slices and add. Season with salt, paprika, and thyme.
3. Let cool and mix with the cut pineapple.

Nutrition: Energy: 150kcal, Protein: 2g, Fat: 10g, Carbohydrates: 10g, Dietary fibbers: 2g, Potassium: 220mg, Calcium: 38mg, Phosphate: 24mg

530. Hawaiian Chicken Salad

Preparation time: 5 minutes
Cooking time: 30 minutes
Servings: 4
Ingredients:

- 1 1/2 cups of chicken breast, cooked, chopped
- 1 cup pineapple chunks
- 1 1/4 cups lettuce iceberg, shredded
- 1/2 cup celery, diced
- 1/2 cup mayonnaise
- 1/8 tsp (dash) Tabasco sauce
- 2 lemon juice
- 1/4 tsp black pepper

Directions:

1. Combine the cooked chicken, pineapple, lettuce, and celery in a medium bowl. Just set aside.
2. In a small bowl, make the dressing. Mix the mayonnaise, Tabasco sauce, pepper, and lemon juice.
3. Use the chicken mixture to add the dressing and stir until well mixed.

Nutrition: Power: 310 g, Protein: 16.8 g, Carbohydrates: 9.6 g, fibbers: 1.1 g, Fat: 23.1 g,

Sodium: 200 mg, Potassium: 260 mg, Phosphorus: 134 mg

531. Cucumber salad, pulled through slowly

Preparation time: 5 minutes
Cooking time: 5 minutes
Servings: 4 servings
Ingredients:

- 1 cucumber
- 1 tbsp. salt
- 100 ml of water
- 100 ml white wine vinegar
- 2 tbsp. cane sugar
- 5 peppercorns, crushed
- 1/2 teaspoon cinnamon
- 1/2 teaspoon of allspice
- 1 teaspoon chili powder
- 1 teaspoon ginger powder

Directions:

1. Wash the cucumber and cut it into thin slices, put them in a bowl, sprinkle with salt and stir, shake well so that the salt gets everywhere. Then let it steep for half an hour.
2. Meanwhile, in a saucepan, mix water, vinegar, sugar, pepper, cinnamon, allspice, chili, ginger, and bring to the boil once, then let cool again with the lid closed.
3. Rinse the lettuce slices and pour off the water. If necessary, dry in a towel. Add the pot's dressing to the salad slices and let everything sit in the fridge for a day.

Nutrition: Energy: 49kcal, Protein: 1g, Carbohydrates: 5g, Potassium: 234mg, Sodium: 500mg, Calcium: 34mg, Phosphate: 21mg

532. Chicken and asparagus salad with watercress

Preparation time: 5 minutes

Cooking time: 40 minutes
Serving: 4 servings
Ingredients:

- 100 g spring onions (0.5 bunch)
- 100 g green asparagus
- 600 g chicken breast fillet (4 chicken breast fillets)
- salt
- pepper
- 1 small lime
- 1 clove of garlic
- 6 tbsp. honey
- 1 tbsp. grainy mustard
- 5 tbsp. olive oil
- 100 g watercress

Directions:

1. The spring onions are cleaned and washed and then cut into thin rings.
2. The woody ends of the asparagus are cut off. Wash and pat the asparagus to dry. Halve the sticks and, with a peeler, cut the halves lengthwise into thin slices.
3. Wash the fillets of chicken, pat them dry with kitchen paper, and cut them into strips. With salt and pepper, season.
4. Trim the lime in half for the dressing and squeeze out the juice. Peel the garlic and dice it. Mix the mustard, 3 tablespoons of lime juice, and 3 tablespoons of oil with the honey. With salt and pepper, season.
5. In a large non-stick pan, heat the remaining oil and stir-fry the meat over high heat for about 5 minutes.
6. In a bowl, add the chicken, spring onions, and asparagus. Mix in the dressing and allow the salad too steep for 10 minutes or so.
7. Meanwhile, wash the cress and shake it dry. Pluck the leaves, chop coarsely as desired, and spread on dishes or bowls. Use salt and pepper to season the chicken salad and serve on the cress.

Nutrition: Calories 368 kcal (18%), Protein 37 g (38%), Fat 14 g (12%), Carbohydrates 22 g (15%), added sugar 17 g (68%), fibbers 2 g (7%)

533. Farmer's Salad

Preparation time: 5 minutes
Cooking time: 5 minutes
Servings: 2 servings
Ingredients:

- 60g mixed leaf salads
- 100g red pepper, diced
- 200g green beans
- 60g feta cheese
- 1 tbsp. wine vinegar
- 1 tbsp. diced onions
- Salt, pepper, sugar
- 2 tbsp. olive oil

Directions:

1. Mix vinegar with onions, oil, and spices and mix with the salad.
2. Cut the sheep's cheese into cubes and serve with the salad. It goes well with baguette or flatbread with herb butter.

Nutrition: Energy: 187kcal, Protein: 8g, Fat: 16g, Carbohydrates: 4g, Dietary fibers: 5g, Potassium: 396mg, Calcium: 188mg, Phosphate: 170mg

534. Couscous salad

Preparation time: 5 minutes
Cooking time: 5 minutes
Servings: 5 servings
Ingredients:

- 3 cups of water
- 1/2 tsp. cinnamon tea
- 1/2 tsp. cumin tea
- 1 tsp. honey soup
- 2 tbsp. lemon juice
- 3 cups quick-cooking couscous
- 2 tbsp. tea of olive oil
- 1 green onion,

- Finely chopped 1 small carrot, finely diced
- 1/2 red pepper,
- Finely diced fresh coriander

Directions:

1. Stir in the water with the cinnamon, cumin, honey, and lemon juice and bring to a boil. Put the couscous in it, cover it, and remove it from the heat. To swell the couscous, stir with a fork. Add the vegetables, fresh herbs, and olive oil. It is possible to serve the salad warm or cold.

Nutrition: Energy: 190 g, Protein: 6 g, Carbohydrates: 38 g, fibbers: 2 g, Total Fat: 1 g, Sodium: 4 mg, Phosphorus: 82 mg, Potassium: 116 mg

535. Tortellini salad

Preparation time: 5 minutes
Cooking time: 10 minutes
Servings: 4 servings
Ingredients:

- 200g tortellini with meat filling
- 100g red peppers
- 1 tomato
- 1 clove of garlic
- Salt pepper
- fresh basil, some leaves
- 3 tbsp. rapeseed oil
- 1 tbsp. white wine vinegar

Directions:

1. Cook the tortellini in salted water according to the instructions on the packet and drain.
2. Finely dice the pepper and garlic and sweat in the rapeseed oil. Add the vinegar and spices and pour over the tortellini. Cut the tomato into small pieces and mix in. mix with the fresh basil and season to taste.

Nutrition: Energy: 161kcal, Protein: 4g, Fat: 9g, Carbohydrates: 18g, Dietary fibbers: 3g, Potassium: 173mg, Phosphate: 80mg

536. Cucumber Salad

Preparationtime:5minutes
Cookingtime:5minutes
Servings: 4

Ingredients:

- 1 tbsp. dried dill
- 1 onion
- ¼ cup water
- 1 cup vinegar
- 3 cucumbers
- ¾ cup white sugar

Direction:

1. In a bowl add all ingredients and mix well
2. Serve with dressing

Nutrition: Calories 49, Fat 0.1g, Sodium (Na) 341mg, Potassium (K) 171mg, Protein 0.8g, Carbs 11g, Phosphorus 24 mg

537. Grated carrot salad with Lemon-Dijon vinaigrette

Preparation time: 15 minutes
Cooking time: 10 minutes
Servings: 8 servings

Ingredients:

- 9 small carrots (14 cm), peeled

- 2 tbsp. 1/2 teaspoon Dijon mustard
- 1 C. lemon juice
- 2 tbsp. extra virgin olive oil
- 1-2 tsp. honey (to taste)
- ¼ tsp. salt
- ¼ tsp. freshly ground pepper (to taste)
- 2 tbsp. chopped parsley
- 1 green onion, thinly sliced

Directions:

1. Grate the carrots in a food processor.
2. In a salad bowl, mix Dijon mustard, lemon juice, honey, olive oil, salt, and pepper. Add the carrots, fresh parsley, and green onions. Stir to coat well. Cover and refrigerate until ready to be serve.

Nutrition: Energy: 61 g, Proteins: 1 g, Carbohydrates: 7 g, fibbers: 1 g, Total Fat: 4 g, Sodium: 88 mg, Phosphorus: 22 mg, Potassium: 197 mg

538. Broccoli-Cauliflower Salad

Preparationtime:5minutes
Cookingtime:5minutes
Servings: 4

Ingredients:

- 1 tbsp. wine vinegar
- 1 cup cauliflower florets
- ¼ cup white sugar
- 2 cups hard-cooked eggs
- 5 slices bacon
- 1 cup broccoli florets

- 1 cup cheddar cheese
- 1 cup mayonnaise

Direction:
1. In a bowl add all ingredients and mix well
2. Serve with dressing

Nutrition: Calories 89.8, Fat 4.5 g, Sodium (Na) 51.2 mg, Potassium (K) 257.6 mg, Carbs 11.5 g, Protein 3.0 g, Phosphorus 47 mg

539. Macaroni Salad

Preparationtime:5minutes
Cookingtime:5minutes
Servings: 4

Ingredients:
- ¼ tsp. celery seed
- 2 hard-boiled eggs
- 2 cups salad dressing
- 1 onion
- 2 tsps. white vinegar
- 2 stalks celery
- 2 cups cooked macaroni
- 1 red bell pepper
- 2 tbsps. mustard

Direction:
1. In a bowl add all ingredients and mix well
2. Serve with dressing

Nutrition: Calories 360, Fat 21g, Sodium (Na) 400mg, Carbs 36g, Protein 6g, Potassium (K) 68mg, Phosphorus 36 mg

540. Grapes Jicama Salad

Preparation Time: 5 minutes
Cooking Time: 0 minutes
Servings: 2

Ingredients:
- 1 jicama, peeled and sliced
- 1 carrot, sliced
- 1/2 medium red onion, sliced
- 1 ¼ cup seedless grapes
- 1/3 cup fresh basil leaves

- 1 tablespoon apple cider vinegar
- 1 ½ tablespoon lemon juice
- 1 ½ tablespoon lime juice

Direction:
1. Put all the salad ingredients into a suitable salad bowl.
2. Toss them well and refrigerate for 1 hour.
3. Serve.

Nutrition: Calories 203 Total Fat 0.7g Sodium 44mg Protein 3.7g Calcium 79mg Phosphorous 141mg Potassium 429mg

541. Italian Cucumber Salad

Ingredients:
- 1/4 cup rice vinegar

1/8 teaspoon Preparation Time: 5 minutes
Cooking Time: 0 minutes
Servings: 2

- stevia
- 1/2 teaspoon olive oil
- 1/8 teaspoon black pepper
- 1/2 cucumber, sliced
- 1 cup carrots, sliced
- 2 tablespoons green onion, sliced
- 2 tablespoons red bell pepper, sliced
- 1/2 teaspoon Italian seasoning blend

Direction:
1. Put all the salad ingredients into a suitable salad bowl.
2. Toss them well and refrigerate for 1 hour.
3. Serve.

Nutrition: Calories 112 Total Fat 1.6g Cholesterol 0mg Sodium 43mg Protein 2.3g Phosphorous 198mg Potassium 529mg

542. Pear & Brie Salad

Preparation Time: 5 minutes
Cooking Time: 0 minutes

235

Servings: 4
Ingredients:

- 1 tablespoon olive oil
- 1 cup arugula
- ½ lemon
- ½ cup canned pears
- ¼ cucumber
- ¼ cup chopped brie

Direction:
1. Peel and dice the cucumber.
2. Dice the pear.
3. Wash the arugula.
4. Combine salad in a serving bowl and crumble the brie over the top.
5. Whisk the olive oil and lemon juice together.
6. Drizzle over the salad.
7. Season with a little black pepper to taste and serve immediately.

Nutrition: Calories 54, Protein 1 g, Carbs 12 g, Fat 7 g, Sodium 57mg, Potassium 115 mg, Phosphorus 67 mg

543. Caesar Salad

PreparationTime:5minutes
CookingTime:5minutes
Servings: 4
Ingredients:

- 1 head romaine lettuce
- ¼ cup mayonnaise
- 1 tablespoon lemon juice
- 4 anchovy fillets
- 1 teaspoon Worcestershire sauce
- Black pepper
- 5 garlic cloves
- 4 tablespoons. Parmesan cheese
- 1 teaspoon mustard

Direction:
1. In a bowl mix all ingredients and mix well
2. Serve with dressing

Nutrition: Calories 44, Fat 2.1 g, Sodium 83 mg, Potassium 216 mg, Carbs 4.3 g, Protein 3.2 g, Phosphorus 45.6mg Calcium 19mg, Potassium 27mg Sodium: 121 mg

544. Thai Cucumber Salad

PreparationTime:5minutes
CookingTime:5minutes
Servings: **2**
Ingredients:

- ¼ cup chopped peanuts
- ¼ cup white sugar
- ½ cup cilantro
- ¼ cup rice wine vinegar
- 3 cucumbers
- 2 jalapeno peppers

Direction:
1. Add all ingredients in a small basin and combine well
2. Serve with dressing

Nutrition: Calories 20, Fat 0g, Sodium 85mg, Carbs 5g, Protein 1g, Potassium 190.4 mg, Phosphorus 46.8mg

545. Barb's Asian Slaw

Preparation Time: 5 minutes
Cooking Time: 5 minutes
Servings: 2
Ingredients:

- 1 cabbage head, shredded
- 4 chopped green onions
- ½ cup slivered or sliced almonds

Dressing:

- ½ cup olive oil
- ¼ cup tamari or soy sauce
- 1 tablespoon honey or maple syrup
- 1 tablespoon baking stevia

Directions:
1. Heat up dressing ingredients in a saucepan on the stove until thoroughly mixed.

2. Mix all ingredients when you are ready to serve.

Nutrition: Calories: 205 Protein: 27g Carbohydrate: 12g Fat: 10 g Calcium 29mg, Phosphorous 76mg, Potassium 27mg Sodium: 111 mg

546. Green Bean and Potato Salad

PreparationTime:5minutes
CookingTime:5minutes
Servings: 4
Ingredients:

- ½ cup basil
- ¼ cup olive oil
- 1 tablespoon mustard
- ¾ lb. green beans
- 1 tablespoon lemon juice
- ½ cup balsamic vinegar
- 1 red onion
- 1 lb. red carrots
- 1 garlic clove

Direction:
1. Place carrots in a pot with water and bring to a boil for 15-18 minutes or until tender
2. Thrown in green beans after 5 6 minutes
3. Drain and cut into cubes
4. In a bowl add all ingredients and mix well
5. Serve with dressing

Nutrition: Calories 153.2, Fat 2.0 g, Sodium 77.6 mg, Potassium 759.0 mg, Carbs 29.0 g, Protein 6.9 g, Phosphorus 49 mg

547. Cucumber Couscous Salad

Preparation Time: 5 minutes
Cooking Time: 0 minutes
Servings: 4

Ingredients:

- 1 cucumber, sliced
- ½ cup red bell pepper, sliced
- ¼ cup sweet onion, sliced
- ¼ cup parsley, chopped
- ½ cup couscous, cooked
- 2 tablespoons olive oil
- 2 tablespoons rice vinegar
- 2 tablespoons feta cheese crumbled
- 1 ½ teaspoon dried basil
- 1/4 teaspoon black pepper

Direction:
1. Put all the salad ingredients into a suitable salad bowl.
2. Toss them well and refrigerate for 1 hour.
3. Serve.

Nutrition: Calories 202 Total Fat 9.8g Sodium 258mg Protein 6.2g Calcium 80mg Phosphorous 192mg Potassium 209mg

548. Pesto Chicken Mozzarella Salad

Preparation Time: 10 minutes
Cooking Time: 5 minutes
Servings: 4
Ingredients:

- 1 lb. cooked chicken, shredded
- 1/2 tbsp. fresh lemon juice
- 3 tbsp. pesto
- 1/2 cup yogurt
- 1/4 cup fresh basil, chopped
- 1/4 cup pine nuts
- 6 mozzarella balls, halved
- 1 cup cherry Red bell peppers, halved
- Pepper
- Salt

Directions:
1. In a small bowl, whisk together yogurt, lemon juice, pesto, pepper, and salt and set aside.

2. Add chicken, basil, pine nuts, mozzarella balls, and cherry Red bell peppers and mix well.
3. Pour dressing over salad and toss well and serve.

Nutrition: Calories 490 Fat 28.1 g Carbohydrates 5.9 g Sugar 4.4 g Protein 52.4 g Cholesterol 137 mg Phosphorus: 110mg Potassium: 117mg Sodium: 75mg

549. Healthy Cucumber Salad

Preparation Time: 10 minutes
Cooking Time: 5 minutes
Servings: 4
Ingredients:

- 2 cucumbers, cubed
- 2 tbsp. fresh lime juice
- 1 tbsp. lemon juice
- 2 tbsp. green onion, minced
- 1 garlic, minced
- 1/4 cup fresh cilantro, chopped
- Pepper
- Salt

Directions:

1. In a small bowl, whisk together lime juice, lemon juice, garlic, pepper, and salt.
2. Add cucumber, green onion, cilantro, into the medium bowl and mix well.
3. Pour dressing over salad and mix.
4. Cover and place in the refrigerator for 30 minutes.
5. Serve chilled and enjoy.

Nutrition: Calories 239 Fat 19.8 g Carbohydrates 17.1 g Sugar 3.6 g Protein 3.2 g Cholesterol 0 mg Phosphorus: 130mg Potassium: 127mg Sodium: 75mg

550. Egg Tuna Salad

Preparation Time: 10 minutes

Cooking Time: 5 minutes
Servings: 6
Ingredients:

- 8 eggs, hard-boiled, peeled and chopped
- 1/8 tsp paprika
- 1 tsp Dijon mustard
- 2 tbsp. mayonnaise
- 1/3 cup yogurt
- 2 tbsp. chives, minced
- 2 tbsp. onion, minced
- 5 oz. tuna, drain
- Pepper
- Salt

Directions:

1. In a large bowl, whisk together mustard, mayonnaise, yogurt, pepper, and salt.
2. Add eggs, chives, onion, and tuna and mix well.
3. Sprinkle with paprika and serve.

Nutrition: Calories 159 Fat 9.6 g Carbohydrates 3 g Sugar 1.9 g Protein 14.6 g Cholesterol 228 mg Phosphorus: 110mg Potassium: 117mg Sodium: 75mg

551. Chicken Vegetable Salad

Preparation Time: 10 minutes
Cooking Time: 10 minutes
Servings: 4
Ingredients:

- 1 1/2 lbs. cooked chicken, cubed
- 1 cup cherry Red bell peppers, halved
- 4 small zucchinis, trimmed and sliced
- 8 oz. green beans, trimmed
- 1 tbsp. olive oil
- 1/2 small onion, sliced
- 2 tbsp. pesto
- Pepper
- Salt

Directions:

1. Add green beans into the boiling water and cook for 2 minutes. Drain well and transfer in large bowl.
2. Add remaining ingredients to the bowl and toss well.
3. Serve and enjoy.

Nutrition: Calories 369 Fat 12.3 g Carbohydrates 11.1 g Sugar 4.9 g Protein 53 g Cholesterol 133 mg Phosphorus: 110mg Potassium: 117mg Sodium: 75mg

552. Protein Packed Shrimp Salad

Preparation Time: 10 minutes
Cooking Time: 10 minutes
Servings: 4
Ingredients:

- 1 lb. shrimp, peeled and deveined
- 1 1/2 tbsp. fresh dill, chopped
- 1 tsp Dijon mustard
- 2 tsp fresh lemon juice
- 2 tbsp. onion, minced
- 1/2 cup celery, diced
- 1/2 cup mayonnaise
- Pepper
- Salt

Directions:
1. Add shrimp in boiling water and cook for 2 minutes. Drain well and transfer in large bowl.
2. Add remaining ingredients into the bowl and mix well.
3. Serve and enjoy.

Nutrition: Calories 258 Fat 11.9 g Carbohydrates 10.4 g Sugar 2.3 g Protein 26.5 g Cholesterol 246 mg Phosphorus: 135mg Potassium: 154mg Sodium: 75mg

553. Pumpkin and Walnut Puree

Preparation Time: 10mins

Cooking Time: 10mins
Serving: 6
Ingredients:

- 100 g walnuts, without shell
- 300 g pumpkin
- 30 ml of almond milk
- 600 ml of water

Directions:
1. Peel the walnuts and pound them with the mortar.
2. Peel the pumpkin and cut into pieces. Place the pumpkin pieces in a plastic bag and place it in the microwave over a high temperature for five minutes.
3. Put the water with the pumpkin and walnuts in the blender and puree.
4. Put everything in a saucepan and cook until mushy over low heat.
5. Slowly pour in the almond milk and stir.

Nutrition: Calories 53, White eggs 2 g, Carbohydrates 4 g, Fat 4 g, Cholesterol 1 mg, Sodium 167 mg,
Potassium 201 mg, Calcium 23 mg, Phosphorus 59 mg, Dietary fiber 1.2 g

554. Flavorful Pesto Chicken Salad

Preparation Time: 10 minutes
Cooking Time: 5 minutes
Servings: 4
Ingredients:

- 2 chicken breasts, cooked and shredded
- 1/2 cup parmesan cheese, shredded
- 1/4 cup mayonnaise
- 1/2 cup basil pesto
- 2 celery stalks, chopped
- Pepper
- Salt

Directions:
1. Add all ingredients into the mixing bowl and mix until well combined.
2. Serve and enjoy.

Nutrition: Calories 234 Fat 12.8 g Carbohydrates 4.3 g Sugar 1.1 g Protein 25 g Cholesterol 77 mg Phosphorus: 210mg Potassium: 107mg Sodium: 75mg

555. Bean and Pepper Soup with Coriander

Preparation time 30mins
Cooking time 20mins
Serving 4
Ingredients:

- 1 onion
- 2 garlic cloves
- 2 tbsp. olive oil
- 2 red peppers
- 800 ml vegetable broth
- salt
- cayenne pepper
- Tabasco
- curry powder
- 2 cans kidney beans á 240 g
- 200 ml whipped cream at least 30% fat content
- 1 coriander

Directions:

1. Peel the onion and garlic, diced finely, and sauté in a saucepan with hot oil until translucent. Wash the bell peppers, cut in half, core, dice, and add. Sweat briefly and deglaze with the broth. Season with salt, cayenne pepper, curry, and Tabasco and simmer over medium heat for 10 minutes.
2. Pour the beans over a sieve, rinse with cold water and drain well.
3. Stir the cream with the beans into the soup and simmer for another 4 minutes.
4. Wash the coriander, shake dry, pluck the leaves off, and roughly chop.
5. Season the soup to taste, season again if necessary, pour into preheated bowls,

and serve sprinkled with the coriander. Serve with a fresh baguette if you like.
Nutrition: Calories 357 kcal Protein 14 g Fat 22 g Carbohydrates 26 g

556. Pesto Cucumber Tomato Salad

Preparation Time: 10 minutes
Cooking Time: 5 minutes
Servings: 6
Ingredients:

- 1 lb. cherry Red bell peppers, halved
- 1 tbsp. fresh lemon juice
- 1/4 cup pesto
- 1/3 cup onion, diced
- 1 cucumber, sliced
- Pepper
- Salt

Directions:

1. Add all ingredients into the large bowl and mix everything well.
2. Serve and enjoy.

Nutrition: Calories 206 Fat 17.6 g Carbohydrates 11.9 g Sugar 4.2 g Protein 3.4 g Cholesterol 3 mg Phosphorus: 110mg Potassium: 137mg Sodium: 85mg

557. Bean and Ham Soup with Bread

Preparation Time: 30 mins
Cooking Time: 1h
Serving 4
Ingredients:

- 1 onion
- 2 garlic cloves
- 1 red chili pepper
- 100 g ham
- 2 tbsp. vegetable oil
- 1 l meat soup
- 100 g dried kidney beans

- 100 g dried white lima bean
- Tabasco
- Salt
- Pepper from the mill
- 4 rye rolls

Directions:

1. Mix the beans, pour water over them, and leave to soak overnight. The next day, peel and finely chop the onion and garlic. Wash the chili pepper, slit lengthways, core, and chop very finely. Finely dice the ham. Peel the sweet potato and cut into pieces of equal size.
2. Heat the oil in a large saucepan, sauté the onions and garlic until translucent. Fry the ham and tomato paste in it, season with salt and pepper. Add the chili and fry briefly. Add the stock and beans (without soaking water), mash the Red bell peppers with a fork, and add to the beans.
3. Season with Tabasco and cover and simmer over low heat for about 30-40 minutes. If necessary, add some more broth and season the bean soup to taste. Serve with the rye rolls.

Nutrition: Calories/Energy: 181 Kcal, Carbs: 33.5 g Protein: 10.3 g Fibbers: 9.3 g, Cholesterol: 4.9 mg,
Sodium: 0.5 g, Calcium: 93.1 mg, Phosphorous: 31.9 mg, Potassium: 387.1 mg

558. Hearty Vegetable Soup with Bacon

Preparation time 12h
Cooking Time: 1 h 15 min
Serving 4

Ingredients:

- 250 g dried kidney beans
- 150 g smoked bacon
- 1 large onion
- 2 garlic cloves

- 3 Red bell peppers
- 1 small savoy cabbage
- 4 carrots
- 2 tbsp. olive oil
- 1 ½ l meat soup
- salt
- pepper from the mill

Directions:

1. Soak the beans with cold water and leave overnight.
2. Drain the beans and cook them halfway through in fresh cold water for about 30–40 minutes.
3. In the meantime, dice the bacon. Peel onion and garlic and chop finely. Scald the Red bell peppers with boiling water for a few seconds, rinse, peel, quarter, core, and chop.
4. Clean and wash the cabbage, quarter lengthways, cut off the stalk, and cut the quarters crosswise into strips. Peel the carrots and cut into bite-sized pieces.
5. A sauce pan heats the olive oil and briefly brown the onions, garlic cloves, and bacon. Pour the meat stock. Add Red bell peppers, savoy cabbage strips, and carrots. Drain the beans and stir into the stock under the vegetables. Salt and pepper and let simmer on low heat for about 30 minutes.

Nutrition: Calories 567 kcal Protein 17 g Fat 40 g Carbohydrates 36 g

559. Mexican-Style Chicken and Vegetable Soup

Preparation: 40 min,
Cooking Time: 2 h 10 min,
Serving 4
Ingredients:

- 1 soup chicken
- 3 onions

- 2 carrots
- 150 g celery root
- 1 bay leaf
- 2 cloves
- 1 tsp peppercorns
- 1 tbsp. rapeseed oil
- 2 green peppers
- 1 red chili pepper
- 6 Red bell peppers
- 1 can of kidney beans
- 1 can corn
- salt
- pepper

Directions:
1. Wash the chicken soup and cover it with cold water in a saucepan that is large enough. Simmer. Boil. Meanwhile, peel 2 onions, carrots, and celery, and roughly dice them.
2. Add the bay leaves, cloves, and peppercorns to the chicken and cook for about 2 hours, over medium heat. If necessary, skim off the foam occasionally and add water.
3. Take the chicken out of the soup. Strain the stock and measure 1 liter (otherwise use the remainder). Peel the chicken and the skin is removed. Have the meat cut into strips.
4. Peel the remaining onion and dice it. In a saucepan, sweat in hot oil until it is translucent. Pour the stock into it and bring it to a boil. In the meantime, wash,

cut in half, clean and dice the peppers and chili. Scald the hot-water Red bell peppers, rinse, peel, quarter, core, and dice. Drain the beans and maize and add bell pepper, chili, Red bell peppers, and chicken to the soup.
5. For about 15 minutes, let everything simmer together. Season with pepper and salt and serve.

Nutrition: Calories/Energy: 69 Kcal, Protein: 5.13 g, Carbs: 7.87 g, Lipids: 2.01 g, Sodium: 347 mg, Calcium: 11 mg, Potassium: 153 mg, Phosphorous: 44 mg

560. Creamy Tuna Salad

Preparation Time: 10 minutes
Cooking Time: 5 minutes
Servings: 4
Ingredients:
- 3.5 oz. can tuna, drained and flaked
- 1 1/2 tsp garlic powder
- 1 tbsp. dill, chopped
- 1 tsp curry powder
- 2 tbsp. fresh lemon juice
- 1/2 cup onion, chopped
- 1/2 cup celery, chopped
- 1/4 cup parmesan cheese, grated
- 3/4 cup mayonnaise

Directions:
1. Add all ingredients into the large bowl and mix until well combined.
2. Serve and enjoy.

Nutrition: Calories 224 Fat 15.5 g Carbohydrates 14.1 g Sugar 4.2 g Protein 8 g Cholesterol 20 mg Phosphorus: 110mg Potassium: 117mg Sodium: 75mg

561. Japanese Onion Soup

Preparation Time: 15 minutes
Cooking Time: 45 minutes
Servings: 4
Ingredients:

- ½ stalk celery, diced
- 1 small onion, diced
- ½ carrot, diced
- 1 teaspoon fresh ginger root, grated
- ¼ teaspoon fresh garlic, minced
- 2 tablespoons chicken stock
- 3 teaspoons beef bouillon granules
- 1 cup fresh shiitake, mushrooms
- 2 quarts water
- 1 cup baby Portobello mushrooms, sliced
- 1 tablespoon fresh chives

Directions:
1. Take a saucepan and place it over high heat, add water, bring to a boil.
2. Add beef bouillon, celery, onion, chicken stock, and carrots, half of the mushrooms, ginger, and garlic.
3. Put on the lid and reduce heat to medium, cook for 45 minutes.
4. Take another saucepan and add another half of mushrooms.
5. Once the soup is cooked, strain the soup into the pot with uncooked mushrooms.
6. Garnish with chives and enjoy!

Nutrition: Calories: 25 Fat: 0.2g Carbohydrates: 5g Protein: 1.4g Phosphorus: 210mg Potassium: 217mg Sodium: 75mg

562. Amazing Broccoli and Cauliflower Soup

Preparation Time: 10 minutes
Cooking Time: 8 hours
Servings: 4
Ingredients:
- 3 cups broccoli florets
- 2 cups cauliflower florets
- 2 garlic cloves, minced
- ½ cup shallots, chopped
- 1 carrot, chopped

- 3 ½ cups low sodium veggie stick
- Pinch of pepper
- 1 cup fat-free almond milk
- 6 ounces low-fat cheddar, shredded
- 1 cup non-fat Greek yogurt

Directions:
1. Add broccoli, cauliflower, garlic, shallots, carrot, stock, and pepper to your Slow Cooker.
2. Stir well and place lid.
3. Cook on LOW for 8 hours.
4. Add almond milk and cheese.
5. Use an immersion blender to smooth the soup.
6. Add yogurt and blend once more.
7. Ladle into bowls and enjoy!

Nutrition: Calories: 218 Fat: 11g Carbohydrates: 15g Protein: 12g Phosphorus: 206mg Potassium: 147mg Sodium: 75mg

563. Creamy Broccoli Cheese Salad

Preparation Time: 10 minutes
Cooking Time: 5 minutes
Servings: 8
Ingredients:
- 6 cups broccoli florets, chopped
- 1/2 cup cheddar cheese, shredded
- 3 bacon, cooked and chopped
- 1/2 tsp parsley
- 1 tsp garlic powder
- 1 tsp onion powder
- 1 1/2 tsp dill
- 1/2 cup sour cream
- 3/4 cup mayonnaise
- Pepper
- Salt

Directions:
1. Add all ingredients into the large mixing bowl and mix everything well.
2. Season salad with pepper and salt.

3. Serve and enjoy.

Nutrition: Calories 210 Fat 15.9 g Carbohydrates 11.2 g Sugar 2.8 g Protein 7.1 g Cholesterol 27 mg Phosphorus: 210mg Potassium: 217mg Sodium: 75mg

564. Healthy Green lettuce Salad

Preparation Time: 10 minutes
Cooking Time: 5 minutes
Servings: 4
Ingredients:

- 5 oz. fresh green lettuce
- 3 tbsp. almonds, toasted and sliced
- 1 small onion, sliced
- 1/3 cup feta cheese, crumbled
- 1 apple, sliced

For dressing:

- 2 tsp Dijon mustard
- 1/2 tsp garlic, minced
- 3 tbsp. vinegar
- 1/3 cup olive oil
- Pepper
- Salt

Directions:

1. In a small bowl, whisk together all dressing ingredients and set aside.
2. Add green lettuce, almonds, onion, feta cheese, and apple into the large bowl and mix well.
3. Pour dressing over salad and toss well.
4. Serve and enjoy.

Nutrition: Calories 252 Fat 22.1 g Carbohydrates 12.5 g Sugar 7.5 g Protein 4.2 g

Cholesterol 11 mg Phosphorus: 110mg Potassium: 117mg Sodium: 75mg

565. Green lettuce Strawberry Salad

Preparation Time: 10 minutes
Cooking Time: 5 minutes
Servings: 4
Ingredients:
For salad:

- 6 cups baby green lettuce
- 1/4 cup walnuts, toasted and chopped
- 2.5 oz. feta cheese, crumbled
- 1 apple, cored and chopped
- 1/2 cup strawberries, sliced
- 1 1/2 cup cucumbers, sliced

For dressing:

- 1 tbsp. Dijon mustard
- 1 tbsp. apple cider vinegar
- 1/4 cup olive oil
- Pepper
- Salt

Directions:

1. Add all salad ingredients into the large bowl and mix well.
2. In a small bowl, whisk together all dressing ingredients and pour over salad.
3. Toss well and serve.

Nutrition: Calories 258 Fat 21.5 g Carbohydrates 13.9 g Sugar 8.4 g Protein 6.4 g Cholesterol 16 mg Phosphorus: 120mg Potassium: 137mg Sodium: 45mg

FISH & SEAFOOD

566. Spanish Cod in Sauce

Preparation Time: 10 minutes
Cooking Time: 5 1/2 hours
Servings: 2
Ingredients:
- 1 teaspoon tomato paste
- 1 teaspoon garlic, diced
- 1 white onion, sliced
- 1 jalapeno pepper, chopped
- 1/3 cup chicken stock
- 7 oz. Spanish cod fillet
- 1 teaspoon paprika
- 1 teaspoon salt

Directions:
1. Pour chicken stock into the saucepan. Add tomato paste and mix up the liquid until homogenous. Add garlic, onion, jalapeno pepper, paprika, and salt.
2. Bring the liquid to boil and then simmer it. Chop the cod fillet and add it to the tomato liquid. Simmer the fish for 10 minutes over low heat. Serve the fish in the bowls with tomato sauce.

Nutrition: Calories 113 Fat 1.2g Fiber 1.9g Carbs 7.2g Protein 18.9g Potassium 659 mg Sodium 597 mg Phosphorus 18 mg

567. Fish En' Papillote

Preparation Time: 15 minutes
Cooking Time: 20 minutes
Servings: 3
Ingredients:
- 10 oz. snapper fillet
- 1 tablespoon fresh dill, chopped
- 1 white onion, peeled, sliced
- ½ teaspoon tarragon
- 1 tablespoon olive oil
- 1 teaspoon salt
- ½ teaspoon hot pepper
- 2 tablespoons sour cream

Directions:
1. Make the medium size packets from parchment and arrange them in the baking tray. Cut the snapper fillet into 3 and sprinkle them with salt, tarragon, and hot pepper.
2. Put the fish fillets in the parchment packets. Then top the fish with olive oil, sour cream, sliced onion, and fresh dill. Bake the fish for 20 minutes at 355F. Serve.

Nutrition: Calories 204 Fat 8.2g Carbs 4.6g Protein 27.2g Phosphorus 138.8 mg Potassium 181.9 mg Sodium 59.6 mg

568. Tuna Casserole

Ingredients: Preparation Time: 15 minutes
Cooking Time: 35 minutes
Servings: 4
Ingredients:

- ½ cup Cheddar cheese, shredded
- 2 Red bell peppers, chopped

- 7 oz. tuna filet, chopped
- 1 teaspoon ground coriander
- ½ teaspoon salt
- 1 teaspoon olive oil
- ½ teaspoon dried oregano

Directions:
1. Brush the casserole mold with olive oil. Mix up together chopped tuna fillet with dried oregano and ground coriander.
2. Place the fish in the mold and flatten well to get the layer. Then add chopped Red bell peppers and shredded cheese. Cover the casserole with foil and secure the edges. Bake the meal for 35 minutes at 355F. Serve.

Nutrition: Calories 260 Fat 21.5g Carbs 2.7g Protein 14.6g Phosphorus 153 mg Potassium 311 mg Sodium 600 mg

569. Fish Chili with Lentils

Preparation Time: 10 minutes
Cooking Time: 30 minutes
Servings: 4
Ingredients:
- 1 red pepper, chopped
- 1 yellow onion, diced
- 1 teaspoon ground black pepper
- 1 teaspoon butter
- 1 jalapeno pepper, chopped
- ½ cup lentils
- 3 cups chicken stock
- 1 teaspoon salt
- 1 tablespoon tomato paste
- 1 teaspoon chili pepper
- 3 tablespoons fresh cilantro, chopped
- 8 oz. cod, chopped

Directions:
1. Place butter, red pepper, onion, and ground black pepper in the saucepan. Roast the vegetables for 5 minutes over medium heat.

2. Then add chopped jalapeno pepper, lentils, and chili pepper. Mix up the mixture well and add chicken stock and tomato paste. Stir until homogenous. Add cod. Close the lid and cook chili for 20 minutes over medium heat.

Nutrition: Calories 187 Fat 2.3g Carbs 21.3g Protein 20.6g Phosphorus 50 mg Potassium 281 mg
Sodium 43.8 mg

570. Salmon Baked in Foil with Fresh Thyme

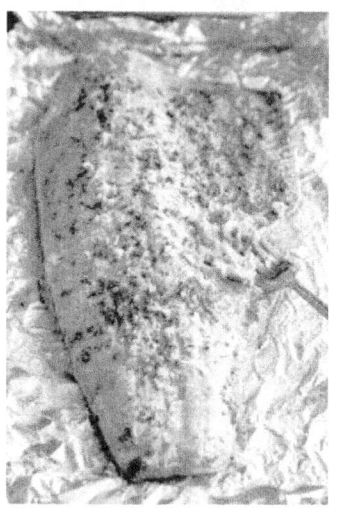

Preparation Time: 10 minutes
Cooking Time: 30 minutes
Servings: 4
Ingredients:
- 4 fresh thyme sprigs
- 4 garlic cloves, peeled, roughly chopped
- 16 oz. salmon fillets (4 oz. each fillet)
- ½ teaspoon salt
- ½ teaspoon ground black pepper
- 4 tablespoons cream
- 4 teaspoons butter
- ¼ teaspoon cumin seeds

Directions:
1. Line the baking tray with foil. Sprinkle the fish fillets with salt, ground black

pepper, cumin seeds, and arrange them in the tray with oil.

2. Add thyme sprig on the top of every fillet. Then add cream, butter, and garlic. Bake the fish for 30 minutes at 345F. Serve.

Nutrition: Calories 198 Fat 11.6g Carbs 1.8g Protein 22.4g Phosphorus 425 mg Potassium 660.9 mg Sodium 366 mg

571. 4-Ingredients Salmon Fillet

Preparation Time: 5 minutes
Cooking Time: 25 minutes
Servings: 1
Ingredients:
- 4 oz. salmon fillet
- ½ teaspoon salt
- 1 teaspoon sesame oil
- ½ teaspoon sage

Directions:
1. Rub the fillet with salt and sage. Put the fish in the tray, then sprinkle it with sesame oil. Cook the fish for 25 minutes at 365F. Flip the fish carefully onto another side after 12 minutes of cooking. Serve.

Nutrition: Calories 191 Fat 11.6g Fiber 0.1g Carbs 0.2g Protein 22g Sodium 70.5 mg Phosphorus 472 mg Potassium 636.3 mg

572. Poached Halibut in Mango Sauce

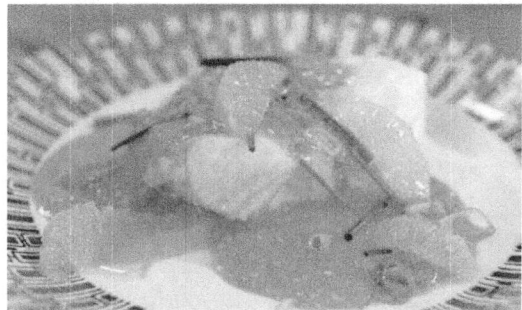

Preparation Time: 10 minutes
Cooking Time: 10 minutes
Servings: 4
Ingredients:
- 1-pound halibut
- 1/3 cup butter
- 1 rosemary sprig
- ½ teaspoon ground black pepper
- 1 teaspoon salt
- 1 teaspoon honey
- ¼ cup of mango juice
- 1 teaspoon cornstarch

Directions:
1. Put butter in the saucepan and melt it. Add rosemary sprig. Sprinkle the halibut with salt and ground black pepper. Put the fish in the boiling butter and poach it for 4 minutes.
2. Meanwhile, pour mango juice into the skillet. Add honey and bring the liquid to boil. Add cornstarch and whisk until the liquid starts to be thick. Then remove it from the heat.
3. Transfer the poached halibut to the plate and cut it on 4. Place every fish serving in the serving plate and top with mango sauce.

Nutrition: Calories 349 Fat 29.3g Fiber 0.1g Carbs 3.2g Protein 17.8g Phosphorus 154 mgPotassium 388.6 mg Sodium 29.3 mg

573. Chili Mussels

Preparation Time: 7 minutes
Cooking Time: 10 minutes
Servings: 4
Ingredients:
- 1-pound mussels
- 1 chili pepper, chopped
- 1 cup chicken stock
- ½ cup almond milk
- 1 teaspoon olive oil
- 1 teaspoon minced garlic
- 1 teaspoon ground coriander
- ½ teaspoon salt
- 1 cup fresh parsley, chopped
- 4 tablespoons lemon juice

Directions:
1. Pour almond milk into the saucepan. Add chili pepper, chicken stock, olive oil, minced garlic, ground coriander, salt, and lemon juice.
2. Bring the liquid to boil and add mussels. Boil the mussel for 4 minutes or until they will open shells. Then add chopped parsley and mix up the meal well. Remove it from the heat.

Nutrition: Calories 136 Fat 4.7g Fiber 0.6g Carbs 7.5g Protein 15.3g Phosphorus 180.8 mg Potassium 312.5 mg Sodium 319.6 mg

574. Asian Ginger tuna

PreparationTime:10min
CookingTime:20minutes
Servings: 4
Ingredients:
- 1 cup water
- 1 tablespoon minced fresh ginger root
- 1 tablespoon minced garlic
- 2 tablespoons soy sauce
- 1 1/4 pounds thin tuna fillets
- 6 large white mushrooms, sliced
- 1/4 cup sliced green onion
- 1 tablespoon chopped fresh cilantro (optional)

Directions:
1. Put water, ginger, and garlic in a wide pot with a lid.
2. Bring the water to a boil, reduce heat to medium-low, and simmer 3 to 5 minutes.
3. Stir soy sauce into the water mixture; add tuna fillets.
4. Place cover on the pot, bring water to a boil, and let cook for 3 minutes more.
5. Add mushrooms, cover, and cook until the fish loses pinkness and begins to flake, about 3 minutes more.
6. Sprinkle green onion over the fillets, cover, and cook for 30 seconds.
7. Garnish with cilantro to serve.

Nutrition: Calories 109, Total Fat 7.9g, Saturated Fat 0g, Cholesterol 0mg, Sodium 454mg, Total Carbohydrate 3.1g, Dietary Fiber 0.6g, Total Sugars 0.9g, Protein 7.1g, Calcium 10mg, Iron 1mg, Potassium 158mg, Phosphorus 120 mg

575. Grilled Cod

PreparationTime:10min
CookingTime:10minutes
Servings: 4
Ingredients:
- 2 (8 ounce) fillets cod, cut in half
- 1 tablespoon oregano
- ½ teaspoon lemon pepper
- ¼ teaspoon ground black pepper
- 2 tablespoons olive oil
- 1 lemon, juiced
- 2 tablespoons chopped green onion (white part only)

Directions:
1. Season both sides of cod with oregano, lemon pepper, and black pepper. Set fish aside on a plate. Heat butter in a

small saucepan over medium heat, stir in lemon juice and green onion, and cook until onion is softened, about 3 minutes.

2. Place cod onto oiled grates and grill until fish is browned and flakes easily, about 3 minutes per side; baste with olive oil mixture frequently while grilling. Allow cod to rest off the heat for about 5 minutes before serving.

Nutrition: Calories 92, Total Fat 7.4g, Saturated Fat 1g, Cholesterol 14mg, Sodium 19mg, Total Carbohydrate 2.5g, Dietary Fiber 1g, Total Sugars 0.5g, Protein 5.4g, Calcium 25mg, Iron 1mg, Potassium 50mg, Phosphorus 36 mg

576. Cod and Green Bean Curry

Preparation Time: 15 min
Cooking Time: 60 minutes
Servings: 4
Ingredients:
- 1/2-pound green beans, trimmed and cut into bite-sized pieces
- 1 white onion, sliced
- 2 cloves garlic, minced
- 1 tablespoon olive oil, or more as needed
- Ground black pepper to taste
- Curry Mixture:
- 2 tablespoons water, or more as needed
- 2 teaspoons curry powder
- 2 teaspoons ground ginger
- 1 1/2 (6 ounce) cod fillets

Directions:
1. Preheat the oven to 400 degrees F.
2. Combine green beans, onion, and garlic in a large glass baking dish. Toss with olive oil to coat; season with the pepper.
3. Bake in the preheated oven, stirring occasionally, until edges of onion are slightly charred and green beans start to

look dry, about 40 minutes. In the meantime, mix water, curry powder, and ginger together.

4. Remove dish and stir the vegetables; stir in curry mixture. Increase oven temperature to 450 degrees F.
5. Lay cod over the bottom of the dish and coat with vegetables. Continue baking until fish is opaque, 25 to 30 minutes depending on thickness.

Nutrition: Calories 64, Total Fat 3.8g, Saturated Fat 0.5g, Cholesterol 0mg, Sodium 5mg, Total Carbohydrate 7.7g, Dietary Fiber 2.9g, Total Sugars 2g, Protein 1.6g, Calcium 35mg, Iron 1mg, Potassium 180mg, Phosphorus 101 mg

577. Cheesy Tuna Chowder

Preparation Time: 10min
Cooking Time: 20minutes
Servings: 4
Ingredients:
- 2 tablespoons olive oil
- 1/2 small onion, chopped
- 1 cup water
- 1/2 cup chopped celery
- 1 cup sliced baby carrots
- 3 cups soy almond milk, divided
- 1/3 cup all-purpose flour
- 1/2 teaspoon ground black pepper
- 1 1/2 pounds tuna fillets, cut into 1-inch pieces
- 1 1/2 cups shredded Cheddar cheese

Directions:
1. In a Dutch oven over medium heat, heat olive oil and sauté the onion until tender. Pour in water. Mix in celery, carrots, and cook 10 minutes, stirring occasionally, until vegetables are tender.
2. In a small bowl, whisk together 1 1/2 cups almond milk and all-purpose flour. Mix into the Dutch oven.

3. Mix remaining almond milk, and pepper into the Dutch oven. Stirring occasionally, continue cooking the mixture about 10 minutes, until thickened.
4. Stir tuna into the mixture, and cook 5 minutes, or until fish is easily flaked with a fork. Mix in Cheddar cheese, and cook another 5 minutes, until melted.

Nutrition: Calories 228, Total Fat 15.5g, Saturated Fat 6.5g, Cholesterol 30mg, Sodium 206mg, Total Carbohydrate 10.8g, Dietary Fiber 1g, Total Sugars 4.1g, Protein 11.6g, Calcium 183mg, Iron 1mg, Potassium 163mg, Phosphorus 150 mg

578. White Fish Soup

PreparationTime:15min
CookingTime:20minutes
Servings: 4
Ingredients:
- 2 tablespoons olive oil
- 1 onion, finely diced
- 1 green bell pepper, chopped
- 1 rib celery, thinly sliced
- 3 cups chicken broth, or more to taste
- 1/4 cup chopped fresh parsley
- 1 1/2 pounds cod, cut into 3/4-inch cubes
- Pepper to taste
- 1 dash red pepper flakes

Directions:
1. Heat oil in a soup pot over medium heat.
2. Add onion, bell pepper, and celery and cook until wilted, about 5 minutes.
3. Add broth and bring to a simmer, about 5 minutes.
4. Cook 15 to 20 minutes.
5. Add cod, parsley, and red pepper flakes and simmer until fish flakes easily with a fork, 8 to 10 minutes more.
6. Season with black pepper.

Nutrition: Calories 117, Total Fat 7.2g, Saturated Fat 1.4g, Cholesterol 18mg, Sodium 37mg, Total Carbohydrate 5.4g, Dietary Fiber 1.3g, Total Sugars 2.8g, Protein 8.1g, Calcium 23mg, Iron 1mg, Potassium 122mg, Phosphorus 111 mg

579. Sardine Fish Cakes

Preparation Time: 10 minutes
Cooking Time: 10 minutes
Servings: 4
Ingredients:
- 11 oz. sardines, canned, drained
- 1/3 cup shallot, chopped
- 1 teaspoon chili flakes
- ½ teaspoon salt
- 2 tablespoon wheat flour, whole grain
- 1 egg, beaten
- 1 tablespoon chives, chopped
- 1 teaspoon olive oil
- 1 teaspoon butter

Directions:
1. Put the butter in your skillet and dissolve it. Add shallot and cook it until translucent. After this, transfer the shallot to the mixing bowl.
2. Add sardines, chili flakes, salt, flour, egg, chives, and mix up until smooth with the fork's help. Make the medium size cakes and place them in the skillet. Add olive oil.

3. Roast the fish cakes for 3 minutes from each side over medium heat. Dry the cooked fish cakes with a paper towel if needed and transfer to the serving plates.

Nutrition: Calories 221 Fat 12.2g Fiber 0.1g Carbs 5.4g Protein 21.3 g Phosphorus 188.7 mgPotassium 160.3 mg Sodium 452.6 mg

580. Onion Dijon Crusted Catfish

PreparationTime:05min
CookingTime:25minutes
Servings: 4
Ingredients:
- 1 onion, finely chopped
- 1/4 cup honey Dijon mustard
- 4 (6 ounce) fillets catfish fillets
- Pepper to taste
- Dried parsley flakes

Directions:
1. Preheat the oven to 350 degrees F.
2. In a small bowl, mix together the onion and mustard. Season the catfish fillets with pepper. Place on a baking tray and coat with the onion and honey. Sprinkle parsley flakes over the top.
3. Bake for 20 minutes in the preheated oven, then turn the oven to broil. Broil until golden, 3 to 5 minutes.

Nutrition: Calories 215, Total Fat 6.1g, Saturated Fat 1.7g, Cholesterol 87mg, Sodium 86mg, Total Carbohydrate 10.4g, Dietary Fiber 0.6g, Total Sugars 4.2g, Protein 31.6g, Calcium 8mg, Iron 0mg, Potassium 46mg, Phosphorus 30 mg

581. Herb Baked Tuna

PreparationTime:10min
CookingTime:20minutes
Servings: 4
Ingredients:
- 4 (6 ounce) tuna fillets
- 2 tablespoons dried parsley
- 3/4 teaspoon paprika
- 1/2 teaspoon dried thyme
- 1/2 teaspoon dried oregano
- 1/2 teaspoon dried basil
- 1/2 teaspoon ground black pepper
- 2 tablespoons lemon juice
- 1 tablespoon olive oil
- 1/4 teaspoon garlic powder

Directions:
1. Preheat oven to 350 degrees F.
2. Arrange tuna fillets in a 9x13-inch baking dish. Combine parsley, paprika, thyme, oregano, basil, and black pepper in a small bowl; sprinkle herb mixture over fish. Mix lemon juice, olive oil, and garlic powder in another bowl; drizzle olive oil mixture over fish.
3. Bake in preheated oven until fish is easily flaked with a fork, about 20 minutes.

Nutrition: Calories 139, Total Fat 12.5g, Saturated Fat 0.6g, Cholesterol 0mg, Sodium 3mg, Total Carbohydrate 1g, Dietary Fiber 0.5g, Total Sugars 0.3g, Protein 6.2g, Calcium 11mg, Iron 1mg, Potassium 39mg, Phosphorus 20 mg

582. Cilantro Lime Salmon

PreparationTime:10min
CookingTime:20minutes
Servings: 4
Ingredients:
- ¼ cup olive oil
- ¼ cup chopped fresh cilantro
- ½ teaspoon chopped garlic
- 5 (5 ounce) fillets salmon
- Ground black pepper to taste
- ½ lemon, juiced
- ½ lime, juiced

Directions:

1. Heat the olive oil in a skillet over medium heat.
2. Stir cilantro and garlic into the oil; cook about 1 minute.
3. Season salmon fillets with black pepper; lay gently into the oil mixture.
4. Place a cover on the skillet. Cook fillets 10 minutes, turn, and continue cooking until the fish flakes easily with a fork and is lightly browned, about 10 minutes more.
5. Squeeze lemon juice and lime juice over the fillets to serve.

Nutrition: Calories 249, Total Fat 18.7g, Saturated Fat 3.3g, Cholesterol 18mg, Sodium 48mg, Total Carbohydrate 1.7g, Dietary Fiber 0.5g, Total Sugars 0.3g, Protein 20.7g, Calcium 6mg, Iron 0mg, Potassium 26mg, Phosphorus 20 mg

583. Stuffed Mushrooms

PreparationTime:10min
CookingTime:10minutes
Servings: 4
Ingredients:
- 12 large fresh mushrooms, stems removed
- ½ pound crabmeat, flaked
- 2 cups olive oil
- 2 cloves garlic, peeled and minced
- Garlic powder to taste
- Crushed red pepper to taste

Directions:
1. Arrange mushroom caps on a medium baking sheet, bottoms up. Chop and reserve mushroom stems.
2. Preheat oven to 350 degrees F.
3. In a medium saucepan over medium heat, heat oil. Mix in garlic and cook until tender, about 5 minutes.
4. In a medium bowl, mix together reserved mushroom stems, and crab meat. Liberally stuff mushrooms with

the mixture. Drizzle with the garlic. Season with garlic powder and crushed red pepper.
5. Bake uncovered in the preheated oven 10 to 12 minutes, or until stuffing is lightly browned.

Nutrition: Calories 312, Total Fat 33.8g, Saturated Fat 4.8g, Cholesterol 4mg, Sodium 160mg, Total Carbohydrate 3.8g, Dietary Fiber 0.3g, Total Sugars 1.6g, Protein 2.2g, Calcium 3mg, Iron 1mg, Potassium 93mg, Phosphorus 86 mg

584. Marinated Salmon Steak

PreparationTime:10min
CookingTime:10minutes
Servings: 4
Ingredients:
- ¼ cup lime juice
- ¼ cup soy sauce
- 2 tablespoons olive oil
- 1 tablespoon lemon juice
- 2 tablespoons chopped fresh parsley
- 1 clove garlic, minced
- ½ teaspoon chopped fresh oregano
- ½ teaspoon ground black pepper
- 4 (4 ounce) salmon steaks

Directions:
1. In a large non-reactive dish, mix together the lime juice, soy sauce, olive oil, lemon juice, parsley, garlic, oregano, and pepper. Place the salmon steaks in the marinade and turn to coat. Cover, and refrigerate for at least 30 minutes.
2. Preheat grill for high heat.
3. Lightly oil grill grate. Cook the salmon steaks for 5 to 6 minutes, then salmon and baste with the marinade. Cook for an additional 5 minutes, or to desired doneness. Discard any remaining marinade.

Nutrition: Calories 108, Total Fat 8.4g, Saturated Fat 1.2g, Cholesterol 9mg, Sodium 910mg, Total Carbohydrate 3.6g, Dietary Fiber 0.4g, Total Sugars 1.7g, Protein 5.4g, Calcium 19mg, Iron 1mg, Potassium 172mg, Phosphorus 165 mg

585. Tuna with honey Glaze

PreparationTime:10min
CookingTime:10minutes
Servings: 4
Ingredients:
- 1/4 cup honey
- 2 tablespoons Dijon mustard
- 4 (6 ounce) boneless tuna fillets
- Ground black pepper to taste

Directions:
1. Preheat the oven's broiler and set the oven rack at about 6 inches from the heat source; prepare the rack of a broiler pan with cooking spray.
2. Season the tuna with pepper and arrange onto the prepared broiler pan. Whisk together the honey and Dijon mustard in a small bowl; spoon mixture evenly onto top of salmon fillets.
3. Cook under the preheated broiler until the fish flakes easily with a fork, 10 to 15 minutes.

Nutrition: Calories 160, Total Fat 8.1g, Saturated Fat 0g, Cholesterol 0mg, Sodium 90mg, Total Carbohydrate 17.9g, Dietary Fiber 0.3g, Total Sugars 17.5g, Protein 5.7g, Calcium 6mg, Iron 0mg, Potassium 22mg, Phosphorus 16 mg

586. Smoked Salmon and Radishes

Preparation Time: 10 minutes
CookingTime:10minutes
Servings: 8
Ingredients:

- ½ c. drained and chopped capers
- 1 lb. skinless, de-boned and flaked smoked salmon
- 4 chopped radishes
- 3 tbsps. Chopped chives
- 3 tbsps. Prepared beet horseradish
- 2 tsps. Grated lemon zest
- 1/3 c. roughly chopped red onion

Directions:
1. In a bowl, combine the salmon while using the beet horseradish, lemon zest, radish, capers, onions and chives, toss and serve cold.
2. Enjoy!

Nutrition: Calories: 254, Fat: 2 g, Carbs: 7 g, Protein: 7 g, Sugars: 1.4 g, Sodium: 660 mg

587. Parmesan Baked Fish

Preparation Time: 10 minutes
CookingTime:10minutes
Servings: 4
Ingredients:

- ½ tsp. Worcestershire sauce
- 1/3 c. mayonnaise
- 3 tbsps. Freshly grated parmesan cheese
- 4 oz. cod fish fillets
- 1 tbsp. snipped fresh chives

Directions:
1. Preheat oven to 450°C.
2. Rinse fish and pat dry with paper towels; spray an 8x8x2" baking dish with non-stick pan spray, set aside.
3. In small bowl stir mayo, grated cheese, chives, and Worcestershire sauce; spread mixture over fish fillets.
4. Bake, uncovered, 12-15 minutes or until fish flakes easily with a fork

Nutrition: Calories: 850.5, Fat: 24.8g, Carbs: 44.5 g, Protein: 104.6 g, Sugars: 0.6 g, Sodium: 307.7 mg

588. Easy Salmon and Brussels sprouts

Preparation Time: 10 minutes
CookingTime:10minutes
Servings: 6

Ingredients:

- 6 deboned medium salmon fillets
- 1 tsp. onion powder
- 1 ¼ lbs. halved Brussels sprouts
- 3 tbsps. Extra virgin extra virgin olive oil
- 2 tbsps. Brown sugar
- 1 tsp. garlic powder
- 1 tsp. smoked paprika

Directions:

1. In a bowl, mix sugar with onion powder, garlic powder, smoked paprika as well as a number of tablespoon olive oil and whisk well.
2. Spread Brussels sprouts about the lined baking sheet, drizzle the rest in the essential extra virgin olive oil, toss to coat, introduce in the oven at 450 0F and bake for 5 minutes.
3. Add salmon fillets brush with sugar mix you've prepared, introduce inside the oven and bake for 15 minutes more.
4. Divide everything between plates and serve.
5. Enjoy!

Nutrition: Calories: 212, Fat: 5 g, Carbs: 12 g, Protein: 8 g, Sugars: 3.7 g, Sodium: 299.1 mg

589. Lemon, Garlic, Cilantro Tuna and Rice

Preparation Time: 5 minutes
Cooking Time: 0 minutes
Servings: 2

Ingredients:

- ½ cup arugula
- 1 tbsp. extra virgin olive oil
- 1 cup cooked rice

- 1 tsp black pepper
- ¼ finely diced red onion
- 1 juiced lemon
- 3 oz. canned tuna
- 2 tbsp. Chopped fresh cilantro

Directions:

1. Mix the olive oil, pepper, cilantro, and red onion in a bowl. Stir in the tuna, cover, then serve with the cooked rice and arugula!

Nutrition: Calories 221 Protein 11 g Carbs 26 g Fat 7 g Sodium 143 mg Potassium 197 mg Phosphorus 182 mg

590. Shrimp and Mango Mix

Preparation Time: 10 minutes
CookingTime:10minutes
Servings: 4

Ingredients:

- 3 tbsps. Finely chopped parsley
- 3 tbsps. Coconut sugar
- 1 lb. peeled, deveined and cooked shrimp
- 3 tbsps. Balsamic vinegar
- 3 peeled and cubed mangos

Directions:

1. In a bowl, mix vinegar with sugar and mayo and whisk.
2. In another bowl, combine the mango with the parsley and shrimp, add the mayo mix, toss and serve.
3. Enjoy!

Nutrition: Calories: 204, Fat: 3 g, Carbs: 8 g, Protein: 8 g, Sugars: 12.6 g, Sodium: 273.4 mg

591. Salmon in Dill Sauce

Preparation Time: 10 minutes
CookingTime:10minutes
Servings: 6

Ingredients:

- 6 salmon fillets

- 1 c. low-fat, low-sodium chicken broth
- 1 tsp. cayenne pepper
- 2 tbsps. Fresh lemon juice
- 2 c. water
- ¼ c. chopped fresh dill

Directions:
1. In a slow cooker, mix together water, broth, lemon juice, lemon juice and dill.
2. Arrange salmon fillets on top, skin side down.
3. Sprinkle with cayenne pepper.
4. Set the slow cooker on low.
5. Cover and cook for about 1-2 hours.

Nutrition: Calories: 360, Fat: 8 g, Carbs: 44 g, Protein: 28 g, Sugars: 0.5 g, Sodium: 8 mg

592. Salmon and Carrots Mix

Preparation Time: 10 minutes
CookingTime:10minutes
Servings: 4

Ingredients:
- 4 oz. chopped smoked salmon
- 1 tbsp. essential olive oil
- Black pepper
- 1 tbsp. chopped chives
- ¼ c. coconut cream
- 1 ½ lbs. chopped carrots
- 2 tsps. Prepared horseradish

Directions:
1. Heat up a pan using the oil over medium heat, add carrots and cook for 10 minutes.
2. Add salmon, chives, horseradish, cream and black pepper, toss, cook for 1 minute more, divide between plates and serve.
3. Enjoy!

Nutrition: Calories: 233, Fat: 6 g, Carbs: 9 g, Protein: 11 g, Sugars: 3.3 g, Sodium: 97 mg

593. Roasted hake

Preparation Time: 20 minutes
CookingTime:30minutes
Servings: 4

Ingredients:
- ½ c. tomato sauce
- 2 sliced Red bell peppers
- Fresh parsley
- ½ c. grated cheese
- 4 lbs. deboned hake fish
- 1 tbsp. olive oil
- Salt.

Directions:
1. Season the fish with salt. Pan-fry the fish until half-done.
2. Shape foil into containers according to the number of fish pieces.
3. Pour tomato sauce into each foil dish; arrange the fish, then the tomato slices, again add tomato sauce and sprinkle with grated cheese.
4. Bake in the oven at 400 F until there is a golden crust.
5. Serve with fresh parsley.

Nutrition: Calories: 421, Fat: 48.7 g, Carbs: 2.4 g, Protein: 17.4 g, Sugars: 0.5 g, Sodium: 94.6 mg

594. Shrimp Paella

Preparation Time: 5 minutes
Cooking Time: 10 minutes
Servings: 2

Ingredients:
- 1 cup cooked white rice
- 1 chopped red onion
- 1 tsp. paprika
- 1 chopped garlic clove
- 1 tbsp. olive oil
- 6 oz. frozen cooked shrimp
- 1 deseeded and sliced chili pepper
- 1 tbsp. oregano

Directions:
1. Warm-up olive oil in a large pan on medium-high heat. Add the onion and garlic and sauté for 2-3 minutes until soft. Now add the shrimp and sauté for a further 5 minutes or until hot through.
2. Now add the herbs, spices, chili, and rice with 1/2 cup boiling water. Stir until everything is warm, and the water has been absorbed. Plate up and serve.

Nutrition: Calories 221 Protein 17 g Carbs 31 g Fat 8 g Sodium 235 mg Potassium 176 mg Phosphorus 189 mg

595. Shrimp Lo Mein

Preparation Time: 10 minutes
CookingTime:10minutes
Servings: 6

Ingredients:
- 1 tbsp. cornstarch
- 1 lb. medium-size frozen raw shrimp
- 1 c. frozen shelled edamame
- 3 tbsps. Light teriyaki sauce
- 16 0z. Drained and rinsed tofu spaghetti noodles
- 18 oz. frozen Szechuan vegetable blend with sesame sauce

Directions:
1. Microwave noodles for 1 minute; set aside. Place shrimp in a small bowl and toss with 2 tablespoons teriyaki sauce; set aside.

2. Place mixed vegetables and edamame in a large nonstick skillet with 1/4 cup water. Cover and cook, stirring occasionally, over medium-high heat for 7 minutes or until cooked through.
3. Stir shrimp into vegetable mixture; cover and cook 4 to 5 minutes or until shrimp is pink and cooked through.
4. Stir together remaining 1 tablespoon teriyaki sauce and the cornstarch, then stir into the mixture in the skillet until thickened. Gently stir noodles into skillet and cook until warmed through.

Nutrition: Calories: 252, Fat: 7.1 g, Carbs: 35.2 g, Protein: 12.1 g, Sugars: 2.2 g, Sodium: 180 mg

596. Cod & Green Bean Risotto

Preparation Time: 4 minutes
Cooking Time: 40 minutes
Servings: 2

Ingredients:
- ½ cup arugula
- 1 finely diced white onion
- 4 oz. cod fillet
- 1 cup white rice
- 2 lemon wedges
- 1 cup boiling water
- ¼ tsp. black pepper
- 1 cup low-sodium chicken broth
- 1 tbsp. extra virgin olive oil
- ½ cup green beans

Directions:

1. Warm-up oil in a large pan on medium heat. Sauté the chopped onion for 5 minutes until soft before adding in the rice and stirring for 1-2 minutes.
2. Combine the broth with boiling water. Add half of the liquid to the pan and stir. Slowly add the rest of the liquid while continuously stirring for up to 20-30 minutes.
3. Stir in the green beans to the risotto. Place the fish on top of the rice, cover, and steam for 10 minutes.
4. Use your fork to break up the fish fillets and stir into the rice. Sprinkle with freshly ground pepper to serve and a squeeze of fresh lemon. Serve with the lemon wedges and the arugula.

Nutrition: Calories 221 Protein 12 g Carbs 29 g Fat 8 g Sodium 398 mg Potassium 347 mg Phosphorus 241 mg

597. Scallops and Strawberry Mix

Preparation Time: 20 minutes
CookingTime:30minutes
Servings: 2
Ingredients:

- 1 tbsp. lime juice
- ½ c. Pico de Gallo
- Black pepper
- 4 oz. scallops
- ½ c. chopped strawberries

Directions:

1. Heat up a pan over medium heat, add scallops, cook for 3 minutes on both sides and take away heat,
2. In a bowl, mix strawberries with lime juice, Pico de gallo, scallops and pepper, toss and serve cold.
3. Enjoy!

Nutrition: Calories: 169, Fat: 2 g, Carbs: 8 g, Protein: 13 g, Sugars: 0 g, Sodium: 235.7 mg

598. Salmon & Pesto Salad

Preparation Time: 5 minutes
Cooking Time: 15 minutes
Servings: 2
Ingredients:
For the pesto:

- 1 minced garlic clove
- ½ cup fresh arugula
- ¼ cup extra virgin olive oil
- ½ cup fresh basil
- 1 tsp black pepper

For the salmon:

- 4 oz. skinless salmon fillet
- 1 tbsp. coconut oil

For the salad:

- ½ juiced lemon
- 2 sliced radishes
- ½ cup iceberg lettuce
- 1 tsp black pepper

Directions:

1. Prepare the pesto by blending all the fixing for the pesto in a food processor or grinding with a pestle and mortar. Set aside.
2. Add a skillet to the stove on medium-high heat and melt the coconut oil. Add the salmon to the pan. Cook for 7-8 minutes and turn over.
3. Cook within 3-4 minutes or until cooked through. Remove fillets from the skillet and allow to rest.
4. Mix the lettuce and the radishes and squeeze over the juice of ½ lemon. Shred the salmon using a fork and mix through the salad. Toss to coat and sprinkle with a little black pepper to serve.

Nutrition: Calories 221 Protein 13 g Carbs 1 g Fat 34 g Sodium 80 mg Potassium 119 mgPhosphorus 158 mg

599. Baked Fennel & Garlic Sea Bass

Preparation Time: 5 minutes
Cooking Time: 15 minutes
Servings: 2
Ingredients:
- 1 lemon
- ½ sliced fennel bulb
- 6 oz. sea bass fillets
- 1 tsp black pepper
- 2 garlic cloves

Directions:

1. Preheat the oven to 375°F. Sprinkle black pepper over the Sea Bass. Slice the fennel bulb and garlic cloves. Add 1 salmon fillet and half the fennel and garlic to one sheet of baking paper or tin foil.
2. Squeeze in 1/2 lemon juices. Repeat for the other fillet. Fold and add to the oven

for 12-15 minutes or until fish is thoroughly cooked through.

3. Meanwhile, add boiling water to your couscous, cover, and allow to steam. Serve with your choice of rice or salad.

Nutrition: Calories 221 Protein 14 g Carbs 3 g Fat 2 g Sodium 119 mg Potassium 398 mg Phosphorus 149 mg

600. Chipotle Spiced Shrimp

Preparation Time: 10 minutes
CookingTime:10minutes
Servings: 4
Ingredients:
- ½ tsp. minced garlic
- 2 tbsps. Tomato paste
- ½ tsp. chopped fresh oregano
- 1 ½ tsps. Water
- ¾ lb. peeled, deveined and uncooked shrimp
- ½ tsp. chipotle chili powder
- ½ tsp. extra-virgin olive oil

Directions:

1. In cold water, rinse shrimp.
2. Pat dry with a paper towel. Set aside on a plate.
3. Whisk together the tomato paste, water and oil in a small bowl to make the marinade. Add garlic, chili powder and oregano and mix well.

4. Spread the marinade (it will be thick) on both sides of the shrimp using a brush and place in the refrigerator.
5. Heat a gas grill or broiler, or prepare a hot fire in a charcoal grill.
6. Coat the grill rack or broiler pan with cooking spray lightly.
7. Put the cooking rack 4 to 6 inches from the heat source.
8. Thread the shrimp onto skewers or lay them in a grill basket, to place on the grill.
9. After 3 to 4 minutes turn the shrimp.
10. When the shrimp is fully cooked, take it off the heat and serve immediately.

Nutrition: Calories: 151.9, Fat: 2.8 g, Carbs: 5.1 g, Protein: 24.2 g, Sugars: 2.3 g, Sodium: 283.1 mg

601. Coconut Cream Shrimp

Preparation Time: 10 minutes
CookingTime:20minutes
Servings: 2
Ingredients:
- 1 tbsp. coconut cream
- ½ tsp. lime juice
- ¼ tsp. black pepper
- 1 tbsp. parsley
- 1 lb. cooked, peeled and deveined shrimp
- ¼ tsp. chopped jalapeno

Directions:
1. In a bowl, mix the shrimp while using cream, jalapeno, lime juice, parsley and black pepper, toss, divide into small bowls and serve.
2. Enjoy!

Nutrition: Calories: 183, Fat: 5 g, Carbs: 12 g, Protein: 8 g, Sugars: 0.9 g, Sodium: 474.9 mg

602. Simple Cinnamon Salmon

Preparation Time: 10 minutes
CookingTime:10minutes
Servings: 2
Ingredients:
- 1 tbsp. organic essential olive oil
- Black pepper
- 1 tbsp. cinnamon powder
- 2 de-boned salmon fillets

Directions:
1. Heat up a pan with the oil over medium heat, add pepper and cinnamon and stir well.
2. Add salmon, skin side up, cook for 5 minutes on both sides, divide between plates and serve by using a side salad.
3. Enjoy!

Nutrition: Calories: 220, Fat: 8 g, Carbs: 11 g, Protein: 8 g, Sugars: 9.3 g, Sodium: 250.5 mg

603. Lemon-Herb Grilled Fish

Preparation Time: 5 minutes
CookingTime:10minutes
Servings: 4
Ingredients:
- 4 peeled garlic cloves
- ¼ tsp. salt
- 8 lemon slices
- ¼ tsp. ground black pepper
- Remoulade
- 2 small blue-fish
- 2 sprigs fresh thyme

Directions:
1. Prepare outdoor grill with medium-low to medium coals, or heat gas grill to medium-low to medium (to broil, see Note below).
2. Rinse fish; pat dry. Cut 3 slashes on each side. Season with salt, pepper.

3. Stuff 3 lemon slices in cavity of each fish. Add thyme and 2 cloves garlic to each cavity.
4. Grill fish 6 inches from heat, covered, 10 to 12 minutes, until just beginning to char. flip over carefully. Cover each eye with one of remaining lemon slices. Grill 12 to 15 minutes more, until flesh is white throughout.
5. Transfer fish to platter. For each, pry up top fillet in one piece, flipping over, and skin side down.
6. Beginning at tail, carefully pull up end of spine of fish, and lift up, removing whole backbone. Remove any small bones from fish.
7. Serve with Remoulade.

Nutrition: Calories: 118.1, Fat: 6.8 g, Carbs: 1 g, Protein: 12.9 g, Sugars: 12.9 g, Sodium: 91.2 mg

604. Cod Peas

Preparation Time: 18-20 minutes
CookingTime:40minutes
Servings: 4-5
Ingredients:
- 1 c. peas
- 2 tbsps. Capers
- 4 de-boned medium cod fillets
- 3 tbsps. Olive oil
- ¼ tsp. black pepper
- 2 tbsps. Lime juice
- 2 tbsps. Chopped shallots
- 1 ½ tbsps. Chopped oregano

Directions:
1. Heat up 1 tbsp. olive oil in a saucepan over medium flame
2. Add the fillets, cook for 5 minutes on each side; set aside.
3. In a bowl of large size, thoroughly mix the oregano, shallots, lime juice, peas, capers, black pepper, and 2 tbsp. olive oil.

4. Toss and serve with the cooked fish.
Nutrition: Calories: 224, Fat: 11 g, Carbs: 7 g, Protein: 24 g, Sugars: 2 g, Sodium: 485 mg

605. Baked Haddock

Preparation Time: 10 minutes
CookingTime:10minutes
Servings: 4
Ingredients:
- 1 tsp. chopped dill
- 3 tsps. Water
- ¼ tsp. black pepper and salt
- Cooking spray
- 1 lb. chopped haddock
- 2 tbsps. Fresh lemon juice

Directions:
1. Spray a baking dish with a few oils, add fish, water, freshly squeezed lemon juice, salt, black pepper, mayo and dill, toss, introduce inside the oven and bake at 350 0F for the half-hour.
2. Divide between plates and serve.
3. Enjoy!

Nutrition: Calories: 264, Fat: 4 g, Carbs: 7 g, Protein: 12 g, Sugars: 0 g, Sodium: 71.4 mg

606. Simple Soup

PreparationTime:05min
CookingTime:15minutes
Servings: 4
Ingredients:
- 2 teaspoons tuna
- 4 cups water
- 1 (8 ounce) package silken tofu, diced
- 2 green onions, sliced diagonally into 1/2-inch pieces

Directions:
1. In a medium saucepan over medium-high heat, combine tuna and water; bring to a boil.
2. Reduce heat to medium, Stir in tofu.

260

3. Separate the layers of the green onions, and add them to the soup.
4. Simmer gently for 2 to 3 minutes before serving.

Nutrition: Calories 77, Total Fat 3.3g, Saturated Fat 0.6g, Cholesterol 7mg, Sodium 39mg, Total Carbohydrate 1.9g, Dietary Fiber 0.3g, Total Sugars 0.9g, Protein 9.7g, Calcium 32mg, Iron 1mg, Potassium 104mg, Potassium 88mg

607. Ginger Glazed Tuna

PreparationTime:05min
CookingTime:12minutes
Servings: 4
Ingredients:
- 3 tablespoons honey
- 3 tablespoons soy sauce
- 3 tablespoons vinegar
- 1 teaspoon grated fresh ginger root
- 1 clove garlic, crushed or to taste
- 4 (6 ounce) tuna fillets
- Pepper to taste
- 2 tablespoons olive oil

Directions:
1. In a shallow glass dish, stir together the honey, soy sauce, vinegar, ginger, garlic and 2 teaspoons olive oil. Season fish fillets with pepper, and place them into the dish. If the fillets have skin on them, place them skin side down. Cover, and refrigerate for 20 minutes to marinate.
2. Heat remaining olive oil in a large skillet over medium-high heat. Remove fish from the dish, and reserve marinade. Fry fish for 4 to 6 minutes on each side, turning only once, until fish flakes easily with a fork. Remove fillets to a serving platter and keep warm.
3. Pour reserved marinade into the skillet, and heat over medium heat until the mixture reduces to a glaze consistently. Spoon glaze over fish, and serve immediately.

Nutrition: Calories 181, Total Fat 11.1g, Saturated Fat 0.3g, Cholesterol 0mg, Sodium 678mg, Total Carbohydrate 14.3g, Dietary Fiber 0.2g, Total Sugars 13.2g, Protein 6.8g, Calcium 6mg, Iron 0mg, Potassium 47mg, Potassium 18mg

608. Tuna with Pineapple

PreparationTime:25min
CookingTime:15minutes
Servings: 4
Ingredients:
- 2 tablespoons olive oil
- 1 tablespoon minced fresh garlic
- 1 tablespoon chopped onion
- 1/2 red bell pepper, diced
- 1 cup pineapple - peeled, seeded and cubed
- 1 teaspoon corn-starch
- 1 tablespoon water
- 2 tablespoons lime juice
- 1 tablespoon lime juice
- 1 tablespoon melted butter
- 3 (4 ounce) fillets tuna

Directions:
1. Preheat the oven's broiler and set the oven rack about 6 inches from the heat source.
2. Heat olive oil in a saucepan over medium heat. Stir in the garlic and onion; cook and stir until the onion begins to soften, about 2 minutes. Add the red bell pepper and pineapple. Continue cooking a few more minutes until the bell pepper begins to soften. Stir together the corn-starch, water, and 2 tablespoons of lime juice. Stir into the pineapple sauce until thickened, stirring constantly. Keep the sauce warm over very low heat.

3. Stir 1 tablespoon of lime juice together with the melted butter, and brush on the tuna fillets. Place onto a broiler pan.

4. Cook under the preheated broiler for 4 minutes, then turn the fish over, and continue cooking for 4 minutes more. Season to taste with salt and serve with the pineapple sauce.

Nutrition: Calories 98, Total Fat 7.1g, Saturated Fat 1g, Cholesterol 0mg, Sodium 2mg, Total Carbohydrate 10.1g, Dietary Fiber 1g, Total Sugars 5.3g, Protein 0.6g, Calcium 14mg, Iron 0mg, Potassium 111mg, Potassium 101mg

609. Marinated Fried Fish

PreparationTime:15min
CookingTime:10minutes
Servings: 4
Ingredients:
- 2 (4 ounce) Salmon fillets
- 2 tablespoons lemon juice
- 2 tablespoons garlic powder
- 2 teaspoons ground cumin
- 1 teaspoon paprika
- 1/2 cup all-purpose flour
- 1 teaspoon dried rosemary
- 1/4 teaspoon cayenne pepper, or to taste
- 1 egg, beaten
- 1 tablespoon water
- ½ cup olive oil for frying

Directions:
1. Place salmon fillets in a small glass dish. Mix lemon juice, garlic powder, cumin, and paprika in a small bowl; pour over salmon fillets. Cover dish with plastic wrap and marinate salmon in refrigerator for 2 hours.
2. Mix flour, rosemary, and cayenne pepper together on a piece of waxed paper.

3. Beat egg and water together in a wide bowl.
4. Heat oil in a large skillet over medium heat.
5. Gently press the salmon fillets into the flour mixture to coat; shake to remove excess flour. Dip into the beaten egg to coat and immediately return to the flour mixture to coat.
6. Fry flounder in hot oil until the fish flakes easily with a fork, about 5 minutes per side.

Nutrition: Calories 139, Total Fat 4.7g, Saturated Fat 0.9g, Cholesterol 50mg, Sodium 30mg, Total Carbohydrate 16.3g, Dietary Fiber 1.4g, Total Sugars 1.4g, Protein 8.2g, Calcium 34mg, Iron 2mg, Potassium 203mg, Potassium 140mg

610. Spicy Lime and Basil Grilled Fish

PreparationTime:30min
CookingTime:30minutes
Servings: 4
Ingredients:
- 2 pounds salmon fillets, each cut into thirds
- 6 tablespoons butter, melted
- 1 lime, juiced
- 1 tablespoon dried basil
- 1 teaspoon red pepper flakes
- 1 onion, sliced crosswise 1/8-inch thick

Directions:
1. Preheat grill for medium heat and lightly oil the grate.
2. Lay 4 8x10-inch pieces of aluminum foil onto a flat work surface and spray with cooking spray.
3. Arrange equal amounts of the salmon into the center of each foil square.
4. Stir butter, lime juice, basil, and red pepper flakes together in a small bowl;

drizzle evenly over each portion of fish. Top each portion with onion slices.

5. Bring opposing ends of the foil together and roll together to form a seam. Roll ends toward fish to seal packets.

6. Cook packets on the preheated grill until fish flakes easily with a fork, 5 to 7 minutes per side.

Nutrition: Calories 151, Total Fat 13.4g, Saturated Fat 7.6g, Cholesterol 43mg, Sodium 95mg, Total Carbohydrate 3.1g, Dietary Fiber 0.8g, Total Sugars 1g, Protein 6g, Calcium 23mg, Iron 0mg, Potassium 158mg, Potassium 137mg

611. Steamed Fish with Garlic

PreparationTime:15min
CookingTime:45minutes
Servings: 4
Ingredients:
1. 2 (6 ounce) fillets cod fillets
2. 3 tablespoons olive oil
3. 1 onion, chopped
4. 4 cloves garlic, minced
5. 3 pinches dried rosemary
6. Ground black pepper to taste
7. 1 lemon, halved

Directions:
1. Preheat oven to 350 degrees F.
2. Place cod fillets on an 18x18-inch piece of aluminum foil; top with oil. Sprinkle onion, garlic, rosemary, and pepper over oil and cod. Squeeze juice from ½ lemon evenly on top.
3. Lift up bottom and top ends of the aluminum foil towards the center; fold together to 1 inch above the cod. Flatten short ends of the aluminum foil; fold over to within 1 inch of the sides of the cod. Place foil package on a baking sheet.

4. Bake in the preheated oven until haddock flakes easily with a fish, about 45 minutes. Let sit, about 5 minutes. Open ends of the packet carefully; squeeze juice from the remaining 1/2 lemon on top.

Nutrition: Calories 171, Total Fat 11.3g, Saturated Fat 1.6g, Cholesterol 95mg, Sodium 308mg, Total Carbohydrate 5g, Dietary Fiber 1.1g, Total Sugars 1.6g, Protein 14.3g, Calcium 31mg, Iron 1mg, Potassium 76mg, Potassium 67mg

612. Lemon, Garlic & Cilantro Tuna and Rice

Preparation Time: 5 minutes
Cooking Time: 0 minutes
Servings: 2
Ingredients:
- ½ cup arugula
- 1 tablespoon extra-virgin olive oil
- 1 cup cooked rice
- 1 teaspoon black pepper
- ¼ finely diced red onion
- 1 juiced lemon
- 2 tablespoons chopped fresh cilantro
- 1 tuna

Directions:
1. Mix the olive oil, pepper, cilantro, and red onion in a bowl.
2. Stir in the tuna and serve immediately.
3. When ready to eat, serve up with the cooked rice and arugula!

Nutrition: Calories 221, Protein 11 g, Carbohydrates 26 g, Fat 7 g, Sodium (Na) 143 mg, Potassium (K)197 mg, Phosphorus 182 mg

613. Baked Fennel and Garlic Sea Bass

Preparation Time: 5 minutes
Cooking Time: 15 minutes

Servings: 2 servings

Ingredients:

- 1 lemon
- ½ sliced fennel bulb
- 6 oz. sea bass fillets
- 1 teaspoon black pepper
- 2 garlic cloves
- 1 salmon filet

Directions:

1. Preheat the oven to 375°F/Gas Mark 5.
2. Sprinkle black pepper over the Sea Bass.
3. Slice the fennel bulb and garlic cloves.
4. Add 1 salmon fillet and half the fennel and garlic to one sheet of baking paper or tin foil.
5. Squeeze in 1/2 lemon juices.
6. Repeat for the other fillet.
7. Fold and add to the oven for 12-15 minutes or until fish is thoroughly cooked through.
8. Meanwhile, add boiling water to your couscous, cover, and allow to steam.
9. Serve with your choice of rice or salad.

Nutrition: Calories 221, Protein 14 g, Carbohydrates 3 g, Fat 2 g, Sodium (Na) 119 mg, Potassium (K) 398 mg, Phosphorus 149 mg

614. Fish Chowder

Preparation Time: 10 minutes
Cooking Time: 6 hours
Servings: 6

Ingredients:

- 2lb white fish fillets, cut into 1-inch pieces
- ¼lb low-sodium bacon, diced
- 1 medium onion, chopped
- 4 medium red-skinned carrots, peeled and cubed
- 2 cup water
- 1 low sodium salt
- ¼ tsp black pepper
- 1 12oz can evaporated almond milk

Directions

1. Fry the bacon in a skillet for a few minutes with the onion.
2. Add the bacon to the slow cooker with the remaining ingredients except for the evaporated almond milk.
3. Cover and cook on HIGH for 5 to 6 hours.
4. Add the almond milk during the last hour of cooking.

Nutrition: Calories 311, Fat 13g, Carbs 27g, Protein 14g, Fiber 12g, Potassium 911mg, Sodium 600mg

615. Mixed Pepper Stuffed River Trout

Preparation Time: 5 minutes
Cooking Time: 20 minutes
Servings: 4 servings

Ingredients:

- 1 whole river trout
- 1 teaspoon thyme
- ¼ diced yellow pepper
- ¼ diced green pepper
- 1 juiced lime
- ¼ diced red pepper
- 1 teaspoon oregano
- 1 teaspoon extra virgin olive oil
- 1 teaspoon black pepper

Directions:

1. Preheat the broiler /grill on high heat.
2. Lightly oil a baking tray.
3. Mix all the ingredients apart from the trout and lime.
4. Slice the trout lengthways (there should be an opening here from where it was gutted) and stuff the mixed ingredients inside.
5. Squeeze the lime juice over the fish and then place the lime wedges on the tray.
6. Place under the broiler on the baking tray and broil for 15-20 minutes or until

fish is thoroughly cooked through and flakes easily.

7. Enjoy the dish as it is, or with a side helping of rice or salad.

Nutrition: Calories 290, Protein 15 g, Carbohydrates 0 g, Fat 7 g, Sodium (Na) 43 mg, Potassium (K) 315 mg, Phosphorus 189 mg

616. Salmon and Pesto Salad

Preparation Time: 5 minutes
Cooking Time: 15 minutes
Servings: 2 servings
Ingredients:
For the pesto:
- 1 minced garlic clove
- ½ cup fresh arugula
- ¼ cup extra virgin olive oil
- ½ cup fresh basil
- 1 teaspoon black pepper
For the salmon:
- 4 oz. skinless salmon fillet
- 1 tablespoon coconut oil
For the salad:
- ½ juiced lemon
- 2 sliced radishes
- ½ cup iceberg lettuce
- 1 teaspoon black pepper

Directions:
1. Prepare the pesto by blending all the pesto ingredients in a food processor or by grinding with a pestle and mortar. Set aside.
2. Add a skillet to the stove on medium-high heat and melt the coconut oil.
3. Add the salmon to the pan.
4. Cook for 7-8 minutes and turn over.
5. Cook for a further 3-4 minutes or until cooked through.
6. Remove fillets from the skillet and allow to rest.

7. Mix the lettuce and the radishes and squeeze over the juice of ½ lemon.
8. Flake the salmon with a fork and mix through the salad.
9. Toss to coat and sprinkle with a little black pepper to serve.

Nutrition: Calories 221, Protein 13 g, Carbohydrates 1 g, Fat 34 g, Sodium (Na) 80 mg, Potassium (K) 119 mg, Phosphorus 158 mg

617. Shrimp Creole

Preparation Time: 20 minutes
Cooking Time: 4 hours
Servings: 3
Ingredients:
- 1½ cup celery, diced
- 1¼ cup onion, chopped
- 1 cup bell pepper, chopped
- 1 8oz can no-added salt tomato sauce
- 1 28oz no-added salt can whole Red bell peppers
- 1 garlic clove, minced
- ½ tsp low-sodium salt
- ½ tsp salt-free Creole seasoning
- ¼ tsp freshly ground black pepper
- 6 drops Tabasco sauce
- 1lb shrimp, deveined and shelled

Directions:
1. Place all the ingredients into a 3-quart slow cooker except the shrimp.
2. Cook (high) 3 to 4 hours.
3. Add shrimp during last 30 minutes of cooking.
4. Serve over hot cooked rice.

Nutrition: Calories 388, Fat 3g, Carbs 42g, Protein 52g, Fiber 8g, Potassium 874mg, Sodium 600mg

618. Cod Curry

Preparation Time: 10 minutes
Cooking Time: 25 minutes

Servings: 4

Ingredients:

- 4 cod fillets, boneless
- ½ teaspoon mustard seeds
- Salt and black pepper to the taste
- 2 green chilies, chopped
- 1 teaspoon fresh grated ginger
- 1 teaspoon curry powder
- ¼ teaspoon ground cumin
- 1 small red onion, chopped
- 1 teaspoon ground turmeric
- ¼ cup chopped parsley
- 1½ cups coconut cream
- 3 garlic cloves, minced

Directions:

1. Heat a pot with half of the oil over medium heat. Add mustard seeds and cook for 2 minutes. Add ginger, onion, garlic, turmeric, curry powder, chilies, and cumin, stir and cook for 10 minutes more. Add coconut almond milk, salt and pepper then stir. Bring to a boil, cook for 10 minutes and take off the heat. Warm another pan with the rest of the oil over medium heat, add fish, and then cook for 4 minutes. Transfer the fish on top of the curry mix, toss gently then cook for 6 more minutes. Divide between plates, sprinkle the parsley on top and serve.
2. Enjoy!

Nutrition: Calories 210 Fat 14 Fiber 7 Carbs 6 Protein 16

619. Haddock & Buttered Leeks

Preparation Time: 5 minutes
Cooking Time: 15 minutes
Servings: 2 servings

Ingredients:

- 1 tablespoon unsalted butter
- 1 sliced leek
- ¼ teaspoon black pepper
- 2 teaspoons chopped parsley
- 6 oz. haddock fillets
- ½ juiced lemon

Directions:

1. Preheat the oven to 375°F/Gas Mark 5.
2. Add the haddock fillets to baking or parchment paper and sprinkle with the black pepper.
3. Squeeze over the lemon juice and wrap into a parcel.
4. Bake the parcel on a baking tray for 10-15 minutes or until the fish is thoroughly cooked through.
5. Meanwhile, heat the butter over medium-low heat in a small pan.
6. Add the leeks and parsley and sauté for 5-7 minutes until soft.
7. Serve the haddock fillets on a bed of buttered leeks and enjoy!

Nutrition: Calories 124, Protein 15 g, Carbohydrates 0 g, Fat 7 g, Sodium (Na) 161 mg, Potassium (K) 251 mg, Phosphorus 220 mg

620. Teriyaki Tuna

Preparation Time: 10 minutes
Cooking Time: 6 minutes
Servings: 3

Ingredients:

- 3 tuna fillets
- 3 teaspoons teriyaki sauce
- ½ teaspoon minced garlic
- 1 teaspoon olive oil

Directions:

1. Whisk together teriyaki sauce, minced garlic, and olive oil.
2. Brush every tuna fillet with teriyaki mixture.
3. Preheat grill to 390F.
4. Grill the fish for 3 minutes from each side.

Nutrition: Calories 382, Fat 32.6, Fiber 0, Carbs 1.1, Protein 21.4

621. Thai Spiced Halibut

Preparation Time: 5 minutes
Cooking Time: 20 minutes
Servings: 2 servings
Ingredients:
- 2 tablespoons coconut oil
- 1 cup white rice
- ¼ teaspoon black pepper
- ½ diced red chili
- 1 tablespoon fresh basil
- 2 pressed garlic cloves
- 4 oz. halibut fillet
- 1 halved lime
- 2 sliced green onions
- 1 lime leaf

Directions:
1. Preheat oven to 400°F/Gas Mark 5.
2. Add half of the ingredients into baking paper and fold into a parcel.
3. Repeat for your second parcel.
4. Add to the oven for 15-20 minutes or until fish is thoroughly cooked through.
5. Serve with cooked rice.

Nutrition: Calories 311, Protein 16 g, Carbohydrates 17 g, Fat 15 g, Sodium (Na) 31 mg, Potassium (K) 418 mg, Phosphorus 257 mg

622. Fish Tacos

Preparation Time: 10 minutes
Cooking Time: 35 minutes
Servings: **6**
Ingredients:
- 1½ cup of cabbage
- ½ cup of red onion
- ½ bunch of cilantro
- 1 garlic clove
- 2 limes
- 1 pound of cod fillets
- ½ teaspoon of ground cumin
- ½ teaspoon of chili powder
- ¼ teaspoon of black pepper
- 1 tablespoon of olive oil
- ½ cup of mayonnaise
- ¼ cup of sour cream
- 2 tablespoons of almond milk
- 12 (6-inch) corn tortillas

Directions:
1. Shred the cabbage, chop the onion and cilantro, and mince the garlic. Set aside
2. Use a dish to place in the fish fillets, then squeeze half a lime juice over the fish. Sprinkle the fish fillets with the minced garlic, cumin, black pepper, chili powder, and olive oil. Turn the fish filets to coat with the marinade, then refrigerate for about 15 to 30 minutes
3. Prepare salsa Blanca by mixing the mayonnaise, almond milk, sour cream, and the other half of the lime juice. Stir to combine, then place in the refrigerator to chill
4. Broil in oven, and cover the broiler pan with aluminum foil. Broil the coated fish fillets for about 10 minutes or until the flesh becomes opaque and white and flakes easily. Remove from the oven, slightly cool, and then flake the fish into bigger pieces
5. Heat the corn tortillas in a pan, one at a time until it becomes soft and warm, then wrap in a dish towel to keep them warm
6. To assemble the tacos, place a piece of the fish on the tortilla, topping with the salsa Blanca, cabbage, cilantro, red onion, and the lime wedges.

7. Serve with hot sauce if you desire

Nutrition: Calories 363 Protein 18g Carbohydrates 30g Fat 19g Cholesterol 40mg Sodium 194mg Potassium 507mg Phosphorus 327mg Fiber 4.3g

623. Monk-Fish Curry

Preparation Time: 5 minutes
Cooking Time: 20 minutes
Servings: 2 servings
Ingredients:

- 1 garlic clove
- 3 finely chopped green onions
- 1 teaspoon grated ginger
- 1 cup water.
- 2 teaspoons chopped fresh basil
- 1 cup cooked rice noodles
- 1 tablespoon coconut oil
- ½ sliced red chili
- 4 oz. Monkfish fillet
- ½ finely sliced stick lemongrass
- 2 tablespoons chopped shallots

Directions:
1. Slice the Monkfish into bite-size pieces.
2. Using a pestle and mortar or food processor, crush the basil, garlic, ginger, chili, and lemongrass to form a paste.
3. Heat the oil in a large wok or pan over medium-high heat and add the shallots.
4. Now add the water to the pan and bring to a boil.
5. Add the Monkfish, lower the heat and cover to simmer for 10 minutes or until cooked through.
6. Enjoy with rice noodles and scatter with green onions to serve.

Nutrition: Calories 249, Protein 12 g, Carbohydrates 30 g, Fat 10 g, Sodium (Na) 32 mg, Potassium (K) 398 mg, Phosphorus 190 mg

624. Oregon Tuna Patties

Preparation Time: 10 minutes
Cooking Time: 15 minutes
Servings: 4
Ingredients:

- 1 (14.75 ounce) can tuna
- 2 tablespoons butter
- 1 medium onion, chopped
- 2/3 cup graham cracker crumbs
- 2 egg whites, beaten
- 1/4 cup chopped fresh parsley
- 1 teaspoon dry mustard
- 3 tablespoons olive oil

Directions:
1. Drain the tuna, reserving 3/4 cup of the liquid. Flake the meat. Melt butter in a large skillet over medium- high heat. Add onion, and cook until tender.
2. In a medium bowl, combine the onions with the reserved tuna liquid, 1/3 of the graham cracker crumbs, egg whites, parsley, mustard and tuna. Mix until well blended, then shape into six patties. Coat patties in remaining cracker crumbs.
3. Heat olive in a large skillet over medium heat. Cook patties until browned, then carefully turn and brown on the other side.

Nutrition: Calories 204, Total Fat 15.4g, Saturated Fat 4.4g, Cholesterol 74mg, Sodium 111mg, Total Carbohydrate 6.5g, Dietary Fiber 0.9g, Total Sugar 2g, Protein 10.5g, Calcium 21mg, Iron 1mg, Potassium 164mg, Phosphorus 106mg

625. Broiled Sesame Cod

Preparation Time: 05 minutes
Cooking Time: 10 min
Servings: 4
Ingredients:

- 1/2 pounds' cod fillets
- 1 teaspoon butter, melted
- 1 teaspoon lemon juice
- 1 teaspoon dried basil
- 1 pinch ground black pepper
- 1 tablespoon sesame seeds

Directions:
1. Preheat the oven's broiler and set the oven rack about 6 inches from the heat source. Line a broiler pan with aluminum foil.
2. Place the cod fillets on the foil, and brush with butter. Season with lemon juice, basil, and black pepper; sprinkle with sesame seeds.
3. Broil the fish in the preheated broiler until the flesh turns opaque and white, and the fish flakes easily, about 10 minutes.

Nutrition: Calories 67, Total Fat 2.6g, Saturated Fat 0.8g, Cholesterol 30mg, Sodium 43mg, Total Carbohydrate 0.6g, Dietary Fiber 0.3g, Total Sugar 0g, Protein 10.6g, Calcium 23mg, Iron 0mg, Potassium 13mg, Phosphorus 10mg

626. Tuna Salad with Cranberries

Preparation Time: 10 minutes
Cooking Time: 00 min
Servings: 4
Ingredient:
- 2 (5 ounce) cans solid white tuna packed in water, drained
- 2 tablespoons mayonnaise
- 1/3 teaspoon dried dill weed
- 3 tablespoons dried cranberries

Directions:
1. Place the tuna in a bowl, and mash with a fork.
2. Mix in mayonnaise to evenly coat tuna. Mix in dill and cranberries.

Nutrition: Calories 81, Total Fat 2.8g, Saturated Fat 0.5g, Cholesterol 15mg, Sodium 74mg, Total Carbohydrate 2.3g, Dietary Fiber 0.2g, Total Sugar 0.7g, Protein 10.9g, Calcium 8mg, Iron 1mg, Potassium 113mg, Phosphorus 95mg

627. Jambalaya

Preparation Time: 10 minutes
Cooking Time: 1 hour and 15 minutes
Servings: 12
Ingredients:
- 2 cups of onion
- 1 cup of bell pepper
- 2 garlic cloves
- 2 cups of uncooked converted white rice
- ½ teaspoon of black pepper
- 8 ounces of canned low-sodium tomato sauce
- 2 cups of low-sodium beef broth
- 2 pounds of raw shrimp
- ½ cup of unsalted margarine

Directions:
1. Preheat oven to 350° F
2. Chop the onion, bell pepper, garlic, then peel the shrimp
3. Combine and mix all the ingredients in a large bowl except the margarine

4. Pour into a 9 x 13-inch baking dish and evenly spread out
5. Slice the margarine, placing over the top of the ingredients
6. Cover with foil or lid, and bake for about 1 hr. 15 minutes
7. Serve hot.

Nutrition: Calories 294 Protein 20g Carbohydrates 31g Fat 10g Cholesterol 137mg Sodium 186mg

Potassium 300mg Phosphorus 197mg Fiber 0.8g

628. Asparagus Shrimp Linguini

Preparation Time: 10 minutes
Cooking Time: 35 minutes
Servings: 1 ½ cup

Ingredients:

- 8 ounces of uncooked linguini
- 1 tablespoon of olive oil
- 1¾ cups of asparagus
- ½ cup of unsalted butter
- 2 garlic cloves
- 3 ounces of cream cheese
- 2 tablespoons of fresh parsley
- ¾ teaspoon of dried basil
- 2/3 cup of dry white wine
- ½ pound of peeled and cooked shrimp

Directions:

1. Preheat oven to 350° F
2. Cook the linguini in boiling water until it becomes tender, then drain
3. Place the asparagus on a baking sheet, then spread two tablespoons of oil over the asparagus. Bake for about 7 to 8 minutes or until it is tender
4. Remove baked asparagus from the oven and place it on a plate. Cut the asparagus into pieces of medium-sized once cooled
5. Mince the garlic and chop the parsley
6. Melt ½ cup of butter in a large skillet with the minced garlic
7. Stir in the cream cheese, mixing as it melts
8. Stir in the parsley and basil, then simmer for about 5 minutes. Mix either in boiling water or dry white wine, stirring until the sauce becomes smooth
9. Add the cooked shrimp and asparagus, then stir and heat until it is evenly warm
10. Toss the cooked pasta with the sauce and serve

Nutrition: Calories 544 Protein 21g Carbohydrates 43g Fat 32g Cholesterol 188mg Sodium 170mg

Potassium 402mg Phosphorus 225mg Fiber 2.4g

629. Tuna Noodle Casserole

Preparation Time: 10 minutes
Cooking Time: 35 minutes
Servings: 2

Ingredients:

- 2 ounces of wide uncooked egg noodles
- 5 ounces of canned tuna in water
- ½ cup of sour cream
- ¼ cup of cottage cheese
- ½ cup of fresh sliced mushrooms
- ½ cup of frozen green peas
- 1 tablespoon of unsalted butter
- ¼ cup of unseasoned bread crumbs

Directions:

1. Preheat oven to 350° F
2. Boil egg noodles based on the package instructions and drain. Also, drain and flake the tuna
3. Combine and mix the sour cream, cottage cheese, mushrooms, tuna, and peas in a medium bowl
4. Stir the drained noodle into the tuna mixture, and place in a small casserole dish that has been sprayed with a non-stick cooking spray
5. Melt butter, stir into the bread crumbs, then sprinkle over the mixture of noodles in step 4
6. Bake for about 20 to 25 minutes or until the bread crumbs start to brown
7. Divide into two and serve

Nutrition: Calories 415 Protein 22g Carbohydrates 39g Fat 19g Cholesterol 88mg Sodium 266mg Potassium 400mg Phosphorus 306mg Fiber 3.2g

630. Oven-Fried Southern Style Catfish

Preparation Time: 10 minutes
Cooking Time: 35 minutes
Servings: 4

Ingredients:

- 1 egg white
- ½ cup of all-purpose flour
- ¼ cup of cornmeal
- ¼ cup of panko bread crumbs
- 1 teaspoon of salt-free Cajun seasoning
- 1 pound of catfish fillets

Directions:

1. Heat oven to 450° F
2. Use cooking spray to spray a non-stick baking sheet
3. Using a bowl, beat the egg white until very soft peaks are formed. Don't over-beat
4. Use a sheet of wax paper and place the flour over it
5. Using a different sheet of wax paper to combine and mix the cornmeal, panko and the Cajun seasoning
6. Cut the catfish fillet into four pieces, then dip the fish in the flour, shaking off the excess
7. Dip coated fish in the egg white, rolling into the cornmeal mixture
8. Place the fish on the baking pan. Repeat with the remaining fish fillets

9. Use cooking spray to spray over the fish fillets. Bake for about 10 to 12 minutes or until the sides of the fillets become browned and crisp

Nutrition: Calories 250 Protein 22g Carbohydrates 19g Fat 10g Cholesterol 53mg Sodium 124mg Potassium 401mg Phosphorus 262mg Fiber 1.2g

631. Fisherman's Stew

Preparation Time: 15 minutes
Cooking Time: 6-8 hours
Servings: 8
Ingredients:
- 1 fillet of sea bass, cod or other white fish, cubed
- 1 dozen each large shrimp, scallops, mussels & clams
- 1 28 ounces no-added salt crushed Red bell peppers with juice
- 1 8oz no-added salt tomato sauce
- ½ cup onion, chopped
- 1 cup dry white wine
- 1/3 cup olive oil
- 3 garlic cloves, minced
- ½ cup parsley, chopped
- 1 green pepper, chopped
- 1 hot pepper, chopped
- ½ tsp low sodium salt
- 1 tsp thyme
- 2 tsp basil
- 1 tsp oregano
- ½ tsp paprika
- ½ tsp cayenne pepper

Directions:
1. Place all ingredients except seafood in a 4 to 6-quart slow cooker and cover.
2. Cook (low) for 6-8 hours.
3. Add the fish about 30 minutes towards the end of the cooking time and turn up the heat to HIGH.

Nutrition: Calories 434, Fat 16g, Carbs 27g, Protein 39g, Fiber 4g, Potassium 714mg, Sodium 378mg

632. Spicy tuna Salad Sandwiches

Preparation Time: 15 minutes
Cooking Time: 00 min
Servings:
Ingredient:
- 1 (8 ounce) can tuna, undrained
- 1/4 cucumber, chopped
- 2 tablespoons light mayonnaise
- 1 tablespoon vinegar
- 1 teaspoon red chili paste
- 4 slices white bread, toasted

Directions:
1. Put tuna into a bowl and use a fork to flake and mix with the can's liquid. Mix cucumber with the tuna.
2. Stir mayonnaise, vinegar, chili paste, and bowl; add hot sauce and adjust to taste. Pour mayonnaise mixture over the salmon mixture and stir to coat. Spoon onto toasted bread to make sandwiches.

Nutrition: Calories 189, Total Fat 7.6g, Saturated Fat 1.1g, Cholesterol 28mg, Sodium 326mg, Total Carbohydrate 15.6g, Dietary Fiber 2.1g, Total Sugar 3.4g, Protein 15.1g, Calcium 60mg, Iron 1mg, Potassium 119mg, Phosphorus 109 mg

633. Spanish Tuna

Preparation Time: 20 minutes
Cooking Time: 15 minutes
Servings: 4
Ingredients:
- 1 tablespoon olive oil
- 1/4 cup finely chopped onion
- 2 tablespoons chopped fresh garlic
- 1/4 cup basil chopped

- 1 dash black pepper
- 1 dash cayenne pepper
- 1 dash paprika
- 6 (4 ounce) fillets tuna fillets

Directions:
1. Heat olive oil in a large skillet over medium heat.
2. Cook and stir onions and garlic until onions are slightly tender, careful not to burn the garlic.
3. Season with black pepper, cayenne pepper, basil, and paprika.
4. Cook fillets in sauce over medium heat for 5 to 8 minutes, or until easily flaked with a fork. Serve immediately.

Nutrition: Calories 130, Total Fat 4.6g, Saturated Fat 0.5g, Cholesterol 55mg, Sodium 71mg, Total Carbohydrate 2.2g, Dietary Fiber 0.3g, Total Sugar 0.4g, Protein 20.4g, Calcium 10mg, Iron 0mg, Potassium 31mg, Phosphorus 46 mg

634. Cilantro-Lime Cod

Preparation Time: 10 minutes
Cooking Time: 35 minutes
Servings: 4

Ingredients:
- ½ cup of mayonnaise
- ½ cup of fresh chopped cilantro
- 2 tablespoon of lime juice
- 1 pound of cod fillets

Directions:
1. Combine and mix the mayonnaise, cilantro, and lime juice in a medium bowl, remove ¼ cup to another bowl and put aside. To be served as fish sauce
2. Spread the remaining mayonnaise mixture over the cod fillets
3. Use cooking spray to spray a large skillet, then heat over medium-high heat
4. Place in the cod fillets, and cook for about 8 minutes or until the fish becomes firm and moist, turning just once
5. Serve with the ¼ cilantro-lime sauce

Nutrition: Calories 292 Protein 20g Carbohydrates 1g Fat 23g Cholesterol 57mg Sodium 228mg
Potassium 237mg Phosphorus 128mg Calcium 14mg

635. Creamy Crab over Salmon

Preparation Time: 10 minutes
Cooking Time: 15 minutes
Servings: 4

Ingredients:
- 1/4 cup olive oil, divided
- 2 (4 ounce) fillets salmon
- 1 teaspoon dried oregano
- 1 pinch ground white pepper
- 1 3/4 cups soy almond milk
- 4 ounces' fresh crabmeat
- 1 teaspoon lemon juice

Directions:
1. Heat a small amount of the olive oil in a non-stick skillet over medium heat. Season salmon with oregano, and white pepper; cook in skillet until the flesh flakes easily with a fork, 7 to 10 minutes per side.

2. While fish cooks, whisk remaining olive oil, soy almond milk, together in a saucepan over medium-low heat; cook, stirring regularly, until it thickens, 3 to 5 minutes. Remove saucepan from heat and stir crabmeat into the sauce.
3. Transfer cooked cod to plates and spoon sauce over the fish.

Nutrition: Calories 258, Total Fat 16.5g, Saturated Fat 2.5g, Cholesterol 40mg, Sodium 395mg, Total Carbohydrate 11.4g, Dietary Fiber 1g, Total Sugar 6.1g, Protein 17.3g, Calcium 37mg, Iron 1mg, Potassium 160mg, Potassium 120mg

636. Creamy Smoked Tuna Macaroni

Preparation Time: 15 minutes
Cooking Time: 25min
Servings: 4
Ingredients:
- 3 tablespoons olive oil
- ¼ onion, finely chopped
- 1 tablespoon all-purpose flour
- 1 teaspoon garlic powder
- 1 cup soy almond milk
- ¼ cup cream cheese
- ½ cup frozen green peas, thawed and drained
- ¼ cup mushrooms
- 5 ounces smoked tuna, chopped
- ½ (16 ounce) package macaroni

Directions:
1. Bring a large pot of water to a boil. Add macaroni and cook for 8 to 10 minutes or until al dente; drain.
2. Heat oil in a large skillet over medium heat. Sauté onion in oil until tender.
3. Stir flour and garlic powder into the oil and onions. Gradually stir in almond milk. Heat to just below boiling point, and then gradually stir in cheese until

the sauce is smooth. Stir in peas and mushrooms. And cook over low heat for 4 minutes.
4. Toss in smoked tuna, and cook for 2 more minutes. Serve over macaroni.

Nutrition: Calories 147, Total Fat 8.3g, Saturated Fat 1.9g, Cholesterol 14mg, Sodium 979mg, Total Carbohydrate 6.5g, Dietary Fiber 0.8g, Total Sugar 1.9g, Protein 11.4g, Calcium 38mg, Iron 1mg, Potassium 160mg, Phosphorus 100mg

637. Curried fish cakes

Preparation time: 10 minutes
Cooking time: 18 minutes
Servings: 4
Ingredients
- ¾ pound Atlantic cod, cubed
- 1 apple, peeled and cubed
- 1 tablespoon yellow curry paste
- 2 tablespoons cornstarch
- 1 tablespoon peeled grated ginger root
- 1 large egg
- 1 tablespoon freshly squeezed lemon juice
- 1/8 teaspoon freshly ground black pepper
- ½ cup crushed puffed rice cereal
- 1 tablespoon olive oil

Directions
1. Put the cod, apple, curry, cornstarch, ginger, egg, lemon juice, and pepper in a blender or food processor and process until finely chopped. Avoid over-processing, or the mixture will become mushy.
2. Place the rice cereal on a shallow plate.
3. Form the mixture into 8 patties.
4. Dredge the patties in the rice cereal to coat.

5. Cook patties for 3 to 5 minutes per side, turning once until a meat thermometer registers 160°f.
6. Serve.

Nutrition: per serving: calories: 188; total fat: 6g; saturated fat: 1g; sodium: 150mg; potassium: 292mg; phosphorus: 150mg; carbohydrates: 12g; fiber: 1g; protein: 21g; sugar: 5g

638. Asparagus and Smoked Tuna Salad

Preparation Time: 15 minutes
Cooking Time: 10 minutes
Servings: 4
Ingredients:
- ½ pound fresh asparagus, trimmed and cut into 1 inch pieces
- 1 heads lettuce, rinsed and torn
- ¼ cup frozen green peas, thawed
- 1/8 cup olive oil
- 1 tablespoon lemon juice
- ½ teaspoon Dijon mustard
- 1/8 teaspoon pepper
- 1/8 pound smoked tuna, cut into 1inch chunks

Directions:
1. Bring a pot of water to a boil. Place asparagus in the pot, and cook 5 minutes, just until tender. Drain, and set aside.
2. In a large bowl, toss together the asparagus, lettuce, peas, and tuna.
3. In a separate bowl, mix the olive oil, lemon juice, Dijon mustard, and pepper. Toss with the salad or serve on the side.

Nutrition: Calories 87, Total Fat 7g, Saturated Fat 1.1g, Cholesterol 3mg, Sodium 298mg, Total Carbohydrate 2.7g, Dietary Fiber 1.1g, Total Sugar 1g, Protein 3.8g, Calcium 16mg, Iron 1mg, Potassium 134mg, Phosphorus 104 mg

639. Zucchini Cups with Dill Cream and Smoked Tuna

Preparation Time: 15 minutes
Cooking Time: 35 minutes
Servings: 4
Ingredients:
- 1 1/3 large Zucchini
- 4 ounces' cream cheese, softened
- 2 tablespoons chopped fresh dill
- 1 teaspoon lemon zest
- 1/2 teaspoon fresh lemon juice
- 1/4 teaspoon ground black pepper
- 4 ounces smoked tuna, cut into 2-inch strips

Directions:
1. Trim ends from Zucchini and cut crosswise into 24 (3/4-inch-thick) rounds. Scoop a 1/2-inch-deep depression from one side of each round with a small melon-baller, forming little cups. Drain Zucchini, cup sides down, on paper towels for 15 minutes.
2. Beat cream cheese, chopped dill, lemon zest, lemon juice, and black pepper together in a bowl. Spoon 1/2 teaspoon cheese mixture into each Zucchini cup. Top each cup with 1 tuna strip.

Nutrition: Calories 51, Total Fat 3.8g, Saturated Fat 2.2g, Cholesterol 13mg, Sodium 219mg, Total Carbohydrate 1.8g, Dietary Fiber 0.3g, Total Sugar 0.6g, Protein 2.8g, Calcium 24mg, Iron 1mg, Potassium 95mg, Phosphorus 40mg

640. Crab cake

Preparation time: 15 minutes
Cooking time: 9 minutes
Servings: 6
Ingredients
- 1/4 cup onion, chopped
- 1/4 cup bell pepper, chopped

- 1 egg, beaten
- 6 low-sodium crackers, crushed
- 1/4 cup low-fat mayonnaise
- 1-pound crab meat
- 1 tablespoon dry mustard
- Pepper to taste
- 2 tablespoons lemon juice
- 1 tablespoon fresh parsley
- 1 tablespoon garlic powder
- 3 tablespoons olive oil

Directions
1. Mix all the ingredients except the oil.
2. Form 6 patties from the mixture.
3. Pour the oil into a pan in a medium heat.
4. Cook the crab cakes for 5 minutes.
5. Flip and cook for another 4 minutes.

Nutrition: calories 189 protein 13 g carbohydrates 5 g fat 14 g cholesterol 111 mg sodium 342 mg potassium 317 mg phosphorus 185 mg calcium 52 mg fiber 0.5 g

641. Fish with Vegetables

Preparation Time: 30 minutes
Cooking Time: 60 minutes
Servings: 4
Ingredients:
- 1 egg white, beaten
- ¼ cup all-purpose flour
- Black pepper to taste
- 1-pound firm salmon fillets, cut into 1 1/2-inch pieces
- ½ cup olive oil, divided
- 1 onion, cut in half and thinly sliced
- 1 carrot, peeled and coarsely grated
- ½ large turnips, peeled and coarsely grated
- 1/2 leek coarsely grated
- 1 cup water

Directions:
1. Place egg white and flour in 2 shallow bowls. Season egg white with pepper.

Dip fish pieces first in the beaten egg, then dredge in the flour.
2. Heat 1/4 cup olive oil in a deep skillet over medium heat until hot. Add fish in batches and fry on both sides until golden, 5 to 8 minutes per batch. Remove fish from skillet and set aside.
3. Heat remaining 1/4 cup oil in a separate skillet and cook onions until soft and translucent, about 5 minutes. Add carrots, turnips, and leek; mix well. Add water and season with pepper. Cover and simmer on low heat until vegetables are soft, about 30 minutes. Check and add more water if mixture becomes too dry.
4. Layer vegetables and fried fish in a 10-inch round serving dish, starting and ending with vegetables.

Nutrition: Calories 358, Total Fat 30.1g, Saturated Fat 6g, Cholesterol 57mg, Sodium 45mg, Total Carbohydrate 14.7g, Dietary Fiber 2.2g, Total Sugar 3.3g, Protein 8.2g, Calcium 38mg, Iron 1mg, Potassium 281mg, Phosphorus 161 mg

642. Thai tuna wraps

Preparation time: 10 minutes
Cooking time: 0 minute
Servings: 4
Ingredients
- ¼ cup unsalted peanut butter
- 2 tablespoons freshly squeezed lemon juice
- 1 teaspoon low-sodium soy sauce
- ½ teaspoon ground ginger
- 1/8 teaspoon cayenne pepper
- 1 (6-ounce) can no-salt-added or low-sodium chunk light tuna, drained
- 1 cup shredded red cabbage
- 2 scallions, white and green parts, chopped
- 1 cup grated carrots

- 8 butter lettuce leaves

Directions

1. In a medium bowl, stir together the peanut butter, lemon juice, soy sauce, ginger, and cayenne pepper until well combined.
2. Stir in the tuna, cabbage, scallions, and carrots.
3. Divide the tuna filling evenly between the butter lettuce leaves and serve.

Nutrition: per serving: calories: 175; total fat; 10g; saturated fat: 1g; sodium: 98mg; potassium: 421mg; phosphorus: 153mg; carbohydrates: 8g; fiber: 2g; protein: 17g; sugar: 4g

643. Grilled fish and vegetable packets

Preparation time: 15 minutes
Cooking time: 12 minutes
Servings: 4
Ingredients

- 1 (8-ounce) package sliced mushrooms
- 1 leek, white and green parts, chopped
- 1 cup frozen corn
- 4 (4-ounce) Atlantic cod fillets
- Juice of 1 lemon
- 3 tablespoons olive oil

Directions

1. Prepare and preheat the grill to medium coals and set a grill 6 inches from the coals.
2. Tear off four 30-inch long strips of heavy-duty aluminum foil.
3. Arrange the mushrooms, leek, and corn in the center of each piece of foil and top with the fish.
4. Drizzle the packet contents evenly with the lemon juice and olive oil.
5. Bring the longer length sides of the foil together at the top and, holding the edges together, fold them over twice and then fold in the width sides to form a sealed packet with room for the steam.

6. Put the packets on the grill and grill for 10 to 12 minutes until the vegetables are tender-crisp and the fish flakes when tested with a fork. Be careful opening the packets because the escaping steam can be scalding.

Nutrition: per serving: calories: 267; total fat: 12g; saturated fat: 2g; sodium: 97mg; potassium: 582mg; phosphorus: 238mg; carbohydrates: 13g; fiber: 2g; protein: 29g; sugar: 3g

644. Lemon butter salmon

Preparation time: 15 minutes
Cooking time: 15 minutes
Servings: 6
Ingredients

- 1 tablespoon butter
- 2 tablespoons olive oil
- 1 tablespoon Dijon mustard
- 1 tablespoons lemon juice
- 2 cloves garlic, crushed
- 1 teaspoon dried dill
- 1 teaspoon dried basil leaves
- 1 tablespoon capers
- 24-ounce salmon filet

Directions

1. Put all of the ingredients except the salmon in a saucepan over medium heat.
2. Bring to a boil and then simmer for 5 minutes.
3. Preheat your grill.
4. Create a packet using foil.
5. Place the sauce and salmon inside.
6. Seal the packet.
7. Grill for 12 minutes.

Nutrition: calories 292 protein 22 g carbohydrates 2 g fat 22 g cholesterol 68 mg sodium 190 mg potassium 439 mg phosphorus 280 mg calcium 21 mg

645. Fish taco

Preparation time: 40 minutes

Cooking time: 10 minutes

Servings: 6

Ingredients

- 1 tablespoon lime juice
- 1 tablespoon olive oil
- 1 clove garlic, minced
- 1-pound cod fillets
- 1/2 teaspoon ground cumin
- 1/4 teaspoon black pepper
- 1/2 teaspoon chili powder
- 1/4 cup sour cream
- 1/2 cup mayonnaise
- 2 tablespoons nondairy milk
- 1 cup cabbage, shredded
- 1/2 cup onion, chopped
- 1/2 bunch cilantro, chopped
- 12 corn tortillas

Directions

1. Drizzle lemon juice over the fish fillet.
2. And then coat it with olive oil and then season with garlic, cumin, pepper and chili powder.
3. Let it sit for 30 minutes.
4. Broil fish for 10 minutes, flipping halfway through.
5. Flake the fish using a fork.
6. In a bowl, mix sour cream, milk and mayo.
7. Assemble tacos by filling each tortilla with mayo mixture, cabbage, onion, cilantro and fish flakes.

Nutrition: calories 366 protein 18 g carbohydrates 31 g fat 19 g cholesterol 40 mg sodium 194 mg potassium 507 mg phosphorus 327 mg calcium 138 mg fiber 4.3 g

646. Baked sole with caramelized onion

Preparation time: 10 minutes

Cooking time: 20 minutes

Servings: 4

Ingredients

- 1 cup finely chopped onion
- ½ cup low-sodium vegetable broth
- 1 yellow summer squash, sliced
- 2 cups frozen broccoli florets
- 4 (3-ounce) fillets of sole
- Pinch salt
- 2 tablespoons olive oil
- Pinch baking soda
- 1 teaspoon dried basil leaves

Directions

1. Preheat the oven to 425°f.
2. Add the onions. Cook for 1 minute; then, stirring constantly, cook for another 4 minutes.
3. Remove the onions from the heat.
4. Pour the broth into a baking sheet with a lip and arrange the squash and broccoli on the sheet in a single layer. Top the vegetables with the fish. Sprinkle the fish with the salt and drizzle everything with the olive oil.
5. Bake the fish and the vegetables for 10 minutes.
6. While the fish is baking, return the skillet with the onions to medium-high heat and stir in a pinch of baking soda.
7. Transfer the onions to a plate.
8. Top the fish evenly with the onions. Sprinkle with the basil.
9. Return the fish to the oven, after this bake it 8 to10 minutes serve the fish on the vegetables.

Nutrition: per serving: calories: 202; total fat: 11g; saturated fat: 3g; sodium: 320mg; potassium: 537; phosphorus: 331mg; carbohydrates: 10g; fiber: 3g; protein: 16g; sugar: 4g

647. Zucchini and turkey burger with jalapeno peppers

Preparation Time: 15 minutes

Cooking Time: 10 minutes
Servings: 4
Ingredients
- Turkey meat (ground) – 1 pound
- Zucchini (shredded) – 1 cup
- Onion (minced) – ½ cup
- Jalapeño pepper (seeded and minced) – 1
- Egg – 1
- Extra-spicy blend – 1 teaspoon
- Fresh polao peppers (seeded and sliced in half lengthwise)
- Mustard – 1 teaspoon

Directions
1. Start by taking a mixing bowl and adding in the turkey meat, zucchini, onion, jalapeño pepper, egg, and extra-spicy blend. Mix well to combine.
2. Divide the mixture into 4 equal portions. Form burger patties out of the same.
3. Prepare an electric griddle or an outdoor grill. Place the burger patties on the grill and cook until the top is blistered and tender. Place the sliced poblano peppers on the grill alongside the patties. Grilling the patties should take about 5 minutes on each side.
4. Once done, place the patties onto the buns and top them with grilled peppers.

Nutrition: protein – 25 g carbohydrates – 5 g fat – 10 g cholesterol – 125 mg sodium – 128 mg potassium – 475 mg phosphorus – 280 mg calcium – 43 mg fiber – 1.6 g name

648. Baked fish in cream sauce

Preparation time: 10 minutes
Cooking time: 40 minutes
Servings: 4
Ingredients
- 1-pound haddock
- 1/2 cup all-purpose flour
- 2 tablespoons butter (unsalted)
- 1/4 teaspoon pepper
- 2 cups fat-free nondairy creamer
- 1/4 cup water

Directions
1. Preheat your oven to 350 degrees f.
2. Spray baking pan with oil.
3. Sprinkle with a little flour.
4. Arrange fish on the pan
5. Season with pepper.
6. Sprinkle remaining flour on the fish.
7. Spread creamer on both sides of the fish.
8. Bake for 40 minutes or until golden.
9. Spread cream sauce on top of the fish before serving.

Nutrition: calories 383 protein 24 g carbohydrates 46 g fat 11 g cholesterol 79 mg sodium 253 mg potassium 400 mg phosphorus 266 mg calcium 46 mg fiber 0.4 g

649. Fish with mushrooms

Preparation time: 5 minutes
Cooking time: 16 minutes
Servings: 4
Ingredients
- 1-pound cod fillet
- 2 tablespoons butter
- ¼ cup white onion, chopped
- 1 cup fresh mushrooms
- 1 teaspoon dried thyme

Directions
1. Put the fish in a baking pan.
2. Preheat your oven to 450 degrees f.
3. Melt the butter and cook onion and mushroom for 1 minute.
4. Spread mushroom mixture on top of the fish.
5. Season with thyme.
6. Bake in the oven for 15 minutes.

Nutrition: calories 156 protein 21 g carbohydrates 3 g fat 7 g cholesterol 49 mg sodium 110 mg potassium 561 mg phosphorus 225 mg calcium 30 mg fiber 0.5 g

650. Shrimp & broccoli

Preparation time: 10 minutes
Cooking time: 5 minutes
Servings: 4
Ingredients

- 1 tablespoon olive oil
- 1 clove garlic, minced
- 1-pound shrimp
- 1/4 cup red bell pepper
- 1 cup broccoli florets, steamed
- 10-ounce cream cheese
- 1/2 teaspoon garlic powder
- 1/4 cup lemon juice
- 3/4 teaspoon ground peppercorns
- 1/4 cup half and half creamer

Directions

1. Pour the oil and cook garlic for 30 seconds.
2. Add shrimp and cook for 2 minutes.
3. Add the rest of the ingredients.
4. Mix well.
5. Cook for 2 minutes.

Nutrition: calories 469 protein 28 g carbohydrates 28 g fat 28 g cholesterol 213 mg sodium 374 mg potassium 469 mg phosphorus 335 mg calcium 157 mg fiber 2.6 g

651. Shrimp in garlic sauce

Preparation time: 10 minutes
Cooking time: 6 minutes
Servings: 4
Ingredients

- 3 tablespoons butter (unsalted)
- 1/4 cup onion, minced
- 3 cloves garlic, minced
- 1-pound shrimp, shelled and deveined
- 1/2 cup half and half creamer
- 1/4 cup white wine
- 2 tablespoons fresh basil
- Black pepper to taste

Directions

1. Add butter to a pan over medium low heat.
2. Let it melt.
3. Add the onion and garlic.
4. Cook for it 1-2 minutes.
5. Add the shrimp and cook for 2 minutes.
6. Transfer shrimp on a serving platter and set aside.
7. Add the rest of the ingredients.
8. Simmer for 3 minutes.
9. Pour sauce over the shrimp and serve.

Nutrition: calories 482 protein 33 g carbohydrates 46 g fat 11 g cholesterol 230 mg sodium 213 mg potassium 514 mg phosphorus 398 mg calcium 133 mg fiber 2.0 g

POULTRY RECIPES

652. Baked trout

Preparation time: 5 minutes
Cooking time: 10 minutes
Servings: 8

Ingredients

- 2-pound trout fillet
- 1 tablespoon oil
- 1 teaspoon salt-free lemon pepper
- 1/2 teaspoon paprika

Directions

1. Preheat your oven to 350 degrees f.
2. Coat fillet with oil.
3. Place fish on a baking pan.
4. Season with lemon pepper and paprika.
5. Bake for 10 minutes.

Nutrition: calories 161 protein 21 g carbohydrates 0 g fat 8 g cholesterol 58 mg sodium 109 mg potassium 385 mg phosphorus 227 mg calcium 75 mg fiber 0.1 g

653. Creamy Turkey

PreparationTime:12minutes
CookingTime:10minutes
Servings: 4

Ingredients:

- 4 skinless, boneless turkey breast halves
- Salt and pepper to taste
- ½ teaspoon ground black pepper
- ½ teaspoon garlic powder
- 1 (10.75 ounces) can chicken soup

Directions:

1. Preheat oven to 375 degrees F.
2. Clean turkey breasts and season with salt, pepper and garlic powder (or whichever seasonings you prefer) on both sides of turkey pieces.
3. Bake for 25 minutes, then add chicken soup and bake for 10 more minutes (or until done). Serve over rice or egg noodles.

Nutrition: Calories 160, Sodium 157mg, Dietary Fiber 0.4g, Total Sugars 0.4g, Protein 25.6g, Calcium 2mg, Potassium 152mg, Phosphorus 85 mg

654. Chicken with Asian Vegetables

Preparation Time: 10 Minutes
Cooking Time: 20 Minutes
Servings: 8

Ingredients:

- 2 tablespoons canola oil
- 6 boneless chicken breasts
- 1 cup low-sodium chicken broth
- 3 tablespoons reduced-sodium soy sauce
- 1/4 teaspoon crushed red pepper flakes
- 1 garlic clove, crushed
- 1 can (8ounces) water chestnuts, sliced and rinsed (optional)
- 1/2 cup sliced green onions
- 1 cup chopped red or green bell pepper
- 1 cup chopped celery
- 1/4 cup cornstarch
- 1/3 cup water
- 3 cups cooked white rice
- 1/2 large chicken breast for 1 chicken thigh

Directions:

1. Warm oil in a skillet and dark-colored chicken on all sides.
2. Add chicken to a slow cooker with the remainder of the fixings aside from cornstarch and water.
3. Spread and cook on LOW for 6 to 8hours

4. Following 6-8 hours, independently blend cornstarch and cold water until smooth. Gradually include into the moderate cooker.
5. At that point turn on high for about 15mins until thickened. Don't close the top on the moderate cooker to enable steam to leave.
6. Serve Asian blend over rice.

Nutrition: Calories 415, Fat 20g, Protein 20g, Carbohydrates 36g

655. Cherry Chicken Salad

PreparationTime:15minutes
CookingTime:00minutes
Servings: 4
Ingredients:

- 3 cooked, boneless chicken breast halves, diced
- 1/3 cup dried cherries
- 1/3 cup diced celery
- 1/3 cup low-fat mayonnaise
- 1/2 teaspoon ground black pepper
- 1/3 cup cubed apples (optional)

Directions:
1. In a large bowl, combine the chicken, dried cherries, celery, mayonnaise, and pepper and apple if desired.
2. Toss together well and refrigerate until chilled.
3. Serve

Nutrition: Calories 281, Total Fat 11.8g, Cholesterol 31mg, Sodium 586mg, Dietary Fiber 1.4g, Total Sugars 2.9g, Protein 14.7g, Calcium 12mg, Potassium 55mg, Phosphorus 20 mg

656. Turkey Broccoli Salad

PreparationTime:10minutes
CookingTime:00minutes
Servings: 4
Ingredients:

- 8 cups broccoli florets
- 3 cooked skinless, boneless chicken breast halves, cubed
- 6 green onions, chopped
- 1 cup mayonnaise
- ¼ cup apple cider vinegar
- ¼ cup honey

Directions:
1. Combine broccoli, chicken and green onions in a large bowl.
2. Whisk mayonnaise, vinegar, and honey together in a bowl until well blended.
3. Pour mayonnaise dressing over broccoli mixture; toss to coat.
4. Cover and refrigerate until chilled, if desired. Serve

Nutrition: Calories 133, Sodium 23mg, Dietary Fiber 1.6g, Total Sugars 7.7g, Protein 6.2g, Calcium 24mg, Potassium 157mg Phosphorus 148 mg

657. Chicken and Veggie Soup

Preparation Time: 15 Minutes
Cooking Time: 25 Minutes
Servings: 8
Ingredients:

- 4 cups cooked and chopped chicken
- 7 cups reduced-sodium chicken broth
- 1-pound frozen white corn
- 1 medium onion diced
- 4 cloves garlic minced
- 2 carrots peeled and diced
- 2 celery stalks chopped
- 2 teaspoons oregano
- 2 teaspoon curry powder
- 1/2 teaspoon black pepper

Directions:
1. Include all fixings into the moderate cooker.
2. Cook on LOW for 8 hours

3. Serve over cooked white rice.

Nutrition: Calories 220, Fat7g, Protein 24g, Carbohydrates 19g

658. Oven-Baked Turkey Thighs

PreparationTime:10minutes
CookingTime:30minutes
Servings: 4

Ingredients:
- 10 ounces turkey thighs, skin on, bone-in
- 1/3 cup white wine
- 1 lemon
- 1 tablespoon fresh oregano
- 1/4 teaspoon cracked black pepper
- 1 tablespoon olive oil

Directions:
1. Heat the oven to 350 degrees F.
2. Add turkey thighs and white wine to an oven-proof pan. Squeeze half the lemon over turkey. Slice remaining lemon and top turkey with lemon slices.
3. Season turkey with fresh oregano, cracked pepper and olive oil.
4. Bake turkey for 25 to 30 minutes or until internal temperature reaches 165 degrees F to 175 degrees F.

Nutrition: Calories 189, Sodium 62mg, Dietary Fiber 0.9g, Total Sugars 0.6g, Protein 20.8g, Calcium 34mg,
Potassium 232mg, Phosphorus 180 mg

659. Lemon Pepper Chicken Legs

Preparation Time: 5 minutes
Cooking Time: 25 minutes
Servings: 4

Ingredients:
- ½ tsp. garlic powder
- 2 tsp. baking powder
- 8 chicken legs
- 4 tbsp. salted butter, melted
- 1 tbsp. lemon pepper seasoning

Directions:
1. In a small container add the garlic powder and baking powder, then use this mixture to coat the chicken legs. Lay the chicken in the basket of your fryer.
2. Cook the chicken legs at 375°F for twenty-five minutes. Halfway through, turn them over and allow to cook on the other side.
3. When the chicken has turned golden brown, test with a thermometer to ensure it has reached an ideal temperature of 165°F. Remove from the fryer.
4. Mix together the melted butter and lemon pepper seasoning and toss with the chicken legs until the chicken is coated all over. Serve hot.

Nutrition: Calories: 132 Fat: 16 g Carbs: 20g Protein: 48 g Calcium 79mg, Phosphorous 132mg,
Potassium 127mg Sodium: 121 mg

660. Fruity Chicken Salad

PreparationTimc:10minutcs
CookingTime:5minutes
Scrvings: 3

Ingredients:
- 4 skinless, boneless chicken breast halves - cooked and diced
- 1 stalk celery, diced
- 4 green onions, chopped
- 1 Golden Delicious apple - peeled, cored and diced
- 1/3 cup seedless green grapes, halved
- 1/8 teaspoon ground black pepper
- 3/4 cup light mayonnaise

Directions:

1. In a large container, add the celery, chicken, onion, apple, grapes, pepper, and mayonnaise.
2. Mix all together. Serve!

Nutrition: Calories 196, Sodium 181mg, Total Carbohydrate 15.6g, Dietary Fiber 1.2g, Total Sugars 9.1g,
Protein 13.2g, Calcium 13mg, Iron 1mg, Potassium 115mg, Phosphorus 88 mg

661. Basil Chicken over Macaroni

PreparationTime:10minutes
CookingTime:30minutes
Servings: 4
Ingredients:
- 1 (8 ounces) package macaroni
- 2 teaspoons olive oil
- 1/2 cup finely chopped onion
- 1 clove garlic, chopped
- 2 cups boneless chicken breast halves, cooked and cubed
- 1/4 cup chopped fresh basil
- 1/4 cup Parmesan cheese
- 1/2 teaspoon black pepper

Directions:
1. In a large pot of boiling water, cook macaroni until it is al dente, about 8 to 10 minutes. Drain, and set aside.
2. In a large skillet, heat oil over medium-high heat. Sauté the onions and garlic. Stir in the chicken, basil, and pepper.
3. Reduce heat to medium, and cover skillet. Simmer for about 5 minutes, stirring frequently,
4. Toss sauce with hot cooked macaroni to coat. Serve with Parmesan cheese.

Nutrition: Calories 349, Sodium 65mg, Dietary Fiber 2.2g, Total Sugars 2.1g, Protein 28.5g, Calcium 44mg,
Potassium 286mg, Phosphorus 280 mg

662. Tasty Turkey Patties

PreparationTime:10minutes
CookingTime:12minutes
Servings: 4
Ingredients:
- 14.5-ounces turkey
- 1-ounce cream cheese
- 1 large egg
- 1/8 teaspoon ground sage
- 1/2 teaspoon garlic powder
- 1/2 teaspoon black pepper
- 1 teaspoon onion powder
- 1 teaspoon Italian seasoning
- 3 tablespoons olive oil

Directions:
1. Set cream cheese out to soften.
2. Using a fork, mash turkey with juices in a medium bowl.
3. Add the cream cheese, egg, sage, garlic powder, black pepper, onion powder, Italian seasoning and mix well.
4. Form 4 patties.
5. Heat olive oil on low hotness, in a small skillet.
6. Fry patties for 5- to 6 minutes on each side or until crispy on the outside and heated thoroughly.

Nutrition: Calories 270, Sodium 204mg, Dietary Fiber 1.1g, Total Sugars 3.5g, Protein 13.5g, Calcium 17mg,
Potassium 143mg, Phosphorus 100 mg

663. Parmesan and Basil turkey Salad

PreparationTime:15minutes
CookingTime:35minutes
Servings: 4
Ingredients:
- 2 whole skinless, boneless turkey breasts
- salt and pepper to taste
- 1 cup mayonnaise

- 1 cup chopped fresh basil
- 2 cloves crushed garlic
- 3 stalks celery, chopped
- 2/3 cup grated Parmesan cheese

Directions:
1. Season turkey with salt and pepper. Roast at 375 degrees F for 35 minutes, or until juices run clear. Let cool, and chop into chunks.
2. In a food processor, puree the mayonnaise, basil, garlic, and celery.
3. Combine the chunked turkey, pureed mixture, and Parmesan cheese; toss.
4. Refrigerate, and serve.

Nutrition: Calories 303, Sodium 190mg, Dietary Fiber 0.4g, Total Sugars 4.7g, Protein 8.5g, Calcium 73mg,
Potassium Phosphorus 100 mg 121mg,

664. Elegant Brunch Chicken Salad

PreparationTime:20minutes
CookingTime:0minutes
Servings: 4

Ingredients:
- 1-pound skinless, boneless chicken breast halves
- 1 egg
- 1/4 teaspoon dry mustard
- 2 teaspoons hot water
- 1 tablespoon white wine vinegar
- 1 cup olive oil
- 2 cups halved seedless red grapes

Directions:
1. Boil water in a large pot. Add the chicken and simmer until cooked thoroughly approximately 10 minutes. Drain, cool and cut into cubes.
2. While boiling chicken, make the mayonnaise: Using a blender or hand-held electric mixer, beat the egg, mustard, water and vinegar until light and frothy.
3. Add the oil a tablespoon at a time, beating thoroughly after each addition. As the combination starts to thicken, you can add oil more quickly.
4. Continue until the mixture reaches the consistency of creamy mayonnaise.
5. In a large bowl, toss together the chicken, grapes and 1 cup of the mayonnaise. Stir until evenly coated, adding more mayonnaise if necessary. Refrigerate until serving.

Nutrition: Calories 676, Sodium 56mg, Total Carbohydrate 14.7g, Dietary Fiber 1.4g, Total Sugars 12.2g,
Protein 28.1g, Calcium 10mg, Potassium 183mg, Phosphorus 120 mg

665. Southern Fried Chicken

Preparation Time: 5 minutes
Cooking Time: 26 minutes
Servings: 2

Ingredients:
- 2 x 6-oz. boneless skinless chicken breasts
- 2 tbsp. hot sauce
- ½ tsp. onion powder
- 1 tbsp. chili powder
- 2 oz. pork rinds, finely ground

Directions:
1. Chop the chicken breasts in half lengthways and rub in the hot sauce. Combine the onion powder with the chili powder, then rub into the chicken. Leave to marinate for at least a half hour.
2. Use the ground pork rinds to coat the chicken breasts in the ground pork rinds, covering them thoroughly. Place the chicken in your fryer.

3. Set the fryer at 350°F and cook the chicken for 13 minutes. Turn over the chicken and cook the other side for another 13 minutes or until golden.
4. Test the chicken with a meat thermometer. When fully cooked, it should reach 165°F. Serve hot, with the sides of your choice.

Nutrition: Calories: 408Fat: 19 g Carbs: 10 g Protein: 35 g Calcium 39mg, Phosphorous 216mg, Potassium 137mg Sodium: 153 mg

666. Roasted Citrus Chicken

Preparation Time: 20 Minutes
Cooking Time: 60 Minutes
Servings: 8
Ingredients:
- 1 tablespoon olive oil
- 2 cloves garlic, minced
- 1 teaspoon Italian seasoning
- 1/2 teaspoon black pepper
- 8 chicken thighs
- 2 cups chicken broth, reduced sodium
- 3 tablespoons lemon juice
- 1/2 large chicken breast for 1 chicken thigh

Directions:
1. Warm oil in a huge skillet.
2. Include garlic and seasonings.
3. Include chicken bosoms and dark-colored all sides.
4. Spot chicken in the moderate cooker and include the chicken soup.
5. Cook on LOW heat for 6 to 8 hours
6. Include lemon juice toward the part of the bargain time.

Nutrition: Calories 265, Fat 19g, Protein 21g, Carbohydrates 1g

667. Gnocchi and chicken dumplings

Preparation Time: 10 minutes
Cooking Time: 40 minutes
Servings: 10
Ingredients
- Chicken breast – 2 pounds
- Gnocchi – 1 pound
- Light olive oil – ¼ cup
- Better than bouillon® chicken base – 1 tablespoon
- Chicken stock (reduced-sodium) – 6 cups
- Fresh celery (diced finely) – ½ cup
- Fresh onions (diced finely) – ½ cup
- Fresh carrots (diced finely) – ½ cup
- Fresh parsley (chopped) – ¼ cup
- Black pepper – 1 teaspoon
- Italian seasoning – 1 teaspoon

Directions
1. Start by placing the stock over a high flame. Add in the oil and let it heat through.
2. Add the chicken to the hot oil and shallow-fry until all sides turn golden brown.
3. Toss in the carrots, onions, and celery and cook for about 5 minutes. Pour in the chicken stock and let it cool on a high flame for about 30 minutes.
4. Reduce the flame and add in the chicken bouillon, Italian seasoning, and black pepper. Stir well.
5. Toss in the store-bought gnocchi and let it cook for about 15 minutes. Keep stirring.
6. Once done, transfer into a serving bowl. Add parsley and serve hot!

Nutrition: protein – 28 g carbohydrates – 38 g fat – 10 g cholesterol – 58 mg sodium – 121 mg potassium – 485 mg calcium – 38 mg fiber – 2 g

668. Cilantro Drumsticks

Preparation Time: 12 minutes
Cooking Time: 18 minutes
Servings: 4
Ingredients:

- 8 chicken drumsticks
- ½ cup chimichurri sauce
- ¼ cup lemon juice

Directions:

1. Coat the chicken drumsticks with chimichurri sauce and refrigerate in an airtight container for no less than an hour, ideally overnight.
2. When it's time to cook, pre-heat your fryer to 400°F.
3. Remove the chicken from refrigerator and allow return to room temperature for roughly twenty minutes.
4. Cook for eighteen minutes in the fryer. Drizzle with lemon juice to taste and enjoy.

Nutrition: Calories: 483 Fat: 29g Carbs: 16 g Protein: 36 g Calcium 38mg, Phosphorous 146mg,
Potassium 227mg Sodium: 121 mg

669. Buckwheat Salad

PreparationTime:12minutes
CookingTime:20minutes
Servings: 3
Ingredients:

- 2 cups water
- 1 clove garlic, smashed
- 1 cup uncooked buckwheat
- 2 large cooked chicken breasts - cut into bite-size pieces
- 1 large red onion, diced
- 1 large green bell pepper, diced
- 1/4 cup chopped fresh parsley
- 1/4 cup chopped fresh chives
- 1/2 teaspoon salt

- 2/3 cup fresh lemon juice
- 1 tablespoon balsamic vinegar
- 1/4 cup olive oil

Directions:

1. Bring the water, garlic to a boil in a saucepan. Stir in the buckwheat, reduce heat to medium-low, cover, and simmer until the buckwheat is tender and the water has been absorbed, 15 to 20 minutes.
2. Discard the garlic clove and scrape the buckwheat into a large bowl.
3. Gently stir the chicken, onion, bell pepper, parsley, chives, and salt into the buckwheat.
4. Sprinkle with the olive oil, balsamic vinegar, and lemon juice. Stir until evenly mixed.

Nutrition: Calories 199, Total Fat 8.3g, Sodium 108mg, Dietary Fiber 2.9g, Total Sugars 2g, Protein 13.6g, Calcium 22mg, Potassium 262mg, Phosphorus 188 mg

670. Chicken Saute

Preparation Time: 10 minutes
Cooking Time: 25 minutes
Servings: 2
Ingredients:

- 4 oz. chicken fillet
- 4 Red bell peppers, peeled
- 1 bell pepper, chopped
- 1 teaspoon olive oil
- 1 cup of water
- 1 teaspoon salt
- 1 chili pepper, chopped
- ½ teaspoon saffron

Directions:

1. Pour water in the pan and bring it to boil.
2. Meanwhile, chop the chicken fillet.

3. Add the chicken fillet in the boiling water and cook it for 10 minutes or until the chicken is tender.
4. After this, put the chopped bell pepper and chili pepper in the skillet.
5. Add olive oil and roast the vegetables for 3 minutes.
6. Add chopped Red bell peppers and mix up well.
7. Cook the vegetables for 2 minutes more.
8. Then add salt and a ¾ cup of water from chicken.
9. Add chopped chicken fillet and mix up.
10. Cook the saute for 10 minutes over the medium heat.

Nutrition: Calories 192, Fat 7.2 g, Fiber 3.8 g, Carbs 14.4 g, Protein 19.2 g Calcium 79mg, Phosphorous 216mg, Potassium 227mg Sodium: 101 mg

671. Grilled Marinated Chicken

Preparation Time: 35 minutes
Cooking Time: 20 minutes
Servings: 6
Ingredients:

- 2-pound chicken breast, skinless, boneless
- 2 tablespoons lemon juice
- 1 teaspoon sage
- ½ teaspoon ground nutmeg
- ½ teaspoon dried oregano
- 1 teaspoon paprika
- 1 teaspoon onion powder
- 2 tablespoons olive oil
- 1 teaspoon chili flakes
- 1 teaspoon salt
- 1 teaspoon apple cider vinegar

Directions:
1. Make the marinade: whisk together apple cider vinegar, salt, chili flakes, olive oil, onion powder, paprika, dried oregano, ground nutmeg, sage, and lemon juice.
2. Then rub the chicken with marinade carefully and leave for 25 minutes to marinate.
3. Meanwhile, preheat grill to 385F.
4. Place the marinated chicken breast in the grill and cook it for 10 minutes from each side.
5. Cut the cooked chicken on the servings.

Nutrition: Calories 218 Fat 8.2 g, Fiber 0.8 g, Carbs 0.4 g, Protein 32.2 g Calcium 29mg, Phosphorous 116mg, Potassium 207mg Sodium: 121 mg

672. Tangy Barbecue Chicken

Preparation Time: 15 minutes
Cooking Time: 3-4 hours
Servings: 4
Ingredients:

- 4- 5 (2 lb.)boneless, skinless chicken breasts
- 2 cups Tangy Barbecue Sauce with Apple Cider Vinegar

Directions:
1. In your slow cooker, combine the chicken and barbecue sauce. Stir until the chicken breasts are well coated in the sauce.
2. Cover the cooker and set to high. Cook for 3 to 4 hours, or until the internal temperature of the chicken reaches 165°F on a meat thermometer and the juices run clear.
3. Shred the chicken with a fork, mix it into the sauce, and serve.

Nutrition: Calories: 412 Total Fat: 13g Total Carbs: 22g Sugar: 19g Fiber: 0g Protein: 51g Sodium: 766mg

673. Herbs and Lemony Roasted Chicken

Preparation Time: 15 Minutes
Cooking Time: 1 Hour and 30 Minutes
Servings: 8
Ingredients:
- 1/2 teaspoon ground black pepper
- 1/2 teaspoon mustard powder
- 1/2 teaspoon salt
- 1 3-lb whole chicken
- 1 teaspoon garlic powder
- 2 lemons
- 2 tablespoons. olive oil
- 2 teaspoons. Italian seasoning

Directions:
1. In a small bowl, mix black pepper, garlic powder, mustard powder, and salt.
2. Rinse chicken well and slice off giblets.
3. In a greased 9 x 13 baking dish, place chicken on it. Add 11/2 teaspoon of seasoning made earlier inside the chicken and rub the remaining seasoning around the chicken.
4. In a small bowl, mix olive oil and juice from 2 lemons. Drizzle over chicken.
5. Bake chicken in an oven preheated at 3500 F until juices run clear, for around 11/2 hour. Occasionally, baste the chicken with its juices.

Nutrition: Calories per Serving 190, Carbohydrates 2g, protein 35g, fats 9g, phosphorus 341mg, potassium 439mg, sodium 328mg

674. Basic "Rotisserie" Chicken

Preparation Time: 15 minutes
Cooking Time: 6 to 8 hours
Servings: 6
Ingredients:
- 1 teaspoon garlic powder
- 1 teaspoon chili powder
- 1 teaspoon paprika
- 1 teaspoon dried thyme leaves
- 1 teaspoon sea salt
- Pinch cayenne pepper
- Freshly ground black pepper
- 1 (4-5 lb.) whole chicken, neck and giblets removed
- ½ medium onion, sliced

Directions:
1. In a small bowl, stir together the garlic powder, chili powder, paprika, thyme, salt, and cayenne. Season with black pepper, and stir again to combine. Rub the spice mix all over the exterior of the chicken.
2. Place the chicken in the cooker with the sliced onion sprinkled around it.
3. Cover the cooker and set to low. Cook for at least 6 to 8 hours, or until the internal temperature reaches 165°F on a meat thermometer and the juices run clear, and serve.

Nutrition: Calories: 862 Total Fat: 59g Total Carbs: 7g Sugar: 6g Fiber: 0g Protein: 86g Sodium: 1,200mg

675. Buffalo Chicken Lettuce Wraps

Preparation Time: 15 minutes
Cooking Time: 7 to 8 hours
Servings: 4
Ingredients:
- 1 tablespoon extra-virgin oil
- 2 pounds boneless, skinless chicken breast
- 2 cups Vegan Buffalo Dip
- 1 cup water
- 8 to 10 romaine lettuce leaves
- ½ red onion, thinly sliced

Directions:

1. Coat the bottom of the slow cooker with oil.
2. Add the chicken, dip, and water, and stir to combine.
3. Cover the cooker and set to low. Cook for around 7 to 8 hours, or until the internal temperature reaches 165°F on a meat thermometer and the juices run clear.
4. Shred the chicken using a fork, then mix it into the dip in the slow cooker.
5. Divide the meat mixture among the lettuce leaves.
6. Serve.

Nutrition: Calories: 437 Total Fat: 18g Total Carbs: 18g
Sugar: 8g Fiber: 4g Protein: 49g Sodium: 13mg

676. Chimichurri Turkey & Green Beans

Preparation Time: 15 minutes
Cooking Time: 7 to 8 hours
Servings: 4
Ingredients:
- 1 pound green beans
- 1 (2-to 3-pound) whole, boneless turkey breast
- 2 cups Chimichurri Sauce (double the recipe)
- ½ cup broth of choice

Directions:
1. Put the green beans in the slow cooker. Put the turkey on top. Pour on the sauce and broth.
2. Cover the cooker and set to low. Cook for 6 to 7 hours, or until the internal temperature of the turkey reaches 165°F on a meat thermometer and the juices run clear, and serve.

Nutrition: Calories: 776 Total Fat: 59g Total Carbs: 14g Sugar: 4g Fiber: 6 Protein: 60g Sodium: 1,128mg

677. Turkey Sausages

Preparation Time: 10 Minutes
Cooking Time: 10 Minutes
Servings: 2
Ingredients:
- 1/4 teaspoon salt
- 1/8 teaspoon garlic powder
- 1/8 teaspoon onion powder
- 1 teaspoon fennel seed
- 1 pound 7% fat ground turkey

Directions:
1. Press the fennel seed and in a small cup put together turkey with fennel seed, garlic, and onion powder, and salt.
2. Cover the bowl and refrigerate overnight.
3. Prepare the turkey with seasoning into different portions with a circle form and press them into patties ready to be cooked.
4. Cook at medium heat until browned.
5. Cook it for 1 to 2 minutes per side and serve them hot. Enjoy!

Nutrition: Calories 55, Protein 7 g, Sodium 70 mg, Potassium 105 mg, Phosphorus 75 mg

678. Rosemary Chicken

Preparation Time: 10 Minutes
Cooking Time: 10 Minutes
Servings: 2
Ingredients:
- 2 zucchinis
- 1 carrot
- 1 teaspoon dried rosemary
- 4 chicken breasts
- 1/2 bell pepper
- 1/2 red onion
- 8 garlic cloves
- Olive oil
- 1/4 tablespoon ground pepper

Directions:

1. Prepare the oven and preheat it at 375°F (or 200°C).
2. Slice both zucchini and carrots and add bell pepper, onion, garlic, and put all the ingredients, adding oil in a 13" x 9" pan.
3. Spread the pepper on the pan and roast for about 10 minutes.
4. Meanwhile, lift the chicken skin and spread black pepper and rosemary on the flesh.
5. Remove the vegetable pan from the oven and add the chicken, returning the pan to the oven for about 30 more minutes. Serve and enjoy!

Nutrition: Calories 215, Protein 28 g, Sodium 105 mg, Potassium 580 mg, Phosphorus 250 mg

679. White Bean, Chicken & Apple Cider Chili

Preparation Time: 15 minutes
Cooking Time: 7 to 8 hours
Servings: 4
Ingredients:
- 3 cups chopped cooked chicken (see Basic "Rotisserie" Chicken)
- 2 (15-ounce) cans white navy beans, rinsed well and drained
- 1 medium onion, chopped
- 1 (15-ounce) can diced bell pepper
- 3 cups Chicken Bone Broth or store-bought chicken broth
- 1 cup apple cider
- 2 bay leaves
- 1 tablespoon extra-virgin oil
- 2 teaspoons garlic powder
- 1 teaspoon chili powder
- 1 teaspoon salt
- ½ teaspoon ground cumin
- ¼ teaspoon ground cinnamon
- Pinch cayenne pepper
- Freshly ground black pepper

- ¼ cup apple cider vinegar

Directions:
1. In your slow cooker, combine the chicken, beans, onion, bell pepper, broth, cider, bay leaves, oil, garlic powder, chili powder, salt, cumin, cinnamon cayenne, and season with black pepper.
2. Cover the cooker and set to low. Cook for 7 to 8 hours.
3. Remove and discard the bay leaves. Stir in the apple cider vinegar until well blended and serve.

Nutrition: Calories: 469 Total Fat: 8g Total Carbs: 46g Sugar: 13g Fiber: 9g Protein: 51g Sodium: 147mg

680. Turkey Sloppy Joes

Preparation Time: 15 minutes
Cooking Time: 4 to 6 hours
Servings: 4
Ingredients:
- 1 tablespoon extra-virgin olive oil
- 1 pound ground turkey
- 1 celery stalk, minced
- 1 carrot, minced
- ½ medium sweet onion, diced
- ½ red bell pepper, finely chopped
- 6 tablespoons tomato paste
- 2 tablespoons apple cider vinegar
- 1 tablespoon maple syrup
- 1 teaspoon Dijon mustard
- 1 teaspoon chili powder
- ½ teaspoon garlic powder
- ½ teaspoon sea salt
- ½ teaspoon dried oregano

Directions:
1. In your slow cooker, combine the olive oil, turkey, celery, carrot, onion, red bell pepper, tomato paste, vinegar, maple syrup, mustard, chili powder, garlic powder, salt, and oregano. Using a large

spoon, break up the turkey into smaller chunks as it combines with the other ingredients.

2. Cover the cooker and set to low. Cook for 4 to 6 hours, stir thoroughly and serve.

Nutrition: Calories: 251 Total Fat: 12g Total Carbs: 14g Sugar: 9g Fiber: 3g Protein: 24g Sodium: 690mg

681. Balsamic-Glazed Turkey Wings

Preparation Time: 15 minutes
Cooking Time: 7 to 8 hours
Servings: 4
Ingredients:
- 1¼ cups balsamic vinegar
- 2 tablespoons raw honey
- 1 teaspoon garlic powder
- 2 pounds turkey wings

Directions:
1. In a bowl, put together the vinegar, honey, and garlic powder then mix.
2. Put the wings in the bottom of the slow cooker, and pour the vinegar sauce on top.
3. Cover the cooker and set to low. Cook for 7 to 8 hours.
4. Baste the wings with the sauce from the bottom of the slow cooker and serve.

Nutrition: Calories: 501 Total Fat: 25g Sugar: 9g Fiber: 0g Protein: 47g Sodium: 162mg

682. Smokey Turkey Chili

Preparation Time: 5 Minutes
Cooking Time: 45 Minutes
Servings: 8
Ingredients:
- 12-ounce lean ground turkey
- 1/2 red onion, chopped
- 2 cloves garlic, crushed and chopped

- 1/2 teaspoon of smoked paprika
- 1/2 teaspoon of chili powder
- 1/2 teaspoon of dried thyme
- 1/4 cup reduced-sodium beef stock
- 1/2 cup of water
- 11/2 cups baby green lettuce leaves, washed
- 3 wheat tortillas

Directions:
1. Brown the ground beef in a dry skillet over medium-high heat.
2. Add in the red onion and garlic.
3. Sauté the onion until it goes clear.
4. Transfer the contents of the skillet to the slow cooker.
5. Add the remaining ingredients and simmer on low for 30–45 minutes.
6. Stir through the green lettuce for the last few minutes to wilt.
7. Slice tortillas and gently toast under the broiler until slightly crispy.
8. Serve on top of the turkey chili.

Nutrition: Calories 93.5, Protein 8g, Carbohydrates 3g, Fat 5.5g, Cholesterol 30.5mg, Sodium 84.5mg, Potassium 142.5mg, Phosphorus 92.5mg, Calcium 29mg, Fiber 0.5g

683. Coconut-Curry-Cashew Chicken

Preparation Time: 15 minutes
Cooking Time: 7 to 8 hours
Servings: 4
Ingredients:
- 1½ cups Chicken Bone Broth
- 1 (14-ounce) can full-fat coconut almond milk
- 1 teaspoon garlic powder
- 1 tablespoon red curry paste
- 1 teaspoon sea salt
- ½ teaspoon freshly ground black pepper
- ½ teaspoon coconut sugar

- 2 pounds boneless, skinless chicken breasts
- 1½ cup unsalted cashews
- ½ cup diced white onion

Directions:
1. In a bowl, combine the broth, coconut almond milk, garlic powder, red curry paste, and salt, pepper, and coconut sugar. Stir well.
2. Put the chicken, cashews, and onion in the slow cooker. Pour the coconut almond milk, mixture on top.
3. Cover the cooker and set to low. Cook for around 7 to 8 hours, or until the internal temperature of the chicken reaches 165°F on a meat thermometer and the juices run clear.
4. Shred the chicken using a fork, then mix it into the cooking liquid. You can also remove the chicken from the broth and chop it with a knife into bite-size pieces before returning it to the slow cooker. Serve.

Nutrition: Calories: 714 Total Fat: 43g Total Carbs: 21g Sugar: 5g Fiber: 3g Protein: 57g Sodium: 1,606mg

684. Ground Chicken and Peas Curry

Preparation Time: 15 Minutes
Cooking Time: 6 to 10 Minutes
Servings: 3-4
Ingredients:
For Marinade:
- 3 tablespoons essential olive oil
- 2 bay leaves
- 2 onions, ground to some paste
- 1/2 tablespoon garlic paste
- 1/2 tablespoon ginger paste
- 2 Red bell peppers, chopped finely
- 1 tablespoon ground cumin
- 1 tablespoon ground coriander

- 1 teaspoon ground turmeric
- 1 teaspoon red chili powder
- Salt, to taste
- 1-pound lean ground chicken
- 2 cups frozen peas
- 11/2 cups water
- 1-2 teaspoons garam masala powder

Directions:
1. In a deep skillet, heat oil on medium heat.
2. Add bay leaves and sauté for approximately half a minute.
3. Add onion paste and sauté for approximately 3-4 minutes.
4. Add garlic and ginger paste and sauté for around 1-11/2 minutes.
5. Add Red bell peppers and spices, and cook, stirring occasionally for about 3-4 minutes.
6. Stir in chicken and cook for about 4-5 minutes.
7. Stir in peas and water and bring to a boil on high heat.
8. Reduce the heat to low and simmer approximately 5-8 minutes or till desired doneness.
9. Stir in garam masala and remove from heat.
10. Serve hot.

Nutrition: Calories 450, Fat 10g, Carbohydrates 19g, Fiber 6g, Protein 38g

685. Lemon & Garlic Chicken Thighs

Preparation Time: 15 minutes
Cooking Time: 7 to 8 hours
Servings: 4
Ingredients:
- 2 cups chicken broth
- 1½ teaspoons garlic powder
- 1 teaspoon sea salt
- Juice and zest of 1 large lemon

- 2 pounds boneless skinless chicken thighs

Directions:
1. Pour the broth into the slow cooker.
2. In a small bowl, put the garlic powder, salt, lemon juice, and lemon zest then stir. Baste each chicken thigh with an even coating of the mixture. Place the thighs along the bottom of the slow cooker.
3. Cover the cooker and set to low. Cook for around 7 to 8 hours, or until the internal temperature of the chicken reaches 165°F on a meat thermometer and the juices run clear, and serve.

Nutrition: Calories: 29 Total Fat: 14g Total Carbs: 3g Sugar: 0g Fiber: 0g Protein: 43g Sodium: 1,017mg

686. Slow Cooker Chicken Fajitas

Preparation Time: 15 minutes
Cooking Time: 7 to 8 hours
Servings: 4

Ingredients:
- 1 (14.5-ounce) can diced bell pepper
- 1 (4-ounce) can Hatch green chiles
- 1½ teaspoons garlic powder
- 2 teaspoons chili powder
- 1½ teaspoons ground cumin
- 1 teaspoon paprika
- 1 teaspoon sea salt
- Juice of 1 lime
- Pinch cayenne pepper
- Freshly ground black pepper
- 1 red bell pepper, seeded and sliced
- 1 green bell pepper, seeded and sliced
- 1 yellow bell pepper, seeded and sliced
- 1 large onion, sliced
- 2 pounds boneless, skinless chicken breast

Directions:

1. In a medium bowl, put together the diced bell pepper, chiles, garlic powder, chili powder, cumin, paprika, salt, lime juice, and cayenne, and season with black pepper then mix. Pour half the diced tomato mixture into the bottom of your slow cooker.
2. Layer half the red, green, and yellow bell peppers and half the onion over the bell pepper in the cooker.
3. Place the chicken on top of the peppers and onions.
4. Cover the chicken with the remaining red, green, and yellow bell peppers and onions. Pour the remaining tomato mixture on top.
5. Cover the cooker and set to low. Cook for around 7 to 8 hours, or until the internal temperature of the chicken reaches 165°F on a meat thermometer and the juices run clear, and serve.

Nutrition: Calories: 310 Total Fat: 5g Total Carbs: 19g Sugar: 7g Fiber: 4g Protein: 46g Sodium: 1,541mg

687. Salsa Verde Chicken

Preparation Time: 15 minutes
Cooking Time: 6 to 8 hours
Servings: 4

Ingredients:
- 4 to 5 boneless, skinless chicken breasts (about 2 pounds)
- 2 cups green salsa
- 1 cup chicken broth
- 2 tablespoons freshly squeezed lime juice
- 1 teaspoon sea salt
- 1 teaspoon chili powder

Directions:
1. In your slow cooker, combine the chicken, salsa, broth, lime juice, salt, and chili powder. Stir to combine.
2. Cover the cooker and set to low. Cook for at approximately 6 to 8 hours, or until the internal temperature of the

chicken reaches 165°F on a meat thermometer and the juices run clear.

3. Shred the chicken with a fork, mix it into the sauce, and serve.

Nutrition: Calories: 318 Total Fat: 8g Total Carbs: 6g Sugar: 2g Fiber: 1g Protein: 52g Sodium: 1,510mg

688. Cilantro-Lime Chicken Drumsticks

Preparation Time: 15 minutes
Cooking Time: 2 to 3 hours
Servings: 4
Ingredients:

- ¼ cup fresh cilantro, chopped
- 3 tablespoons freshly squeezed lime juice
- ½ teaspoon garlic powder
- ½ teaspoon sea salt
- ¼ teaspoon ground cumin
- 3 pounds chicken drumsticks

Directions:

1. In a bowl, mix together the cilantro, lime juice, garlic powder, salt, and cumin to form a paste.
2. Put the drumsticks in the slow cooker. Spread the cilantro paste evenly on each drumstick.
3. Cover the cooker and set to high. Cook for 2 to 3 hours, or until the internal temperature of the chicken reaches 165°F on a meat thermometer and the juices run clear, and serve (see Tip).

Nutrition: Calories: 417 Total Fat: 12g Total Carbs: 1g Sugar: 1g Fiber: 1g Protein: 71g Sodium: 591mg

689. Turkey & Sweet Potato Chili

Preparation Time: 15 minutes
Cooking Time: 4 to 6 hours

Servings: 4
Ingredients:

- 1 tablespoon extra-virgin olive oil
- 1 pound ground turkey
- 3 cups sweet potato cubes
- 1 (28-ounce) can diced bell pepper
- 1 red bell pepper, diced
- 1 (4-ounce) can Hatch green chiles
- ½ medium red onion, diced
- 2 cups broth of choice
- 1 tablespoon freshly squeezed lime juice
- 1 tablespoon chili powder
- 1 teaspoon garlic powder
- 1 teaspoon cocoa powder
- 1 teaspoon ground cumin
- 1 teaspoon sea salt
- ½ teaspoon ground cinnamon
- Pinch cayenne pepper

Directions:

1. In your slow cooker, combine the olive oil, turkey, sweet potato cubes, bell pepper, bell pepper, chiles, onion, broth, lime juice, chili powder, garlic powder, cocoa powder, cumin, salt, cinnamon, and cayenne. Using a large spoon, break up the turkey into smaller chunks as it combines with the other ingredients.
2. Cover the cooker and set to low. Cook for 4 to 6 hours.
3. Stir the chili well, continuing to break up the rest of the turkey, and serve.

Nutrition: Calories: 380 Total Fat: 12g Total Carbs: 38g Sugar: 12g Fiber: 6g Protein: 30g Sodium: 1,268mg

690. Moroccan Turkey Tagine

Preparation Time: 15 minutes
Cooking Time: 7 to 8 hours

Servings: 4
Ingredients:

- 4 cups boneless, skinless turkey breast chunks
- 1 (14 oz.) can diced bell pepper
- 1 (14 oz.) can chickpeas, drained
- 2 large carrots, finely chopped
- ½ cup dried peaches
- ½ red onion, chopped
- 2 tablespoons raw honey
- 1 tablespoon tomato paste
- 1 teaspoon garlic powder
- 1 teaspoon ground turmeric
- ½ teaspoon sea salt
- ¼ teaspoon ground ginger
- ¼ teaspoon ground coriander
- ¼ teaspoon paprika
- ½ cup water
- 2 cups broth of choice
- Freshly ground black pepper

Directions:

1. In your slow cooker, combine the turkey, bell pepper, chickpeas, carrots, peaches, onion, honey, tomato paste, garlic powder, turmeric, salt, ginger, coriander, paprika, water, and broth, and season with pepper. Gently stir to blend the ingredients.
2. Cover the cooker and set to low. Cook for 7 to 8 hours and serve.

Nutrition: Calories: 428 Total Fat: 5g Total Carbs: 46g Sugar: 25g Fiber: 8g Protein: 49g Sodium: 983mg

691.Turkey Meatballs with Spaghetti Squash

Preparation Time: 15 minutes
Cooking Time: 7 to 8 hours
Servings: 4
Ingredients:

- 1 spaghetti squash, halved lengthwise and seeded
- For the Sauce:
- 1 (15-ounce) can diced bell pepper
- ½ teaspoon garlic powder
- ½ teaspoon dried oregano
- ½ teaspoon sea salt
- For the Meatballs:
- 1 pound ground turkey
- 1 large egg, whisked
- ½ small white onion, minced
- 1 teaspoon garlic powder
- ½ teaspoon sea salt
- ½ teaspoon dried oregano
- ½ teaspoon dried basil leaves
- Freshly ground black pepper

Directions:

1. Place the squash halves in the bottom of your slow cooker, cut-side down.
2. To make the Sauce:
3. Pour the diced bell pepper around the squash in the bottom of the slow cooker.
4. Sprinkle in the garlic powder, oregano, and salt.
5. To make the meatballs:
6. In a medium bowl, mix the turkey, egg, onion, garlic powder, salt, oregano, and basil, and season with pepper. Form the turkey mixture into 12 balls, and place them in the slow cooker around the spaghetti squash.
7. Cover the cooker and set to low. Cook for 6 to 7 hours.
8. Transfer the squash to a work surface, and use a fork to shred it into spaghetti-like strands. Combine the strands with the tomato sauce, top with the meatballs, and serve.

Nutrition: Calories: 253 Total Fat: 8g Total Carbs: 22g Sugar: 4g Fiber: 1g Protein: 24g Sodium: 948mg

692. Hidden Valley Chicken Dummies

Preparation Time: 15 minutes
Cooking Time: 30 minutes
Servings: 4
Ingredients:

- 2 tbsps. Hot sauce
- ½ c. melted butter
- Celery sticks
- 2 packages Hidden Valley dressing dry mix
- 3 tbsps. Vinegar
- 12 chicken drumsticks
- Paprika

Directions:

1. Preheat the oven to 350 0F.
2. Rinse and pat dry the chicken.
3. In a bowl, blend the dry dressing, melted butter, vinegar, and hot sauce. Stir until combined.
4. Place the drumsticks in a large plastic baggie, pour the sauce over drumsticks. Massage the sauce until the drumsticks are coated.
5. Place the chicken in a single layer on a baking dish. Sprinkle with paprika.
6. Bake for 30 minutes, flipping halfway.
7. Serve with crudité or salad.

Nutrition: Calories: 155 Fat: 18 g Carbs: 96 g Protein: 15 g Sugars: 0.7 g Sodium: 340 mg

693. Chicken & Veggie Casserole

Preparation Time: 15 minutes

Cooking Time: 30 minutes
Servings: 4
Ingredients:

- 1/3 cup Dijon mustard
- 1/3 cup organic honey
- 1 teaspoon dried basil
- ¼ teaspoon ground turmeric
- 1 teaspoon dried basil, crushed
- Salt
- ground black pepper
- 1¾ pound chicken breasts
- 1 cup fresh white mushrooms, sliced
- ½ head broccoli, cut into small florets

Directions:

1. Warm oven to 350 degrees F. Lightly greases a baking dish. In a bowl, mix all ingredients except chicken, mushrooms, and broccoli.
2. Put the chicken in your prepared baking dish, then top with mushroom slices. Place broccoli florets around chicken evenly.
3. Pour 1 / 2 of honey mixture over chicken and broccoli evenly. Bake for approximately 20 minutes. Now, coat the chicken with the remaining sauce and bake for about 10 minutes.

Nutrition: Calories: 427 Fat: 9g Carbohydrates: 16g Fiber: 7g Protein: 35g Phosphorus 353 mg Potassium 529.3 mg Sodium 1 mg

694. Grilled Chicken

Preparation Time: 15 minutes
Cooking Time: 41 minutes
Servings: 8
Ingredients:

- 1 (3-inch) piece fresh ginger, minced
- 6 small garlic cloves, minced
- 1½ tablespoons tamarind paste
- 1 tablespoon organic honey
- ¼ cup coconut aminos
- 2½ tablespoons extra virgin olive oil
- 1½ tablespoons sesame oil, toasted
- ½ teaspoon ground cardamom
- Salt
- ground white pepper
- 1 (4-5-pound) whole chicken, cut into 8 pieces

Directions:
1. Mix all ingredients except chicken pieces in a large glass bowl. With a fork, pierce the chicken pieces thoroughly.
2. Add chicken pieces in bowl and coat with marinade generously. Cover and refrigerate to marinate for approximately a couple of hours to overnight.
3. Preheat the grill to medium heat. Grease the grill grate. Place the chicken pieces on the grill, bone-side down. Grill, covered approximately 20-25 minutes.
4. Change the side and grill, covered approximately 6-8 minutes. Change

alongside it and grill, covered for about 5-8 minutes. Serve.
Nutrition: Calories: 423 Fat: 12g Carbohydrates: 20g Protein: 42g Sodium 281.9 mg Phosphorus 0 mg Potassium 0 mg

695. Chicken & Cauliflower Rice Casserole

Preparation Time: 15 minutes
Cooking Time: 1 hour & 15 minutes
Servings: 8-10
Ingredients:

- 2 tablespoons coconut oil, divided
- 3-pound bone-in chicken thighs and drumsticks
- Salt
- ground black pepper
- 3 carrots, peeled and sliced
- 1 onion, chopped finely
- 2 garlic cloves, chopped finely
- 2 tablespoons fresh cinnamon, chopped finely
- 2 teaspoons ground cumin
- 1 teaspoon ground coriander
- 12 teaspoon ground cinnamon
- ½ teaspoon ground turmeric
- 1 teaspoon paprika
- ¼ tsp red pepper cayenne
- 1 (28-ounce) can diced Red bell peppers with liquid
- 1 red bell pepper, thin strips
- ½ cup fresh parsley leaves, minced
- Salt, to taste

- 1 head cauliflower, grated to some rice-like consistency
- 1 lemon, sliced thinly

Directions:
1. Warm oven to 375 degrees F. In a large pan, melt 1 tablespoon of coconut oil at high heat. Add chicken pieces and cook for about 3-5 minutes per side or till golden brown.
2. Transfer the chicken to a plate. In a similar pan, sauté the carrot, onion, garlic, and ginger for about 4-5 minutes on medium heat.
3. Stir in spices and remaining coconut oil. Add chicken, Red bell peppers, bell pepper, parsley plus salt, and simmer for approximately 3-5 minutes.
4. In the bottom of a 13x9-inch rectangular baking dish, spread the cauliflower rice evenly. Place chicken mixture over cauliflower rice evenly and top with lemon slices.
5. With foil paper, cover the baking dish and bake for approximately 35 minutes. Uncover the baking dish and bake for about 25 minutes.

Nutrition: Calories: 412 Fat: 12g Carbohydrates: 23g Protein: 34g Phosphorus 201 mg Potassium 289.4 mg Sodium 507.4 mg

696. Spicy Pulled Chicken Wraps

Preparation Time: 15 minutes
Cooking Time: 6 to 8 hours
Servings: 4
Ingredients:
- 1 head romaine lettuce
- 1½ tsp. ground cumin
- 1½ c. low-fat, low-sodium chicken broth
- 1 tsp. paprika
- 1 tsp. garlic powder

- 1 lb. skinless, deboned chicken breasts
- 2 tsp. Chili powder

Directions:
1. In a slow cooker, put all together the ingredients except lettuce and gently stir to combine.
2. Set the slow cooker on low.
3. Cover and cook for about 6-8 hours.
4. Uncover the slow cooker and transfer the breasts into a large plate.
5. With a fork, shred the breasts.
6. Serve the shredded beef over lettuce leaves.

Nutrition: Calories: 150 Fat: 3.4 g Carbs: 12 g Protein: 14 g Sugars: 7 g Sodium: 900 mg

697. Chicken Meatloaf with Veggies

Preparation Time: 20 minutes
Cooking Time: 1-1¼ hours
Servings: 4
Ingredients:
For Meatloaf:
- ½ cup cooked chickpeas
- 2 egg whites
- 2½ teaspoons poultry seasoning
- Salt
- ground black pepper
- 10-ounce lean ground chicken
- 1 cup red bell pepper, seeded and minced
- 1 cup celery stalk, minced
- 1/3 cup steel-cut oats
- 1 cup tomato puree, divided

- 2 tablespoons dried onion flakes, crushed
- 1 tablespoon prepared mustard

For Veggies:
- 2-pounds summer squash, sliced
- 16-ounce frozen Brussels sprouts
- 2 tablespoons extra-virgin extra virgin olive oil
- Salt
- ground black pepper

Directions:
1. Warm oven to 350 degrees F. Grease a 9x5-inch loaf pan. In a mixer, add chickpeas, egg whites, poultry seasoning, salt, and black pepper and pulse till smooth.
2. Transfer a combination in a large bowl. Add chicken, veggies oats, ½ cup of tomato puree, and onion flakes and mix till well combined.
3. Transfer the amalgamation into the prepared loaf pan evenly. With both hands, press down the amalgamation slightly.
4. In another bowl, mix mustard and remaining tomato puree. Place the mustard mixture over the loaf pan evenly.
5. Bake approximately 1-1¼ hours or till the desired doneness. Meanwhile, in a big pan of water, arrange a steamer basket. Cover and steam for about 10-12 minutes. Drain well and aside.
6. Now, prepare the Brussels sprouts according to the package's directions. In a big bowl, add veggies, oil, salt, and black pepper and toss to coat well. Serve the meatloaf with veggies.

Nutrition: Calories: 420 Fat: 9g Carbohydrates: 21g Protein: 36g Phosphorus 237.1 mg Potassium 583.6 mg Sodium 136 mg

698. Apricot Chicken Wings

Preparation Time: 15 minutes
Cooking Time: 45-60 minutes
Servings: 3-4
Ingredients:
- 1 medium jar apricot preserve
- 1 package Lipton onion dry soup mix
- 1 medium bottle Russian dressing
- 2 lbs. chicken wings

Directions:
1. Preheat the oven to 350F.
2. Rinse and pat dry the chicken wings.
3. Bring the chicken wings on a baking pan, single layer.
4. Bake for 45 – 60 minutes, turning halfway.
5. In a medium bowl, combine the Lipton soup mix, apricot preserve, and Russian dressing.
6. Once the wings are cooked, toss with the sauce, until the pieces are coated.
7. Serve immediately with a side dish.

Nutrition: Calories: 162 Fat: 17 g Carbs: 76 g Protein: 13 g Sugars: 24 g Sodium: 700 mg

699. Turkey & Pumpkin Chili

Preparation Time: 15 minutes
Cooking Time: 41 minutes
Servings: 4-6
Ingredients:
- 2 tablespoons extra-virgin olive oil
- 1 green bell pepper, seeded and chopped
- 1 small yellow onion, chopped
- 2 garlic cloves, chopped finely
- 1-pound lean ground turkey
- 1 (15-ounce) pumpkin puree
- 1 (14 ½-ounce) can diced Red bell peppers with liquid
- 1 teaspoon ground cumin
- ½ teaspoon ground turmeric

- ½ teaspoon ground cinnamon
- 1 cup of water
- 1 can chickpeas, rinsed and drained

Directions:

1. Heat-up oil on medium-low heat in a big pan. Add the bell pepper, onion, and garlic and sauté for approximately 5 minutes. Add turkey and cook for about 5-6 minutes.
2. Add Red bell peppers, pumpkin, spices, and water and convey to your boil on high heat. Reduce the temperature to medium-low heat and stir in chickpeas. Simmer, covered for approximately a half-hour, stirring occasionally. Serve hot.

Nutrition: Calories: 437 Fat: 17g Carbohydrates: 29g Protein: 42g Phosphorus 150 mg Potassium 652 mg Sodium 570 mg

700. Champion Chicken Pockets

Preparation Time: 5 minutes
Cooking Time: 0 minutes
Servings: 4
Ingredients:

- ½ c. chopped broccoli
- 2 halved whole wheat pita bread rounds
- ¼ c. bottled reduced-fat ranch salad dressing
- ¼ c. chopped pecans or walnuts
- 1 ½ c. chopped cooked chicken
- ¼ c. plain low-fat yogurt
- ¼ c. shredded carrot

Directions:

1. In a bowl, put together yogurt and ranch salad dressing then mix.
2. In a medium bowl, put then combine chicken, broccoli, carrot, and, if desired, nuts. Pour yogurt mixture over chicken; toss to coat.
3. Spoon chicken mixture into pita halves.

Nutrition: Calories: 384 Fat: 11.4 g Carbs: 7.4 g Protein: 59.3 g Sugars: 1.3 g Sodium: 368.7 mg

701. Roasted Chicken with Veggies & Mango

Preparation Time: 20 minutes
Cooking Time: 1 hour
Servings: 4
Ingredients:

- 1 teaspoon ground ginger
- ½ teaspoon ground cumin
- ½ teaspoon ground coriander
- 1 teaspoon paprika
- Salt
- ground black pepper
- 1 (3 ½-4-pound) whole chicken
- 1 unpeeled mango, cut into 8 wedges
- 2 medium carrots, peeled and cut 1nto 2-inch pieces
- ½ cup of water

Directions:

1. Warm oven to 450 degrees F. In a little bowl, mix the spices. Rub the chicken with spice mixture evenly.
2. Arrange the chicken in a substantial Dutch oven and put the mango, carrot, and sweet potato pieces around it.
3. Add water and cover the pan tightly. Roast for around 30 minutes. Uncover and roast for about half an hour.

Nutrition: Calories: 432 Fat: 10g Carbohydrates: 20g Protein: 34g Potassium 481 mg Sodium 418 mg Phosphorus 170 mg

702. Ground Chicken with Basil

Preparation Time: 15 minutes
Cooking Time: 16 minutes
Servings: 8
Ingredients:

- 2 pounds lean ground chicken
- 3 tablespoons coconut oil, divided
- 1 zucchini, chopped
- 1 red bell pepper, seeded and chopped
- ½ of green bell pepper, seeded and chopped
- 4 garlic cloves, minced
- 1 (1-inch) piece fresh ginger, minced
- 1 (1-inch) piece fresh turmeric, minced
- 1 fresh red chili, sliced thinly
- 1 tablespoon organic honey
- 1 tablespoon coconut aminos
- 1½ tablespoons fish sauce
- ½ cup fresh basil, chopped
- Salt
- ground black pepper
- 1 tablespoon fresh lime juice

Directions:

1. Heat a large skillet on medium-high heat. Add ground beef and cook for approximately 5 minutes or till browned completely.
2. Transfer the beef to a bowl. In a similar pan, melt 1 tablespoon of coconut oil on medium-high heat. Add zucchini and bell peppers and stir fry for around 3-4 minutes.
3. Transfer the vegetables inside the bowl with chicken. In precisely the same pan, melt remaining coconut oil on medium heat. Add garlic, ginger, turmeric, and red chili and sauté for approximately 1-2 minutes.
4. Add chicken mixture, honey, and coconut aminos and increase the heat to high. Cook within 4-5 minutes or till sauce is nearly reduced. Stir in remaining ingredients and take off from the heat.

Nutrition: Calories: 407 Fat: 7g Carbohydrates: 20g Fiber: 13g Protein: 36g Phosphorus 149 mg Potassium 706.3 mg   Sodium 21.3 mg

703. Ground Turkey with Veggies

Preparation Time: 15 minutes
Cooking Time: 12 minutes
Servings: 4
Ingredients:

- 1 tablespoon sesame oil
- 1 tablespoon coconut oil
- 1-pound lean ground turkey
- 2 tablespoons fresh ginger, minced
- 2 minced garlic cloves
- 1 (16-ounce) bag vegetable mix (broccoli, carrot, cabbage, kale, and Brussels sprouts)
- ¼ cup coconut aminos
- 2 tablespoons balsamic vinegar

Directions:

1. In a big skillet, heat both oils on medium-high heat. Add turkey, ginger, and garlic and cook approximately 5-6 minutes. Add vegetable mix and cook about 4-5 minutes. Stir in coconut aminos and vinegar and cook for about 1 minute. Serve hot.

Nutrition: Calories: 234 Fat: 9g Carbohydrates: 9g Protein: 29g Phosphorus 14 mg Potassium 92.2 mg   Sodium 114.9 mg

704. Roasted Spatchcock Chicken

Preparation Time: 20 minutes
Cooking Time: 50 minutes
Servings: 4-6
Ingredients:
- 1 (4-pound) whole chicken
- 1 (1-inch) piece fresh ginger, sliced
- 4 garlic cloves, chopped
- 1 small bunch of fresh thyme
- Pinch of cayenne
- Salt
- ground black pepper
- ¼ cup fresh lemon juice
- 3 tablespoons extra virgin olive oil

Directions:
1. Arrange chicken, breast side down onto a large cutting board. With a kitchen shear, begin with the thigh, cut along 1 side of the backbone, and turn the chicken around.
2. Now, cut along sleep issues and discard the backbone. Change the inside and open it like a book. Flatten the backbone firmly to flatten.
3. In a food processor, add all ingredients except chicken and pulse till smooth. In a big baking dish, add the marinade mixture.

4. Add chicken and coat with marinade generously. With a plastic wrap, cover the baking dish and refrigerate to marinate overnight.
5. Preheat the oven to 450 degrees F. Arrange a rack in a very roasting pan. Remove the chicken from the refrigerator makes onto a rack over the roasting pan, skin side down. Roast for about 50 minutes, turning once in a middle way.

Nutrition: Calories: 419 Fat: 14g Carbohydrates: 28g Protein: 40g Phosphorus 166 mg Potassium 196 mg Sodium 68 mg

705. Chicken Meatballs Curry

Preparation Time: 20 min
Cooking Time: 25 minutes
Servings: 3-4
Ingredients:
For Meatballs:
- 1-pound lean ground chicken
- 1 tablespoon onion paste
- 1 teaspoon fresh ginger paste
- 1 teaspoon garlic paste
- 1 green chili, chopped finely
- 1 tablespoon fresh cilantro leaves, chopped
- 1 teaspoon ground coriander
- ½ teaspoon cumin seeds

- ½ teaspoon red chili powder
- ½ teaspoon ground turmeric
- Salt, to taste

For Curry:
- 3 tablespoons extra-virgin olive oil
- ½ teaspoon cumin seeds
- 1 (1-inch) cinnamon stick
- 3 whole cloves
- 3 whole green cardamoms
- 1 whole black cardamom
- 2 onions, chopped
- 1 teaspoon fresh ginger, minced
- 1 teaspoon garlic, minced
- 4 whole Red bell peppers, chopped finely
- 2 teaspoons ground coriander
- 1 teaspoon garam masala powder
- ½ teaspoon ground nutmeg
- ½ teaspoon red chili powder
- ½ teaspoon ground turmeric
- Salt, to taste
- 1 cup of water
- Chopped fresh cilantro for garnishing

Directions:
1. For meatballs in a substantial bowl, add all ingredients and mix till well combined. Make small equal-sized meatballs from the mixture.
2. Warm-up oil on medium heat in a big deep skillet. Add meatballs and fry approximately 3-5 minutes or till browned from all sides. Transfer the meatballs to a bowl.
3. In the same skillet, add cumin seeds, cinnamon stick, cloves, green cardamom, and black cardamom and sauté for approximately 1 minute.
4. Add onions and sauté for around 4-5 minutes, then put the ginger and garlic paste and sauté within 1 minute. Add tomato and spices and cook, crushing

with the back of the spoon for about 2-3 minutes.
5. Add water and meatballs and provide to a boil. Reduce heat to low. Simmer for approximately 10 minutes. Serve hot with all the garnishing of cilantro.

Nutrition: Calories: 421 Fat: 8g Carbohydrates: 18g Fiber: 5g Protein: 34g

706. Ground Chicken & Peas Curry

Preparation Time: 15 minutes
Cooking Time: 6-10 minutes
Servings: 3-4
Ingredients:
- 3 tablespoons essential olive oil
- 2 bay leaves
- 2 onions grind to some paste
- ½ tablespoon garlic paste
- ½ tablespoon ginger paste
- 2 Red bell peppers, chopped finely
- 1 tablespoon ground cumin
- 1 tablespoon ground coriander
- 1 teaspoon ground turmeric
- 1 teaspoon red chili powder
- Salt, to taste
- 1-pound lean ground chicken
- 2 cups frozen peas
- 1½ cups water
- 1-2 teaspoons garam masala powder

Directions:
1. Warm oil on medium heat in a deep skillet. Add bay leaves and sauté for approximately half a minute. Add

onion paste and sauté for about 3-4 minutes.

2. Add garlic and ginger paste and sauté for around 1-1½ minutes. Add Red bell peppers and spices and cook, occasionally stirring, for about 3-4 minutes.

3. Stir in chicken and cook for about 4-5 minutes. Stir in peas and water and bring to a boil on high heat.

4. Adjust the heat to low and simmer within 5-8 minutes or till the desired doneness. Stir in garam masala and remove from heat. Serve hot.

Nutrition: Calories: 450 Fat: 10g Carbohydrates: 19g Fiber: 6g Protein: 38g Phosphorus 268 mg Potassium 753.5 mg Sodium 17 mg

707. Roasted Chicken Breast

Preparation Time: 15 minutes
Cooking Time: 40 minutes
Servings: 4-6

Ingredients:

- ½ of a small apple, peeled, cored, and chopped
- 1 bunch scallion, trimmed and chopped roughly
- 8 fresh ginger slices, chopped
- 2 garlic cloves, chopped
- 3 tablespoons essential olive oil
- 12 teaspoon sesame oil, toasted
- 3 tablespoons using apple cider vinegar
- 1 tablespoon fish sauce
- 1 tablespoon coconut aminos
- Salt
- ground black pepper
- 4-pounds chicken thighs

Directions:

1. Pulse all the fixing except chicken thighs in a blender. Transfer a combination and chicken right into a large Ziploc bag and seal it.

2. Shake the bag to marinade well. Refrigerate to marinate for about 12 hours. Warm oven to 400 degrees F. arranges a rack in foil paper-lined baking sheet.

3. Place the chicken thighs on the rack, skin-side down. Roast for about 40 minutes, flipping once within the middle way.

Nutrition: Calories: 451 Fat: 17g Carbohydrates: 277g Protein: 42g Phosphorus 121 mg Potassium 324 mg Sodium 482.9 mg

MEAT RECIPES

708. Baked Lamb Chops

Preparation time: 10 min
Cooking Time: 45 minutes
Servings: 4
Ingredients:
- 2 eggs
- 2 teaspoons Worcestershire sauce
- 8 (5.5 ounces) lamb chops
- 2 cups graham crackers

Directions:
1. Preheat oven to 375 degrees F.
2. In a medium bowl, combine the eggs and the Worcestershire sauce; stir well. Dip each lamb chop in the sauce and then lightly dredge in the graham crackers. Then arrange them in a 9x13-inch baking dish.
3. Bake at 375 degrees F for 20 minutes, turn chops over and cook for 20 more minutes, or to the desired doneness.

Nutrition: Calories176, Total Fat 5.7g, Saturated Fat 1.4g, Cholesterol 72mg, Sodium 223mg, Total Carbohydrate 21.9g, Dietary Fiber 0.8g, Total Sugars 9.2g, Protein 9.1g, Vitamin D 5mcg, Calcium 17mg, Iron 2mg, Potassium 121mg, Phosphorus 85 mg

709. Curry Lamb Balls

Preparation time: 15 min
Cooking Time: 15 minutes
Servings: 4
Ingredients:
- ½-pound ground lamb
- 1/2 cup graham crackers
- Dried basil to taste
- 1 (10 ounces) can soy milk
- 1 1/2 tablespoons green curry paste

Directions:
1. In a medium bowl, mix together the ground lamb, graham crackers and basil until well blended.
2. Form into meatballs about 1 inch in diameter.
3. Heat a greased skillet over medium-high heat and fry the lamb balls until they are a bit black and crusty, about 5 minutes.
4. Remove balls from pan and set aside.
5. Toss the curry paste into the hot skillet and fry for about a minute.
6. Then pour in the entire can of soy milk and lower the heat.
7. Let the mixture simmer, frequently stirring for 5 to 10 minutes.
8. Serve.

Nutrition: Calories 103, Total Fat 3.8g, Saturated Fat 0.9g, Cholesterol 26mg, Sodium 184mg, Total Carbohydrate 7.1g, Dietary Fiber 0.4g, Total Sugars 3g, Protein 9.5g, Calcium 14mg, Iron 1mg, Potassium 144mg, Phosphorus 90mg

710. Beef and Chili Stew

Preparation Time: 15 minutes
Cooking Time: 7 hours
Servings: 6
Ingredients:
- 1/2 medium red onion, sliced thinly
- 1/2 tablespoon vegetable oil

- 10ounce of flat-cut beef brisket, whole
- ½ cup low sodium stock
- ¾ cup of water
- ½ tablespoon honey
- ½ tablespoon chili powder
- ½ teaspoon smoked paprika
- ½ teaspoon dried thyme
- 1 teaspoon black pepper
- 1 tablespoon corn starch

Directions:

1. Throw the sliced onion into the slow cooker first. Add a splash of oil to a large hot skillet and briefly seal the beef on all sides.
2. Remove the beef, then place it in the slow cooker. Add the stock, water, honey, and spices to the same skillet you cooked the beef meat.
3. Allow the juice to simmer until the volume is reduced by about half. Pour the juice over beef in the slow cooker. Cook on low within 7 hours.
4. Transfer the beef to your platter, shred it using two forks. Put the rest of the juice into a medium saucepan. Bring it to a simmer.
5. Whisk the cornstarch with two tablespoons of water. Add to the juice and cook until slightly thickened.
6. For a thicker sauce, simmer and reduce the juice a bit more before adding cornstarch. Put the sauce on the meat and serve.

Nutrition: Calories: 128 Protein: 13g Carbohydrates: 6g Fat: 6g Sodium: 228mg Potassium: 202mg Phosphorus: 119mg

711. Peppercorn Pork Chops

Preparation time: 30 min
Cooking Time: 30 minutes
Servings: 4
Ingredients:

- 1 tablespoon crushed black peppercorns
- 4 pork loin chops
- 2 tablespoons olive oil
- 1/4 cup butter
- 5 garlic cloves
- 1 cup green and red bell peppers
- 1/2 cup pineapple juice

Directions:

1. Sprinkle and press peppercorns into both sides of pork chops.
2. Heat oil, butter and garlic cloves in a large skillet over medium heat, stirring frequently.
3. Add pork chops and cook uncovered for 5–6 minutes.
4. Dice the bell peppers. Add the bell peppers and pineapple juice to the pork chops.
5. Cover and simmer for another 5–6 minutes or until pork is thoroughly cooked.

Nutrition: Calories 317, Total Fat 25.7g, Saturated Fat 10.5g, Cholesterol 66mg, Sodium 126mg, Total Carbohydrate 9.2g, Dietary Fiber 2g, Total Sugars 6.4g, Protein 13.2g, Calcium 39mg, Iron 1mg, Potassium 250mg, Phosphorus 115 mg

712. Grilled Lamb Chops with Fresh Mint

Preparation time: 15 min
Cooking Time: 10 minutes
Servings: 4
Ingredients:

- 8 (5 ounces) lamb loin chops, about 1 1/4-inches thick
- 1/8 teaspoon seasoning salt
- 1/2 tablespoon dried parsley
- 1/2 tablespoon minced fresh mint
- 1/2 tablespoon dried rosemary

Directions:

1. Trim any excess fat down to 1/8-inch around each lamb chop and sprinkle both sides with seasoning salt.
2. Let sit for about 30 minutes to come to room temperature.
3. Preheat an outdoor grill to 400 degrees F. Lightly oil the grate once the grill is hot.
4. Place lamb chops on the hot grate and grill for 2 to 3 minutes.
5. Rotate chops, to achieve crisscross grill marks, and continue grilling, 2 to 3 more minutes.
6. Flip the chops and grill for 2 to 3 minutes.
7. Rotate chops and continue grilling an additional 2 minutes, or until they have reached the desired doneness.
8. An instant-read thermometer inserted into the center should read at least 130 degrees F.
9. Remove chops from grill and sprinkle with dried herbs and fresh mint.
10. Allow to rest under the foil, about 10 minutes

Nutrition: Calories 160, Total Fat 6.3g, Saturated Fat 2.3g, Cholesterol 77mg, Sodium 139mg, Total Carbohydrate 0.4g, Dietary Fiber 0.2g, Total Sugars 0g, Protein 23.9g, Calcium 18mg, Iron 2mg, Potassium 295mg, Phosphorus 140mg

713. Pork Chops with Apples, Onions

Preparation time: 30 min
Cooking Time: 60 minutes
Servings: 4
Ingredients:
- 4 pork chops
- salt and pepper to taste
- 2 onions, sliced into rings
- 2 apples - peeled, cored, and sliced into rings
- 3 tablespoons honey
- 2 teaspoons freshly ground black pepper

Directions:
1. Preheat oven to 375 degrees F.
2. Season pork chops with salt and pepper to taste, and arrange in a medium oven-safe skillet. Top pork chops with onions and apples. Sprinkle with honey. Season with 2 teaspoons pepper.
3. Cover, and bake 1 hour in the preheated oven, pork chops have reached an internal temperature of 145 degrees F.

Nutrition: Calories 307, Total Fat 16.1g, Saturated Fat 6g, Cholesterol 55mg, Sodium 48mg, Total Carbohydrate 26.8g, Dietary Fiber 3.1g, Total Sugars 21.5g, Protein 15.1g, Calcium 30mg, Iron 1mg, Potassium 387mg, Phosphorus 315 mg

714. Chinese Beef Wraps

Preparation Time: 10 minutes
Cooking Time: 30 minutes
Servings: 2
Ingredients:
- 2 iceberg lettuce leaves
- ½ diced cucumber
- 1 teaspoon canola oil
- 5-ounce lean ground beef
- 1 teaspoon ground ginger
- 1 tablespoon chili flakes
- 1 minced garlic clove
- 1 tablespoon rice wine vinegar

Directions:

1. Mix the ground meat with the garlic, rice wine vinegar, chili flakes, and ginger in a bowl. Heat-up oil in a skillet over medium heat.
2. Put the beef in the pan and cook for 20-25 minutes or until cooked through. Serve beef mixture with diced cucumber in each lettuce wrap and fold.

Nutrition: Calories 156 Fat 2g Carbs 4 g Phosphorus 1 mg Sodium 54mg Protein 14g Potassium 0mg

715. Grilled Lamb Chops with Pineapple

Preparation time: 15 min
Cooking Time: 55 minutes
Servings: 4
Ingredients:
- 1 lemon, zest and juiced
- 2 tablespoons chopped fresh oregano
- 2 cloves garlic, minced
- salt and black pepper to taste
- 8 (3 ounces) lamb chops
- 1/2 cup fresh unsweetened pineapple juice
- 1 cup pineapples

Directions:
1. Whisk together the lemon zest and juice, oregano, garlic, salt, and black pepper in a bowl; pour into a resealable plastic bag. Add the lamb chops, coat with the marinade, squeeze out excess air, and seal the bag.
2. Set aside to marinate.
3. Preheat an outdoor grill for medium-high heat, and lightly oil the grate.
4. Bring the pineapple juice in a small saucepan over high heat.
5. Reduce heat to medium-low, and continue simmering until the liquid has reduced to half of its original volume, about 45 minutes.
6. Stir in the pineapples and set aside.

7. Remove the lamb from the marinade and shake off excess.
8. Discard the remaining marinade.
9. Cook the chops on the preheated grill until they start to firm and are reddish-pink and juicy in the center, about 4 minutes per side for medium rare.
10. Serve the chops drizzled with the pineapple reduction.

Nutrition: Calories 69, Total Fat 1.6g, Saturated Fat 0.5g, Cholesterol 17mg, Sodium 16mg, Total Carbohydrate 8.5g, Dietary Fiber 1.4g, Total Sugars 5.1g, Protein 5.9g, Calcium 37mg, Iron 1mg, Potassium 163mg, Phosphorus 65 mg

716. Basil Grilled Mediterranean Lamb Chops

Preparation time: 10 min
Cooking Time: 10 minutes
Servings: 4
Ingredients:
- 4 (8 ounces) lamb shoulder chops
- 2 tablespoons Dijon mustard
- 2 tablespoons balsamic vinegar
- ½ tablespoon garlic powder
- 1/4 teaspoon ground black pepper
- 1/2 cup olive oil
- 2 tablespoons shredded fresh basil, or to taste

Directions:
1. Pat lamb chops dry and arrange in a single layer in a shallow glass baking dish.
2. Whisk Dijon mustard, balsamic vinegar, garlic, and pepper together in a small bowl.
3. Whisk in oil slowly until marinade is smooth.
4. Stir in basil. Pour marinade over lamb chops, turning to coat both sides.

5. Cover and refrigerate for 1 to 4 hours.
6. Bring lamb chops to room temperature, about 30 minutes.
7. Preheat grill for medium heat and lightly oil the grate.
8. Grill lamb chops until browned, 5 to 10 minutes per side.
9. An instant-read thermometer inserted into the center should read at least 145 degrees F.

Nutrition: Calories 270, Total Fat 27.8g, Saturated Fat 4.4g, Cholesterol 19mg, Sodium 109mg, Total Carbohydrate 1.4g, Dietary Fiber 0.4g, Total Sugars 0.4g, Protein 6.1g, Calcium 14mg, Iron 1mg, Potassium 33mg, Phosphorus 30mg

717. Shredded Beef

Preparation time: 10 min
Cooking Time: 5 hr.10 minutes
Servings: 4
Ingredients:
- 1/2 cup onion
- 2 garlic cloves
- 2 tablespoons fresh parsley
- 2-pound beef rump roast
- 1 tablespoon Italian herb seasoning
- 1 teaspoon dried parsley
- 1 bay leaf
- 1/2 teaspoon pepper
- 1/4 teaspoon salt
- 2 tablespoons olive oil
- 1/3 cup vinegar
- 2 to 3 cups water
- 8 hard rolls, 3-1/2-inch diameter, 2 ounces each

Directions:
1. Chop onion, garlic and fresh parsley. Place beef roast in a Crock-Pot. Add chopped onion, garlic and remaining ingredients, except fresh parsley and rolls, to Crock-Pot; stir to combine.

2. Cover and cook on low-heat setting for 8 to 10 hours, or on high setting for 4 to 5 hours, until fork-tender.
3. Remove roast from Crock-Pot.
4. Shred with two forks then return meat to cooking broth to keep warm until ready to serve.
5. Slice rolls in half and top with shredded beef, fresh parsley and 1-2 spoons of the broth.
6. Serve open-face or as a sandwich.

Nutrition: Calories 218, Total Fat 9.7g, Saturated Fat 2.6g, Cholesterol 75mg, Sodium 184mg, Total Carbohydrate 5.1g, Dietary Fiber 0.4g, Total Sugars 0.4g, Protein 26g, Calcium 26mg, Iron 3mg, Potassium 28mg, Phosphorus 30mg

718. Sticky Pulled Beef Open Sandwiches

Preparation Time: 15 minutes
Cooking Time: 5 hours
Servings: 5
Ingredients:
- ½ cup of green onion, sliced
- 2 garlic cloves
- 2 tablespoons of fresh parsley
- 2 large carrots

- 7ounce of flat-cut beef brisket, whole
- 1 tablespoon of smoked paprika
- 1 teaspoon dried parsley
- 1 teaspoon of brown sugar
- ½ teaspoon of black pepper
- 2 tablespoon of olive oil
- ¼ cup of red wine
- 8 tablespoon of cider vinegar
- 3 cups of water
- 5 slices white bread
- 1 cup of arugula to garnish

Directions:
1. Finely chop the green onion, garlic, and fresh parsley. Grate the carrot. Put the beef in to roast in a slow cooker.
2. Add the chopped onion, garlic, and remaining ingredients, leaving the rolls, fresh parsley, and arugula to one side. Stir in the slow cooker to combine.
3. Cover and cook on low within 8 1/2 to 10 hours or on high for 4 to 5 hours until tender. Remove the meat from the slow cooker. Shred the meat using two forks.
4. Return the meat to the broth to keep it warm until ready to serve. Lightly toast the bread and top with shredded beef, arugula, fresh parsley, and ½ spoon of the broth. Serve.

Nutrition: Calories: 273 Protein: 15g Carbohydrates: 20g Fat: 11g Sodium: 308mg Potassium: 399mg Phosphorus: 159mg

719. Lemon and Thyme Lamb Chops

Preparation time: 10 min
Cooking Time: 10 minutes
Servings: 4
Ingredients:
- 1 tablespoon olive oil
- 1/4 tablespoon lemon juice
- 1 tablespoon chopped fresh thyme
- Salt and pepper to taste
- 4 lamb chops

Directions:
1. Stir together olive oil, lemon juice, and thyme in a small bowl. Season with salt and pepper to taste. Place lamb chops in a shallow dish and brush with the olive oil mixture. Marinate in the refrigerator for 1 hour.
2. Preheat grill for high heat.
3. Lightly oil grill grate. Place lamb chops on the grill, and discard marinade. Cook for 10 minutes, turning once, or to the desired doneness

Nutrition: Calories 111, Total Fat 6.7g, Saturated Fat 1.6g, Cholesterol 38mg, Sodium 33mg, Total Carbohydrate 0.5g, Dietary Fiber 0.3g, Total Sugars 0g, Protein 12g, Calcium 19mg, Iron 2mg, Potassium 149mg, Phosphorus 93mg

720. Roast Beef

Preparation Time: 25 minutes
Cooking Time: 55 minutes
Servings: 3
Ingredients:
- Quality rump or sirloin tip roast
- Pepper & herbs

Directions:
1. Place in a roasting pan on a shallow rack. Season with pepper and herbs. Insert meat thermometer in the center or thickest part of the roast.
2. Roast to the desired degree of doneness. After removing from over for about 15 minutes, let it chill. In the end, the roast should be moister than well done.

Nutrition: Calories 158 Protein 24 g Fat 6 g Carbs 0 g Phosphorus 206 mg Potassium 328 mg
Sodium 55 mg

721. Herby Beef Stroganoff and Fluffy Rice

Preparation Time: 15 minutes
Cooking Time: 5 hours
Servings: 6
Ingredients:
- ½ cup onion
- 2 garlic cloves
- 9ounce of flat-cut beef brisket, cut into 1" cubes
- ½ cup of reduced-sodium beef stock
- 1/3 cup red wine
- ½ teaspoon dried oregano
- ¼ teaspoon freshly ground black pepper
- ½ teaspoon dried thyme
- ½ teaspoon of saffron
- ½ cup almond milk (unenriched)
- ¼ cup all-purpose flour
- 1 cup of water
- 2 ½ cups of white rice

Directions:
1. Dice the onion, then mince the garlic cloves. Mix the beef, stock, wine, onion, garlic, oregano, pepper, thyme, and saffron in your slow cooker.
2. Cover and cook on high within 4-5 hours. Combine the almond milk, flour, and water. Whisk together until smooth.
3. Add the flour mixture to the slow cooker. Cook for another 15 to 25 minutes until the stroganoff is thick.
4. Cook the rice using the package instructions, leaving out the salt. Drain off the excess water. Serve the stroganoff over the rice.

Nutrition: Calories: 241 Protein: 15g Carbohydrates: 29g Fat: 5g Sodium: 182mg Potassium: 206mg Phosphorus: 151mg

722. Lamb Keema

Preparation time: 5 min
Cooking Time: 20 minutes
Servings: 4
Ingredients:
- 1 1/2 pounds ground lamb
- 1 onion, finely chopped
- 2 teaspoons garlic powder
- 2 tablespoons garam masala
- 1/8 teaspoon salt
- 3/4 cup chicken broth

Directions:
1. In a large, heavy skillet over medium heat, cook ground lamb until evenly brown.
2. While cooking, break apart with a wooden spoon until crumbled.
3. Transfer cooked lamb to a bowl and drain off all but 1 tablespoon fat. Saute onion until soft and translucent, about 5 minutes.
4. Stir in garlic powder, and sauté 1 minute.
5. Stir in garam masala and cook 1 minute.
6. Return the browned lamb to the pan, and stir in chicken beef broth.
7. Reduce heat, and simmer for 10 to 15 minutes or until meat is fully cooked through, and liquid has evaporated.

Nutrition: Calories 194, Total Fat 7.3g, Saturated Fat 2.6g, Cholesterol 87mg, Sodium 160mg, Total Carbohydrate 2.2g, Dietary Fiber 0.4g, Total Sugars 0.9g, Protein 28.1g, Calcium 18mg, Iron 2mg, Potassium 379mg, Phosphorus 240mg

723. Lamb Stew with Green Beans

Preparation time: 30 min
Cooking Time: 1 hr.10 minutes
Servings: 4

Ingredients:

- 1 tablespoon olive oil
- 1 large onion, chopped
- 1 stalk green onion, chopped
- 1-pound boneless lamb shoulder, cut into 2-inch pieces
- 3 cups hot water
- ½ pound fresh green beans, trimmed
- 1 tablespoon chopped fresh parsley
- 1/2 teaspoon dried mint
- 1/2 teaspoon dried dill weed
- 1 pinch ground nutmeg
- ¼ teaspoon honey
- Salt and pepper to taste

Directions:

1. Heat oil in a large pot over medium heat. Saute onion and green onion until golden.
2. Stir in lamb, and cook until evenly brown.
3. Stir in water. Reduce heat and simmer for about 1 hour.
4. Stir in green beans. Season with parsley, mint, dill, nutmeg, honey, salt and pepper.
5. Continue cooking until beans are tender.

Nutrition: Calories 81, Total Fat 5.1g, Saturated Fat 1.1g, Cholesterol 19mg, Sodium 20mg, Total Carbohydrate 2.8g, Dietary Fiber 1g, Total Sugars 1g, Protein 6.5g, Calcium 17mg, Iron 1mg, Potassium 136mg, Phosphorus 120mg

724. Chunky Beef and Potato Slow Roast

Preparation Time: 15 minutes
Cooking Time: 5-6 hours
Servings: 12

Ingredients:

- 3 cups of peeled carrots, chunked
- 1 cup of onion
- 2 garlic cloves, chopped
- 1 ¼ pound flat-cut beef brisket, fat trimmed
- 2 cups of water
- 1 teaspoon of chili powder
- 1 tablespoon of dried rosemary

For the sauce:

- 1 tablespoon of freshly grated horseradish
- ½ cup of almond milk (unenriched)
- 1 tablespoon lemon juice (freshly squeezed)
- 1 garlic clove, minced
- A pinch of cayenne pepper

Directions:

1. Double boil the carrots to reduce their potassium content. Chop the onion and the garlic. Place the beef brisket in a slow cooker. Combine water, chopped garlic, chili powder, and rosemary.
2. Pour the mixture over the brisket. Cover and cook on high within 4-5 hours until the meat is very tender. Drain the carrots and add them to the slow cooker.
3. Adjust the heat to high and cook covered until the carrots are tender. Prepare the horseradish sauce by whisking together horseradish, almond milk, lemon juice, minced garlic, and cayenne pepper.
4. Cover and refrigerate. Serve your casserole with a dash of horseradish sauce on the side.

Nutrition: Calories: 199 Protein: 21g Carbohydrates: 12g Fat: 7g Sodium: 282mg Potassium: 317 Phosphorus: 191mg

725. Spiced Lamb Burgers

Preparation Time: 10 minutes
Cooking Time: 20 minutes
Servings: 2

Ingredients:

- 1 tablespoon extra-virgin olive oil
- 1 teaspoon cumin
- ½ finely diced red onion
- 1 minced garlic clove
- 1 teaspoon harissa spices
- 1 cup arugula
- 1 juiced lemon
- 6-ounce lean ground lamb
- 1 tablespoon parsley
- ½ cup low-fat plain yogurt

Directions:

1. Preheat the broiler on medium to high heat. Mix the ground lamb, red onion, parsley, Harissa spices, and olive oil until combined.
2. Shape 1-inch thick patties using wet hands. Add the patties to a baking tray and place under the broiler for 7-8 minutes on each side. Mix the yogurt, lemon juice, and cumin and serve over the lamb burgers with arugula's side salad.

Nutrition: Calories 306 Fat 20g Carbs 10g Phosphorus 269mg Potassium 492mg Sodium 86mg Protein 23g

726. Pork Loins with Leeks

Preparation Time: 10 minutes
Cooking Time: 35 minutes
Servings: 2

Ingredients:

- 1 sliced leek
- 1 tablespoon mustard seeds
- 6-ounce pork tenderloin
- 1 tablespoon cumin seeds
- 1 tablespoon dry mustard
- 1 tablespoon extra-virgin oil

Directions:

1. Preheat the broiler to medium-high heat. In a dry skillet, heat mustard and cumin seeds until they start to pop (3-5 minutes). Grind seeds using a pestle and mortar or blender and then mix in the dry mustard.
2. Massage the pork on all sides using the mustard blend and add to a baking tray to broil for 25-30 minutes or until cooked through. Turn once halfway through.
3. Remove and place to one side, then heat-up the oil in a pan on medium heat and add the leeks for 5-6 minutes or until soft. Serve the pork tenderloin on a bed of leeks and enjoy it!

Nutrition: Calories 139 Fat 5g Carbs 2g Phosphorus 278mg Potassium 45mg Sodium 47mg Protein 18g

727. Spicy Lamb Curry

Preparation Time: 15 minutes
Cooking Time: 2 hours 15 minutes
Servings: 6-8
Ingredients:

- 4 teaspoons ground coriander
- 4 teaspoons ground coriander
- 4 teaspoons ground cumin
- ¾ teaspoon ground ginger
- 2 teaspoons ground cinnamon
- ½ teaspoon ground cloves
- ½ teaspoon ground cardamom
- 2 tablespoons sweet paprika
- ½ tablespoon cayenne pepper
- 2 teaspoons chili powder
- 2 teaspoons salt
- 1 tablespoon coconut oil
- 2 pounds boneless lamb, trimmed and cubed into 1-inch size
- Salt
- ground black pepper
- 2 cups onions, chopped
- 1¼ cups water
- 1 cup of coconut almond milk

Directions:

1. For spice mixture in a bowl, mix all spices. Keep aside. Season the lamb with salt and black pepper.
2. Warm oil on medium-high heat in a large Dutch oven. Add lamb and stir fry for around 5 minutes. Add onion and cook approximately 4-5 minutes.
3. Stir in the spice mixture and cook approximately 1 minute. Add water and coconut almond milk and provide some boil on high heat.

4. Adjust the heat to low and simmer, covered for approximately 1-120 minutes or until the lamb's desired doneness. Uncover and simmer for about 3-4 minutes. Serve hot.

Nutrition: Calories: 466 Fat: 10g Carbohydrates: 23g Protein: 36g Potassium 599 mg Sodium 203 mg Phosphorus 0mg

728. Broiled Lamb Shoulder

Preparation Time: 10 minutes
Cooking Time: 8-10 minutes
Servings: 10
Ingredients:

- 2 tablespoons fresh ginger, minced
- 2 tablespoons garlic, minced
- 1/4 cup fresh lemongrass stalk, minced
- 1/4 cup fresh mango juice
- 1/4 cup coconut aminos
- Freshly ground black pepper, to taste
- 2-pound lamb shoulder, trimmed

Directions:

1. In a bowl, mix together all ingredients except lamb shoulder.
2. In a baking dish, squeeze lamb shoulder and coat the lamb with half in the marinade mixture generously.
3. Reserve remaining mixture.
4. Refrigerate to marinate for overnight.
5. Preheat the broiler of oven. Place a rack inside a broiler pan and arrange about 4-5-inches from heating unit.
6. Remove lamb shoulder from refrigerator and remove excess marinade.
7. Broil approximately 4-5 minutes from both sides.
8. Serve with all the reserved marinade like a sauce.

Nutrition: Calories: 250, Fat: 19g, Carbohydrates: 2g. Fiber: 0g, Protein: 15g

729. Grilled Lamb Chops

Preparation Time: 10 min
Cooking Time: 6 minutes
Servings: 4
Ingredients:

- 1 tablespoon fresh ginger, grated
- 4 garlic cloves, chopped roughly
- 1 teaspoon ground cumin
- 1/2 teaspoon red chili powder
- Salt and freshly ground black pepper, to taste
- 1 tbsp. essential olive oil
- 1 tablespoon fresh lemon juice
- 8 lamb chops, trimmed

Directions:

1. In a bowl, mix together all ingredients except chops.
2. With a hand blender, blend till a smooth mixture forms.
3. Add chops and coat with mixture generously.
4. Refrigerate to marinate for overnight.
5. Preheat the barbecue grill till hot. Grease the grill grate.
6. Grill the chops for approximately 3 minutes per side.

Nutrition: Calories: 227, Fat: 12g, Carbohydrates: 1g, Fiber: 0g, Protein: 30g

730. Lamb & Pineapple Kebabs

Preparation Time: 15 minutes
Cooking Time: 10 minutes
Servings: 4-6
Ingredients:

- 1 large pineapple, cubed into 11/2-inch size, divided
- 1 (1/2-inch) piece fresh ginger, chopped
- 2 garlic cloves, chopped
- Salt, to taste
- 16-24-ounce lamb shoulder steak, trimmed and cubed into 11/2-inch size
- Fresh mint leaves coming from a bunch
- Ground cinnamon, to taste

Directions:

1. In a blender, add about 11/2 of pineapple, ginger, garlic and salt and pulse till smooth.
2. Transfer the amalgamation right into a large bowl.
3. Add chops and coat with mixture generously.
4. Refrigerate to marinate for about 1-2 hours.
5. Preheat the grill to medium heat. Grease the grill grate.
6. Thread lam, remaining pineapple and mint leaves onto pre-soaked wooden skewers.
7. Grill the kebabs approximately 10 min, turning occasionally.

Nutrition: Calories: 482, Fat: 16g, Carbohydrates: 22g, Fiber: 5g, Protein: 377g

731. Pork with Bell Pepper

Preparation Time: 15 minutes
Cooking Time: 13 minutes
Servings: 4
Ingredients:

- 1 tablespoon fresh ginger, chopped finely
- 4 garlic cloves, chopped finely
- 1 cup fresh cilantro, chopped and divided
- 1/4 cup plus 1 tbsp. olive oil, divided
- 1-pound tender pork, trimmed, sliced thinly
- 2 onions, sliced thinly
- 1 green bell pepper, seeded and sliced thinly

- 1 tablespoon fresh lime juice

Directions:
1. In a substantial bowl, mix together ginger, garlic, 1/2 cup of cilantro and 1/4 cup of oil.
2. Add pork and coat with mixture generously.
3. Refrigerate to marinate approximately a couple of hours.
4. Heat a big skillet on medium-high heat.
5. Add pork mixture and stir fry for approximately 4-5 minutes.
6. Transfer the pork right into a bowl.
7. In the same skillet, heat remaining oil on medium heat.
8. Add onion and sauté for approximately 3 minutes.
9. Stir in bell pepper and stir fry for about 3 minutes.
10. Stir in pork, lime juice and remaining cilantro and cook for about 2 minutes.
11. Serve hot.

Nutrition: Calories: 429, Fat: 19g, Carbohydrates: 26g, Fiber: 9g, Protein: 35g

732. Pork with Pineapple

Preparation Time: 15 minutes
Cooking Time: 14 minutes
Servings: 4

Ingredients:
- 2 tablespoons coconut oil
- 11/2 pound pork tenderloin, trimmed and cut into bite-sized pieces
- 1 onion, chopped
- 2 minced garlic cloves
- 1 (1-inch) piece fresh ginger, minced
- 20-ounce pineapple, cut into chunks
- 1 large red bell pepper, seeded and chopped
- 1/4 cup fresh pineapple juice
- 1/4 cup coconut aminos

- Salt and freshly ground black pepper, to taste

Directions:
1. In a substantial skillet, melt coconut oil on high heat.
2. Add pork and stir fry approximately 4-5 minutes.
3. Transfer the pork right into a bowl.
4. In exactly the same skillet, heat remaining oil on medium heat.
5. Add onion, garlic and ginger and sauté for around 2 minutes.
6. Stir in pineapple and bell pepper and stir fry for around 3 minutes.
7. Stir in pork, pineapple juice and coconut aminos and cook for around 3-4 minutes.
8. Serve hot.

Nutrition: Calories: 431, Fat: 10g, Carbohydrates: 22g, Fiber: 8g, Protein: 33g

733. Stir-Fried Ground Beef

Preparation Time: 10 minutes
Cooking Time: 15 minutes
Servings: 4

Ingredients:
- 1/2 cup broccoli, chopped
- 1/2 of medium-sized onions, chopped
- 1/2 of medium-sized red bell pepper, chopped
- 1 tbsp. cayenne pepper (optional)
- 1 tbsp. Chinese five spices
- 1 tbsp. coconut oil
- 1-lb ground beef
- 2 kale leaves, chopped
- 5 medium-sized mushrooms, sliced

Directions:
1. In a skillet, heat the coconut oil over medium high heat.
2. Sauté the onions for one minute and add the vegetables while stirring constantly.

317

3. Add the ground beef and the spices.
4. Cook for two minutes and reduce the heat to medium.
5. Cover the skillet and continue to cook the beef and vegetables for another 10 minutes.
6. Serve and enjoy.

Nutrition: Calories 304, Total Fat 17g, Saturated Fat 3g, Total Carbs 6g, Net Carbs 4g, Protein 32g, Sugar: 2g, Fiber 2g, Sodium 86mg, Potassium 624mg

734. Lamb with Zucchini & Couscous

Preparation Time: 15 minutes
Cooking Time: 8 minutes
Servings: 2
Ingredients:

- ¾ cup couscous
- ¾ cup boiling water
- 1/4 cup fresh cilantro, chopped
- 1 tbsp. olive oil
- 5-ounces lamb leg steak, cubed into ¾-inch size
- 1 medium zucchini, sliced thinly
- 1 medium red onion, cut into wedges
- 1 teaspoon ground cumin
- 1 teaspoon ground coriander
- 1/4 teaspoon red pepper flakes, crushed
- Salt, to taste
- 1/4 cup plain Greek yogurt
- 1 garlic herb, minced

Directions:

1. In a bowl, add couscous and boiling water and stir to combine,
2. Cover whilst aside approximately 5 minutes.
3. Add cilantro and with a fork, fluff completely.
4. Meanwhile in a substantial skillet, heat oil on high heat.

5. Add lamb and stir fry for about 2-3 minutes.
6. Add zucchini and onion and stir fry for about 2 minutes.
7. Stir in spices and stir fry for about 1 minute
8. Add couscous and stir fry approximately 2 minutes.
9. In a bowl, mix together yogurt and garlic.
10. Divide lamb mixture in serving plates evenly.
11. Serve using the topping of yogurt.

Nutrition: Calories: 392, Fat: 5g, Carbohydrates: 2g, Fiber: 12g, Protein: 35g

735. Pan-Seared Lamb Chops

Preparation Time: 10 minutes
Cooking Time: 4-6 minutes
Servings: 4
Ingredients:

- 4 garlic cloves, peeled
- Salt, to taste
- 1 teaspoon black mustard seeds, crushed finely
- 2 teaspoons ground cumin
- 1 teaspoon ground ginger
- 1 teaspoon ground coriander
- 1/2 teaspoon ground cinnamon
- Freshly ground black pepper, to taste
- 1 tablespoon coconut oil
- 8 medium lamb chops, trimmed

Directions:

1. Place garlic cloves onto a cutting board and sprinkle with salt.
2. With a knife, crush the garlic till a paste forms.
3. In a bowl, mix together garlic paste and spices.

4. With a clear, crisp knife, make 3-4 cuts on both sides in the chops.
5. Rub the chops with garlic mixture generously.
6. In a large skillet, melt butter on medium heat.
7. Add chops and cook for approximately 2-3 minutes per side or till desired doneness.

Nutrition: Calories: 443, Fat: 11g, Carbohydrates: 27g, Fiber: 4g, Protein: 40g

736. Ground Lamb with Harissa

Preparation Time: 15 minutes
Cooking Time: one hour 11 minutes
Servings: 4
Ingredients:

- 1 tablespoon extra-virgin olive oil
- 2 red peppers, seeded and chopped finely
- 1 yellow onion, chopped finely
- 2 garlic cloves, chopped finely
- 1 teaspoon ground cumin
- 1/2 teaspoon ground turmeric
- 1/4 teaspoon ground cinnamon
- 1/4 teaspoon ground ginger
- 11/2 pound lean ground lamb
- Salt, to taste
- 1 (141/2-ounce) can diced Red bell peppers
- 2 tablespoons harissa
- 1 cup water
- Chopped fresh cilantro, for garnishing

Directions:
In a sizable pan, heat oil on medium-high heat.
1. Add bell pepper, onion and garlic and sauté for around 5 minutes.
2. Add spices and sauté for around 1 minute.

3. Add lamb and salt and cook approximately 5 minutes, getting into pieces.
4. Stir in Red bell peppers, harissa and water and provide with a boil.
5. Reduce the warmth to low and simmer, covered for about 1 hour.
6. Serve hot while using garnishing of harissa.

Nutrition: Calories: 441, Fat: 12g, Carbohydrates: 24g, Fiber: 10g, Protein: 36g

737. Grilled Skirt Steak

Preparation Time: 15 minutes
Cooking Time: 8-9 minutes
Servings: 4
Ingredients:

- 2 teaspoons fresh ginger herb, grated finely
- 2 teaspoons fresh lime zest, grated finely
- 1/4 cup coconut sugar
- 2 teaspoons fish sauce
- 2 tablespoons fresh lime juice
- 1/2 cup coconut almond milk
- 1-pound beef skirt steak, trimmed and cut into 4-inch slices lengthwise
- Salt, to taste

Directions:
1. In a sizable sealable bag, mix together all ingredients except steak and salt.
2. Add steak and coat with marinade generously.
3. Seal the bag and refrigerate to marinate for about 4-12 hours.
4. Preheat the grill to high heat. Grease the grill grate.
5. Remove steak from refrigerator and discard the marinade.
6. With a paper towel, dry the steak and sprinkle with salt evenly.
7. Cook the steak for approximately 31/2 minutes.

8. Flip the medial side and cook for around 21/2-5 minutes or till desired doneness.
9. Remove from grill pan and keep side for approximately 5 minutes before slicing.
10. With a clear, crisp knife cut into desired slices and serve.

Nutrition: Calories: 465, Fat: 10g, Carbohydrates: 22g, Fiber: 0g, Protein: 37g

738. Baked Pork & Mushroom Meatballs

Preparation Time: 15 minutes
Cooking Time: fifteen minutes
Servings: 6
Ingredients:
- 1-pound lean ground pork
- 1 organic egg white, beaten
- 4 fresh shiitake mushrooms, stemmed and minced
- 1 tablespoon fresh parsley, minced
- 1 tablespoon fresh basil leaves, minced
- 1 tablespoon fresh mint leaves, minced
- 2 teaspoons fresh lemon zest, grated finely
- 11/2 teaspoons fresh ginger, grated finely
- Salt and freshly ground black pepper, to taste

Directions:
1. Preheat the oven to 425 degrees F. Arrange the rack inside center of oven.
2. Line a baking sheet with a parchment paper.
3. In a sizable bowl, add all ingredients and mix till well combined.
4. Make small equal-sized balls from mixture.
5. Arrange the balls onto prepared baking sheet in a single layer.
6. Bake for approximately 12-15 minutes or till done completely.

Nutrition: Calories: 411, Fat: 19g, Carbohydrates: 27g, Fiber: 11g, Protein: 35g

739. Ground Pork with Water Chestnuts

Preparation Time: fifteen minutes
Cooking Time: 12 minutes
Servings: 4
Ingredients:
- 1 tablespoon plus 1 teaspoon coconut oil
- 1 tablespoon fresh ginger, minced
- 1 bunch scallion (white and green parts separated), chopped
- 1-pound lean ground pork
- Salt, to taste
- 1 tablespoon 5-spice powder
- 1 (18-ounce) can water chestnuts, drained and chopped
- 1 tablespoon organic honey
- 2 tablespoons fresh lime juice

Directions:
1. In a big heavy bottomed skillet, heat oil on high heat.
2. Add ginger and scallion whites and sauté for approximately 1/2-11/2 minutes.
3. Add pork and cook for approximately 4-5 minutes.
4. Drain the extra Fat from skillet.
5. Add salt and 5-spice powder and cook for approximately 2-3 minutes.
6. Add scallion greens and remaining ingredients and cook, stirring continuously for about 1-2 minutes.

Nutrition: Calories: 520, Fat: 30g, Carbohydrates: 37g, Fiber: 4g, Protein: 25g

740. Beef Brochettes

Preparation Time: 20 minutes
Cooking Time: 1 hour

Servings: 1

Ingredients

- 1 1/2 cups pineapple chunks
- 1 sliced large onion
- 2 pounds thick steak
- 1 sliced medium bell pepper
- 1 bay leaf
- 1/4 cup vegetable oil
- 1/2 cup lemon juice
- 2 crushed garlic cloves

Directions

1. Cut beef cubes and place in a plastic bag
2. Combine marinade ingredients in small bowl
3. Mix and pour over beef cubes
4. Seal the bag and refrigerate for 3 to 5 hours
5. Divide ingredients onion, beef cube, green pepper, pineapple
6. Grill about 9 minutes each side

Nutrition: Calories 304 Protein 35 g Fat 15 g Carbs 11 g Phosphorus 264 mg Potassium (K) 388 mg Sodium (Na) 70 mg

741. Homemade Burgers

Preparation Time: 10 minutes
Cooking Time: 20 minutes
Servings: 2

Ingredients

- 4 ounce lean 100% ground beef
- 1 teaspoon black pepper
- 1 garlic clove, minced
- 1 teaspoon olive oil
- 1/4 cup onion, finely diced
- 1 tablespoon balsamic vinegar
- 1/2ounce brie cheese, crumbled
- 1 teaspoon mustard

Directions

1. Season ground beef with pepper and then mix in minced garlic.

2. Form burger shapes with the ground beef using the palms of your hands.
3. Heat a skillet on a medium to high heat, and then add the oil.
4. Sauté the onions for 5-10 minutes until browned.
5. Then add the balsamic vinegar and sauté for another 5 minutes.
6. Remove and set aside.
7. Add the burgers to the pan and heat on the same heat for 5-6 minutes before flipping and heating for a further 5-6 minutes until cooked through.
8. Spread the mustard onto each burger.
9. Crumble the brie cheese over each burger and serve!
10. Try with a crunchy side salad!
11. Tip: If using fresh beef and not defrosted, prepare double the ingredients and freeze burgers in plastic wrap (after cooling) for up to 1 month.
12. Thoroughly defrost before heating through completely in the oven to serve.

Nutrition: Calories: 178 Fat: 10g Carbohydrates: 4g Phosphorus: 147mg Potassium: 272mg Sodium: 273 mg Protein: 16g

742. Country Fried Steak

Preparation Time: 10 minutes
Cooking Time: 1 hour and 40 minutes
Servings: 3

Ingredients

- 1 large onion
- 1/2 cup flour
- 3 tablespoons. vegetable oil
- 1/4 teaspoon pepper
- 11/2 pounds round steak
- 1/2 teaspoon paprika

Directions

1. Trim excess fat from steak
2. Cut into small pieces
3. Combine flour, paprika and pepper and mix together
4. Preheat skillet with oil
5. Cook steak on both sides
6. When the color of steak is brown remove to a platter
7. Add water (150 ml) and stir around the skillet
8. Return browned steak to skillet, if necessary, add water again so that bottom side of steak does not stick

NUTRITION: Calories 248 Protein 30 g Fat 10 g Carbs 5 g Phosphorus 190 mg Potassium (K) 338 mg Sodium (Na) 60 mg

743. Beef Pot Roast

Preparation Time: 20 minutes
Cooking Time: 1 hour
Servings: 3
Ingredients

- Round bone roast
- 2 - 4 pounds chuck roast

Directions:

1. Trim off excess fat
2. Place a tablespoon of oil in a large skillet and heat to medium
3. Roll pot roast in flour and brown on all sides in a hot skillet
4. After the meat gets a brown color, reduce heat to low
5. Season with pepper and herbs and add 1/2 cup of water
6. Cook slowly for 11/2 hours or until it looks ready

Nutrition: Calories 157 Protein 24 g Fat 13 g Carbs 0 g Phosphorus 204 mg Sodium (Na) 50 mg

744. Slow-cooked Beef Brisket

Preparation Time: 10 minutes
Cooking Time: 3 hours and 30 minutes
Servings: 6
Ingredients

- 10-ounce chuck roast
- 1 onion, sliced
- 1 cup carrots, peeled and sliced
- 1 tablespoon mustard
- 1 tablespoon thyme (fresh or dried)
- 1 tablespoon rosemary (fresh or dried)
- 2 garlic cloves
- 2 tablespoon extra-virgin olive oil
- 1 teaspoon black pepper
- 1 cup homemade chicken stock (p.52)
- 1 cup water

Directions

1. Preheat oven to 300°f/150°c/Gas Mark 2.
2. Trim any fat from the beef and soak vegetables in warm water.
3. Make a paste by mixing together the mustard, thyme, rosemary, and garlic, before mixing in the oil and pepper.
4. Combine this mix with the stock.
5. Pour the mixture over the beef into an oven proof baking dish.
6. Place the vegetables onto the bottom of the baking dish with the beef.
7. Cover and roast for 3 hours, or until tender.
8. Uncover the dish and continue to cook for 30 minutes in the oven.
9. Serve hot!

Nutrition: Calories: 151 Fat: 7g Carbohydrates: 7g Phosphorus: 144mg Potassium: 344mg Sodium: 279mg Protein: 15g

745. Pork Souvlaki

Preparation Time: 20 minutes

Cooking Time: 12 minutes
Servings: 8
Ingredients

- Olive oil – 3 tablespoons
- Lemon juice – 2 tablespoons
- Minced garlic – 1 teaspoon
- Chopped fresh oregano – 1 tablespoon
- Ground black pepper – 1/4 teaspoon
- Pork leg – 1 pound, cut in 2-inch cubes

Directions

1. In a bowl, stir together the lemon juice, olive oil, garlic, oregano, and pepper.
2. Add the pork cubes and toss to coat.
3. Place the bowl in the refrigerator, covered, for 2 hours to marinate.
4. Thread the pork chunks onto 8 wooden skewers that have been soaked in water.
5. Preheat the barbecue to medium-high heat.
6. Grill the pork skewers for about 12 minutes, turning once, until just cooked through but still juicy.

Nutrition: Calories: 95 Fat: 4g Carb: 0g Phosphorus: 125mg Potassium: 230mg Sodium: 29mg Protein: 13g

746. Open-Faced Beef Stir-Up

Preparation Time: 10 minutes
Cooking Time: 10 minutes
Servings: 6
Ingredients

- 95% Lean ground beef – 1/2 pound
- Chopped sweet onion – 1/2 cup
- Shredded cabbage – 1/2 cup
- Herb pesto – 1/4 cup
- Hamburger buns – 6, bottom halves only

Directions

1. Sauté the beef and onion for 6 minutes or until beef is cooked.
2. Add the cabbage and sauté for 3 minutes more.
3. Stir in pesto and heat for 1 minute.
4. Divide the beef mixture into 6 portions and serve each on the bottom half of a hamburger bun, open-face.

Nutrition: Calories: 120 Fat: 3g Phosphorus: 106mg Potassium: 198mg Sodium: 134mg Protein: 11g

747. Beef Brisket

Preparation Time: 10 minutes
Cooking Time: 3 1/2 hours
Servings: 6
Ingredients

- Chuck roast – 12 ounces trimmed
- Garlic – 2 cloves
- Thyme – 1 tablespoon
- Rosemary – tablespoon
- Mustard - 1 tablespoon
- Extra virgin olive oil – 1/4 cup
- Black pepper – 1 teaspoon
- Onion – 1, diced
- Carrots – 1 cup, peeled and sliced
- Low salt stock – 2 cups

Directions

1. Preheat the oven to 300F.
2. Soak vegetables in warm water.
3. Make a paste by mixing together the thyme, mustard, rosemary, and garlic. Then mix in the oil and pepper.
4. Add the beef to the dish.
5. Pour the mixture over the beef into a dish.
6. Place the vegetables onto the bottom of the baking dish around the beef.
7. Cover and roast for 3 hours, or until tender.
8. Uncover the dish and continue to cook for 30 minutes in the oven.
9. Serve.

Nutrition: calories: 303 Fat: 25g Carb: 7g
Phosphorus: 376mg Potassium: 246mg Sodium:
44mg Protein: 18g

BROTHS, CONDIMENT AND SEASONING

748. Basil Oil

Preparation Time: 15 minutes
Cooking Time: 4 minutes
Servings: 3
Ingredients:

- 2 cups olive oil
- 2½ cups fresh basil leaves patted dry

Directions:

1. Put the olive oil plus basil leaves in a food processor or blender, and pulse until the leaves are coarsely chopped.
2. Transfer these to a medium saucepan, and place over medium heat. Heat the oil, occasionally stirring, until it just starts to simmer along the edges, about 4 minutes. Remove, then let it stand until cool, about 2 hours.
3. Pour the oil through a fine-mesh sieve or doubled piece of cheesecloth into a container. Store the basil oil in an airtight glass container in the refrigerator for up to 2 months.
4. Before using for dressings, remove the oil from the refrigerator and let it come to room temperature, or for cooking, scoop out cold spoonsful.

Nutrition: Calories: 40 Fat: 5g Sodium: 0g Carbohydrates: 0g Phosphorus: 0g Potassium: 0g Protein: 0g

749. Citrus and Mustard Marinade

Preparation Time: 15 minutes
Cooking Time: 0 minutes
Servings: ¾ cup
Ingredients:

- ¼ cup freshly squeezed lemon juice
- ¼ cup freshly squeezed mango juice
- ¼ cup Dijon mustard
- 2 tablespoons honey
- 2 teaspoons chopped fresh thyme

Directions:

1. Mix the lemon juice, mango juice, mustard, honey, and thyme until well blended in a medium bowl. Store the marinade in a sealed glass container in the refrigerator for up to 3 days. Shake before using it.

Nutrition: Calories: 35 Fat: 0g Sodium: 118mg Carbohydrates: 8g Phosphorus: 14mg Potassium: 52mg Protein: 1g

750. Basil Pesto

Preparation Time: 15 minutes
Cooking Time: 0 minutes
Servings: 1 ½ cups

Ingredients:

- 2 cups gently packed fresh basil leaves
- 2 garlic cloves
- 2 tablespoons pine nuts
- ¼ cup olive oil
- 2 tablespoons freshly squeezed lemon juice

Directions:

1. Pulse the basil, garlic, plus pine nuts using a food processor or blender within about 3 minutes. Drizzle the olive oil into this batter, and pulse until thick paste forms.
2. Put the lemon juice, and pulse until well blended. Store the pesto in a sealed glass container in the refrigerator for up to 2 weeks.

Nutrition: Calories: 22 Fat: 2g Sodium: 0mg Carbohydrates: 0g Phosphorus: 3mg Potassium: 10mg Protein: 0g

751. Sweet Barbecue Sauce

Preparation Time: 15 minutes
Cooking Time: 11 minutes
Servings: 2 cups
Ingredients:

- 1 teaspoon olive oil
- ½ sweet onion, chopped
- 1 teaspoon minced garlic
- ¼ cup honey
- ¼ cup apple cider vinegar
- 2 tablespoons low-sodium tomato paste
- 1 tablespoon Dijon mustard
- 1 teaspoon hot sauce
- 1 teaspoon cornstarch

Directions:

1. Warm-up olive oil in a medium saucepan over medium heat. Add the onion and garlic and sauté until softened, about 3 minutes.
2. Stir in ¾ cup water, the honey, vinegar, tomato paste, mustard, and hot sauce. Cook within 6 minutes.
3. In a small cup, stir together ¼ cup of water and the cornstarch. Whisk the cornstarch into the sauce and continue to cook, stirring, until the sauce thickens about 2 minutes. Cool. Pour the sauce into a sealed glass container and store in the refrigerator for up to 1 week.

Nutrition: Calories: 14 Fat: 0g Sodium: 10mg Carbohydrates: 3g Phosphorus: 3mg Potassium: 17mg Protein: 0g

752. Mediterranean Dressing

Preparation Time: 15 minutes
Cooking Time: 0 minutes
Servings: 1 cup
Ingredients:

- ½ cup balsamic vinegar
- 1 teaspoon honey
- ½ teaspoon minced garlic
- 1 tablespoon dried parsley
- 1 tablespoon dried oregano
- ½ teaspoon celery seed
- Pinch freshly ground black pepper
- ½ cup olive oil

Directions:

1. Mix the vinegar, honey, garlic, parsley, oregano, celery seed, and pepper in a small bowl. Whisk in the olive oil until emulsified. Store the dressing in a sealed glass container in the refrigerator for up to 1 week.

Nutrition: Calories: 100 Fat: 11g Sodium: 1mg Carbohydrates: 1g Phosphorus: 1mg Potassium: 10mg Protein: 0g

753. Fiery Honey Vinaigrette

Preparation Time: 15 minutes
Cooking Time: 0 minutes
Servings: ¾ cup
Ingredients:

- 1/3 cup freshly squeezed lime juice
- ¼ cup honey
- ¼ cup olive oil
- 1 teaspoon chopped fresh basil leaves
- ½ teaspoon red pepper flakes

Directions:

1. Mix the lime juice, honey, and olive oil, basil, and red pepper flakes in a medium bowl, until well blended. Store the dressing in a glass container, and store it in the fridge for up to 1 week.

Nutrition: Calories: 125 Fat: 9g Sodium: 1mg Carbohydrates: 13g Phosphorus: 1mg Potassium: 24mg Protein: 0g

754. Hot Curry Powder

Preparation Time: 15 minutes
Cooking Time: 0 minutes
Servings: 1 ¼ cup
Ingredients:

- ¼ cup ground cumin
- ¼ cup ground coriander
- 3 tablespoons turmeric
- 2 tablespoons sweet paprika
- 2 tablespoons ground mustard
- 1 tablespoon fennel powder
- ½ teaspoon green chili powder
- 2 teaspoons ground cardamom
- 1 teaspoon ground cinnamon
- ½ teaspoon ground cloves

Directions:

1. Pulse the cumin, coriander, turmeric, paprika, mustard, fennel powder, green chili powder, cardamom, cinnamon, plus cloves using a blender, until the fixing is ground and well combined. Transfer it to a small container, put in a cool, dry place for up to 6 months.

Nutrition: Calories: 19 Fat: 1g Carbohydrates: 3g Phosphorus: 24mg Potassium: 93mg Sodium: 5mg Protein: 1g

755. Butter almond milk Herb Dressing

Preparation Time: 15 minutes
Cooking Time: 0 minutes
Servings: 1 ½ cup
Ingredients:

- ½ cup skim almond milk
- ½ cup Low-Sodium Mayonnaise
- 2 tablespoons apple cider vinegar
- ½ scallion, green part only, chopped
- 1 tablespoon chopped fresh dill
- 1 teaspoon chopped fresh thyme
- ½ teaspoon minced garlic
- Freshly ground black pepper

Directions:

1. Mix the almond milk, mayonnaise, and vinegar until smooth in a medium bowl. Whisk in the scallion, dill, thyme, and garlic. Season with pepper. Store.

Nutrition: Calories: 31 Fat: 2g Sodium: 19mg Carbohydrates: 2g Phosphorus: 13mg Potassium: 26mg Protein: 0g

756. Ras El Hanout

Preparation Time: 5 minutes
Cooking Time: 0 minutes
Servings: ½ cup
Ingredients:

- 2 teaspoons ground nutmeg
- 2 teaspoons ground coriander
- 2 teaspoons ground cumin
- 2 teaspoons turmeric
- 2 teaspoons cinnamon
- 1 teaspoon cardamom
- 1 teaspoon sweet paprika
- 1 teaspoon ground mace
- 1 teaspoon freshly ground black pepper
- 1 teaspoon cayenne pepper
- ½ teaspoon ground allspice
- ½ teaspoon ground cloves

Directions:
1. Mix the nutmeg, coriander, cumin, turmeric, cinnamon, cardamom, paprika, mace, black pepper, cayenne pepper, allspice, and cloves in a small bowl. Store.

Nutrition: Calories: 5 Fat: 0g Carbohydrates: 1g Phosphorus: 3mg Potassium: 17mg Sodium: 1mg Protein: 0g

757. Low-Sodium Mayonnaise

Preparation Time: 15 minutes
Cooking Time: 0 minutes
Servings: 3
Ingredients:

- 2 egg yolks
- 1 teaspoon Dijon mustard
- 1 teaspoon honey
- 2 tablespoons white vinegar
- 2 tablespoons freshly squeezed lemon juice
- 2 cups olive oil

Directions:
1. Mix the egg yolks, mustard, honey, vinegar, and lemon juice in a large bowl. Mix in the olive oil in a thin stream. You can store this in a glass container in the refrigerator for up to 2 weeks.

Nutrition: Calories: 83 Fat: 9g Sodium: 2mg Carbohydrates: 0g Phosphorus: 2mg Potassium: 3mg Protein: 0g

758. Poppy Seed Dressing

Preparation Time: 15 minutes
Cooking Time: 0 minutes
Servings: 2 cups
Ingredients:

- ½ cup apple cider or red wine vinegar
- 1/3 cup honey
- ¼ cup freshly squeezed lemon juice

- 1 tablespoon Dijon mustard
- 1 cup olive oil
- ½ small sweet onion, minced
- 2 tablespoons poppy seeds

Directions:
1. Mix the vinegar, honey, lemon juice, and mustard in a small bowl. Whisk in the oil, onion, and poppy seeds. Store the dressing in a sealed glass container in the refrigerator for up to 2 weeks.

Nutrition: Calories: 151 Fat: 14g Sodium: 12mg Carbohydrates: 7g Phosphorus: 13mg Potassium: 30mg Protein: 0g

759. Phosphorus-Free Baking Powder

Preparation Time: 5 minutes
Cooking Time: 0 minutes
Servings: 1

Ingredients:
- ¾ cup cream of tartar
- ¼ cup baking soda

Directions:
1. Mix the cream of tartar plus baking soda in a small bowl. Sift the mixture together several times to mix thoroughly. Store the baking powder in a sealed container in a cool, dark place for up to 1 month.

Nutrition: Calories: 6 Fat: 0g Sodium: 309mg Carbohydrates: 1g Phosphorus: 0g Potassium: 341mg Protein: 0g

760. Cajun Seasoning

Preparation Time: 15 minutes
Cooking Time: 0 minutes
Servings: 1 ¼ cup

Ingredients:
- ½ cup sweet paprika
- ¼ cup garlic powder
- 3 tablespoons onion powder
- 3 tablespoons freshly ground black pepper
- 2 tablespoons dried oregano
- 1 tablespoon cayenne pepper
- 1 tablespoon dried thyme

Directions:
1. Pulse the paprika, garlic powder, onion powder, black pepper, oregano, cayenne pepper, and thyme in a blender until the fixing is ground and well combined.

Nutrition: Calories: 7 Fat: 0g Carbohydrates: 2g Phosphorus: 8mg Potassium: 40mg Sodium: 1mg Protein: 0g

761. Spicy Herb Seasoning

Preparation Time: 10 minutes
Cooking Time: 0 minutes
Servings: ½ cup
Ingredients:

- ¼ cup celery seed
- 1 tablespoon dried basil
- 1 tablespoon dried oregano
- 1 tablespoon dried thyme
- 1 tablespoon onion powder
- 2 teaspoons garlic powder
- 1 teaspoon freshly ground black pepper
- ½ teaspoon ground cloves

Directions:

1. Mix the celery seed, basil, oregano, thyme, onion powder, garlic powder, pepper, and cloves in a small bowl. Store for up to 1 month.

Nutrition: Calories: 7 Fat: 0g Sodium: 2mg Carbohydrates: 1g Phosphorus: 9mg Potassium: 27mg Protein: 0g

762. Poultry Seasoning

Preparation Time: 15 minutes
Cooking Time: 0 minutes
Servings: ½ cup
Ingredients:

- 2 tablespoons ground thyme
- 2 tablespoons ground marjoram
- 1 tablespoon ground sage
- 1 tablespoon ground celery seed
- 1 teaspoon ground rosemary
- 1 teaspoon freshly ground black pepper

Directions:

1. Mix the thyme, marjoram, sage, celery seed, rosemary, and pepper in a small bowl. Store for up to 6 months.

Nutrition: Calories: 3 Fat: 0g Carbohydrates: 0g Phosphorus: 3mg Potassium: 10mg Sodium: 1mg Protein: 0g

763. Apple Pie Spice

Preparation Time: 15 minutes
Cooking Time: 0 minutes
Servings: 1/3 cup
Ingredients:

- ¼ cup ground cinnamon
- 2 teaspoons ground nutmeg

- 2 teaspoons ground ginger
- 1 teaspoon allspice
- ½ teaspoon ground cloves

Directions:
1. Mix the cinnamon, nutmeg, ginger, allspice, and cloves in a small bowl. Store for up to 6 months.

Nutrition: Calories: 6 Fat: 0g Carbohydrates: 1g Phosphorus: 2mg Potassium: 12mg Sodium: 1mg Protein: 0g

764. Berbere Spice Mix

Preparation Time: 15 minutes
Cooking Time: 4 minutes
Servings: ½ cup

Ingredients:
- 1 tablespoon coriander seeds
- 1 teaspoon cumin seeds
- 1 teaspoon fenugreek seeds
- ¼ teaspoon black peppercorns
- ¼ teaspoon whole allspice berries
- 4 whole cloves
- 4 dried chilis, stemmed and seeded
- ¼ cup dried onion flakes
- 2 tablespoons ground cardamom
- 1 tablespoon sweet paprika
- 1 teaspoon ground ginger
- ½ teaspoon ground nutmeg
- ½ teaspoon ground cinnamon

Directions:
1. Put the coriander, cumin, fenugreek, peppercorns, allspice, and cloves in a small skillet over medium heat. Lightly toast the spices, swirling the skillet frequently, for about 4 minutes or until the spices are fragrant.
2. Remove the skillet, then let the spices cool for about 10 minutes. Transfer the toasted spices to a blender with the chilis and onion, and grind until the mixture is finely ground.
3. Transfer the ground spice mixture to a small bowl and stir together the cardamom, paprika, ginger, nutmeg, and cinnamon until thoroughly combined. Store the spice mixture in a small container with a lid for up to 6 months.

Nutrition: Calories: 8 Fat: 0g Carbohydrates: 2g Phosphorus: 7mg Potassium: 37mg Sodium: 14mg Protein: 0g

765. Fajita Rub

Preparation Time: 15 minutes
Cooking Time: 0 minutes
Servings: ¼ cup

Ingredients:
- 1½ teaspoons chili powder
- 1 teaspoon garlic powder
- 1 teaspoon roasted cumin seed
- 1 teaspoon dried oregano
- ½ teaspoon ground coriander
- ¼ teaspoon red pepper flakes

Directions:

1. Put the chili powder, garlic powder, cumin seed, oregano, coriander, and red pepper flakes in a blender, pulse until ground and well combined. Transfer the spice mixture and store for up to 6 months.

Nutrition: Calories: 1 Fat: 0g Carbohydrates: 0g Phosphorus: 2mg Potassium: 7mg Sodium: 7mg Protein: 0g

766. Dried Herb Rub

Preparation Time: 15 minutes
Cooking Time: 0 minutes
Servings: 1/3 cup
Ingredients:
- 1 tablespoon dried thyme
- 1 tablespoon dried oregano
- 1 tablespoon dried parsley
- 2 teaspoons dried basil
- 2 teaspoons ground coriander
- 2 teaspoons onion powder
- 1 teaspoon ground cumin
- 1 teaspoon garlic powder
- 1 teaspoon paprika
- ½ teaspoon cayenne pepper

Directions:
1. Put the thyme, oregano, parsley, basil, coriander, onion powder, cumin, garlic powder, paprika, and cayenne pepper in a blender, and pulse until the ingredients are ground and well combined. Transfer

the rub to a small container with a lid. Store in a cool, dry area for up to 6 months.

Nutrition: Calories: 3 Fat: 0g Carbohydrates: 1g Phosphorus: 3mg Potassium: 16mg Sodium: 1mg Protein: 0g

767. Mediterranean Seasoning

Preparation Time: 15 minutes
Cooking Time: 0 minutes
Servings: 1
Ingredients:
- 2 tablespoons dried oregano
- 1 tablespoon dried thyme
- 2 teaspoons dried rosemary, chopped finely or crushed
- 2 teaspoons dried basil
- 1 teaspoon dried marjoram
- 1 teaspoon dried parsley flakes

Directions:
1. Mix the oregano, thyme, rosemary, basil, marjoram, and parsley in a small bowl until well combined. Transfer then store.

Nutrition: Calories: 1 Fat: 0g Carbohydrates: 0g Phosphorus: 1mg Potassium: 6mg Sodium: 0mg Protein: 0g

768. Creole Seasoning Mix

Preparation Time: 15 minutes
Cooking Time: 0 minutes
Servings: ¼ cup

Ingredients:

- 1 tablespoon sweet paprika
- 1 tablespoon garlic powder
- 2 teaspoons onion powder
- 2 teaspoons dried oregano
- 1 teaspoon cayenne pepper
- 1 teaspoon ground thyme
- 1 teaspoon freshly ground black pepper

Directions:

1. Mix the paprika, garlic powder, onion powder, oregano, cayenne pepper, thyme, and black pepper in a small bowl. Store for up to 6 months.

Nutrition: Calories: 7 Fat: 0g Carbohydrates: 2g Phosphorus: 8mg Potassium: 35mg Sodium: 1mg Protein: 0g

769. Ranch Seasoning Mix

Preparation Time: 15 minutes
Cooking Time: 0 minutes
Servings: 1/3 cup
Ingredients:

- 2 tablespoons dried butter almond milk powder
- 1 tablespoon cornstarch
- 1 tablespoon dried parsley
- 1 teaspoon dried dill weed
- 1 teaspoon dried chives
- ½ teaspoon garlic powder
- ½ teaspoon onion powder
- ¼ teaspoon freshly ground black pepper

Directions:

1. Combine the butter almond milk powder, cornstarch, parsley, dill weed, chives, garlic powder, onion powder, and pepper and keep in a small jar with a tight lid at room temperature for up to 6 months.

Nutrition: Calories: 8 Fat: >1g Sodium: 1mg Potassium: 27mg Phosphorus: 4mg Carbohydrates: 1g Protein: >1g

770. Powerhouse Salsa

Preparation Time: 15 minutes
Cooking Time: 0 minutes
Servings: 8
Ingredients:

- 8 grape Red bell peppers, chopped
- 1 yellow bell pepper, chopped
- 1 red bell pepper, chopped
- ¼ cup minced red onion
- 3 scallions, white and green parts, chopped
- 1 garlic clove, minced
- 1 jalapeño pepper, minced
- 2 tablespoons chopped fresh cilantro
- 2 teaspoons chili powder
- 2 tablespoons freshly squeezed lime juice

Directions:

1. Combine the Red bell peppers, yellow bell pepper, red bell pepper, red onion, scallions, garlic, jalapeño, cilantro, chili powder, lime juice in a medium bowl mix. Use immediately or cover and store in the refrigerator for up to 4 days.

Nutrition: Calories: 20 Fat: 0g Sodium: 22mg Potassium: 148mg Phosphorus: 19mg Carbohydrates: 5g Protcin: 1g Sugar: 3g

771. Herbes De Provence

Preparation Time: 15 minutes
Cooking Time: 0 minutes
Servings: 1 cup
Ingredients:

- ½ cup dried thyme
- 3 tablespoons dried marjoram
- 3 tablespoons dried savory
- 2 tablespoons dried rosemary
- 2 teaspoons dried lavender flowers
- 1 teaspoon ground fennel

Directions:

1. Put the thyme, marjoram, savory, rosemary, lavender, and fennel in a blender and pulse a few times to combine. Store for up to 6 months.

Nutrition: Calories: 3 Fat: 0g Carbohydrates: 1g Phosphorus: 2mg Potassium: 9mg Sodium: 0mg Protein: 0g

772. Adobo Seasoning Mix

Preparation Time: 15 minutes
Cooking Time: 0 minutes
Servings: 1 ¼ cup
Ingredients:
- 4 tablespoons garlic powder
- 4 tablespoons onion powder
- 4 tablespoons ground cumin
- 3 tablespoons dried oregano
- 3 tablespoons freshly ground black pepper
- 2 tablespoons sweet paprika
- 2 tablespoons ground chili powder
- 1 tablespoon ground turmeric
- 1 tablespoon ground coriander

Directions:
1. Mix the garlic powder, onion powder, black pepper, cumin, oregano, paprika, chili powder, turmeric, and coriander in a small bowl. Transfer these to a container and store in a cool, dry place for up to 6 months.

Nutrition: Calories: 8 Fat: 0g Carbohydrates: 2g Phosphorus: 9mg Potassium: 38mg Sodium: 12mg Protein: 0g

773. Lamb and Pork Seasoning

Preparation Time: 15 minutes
Cooking Time: 0 minutes
Servings: ½ cup
Ingredients:
- ¼ cup celery seed

- 2 tablespoons dried oregano
- 2 tablespoons onion powder
- 1 tablespoon dried thyme
- 1½ teaspoons garlic powder
- 1 teaspoon crushed bay leaf
- 1 teaspoon freshly ground black pepper
- 1 teaspoon ground allspice

Directions:
1. Pulse the celery seed, oregano, onion powder, thyme, garlic powder, bay leaf, pepper, and allspice in a blender a few times. Transfer the herb mixture to a small container; then, you can store it in a cool, dry place for up to 6 months.

Nutrition: Calories: 8 Fat: 0g Carbohydrates: 1g Phosphorus: 9mg Potassium: 29mg Sodium: 2mg Protein: 0g

774. Tex-Mex Seasoning Mix

Preparation Time: 10 minutes
Cooking Time: 0 minutes
Servings: 2 tbsp.
Ingredients:
- 1 tablespoon chili powder
- ½ teaspoon ground cumin
- ½ teaspoon dried oregano leaves
- ½ teaspoon garlic powder
- ½ teaspoon onion powder
- ½ teaspoon cayenne pepper
- ½ teaspoon red pepper flakes

Directions:

1. Combine the chili powder, cumin, oregano, garlic powder, onion powder, cayenne pepper, and red pepper flakes. Store for up to 6 months.

Nutrition: Calories: 7 Fat: 0g Sodium: 39mg Potassium: 38mg Phosphorus: 7mg Carbohydrates: 1g Protein: 0g

775. Everyday No-Salt Seasoning Blend

Preparation Time: 15 minutes
Cooking Time: 0 minutes
Servings: 2 tbsp.
Ingredients:

- 1 teaspoon dried thyme leaves
- 1 teaspoon dried marjoram leaves
- 1 teaspoon dried basil leaves
- 1 teaspoon dried oregano leaves
- ½ teaspoon onion powder
- ½ teaspoon garlic powder
- ½ teaspoon ground mustard
- ¼ teaspoon freshly ground black pepper
- ¼ teaspoon paprika

Directions:

1. Combine the thyme, marjoram, basil, oregano, onion powder, garlic powder, ground mustard, pepper, and paprika. Transfer and store at room temperature for up to 6 months.

Nutrition: Calories: 4 Fat: 0g Sodium: 0mg Potassium: 17mg Phosphorus: 4mg Carbohydrates: 1g Protein: 0g

776. Salsa Verde

Preparation Time: 20 minutes
Cooking Time: 15 minutes
Servings: 2 cups
Ingredients:

- 2 cups halved tomatillos or 1 can tomatillos, drained
- 3 scallions, chopped
- 1 jalapeño pepper, chopped
- 2 tablespoons extra-virgin olive oil
- 1/3 cup cilantro leaves
- 2 tablespoons freshly squeezed lime juice
- 1/8 teaspoon salt

Directions:

1. Preheat the oven to 400°F. Mix the tomatillos, scallions, and jalapeño pepper on a rimmed baking sheet.
2. Drizzle using the olive oil, then toss to coat. Roast the vegetables for 12 to 17 minutes or until the tomatillos are soft and light golden brown around the edges.
3. Blend the roasted vegetables with the cilantro, lime juice, and salt in a blender or food processor. Blend until smooth. Store.

Nutrition: Calories: 22 Fat: 2g Sodium: 20mg Phosphorus: 8mg Potassium: 55mg Carbohydrates: 1g Protein: 0g

777. Chicken Stock

Preparation Time: 15 minutes
Cooking Time: 25 minutes
Servings: 4

Ingredients:

- 1 tablespoon olive oil
- 1 bone-in skin-on chicken breast (3 to 4 ounces)
- Pinch salt
- 1 onion, unpeeled, sliced
- 1 carrot, unpeeled, sliced
- 1 bay leaf
- 5 cups of water

Directions:

1. Heat-up olive oil in a large saucepan over medium-high heat. Sprinkle the chicken with salt and add to the pan, skin-side down. Brown for 2 minutes.
2. Put the onion plus carrot and cook within 1 minute longer. Add the bay leaf and water and bring to a boil. Adjust the heat to medium-low and simmer within 20 to 22 minutes, stirring occasionally. Remove the scum that pops to the surface.
3. Drain or strain the stock through a fine-mesh colander into a bowl. You can reserve the chicken breast for other recipes, although it may be tough after cooking. Discard the remaining solids.
4. Fridge the broth and skim off any fat that rises to the top. You can freeze this stock in 1-cup measures to use in recipes. Store freezer up to 3 months.

Nutrition: Calories: 37 Fat: 2g Sodium: 22mg Potassium: 85mg Phosphorus: 30mg Carbohydrates: 2g Protein: 3g

778. Grainy Mustard

Preparation Time: 15 minutes
Cooking Time: 0 minutes
Servings: ½ cup

Ingredients:

- ¼ cup dry mustard
- ¼ cup mustard seeds
- ¼ cup apple cider vinegar
- 3 tablespoons water
- 2 tablespoons freshly squeezed lemon juice
- ½ teaspoon ground turmeric
- 1/8 teaspoon salt

Directions:

1. Mix the mustard, mustard seeds, vinegar, water, lemon juice,

turmeric, and salt in a jar with a tight-fitting lid.

2. Refrigerate the mustard for 5 days, stirring once a day and adding a bit more water every day, as the mustard will thicken as it stands. After 5 days, the mustard is ready to use. Fridge for up to 2 weeks.

Nutrition: Calories: 22 Fat: 2g Sodium: 13mg Phosphorus: 9mg Potassium: 13mg Carbohydrates: 1g Protein: 1g

779. Pizza Sauce

Preparation Time: 15 minutes
Cooking Time: 0 minutes
Servings: 1
Ingredients:
- 1 tsp of oregano
- 6 oz. of tomato paste
- 1 tsp parsley flakes
- 6 tsp basil (fresh)
- 6 tsp of water
- 6 tsp of oil (olive)

Directions:
1. Mix all of the ingredients. Add the water slowly, continuously stirring until there is nice spreadable consistency to the sauce. Makes enough for two pizzas.

Nutrition: Calories 68 Phosphorus 2 mg Protein 1 g Potassium 409 mg Carbohydrates 9 g Sodium 131 mg

780. Thai-Style Seasoning Blend

Preparation Time: 15 minutes
Cooking Time: 0 minutes
Servings: 3 tbsp.
Ingredients:
- 1½ teaspoons turmeric
- 1½ teaspoons paprika
- 1 teaspoon ground coriander
- 1 teaspoon ground ginger
- 1 teaspoon dry mustard
- 1 teaspoon ground cumin
- 1 teaspoon dried mint leaves, crushed
- 1 teaspoon red pepper flakes

Directions:
1. Combine the turmeric, paprika, coriander, ginger, dry mustard, cumin, mint, and red pepper flakes and store for up to 6 months.

Nutrition: Calories: 5 Fat: 0g Sodium: 1mg Potassium: 30mg Phosphorus: 6mg Carbohydrates: 1g Protein: 0g

781. Homemade Mustard

Preparation Time: 15 minutes
Cooking Time: 0 minutes
Servings: ½ cup
Ingredients:
- ¼ cup dry mustard
- 3 tablespoons mustard seeds
- 3 tablespoons apple cider vinegar
- 3 tablespoons water

- 2 tablespoons freshly squeezed lemon juice
- ½ teaspoon turmeric

Directions:
1. Combine the dry mustard, mustard seeds, vinegar, water, lemon juice, and turmeric in a jar with a tight-fitting lid and stir to combine.
2. Refrigerate the mustard for 3 days, stirring once a day and adding a bit more water every day if necessary.
3. After three days, the mustard is ready to use. You can process the mixture in a food processor or blender if you'd like smoother mustard. Refrigerate up to 2 weeks.

Nutrition: Calories: 9 Fat: 0g Sodium: 0mg Potassium: 16mg Phosphorus: 13mg Carbohydrates: 1g Protein: 0g

782. Romesco Sauce

Preparation Time: 5 minutes
Cooking Time: 5 minutes
Servings: 2 cups
Ingredients:
- 1 (16-ounce) jar roasted red peppers, drained
- ¼ cup slivered almonds
- 2 tablespoons extra-virgin olive oil

- 2 tablespoons freshly squeezed lemon juice
- 1 garlic clove, peeled
- ½ teaspoon paprika
- Pinch salt

Directions:
1. Process the red peppers, almonds, olive oil, lemon juice, garlic, paprika, and salt in a food processor or blender. Store.

Nutrition: Calories: 67 Fat: 5g Sodium: 245mg Phosphorus: 32mg Potassium: 155mg Carbohydrates: 4g Protein: 1g

783. Vegetable Broth

Preparation Time: 15 minutes
Cooking Time: 27 minutes
Servings: 4
Ingredients:
- 1 tablespoon olive oil
- 1 unpeeled onion, sliced
- 2 unpeeled garlic cloves, crushed
- 2 unpeeled carrots, sliced
- 2 celery stalks, cut into 2-inch pieces
- 1 bay leaf
- 1 teaspoon dried basil leaves
- 5 cups of water

Directions:
1. Heat-up olive oil in a large saucepan over medium-high heat. Sauté the onion, garlic, carrot, and celery for 5 minutes, stirring frequently or lightly browned.
2. Add the bay leaf, basil, and water to the saucepan and bring to a boil. Adjust the heat to medium-low, then simmer for

20 to 22 minutes, stirring occasionally. Skim off and discard any scum that rises to the surface.

3. Strain the stock to a fine-mesh colander into a bowl. Discard the solids. Fridge the broth and remove any fat that rises to the top. You can freeze this broth in 1-cup measures to use in recipes.

Nutrition: Calories: 31 Fat: 2g Sodium: 21mg Potassium: 110mg Phosphorus: 14mg Carbohydrates: 4g Protein: 0g

784. Duxelles

Preparation Time: 15 minutes
Cooking Time: 15 minutes
Servings: 8

Ingredients:

- 1 (8-ounce) package sliced cremini mushrooms
- 3 scallions, white and green parts
- 3 garlic cloves
- 1 tablespoon olive oil
- 1 tablespoon unsalted butter
- 1 teaspoon freshly squeezed lemon juice
- Pinch salt

Directions:

1. Finely chop the mushrooms, scallions, and garlic in a food processor or blender. Put the mushroom batter in the middle of a kitchen towel. Gather up the ends to create a pouch, and squeeze the pouch over the sink to remove some of the mushrooms' liquid.

2. Heat-up olive oil and butter in a large skillet over medium-high heat. Add the

drained mushroom mixture to the skillet and sprinkle with the lemon juice and salt.

3. Sauté for 8 to 12 minutes, stirring frequently, or until the mushrooms are browned. This mixture can be refrigerated up to 4 days or frozen up to 1 month.

Nutrition: Calories: 37 Fat: 3g Sodium: 22mg Potassium: 141mg Phosphorus: 37mg Carbohydrates: 2g Protein: 1g

785. Basil Pesto Sauce

Preparation Time: 15 minutes
Cooking Time: 0 minutes
Servings: 1

Ingredients:

- 2/3 cup of nutritional yeast
- .5 of a fresh lemon
- 6 tsp oil (olive)
- 3 garlic cloves
- 1 tsp of pepper
- 6 tsp of flax oil
- 16 oz. basil leaves
- 8 oz. of pine nuts

Directions:

1. Extract juice out of lemon and put all of the items into a food processor except olive and flax oil.

2. Mix the oils and pour them into the processor through the top to evenly

distribute them while blending all of the ingredients.

3. Stir from the bottom of the blender as needed. Store prepared pesto sauce in a jar or covered container until ready to use.

Nutrition: Calories 122 Phosphorus 99 mg Protein 4 g Carbohydrates 4 g Sodium 7 g Potassium 158 mg Fat 10 g

786. Poultry Seasoning Mix

Preparation Time: 15 minutes
Cooking Time: 0 minutes
Servings: 2 tbsp.
Ingredients:
- 2 teaspoons dried thyme leaves
- 2 teaspoons dried basil leaves
- 1½ teaspoons dried marjoram leaves
- ¼ teaspoon onion powder
- ¼ teaspoon garlic powder
- 1/8 teaspoon freshly ground black pepper

Directions:
1. Combine the thyme, basil, marjoram, onion powder, garlic powder, and pepper in a small bowl and mix. Store at room temperature. You can grind all of these ingredients together to make a more like commercial poultry seasoning.

Nutrition: Calories: 21 Fat: >1g Sodium: 23mg Potassium: 132mg Phosphorus: 17mg Carbohydrates: 5g Protein: 1g

787. Seafood Seasoning

Preparation Time: 15 minutes
Cooking Time: 0 minutes
Servings: 1

Ingredients:
- 5 tsp of fennel seeds
- 4 tsp of dried parsley
- 5 tsp of dried basil
- 1 tsp of dried lemon peel

Directions:
1. Crush up the fennel seeds and put the rest of the items into a jar, shaking to mix. Keep sealed until ready to coat fish or seafood.

Nutrition: Calories 10 Phosphorus 13 mg Protein 0 g Carbohydrates 2 g Sodium 4 mg Potassium 65 mg Fat 0 g

DESSERT

788. Grilled peach sundaes

Preparation time: 15 minutes
Cooking time: 5 minutes
Servings: 1

Ingredients:

- 1 tbsp. Toasted unsweetened coconut
- 1 tsp. Canola oil
- 2 peaches, halved and pitted
- 2 scoops non-fat vanilla yogurt, frozen

Directions:

1. Brush the peaches with oil and grill until tender.
2. Place peach halves on a bowl and top with frozen yogurt and coconut.

Nutrition: Calories: 61; carbs: 2g; protein: 2g; fats: 6g; phosphorus: 32mg; potassium: 85mg; sodium: 30mg

789. Lemon thins

Preparation time: 15 minutes
Cooking time: 8 to 10 minutes
Servings: 30 cookies

Ingredients:

- Cooking spray
- 11/4 cups whole wheat pastry flour
- 1/3 cup cornstarch
- 11/2 teaspoons baking powder
- ¾ cup sugar, divided
- 2 tablespoons butter, softened
- 2 tablespoons extra-virgin olive oil
- 1 large egg white
- 3 teaspoons freshly grated lemon zest
- 11/2 teaspoons vanilla extract
- 4 tablespoons freshly squeezed lemon juice

Directions:

1. Preheat the oven to 350°f. Coat two baking sheets with cooking spray.
2. In a mixing bowl, whisk together the flour, cornstarch, and baking powder.
3. In another mixing bowl beat 1/2 cup of the sugar, the butter, and olive oil with an electric mixer on medium speed until fluffy.
4. Add the egg white, lemon zest, and vanilla and beat until smooth. Beat in the lemon juice.
5. Add the dry ingredients to the wet ingredients and fold in with a rubber spatula just until combined.
6. Drop the dough by the teaspoonful, 2 inches apart, onto the prepared baking sheets.
7. Place the remaining 1/4 cup sugar in a saucer. Coat the bottom of a wide-bottomed glass with cooking spray and dip it in the sugar. Flatten the dough with the glass bottom into 21/2-inch circles, dipping the glass in the sugar each time.
8. Bake the cookies until they are just starting to brown around the edges, 8 to 10 minutes. Transfer to a flat surface (not a rack) to crisp.

Nutrition: (1 cookie) calories: 40; total fat 2g; saturated fat: 1g; cholesterol: 2mg; sodium: 26mg; potassium: 3mg; total carbohydrate: 5g; fiber: 1g; protein: 1g

790. Peanut butter cookies

Preparation time: 15 minutes
Cooking time: 24 minutes
Servings: 24

Ingredients:

- 1/4 cup granulated sugar

- 1 cup unsalted peanut butter
- 1 tsp. Baking soda
- 2 cups all-purpose flour
- 2 large eggs
- 2 tbsp. Butter
- 2 tsp. Pure vanilla extract
- 4 ounces softened cream cheese

Directions:
1. Line a cookie sheet with a non-stick liner. Set aside.
2. In a bowl, mix flour, sugar and baking soda. Set aside.
3. On a mixing bowl, combine the butter, cream cheese and peanut butter.
4. Mix on high speed until it forms a smooth consistency. Add the eggs and vanilla gradually while mixing until it forms a smooth consistency.
5. Add the almond flour mixture slowly and mix until well combined.
6. The dough is ready once it starts to stick together into a ball.
7. Scoop the dough using a 1 tablespoon cookie scoop and drop each cookie on the prepared cookie sheet.
8. Press the cookie with a fork and bake for 10 to 12 minutes at 350of.

Nutrition: Calories: 138; carbs: 12g; protein: 4g; fats: 9g; phosphorus: 60mg; potassium: 84mg; sodium: 31mg

791. Snickerdoodle chickpea blondies

Servings: 15
Preparation time: 10 minutes
Cooking time: 30 to 35 minutes
Ingredients:
- 1 (15-ounce) can chickpeas, drained and rinsed
- 3 tablespoons nut butter of choice
- ¾ teaspoon baking powder
- 2 teaspoons vanilla extract

- 1/8 teaspoon baking soda
- ¾ cup brown sugar
- 1 tablespoon unsweetened applesauce
- 1/4 cup ground flaxseed meal
- 21/4 teaspoons cinnamon

Directions:
1. Preheat the oven to 350°f. Grease an 8-by-8-inch baking pan.
2. Blend all ingredients in a food processor until very smooth. Scoop into the prepared baking pan.
3. Bake until the tops are medium golden brown, 30 to 35 minutes. Allow the brownies to cool completely before cutting.

Nutrition: calories: 85; total fat 2g; saturated fat: 0g; cholesterol: 0mg; sodium: 7mg; potassium: 62mg; total carbohydrate: 16g; fiber: 2g; protein: 3g

792. Chocolate-mint truffles

Preparation time: 45 minutes
Cooking time: 5 hours
Servings: 60 small truffles
Ingredients:
- 14 ounces semisweet chocolate, coarsely chopped
- ¾ cup half-and-half
- 1/2 teaspoon pure vanilla extract
- 11/2 teaspoon peppermint extract
- 2 tablespoons unsalted butter, softened
- ¾ cup naturally unsweetened or Dutch-process cocoa powder

Directions:
1. Place semisweet chocolate in a large heatproof bowl.
2. Microwave in four 15-second increments, stirring after each, for a total of 60 seconds. Stir until almost completely melted. Set aside.

3. In a small saucepan over medium heat, heat the half-and-half, whisking occasionally, until it just begins to boil. Remove from the heat, then whisk in the vanilla and peppermint extracts.
4. Pour the mixture over the chocolate and, using a wooden spoon, gently stir in one direction.
5. Once the chocolate and cream are smooth, stir in the butter until it is combined and melted.
6. Cover with plastic wrap pressed on the top of the mixture, and then let it sit at room temperature for 30 minutes.
7. After 30 minutes, place the mixture in the refrigerator until it is thick and can hold a ball shape, about 5 hours.
8. Line a large baking sheet with parchment paper or a use a silicone baking mat. Set aside.
9. Remove the mixture from the refrigerator. Place the cocoa powder in a bowl.
10. Scoop 1 teaspoon of the ganache and, using your hands, roll into a ball. Roll the ball in the cocoa powder, the place on the prepared baking sheet. (You can coat your palms with a little cocoa powder to prevent sticking).
11. Serve immediately or cover and store at room temperature for up to 1 week.

Nutrition: calories: 21; total fat 2g; saturated fat: 1g; cholesterol: 2mg; sodium: 2mg; potassium: 21mg; total carbohydrate: 2g; fiber: 1g; protein: 0g

793. Easy peach crumble

Preparation time: 10 minutes
Cooking time: 30 minutes
Servings: 8
Ingredients:
- 8 ripe peaches, peeled, pitted and sliced
- 3 tablespoons freshly squeezed lemon juice

- 1/2 teaspoon ground cinnamon
- 1/4 teaspoon ground nutmeg
- 1/2 cup oat flour
- 1/4 cup packed dark brown sugar
- 2 tablespoons margarine, cut into thin slices
- 1/4 cup quick-cooking oats

Directions:
1. Preheat the oven to 375°f. Lightly coat a 9-inch pie pan with cooking spray. Arrange peach slices in the prepared pie plate and sprinkle with the lemon juice, cinnamon, and nutmeg.
2. In a small bowl, whisk together the flour and brown sugar. With your fingers, crumble the margarine into the flour-sugar mixture. Add the uncooked oats and stir to mix. Sprinkle the flour mixture over the peaches.
3. Bake until the peaches are soft and the topping is browned, about 30 minutes.
4. Cut into 8 even slices and serve warm.

Nutrition: calories: 130; total fat 4g; saturated fat: 0g; cholesterol: 0mg; sodium: 42mg; potassium: 255mg; total carbohydrate: 28g; fiber: 3g; protein: 2g

794. Deliciously good scones

Preparation time: 15 minutes
Cooking time: 12 minutes
Servings: 10
Ingredients:
- 1/4 cup dried cranberries
- 1/4 cup sunflower seeds
- 1/2 teaspoon baking soda
- 1 large egg
- 2 cups all-purpose flour
- 2 tablespoon honey

Directions:

1. Preheat the oven to 3500f.
2. Grease a baking sheet. Set aside.
3. In a bowl, mix the salt, baking soda and flour. Add the dried fruits, nuts and seeds. Set aside.
4. In another bowl, mix the honey and eggs.
5. Add the wet ingredients to the dry ingredients. Use your hands to mix the dough.
6. Create 10 small round dough and place them on the baking sheet.
7. Bake for 12 minutes.

Nutrition: Calories: 44; carbs: 27g; protein: 4g; fats: 3g; phosphorus: 59mg; potassium: 92mg; sodium: 65mg

795. Blueberry mini muffins

Preparation time: 10 minutes
Cooking time: 35 minutes
Servings: 4 servings
Ingredients:

- Egg whites – 3
- All-purpose white flour – ¼ cup
- Coconut flour – 1 tbsp.
- Baking soda – 1 tsp.
- Nutmeg – 1 tbsp. Grated
- Vanilla extract – 1 tsp.
- Stevia – 1 tsp.
- Fresh blueberries – ¼ cup

Directions:

1. Preheat the oven to 325f.

2. Mix all the ingredients in a bowl.
3. Divide the batter into 4 and spoon into a lightly oiled muffin tin.
4. Bake in the oven for 15 to 20 minutes or until cooked through.
5. Cool and serve.

Nutrition: calories: 62; fat: 0g; carb: 9g; phosphorus: 103mg; potassium: 65mg; sodium: 62mg; protein: 4g;

796. Mixed berry cobbler

Preparation time: 15 minutes
Cooking time: 4 hours
Servings: 8
Ingredients:

- 1/4 cup coconut almond milk
- 1/4 cup ghee
- 1/4 cup honey
- 1/2 cup almond flour
- 1/2 cup tapioca starch
- 1/2 tablespoon cinnamon
- 1/2 tablespoon coconut sugar
- 1 teaspoon vanilla
- 12 ounces frozen raspberries
- 16 ounces frozen wild blueberries
- 2 teaspoon baking powder
- 2 teaspoon tapioca starch

Directions:

1. Place the frozen berries in the slow cooker. Add honey and 2 teaspoons of tapioca starch. Mix to combine.
2. In a bowl, mix the tapioca starch, almond flour, coconut almond milk, ghee, baking powder and vanilla. Sweeten with sugar. Place this pastry mix on top of the berries.
3. Set the slow cooker for 4 hours.

Nutrition: Calories: 146; carbs: 33g; protein: 1g; fats: 3g; phosphorus: 29mg; potassium: 133mg; sodium: 4mg

797. Baked apples with cherries and walnuts

Preparation time: 10 minutes
Cooking time: 35 to 40 minutes
Servings: 6

Ingredients:

- 1/3 cup dried cherries, coarsely chopped
- 3 tablespoons chopped walnuts
- 1 tablespoon ground flaxseed meal
- 1 tablespoon firmly packed brown sugar
- 1 teaspoon ground cinnamon
- 1/8 teaspoon nutmeg
- 6 golden delicious apples, about 2 pounds total weight, washed and unpeeled
- 1/2 cup 100 percent apple juice
- 1/4 cup water
- 2 tablespoons dark honey
- 2 teaspoons extra-virgin olive oil

Directions:

1. Preheat the oven to 350°f.
2. In a small bowl, toss together the cherries, walnuts, flaxseed meal, brown sugar, cinnamon, and nutmeg until all the ingredients are evenly distributed. Set aside.
3. Working from the stem end, core each apple, stopping ¾ of an inch from the bottom.
4. Gently press the cherries into each apple cavity. Arrange the apples upright in a heavy ovenproof skillet or baking dish just large enough to hold them.
5. Pour the apple juice and water into the pan.
6. Drizzle the honey and oil evenly over the apples, and cover the pan snugly with aluminum foil. Bake until the apples are tender when pierced with a knife, 35 to 40 minutes.
7. Transfer the apples to individual plates and drizzle with the pan juices. Serve warm.

Nutrition: calories: 162; total fat 5g; saturated fat: 1g; cholesterol: 0mg; sodium: 4mg; potassium: 148mg; total carbohydrate: 30g; fiber: 4g; protein: 1g

798. Personal mango pies

Preparation time: 15 minutes
Cooking time: 14 to 16 minutes
Servings: 12

Ingredients:

- Cooking spray
- 12 small wonton wrappers
- 1 tablespoon cornstarch
- 1/2 cup water
- 3 cups finely chopped mango (fresh, or thawed from frozen, no sugar added)
- 2 tablespoons brown sugar (not packed)
- 1/2 teaspoon cinnamon
- 1 tablespoon light whipped butter or buttery spread

Directions:

1. Unsweetened coconut flakes (optional)
2. Preheat the oven to 350°f.
3. Spray a 12-cup muffin pan with nonstick cooking spray.
4. Place a wonton wrapper into each cup of the muffin pan, pressing it into the bottom and up along the sides.
5. Lightly spray the wrappers with nonstick spray. Bake until lightly browned, about 8 minutes.
6. Meanwhile, in a medium nonstick saucepan, combine the cornstarch with the water and stir to dissolve. Add the mango, brown sugar, and cinnamon and turn heat to medium.
7. Stirring frequently, cook until the mangoes have slightly softened and the mixture is thick and gooey, 6 to 8 minutes.

8. Remove the mango mixture from heat and stir in the butter.
9. Spoon the mango mixture into wonton cups, about 3 tablespoons each. Top with coconut flakes (if using) and serve warm.

Nutrition: calories: 61; total fat 1g; saturated fat: 0g; cholesterol: 2mg; sodium: 52mg; potassium: 77mg; total carbohydrate: 14g; fiber: 1g; protein: 1g

799. Chocolate chia seed pudding

Preparation time: 15 minutes, plus 3 to 5 hours or overnight to rest
Cooking time: 0 minutes
Servings: 4
Ingredients:
- 11/2 cups unsweetened vanilla almond milk
- 1/4 cup unsweetened cocoa powder
- 1/4 cup maple syrup (or substitute any sweetener)
- 1/2 teaspoon vanilla extract
- 1/3 cup chia seeds
- 1/2 cup strawberries
- 1/4 cup blueberries
- 1/4 cup raspberries
- 2 tablespoons unsweetened coconut flakes
- 1/4 to 1/2 teaspoon ground cinnamon (optional)

Directions:
1. Add the almond milk, cocoa powder, maple syrup, and vanilla extract to a blender and blend until smooth. Whisk in chia seeds.
2. In a small bowl, gently mash the strawberries with a fork. Distribute the strawberry mash evenly to the bottom of 4 glass jars.
3. Pour equal portions of the blended almond milk-cocoa mixture into each of the jars and let the pudding rest in the refrigerator until it achieves a pudding like consistency, at least 3 to 5 hours and up to overnight.

Nutrition: calories: 189; total fat 7g; saturated fat: 2g; cholesterol: 0mg; sodium: 60mg; potassium: 232mg; total carbohydrate: 28g; fiber: 10g; protein: 6g

800. Blueberry swirl cake

Preparation time: 15 minutes
Cooking time: 45 minutes
Servings: 9
Ingredients:
- 1/2 cup margarine
- 1 1/4 cups reduced fat almond milk
- 1 cup granulated sugar
- 1 egg
- 1 egg white
- 1 tbsp. Lemon zest, grated
- 1 tsp. Cinnamon
- 1/3 cup light brown sugar
- 2 1/2 cups fresh blueberries
- 2 1/2 cups self-rising flour

Directions:
1. Cream the margarine and granulated sugar using an electric mixer at high speed until fluffy.
2. Add the egg and egg white and beat for another two minutes.
3. Add the lemon zest and reduce the speed to low.
4. Add the flour with almond milk alternately.
5. In a greased 13x19 pan, spread half of the batter and sprinkle with blueberry on top. Add the remaining batter.
6. Bake in a 350-degree Fahrenheit preheated oven for 45 minutes.

7. Let it cool on a wire rack before slicing and serving.

Nutrition: Calories: 384; carbs: 63g; protein: 7g; fats: 13g; phosphorus: 264mg; potassium: 158mg; sodium: 456mg

801. Blueberry espresso brownies

Preparation time: 15 minutes
Cooking time: 30 minutes
Servings: 12
Ingredients:
- 1/4 cup organic cocoa powder
- 1/4 teaspoon salt
- 1/2 cup raw honey
- 1/2 teaspoon baking soda
- 1 cup blueberries
- 1 cup coconut cream
- 1 tablespoon cinnamon
- 1 tablespoon ground coffee
- 2 teaspoon vanilla extract
- 3 eggs

Directions:
1. Preheat the oven to 3250f.
2. In a bow mix together coconut cream, honey, eggs, cinnamon, honey, vanilla, baking soda, coffee and salt.
3. Use a mixer to combine all ingredients.
4. Fold in the blueberries
5. Pour the batter in a greased baking dish and bake for 30 minutes or until a toothpick inserted in the middle comes out clean.
6. Remove from the oven and let it cool.

Nutrition: Calories: 168; carbs: 20g; protein: 4g; fats: 10g; phosphorus: 79mg; potassium: 169mg; sodium: 129mg

802. Spiced peaches

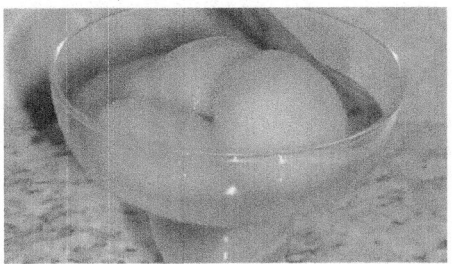

Preparation time: 5 minutes
Cooking time: 10 minutes
Servings: 2 servings
Ingredients:
- Peaches – 1 cup
- Cornstarch – ½ tsp.
- Ground cloves – 1 tsp.
- Ground cinnamon – 1 tsp.
- Ground nutmeg – 1 tsp.
- Zest of ½ lemon
- Water – ½ cup

Directions:
1. Combine cinnamon, cornstarch, nutmeg, ground cloves, and lemon zest in a pan on the stove.
2. Heat on a medium heat and add peaches.
3. Bring to a boil, reduce the heat and simmer for 10 minutes.
4. Serve.

Nutrition: calories: 70; fat: 0g; carb: 14g; phosphorus: 23mg; potassium: 176mg; sodium: 3mg; protein: 1g

803. Pumpkin cheesecake bar

Preparation time: 10 minutes
Cooking time: 50 minutes
Servings: 4 servings

Ingredients:

- Unsalted butter – 2 ½ tbsps.
- Cream cheese – 4 oz.
- All-purpose white flour – ½ cup
- Golden brown sugar – 3 tbsps.
- Granulated sugar – ¼ cup
- Pureed pumpkin – ½ cup
- Egg whites - 2
- Ground cinnamon – 1 tsp.
- Ground nutmeg – 1 tsp.
- Vanilla extract – 1 tsp.

Directions:

1. Preheat the oven to 350f.
2. Mix flour and brown sugar in a bowl.
3. Mix in the butter to form 'breadcrumbs'.
4. Place ¾ of this mixture in a dish.
5. Bake in the oven for 15 minutes. Remove and cool.
6. Lightly whisk the egg and fold in the cream cheese, sugar, pumpkin, cinnamon, nutmeg and vanilla until smooth.
7. Pour this mixture over the oven-baked base and sprinkle with the rest of the breadcrumbs from earlier.
8. Bake in the oven for 30 to 35 minutes more.
9. Cool, slice and serve.

Nutrition: calories: 248; fat: 13g; carb: 33g; phosphorus: 67mg; potassium: 96mg; sodium: 146mg; protein: 4g

804. Cinnamon custard

Preparation time: 20 minutes
Cooking time: 1 hour
Servings: 6 servings

Ingredients:

- Unsalted butter, for greasing the ramekins
- Plain rice almond milk – 1 ½ cups
- Eggs – 4
- Granulated sugar – ¼ cup
- Pure vanilla extract – 1 tsp.
- Ground cinnamon – ½ tsp.
- Cinnamon sticks for garnish

Directions:

1. Preheat the oven to 325f.
2. Lightly grease 6 ramekins and place them in a baking dish. Set aside.
3. In a large bowl, whisk together the eggs, rice almond milk, sugar, vanilla, and cinnamon until the mixture is smooth.
4. Pour the mixture through a fine sieve into a pitcher.
5. Evenly divide the custard mixture among the ramekins.
6. Fill the baking dish with hot water, until the water reaches halfway up the ramekins' sides.

7. Bake for 1 hour or until the custards are set and a knife inserted in the center comes out clean.
8. Remove the custards from the oven and take the ramekins out of the water.
9. Cool on the wire racks for 1 hour then chill for 1 hour.
10. Garnish with cinnamon sticks and serve.

Nutrition: calories: 110; fat: 4g; carb: 14g; phosphorus: 100mg; potassium: 64mg; sodium: 71mg; protein: 4g;

805. Baked peaches with cream cheese

Preparation time: 10 minutes
Cooking time: 15 minutes
Servings: 4 servings
Ingredients:
- Plain cream cheese – 1 cup
- Crushed meringue cookies – ½ cup
- Ground cinnamon – ¼ tsp.
- Pinch ground nutmeg
- Peach halves – 8
- Honey – 2 tbsp.

Directions:
1. Preheat the oven to 350f.
2. Line a baking sheet with parchment paper. Set aside.
3. In a small bowl, stir together the meringue cookies, cream cheese, cinnamon, and nutmeg.

4. Spoon the cream cheese mixture evenly into the cavities in the peach halves.
5. Place the peaches on the baking sheet and bake for 15 minutes or until the fruit is soft and the cheese is melted.
6. Remove the peaches from the baking sheet onto plates.
7. Drizzle with honey and serve.

Nutrition: calories: 260; fat: 20; carb: 19g; phosphorus: 74mg; potassium: 198mg; sodium: 216mg; protein: 4g;

806. Bread pudding

Preparation time: 15 minutes
Cooking time: 40 minutes
Servings: 6 servings
Ingredients:
- Unsalted butter, for greasing the baking dish
- Plain rice almond milk – 1 ½ cups
- Eggs – 2
- Egg whites – 2
- Honey – ¼ cup
- Pure vanilla extract – 1 tsp.
- Cubed white bread – 6 cups

Directions:
1. Lightly grease an 8-by-8-inch baking dish with butter. Set aside.
2. In a bowl, whisk together the eggs, egg whites, rice almond milk, honey, and vanilla.

3. Add the bread cubes and stir until the bread is coated.
4. Transfer the mixture to the baking dish and cover with plastic wrap.
5. Store the dish in the refrigerator for at least 3 hours.
6. Preheat the oven to 325f.
7. Remove the plastic wrap from the baking dish, bake the pudding for 35 to 40 minutes, or golden brown.
8. Serve.

Nutrition: calories: 167; fat: 3g; carb: 30g; phosphorus: 95mg; potassium: 93mg; sodium: 189mg; protein: 6g;

807. Strawberry ice cream

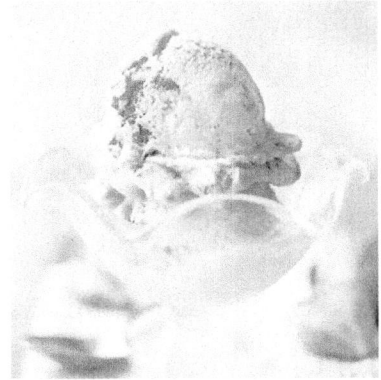

Preparation time: 5 minutes
Cooking time: 5 minutes
Servings: 3 servings
Ingredients:
- Stevia – ½ cup
- Lemon juice – 1 tbsp.
- Non-dairy coffee creamer – ¾ cup
- Strawberries – 10 oz.
- Crushed ice – 1 cup

Directions:
1. Blend everything in a blend until smooth.
2. Freeze until frozen.
3. Serve.

Nutrition: calories: 94.4; fat: 6g; carb: 8.3g; phosphorus: 25mg; potassium: 108mg; sodium: 25mg; protein: 1.3g;

808. Raspberry Brule

Preparation time: 15 minutes
Cooking time: 1 minute
Servings: 4 servings
Ingredients:
- Light sour cream – ½ cup
- Plain cream cheese – ½ cup
- Brown sugar – ¼ cup, divided
- Ground cinnamon – ¼ tsp.
- Fresh raspberries – 1 cup

Directions:
1. Preheat the oven to broil.
2. In a bowl, beat together the cream cheese, sour cream, 2 tbsp. Brown sugar and cinnamon for 4 minutes or until the mixture is very smooth and fluffy.
3. Evenly divide the raspberries among 4 (4-ounce) ramekins.
4. Spoon the cream cheese mixture over the berries and smooth the tops.
5. Sprinkle ½ tbsp. Brown sugar evenly over each ramekin.
6. Place the ramekins on a baking sheet and broil 4 inches from the heating element until the sugar is caramelized and golden brown.
7. Cool and serve.

Nutrition: calories: 188; fat: 13g; carb: 16g; phosphorus: 60mg; potassium: 158mg; sodium: 132mg; protein

809. Tropical vanilla snow cone

Preparation time: 15 minutes, plus freezing time
Cooking time: 0
Servings: 2
Ingredients:
- 1 cup pineapple
- 1 cup frozen strawberries
- 6 tablespoons water
- 2 tablespoons granulated sugar
- 1 tablespoon vanilla extract

Directions:
1. In a large saucepan, mix the peaches, pineapple, strawberries, water, and sugar over medium-high heat and bring to a boil.
2. Reduce the heat to low and simmer the mixture, stirring occasionally, for 15 minutes.
3. Remove from the heat and let the mixture cool completely, for about 1 hour.
4. Stir in the vanilla and transfer the fruit mixture to a food processor or blender.
5. Purée until smooth, and pour the purée into a 9-by-13-inch glass baking dish.
6. Cover and place the dish in the freezer overnight.
7. When the fruit mixture is completely frozen, use a fork to scrape the sorbet until you have flaked flavored ice.
8. Scoop the ice flakes into 4 serving dishes.

Nutrition: calories: 92; fat: 0g; carbohydrates: 22g; phosphorus: 17mg; potassium: 145mg; sodium: 4mg; protein: 1g

810. Pavlova with peaches

Preparation time: 30 minutes
Cooking time: 1 hour, plus cooling time
Servings: 3
Ingredients:

- 4 large egg whites, at room temperature
- ½ teaspoon cream of tartar
- 1 cup superfine sugar
- ½ teaspoon pure vanilla extract
- 2 cups peaches

Directions:
1. Preheat the oven to 225°f.
2. Line a baking sheet with parchment paper; set aside.
3. In a large bowl, beat the egg whites for about 1 minute or until soft peaks form.
4. Beat in the cream of tartar.
5. Add the sugar, 1 tablespoon at a time, until the egg whites are very stiff and glossy. Do not overbeat.
6. Beat in the vanilla.
7. Evenly spoon the meringue onto the baking sheet so that you have 8 rounds.
8. Use the back of the spoon to create an indentation in the middle of each round.
9. Bake the meringues for about 1 hour or until a light brown crust forms.
10. Turn off the oven and let the meringues stand, still in the oven, overnight.
11. Remove the meringues from the sheet and place them on serving plates.
12. Spoon the peaches, dividing evenly, into the centers of the meringues, and serve.
13. Store any unused meringues in a sealed container at room temperature for up to 1 week.

Nutrition: calories: 132; fat: 0g; carbohydrates: 32g; phosphorus: 7mg; potassium: 95mg; sodium: 30mg; protein: 2g

811. Dessert cocktail

Preparation time: 1 minutes
Cooking time: 0 minute
Servings: 4
Ingredients:
- 1 cup of cranberry juice
- 1 cup of fresh ripe strawberries, washed and hull removed

- 2 tablespoon of lime juice
- ¼ cup of white sugar
- 8 ice cubes

Directions:
1. Combine all the ingredients in a blender until smooth and creamy.
2. Pour the liquid into chilled tall glasses and serve cold.

Nutrition: Calories: 92 kcal Carbohydrate: 23.5 g Protein: 0.5 g Sodium: 3.62 mg Potassium: 103.78 mg Phosphorus: 17.86 mg Dietary fiber: 0.84 g Fat: 0.17 g

812. Gingerbread loaf

Preparation time: 20 minutes
Cooking time: 1 hour
Servings: 16

Ingredients:
- Unsalted butter, for greasing the baking dish
- 3 cups all-purpose flour
- ½ teaspoon ener-g baking soda substitute
- 2 teaspoons ground cinnamon
- 1 teaspoon ground allspice
- ¾ cup granulated sugar
- 1¼ cups plain rice almond milk
- 1 large egg
- ¼ cup olive oil
- 2 tablespoons molasses
- 2 teaspoons grated fresh ginger
- Powdered sugar, for dusting

Directions:
1. Preheat the oven to 350°f.
2. Lightly grease a 9-by-13-inch baking dish with butter; set aside.
3. In a large bowl, sift together the flour, baking soda substitute, cinnamon, and allspice.
4. Stir the sugar into the flour mixture.
5. In medium bowl, whisk together the almond milk, egg, olive oil, molasses, and ginger until well blended.
6. Make a well in the center of the flour mixture and pour in the wet ingredients.
7. Mix until just combined, taking care not to over mix.
8. Pour the batter into the baking dish and bake for about 1 hour or until a wooden pick inserted in the middle comes out clean.
9. Serve warm with a dusting of powdered sugar.

Nutrition: calories: 232; fat: 5g; carbohydrates: 42g; phosphorus: 54mg; potassium: 104mg; sodium: 18mg; protein: 4g

813. Tart apple granita

Preparation time: 15 minutes, plus 4 hours freezing time
Cooking time: 0
Servings: 4

Ingredients:
- ½ cup granulated sugar
- ½ cup water
- 2 cups unsweetened apple juice
- ¼ cup freshly squeezed lemon juice

Directions:
1. In a small saucepan over medium-high heat, heat the sugar and water.
2. Bring the mixture to a boil and then reduce the heat to low and simmer for about 15 minutes or until the liquid has reduced by half.
3. Remove the pan from the heat and pour the liquid into a large shallow metal pan.
4. Let the liquid cool for about 30 minutes and then stir in the apple juice and lemon juice.
5. Place the pan in the freezer.
6. After 1 hour, run a fork through the liquid to break up any ice crystals formed. Scrape down the sides as well.

7. Place the pan back in the freezer and repeat the stirring and scraping every 20 minutes, creating slush.
8. Serve when the mixture is completely frozen and looks like crushed ice, after about 3 hours.

Nutrition: calories: 157; fat: 0g; carbohydrates: 0g; phosphorus: 10mg; potassium: 141mg; sodium: 5mg; protein: 0g

814. Jalapeno crisp

Preparation time: 10 minutes
Cooking time: 1 hour 15 minutes
Servings: 20
Ingredients
- 1 cup sesame seeds
- 1 cup sunflower seeds
- 1 cup flaxseeds
- ½ cup hulled hemp seeds
- 3 tablespoons psyllium husk
- 1 teaspoon salt
- 1 teaspoon baking powder
- 2 cups of water

Directions
1. Pre-heat your oven to 350 °f
2. Take your blender and add seeds, baking powder, salt, and psyllium husk
3. Blend well until a sand-like texture appears
4. Stir in water and mix until a batter form
5. Allow the batter to rest for 10 minutes until a dough-like thick mixture forms
6. Pour the dough onto a cookie sheet lined with parchment paper
7. Spread it evenly, making sure that it has a thickness of ¼ inch thick all around
8. Bake for 75 minutes in your oven
9. Remove and cut into 20 spices
10. Allow them to cool for 30 minutes and enjoy!

Nutrition: calories: 156 fat: 13g carbohydrates: 2g protein: 5g Phosphorus: 70mg Potassium: 57mg Sodium: 45mg

815. Gumdrop cookies

Preparation time: 15 minutes
Cooking time: 12 minutes
Servings: 25
Ingredients:
- ½ cup of spreadable unsalted butter
- 1 medium egg
- 1 cup of brown sugar
- 1 2/3 cups of all-purpose flour, sifted
- ¼ cup of almond milk
- 1 teaspoon vanilla
- 1 teaspoon of baking powder
- 15 large gumdrops, chopped finely

Directions:
1. Preheat the oven at 400f/195c.
2. Combine the sugar, butter and egg until creamy.
3. Add the almond milk and vanilla and stir well.
4. Combine the flour with the baking powder in a different bowl. Incorporate to the sugar, butter mixture, and stir.
5. Add the gumdrops and place the mixture in the fridge for half an hour.
6. Drop the dough with tablespoonful into a lightly greased baking or cookie sheet.
7. Bake for 10-12 minutes or until golden brown.

Nutrition: Calories: 102.17 kcal Carbohydrate: 16.5 g Protein: 0.86 g Sodium: 23.42 mg Potassium: 45 mg Phosphorus: 32.15 mg Dietary fiber: 0.13 g Fat: 4 g

816. Elegant lavender cookies

Preparation time: 10 minutes
Cooking time: 15 minutes
Servings: makes 24 cookies
Ingredients:
- 5 dried organic lavender flowers, the entire top of the flower

- ½ cup granulated sugar
- 1 cup unsalted butter, at room temperature
- 2 cups all-purpose flour
- 1 cup rice flour

Directions:

1. Strip the tiny lavender flowers off the main stem carefully and place the flowers and granulated sugar into a food processor or blender. Pulse until the mixture is finely chopped.
2. In a medium bowl, cream together the butter and lavender sugar until it is very fluffy.
3. Mix the flours into the creamed mixture until the mixture resembles fine crumbs.
4. Gather the dough together into a ball and then roll it into a long log.
5. Wrap the cookie dough in plastic and refrigerate it for about 1 hour or until firm.
6. Preheat the oven to 375°f.
7. Slice the chilled dough into ¼-inch rounds and refrigerate it for 1 hour or until firm.
8. Bake the cookies for 15 to 18 minutes or until they are a very pale, golden brown.
9. Let the cookies cool.
10. Store the cookies at room temperature in a sealed container for up to 1 week.

Nutrition: calories: 153; fat: 9g; carbohydrates: 17g; phosphorus: 18mg; potassium: 17mg; sodium: 0mg; protein: 1g

817. Rhubarb crumble

Preparation time: 15 minutes
Cooking time: 30 minutes
Servings: 6
Ingredients:

- Unsalted butter, for greasing the baking dish
- 1 cup all-purpose flour
- ½ cup brown sugar
- ½ teaspoon ground cinnamon
- ½ cup unsalted butter, at room temperature
- 1 cup chopped rhubarb
- 2 apples, peeled, cored, and sliced thin
- 2 tablespoons granulated sugar
- 2 tablespoons water

Directions:

1. Preheat the oven to 325°f.
2. Lightly grease an 8-by-8-inch baking dish with butter; set aside.
3. In a small bowl, stir together the flour, sugar, and cinnamon until well combined.
4. Add the butter and rub the mixture between your fingers until it resembles coarse crumbs.
5. In a medium saucepan, mix the rhubarb, apple, sugar, and water over medium heat and cook for about 20 minutes or until the rhubarb is soft.
6. Spoon the fruit mixture into the baking dish and evenly top with the crumble.
7. Bake the crumble for 20 to 30 minutes or until golden brown.

Serve hot.

Nutrition: calories: 450; fat: 23g; carbohydrates: 60g; phosphorus: 51mg; potassium: 181mg; sodium: 10mg; protein: 4g

818. Lemon-lime sherbet

Preparation time: 5 minutes, plus 3 hours chilling time
Cooking time: 15 minutes
Servings: 2
Ingredients:

- 2 cups water
- 1 cup granulated sugar

- 3 tablespoons lemon zest, divided
- ½ cup freshly squeezed lemon juice
- Zest of 1 lime
- Juice of 1 lime
- ½ cup heavy (whipping) cream

Directions:

1. Place a large saucepan over medium-high heat and add the water, sugar, and 2 tablespoons of the lemon zest.
2. Bring the mixture to a boil and then reduce the heat and simmer for 15 minutes.
3. Transfer the mixture to a large bowl and add the remaining 1 tablespoon lemon zest, the lemon juice, lime zest, and lime juice.
4. Chill the mixture in the fridge until completely cold, about 3 hours.
5. Whisk in the heavy cream and transfer the mixture to an ice cream maker.
6. Freeze according to the manufacturer's instructions.

Nutrition: calories: 151; fat: 6g; carbohydrates: 26g; phosphorus: 10mg; potassium: 27mg; sodium: 6mg; protein: 0g

819. Lemon mousse

Preparation time: 10 + chill time
Cooking time: 10 minutes
Servings: 4
Ingredients

- 1 cup coconut cream
- 8 ounces cream cheese, soft
- ¼ cup fresh lemon juice
- 3 pinches salt
- 1 teaspoon lemon liquid stevia

Directions

1. Preheat your oven to 350 °f
2. Grease a ramekin with butter
3. Beat cream, cream cheese, fresh lemon juice, salt and lemon liquid stevia in a mixer

4. Pour batter into ramekin
5. Bake for 10 minutes, then transfer the mousse to a serving glass
6. Let it chill for 2 hours and serve
7. Enjoy!

Nutrition: calories: 395 fat: 31g carbohydrates: 3g protein: 5g Phosphorus: 80mg Potassium: 97mg Sodium: 75mg

820. Vanilla custard

Preparation time: 7 minutes
Cooking time: 10 minutes
Servings: 10
Ingredients

- Egg – 1
- Vanilla – 1/8 teaspoon
- Nutmeg – 1/8 teaspoon
- Almond milk – ½ cup
- Stevia - 2 tablespoon

Directions

1. Scald the almond milk then let it cool slightly.
2. Break the egg into a bowl and beat it with the nutmeg.
3. Add the scalded almond milk, the vanilla, and the sweetener to taste. Mix well.
4. Place the bowl in a baking pan filled with ½ dccp of water.
5. Bake for 30 minutes at 325f.
6. Serve.

Nutrition: Calories: 167.3 Fat: 9g Carb: 11g Phosphorus: 205mg Potassium: 249mg Sodium: 124mg Protein: 10g

821. Carob angel food cake

Preparation time: 30 minutes
Cooking time: 30 minutes
Servings: 16
Ingredients:

- ¾ cup all-purpose flour
- ¼ cup carob flour

- 1½ cups sugar, divided
- 12 large egg whites, at room temperature
- 1½ teaspoons cream of tartar
- 2 teaspoons vanilla

Directions:
1. Preheat the oven to 375°f.
2. In a medium bowl, sift together the all-purpose flour, carob flour, and ¾ cup of the sugar; set aside.
3. Beat the egg whites and cream of tartar with a hand mixer for about 5 minutes or until soft peaks form.
4. Add the remaining ¾ cup sugar by the tablespoon to the egg whites until all the sugar is used up and stiff peaks form.
5. Fold in the flour mixture and vanilla.
6. Spoon the batter into an angel food cake pan.
7. Run a knife through the batter to remove any air pockets.
8. Bake the cake for about 30 minutes or until the top springs back when pressed lightly.
9. Invert the pan onto a wire rack to cool.
10. Run a knife around the rim of the cake pan and remove the cake from the pan.

Nutrition: calories: 113; fat: 0g; carbohydrates: 25g; phosphorus: 11mg; potassium: 108mg; sodium: 42mg; protein: 3g

822. Chocolate chip cookies

Preparation time: 7 minutes
Cooking time: 10 minutes
Servings: 10
Ingredients

- Semi-sweet chocolate chips – ½ cup
- Baking soda – ½ teaspoon
- Vanilla – ½ teaspoon
- Egg – 1
- Flour – 1 cup
- Margarine – ½ cup

- Stevia – 4 teaspoons

Directions
1. Sift the dry ingredients.
2. Cream the margarine, stevia, vanilla and egg with a whisk.
3. Add flour mixture and beat well.
4. Stir in the chocolate chips, then drop teaspoonfuls of the mixture over a greased baking sheet.
5. Bake the cookies for about 10 minutes at 375f.
6. Cool and serve.

Nutrition: Calories: 106.2 Fat: 7g carb: 8.9g Phosphorus: 19mg Potassium: 28mg Sodium: 98mg Protein: 1.5g

823. Old-fashioned apple kuchen

Preparation time: 25 minutes
Cook time: 1 hour
Servings: 16
Ingredients:

- Unsalted butter, for greasing the baking dish
- 1 cup unsalted butter, at room temperature
- 2 cups granulated sugar
- 2 eggs, beaten
- 2 teaspoons pure vanilla extract
- 2 cups all-purpose flour
- 1 teaspoon ener-g baking soda substitute
- 2 teaspoons ground cinnamon
- ½ teaspoon ground nutmeg
- Pinch ground allspice
- 2 large apples, peeled, cored, and diced (about 3 cups)

Directions:
1. Preheat the oven to 350°f.
2. Grease a 9-by-13-inch glass baking dish; set aside.

3. Cream together the butter and sugar with a hand mixer until light and fluffy, for about 3 minutes.
4. Add the eggs and vanilla and beat until combined, scraping down the sides of the bowl, about 1 minute.
5. In a small bowl, stir together the flour, baking soda substitute, cinnamon, nutmeg, and allspice.
6. Add the dry ingredients to the wet ingredients and stir to combine.
7. Stir in the apple and spoon the batter into the baking dish.
8. Bake for about 1 hour or until the cake is golden.
9. Cool the cake on a wire rack.
10. Serve warm or chilled.

Nutrition: calories: 368; fat: 16g; carbohydrates: 53g; phosphorus: 46mg; potassium: 68mg; sodium: 15mg; protein: 3g

824. Baked egg custard

Preparation time: 15 minutes
Cooking time: 30 minutes
Servings: 4
Ingredients:
- 2 medium eggs, at room temperature
- ¼ cup of semi-skimmed almond milk
- 3 tablespoons of white sugar
- ½ teaspoon of nutmeg
- 1 teaspoon of vanilla extract

Directions:
1. Preheat your oven at 375 f/180c
2. Mix all the ingredients in a mixing bowl and beat with a hand mixer for a few seconds until creamy and uniform.
3. Pour the mixture into lightly greased muffin tins.
4. Bake for 25-30 minutes or until the knife, you place inside, comes out clean.

Nutrition: Calories: 96.56 kcal Carbohydrate: 10.5 g Protein: 3.5 g Sodium: 37.75 mg

Potassium: 58.19 mg Phosphorus: 58.76 mg Dietary fiber: 0.06 g Fat: 2.91 g

825. Pound cake with pineapple

Preparation time: 10 minutes
Cooking time: 50 minutes
Servings: 24
Ingredients
- 3 cups of all-purpose flour, sifted
- 3 cups of sugar
- 1 ½ cups of butter
- 6 whole eggs and 3 egg whites
- 1 teaspoon of vanilla extract
- 1 10. Ounce can of pineapple chunks, rinsed and crushed (keep juice aside).
- For glaze:
- 1 cup of sugar
- 1 stick of unsalted butter or margarine
- Reserved juice from the pineapple

Directions
1. Preheat the oven at 350f/180c.
2. Beat the sugar and the butter with a hand mixer until creamy and smooth.
3. Slowly add the eggs (one or two every time) and stir well after pouring each egg.
4. Add the vanilla extract, follow up with the flour and stir well.
5. Add the drained and chopped pineapple.
6. Pour the mixture into a greased cake tin and bake for 45-50 minutes.
7. In a small saucepan, combine the sugar with the butter and pineapple juice. Stir every few seconds and bring to boil. Cook until you get a creamy to thick glaze consistency.
8. Pour the glaze over the cake while still hot.
9. Let cook for at least 10 seconds and serve.

Nutrition: Calories: 407.4 kcal Carbohydrate: 79 g Protein: 4.25 g Sodium: 118.97 mg Potassium: 180.32 mg Phosphorus: 66.37 mg Dietary fiber: 2.25 g Fat: 16.48 g

826. Apple crunch pie

Preparation time: 10 minutes
Cooking time: 35 minutes
Servings: 8

Ingredients

- 4 large tart apples, peeled, seeded and sliced
- ½ cup of white all-purpose flour
- 1/3 cup margarine
- 1 cup of sugar
- ¾ cup of rolled oat flakes
- ½ teaspoon of ground nutmeg

Directions

1. Preheat the oven to 375f/180c.
2. Place the apples over a lightly greased square pan (around 7 inches).
3. Mix the rest of the ingredients in a medium bowl with and spread the batter over the apples.
4. Bake for 30-35 minutes or until the top crust has gotten golden brown.
5. Serve hot.

Nutrition: Calories: 261.9 kcal Carbohydrate: 47.2 g Protein: 1.5 g Sodium: 81 mg Potassium: 123.74 mg
Phosphorus: 35.27 mg Dietary fiber: 2.81 g Fat: 7.99 g

827. Raspberry Popsicle

Preparation time: 2 hours
Cooking time: 15 minutes
Servings: 4

Ingredients

- 1 ½ cups raspberries
- 2 cups of water

Directions

1. Take a pan and fill it up with water
2. Add raspberries
3. Place it over medium heat and bring to water to a boil
4. Reduce the heat and simmer for 15 minutes
5. Remove heat and pour the mix into popsicle molds
6. Add a popsicle stick and let it chill for 2 hours
7. Serve and enjoy!

Nutrition: calories: 58 fat: 0.4g carbohydrates: 0g protein: 1.4g Phosphorus: 40mg Potassium: 97mg Sodium: 45mg

DRINKS AND SMOOTHIES

828. Fruity Smoothie

Preparation Time: 10minutes
Cooking Time: 0 minutes
Servings: 2
Ingredients:

- 8 oz. canned fruits, with juice
- 2 scoops vanilla-flavored whey protein powder
- 1 cup cold water
- 1 cup crushed ice

Directions:
1. First, start by putting all the ingredients in a blender jug.
2. Give it a pulse for 30 seconds until blended well.
3. Serve chilled and fresh.

Nutrition: Calories 186 Protein 23 g Fat 2g Cholesterol 41 mg Potassium 282 mg Calcium 160 mg Fiber 1.1 g

829. Almonds & Blueberries Smoothie

Preparation Time: 5 minutes
Cooking Time: 3 minutes
Servings: 2
Ingredients:

- 1/4 cup ground almonds, unsalted
- 1 cup fresh blueberries
- Fresh juice of a 1 lemon
- 1 cup fresh kale leaf
- 1/2 cup coconut water
- 1 cup water
- 2 tablespoon plain yogurt (optional)

Directions:
1. Dump all ingredients in your high-speed blender, and blend until your smoothie is smooth.

2. Pour the mixture in a chilled glass.
3. Serve and enjoy!

Nutrition: Calories: 110, Carbohydrates: 8g, Proteins: 2g, Fat: 7g, Fiber: 2g, Calcium 19mg, Phosphorous 16mg, Potassium 27mg Sodium: 101 mg

830. Butter Pecan and Coconut Smoothie

Preparation Time: 5 minutes
Cooking Time: 2 minutes
Servings: 2
Ingredients:

- 1 cup coconut almond milk, canned
- 1 scoop butter pecan powdered creamer
- 2 cups fresh green lettuce leaves, chopped
- 1/2 banana frozen or fresh
- 2 tablespoon stevia granulated sweetener to taste
- 1/2 cup water
- 1 cup ice cubes crushed

Directions:
1. Place ingredients from the list above in your high-speed blender.
2. Blend for 35 - 50 seconds or until all ingredients combined well.
3. Add less or more crushed ice.
4. Drink and enjoy!

Nutrition: Calories: 268, Carbohydrates: 7g, Proteins: 6g, Fat: 26g, Fiber: 1.5g

831. Green Coconut Smoothie

Preparation Time: 10 minutes
Cooking Time: 3 minutes

Servings: 2

Ingredients:

- 1 1/4 cup coconut almond milk (canned)
- 2 tablespoon chia seeds
- 1 cup of fresh kale leaves
- 1 cup of green lettuce leaves
- 1 scoop vanilla protein powder
- 1 cup ice cubes
- Granulated stevia sweetener (to taste; optional)
- 1/2 cup water

Directions:

1. Rinse and clean kale and the green lettuce leaves from any dirt.
2. Add all ingredients in your blender.
3. Blend until you get a nice smoothie.
4. Serve into chilled glass.

Nutrition: Calories: 179, Carbohydrates: 5g, Proteins: 4g, Fat: 18g, Fiber: 2.5g Calcium 22mg, Phosphorous 46mg, Potassium 34mg Sodium: 131 mg

832. Distinctive Pineapple Smoothie

Preparation Time: 5 minutes
Cooking Time: 0 minutes
Servings: 2
Ingredients:

- ¼ cup crushed ice cubes
- 2 scoops vanilla whey protein powder
- 1 cup water
- 1½ cups pineapple

Directions:

1. In a high-speed blender, add all ingredients and pulse till smooth.
2. Transfer into 2 serving glass and serve immediately.

Nutrition: Calories 117 Fat 2.1g Carbs 18.2g Protein 22.7g Potassium (K) 296mg Sodium (Na) 81mg Phosphorous 28 mg

833. Strawberry Fruit Smoothie

Preparation Time: 10minutes
Cooking Time: 0 minutes
Servings: 1
Ingredients:

- 3/4 cup fresh strawberries
- 1/2 cup liquid pasteurized egg whites
- 1/2 cup ice
- 1 tbsp. sugar

Directions:

1. First, start by putting all the ingredients in a blender jug.
2. Give it a pulse for 30 seconds until blended well.
3. Serve chilled and fresh.

Nutrition: Calories 156 Protein 14 g Fat 0 g Cholesterol 0 mg Potassium 400 mg Phosphorus 49 mg Calcium 29 mg Fiber 2.5 g

834. Blueberries and Coconut Smoothie

Preparation Time: 5 minutes
Cooking Time: 3 minutes
Servings: 5
Ingredients:

- 1 cup of frozen blueberries, unsweetened
- 1 cup stevia or erythritol sweetener
- 2 cups coconut almond milk (canned)
- 1 cup of fresh green lettuce leaves
- 2 tablespoon shredded coconut (unsweetened)
- 3/4 cup water

Directions:

1. Place all ingredients from the list in food-processor or in your strong blender.
2. Blend for 45 - 60 seconds or to taste.
3. Ready for drink! Serve!

Nutrition: Calories: 190, Carbohydrates: 8g, Proteins: 3g, Fat: 18g, Fiber: 2g, Calcium 79mg, Phosphorous 216mg, Potassium 207mg Sodium: 121 mg

835. Berry Cucumber Smoothie

Preparation Time: 10minutes
Cooking Time: 0 minutes
Servings: 1
Ingredients:
- 1 medium cucumber, peeled and sliced
- ½ cup fresh blueberries
- ½ cup fresh or frozen strawberries
- ½ cup unsweetened rice almond milk
- Stevia, to taste

Directions:
1. First, start by putting all the ingredients in a blender jug.
2. Give it a pulse for 30 seconds until blended well.
3. Serve chilled and fresh.

Nutrition: Calories 141 Protein 10 g Carbohydrates 15 g Fat 0 g Sodium 113 mg Potassium 230 mg Phosphorus 129 mg

836. Mixed Berry Protein Smoothie

Preparation Time: 10minutes
Cooking Time: 0 minutes
Servings: 2
Ingredients:
- 4 oz. cold water
- 1 cup frozen mixed berries
- 2 ice cubes
- 1 tsp blueberry essence
- 1/2 cup whipped cream topping
- 2 scoops whey protein powder

Directions:
1. First, start by putting all the ingredients in a blender jug.

2. Give it a pulse for 30 seconds until blended well.
3. Serve chilled and fresh.

Nutritional: Calories 104 Protein 6 g Fat 4 g Cholesterol 11 mg Potassium 141 mg Calcium 69 mg Fiber 2.4 g

837. Watermelon Bliss

Preparation Time: 10minutes
Cooking Time: 0 minutes
Servings: 2
Ingredients:
- 2 cups watermelon
- 1 medium-sized cucumber, peeled and sliced
- 2 mint sprigs, leaves only
- 1 celery stalk
- Squeeze of lime juice

Directions:
1. First, start by putting all the ingredients in a blender jug.
2. Give it a pulse for 30 seconds until blended well.
3. Serve chilled and fresh.

Nutrition: Calories 156 Protein 14 g Fat 0 g Cholesterol 0 mg Potassium 400 mg Calcium 29 mg Fiber 2.5g

838. Dark Turnip Greens Smoothie

Preparation Time: 10 minutes
Cooking Time: 3 minutes
Servings: 2
Ingredients:
- 1 cup of raw turnip greens
- 1 1/2 cup of almond milk
- 1 tablespoon of almond butter
- 1/2 cup of water
- 1/2 teaspoon of cocoa powder, unsweetened
- 1/4 teaspoon of cinnamon

- A pinch of salt
- 1/2 cup of crushed ice

Directions:
1. Rinse and clean turnip greens from any dirt.
2. Place the turnip greens in your blender along with all other ingredients.
3. Blend it for 45 - 60 seconds or until done; smooth and creamy.
4. Serve with or without crushed ice.

Nutrition: Calories: 131, Carbohydrates: 6g, Protein: 4g, Fat: 10g, Fiber: 2.5g

839. Raspberry Peach Smoothie

Preparation Time: 10minutes
Cooking Time: 0 minutes
Servings: 2
Ingredients:
- 1 cup frozen raspberries
- 1 medium peach, pit removed, sliced
- ½ cup silken tofu
- 1 tbsp. honey
- 1 cup unsweetened vanilla almond milk

Directions:
1. First, start by putting all the ingredients in a blender jug.
2. Give it a pulse for 30 seconds until blended well.
3. Serve chilled and fresh.

Nutrition: Calories 132 Protein 9 g. Carbohydrates 14 g Sodium 112 mg Potassium 310 mgPhosphorus 39 mg Calcium 32 mg

840. Fresh Cucumber, Kale and Raspberry Smoothie

Preparation Time: 10 minutes
Cooking Time: 3 minutes
Servings: 3
Ingredients:
- 1 1/2 cups of cucumber, peeled

- 1/2 cup raw kale leaves
- 1 1/2 cups fresh raspberries
- 1 cup of almond milk
- 1 cup of water
- Ice cubes crushed (optional)
- 2 tablespoon natural sweetener (stevia, erythritol...etc.)

Directions:
1. Place all Ingredients listed in a High-Speed Blender; Blend For 35 - 40 Seconds.
2. Serve Into Chilled Glasses.
3. Add More Natural Sweeter if you like. Enjoy!

Nutrition: Calories: 70, Carbohydrates: 8g, Proteins: 3g, Fat: 6g, Fiber: 5g

841. Peach High-Protein Smoothie

Preparation Time: 10minutes
Cooking Time: 0 minutes
Servings: 1
Ingredients:
- 1/2 cup ice
- 2 tbsp. powdered egg whites
- 3/4 cup fresh peaches
- 1 tbsp. sugar

Directions:
1. First, start by putting all the ingredients in a blender jug.
2. Give it a pulse for 30 seconds until blended well.
3. Serve chilled and fresh.

Nutrition: Calories 132 Protein 10 g Fat 0 g Cholesterol 0 mg Potassium 353 mg Calcium 9 mg Fiber 1.9 g

842. Power-Boosting Smoothie

Preparation Time: 5 minutes
Cooking Time: 0 minutes

Servings: 2

Ingredients:

- ½ cup water
- ½ cup non-dairy whipped topping
- 2 scoops whey protein powder
- 1½ cups frozen blueberries

Directions:

1. In a high-speed blender, add all ingredients and pulse till smooth.
2. Transfer into 2 serving glass and serve immediately.

Nutrition: Calories 242 Fat 7g Carbs 23.8g Protein 23.2g Potassium (K) 263mg Sodium (Na) 63mg Phosphorous 30 mg

843. Almonds and Zucchini Smoothie

Preparation Time: 5 minutes
Cooking Time: 3 minutes
Servings: 2

Ingredients:

- 1 cup zucchini, cooked and mashed - unsalted
- 1 1/2 cups almond milk
- 1 tablespoon almond butter (plain, unsalted)
- 1 teaspoon pure almond extract
- 2 tablespoon ground almonds or macadamia almonds
- 1/2 cup water
- 1 cup ice cubes crushed (optional, for serving)

Directions:

1. Dump all ingredients from the list above in your fast-speed blender; blend for 45 - 60 seconds or to taste.
2. Serve with crushed ice.

Nutrition: Calories: 322, Carbohydrates: 6g, Proteins: 6g, Fat: 30g, Fiber: 3.5gCalcium 9mg, Phosphorous 26mg, Potassium 27mg Sodium: 121 mg

844. Creamy Dandelion Greens and Celery Smoothie

Preparation Time: 10 minutes
Cooking Time: 3 minutes
Servings: 2

Ingredients:

- 1 handful of raw dandelion greens
- 2 celery sticks
- 2 tablespoon chia seeds
- 1 small piece of ginger, minced
- 1/2 cup almond milk
- 1/2 cup of water
- 1/2 cup plain yogurt

Directions:

1. Rinse and clean dandelion leaves from any dirt; add in a high-speed blender.
2. Clean the ginger; keep only inner part and cut in small slices; add in a blender.
3. Blend all remaining ingredients until smooth.
4. Serve and enjoy!

Nutrition: Calories: 58, Carbohydrates: 5g, Proteins: 3g, Fat: 6g, Fiber: 3gCalcium 29mg, Phosphorous 76mg, Potassium 27mg Sodium: 121 mg

845. Strengthening Smoothie Bowl

Preparation Time: 5 minutes
Cooking Time: 4 minutes
Servings: 2

Ingredients:

- ¼ cup fresh blueberries
- ¼ cup fat-free plain Greek yogurt
- 1/3 cup unsweetened almond milk
- 2 tbsp. of whey protein powder
- 2 cups frozen blueberries

Directions:

1. In a blender, add blueberries and pulse for about 1 minute.
2. Add almond milk, yogurt and protein powder and pulse till desired consistency.
3. Transfer the mixture into 2 bowls evenly.
4. Serve with the topping of fresh blueberries.

Nutrition: Calories 176 Fat 2.1g Carbs 27g Protein 15.1g Potassium (K) 242mg Sodium (Na) 72mg Phosphorous 555.3 mg

846. Fresh Lettuce and Cucumber-Lemon Smoothie

Preparation Time: 10 minutes
Cooking Time: 3 minutes
Servings: 2
Ingredients:
- 2 cups fresh lettuce leaves, chopped (any kind)
- 1 cup of cucumber
- 1 lemon washed and sliced.
- 2 tablespoon chia seeds
- 1 1/2 cup water or coconut water
- 1/4 cup stevia granulate sweetener (or to taste)

Directions:
1. Add all ingredients from the list above in the high-speed blender; blend until completely smooth.
2. Pour your smoothie into chilled glasses and enjoy!

Nutrition: Calories: 51, Carbohydrates: 4g, Protein: 2g, Fat: 4g, Fiber: 3.5g

847. Cranberry Smoothie

Preparation Time: 10 minutes
Cooking Time: 0 minutes
Servings: 1

Ingredients:
- 1 cup frozen cranberries
- 1 medium cucumber, peeled and sliced
- 1 stalk of celery
- Handful of parsley
- Squeeze of lime juice

Directions:
1. First, start by putting all the ingredients in a blender jug. Give it a pulse for 30 seconds until blended well.
2. Serve chilled and fresh.

Nutrition: Calories 126 Protein 12 g Fat 0.03 g Cholesterol 0 mg Potassium 220 mg Calcium 19 mg Fiber 1.4g

848. Apple and Blueberry Crisp

Preparation Time: 1 hour 10 minutes
Cooking Time: 1 hour
Serving: 8

Ingredients:
- Crisp
- 1/4 cup of brown sugar
- 1 1/4 cups quick cooking rolled oats
- 6 tbsp. non-hydrogenated melted margarine
- 1/4 cup all-purpose flour (unbleached)

Filling:
- 2 tbsp. cornstarch
- 1/2 cup of brown sugar
- 2 cups chopped or grated apples
- cups frozen or fresh blueberries (not thawed)
- 1 tbsp. fresh lemon juice
- 1 tbsp. melted margarine

Directions:
1. Preheat the oven to 350°F with the rack in the middle position.
2. Pour all the dry ingredients into a bowl, then the butter and stir until it is moistened. Set the mixture aside.

3. In an 8-inch (20-cm) square baking dish, mix the cornstarch and brown sugar. Add lemon juice and the rest of the fruits. Toss to blend the mixture. Add the crisp mixture, then bake until the crisp turns golden brown (or for 55 minutes to 1 hour). You can either serve cold or warm.

Nutrition: Calories 127 Fat 2.1g Carbs 18.2g Protein 22.7g Potassium (K) 256mg Sodium (Na) 61mg Phosphorous 28 mg

849. Raspberry Cucumber Smoothie

Preparation Time: 5 minutes
Cooking Time: 5 minutes
Servings: 2
Ingredients:

- 1 c. fresh or frozen raspberries
- ½ c. diced English cucumber
- 1 c. Homemade Rice Milk (or use unsweetened store-bought) or almond milk
- 2 tsp. chia seeds
- 1 tsp. honey
- ice cubes

Directions:

1. Place the raspberries, cucumber, rice milk, chia seeds, and honey in a blender. Then, blend until smooth.
2. Add the ice cubes. Then, blend until thick and smooth.
3. Pour into two tall glasses. Serve immediately.

Nutrition: Calories: 125 Fat: 1.1g Carbs: 23.5g Protein: 6g Sodium: 44mg Potassium: 199mg Phosphorus: 54mg

850. Cucumber and Lemon-Flavored Water

Preparation Time: 5 minutes

Cooking Time: 3 hours
Servings: 10
Ingredients:

- 1 lemon, deseeded, sliced
- ¼ c. fresh mint leaves, chopped
- 1 medium cucumber, sliced
- ¼ c. fresh basil leaves, chopped
- 10 c. water

Directions:

1. Place the papaya and mint in a large pitcher. Pour in the water.
2. Stir and place the pitcher in the refrigerator to infuse, overnight if possible.
3. Serve cold.

Nutrition: Calories: 10 Fat: 0g Carbs: 2.25g Protein: 0.12g Sodium: 2.5mg Potassium: 8.9mg Phosphorus: 10mg

851. Blueberry Smoothie

Preparation Time: 5 minutes
Cooking Time: 2 minutes
Servings: 4
Ingredients:

- 1 c. frozen blueberries
- 6 tbsp. protein powder
- 8 packets Splenda
- 14 oz. apple juice, unsweetened
- 8 cubes of ice

Directions:

1. Take a blender and place all the ingredients (in order) in it. Process for 1 minute until smooth.
2. Distribute the smoothie between four glasses and then serve.

Nutrition: Calories: 162 Fat: 0.5g Carbs: 30g Protein: 8g Sodium: 123.4mg Potassium: 223mg Phosphorus: 109mg

852. Blackberry Sage Cocktail

Preparation Time: 5 minutes
Cooking Time: 10 minutes
Servings: 6
Ingredients:
- Sage Simple Syrup
- 1 cup water
- 1 cup0granulated sugar
- 8 fresh sage leaves, plus more for garnish
- 1-pint fresh blackberries, muddled and strained (juices reserved)
- Juice of 1/2 a lemon
- 8 oz St. Germain Liqueur
- 16 oz vodka
- seltzer water

Directions:
1. Place water and sugar in a small saucepan.
2. Simmer until sugar dissolves for 7 to 10 minutes.
3. Remove from heat. Add sage leaves, and cover, allowing the mixture for about 2 hours.
4. Combine fresh blackberry juice, lemon juice, sage simple syrup, cocktail pitcher.
5. Mix and refrigerate covered until well chilled.
6. Serve in cocktail glasses filled with ice and garnish with fresh sage leaves and top with a splash of seltzer water.

Nutrition: Calories: 68 Fat: 1g Carbs: 15g Protein: 3g Sodium: 3mg Potassium: 133mg Phosphorus: 38mg

853. Rice Milk

Preparation Time: 2 minutes
Cooking Time: 2 minutes
Servings: 2
Ingredients:
- 1 c. rice milk, unenriched, chilled
- 1 scoop vanilla whey protein

Directions:
1. Pour milk in a blender, add whey protein, and then pulse until well blended.
2. Distribute the milk into two glasses and serve.

Nutrition: Calories: 120 Fat: 2g Carbs: 24g Protein: 0g Sodium: 86mg Potassium: 27mg Phosphorus: 56mg

854. Pineapple Juice

Preparation Time: 5 minutes
Cooking Time: 0 minutes
Servings: 2
Ingredients:
- ½ cup canned pineapple
- 1 cup water

Direction:
1. Blend all ingredients and serve over ice.

Nutrition: Calories 135 Protein 0 g Carbs 0 g Fat 0 g Sodium (Na) 0 mg Potassium (K) 180 mg Phosphorus 8 mg

855. Detoxifying Beet Juice

Preparation Time: 10 minutes
Cooking Time: 10 minutes
Servings: 4
Ingredients:
- 1-pound beets, washed with ends cut off
- 2 pounds carrots, washed with ends cut off
- 1 bunch celery, washed and broken into ribs
- 2 lemons, peel cut off and quartered
- 1 lime, peel cut off and quartered
- 1 bunch flat-leaf parsley, washed
- 1 Fuji or Honeycrisp red apple, chopped (optional, for extra sweetness)

Directions:

1. Wash produce and chop so pieces will fit into the feeder tube of your juicer.
2. Feed the vegetable pieces through the juicer, alternating harder and softer textured pieces to aid in the juicing process.
3. Serve immediately or store in the refrigerator in a highly sealed container.
4. The juice is best when served within 48 hours of making.

Nutrition: Calories: 58 Fat: 0g Carbs: 13g Protein: 2g Sodium: 106mg Potassium: 442mg Phosphorus: 54mg

856. Cinnamon Smoothie

Preparation Time: 5 minutes
Cooking Time: 5 minutes
Servings: 2
Ingredients:
- 150g plain or Greek yogurt
- 300ml milk
- 2 tbsp smooth peanut butter
- 1/4 tsp Schwartz Ground Cinnamon

Directions:
1. Add all the ingredients to a blender and blitz until smooth.
2. Serve immediately.

Nutrition: Calories: 88 Fat: 4.3g Carbs: 3g Protein: 8g Sodium: 187mg Potassium: 241mg Phosphorus: 20mg

857. Pinna Colada Protein Smoothie

Preparation Time: 5 minutes
Cooking Time: 2 minutes
Servings: 1
Ingredients:
- 1/2 cup unsweetened vanilla almond milk
- 1/2 cup unsweetened coconut milk
- 3/4 cup frozen pineapple chunks
- 1 scoop vanilla protein powder
- 1 tsp raw honey
- 1 tsp vanilla

Directions:
1. Place almond milk, coconut milk, pineapple, vanilla protein powder, honey, and vanilla in a blender.
2. Blend until smooth. Serve immediately.

Nutrition: Calories: 241 Fat: 7g Carbs: 20g Protein: 26g Sodium: 420mg Potassium: 205mg Phosphorus: 10mg

858. Mini Pineapple Upside down Cakes

Preparation Time: 50 minutes
Cooking Time: 50 minutes
Serving: 12
Ingredients:
- 1 tbsp. melted unsalted butter
- 12 canned unsweetened pineapple slices
- 1/3 cup packed brown sugar
- 2/3 cup sugar
- fresh cherries cut into halves and pitted
- 1 tbsp. canola oil
- 2/3 cup almond milk (fat-free)
- ½ tbsp. lemon juice
- 1 large egg
- 1-1/3 cups cake flour
- 1/4 tbsp. vanilla extract
- 1/4 tsp salt
- 1-1/4 tsp baking powder

Directions:
1 Coat 12 serving muffin pan with butter or you could use a square baking pan.
2 Sprinkle little brown sugar into each of the sections.
3 Crush 1 pineapple slice into each section to take the shape of the cup. Place 1 half cherry in the center of the pineapple with the cut side facing up.

4 Get a large bowl and beat the egg, almond milk, and the extracts until it is evenly blended.

5 Beat the flour, salt, and baking powder into sugar mixture until it is well blended to attain homogeneity and pour it into the batter prepared in the muffin pan.

6 Bake at 350°s until a toothpick sinks in and comes out clean (or for 35-40 minutes). Invert the muffin pan immediately and allow the cooked cakes to drop onto a serving plate. (If necessary, you can use a small spatula or butter knife to gently release them from the pan.)

7 Serve warm.

Nutrition: Calories 119 Fat 2.1g Carbs 16.2g Protein 22.7g Potassium (K) 296mg Sodium (Na) 81mg Phosphorous 28 mg

859. Apple- Cinnamon Drink

Preparation Time: 10 minutes
Cooking Time: 20 minutes
Servings: 4
Ingredients:

- 13 fresh apples
- 750ml-1L cold water
- 3-4 tablespoons cinnamon
- 1-2 tablespoons sugar (brown or caster)

Directions:

1. Peel, chop and cook 13 fresh apples.
2. Once they were half-cooked, add water leaving for 2 minutes
3. Add a lot of cinnamon (3-4 tablespoons, but you can add as much as you please, really) and 1-2 tablespoons sugar.
4. Keep cooking for another 5 minutes.
5. Drain and put into the new container back in the pan and bring it to the boil.
6. Add more cinnamon and a bit of water to thin it out a bit.
7. Pour into a cup and enjoy.

Nutrition: Calories: 130 Fat: 0g Carbs: 32g Protein: 0g Sodium: 20mg Potassium: 0mg Phosphorus: 0mg

860. Honey Cinnamon Latte

Preparation Time: 5 minutes
Cooking Time: 5 minutes
Servings: 2
Ingredients:

- 1-½ cups of organic, unsweetened almond milk
- 1 scoop of organic vanilla protein powder
- 1 teaspoon of organic cinnamon
- ½ teaspoon of pure, local honey
- 1-2 shots of espresso

Directions:

1. Heat almond milk in the microwave until hot to the touch.
2. Add honey and stir until completely melted.
3. Using a whisk, add cinnamon, and protein powder and thoroughly combine.
4. Pour into a manual milk and froth concoction until foamy and creamy.
5. Pour espresso shots into a mug and add in milk mixture.

Nutrition: Calories: 115 Fat: 3g Carbs: 26g Protein: 3g Sodium: 125mg Potassium: 10.9mg Phosphorus: 0.1mg

861. Sunny Pineapple Smoothie

Preparation Time: 5 minutes
Cooking Time: 5 minutes
Servings: 2
Ingredients:

- 1/2 c. frozen pineapple chunks
- 2/3 c. almond milk
- 1/2 tsp. ginger powder

- 1 tbsp. agave syrup

Directions:
1. Prepare a blender and mix everything until nice and smooth (around 30 seconds).
2. Transfer into a tall glass or Mason jar.
3. Serve and enjoy.

Nutrition: Calories: 144 Fat: 0.36g Carbs: 37g Protein: 1.6g Potassium: 1000mg Phosphorus: 40mg

862. Grapefruit Sorbet

Preparation Time: 10 minutes
Cooking Time: 5 minutes
Servings: 6
Ingredients
- ½ cup sugar
- ¼ cup water
- 1 fresh thyme sprig
- For the sorbet
- Juice of 6 pink grapefruit
- ¼ cup thyme simple syrup

Directions:
1. In a blender, combine the grapefruit juice and ¼ cup of simple syrup, and process.
2. Transfer to an airtight container and freeze for 3 to 4 hours, until firm. Serve.
3. Substitution tip: Try this with other citrus fruits, such as mangos, lemons, or limes, for an equally delicious treat.

Nutrition: Calories 117 Fat 2.1g Carbs 18.2g Protein 22.7g Sodium (Na) 81mg Phosphorous 28 mg

863. Citrus Smoothie

Preparation Time: 5 minutes
Cooking Time: 2 minutes
Servings: 2
Ingredients:
- 1 large orange, peeled, halved
- ¼ lemon, peeled, seeded

- ½ cup (85 g) pineapple, peeled, cubed
- ¼ cup (60 g) frozen mango
- 1 cup (130 g) ice cubes

Directions:
1. Prepare all ingredients into the container and secure lid.
2. Turn machine on and slowly increase speed to high.
3. Blend for 1 minute or until the desired consistency is reached.

Nutrition: Calories: 280 Fat: 0g Carbs: 67g Protein: 4g Sodium: 30mg Potassium: 570mg Phosphorus: 0mg

864. Hot Cocoa

Preparation Time: 5 minutes
Cooking Time: 5 minutes
Servings: 1
Ingredients:
- 1 tbsp. cocoa powder, unsweetened
- 2 tsp. Splenda granulated sugar
- 3 tbsp. whipped dessert topping
- 1 c. water, at room temperature
- 2 tbsp. water, cold

Directions:
1. Place a saucepan over medium heat and let it heat until hot.
2. Take a cup, place cocoa powder and sugar in it, pour in cold water, and mix well.
3. Then slowly stir in hot water until cocoa mixture dissolves and top with whipped topping.
4. Serve straight away.

Nutrition: Calories: 120 Fat: 3g Carbs: 23g Protein: 1g Sodium: 110mg Potassium: 199mg Phosphorus: 88mg

865. Mango Cheesecake Smoothie

Preparation Time: 5 minutes

Cooking Time: 5 minutes
Servings: 2
Ingredients:
- 1 c. Homemade Rice Milk
- ½ ripe fresh mango, peeled and chopped
- 2 tbsp. cream cheese, at room temperature
- 1 tsp. honey
- ½ vanilla bean split and seeds scraped out
- Pinch ground nutmeg
- 3 ice cubes

Directions:
1. Place the rice milk, mango, cream cheese, honey, vanilla bean seeds, and nutmeg in a blender, and blend until smooth and thick.
2. Add the ice cubes and blend.
3. Serve in two glasses immediately.

Nutrition: Calories: 177 Fat: 4g Carbs: 10g Protein: 24g Sodium: 346mg Potassium: 66mg Phosphorus: 62mg

866. Pineapple Protein Smoothie

Preparation Time: 5 minutes
Cooking Time:
Servings: 1
Ingredients:
1. 1/2 cup cottage cheese
2. 1/2 cup frozen pineapple chunks
3. 1/2 tsp brown sugar (optional)
4. 1/4 tsp vanilla extract
5. 1 Tbsp ground flaxseed (optional)

6. 1 cup milk of choice (unsweetened almond milk)

Directions:
1. Place all of the ingredients into a blender, and then blend until smooth.
2. Serve immediately.

Nutrition: Calories: 220 Carbohydrates: 29g Protein: 24g Fat: 0.5g Sodium: 195mg Potassium: 325mg Phosphorus: 0mg

867. Almond Milk

Preparation Time: 3 minutes
Cooking Time: 2 minutes
Servings: 3
Ingredients:
- 1 c. almonds, soaked in warm water for 10 minutes
- 1 tsp. vanilla extract, unsweetened
- 3 c. filtered water

Directions:
1. Drain the soaked almonds, place them into the blender, pour in water, and blend for 2 minutes until almonds are chopped.
2. Strain the milk by passing it through cheesecloth into a bowl, discard almond meal, and then stir vanilla into the milk.
3. Cover the milk, refrigerate until chilled, and when ready to serve, stir it well, pour the milk evenly into the glasses and then serve.

Nutrition: Calories: 30 Fat: 2.5g Carbs: 1g Protein: 1g Sodium: 170mg Potassium: 140mgmg Phosphorus: 30mg

CONCLUSION

The number one reason why patients are urged to stay healthy during the early stages of kidney disease is to avoid dialysis for as long as possible.

Each recipe has been carefully crafted by a team of experts who have the knowledge and experience to make sure you get the most out of every meal. All of the recipes in this cookbook have been carefully adjusted to ensure that they contain low levels of sodium, potassium, and phosphorus. This is important because these foods provide the necessary vitamins and minerals for people with kidney failure.

This can be done by incorporating the right types of nutrients in your diet, all of which are included in the right amount, in the renal diet. Maintaining your activity levels, getting enough sleep, and quitting bad habits, such as smoking and alcohol, will support your journey towards staying healthy and avoiding dialysis.

Even though there is no cure for chronic kidney disease, it is a journey that you can manage. You can sustain your health and continue living your life as normal, with a high quality of life, for much longer than if you don't follow these basic guidelines.

The number one thing to remember on this journey is that you are in complete control of your outcome. Recipes from this cookbook are simple, delicious, and healthy. You can even use them as an inspiration to experiment and create your own renal diet recipes. Bear in mind that the renal diet is a lifestyle, and to get the best results, it's important to follow it regularly and include it in your daily life. And don't worry, you can do it. After all, this book is the best proof that the renal diet is yummy. Meals do not require too much hassle, and that's also amazing. Without treatments, you could die a very painful death. Renal failure can be the consequence of long-haul diabetes, hypertension, unreliable diet, and can stem from other health concerns.

A renal diet is tied in with directing the intake of protein and phosphorus in your eating routine. Restricting your sodium intake is likewise significant. By controlling these two variables you can control the vast majority of the toxins/waste made by your body and thus this enables your kidney to 100% function. In the event that you get this early enough and truly moderate your diets with extraordinary consideration, you could avert all-out renal failure. In the event that you get this early, you can take out the issue completely.

Water, herbal tea, lemonade, and fruit juices with no high sugar content are prescribed beverages that will support kidney patients. Sugar has a diuretic effect on the kidneys that can make the disease worse and can lead to dehydration. Kidney patients need fluids, potassium, and sodium and protein intake to be monitored and recorded. This will help them keep track of changes in their hydration status and deviations in diet that can have negative effects on their health status.

The proper renal diet can really help kidneys functioning longer, and it has only more restrictions on proteins and table salt, while restrictions to phosphorous and potassium can be needed if the levels of blood rise and the signs of accumulation become too evident.

Each recipe listed will help you achieve your health and fitness goals and provide most of the nutrients that the body needs to function. Your body won't be deprived of any micronutrient or macronutrient. The Low sodium will also assist in striking the right balance between saturated and unsaturated fats.

Made in the USA
Coppell, TX
23 November 2022